ANCIENT COMPLEX SOCIETIES

Ancient Complex Societies examines the archaeological evidence for the rise and functioning of politically and socially "complex" cultures in antiquity. Particular focus is given to civilizations exhibiting positions of leadership, social and administrative hierarchies, emerging and already developed complex religious systems, and economic differentiation. Case studies are drawn from around the globe, including Asia, the Mediterranean region, and the American continents. Using case studies from Africa, Polynesia, and North America, discussion is dedicated to identifying what "complex" means and when it should be applied to ancient systems. Each chapter attempts not only to explore the sociopolitical and economic elements of ancient civilizations, but to also present an overview of what life was like for the later population within each system, sometimes drilling down to individual people living their daily lives. Throughout the chapters, the authors address problems with the idea of complexity, the incomparability of cultures, and the inconsistency of archaeological and historical evidence in reconstructing ancient cultures.

Jennifer C. Ross is a Professor of Art & Archaeology at Hood College in Frederick, MD. She is the Associate Director of the Çadır Höyük excavations and has published on topics ranging from the invention of cuneiform to metallurgical technologies in the ancient Near East.

Sharon R. Steadman is a Professor of Anthropology at the State University of New York College at Cortland. She has published on the subjects of ancient religions in archaeological context and the archaeology of architecture and has edited several volumes on the archaeology of Anatolia.

ANCIENT COMPLEX SOCIETIES

Jennifer C. Ross and Sharon R. Steadman

Routledge
Taylor & Francis Group
NEW YORK AND LONDON

First published 2017
by Routledge
711 Third Avenue, New York, NY 10017

and by Routledge
2 Park Square, Milton Park, Abingdon, Oxon OX14 4RN

Routledge is an imprint of the Taylor & Francis Group, an informa business

© 2017 Taylor & Francis

The right of Jennifer C. Ross and Sharon R. Steadman to be identified as authors of this work has been asserted by them in accordance with sections 77 and 78 of the Copyright, Designs and Patents Act 1988.

All rights reserved. No part of this book may be reprinted or reproduced or utilised in any form or by any electronic, mechanical, or other means, now known or hereafter invented, including photocopying and recording, or in any information storage or retrieval system, without permission in writing from the publishers.

Trademark notice: Product or corporate names may be trademarks or registered trademarks, and are used only for identification and explanation without intent to infringe.

British Library Cataloguing-in-Publication Data
A catalogue record for this book is available from the British Library

Library of Congress Cataloging in Publication Data
Names: Ross, Jennifer C., author. | Steadman, Sharon R., author.
Title: Ancient complex societies / Jennifer C. Ross and Sharon R. Steadman.
Description: Milton Park, Abingdon, Oxon ; New York, NY : Routledge, 2017. | Includes bibliographical references and index.
Identifiers: LCCN 2016030196 | ISBN 9781611321951 (hardback : alk. paper) | ISBN 9781611321968 (pbk. : alk. paper) | ISBN 9781315305639 (ebk)
Subjects: LCSH: Civilization, Ancient. | Social archaeology.
Classification: LCC CB311 .R597 2017 | DDC 930.1—dc23
LC record available at https://lccn.loc.gov/2016030196

ISBN: 978-1-61132-195-1 (hbk)
ISBN: 978-1-61132-196-8 (pbk)
ISBN: 978-1-315-30563-9 (ebk)

Typeset in Bembo
by Apex CoVantage, LLC

Printed in the United Kingdom
by Henry Ling Limited

CONTENTS

List of Figures   *vii*
List of Tables   *x*
Acknowledgments   *xi*

1 Complexity and Its Discontents   1

2 Human Cultural Institutions: Critical Elements in Complex Society   6

3 Ancient Systems: From Forager to State   16

4 Scales of Complexity: Case Studies   28

5 Southwest Asia: Ancient Mesopotamia and Its Neighbors   52

6 The Nile Valley of Egypt   86

7 The Aegean Bronze Age and the Classical World   118

8 The Indus Valley Civilization   173

9 Ancient Chinese Civilizations   204

10 Empires in Southeast Asia   237

11 The Mississippian System in the American Bottom   265

12 Ancient Mesoamerican Cultures   298

13 Andean Civilizations and Empires   327
14 Why Complex Societies Collapse   366

Bibliography   *371*
Index   *414*

FIGURES

4.1	Map of Southern Africa and Sites Discussed in the Text	29
4.2	Sketch Plan of the Great Zimbabwe Hill Complex; Sketch Plan of the Great Enclosure; Photo of the Great Enclosure	30
4.3	Examples of the Great Zimbabwe Bird Carvings on the Hill Complex Structure	32
4.4	Map of American Southwest and Sites Discussed in the Text	33
4.5	Photo of Pueblo Bonito: An Example of a Chacoan Great House	35
4.6	Photo of Kiva (Circular Structure) at Pueblo del Arroyo Great House in Chaco Canyon	36
4.7	Photo of Fajada Butte in Chaco Canyon; Artistic Rendering of the Butte and the "Sun Daggers" at Fajada Butte	37
4.8	Map of Polynesia Including New Zealand and Hawaii	43
4.9	Example of Sacred Hot Spring and Swamp, Whakarewarewa Thermal Valley Near Rotorua, used by the Maori for Deposit of Sacred/Tapu Objects	45
4.10	Example of a Hawaiian Feathered Cape	49
5.1	Map of Regions and Sites Discussed in the Chapter	53
5.2	Plastered Skull from Jericho	57
5.3	Reconstruction of the White Temple at Uruk; Plan of the Eanna Precinct at Uruk	62
5.4	Early Dynastic Votive Figurine from Mari	67
5.5	Naram-Sin Stele	71
5.6	Law Code Stele of Hammurabi	74
5.7	Colossal Winged Lion (*lamassu*) from the Northwest Palace of Assurnasirpal II at Nimrud (Kalhu)	81
6.1	Map of Regions and Sites Discussed in the Chapter	87
6.2	Plan of Tomb U-j at Abydos	95
6.3	Narmer Palette	96
6.4	The Pyramids at Giza	101
6.5	Portrait of Senwosret III as a Sphinx	106
6.6	Plan of the Temple of Amun at Luxor, Showing Additions over Time	109
6.7	Family Scene Depicting Akhenaten, Nefertiti, and Their Daughters	111
6.8	Cat Mummy from Abydos	114
7.1	Map of Regions and Sites Discussed in the Chapter	119

7.2	Standard Megaron Plan	123
7.3	Early Bronze Age: Cycladic Folded-Arm Figurine; Plan of the House of the Tiles at Lerna	124
7.4	Lustral Basin in the Palace at Malia	128
7.5	Knossos Palace Plan	130
7.6	Shaft Graves at Mycenae	136
7.7	Pylos Palace Plan	138
7.8	Map of the Classical World	143
7.9	Geometric Period Art	145
7.10	Plan of Classical Period Athens	147
7.11	Archaic Period Pottery	148
7.12	Kouros From Volomandra, ca. 560 BCE; Peplos Kore, ca. 530 BCE	150
7.13	Etruscan Mural: Detail of a Banqueting Scene, Tomb of the Leopards, Tarquinia, 480–470 BCE	159
7.14	Plan of Rome	161
7.15	Map of the Hellenistic and Roman Empires	163
7.16	Prima Porta statue	168
8.1	Map of Regions and Sites Discussed in the Text	174
8.2	Plan of Mohenjo Daro settlement; Close-up of Structures on the Citadel	181
8.3	Photo of the Great Bath at Mohenjo Daro	182
8.4	Photo of Typical Street at Mohenjo Daro	183
8.5	Sketch Plan of Dholavira Observatory	185
8.6	Example of a Private Well at Mohenjo Daro	187
8.7	Harappan Script on Seals	191
8.8	Example of Harappan Seal With Unicorn	192
8.9	Artistic Reconstruction of the Great Bath	195
8.10	Example of Harappan Female Figurine	196
8.11	Drawing of the So-named "Priest-King" Statue	197
8.12	Drawing of the "Proto-Shiva" Seal	198
8.13	Photo of a Pipal Tree (*Ficus religious*) and Its Heart-shaped Leaves	198
9.1	Map of China and Sites Discussed in the Text	205
9.2	Plan of Jiangzhai Village	209
9.3	Example of an Oracle Bone From the Shang Dynasty	212
9.4	Plan of Sanxingdui Settlement	214
9.5	Example of Sanxingdui *Bianfa* Style Hair Braid on a Figurine	216
9.6	Examples of the *Jia, Jua,* and *He* Decorative Vessels	218
9.7	Plan of Yanshi City and Close-up of Palace Area	220
9.8	Examples of Naturalistic and Stylistic Early Chinese Pictographs	223
9.9	Plan of the Yinxu Settlement Showing Residential and Workshop Areas, Royal Cemetery, and Palatial/Ceremonial Precinct	225
9.10	Plan of the Xibeigang Royal Cemetery at Yinxu	226
9.11	Photo of Eastern Zhou Dynasty Bronze Cauldron Known as a "Ding"	230
9.12	Photo of the Great Wall of China at Badaling	233
9.13	Photo of Terracotta Soldiers in Qin Emperor Shi Huangti's Tomb	235
10.1	Map of Regions and Sites Discussed in the Text	238
10.2	Photo of Cambodian House on Stilts at Kampong Phluk Village Near Tonle Sap Lake	239
10.3	Example of Dong Son Bronze Dagger With Elegant Hilt	245

10.4	Photo of a Lingam Stone in a Hindu Temple (in India) Dedicated to Shiva	248
10.5	Photo of One Heavily Carved Tower Inside the Banteay Srei Temple in Cambodia	254
10.6	Photo of the Five Towers, the Central One Representing Mt. Meru, at Angkor Wat in Cambodia	256
10.7	Photo of Two Apsara Dancers Carved in Stone at Angkor Wat	257
10.8	Photo of Bayon (Three of Four Faces) at Angkor Thom, Cambodia	258
10.9	Stone Carvings at Angkor Thom	259
11.1	Map of Regions and Major Paleoindian, Archaic, and Woodland Period Sites Discussed in the Text	266
11.2	Map of Major Sites in the American Bottom Region Discussed in the Text	267
11.3	Plan of the Watson Brake Mounds	271
11.4	Plan of Poverty Point and Associated Mounds	272
11.5	Examples of Poverty Point Artifacts	274
11.6	Example of Hopewell Period Effigy of a Flat Human Hand Cut From a Sheet of Mica, Excavated From the Hopewell Mound Group	278
11.7	Sketch of Two Causewayed Enclosure Hopewell Sites	279
11.8	Example of Stone Hopewell Effigy Pipe	280
11.9	Sketch of Serpent Mound in Ohio	282
11.10	Artistic Rendering of Monks Mound and Cahokian Center	286
11.11	Example of the Type of Cahokian Figurines That Show Female and Agricultural Symbols	293
12.1	Map of Preclassic and Classic Period Regions and Sites Discussed in the Chapter	299
12.2	Olmec Monuments: Plan of La Venta; Olmec Head	301
12.3	Monte Albán: View; Drawing of Danzante	306
12.4	Teotihuacan: Plan; Feathered Serpent Head, Feathered Serpent Pyramid	308
12.5	Map of Classic Period Maya and Postclassic Period Sites and Regions Discussed in the Chapter	312
12.6	Tikal: Plan of Central Area; Photo of Temples I and II in 1882	316
12.7	Lintel Relief (Lintel 25) Showing Bloodletting Ritual From Yaxchilan, Mexico	319
12.8	Sarcophagus Lid of Pakal	320
12.9	Chichen Itza: Photo of El Castillo; Photo of Chacmool From the Temple of the Warriors	323
13.1	Map of South American Region and Location of Early Preceramic Sites	328
13.2	View of an Andes Volcano (at Villarrica Lake, Chile)	328
13.3	Photo of South American Cuy; Photo of South American Alpacas (Camelids)	331
13.4	Map of Sites Dating From the Preceramic to Nasca Period	332
13.5	Sketch of Real Alto Archaeological Site	333
13.6	Plan of Chavín de Huántar Site and Area	336
13.7	Representation of the Lanzon Stone	337
13.8	Plan of Huacas de Moche	340
13.9	Photo of Nasca Geoglyphs Showing the "Hummingbird"	347
13.10	Map of Sites in Tiwanaku, Wari, Chimú, and Inca Cultures	348
13.11	Sketch Plan of the Chan Chan Capital; Detail of Ciudadela Rivera; Photo of the Administrative Area of Ciudadela Tschudi	353
13.12	Photo of Machu Picchu	358
13.13	Drawing of a Khipu	361
13.14	Artistic Reconstruction of Sacrifice Ritual of Ice Maiden ("Juanita")	363

TABLES

5.1	Chronological Periods and Sites Discussed in Chapter 5	54
6.1	Chronological Periods and Sites Discussed in Chapter 6	88
7.1	Chronological Periods and Sites Discussed in Chapter 7	120
8.1	Chronological Periods and Sites Discussed in Chapter 8	175
9.1	Chronological Periods and Sites Discussed in Chapter 9	206
10.1	Chronological Periods and Sites Discussed in Chapter 10 and List of Khmer Kings	240
11.1	Chronological Periods and Sites Discussed in Chapter 11	268
12.1	Chronological Periods and Sites Discussed in Chapter 12	300
13.1	Chronological Periods and Sites Discussed in Chapter 13	330

ACKNOWLEDGMENTS

This book was begun at the urging and encouragement of Mitch Allen, formerly of Left Coast Press, to whom the authors are immensely indebted. We also thank Caryn Berg, our acquisitions and marketing contact at Left Coast, for her help in the early stages of assembly and editing, and the anonymous reviewers who read the manuscript at that point. Their careful assessments helped reshape the text in important ways.

At Routledge, Lola Harre has helped see the manuscript through its final stages of revision; we are grateful for her aid.

Closer to home, Jennifer Ross would like to thank Aimee Gee and Kaitlyn May, Interlibrary Loan librarians at Hood College, for their patience and perseverance in accessing a variety of obscure materials for this research. Hood College students have test-driven some of the notions from these chapters over the years, and their insights and reactions have provided a thoughtful complement to our ideas.

Sharon Steadman is indebted to Scott Anderson, Wendy Miller, and Benjamin Spencer for their help in creating the maps for this volume. She also thanks Lisi Krall and Scott Moranda for their friendship and support during this and all projects.

To our husbands and families, we cannot put into words our gratitude for their support and patience. Our excavation teams at Çadır Höyük have also put up with high levels of distraction and found ways to rise above our disarray over several years. To all, we owe an enormous debt.

1

COMPLEXITY AND ITS DISCONTENTS

Complexity is a thorny topic. At the start of this book project, the two authors probably did not define it in the same way; in fact, we avoided any discussion of what we meant by "complexity." By the end, we may have come to a common understanding of what complexity means to archaeologists and the methods by which they identify and analyze it. We hope that our readers will see it our way, though we certainly understand that you may not.

How did things get so complicated? In the chapters and case studies that follow, you will encounter cultural diversity in all its splendor. Yet the ancient societies we present are all generally agreed to have been "complex"—that is, archaeologists recognize a common set of institutions beyond kinship or family bonds that guided political, social, economic, and religious organizations. Complex societies typically exhibit centralization of population (but rely on rural members for sustenance) and a hierarchy of economic political positions (but with a variety of mechanisms to level out and disguise differences). Complex political systems integrate numerous interacting social groups so that conflicts of values and goals are avoided and peaceful relationships (on a human and cosmic level) are maintained. Yet conflict and competition fuel innovation and change, producing social dynamics and new formations that may merge the old and the new.

Theories and Theorists of Complexity

Studies of complex society got their start in the 19th century, as scholars in the newly developed fields of anthropology and sociology began to categorize extant societies into types on the basis of population, kinship and religious institutions, economic organization, and political structures. Characteristic of this work were the social evolutionary schemes of Lewis Henry Morgan and Edward Tylor that traced the development of human history from savagery and barbarism to civilization (Trigger 1989). This classificatory passion reached its peak with the work of Marshall Sahlins (1958) and Elman Service (1962), who independently outlined the features of four types of societies: band, tribe, chiefdom, and state. Sahlins and Service understood these categories to be ideal types, each distinct in terms of demography and its social, political, economic, and religious institutions. Still, their work contributed to a pre-existing tendency to see societal types as evolutionary, with a group of people "advancing" from one stage to another in an inevitable progression toward the institutions of modern life. Those that never "rose" to state level might be regarded as maladaptive, and every society was forced into one of the types, even if its components only partially matched the ideals. Numerous scholars in the social sciences have theorized the development and functioning of complexity since this time; we can divide them into those who look at all elements of society and those who see developments in terms of a "prime mover"—a single feature that led to the creation of state-level society.

Big Picture Theorists

One school of theory examines complexity in terms of the interacting and integrated "systems" of a society; these systems are the interwoven economic, social, religious, and political organizations that structure societies. Systems theory in archaeology had its origins in the 1960s, when archaeology as a discipline in the United States and Britain became more closely aligned with anthropology (after several decades of a "culture historical" orientation). Among the most prominent scholars studying the rise of complex societies using a systems framework were Kent V. Flannery and Robert M. Adams. They, and others, regarded every society as comprising a unique combination of interacting systems, on the model of the organs in a body. For example (see Chapter 5 for more detail), 1st millennium BCE Mesopotamia relied on an agricultural economy with a high level of craft specialization, possessed social and administrative hierarchies that divided surplus wealth and distributed power, housed a multiethnic population, featured a polytheistic religion with a warrior god at its head, had a full-time military led by the king, and took an imperial stance that required constant expansion of territory. A change to any element in this overarching system—such as the accession of a weak king, incapable of leading the army or of bringing the priesthood under his control—would lead to changes in all other subsystems, including the loss of territory, military challenges, and social upheavals. The systemic whole might eventually be re-established after temporary instability, or permanent change could ensue that resulted in economic, social, religious, and political reorganization.

Challenges to systems models emerged in the 1980s, as archaeologists criticized them as too mechanistic and not flexible enough to account for human behaviors and social relationships. Still, the idea that culture may be divided into interrelated and interactive subsystems continues to generate theories of culture change, even ones that focus on social relations (Bender 1978; Hayden 1995). Among more recent scholars of culture, studies of power, its development, and its working through the subsystems of culture, have become prevalent. The anthropologist Eric Wolf (1999) and sociologist Michael Mann (1986) fall into this category. These scholars are particularly interested in tracing the causes of changes in the configurations of power and have devised a set of potential "push" factors that would present opportunities for aspiring leaders to acquire permanent powers by attracting increasing numbers of followers who permanently entrust a leader with rights over their labor and resources. Any one of these "sources of social power" (Mann 1986) could arise at any time in a group's history; only under particular social, environmental, and historical circumstances will they become causes for political change. Mann (1986: 22–27) has identified four main potential sources of power, in what he calls his IEMP Model: ideological, economic, military, and political. Typically, no one source develops on its own, but some or all can be intertwined, working in concert to shape societal change.

Mann's delineation of sources of power, and his initial application of the model to a number of ancient societies, generated a great deal of elaboration by scholars, and the refinement of categories and of their connections is ongoing (Yoffee 1993, 2005). Ideological power derives from the capacity to control meaning and perceptions, most often in support of an individual's position. Economic power has a number of potential dimensions, including control over scarce or previously untapped resources (Eerkens 2009), or over property (Earle 1991a). Economic power can also originate in the accumulation of surplus staple goods, mobilized in feasts or at times of food scarcity (Bird and

Bliege Bird 2009), in such a way that fosters a sense of social indebtedness. Control over labor and its products can lead to economic power (Arnold 2000, 2009; Berdan 1989). A number of scholars have investigated the benefits that accrue to individuals who manage long-distance trade, gaining access to particular exotic items (Helms 1993; Kipp and Schortmann 1989).

Military power denotes the management of both defensive protection and offensive territorial expansion. A leader with troops under his or her charge also commands respect and fear within a society, with the potential to recruit additional supporters (Stanish 2009). Finally, political power is the decision-making capacity described earlier and the organizational or management capability to carry decisions out.

Mann's categories serve as ideal formulations, and the precise mechanisms of change in any given society may be difficult to determine, especially when one must rely only on archaeological evidence.

Theorists with Narrower Focus

Even before systems theory became a dominant framework for examining culture and, especially, relations of power, a number of theorists had identified specific elements or subsystems as the ones they thought best explained the development of inequality and of advanced civilizations. We will call these scholars "small picture theorists" because they focus on a much narrower range of cultural components than those described earlier. This does not mean that their ideas have had less impact on our understanding of complexity.

Chief among the theories that one element of culture has been responsible for the rise of civilizations across the globe are those that focus on economy—whether subsistence, technology, or exchange. Beginning in the 1930s, Karl Wittfogel (1957) proposed that, in the great river-based agricultural societies of the Old World (Mesopotamia, Egypt, China, and the Indus Valley), political power was in the hands of individuals and groups who controlled the flow of water through irrigation systems. Wittfogel's "hydraulic hypothesis" envisioned a circumstance in which those who relied on irrigation for survival and prosperity became permanently dependent on the few people who regulated and maintained irrigation canals. Wittfogel's hypothesis obviously does not apply to environments, like Greece and Rome, where agriculture is dependent on rainfall, nor did archaeological evidence for the earliest state organizations support his ideas.

V. Gordon Childe, in the 1920s, also tied the development of state systems to economic concerns. Childe's work was especially focused on major societal shifts in land and labor organization, changes he called, in the Marxist terminology of his day, "revolutions." Both the Neolithic (agricultural) and the Urban Revolutions were topics of Childe's archaeological and theoretical studies (1936, 1950). To explain the origins of agriculture, he posited a major environmental change that brought humans, plants, and animals into proximity. With the development of agriculture, the harvesting of surpluses of food made possible the next step, as some people turned from agricultural pursuits in the countryside to occupational specializations (metallurgy, especially) in towns: the Urban Revolution.

These environmental, subsistence, and labor-related explanations for major transformations in human history are very much in keeping with economic models of human behaviors proposed in later decades. Chief among these is Immanuel Wallerstein's World-Systems theory (1974), first developed to explain the rise and dominance of capitalism over the world's economies. In Wallerstein's view, powerful nation-states impose an extractive economic system on weaker and dependent states. The dominant states form a core, extracting raw materials, subsistence, goods, and labor from their peripheral dependencies, then transforming these materials and selling the finished products back to the peripheral nations. Wallerstein believes that such unequal economic relationships had their origins in Renaissance Europe but that the system spread and expanded into a system of political dominance as western European states sent colonies to Africa, the Americas, and Australia. Since Wallerstein's formulation of World-Systems theory, a number of scholars have attempted to apply its fundamental principles of an unequal set of economic relationships between cores and peripheries to a variety of settings in the ancient world, with varying degrees of success. Perhaps most useful here is the idea that these economic relationships across cultural boundaries have the potential to transform all societies that are part of the network.

While the majority of theorists who focus on just one or two aspects of society as primary factors in major societal changes prefer to see economics as the prime mover in cultural evolution, a few point to non-economic causes. Primary among these is Robert Carneiro (1970), whose "circumscription theory" proposed that, in areas where a populations is geographically circumscribed, meaning that environment and subsistence practices, especially agriculture, prevent people from easily moving away, warfare promotes state development. Because a defeated population is tied to its land, it must submit to its conquerors, thus expanding the amount of land and numbers of people they control. Carneiro applied this theory to early state development in Egypt, China, the Indus Valley, Mesopotamia, and parts of Peru. Scholars have expanded on Carneiro's ideas by suggesting factors beyond geography, such as social and religious ties, as responsible for circumscription.

Critiques of Complexity

Two powerful critiques of the archaeological study of complex society, from the mid-2000s, built on a growing sense of dissatisfaction with the concepts of cultural evolution and the stages proposed by Sahlins and Service. Norman Yoffee's *Myths of the Archaic State* (2005) took on the idea that early states could be characterized by a list of traits; to Yoffee, the word "complexity" itself implies intricacies of interrelationships among people and institutions that elude classification. Timothy Pauketat's *Chiefdoms and other Archaeological Delusions* (2007) makes a similar point about the difficulty and danger of making generalizations about ancient societies. Both Pauketat and Yoffee focus on "difference" as the most characteristic quality of societies; every civilization has a unique set of characteristics, and the impetuses that guided changes in societal organization worked in distinctly different ways. Complex societies can thus be hierarchical or not; hierarchically organized societies may retain and even promote heterarchical or heterogeneous aspects. Regional and historical contingencies play a significant role in the development of every culture; predictable or inevitable trajectories toward complexity are, therefore, nonexistent.

The Book in Your Hands

Keeping in mind these critiques, the book that follows is necessarily detail oriented, with attention to environmental, historical, and socioeconomic conditions that contributed to the development of complex societies. Our approach will be open-ended and bottom-up, emphasizing circumstances and conditions over direction. It is also heavily archaeological, with additional evidence provided by the written record, as these evidentiary sources provide the raw data on which reconstructions of daily life and social relationships depend.

Organization

This book is intended to provide you with a wide array of studies that will present the concepts and data for studying complexity in the ancient world. The two chapters that follow this one (Chapters 2 and 3) introduce much of the terminology of complexity and the cultural institutions (social, economic, and political) that comprise it. Chapter 3 also describes the major political systems, ranging in complexity from forager to state, and the evidentiary basis by which those categories are constructed. A final chapter in this section, Chapter 4, examines several societies whose placement into one of the four main sociopolitical categories is debated. These provide archaeologists with the opportunity to examine variability in the organization of cultural institutions, and to challenge the utility of using the blanket typology of political forms.

The bulk of this book is devoted to case studies of ancient complex societies around the globe. Chapters 5 through 7 look at the geographic regions and cultures of the Middle East and Mediterranean, areas perhaps most often noted as the "cradle(s) of civilization" and of Western political values and institutions. In Chapters 8 through 10, three south and southeast Asian regions are examined, while Chapters 11 to 13 turn to the ancient cultures of the Americas. While these areas are not the only ones that exhibited complexity in antiquity (northern and western Europe are notably absent here, as they fall outside our own areas of expertise), they provide examples from a wide range of physical environments and exhibit significant variability in the configurations of social and political institutions they possessed. A final chapter (Chapter 14), on collapse in complex societies, will make the point that full societal collapse and dissolution is a rare circumstance; more often in the ancient world, the upper echelon of political leaders may have been displaced, and some of the trappings of administration may have disappeared. But cultural systems, values, and populations remained relatively stable.

We hope that this book encourages you to explore these ancient cultures and their institutions further. An extensive bibliography at the end of the book should help.

2

HUMAN CULTURAL INSTITUTIONS

Critical Elements in Complex Society

Introduction

We use the phrase "cultural institutions," which derives from cultural anthropology, to refer to the pillars that combine to create every human culture. Although there are many "cultural institutions," including aspects of human societal structure such as art, marriage and residence patterns, and education, this chapter takes up the components that comprise the societal institutions often cited as the elements of "complexity" in ancient civilizations. Four cultural institutions, central components of human social organization, are explored here: kinship relationships and associated social relationships, religious belief systems, economic systems, including aspects of exchange patterns, and political structures. It is the latter two, economic and political systems, that are most often associated with the development of complex society, and these receive the most discussion here.

Kinship, Social Networks, and Social Differentiation

At the heart of human social institutions is kinship, which embodies far more than just who an individual considers to be "family" and who is not (Foley 2001). Primary to human societies is survival; kinship structure can serve as a critical factor in risk management activities, particularly in highly mobile or small-scale sedentary societies, in which individuals depend on cooperative family relationships for survival. Kinship relationships not only provide social identity and confer status but are also crucial for determining appropriate marriage partners and economic and political allies, and they often dictate proper methods of worship and ritual behaviors. This can then be contrasted with the types of social relationships that are more commonly found in early state societies. Though not universal, it is common for kinship ties to become less influential in state societies, while other factors that define a person's identity become far more important. The reasons for the de-emphasis on kinship are myriad and complicated and are also integrated with many other elements that can be seen as both "causing" and resulting from increasing complexity in a society.

The method of analysis used to assess the role "kinship" plays in less complex versus more complex societies draws upon studies primarily concerned with the use of resources in small scale societies, including foraging groups (Lee and DeVore 1968; but see Arnold 1993). Though there is a constellation of socioeconomic and political elements that might serve as valid comparisons, the following three are, arguably, most closely associated with kinship relations. First is *social identity*;

how is an individual's social standing perceived within a culture, and how does this correlate with kinship affiliation? Does membership in certain families confer privileged standing in the society, or is individual accomplishment (such as becoming very wealthy) of greater import? *Rights to labor and ownership of property/resources* are critical factors for survival; who has access to the products of a person's labor is a strong indicator of how a society is organized socially and economically. In most less complex societies, access to the products resulting from labor is limited to the family and sometimes the surrounding community. In more complex societies, products of labor can be controlled from outside the family circle, indicating a more complex socioeconomic and political system. Finally, kinship sometimes plays an important role in *power and politics*. The role of kinship in the growth of complex society will be explored in more detail in Chapter 3.

Religion and Ritual

Religion operates differently, is practiced differently, and means different things in societies at varying levels of complexity. Religions in less complex societies tend to be more household- and community-based, while those in complex states are usually more centralized and structured. While residents of a state may continue to conduct private rituals in their homes, they are also usually required to acknowledge and respect, and often participate in and contribute to, state rituals conducted by secular and religious elites. It is here that the strong element of control over a population's religious life emerges in the ancient (and modern) state. There is a very strong relationship between the development of the archaic state and the consolidation of power by emerging leaders; quite often some of that power emanates from the ability to control religious beliefs and practices.

Anthropologists and archaeologists have noted that a culture's religion is quite reflective of the culture itself (Steadman 2009: 47–49). For instance, a culture that relies on hunting for a significant portion of its diet, such as the Inuit who live near and within the Arctic Circle, will have a great deal of animal symbolism in their religion (Kluckholm 1942; Pelly 2001); the same would be true of a herding culture such as the Nuer of Africa who care for vast herds of cattle and whose religion revolves around cattle symbolism (Evans-Pritchard 1940). Cultures relying, therefore, on agriculture might emphasize fertility and the growth cycle in their belief system, while cultures that engage in a significant amount of warfare to defend or expand their lands would likely include a supernatural being, or at least rituals, meant to enhance their fighting skills or to protect them against attack. In the same vein, religions reflect not only a culture's subsistence or social interaction strategies but also its social complexity (Steadman 2009: 41–44).

Although not always true, it is often the case that the more stratified (economically and politically complex) a society is, the more stratified the religion, not only in the supernatural realm, but also in the actual practice of worship, ritual, and number and rank of religious leaders. Therefore, while a mobile foraging society may have a religious specialist, known in anthropology as a "shaman," who carries out spiritual activities on a part-time basis (for illness, a request of the spirits to bring rain, etc.), archaic states may practice religions that feature a supernatural pantheon containing dozens, even hundreds, of gods and goddesses all ranked hierarchically, each with their own purview over some element of the human experience. A complicated set of religious specialists, including priests and priestesses, will usually serve as full-time specialists to guide the populace in the religion. This hierarchy of religious specialists often wield a fair amount of power.

Religion is inextricably tied to a culture's other social institutions such as marriage, family, economic subsistence strategies, and, quite often, its political structure. Archaeologists can sometimes trace religion as one important catalyst to the emergence of complex society. In fact, religion can have a rather direct tie to social change (Aldenderfer 1993) and even the emergence of a state. It can be an exceedingly powerful motivator for people to act in ways that are conducive to the development of increasingly complex societies. For instance, a leader may marshal people to build a temple or to attend a ceremony never before open to commoners; at the same time as the leader is publically honoring the deity, he or she is also advancing a level of control over the people, their religion, and how it is conducted. This, in turn, can lead to other instances in which an emergent leader collects more power to accomplish tasks such as territorial enlargement, expansion of trade, control of subsistence production, and other factors that are constituent in establishing an archaic state (e.g., Spencer 2010). The most direct route to acquiring absolute power over a population is for a ruler to not only control the society's religious, political, and economic ideology but to become one with it (Blanton et al. 1996; Knapp 1988). For instance, a thousand years ago, Khmer rulers, who upon ascension to the throne declared themselves one with a Hindu god (usually Shiva or Vishnu), coerced thousands of commoners to build massive stone temples and religious compounds to acknowledge the glory of the living, divine rulers (Chapter 10). Another example comes from ancient Egypt (Chapter 6). Not only did divine pharaohs command their people to build lavish tombs for their eventual deaths, but the pharaohs' ascension to then live among the gods ensured continued worship at religious centers dedicated to them. While it is not necessary for social control to be achieved through an ideology based solely in religion—Joseph Stalin and his terrifying control of the mid-20th-century Soviet culture and its people is an excellent example of a secular ideology allowing a leader to manage every iota of his people's lives—more common is a ruler's use of religious ideology to achieve complete control.

Economic Organization

Economic institutions, like social relations, are at the root of social organization. While the modern academic discipline of economics generally deals with money and finance, the word "economics" derives from the Greek term *oikos*, meaning "household" or "family." The economy, then, is the material foundation for the health and maintenance of the household in every society.

Resources

Fundamental to the economic organization of a society, large or small, are the ways it makes use of the resources at its disposal. Resources include available subsistence goods, ecological and mineralogical materials available on the landscape, and human labor.

Subsistence and Social Complexity

Subsistence economy refers to how a society procures food. Even in the modern world, social groups may pursue a range of strategies of food procurement and production, including farming, herding, foraging, and scavenging. The degree of reliance on wild foods versus domesticated food production is really a continuum and depends on factors such as ecological conditions and environmental change, resource availability, and competition for resources.

Subsistence strategy is connected to mobility or sedentism, but this linkage is not always consistent; foraging groups tend to be more mobile than agriculturalists, but archaeological and ethnographic examples of sedentary foragers and of mobile agriculturalists abound. When foraging groups have made the transition to part- or full-time agriculture and/or pastoralism, their choices weighed factors such as climate change, which affects mobility strategies by eliminating, moving, or making available new food groups, against dietary needs and preferences (Barker 2006). Long-term investment in plots of land for crops requires seed storage for sowing, fallowing, and provision of water. These strategies foster and may grow out of a sense of territoriality or ownership of land or herds.

Raw Materials

Non-subsistence resources are those naturally occurring minerals and other materials that are esteemed as valuable by a group of people. Value is embedded in a culture's ideological and economic systems. High-value or prestige resources may be regarded as derived from gods or ancestors or may be items difficult to obtain or coming from a great distance (Helms 1993). Value may also be externally generated, imposed, or inspired by an outside group. Societies also vary in their perception of who owns natural resources. Among some foraging groups and most agriculturalists, resources belong to either the group or to some subsection of it, whether an individual, a family, occupational specialists, or a class (Ingold 1979). Ownership, as with surplus subsistence resources, can be the foundation for stratification and other forms of power. Differential access to certain materials seems to be universal to human groups but is more firmly held and ideologically supported in regional polities and states (Earle 1987, 2001; Hirth 1978).

Labor

A third category of resources is human labor, mentioned earlier. Labor denotes a social relationship: someone works for himself, or works for another person, often a family member. Although it is nearly impossible to quantify, subsistence-related labor comprises the majority of work in any society; among state-level agricultural societies, estimates run as high as 70% to 90% of total labor (Trigger 2003: 313). Among foragers, most subsistence work is done collectively and its products shared evenly. Among village agriculturalists with some form of land ownership, farming is most often done by kin in shared fields. These circumstances favor larger households, often extended family groups; shared work creates obligations among family members (Arnold 2000; Bernbeck 1995).

In societies with higher levels of complexity, land owned by institutions (royal or temple lands, for instance) will be worked by non-kin. This may require a corvée system, by which tax obligations are met through labor. Institutions might require labor for other purposes as well, including craft production, public works, and military service. These forms of labor stretch back in time as well, but in stratified societies, the products of this labor—from prestige goods to monuments to military conquest—provide ideological support for elite power. Since labor can be in shorter supply than other resources, institutions derive significant power from their ability to coerce or control labor (Arnold 2000).

Technology and Craft Production

The discussion of labor brings up another component of economic organization: the degree of craft specialization and the more general role of technology in a society. Technology may be defined as a set of means and methods to get things done. Archaeologists more often use the term "technology" to describe ways of making things that leave physical evidence, including raw materials, tools and spaces for performing a task, and finished products, which sometimes bear the marks of production processes. Technological production takes place within a cultural context, in which group membership, values, typical ways of doing things, and divisions of labor may be outside the conscious control of the person making a particular item.

Looking at technology in terms of sociopolitical complexity raises the issue of craft specialization, characterized as a person's acquisition of the skills, knowledge, and materials necessary to afford them at least part of their income from pursuits other than subsistence production. Craft specialists occur in every kind of society, but the degree of specialization within a society varies;

among the dimensions of variability are the social identities of craftspeople (sex, age, social class, ethnicity, religion); the types of items made; and the intended consumers. Some of these components are linked to complexity. The number of craft specialists within a society and the intensity of their work largely depend on the market for their products. Specialists may work independently, or be attached to leading institutions. This category (attached vs. unattached) is really a continuum: craft production for an institution may be full-time; it may be seasonal or *ad hoc;* or it could be performed in fulfillment of tax obligations (Brumfiel and Earle 1987).

A large number of productive activities may be practiced by craft specialists, although archaeologists focus on those with the greatest visibility. Ethnographic accounts caution that societies may have included categories of specialization in ritual, communication, fishing and other subsistence pursuits, transportation, music and dance, etc. Those specialties discussed most often in archaeological literature, especially on complex societies, include lithic and ceramic production, weaving and other textile production, architecture and construction, sculpture and other artistic work, woodworking, and basketry. Practitioners vary in the wealth they accrue and the status accorded them by their societies, both among the various specialties and even within a given craft.

A final technological topic to consider is change, and the correlation of technology change with, and impacts on, changes in societies. Technologies may change as part of adaptation to physical and social conditions. Groups and subgroups may invest in technology in an effort to increase their status and political position. But there is no set evolutionary movement from one technology to another, just as there is no single route from one type of social structure to another; the contexts are too variable for predictable patterns of change (Pfaffenberger 1988). Technology solves problems, extending and enhancing the human capacity to accomplish a task, whether that task has a physical or psychological result. Technology change may be imposed on a producer from the outside or developed from the inside.

Exchange

How items circulated will be discussed in each chapter that follows. Ancient methods of exchange were embedded in social relationships, as ancient economies (really, *all* economies) are interconnected with social and political institutions. Mauss's (1967) insight that exchange is a "total social fact"—created, maintained, and undone by means of particular connections among people—remains a central tenet of archaeological studies of exchange today. Compared to a state of general consensus 30 years ago, scholars today are much less willing to assume a linkage of particular methods of exchange to certain stages of sociopolitical complexity. This uncertainty is a result of richer ethnographic and historical studies as well as a more nuanced understanding of the archaeological record and its limitations. Economic transactions are embedded within particular sociopolitical relationships and strategies, no matter how complex or simple a society is judged to be. And political context is key to the determination of value, a major component within any transaction, providing a set of rules and restrictions that constrain how an object is evaluated and who may exchange it (Appadurai 1986). At the highest level of political complexity, the state, multiple types of exchange coexist, and objects may move through all the different types. At lower levels of complexity, fewer options may exist.

Methods of Exchange: Definitions and Evidence

Scholars have delineated three major modes or methods of exchange: reciprocity, redistribution, and market exchange. While most objects can circulate in any one of these ways, there are distinguishing characteristics that justify separating them. Reciprocity, a form of exchange that occurs in all societies, is giving one thing for another. It defines a relationship that is basic to humanity and grounds all social relationships. The things given can be the same or different (food for food, child care for laundry services). It is often embodied in gift-giving, but it requires no special occasion. Reciprocity should not be confused with "generosity"; a reciprocal transaction requires a sacrifice to be made by each side. Nor are the goods and services exchanged necessarily equal in value: reciprocal relationships may be balanced or unbalanced. To give is to expect something in exchange; reciprocity creates and underlies potentially long-term relationships of giving and receiving, as exemplified by the famous Polynesian Kula Ring, wherein named and famed shells are exchanged among powerful men of the islands (Munn 1986). While it usually takes place locally, it may also be the principal method of long-distance trade, especially in valuable and symbolic goods (Hastorf 1990). The Kula Ring is an example of the latter type, as was the royal gift exchange system of the Late Bronze Age eastern Mediterranean region, described in Chapter 5.

Redistribution is typical of societies with some degree of centralization. It is the extraction of subsistence, manufactured goods, and/or labor from a population in order to support the activities of administrators. Taxation is a form of redistribution; funds are collected from a population at large and mobilized, at best, on projects that are agreed upon to serve a public good: health, education, infrastructure, military activities, etc.

The final mode is market exchange, a nebulous concept that was long denied a role in antiquity. Market exchange frequently involves the exchange of goods and services for money, with prices fixed according to supply and demand, and the value of money guaranteed by a state authority. Because coinage was invented only in the mid-1st millennium BCE in the Old World, economic historians once saw no role for market exchange before the Greeks. But in fact, many societies had standard units of currency before that time, so an absence of coinage is not sufficient to deny that market exchange took place in an ancient culture.

This matter of currency is important, however, because it removes the element of trust from the transaction; participants do not have to develop a social relationship with mutual understandings and negotiation for a transaction to take place. This makes the exchange distinct from reciprocity. States may provide locales where buyers and sellers come together (marketplaces), but any physical space can be used for a market-type transaction. Cultural rules may restrict market exchange involving particular types of goods and services, guaranteeing that certain kinds of objects (and people) never become available to populations at large. The degree to which objects are commoditized—i.e., available on the market—varies widely by culture.

Barter is best understood as a variety of market exchange in which two unlike objects, whose value is agreed by the participants to be equivalent, change hands (Appadurai 1986). Like market exchange using currency, the transaction is the point of the exchange; no social relationships are enacted or sustained by the process. Barter transactions take place in nearly all societies, including those that have money and government oversight of currency. It cannot, therefore, be assumed to belong exclusively to less complex societies (Humphrey and Hugh-Jones 1992).

Economic Differentiation and Complexity

The chapters that follow will devote considerable space to the issue of economic differentiation and its ties to political complexity. Differentiation or ranking, which denotes the economic status of one person or group relative to others, combines the concepts of resource extraction (both natural and human resources), production (subsistence and non-subsistence), distribution (exchange systems), and consumption, all of which have been delineated in this section. While there is a relationship between differentiation and complexity, it is not a simple causal relationship: increased differentiation within a society does not bring about a rise in political complexity. Nor is there an easy correlation: a society with a larger number of economic classes is not necessarily more complex than one with fewer.

Built into all human relationships, and therefore all societies, is some degree of wealth inequality. This is true even of small foraging groups. Similarly, groups experience changes over time in their degree of differentiation and often have regulating mechanisms to reduce inequality (Bird and Bliege Bird 2009). Archaeologists study economic differentiation within a society, and between two periods, by using various indicators of wealth: access to rare or high-status resources and items, command over the labor of others, and efforts to display difference, particularly in public events and funerary ritual.

Inequality is rooted in human physical and intellectual differences, as well as in recognized distinctions that come from age and experience. Evidence for age- and sex-based divisions of labor, present in all groups from foragers to states, goes back to the earliest *Homo sapiens*, if not before (Kuhn and Stiner 2006). Wealth inequalities within more complex societies are however distinctly different from these more basic differences. They originate in principles of ownership or possession of land, resources, or the labor of others, which are not features of simpler societies. How these practices came about is probably different for every society (Eerkens 2009). Inequalities may also derive from social relationships, alliances within a group or with outsiders that provide an individual with enhanced access to goods and labor, to be leveraged for wealth and position (Bender 1990).

Accumulation of wealth begins as differentiation within one's kin group and then extends to unequal economic relationships with non-kin. Where it begins to cross over into political power is the capacity of those with wealth to manage, or make decisions about, a group's economic strategies. As noted earlier, power or influence in one cultural sphere (there religion, here economy) does not have to impart power in another, but the categories easily bleed together. The sorts of decisions being made about economic direction include those affecting subsistence (where and what to hunt, what land to farm and how, how much of the yield to store, and how to use surpluses); labor (on what projects to deploy it: subsistence, resource extraction, construction, or military action); technology (what innovations to support); and exchange (who to trade with, what items to make available). In more complex societies, a proportionately smaller number of people manages the economy for a larger number of non-kin (Brumfiel 1994b).

For economic inequality to become a route to political power in a society (i.e., for management of the economy to transition to long-term political leadership), with permanent positions of power, two additional factors must emerge. First, wealth must be inheritable, together with the decision-making capabilities it enables. In societies where wealth is not inherited, positions of influence and leadership are informal and dissipate after the death of their holders. Second, economic power will not be converted to political power—will not be institutionalized—without manipulation of symbols of difference and authority. Leaders must control ideology, the beliefs and representations relating to power, to maintain their positions (Gilman 1991; Hastorf 1990). Economic wherewithal is central to being able to acquire symbols of power.

Political Organization and Complexity

The final element of cultural organization and complexity that runs throughout the case studies in this book is political organization. As noted previously, political structure cannot be separated out from social and economic behaviors. But politics also means leadership, generally defined as the capacity to make and enforce decisions for a segment of society beyond one's immediate kin.

Definitions

Most scholarly studies of power define it as the ability to exert one's will and accomplish one's goals by getting other people to acquiesce. Power is therefore relational and social, and its achievement places one person over another (Foias 2013: 24). All interactions have power embedded in them.

A leader may gain consensus or may coerce others to do his or her will. Leadership requires followers, or "factions," and a leader's power is only as great as his capacity to maintain or add to his followers, rather than losing them. Most often, the decisions made by a leader have to do with the allocation of resources: natural, human, and intellectual (Kantner 2009).

Political units consist of the people who recognize the authority of one or more leaders. Units may be geographically bound, such as the populace of a state. They vary in size and in their degrees of centralization and of hierarchy; ethnographic and historical examples range from leaderless foraging bands, where all decisions are reached by consensus, to highly centralized states, like Shang Dynasty China. A major feature is how long political power may be held by one person or inherited within a dynasty. Inherited political offices are found among ranked societies but rarely among foragers and village agriculturalists.

Dimensions of Political Complexity

Complexity, typically defined in political terms, is a continuum along which societies may be arranged. But no one aspect of political organization provides the definition for complexity. For this reason, complexity may be seen in terms of three axes of variability: centralization, differentiation, and integration. Each feature, while primarily defined in political terms, impacts social and economic systems as well.

Centralization

One component of complexity is the degree of centralization of a society. This refers to the degree to which decision-making power is concentrated in society: invested in a single person or a few or dispersed across society (Foias 2013: 111). Within state-level society decision-making, at least for the state as a whole, is usually concentrated in the ultimate leader's hands (whether a singular individual or a collective entity). Centralization is also measured in terms of the geographical extent of a polity, and its population, although as with urbanism there is no strict number of settlements or people that distinguishes among a village farming group, a ranked society, and a state. More centralized political systems tend to control more land and resources than decentralized ones and have more labor at their disposal. Settlement patterns—the arrangement of sites across a landscape, and their relative sizes—are a frequent source of information for archaeologists.

Archaeologists since the 1960s have examined political organization by delineating settlement hierarchies: distributions of settlements of various sizes clustered around large sites in such a way as to maximize the efficiency of communication and movement of goods across the landscape. We may read that an ancient state society had a site size hierarchy of four or five tiers (with a city or capital at the top), while a less centralized chiefdom had only three levels of site sizes. Sedentary foragers and village agriculturalists may live in small and large villages of up to several hundred people. In ranked societies and states, mechanisms for consensus-building, decision-making, and conflict avoidance allow for the growth of significantly larger settlements (Flannery 1998). The protection offered by central authorities encourages the development of buffer zones between the settlement clusters of rival territories (Algaze 2008). In practice, these size and hierarchical categories have often proven dissatisfying, even assuming perfect representation of site sizes in the archaeological record, because they offer little understanding of practical issues of governance or the lived experience of being governed.

Differentiation

A second component of political complexity is differentiation, which refers to the number and levels of political roles within a society. Often, "differentiation" is used as a near synonym to complexity itself; at other times, scholars use the term "bureaucracy" in reference to political differentiation. At the state level, a hierarchy of political ranks may be centralized or may be spread across the territory of a polity, resulting in a less hierarchized division of roles (Foias 2013: 47).

While economic status and political rank are not the same (women, for example, may be excluded from political office while belonging to the upper class of their society), political leaders have often been drawn from the upper classes, as defined by both wealth and family background. Political ranking frequently derives from competition for prestige among individuals and groups of similar background and wealth; the winners in this competition are those able to accumulate more, and more valuable, resources (staple goods, wealth items, and labor) and to pass these privileges on to their chosen successors (Clark and Blake 1994). As differentiation and hierarchy increase, more limits are placed on who is able to hold political power and on the routes by which one may move through the ranks. Within states, ideological authority and ritual reinforcement are used to legitimate and justify individual achievement of rank (Marcus and Feinman 1998; Rowlands 1987).

Integration

A final dimension of social complexity is "integration": the interconnectedness within and between the social, political, and economic organizations within society (Pool 2012). Management or achievement of integration could also be said to be the main function of government organizations. It is probably more common to think of political leaders and institutions as integrating the economy of a land: this "political economy" would include the collection and redistribution of surplus foods, mobilization of labor, regulation of reciprocal and market exchange systems, acquisition of exotic materials from outside sources, and sponsorship of a variety of craft specialists. But social integration is just as important; political leaders employ a combination of coercive and persuasive means to bring disparate people into cooperative relationships (Sneath 2007). The distances over which leaders can integrate people are limited by topography, transport and communication technologies, and competing interest groups; these factors may have limited the size of early states (Feinman 1998).

Architecture provides a powerful signal for behaviors within a settlement and therefore serves to assimilate populations within a political organization. Monumental building projects are often connected to the emergence of central authorities and typically are carried out by commoner labor (Pauketat 2000). But monumentality is not the only mark of leadership; the presence of a range of architectural types indicates a diverse bureaucratic organization, which may include palaces, temples, and additional public administrative buildings (Redmond and Spencer 2012). Only states could collect taxes and tribute in the form of corvée labor to build palaces for rulers (Flannery 1998). Similarly, temples provided a legitimizing force for leaders (Marcus 1998).

Sociopolitical integration may be achieved by additional means. The use of coercive force—warfare and oppression—is often cited in historical sources, and interpersonal violence is sometimes attested archaeologically by mass graves containing skeletons with traumatic injuries or by incidences of human sacrifice. The threat of coercive force may sometimes be just as effective; one mark of state organization may be the maintenance of a standing army, and leaders may stress their military prowess in artwork and ritual acts. An ideological focus on "order" is the counterpart to coercion; individuals and groups are encouraged to suppress their personal goals for the good of all, guaranteeing the smooth functioning of society and even the cosmos. Social order may be depicted in ritual and art; it can be reinforced in the built environment by the repetition and standardization of buildings and spaces (Earle 1990; Rautman 2013).

Scholars have also pointed to the potential for resistance to power and to political integration. In the absence of coercive forces, people may walk away from situations where their rights are co-opted (Eerkens 2009). Communities are built through consensus, relying on a set of relationships, alliances, and shared beliefs to bring people together (Pauketat 2007: 195). Common labor projects impart material form to a community. To build cohesive larger communities, aspiring leaders must provide opportunities to develop collective identities (Pauketat 2007: 199). Within larger political units, different groups may pursue different strategies, some complying with those in power, and others resisting (Stark and Chance 2012).

Other archaeological evidence exists for integration of populations into a political unit. Writing and other administrative artifacts served to communicate and store economic and other information that was central to the success of a government (Johnson 1973). Writing was, for many societies, a development that followed the growth of a bureaucracy and one that facilitated economic integration (Steinkeller 2004). It was not, however, required, even in societies with state organization: the Inca Empire, notably, did not develop a formal writing system for record-keeping. That does not mean the Inca lacked records or a communication system; they kept elaborate mnemonic records using knotted ropes called *khipu*. In many states, however, writing was a major tool of bureaucracy, facilitating agricultural planning, tax collection, tracking of raw materials and finished products, and promoting communication among trade and political partners and dependents (R. Adams 2004; Steinkeller 2004).

Conclusion

This chapter has outlined the principal cultural institutions of human societies, and identified their main archaeological correlates. In the chapters that follow, evidence for social, religious, economic, and political structures will be highlighted and examined for the contributions each of these systems made to the development, maintenance, and decline of complexity within individual societies.

3
ANCIENT SYSTEMS
From Forager to State

Introduction

The previous chapter outlined in some detail the various human cultural institutions that are the building blocks to ancient, and present-day, societies: kinship and social relations, religion, economy, and political structures. This chapter is devoted to interrogating the role that these human social institutions played in the emergence of civilization. It is too simplistic to say that any given social institutions "caused" civilization to happen; nor is it correct to say they were simply impacted by social factors as more complex societies emerged. Rather, the interactive nature of human actions and perceptions, as they relate to family, belief, economic organization, and political structure, were intricately interwoven into the fabric that made up "civilization" in the ancient world.

Archaeologists continually grapple with the concept of "complex society" and all it entails. When does a society officially become "complex," and what makes it so? In large part, that is a question this book seeks to address. Most anthropologists and archaeologists acknowledge that large regional polities, which can be labeled "chiefdoms" in some contexts, fall into the "complex" category, and of course, archaic states are the epitome of such in the ancient world. Conversely, cultures that practice a hunting-and-gathering economy, also known as "foraging groups," have political and economic structures that are generally viewed as resting at the opposite end of the "complexity" continuum from states. Falling somewhere between foraging group and regional polity are the sociopolitical structures found in cultures living in small and medium villages with economies based on farming and animal husbandry. It is these four very broad socioeconomic and political structures that will be briefly described here.

Chapter 2 outlined the differences between non-centralized and centralized political systems, the former including foragers/hunter-gatherers and village-based societies and the latter including regional polities/chiefdoms and states. Standard anthropological thinking identifies foraging groups as the least complex with regard to these cultural institutions, with states at the opposite end of the complexity spectrum. The following sections explore each of these social institutions as they are constituted in terms of human social structures that range from those typically identified as less, or more, or most, complex.

Mobile Foraging Groups

Societies that practice the hunting and gathering of wild game and plants typically practice some level of mobility so as not to over-exploit any particular landscape. Mobile foraging societies are also usually described as "egalitarian," referring to the practice of complete equality regarding social status and distribution of power; while true on some level, there are various ways to be "egalitarian" and still practice social differentiation. Foraging groups are necessarily small, usually no more than 50 individuals but more usually consisting of 20–30 members, and are typically comprised of extended family groups related through blood and marriage ties.

Kinship and Mobile Foraging Groups

Kinship is the primary social bond between individuals, and it is the main factor determining the formation of a group. Individuals define their own social identity through their kinship ties and gauge their relationship to others according to what is often a complex system of close versus more distant family connections. Even strangers, such as anthropologists, are eventually incorporated into the kinship system (Lee 1984: 56–57). Kinship relations form the basis of survival for all hunter-gatherers in that interdependence on kin members for adequate subsistence provision is at the heart of daily activities.

Economic Strategies and Mobile Foraging Groups

Foraging societies must engage in risk management strategies in order to ensure subsistence provision. Mobility is one key since groups can move more frequently if resource availability (due to drought or other environmental factors) is deficient (Gregg 1988). In truly egalitarian foraging societies, all members have equal rights to every group member's labor. In foraging cultures where close family (nuclear or extended family groups) cooperate more closely within the larger camp, all family members have rights to each other's labor, but the entire camp participates in cooperative relationships to ensure group survival (Leacock 1982). Resources in mobile foraging societies consist of natural food sources (plant and animal) and materials necessary for tools, weapons, and craft-making. Typically in such societies, all members have equal access to any resources, though exploitation may be gender-based, i.e., males hunt the animals and acquire stone for tools and weapons, women gather plants for food and make items such as reed baskets. Surplus is not a factor in mobile foraging societies since it would be a detriment rather than a positive feature. If occasional surpluses are acquired by some, they are then shared by all.

Power, Political Standing, and Mobile Foraging Groups

While the foregoing describes the traditional view of foraging groups, ethnographic work has determined that larger groups of more sedentary "complex foragers" may in fact possess individually owned equipment for food processing technologies and engage in surplus storage (Bettinger 2001). Such practices can result in social inequality even in foraging groups (Flannery and Marcus 2012: 67–74). For instance, if excess food is kept or controlled by one or just a few people, they may choose to deploy it for purposes other than long-term community welfare. A surplus may be used, instead, to create or maintain social relationships outside the community, with prestige accruing to the surplus-holder (Bender 1990; Hayden 1995).

Religion and Mobile Foraging Groups

Religious belief systems in foraging societies are usually tied strongly to subsistence strategies and the elements that are critical to survival. There is little hierarchy in hunter-gatherer religions, in either the supernatural or human worlds. Religious specialists, termed "shamans" by anthropologists, do not necessarily command greater power or prestige than non-shamans, and there is rarely a set of strictly ranked gods or spirits in whom the people believe. The supernatural world is largely reflective of the human one. There may be individualized spirits, or gods, who have duties to perform for the people, and/or collective spirits, who are meant to protect the people and guide their behavior. In general, all of these receive attention through ritual performance and other activities, and all are considered important within the belief system. The type of hierarchical order of supernatural beings found in more complex societies (e.g., Classical Greek religion) is largely lacking in hunter-gatherer societies.

Small-Scale Sedentary Villages

The social dynamics change in significant ways in cultures that typically practice small-scale cultivation as their subsistence practice, accompanied by hunting and sometimes basic animal husbandry. Many cultures that practice horticulture or small-scale farming live in more permanent settings in order to tend their crops. Though they may practice "shifting cultivation" (cultivating different fields every few years, sometimes accompanied by residential relocation), they still live together in small hamlets or villages for extended periods; individual and group mobility is thus reduced significantly (Bocek 1991). While populations in villages vary, the numbers tend to range in the hundreds rather than the dozens. Village structure, organized along kinship lines, consists of households (of either nuclear or extended families) of cooperating individuals who possess a variety of material goods, including cultivation tools, crafts, weapons, and other items associated with sedentary living. These material possessions are essentially owned by the members in each household rather than shared across the village.

Farming societies, as well as nomadic pastoralists, have some degree of complexity. How much depends on group size and mobility and on other resource issues. Decision-making methods vary in these societies; significant subsistence-related choices may include whether to intensify production to cope with increased population and demand or to split a community and relocate at times of food scarcity. The development of leadership structures is rooted in predictable subsistence production, but other features play into it. The foundations of economic inequality among agriculturalists rest, in part, in differences in land and soil quality, which can lead to differences in food production. With better land, some families will be able to produce larger surpluses, and perhaps grow different kinds of crops, producing an advantage over others within the society. This occurs in areas where land is not held in common, but where individual families have rights to specific parcels of land. The environments in which agriculture developed and the particular crops on which it was grounded vary significantly.

Kinship and Small-Scale Sedentary Village Structures

Who your close family is becomes somewhat more important in small-scale sedentary societies than in mobile foraging groups. Family ties are more solidified since people are required to remain permanent members of the household production group (except when adult children, usually daughters, marry and leave for a spouse's household). Village populations often consist of several kinship groups (unilineal descent groups, for instance). Social identity therefore may consist of several levels, the primary being with the family with whom an individual lives and works, secondarily with other kin members living in other households in the village, and finally with other kin members in other villages (Gregg 1988: 24–25). Such ties may be complicated, however, by interpolitical issues where loyalties must lie with the village leader rather than with kin members in outside settings. Coupled with kinship membership is the family's position in the village. The village residents may view a member of the tribal leader's family as possessing greater importance in the village than someone from a different kinship group; the same may be true for a member of a "wealthy" family (possessing more gardens or domesticated animals) than for a member from less fortunate circumstances. In small-scale sedentary villages, therefore, one's social identity is significantly defined by kinship affiliation, but societal position may also confer an element of status to individual social identity.

Economic Strategies and Small-Scale Sedentary Village Structures

Rules of land tenure and ownership vary widely between settled and partially or fully mobile societies. Collective land ownership tends to appear among foragers and village agriculturalists, while private land ownership is a feature of some village agriculturalists, regional polities, and states, as is described later. Risk management strategies are quite different in sedentary villages than in mobile foraging groups. Residents must be careful regarding resource exploitation, leading to a far more rigorous regulation of access to resources. Products from gardens and fields, domestic animals, and hunting expeditions, are typically not shared across the village but rather are individual to each household or kinship group (Hegmon 1991). To this end, family relations become a critical factor for ensuring adequate subsistence and protecting access to vital resources. Most small-scale sedentary villages are made up of family groups with each group cooperating in production and consumption activities. Family members must depend on each other to successfully carry out all subsistence activities as well as to produce household crafts, tools, and weapons. Family cohesion is at the crux of successful risk management.

While the Western concept of real estate ownership is usually absent in small-scale sedentary societies, there are strong notions of territoriality and precedent regarding the kin-group exploitation of certain gardens or crop lands and the products from the animals that they raise (Earle 1991a: 73). There is a strong perception of rights to property and the products from that property as belonging to individual households; sharing may take place between kin-related households but not usually outside of the kin or clan group (Johnson and Earle 1987: 131–52). Surplus is desirable and varied; households with greater access to cultivatable lands and who can raise and keep more domestic animals can generate greater surpluses, making them "wealthier" within the village. Surpluses may be given to non-kin residents in order to facilitate political purposes (feasts, trade, "loans" to create debtors and thus supporters) or may be shared exclusively among kin within the village in order to elevate the standing of the entire kin lineage. Property and resources are an integral element of social identity in sedentary villages.

Power, Political Standing, and Sedentary Village Structures

The political structure in small sedentary villages is often referred to as "tribal" (Parkinson 2002), in which there is an informally acknowledged leader who has no permanent authority but who is considered "exceptional" by fellow residents (Johnson and Earle 1987: 102); the acknowledged leader generally has influence only in his or her own village. Such leaders come to the fore by gaining the respect and trust of their fellow residents and by having attributes that are admired in the culture (e.g., superior warrior skills, a soaring oratory, wealth, and so forth). Problems such as theft, adultery, accusations of sorcery, and other issues may be taken to the tribal leader (and sometimes to a council of elders) for adjudication. Leadership may shift at any time depending on the attitudes of residents and individual abilities of other community members vying for the leadership role.

In villages with tribal political structures, there is some ranking between individuals. The tribal leader and anyone in his or her household tend to have access to somewhat greater levels of power in the village, mainly in the form of influence, and may have greater access to wealth (through gifts, superior trade opportunities, more preferential marriages, etc.). In small-scale villages social differentiation with respect to wealth and power, though at fairly minimal levels, has become a consistent element in the socioeconomic and political fabric of daily life.

Small-Scale Sedentary Villages: Household and Community Religion

Defining a "type" of religion in small-scale sedentary villages is essentially impossible as belief systems are as numerous and diverse as cultures. A few generalities can be sketched here to offer a serviceable outline of religious practices in small-scale societies. Every culture possesses a "worldview," which may also be termed its "cosmology"; a culture's cosmology comprises how the members of that culture perceive the reality of the world around them, how it came into being, and why. In small-scale cultures, such as those that practice herding and horticulture agriculture, anthropologists typically find what can be termed a "naturalistic" worldview, meaning the societal members view themselves as operating within the natural world, which would include the physical world of plants and animals and "supernatural" aspects such as spirits. In a society that possesses a naturalistic worldview, proper behaviors with regard to the natural and supernatural world are absolutely necessary to maintain harmony and balance.

Ritual practices in small-scale society take place both in the natural landscape and within the community. For instance, a household shrine, dedicated to the residents' ancestors, might be found in every home in a farming society; alternatively, a hunter may perform a ritual after a successful kill in order to maintain balance and harmony (Anderson 1991). There is generally little ranking regarding who has access to what ritual activities, with the exception of household ceremonies limited to family members.

Though village residents conduct or participate in much of religious ritual in small-scale societies, as noted earlier, there are usually religious specialists, or shamans, present to aid people in their religious concerns. Some cultures have only one or a few shamans per village or region, and others have as many as wish to engage in shamanistic duties. Shamans are generally residents of the community they serve and usually carry out daily activities just like everyone else; it is only when their services are called upon that they may transform into religious practitioners, often donning a costume, using medicines and potions and possibly musical instruments, and typically entering a trance to carry out their work (Steadman 2009). The shaman's role in small-scale society is diverse; most commonly shamans are called upon to heal illness and to fix problems caused either by the supernatural world or by sorcery cast by enemies (in some societies, shamans also have the ability to cast the sorcerous curse at the bidding of a client or according to the shaman's own agenda). The shaman's role is to serve the community through healing the ill and solving acute problems by interacting with the supernatural world. In small-scale sedentary villages, the practice of religion and ritual is largely undifferentiated among residents; all are eligible to participate (sometimes according to gender- or age-based rules) and all generally do. As will be seen later, religions found in full-fledged archaic states contrast considerably with religious practices described earlier.

The Regional Polity (Chiefdom)

The regional polity—in some parlance, the "supra-local community" (Drennen and Peterson 2012) or the "chiefdom" (Chapman 2003; Earle 1991b; Wright 1977; but see Pauketat 2007)—is a larger and far more populous entity than the sedentary village (Feinman 1998). While the latter is generally autonomous with an informal leader, the regional polity is constituted by a collection of villages and towns, often with one central locale where the acknowledged leader resides. The economic system, however, still relies primarily on agriculture. There is a very wide array of socioeconomic and political structures that can be labeled "chiefdoms" or regional polities, ranging from a system not much larger than a single village to what some would term an agrarian state (e.g., the Mississippian Culture [Chapter 11]; Pauketat 2007). Though wide-ranging in scope and structure, there are some similarities in these systems that will allow a general description here.

Regional polity systems appear to emerge when there are significant economic, environmental, or social problems that need to be resolved on a regular basis (Earle 1991b). Such problems might include population growth and food management, varying climates that threaten drought or reduced agricultural output, concern over hostile attack, or other issues that would affect an entire population. Solutions to such problems, undertaken by emergent leaders, might require the organization of labor beyond household management in order to ensure economic solvency, regular food supplies, a defense system, and so forth (Arnold 1993). This process relates directly to risk management. A community facing widespread crises (crop failures, attack) may turn to the leadership to solve the problems. Once leaders have demonstrated their ability to solve critical societal problems, they can engage in power consolidation that elevates their status in the community and establishes their control over important sociopolitical processes such as goods production, trade, warfare and defense, surplus acquisition and distribution, and religious matters (Carneiro 1981; Chapman 2003; Crumley 1995; Wright 1977).

Regional polities are typically socially stratified, with elites, the clergy, and sometimes warriors and merchants in the upper echelon of society, and craft-makers, farmers, herders, and those encumbered in circumscription (e.g., slavery or other forms of structured servitude) generally in the lower levels. Leaders in such societies may be elected by popular vote, selected by a council, or may attain their position through a hereditary process. Family ties, therefore, can be a critical factor among elites in some regional polities (Johnson and Earle 1987: 225–26).

Kinship and the Regional Polity

Kinship remains important for identity at the regional polity level, but it is joined by other aspects that partially dilute, but simultaneously enhance, the importance of family relations. Population numbers in the thousands, even tens of thousands, preclude everyone knowing everyone else, their family relationships, their status in the village system, and who their marriage connections are. Therefore, when members of a regional polity encounter one another, other identifiers may be as relevant, if not more so, than who one's family is, such as what village, hamlet, or town does one hail from; what work does one perform (farmer, warrior, servant) and thus, perhaps, what social stratum does one inhabit; or what religion does one practice?

However, family relations are critical in polities in which the transmission of critical wealth, property, or power through lines of inheritance is paramount. Similarly, at the upper echelon of the society, one's kinship ties with elites and the ruling class likely confer benefits and thereby stand as an important social identifier, carrying with it access to prestige, power, and most likely wealth. Thus, in the case of this more complex and stratified sociopolitical system, kinship becomes a critical element in social identity for a very few people at the pinnacle of society but is de-emphasized to only one of many elements used to place the majority of individual residents within proper societal context.

Economic Structures and the Regional Polity

Different regional polities treat property and associated labor in different ways; in some societies, the "chief" owns all the property and thus has rights to all the labor carried out upon it (Earle 1991a). It is perhaps best to describe an individual's rights to labor as no longer exclusively within the realm of providing solely for kin relations. Leaving aside those in categories designated as "enslaved" or some other structured servitude, in a broad sense, all members in a regional polity or chiefdom have rights to everyone else's labor; this is effectively carried out in a more narrow process through the payment of tax, tribute, tithe, or donated labor, to the chief, leader(s), or polity (Kristiansen 1991). Rights to labor might include the requirement that farmers, artisans, and other workers give up a portion of their product to the leadership or convert these products to whatever currency operates in that system and hand that over; alternatively, males (or even females) from some or all families may be required to serve the polity as warriors, builders, or in other capacities required by the leaders. This system is termed "redistributive" in that an acknowledged leader gathers donations from all the people in the system and redistributes them according to need. This system allows the leadership to extract surpluses from the population as a whole and to redistribute them as it sees fit; surpluses also support an administrative class that does not produce its own food. While required "donations" are intended to support all members of the polity, they also serve to increase the wealth and power base of the leader(s).

Power, Political Standing, and the Regional Polity

As should be clear at this point, family affiliation for commoners offers little in the way of access to power or status in the regional polity. This is quite different from members of kinship systems in which it is indeed one's position vis-à-vis the leader that determines the possession of power and status within the sociopolitical structure. While there are often descending levels of leadership positions in regional polities, such as a council of elders from outlying regions, the selection of council members may not depend on their family position but rather on their level of wealth or perhaps on whether they offered consistent support to the sitting leader prior to and during attainment of the position. Of critical importance to the attainment of power are strategies designed to illustrate that leaders and elites are in control of the maintenance and success of the regional polity. These methods include collecting tax/tribute to create a surplus, establishing (and controlling) external trade systems, creating methods for defense against attack, establishing regulations to control unwanted and criminal behavior within the polity, and constructing an intimate connection with the religious belief system (Earle 1991b: 5–10; Wright 1977). These strategies not only firmly establish a leader's position but also create opportunities for attaining greater wealth and power.

Religious Systems and the Regional Polity

In regional polities, or chiefdoms, ritual and belief may still be practiced within the homes, but most often, there is also a "public" religion, one that centers on aspects critical to the health of the people and their economy and general welfare. It is usually the case that in the more public religions—which may include community-wide ceremonies and rituals at which all are welcome, or more private rituals in a temple or sacred building carried out *on behalf of* the people—the chief or polity leader either is the lead practitioner at the ceremony or is intimately involved. In fact, religion is often very successfully used as a vehicle to leadership positions (Kantner 2009). There are several examples of such circumstances in this book (e.g., Khmer, Mississippian, Mesoamerican), in which leaders gained ultimate power in part through their role in the religious realm. It is in regional polities/chiefdoms that the groundwork for acquiring leadership positions through religious avenues can often be most clearly seen.

Religion and ritual carried out in the home is often that which is deeply culturally embedded: ancestor veneration, fertility rituals associated with animals or agricultural endeavors, healing rituals, actions that meet the daily needs of the commoners. The more public face of religion, led by the chief or leadership council, or the priests at the behest of the chief, usually deals more specifically with issues that affect the polity. Shamans, far more common in foraging and small-scale agricultural communities as the main religious specialists, are no longer at the center of religious practice in the chiefdom community and have more often been marginalized to become solely the healers or to work with small groups at the household level.

At the public level, ceremonies and rituals, whether held with the intention of community-wide attendance, or privately held but on behalf of the community, are usually dedicated to issues that are of considerable concern to both leaders and community members. For instance, if the practice of warfare, either in a more aggressive, expansionist attitude or in a defensive approach, is of importance to the society, then it is likely that ceremonies and rituals to supernatural deities associated with war will be conducted by the chief and/or upper-echelon priests rather than by people in their homes. Agricultural fertility, while perhaps a household-based matter, may also become a concern of the polity and public, and "important" rituals may be carried out by the chief or priests (see, for instance, the adoption of agricultural ritual by Mississippian leaders in Chapter 11). Chiefs who sit at the pinnacle of the political, economic, and religious roles in their societies can wield a significant amount of power over their own people and even surrounding territories. In some circumstances, a chief who also serves as ritual leader may be more widely known for his religious leadership than for the political control of his chiefdom (Kusimba and Kusimba 2009). He may even be invited to another chiefdom to lead a ceremony if his "expertise" is deemed necessary and desirable. Such fame may even lead to greater political power over larger regions.

The Archaic State

In many ways, a state is an intensified chiefdom/regional polity; the elements present in the regional polity are often larger and more complicated in an archaic state. States are generally the largest political entities, though this is not always the case as a "city-state" may be smaller in area than a regional polity. In nearly all cases, the population is larger than that found in regional polities (see Chapter 5 on Mesopotamia), with numbers ranging in the hundreds of thousands or more (Feinman 1998); anonymity is at far higher levels, and state residents often encounter many more strangers than acquaintances on any given day. There are typically more levels of governance, which may be structured vertically (from leader on down) or more horizontally in that members of administration, clergy, and possibly the military may all be internally ranked. That there is a military or warrior class is nearly a given in a state society, along with all the other occupational groups (merchants, artisans, farmers, etc.) found in the regional polity. Monumental architecture, for both public and private elite use, is common in such societies. Writing or some form of record-keeping is also found, as is a mechanism for recording the acquisition and distribution of goods flowing into and out of major centers, activities that drive a robust market economy.

Kinship and the Archaic State

In a state society, the population density requires frequent interaction with greater numbers of people on a daily basis, but encounters are often more fleeting than in less complex societies (Drennan and Peterson 2012). Maintaining long-term social ties with strangers, merchants, and those encountered on the street, except in the moment of interaction, is unnecessary, and thus recognizing each person's social identity is not relevant. People may be "pegged" as to ethnicity or perhaps class by strangers briefly interacting with them, but their social identity vis-à-vis kin relationships are largely irrelevant. The complex economic and political construction of state societies elevates the importance of what "job" one holds over who one's relations are. Those at the lower echelon of society may simply be "cogs in the wheel" of the state machinery (Wright 1977) with their immediate superiors hardly knowing more than a worker's name and how many days were worked.

In states, who your family is remains an important element in the elite classes since inheritance rights and status may be linked to kinship affiliation, including an eventual pathway to the pinnacle of political power. While inheritance customs surely operated at all levels of society, those who populated the "commoner" classes had far less to pass on, and what was available did not, in most cases, convey power and status to inheritors (in fact, in some states, what they inherited was the burden of continued work as a corvée laborer in the same place as their parent and grandparent). Though kinship is not a major factor in the creation of states, it can be a critical pathway to power once those states are created, but only for elites and leaders. For the commoners, kinship ties become relegated to only one of many aspects of social identity and are often largely nullified as critical factors in property and resource ownership.

Economic Structures and the Archaic State

States emerge for similar reasons to regional polities through a combination of risk management concerns and power accumulation tactics undertaken by elites and leaders (Fargher and Blanton 2007). The redistribution of goods, which is somewhat transparent in a regional polity, becomes far more complicated and opaque in a state system. For instance, one common process in states is the usurpation of benefits originally meant as "insurance" against future crises (Roscoe 2000). Goods and services, originally meant for redistribution to the people, might be absorbed by the state to elevate the wealth and power of the elites who may then extend their power to exploit workers for their own gains or even coerce additional labor for state/elite projects.

Land and property management, and ownership, is incredibly varied in states, but there is some consistency in that elites are often the owners of large tracts of land and vast estates; the state and other institutions, such as temples, generally own or at least manage productive land, and private ownership of land may be limited to those higher up on the political and social hierarchical ladders (Earle 2000). Therefore, those who actually produce subsistence goods often work on lands or live in homes that belong either to the state or to a wealthy elite. Risk management strategies, then, are oriented toward protecting the state against a crisis such as invasion or usurpation of elite power. That everyone may depend on the state for support in lean times is a given within state society and is in essence one of the main reasons for the emergence of the state. However, the state is too large and complicated to keep track of individual household welfare, and many fell into poverty or dependence in ancient agrarian states.

As is essentially the case in nearly every human society, family members within a state maintain the rights to each other's labor to aid in subsistence. However, there may be a number of other individuals or entities who have rights to any given person's labor in a state. The family who farms state- or elite-owned land is obligated to provide products to the owner. A state system that levies a tax on its people has, in effect, rights to their labor; in the same vein, a state system that demands military service in times of crisis also holds rights to the labor of those potential soldiers (Drennan and Peterson 2012). In a state society, any number of people may have claims to the products of an individual's labor far beyond the basic need to provide for kin relations.

Power, Political Standing, and the Archaic State

As was the case in regional polities, except in the elite classes, kin relationships are not a typical pathway to positions of status and power except among elites, especially in dynastic leadership systems. In most state-level societies, the only leadership potential afforded by family relationships is as head of household, which may confer decision-making power about household economics, marriage choices, and household ritual practice, but the only people who are governed by such decisions are family or household members themselves. It is most often the case that, in states, kinship is important only to those one lives with and relies upon within the confines of the household.

Another critical element necessary for measuring the power and the political standing of individuals within an archaic state is that of political scale. Urbanism appears to be a by-product of the centralization of leadership, as leaders provide protection, opportunities for work, materials acquired through trade, and locales for worship (Yoffee 2005: 54). Archaeologically, nucleated settlements may be marked by dense occupation, fortifications, and evidence for economic activities beyond self-sufficient subsistence. The physical grouping of institutions within an urban center increases efficiency and control over the movement of resources and people.

An archaic state generally has at least one urban center at its apex, likely where the supreme leader resides, with a smattering, or sometimes a profusion, of surrounding towns, villages, and hamlets across the landscape, all looking to a central place for leadership in economic, religious, social, and other core elements of society. It is often the case that the larger the geographical extent, the more powerful the archaic state. It stands to reason that the more people living within the confines of that state, the more robust it can potentially be in terms of economic productivity. The more people resident in a state, the greater the variety of activities that can be performed in terms of craft production, trade, subsistence strategies, and service to upper echelons within the society.

A further correlate is that the more individuals present within a state society, the more differentiation there will be within that society. Evidence for differentiation is often quite straightforward in societies with writing, itself a product of state-level political organization. An analysis of Classic-Period Maya inscriptions, for example, reveals a variety of administrative titles and roles, and the principles by which they were ranked and interconnected (Foias 2013). Yet social and economic hierarchies are created in the first place by leaders who reward supporters for loyalty. Material rewards, visible archaeologically, might include larger, more ornate, or better-built residences and symbols of rank, often carried or worn to draw attention to the possessor (DeMarrais, Castillo, and Earle 1996; Foias 2013; Redmond and Spencer 2012). These objects might be created by specialists in prestige goods production, like feather cloak makers in Hawaii (see Chapter 4), metallurgists in early Peru, and painted ceramic specialists among the Maya (Lass 1998).

Related to the notion of differentiation is that of "integration," raised in Chapter 2. This refers to the interconnections between every level of society within an archaic state. For instance, large storage facilities for staple goods, found often in the largest settlement in an area, suggest a central authority that collects taxes and uses the surplus to feed its dependents. In ancient Egypt, royal lands were spread across the country; yields from these lands were kept in the provincial centers in large granaries (Baines and Yoffee 1998). Political leaders may also coordinate trade with outside partners; exotic goods would be found especially in association with palaces and elite buildings. Discovery of craft workshops producing prestige goods indicates an integrative role of political leaders, as can market spaces, often sponsored by elite patrons to serve the provisioning needs of the populace. Aspiring leaders also deploy generosity, often in the form of gift-giving and feast-hosting, to display their largess and worthiness and to gather people to their cause; evidence for feasting includes large deposits of serving and cooking vessels. Integration can also occur in large-scale public secular and religious ceremonies, carried out by leaders and elites, and attended by the populace. This encourages cooperation by the lower classes who may be called upon to help build and maintain public architectural structures dedicated to the good of the society. In fact, the role of religion can be a central element in how a leader, or group of leaders, both maintain and exert control over a vast population across an expansive landscape.

Religion in the Archaic State

Religious practice in state systems is, predictably, far more complicated and often more restrictive than for less complex societies. Differences include the location and structure of rituals, the type of religious specialists typically found, and even the supernatural beings in the cosmology. The best place to begin defining the differences between religions found in small-scale societies and archaic states is perhaps with the worldview. The naturalistic worldview so common in small-scale societies is not typical in state societies; rather state worldviews are far more hierarchical with members of an archaic state identifying their placement within the universe as below their gods but often perceiving themselves as more important than, and even the masters of, the natural environment around them. The worldview defines how the religion in a state system is structured. This hierarchy extends, not only to how the humans see themselves vis-à-vis their gods and their environment, but also to how societal members are ranked as regards social and religious importance.

Religion in a state system usually has exceedingly formalized elements including where and when rituals should take place, who should conduct them (and who may attend), how one may worship, and so forth. In contrast to small-scale societies, many elements in a state religion have undergone a process of "materialization" (DeMarrais, Castillo, and Earle 1996), meaning that visual symbols in the form of monuments, written documents, formalized ceremonies, and icons have become the norm. These manifestations are generated and controlled by the state, either by the rulers themselves, including the elites, or by the high-ranking personnel in charge of religious matters. In this way, religion and ritual may be controlled, and even manipulated, by those in power, and a standard "state" ideology can be proffered to the people. State-sponsored values can be reinforced in the performance of rituals and ceremonies, the display of symbols and icons, and the construction of religious monuments and buildings.

In a state system, there may be several categories of ritual practice, ranging from state-sponsored rituals performed according to a religious calendar, to household-based rituals dedicated to ancestors or other family found in small-scale societies. In many cases, leaders and elites seek to limit private household ritual since it might serve to distract the commoners from religious concerns controlled and managed by the state. For instance, elites in the pre-Columbian Mississippian culture, discussed in Chapter 11, appear to have slowly usurped agrarian fertility rituals, removing them from household performance and placing them under the purview of the leadership structure (Mehrer 1995). Thus, rituals and beliefs once under the control of agrarian farmers in their households and communities became part of a "state-controlled" religious cycle with the most prominent "worshippers" being the elites and leaders (Emerson 1997a).

The theme of the leader and elites being critical players in successful religious ritual and the ultimate success and favor of the supernatural world (and therefore health and security of the human one) is exceedingly common in state religions. A number of examples can be found in this volume: the singular role the Great Zimbabwean leader plays in communicating with the ultimate deity (see Chapter 4), the leading position elites in Mississippian society held in the centralized major rituals (Chapter 11), and the importance of elite blood sacrifice to please Mesoamerican gods (Chapter 12). Perhaps the best illustrations are found in the ancient Khmer and Egyptian Empires in which the kings were divine and could command vast quantities of labor from their peoples to ensure a content supernatural realm (Chapters 6 and 10). In each of these cultures, the role of the elites, and particularly of the state leader(s), is a critical element to the health and welfare of the general population.

Standing alongside leaders in archaic states, and often wielding nearly as much power, are other religious specialists. The anthropological term for practitioners typically operating in state religions is "priests" (or priestesses), which connotes formally trained, permanent religious specialists who often live in or near sacred centers such as temples or shrines (Steadman 2009). Priests are full-time specialists and often wear garb or carry accoutrements that mark them as important religious figures. Priestly duties are often dictated by a proscribed calendar and even a set of written instructions such as might be found in a holy text (if the culture is literate). There are usually multiple priests in a state system overseeing different elements of religious life, and often they are ranked. Priests could, in certain circumstances, wield significant power in guiding critical acts made by a secular leader; decisions dealing with life and death such as whether to wage war, to delay a harvest, or to force commoners to build a major monument could be decided by priests rather than rulers.

The religious systems found in archaic states are, like the sociopolitical systems in the states themselves, usually quite hierarchical, with ranked levels of both deities and religious specialists. The state regulates, through its priests, most if not all of the rituals required to serve the supernatural order, and commoners and elites alike have their proscribed roles to play, guided by the priests, to ensure continued health and welfare of both self and society through ritual participation. Religious monuments are central to the belief system and serve to control the movement and participation of the parishioners, allowing secular and religious leaders to either perform rites in secret or to publically reward commoners, both according to the dictates of the supernatural order and designed to highlight the ultimate importance of state (religious and secular) leaders as intermediaries between the supernatural world and the populace. Control of the religious experience in a state system is firmly in the hands of leaders and elites, with commoners relegated to relying on their leaders to ensure health, welfare, and prosperity for all.

Conclusions

While this chapter has described the particular forms of political organization most often used by archaeologists and anthropologists in categorizing ancient and contemporary societies, it has by no means been exhaustive in attempting to convey the variability provided by archaeological and textual evidence from antiquity and by ethnographic accounts. Precise combinations of political, economic, social, and religious institutions indicate that social life and relationships in the past and present are richly varied. That variability has presented special challenges when turning to "borderline cases" of complexity, as described in the following chapter.

4

SCALES OF COMPLEXITY

Case Studies

Introduction

The previous chapters offered overviews of the components that constitute "complexity" in the context of differing types of societies, ranging from mobile hunter-gatherers to village dwellers and state systems. One of the greatest challenges archaeologists encounter is attempting to define the difference between a complex chiefdom, or, as designated in Chapter 3, a regional polity, and a state-level society. It isn't uncommon for different archaeologists studying the same ancient culture to have differing opinions as to the level of complexity found in an ancient system. The four case studies presented in this chapter serve a dual purpose: they offer descriptions of ancient cultures that fit complexity levels ranging from simple chiefdom to incipient state, and they highlight cultural institutions that allowed leaders to ascend to power and sociopolitical complexity to develop.

Great Zimbabwe in Africa: Religion at the Helm

The Kingdom of Great Zimbabwe, resting on a plateau between the Limpopo and Zambezi Rivers in southeastern Africa (Figure 4.1), is an excellent example of how religion and power are inextricably tied in a regional polity. The previous sentence used both "kingdom," which is the term used in local ethnographic tradition for this ancient culture, and "regional polity," which suggests that Great Zimbabwe was more chiefdom than state. Some have argued that Great Zimbabwe was in fact an early state (Kim and Kusimba 2008; Pikirayi 2001). In part, this assessment is based on the status of Great Zimbabwe as a major trade center in the 14th century CE and the identification of its spectacular stone structures as palaces (Chirikure and Pikirayi 2008; Pikirayi and Chirikure 2011). However, this latter interpretation has been staunchly refuted (Huffman 2010a, 2010b, 2011). It is also argued that, while the king and wealthy elites did indeed direct trade and that the Great Zimbabwe settlement hosted a thriving market economy, the sociopolitical and economic structures, and the class structure, cannot be defined as belonging to a "state-level society" (Huffman 2010a; Pwiti 2004) but rather a complex chiefdom.

Great Zimbabwe Origins

Reaching a zenith in the 14th century CE, Great Zimbabwe is named for the over 300 stone enclosures (Figure 4.2) called *zimbabwe*, which translates to "ritual seat of a king" or, more generally, to

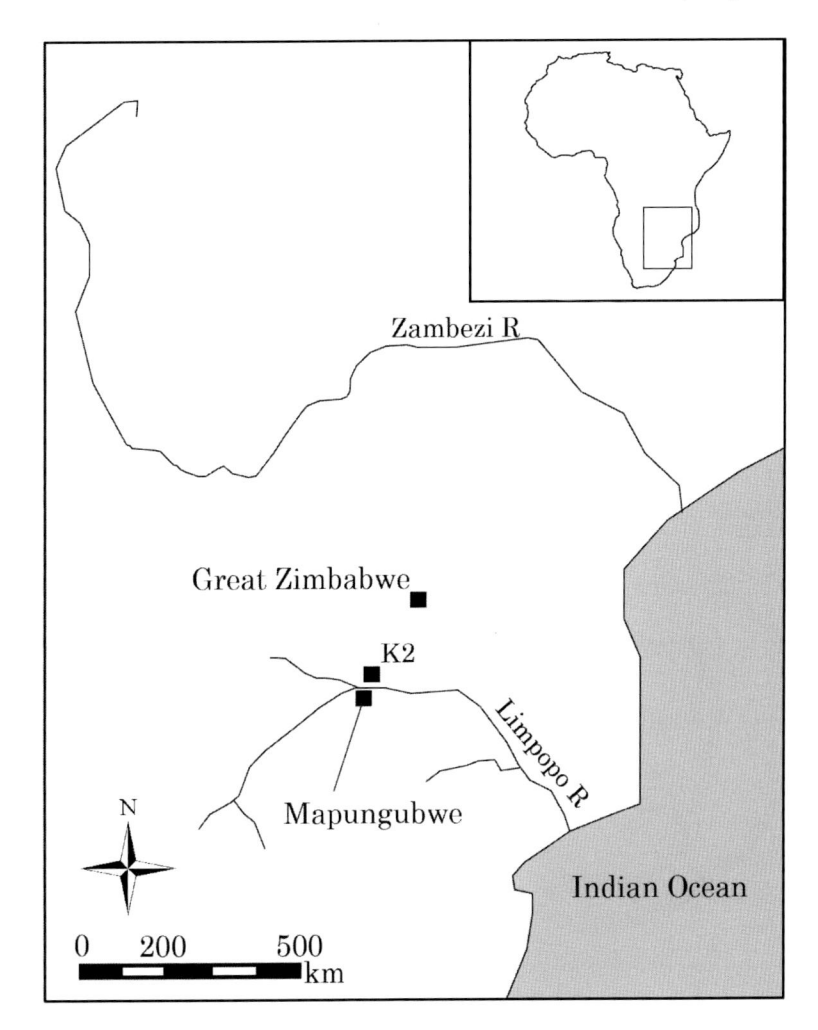

FIGURE 4.1 Map of Southern Africa and Sites Discussed in the Text

Source: S.R. Steadman

"sacred house" (McIntosh 1998). The beauty of the stone buildings at Great Zimbabwe inspired many early visitors to believe they were built by a great and ancient civilization; one of the most popular beliefs, generated by European explorers, was that they were the site of King Solomon's mines, famous from Biblical descriptions (Ndoro 2005).

In approximately 1000 CE, changes in the rainfall pattern allowed larger settlements to emerge in the previously lightly occupied Limpopo-Zambezi region. The first substantial settlement, known as K2, had a population of about 1,500 people by 1200 CE and can be described as a ranked society (Huffman 2009). The K2 chief lived among the people, in a large circular structure with satellite buildings that may have served as kitchens and storage areas (Huffman 2005). K2 residents were involved in both agricultural and pastoralist activities, and thus sufficient rainfall in this dry area was critical. Every fall, important rain-making ceremonies were carried out on hilltop locations (Huffman 2009). At harvest time, the chief presided over a community-wide feast to celebrate the harvest, clearly enacting the redistributive actions common in a chiefdom system.

After 1200 CE the capital moved from K2 across the river to Mapungubwe, encompassing a hill where the important rain-making rituals took place each fall. At Mapungubwe, the chief built his

30 Scales of Complexity: Case Studies

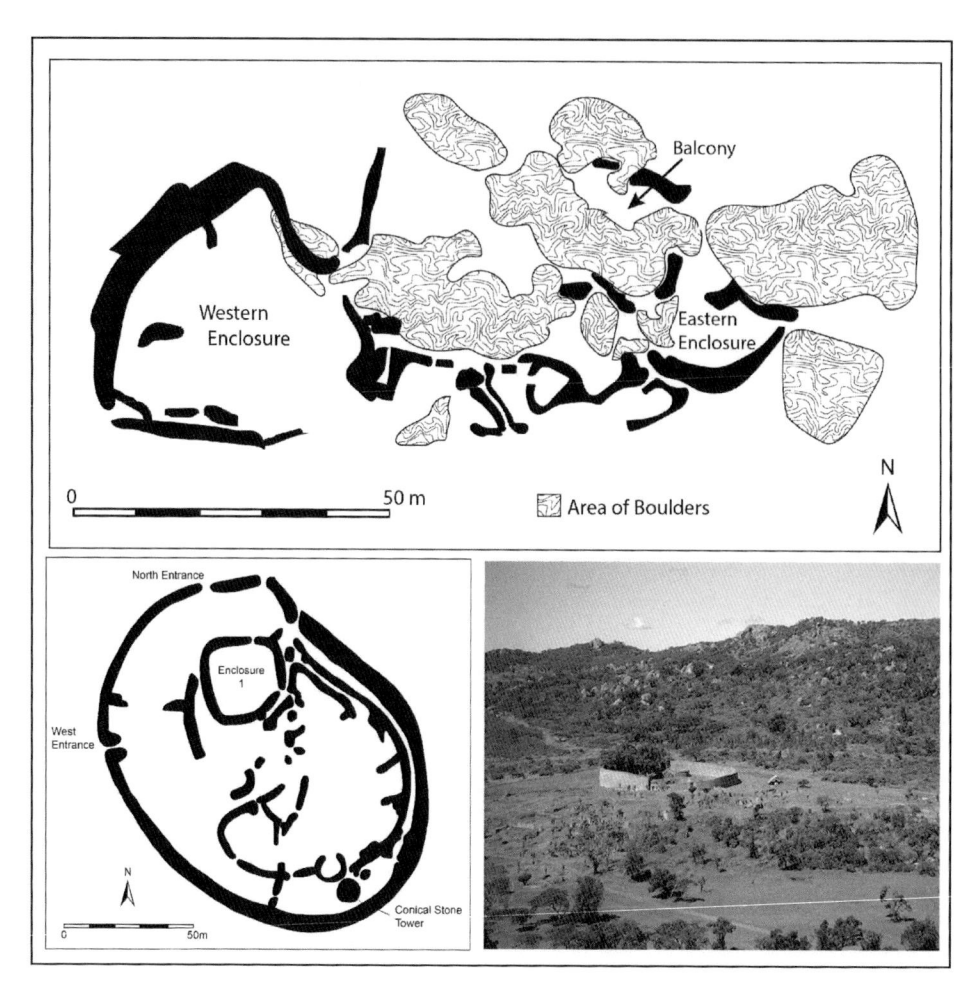

FIGURE 4.2 Top: Sketch Plan of the Great Zimbabwe Hill Complex (after Garlake 1973: 26, fig. 10); Bottom left: Sketch Plan of the Great Enclosure (after Garlake 1973: 28, fig. 11); Bottom right: Photo of the Great Enclosure (by Jan Derk, 1997)

house on the apron of this hill rather than among the people, elevating himself and his home above the residents who lived below (Huffman 2005) and associating him with an important ritual area. The population of Mapungubwe grew to as many as 5,000 over the next several decades, and the chiefly position gained in power. The zimbabwe that was the chief's residence was organized so that he resided at the back, separate from all including his family; public access to him was restricted by a messenger who received potential visitors at the front of the structure. Those given permission to approach the chief (by now referred to as a "king" in ethnographic accounts) were allowed into the audience hall. However, it is likely that visitors never saw the chief but rather spoke to an intermediary; the chief may have been in the audience hall but sequestered behind a wall or curtain, elevating his position as too important to deal with daily matters.

In the late 13th century, a climate shift began to limit water supplies and people abandoned Mapungubwe for the potentially more stable region of Great Zimbabwe (Huffman 2009). Great Zimbabwe had been occupied at least since 1100 and sat at the center of a significant trade network (Ndoro 2005). It may have offered some trade competition with Mapungubwe, contributing to the latter's abandonment. Elites at Great Zimbabwe regulated the external trade network that involved the extraction and export of gold and the acquisition of imported items including ceramics, glass, copper, iron objects, and likely textiles (Pikirayi 2001: 140–47). The ownership and distribution of these luxury goods was in the hands of the elites, contributing to their wealth and social standing; at the pinnacle of this trade nexus was the chief.

Within a few decades, there were as many as 18,000 people living at Great Zimbabwe, which encompassed a 300-foot high granite cliff, upon which the "Hill Complex" was located. Below was where the majority of the population resided and engaged in cattle-herding and agriculture. The Hill Complex featured stone-built enclosures decorated with stone carvings of birds and snakes, both sacred in this culture. A balcony overlooked the valley below, and just beneath the Hill Complex was a cave with acoustical qualities that made it possible for sounds produced in the cave to echo throughout the valley. Below the cliff in the valley stood the Great Enclosure, a vast stone-built circular structure with stone walls reaching heights of 9.7 meters and as thick as 5 meters. Inside the Great Enclosure was a massive stone-built tower about 9 meters high and 5.5 meters in diameter, along with smaller zimbabwes and several stone platforms.

Great Zimbabwean Society and Beliefs

Much of current understanding of Great Zimbabwe religious beliefs comes from ethnographic accounts in the 20th century rather than from materials retrieved at the archaeological sites. Among the supernatural beings in Great Zimbabwean religion, ancestor spirits were considered the most important; they served as guardians of their descendants and endeavored to ensure success and health and to deflect witchcraft and evil sent by enemies (Shoko 2007). In Great Zimbabwe houses, there was usually a stone platform upon which offerings (millet, beer, and other items) to the ancestors were made. Beyond this generally household-based ritual practice, there was a more public belief system that involved critical ceremonies associated with rain-making and agricultural fertility. Ceremonies associated with these life-sustaining elements were conducted by the chief who led the rituals and hosted the feasts.

The chief's role in bringing much needed rain and guaranteeing agricultural fertility was central in Great Zimbabwean culture. His ancestors were considered to have a deep spiritual link to the land and could therefore ensure fertility and successful harvests (Shoko 2007). It was critical, therefore, that the chief maintain strong ties with his ancestors and propitiate them with gifts, feasts, and attention; while most of these ritual performances took place within the Hill Complex, it is possible that some were carried out in the Great Enclosure on the stone platforms (Huffman 1987). When the chief died, and rulership passed to the closest male heir, he then became an important ancestor and thus obedience to him, and, essentially, worship of him during his lifetime was critical in order to ensure his loyalty and aid.

The Hill Complex consisted of a number of enclosures, the most eastern of which was probably where the more public rituals (likely attended only by the Great Zimbabwean elites) were held. This enclosure was decorated with snake and bird imagery (Figure 4.3); snakes were associated with fertility and rain-making, and birds, particularly raptors, were considered the vehicles that carried messages between ancestors and their living descendants (Huffman 2009). Beautifully carved soapstone birds decorated the Eastern Enclosure of the Hill Complex, suggesting the chief had consistent contact with his very important ancestors.

The Great Zimbabweans, based on ethnographic information, likely believed in a supreme deity known as Mwari, who was responsible for the bringing of rain. It was the job of the ancestors, and particularly the chief's ancestors, to communicate to Mwari the need for sufficient rain each season. Mwari could be petitioned at sites sacred to him; one of the most sacred of his sites was the cave located below the Hill Complex. Those wishing to address Mwari about rain, or other issues, could

32 Scales of Complexity: Case Studies

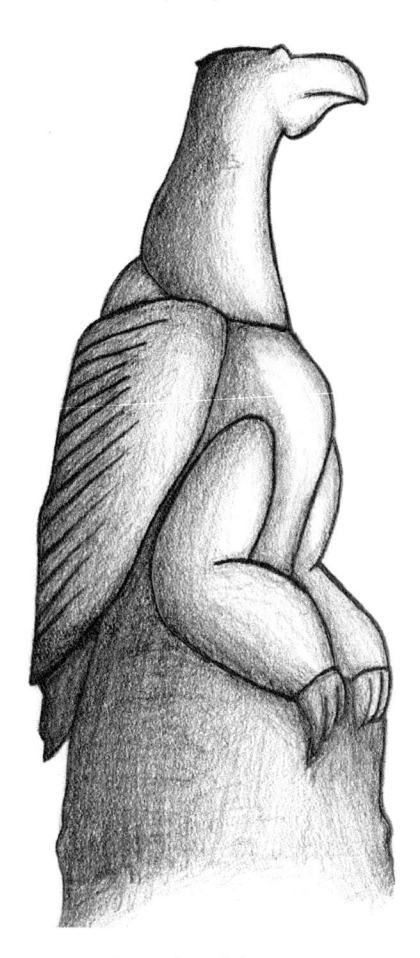

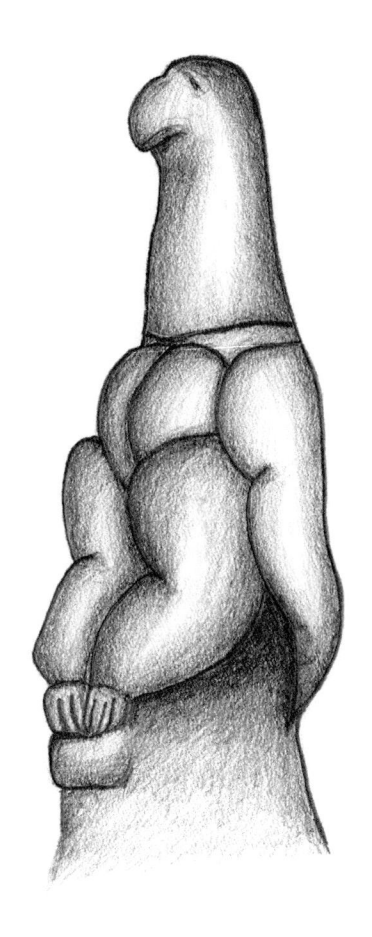

FIGURE 4.3 Examples of the Great Zimbabwe Bird Carvings on the Hill Complex Structure
Source: R. Jennison

approach the cave, and a message would issue from the cave; these messages would be interpreted for the propitiate either by priests who served the chief or perhaps by the chief himself, through an intermediary (Shoko 2007). That the chief resided above a site sacred to the most supreme deity served to illustrate his physical and spiritual proximity to the religious realm.

The Great Zimbabwean chief certainly was deeply involved in political and economic endeavors for his people, but his role as principal religious figure was a primary element in his ability to rule his people. That his ancestors were critical to agricultural fertility, and that upon his death he would ascend to that status as well, was more than enough to keep loyalty and obedience at a very high level. The chief's access to Mwari only added to his status as spiritual leader of his people.

Great Zimbabwean Complexity

The Great Zimbabwe leader clearly held an important religious role, and much of his power derived from the population's belief that he was critical to maintaining the health and well-being of both landscape and people. However, while trade did allow for the acquisition of some luxury goods and artisans crafted beautiful statuary for the chief's residence, the control the leader and elites exerted over craft production and the movement of goods was fairly weak. Most residents were engaged in agricultural or pastoralist pursuits, and most crafts were produced in the household for individual use. Though material remains are minimal, differentiation across Great Zimbabwe houses does not appear to suggest a significant level of social stratification; rather the leader and elites constituted a higher rank and the remaining population filled out a "lower" rank. Warfare, expansionary or defensive, did not appear to consume much of Great Zimbabwe's daily life, nor did the building of monumental structures other than the chief's residence and the Great Enclosure require the services of the population on a grand scale. Given time, changes in technology, and an increase in the control of trade and craft production, Great Zimbabwe may have eventually become one of sub-Saharan Africa's great states. However, by the mid-15th century, rising states in neighboring regions, and the arrival of European colonial powers just a century later, quashed any trajectory Great Zimbabwe may have followed from chiefdom to eventual state.

The American Southwest: Chaco Canyon

Many arguments regarding complexity center on North American societies, with a major example found in discussions regarding the Mississippian culture of the American midwest in Chapter 11. Another is the debate regarding the Chacoan culture of the American southwest (Figure 4.4). In the early decades of archaeological research on Chaco Canyon sites, it was assumed, in part based on ethnographic research on present-day Puebloan communities, that the ancient inhabitants of

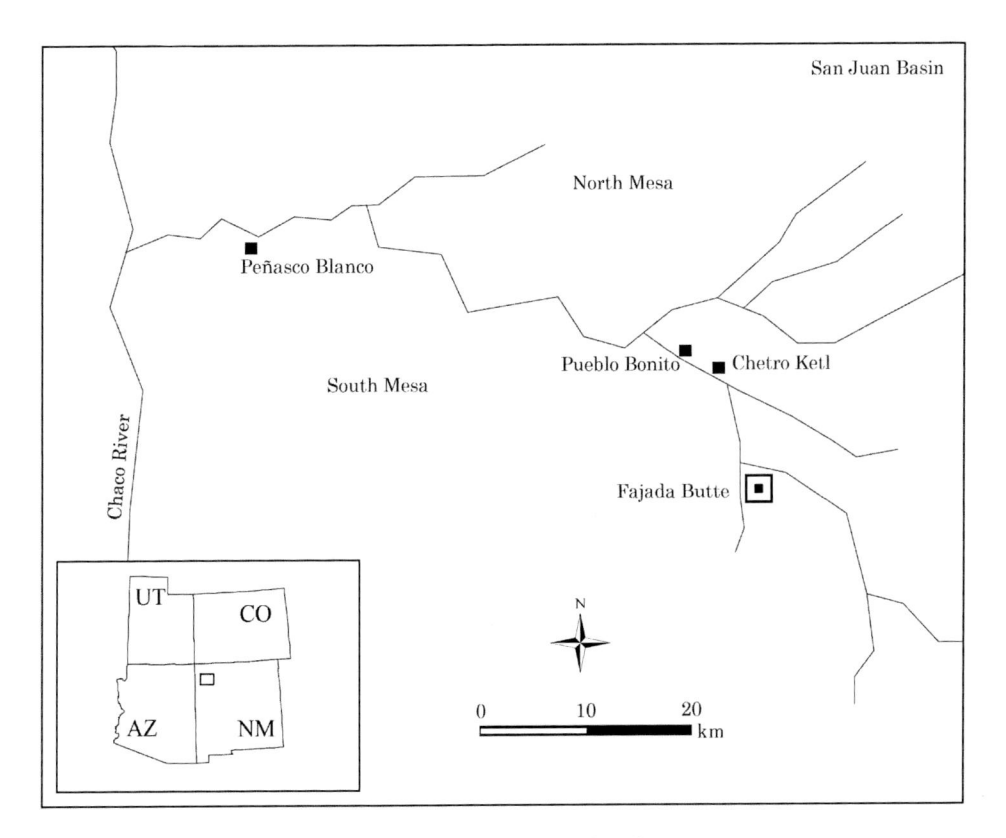

FIGURE 4.4 Map of American Southwest and Sites Discussed in the Text

Source: S.R. Steadman

the region were largely egalitarian, living in cooperative kinship systems and sharing important resources. In recent decades, however, archaeologists have begun to recognize clear signals of hierarchical social organization in the Chaco communities of 1,000 years ago, giving rise to a host of questions about the nature of leadership in Chacoan society. Barbara Mills nicely sums up the debates regarding these issues, which "center on three key variables: whether Chacoan society was organized hierarchically or along more egalitarian lines; whether leadership was centralized or dispersed among a number of different individuals and communities; and what constituted the varied sources of leaders' power" (2004: 124–25). The following case study takes Mills's first variable, hierarchical organization, as a given in ancient Chacoan society (and see Mills 2012; Plog 2015). It is the other two variables, centralized or dispersed leadership and the sources of power that created such leaders, that will form the basis of discussion here.

Chaco Origins

At least two millennia ago, residents of the American southwest were hunter-gatherers archaeologists call the "Basketmaker" cultures. By the Basketmaker III phase of the 8th century CE, more sedentary settlement began to take hold, and Basketmaker cultures produced ceramics and built more substantial structures. The phases that follow the Basketmaker are termed "Pueblo," named after the above-ground style of housing still found in the southwest today. It is during the Pueblo phases, divided into Pueblo I (700–900 CE), Pueblo II (900–1100 CE), and Pueblo III (1100–1300 CE), that major settlement in the San Juan Basin and Chaco Canyon took place.

Now in the state of New Mexico, Chaco Canyon rests at an elevation of approximately 1,220 meters within the San Juan Basin on the Colorado Plateau. It is partially surrounded by mountain ranges, with the San Juan range to the north, the San Pedro range to the east, and the Chuska to the west. Northwest of the canyon is the Chaco River; the canyon was created by a robust wash flowing off this river through time. The canyon walls are cut by cracks created by runoff from springtime rains and snowmelt. Winters can easily reach subzero temperatures, especially on the plateau above the canyon, and summer temperatures can reach over 100 degrees Fahrenheit. The mountain ranges, particularly the Chuska approximately 80 kilometers west, are the closest source of wood for building purposes. As in a desert climate, rainfall on the basin floor is often below 25 centimeters per year, and the climate is extremely arid. While beautiful, the Chaco landscape provided a number of challenges to those who chose to settle there.

In the Pueblo I phase settlement, size increased as much as five-fold over the Basketmaker III; villages held 20 to 30 houses often centered around central plazas and large circular religious buildings termed *kivas* (Young 2012). At this time, residents built their settlements in the higher elevations of the Chaco and San Juan regions where rain-fed agriculture was possible, eschewing the valley floors where water was less available and the growing cycle less certain. By the end of the Pueblo I phase, however, residents in the Chaco region had moved to the valley floor where it was hotter and drier though springtime water runoff allowed for a short but productive growing cycle. Reasons for the move may have been climate change, competition for land, or other motivations as yet unclear to archaeologists, but water management systems allowed residents to grow sufficient crops to sustain substantial settlements (Vivian and Watson 2015). Houses in the smaller villages were detached from one another, but in some of the larger settlements they were also contiguous, with one room or set of rooms sharing walls with neighboring rooms. The Pueblo II phase (900–1100 CE), when the Chaco culture reached its zenith, featured masonry-built structures known as "Great Houses" due to their size and grandeur (Figure 4.5). These Great Houses featured a contiguous attached architectural style and could stand several stories high and contain hundreds of rooms. They were built of a combination of stone and wood, with some adobe components built

FIGURE 4.5 Photo of Pueblo Bonito: An Example of a Chacoan Great House

Source: Photo by J.C. Ross

into some structures. Most, however, consisted of stone masonry, a relatively new building material utilized in Chacoan Great Houses (Windes 2004).

By the beginning of the Pueblo III phase (ca. 1100 CE), alterations in the climate resulted in a falling population and increasing hardships for Puebloan residents in Chaco Canyon and beyond. Food shortages and warfare over resources made daily life nearly unsustainable for residents of the region. No more Great Houses were built, trade connections eroded (Kantner 2004), and starvation diets became the norm. By the end of the Pueblo III phase, Chaco Canyon was largely empty, as were other Great Houses and smaller communities on the bluffs surrounding the canyon. Residents had departed for more well-watered regions to the north and elsewhere, leaving behind the incredible architecture they had worked so hard to build.

Chacoan Society

Kinship played an important role in ancient Puebloan social relationships, particularly in the Basketmaker and early Pueblo phases (Whiteley 2015). Though house size suggests that each household contained a nuclear rather than extended family, clusters of such houses are thought to have belonged to related families working in cooperative kinship networks to secure food and provide safety. Many archaeologists believe that kinship was matrilineal and residence was matrilocal in the Chaco cultures, though other kinship and residence patterns may have been in place as well (Mills 2002; Whiteley 2015). Kinship ties through extended families allowed ancient Puebloans to pool resources, such as food, in lean times and to develop networks of trade linkages for resource acquisition. Throughout the period and even into today's Puebloan cultures, however, family ties retain a core role in social relationships.

There were numerous settlements in Chaco Canyon, some containing just a few houses (often with detached architecture) and others consisting of the Great Houses, massive kivas (Figure 4.6), and other structures. The vast majority of the Chaco Canyon population consisted of commoners, mostly farmers, living in small pueblo villages and hamlets located along the valley floor and above

FIGURE 4.6 Photo of Kiva (Circular Structure) at Pueblo del Arroyo Great House in Chaco Canyon

Source: Photo by S.R. Steadman

the canyon walls. The westernmost Great House is Peñasco Blanco on the southern side of the canyon, and though smaller than some of the other Chaco communities, it still likely boasts dozens of rooms (it is as yet largely unexcavated) and has four great kivas. Near the southeastern end of the canyon is Fajada Butte (Figure 4.7a–b), which features stone carvings on which the sun shines at the solstice points; it was likely an important ritual site for the agricultural cycle (Sofaer 2007). At the center of Chaco Canyon, roughly equidistant from Peñasco Blanco and Fajada Butte, is the site of Pueblo Bonito, the best known of all the Great House communities. It sits, as many have described, at a "center place" (Gabriel 1991; Van Dyke 2004, 2007, 2012) and also rests at the center of controversy concerning the nature of the sociopolitical structure in the Chaco system.

Set against the northern wall of Chaco Canyon, Pueblo Bonito's plan is a massive "D-shape," 4-story structure featuring nearly 700 rooms and over 30 kivas, including at least 2 great kivas, all resting within an enclosed plaza. The first buildings appeared at this site in the 9th century CE, expanding to its monumental size between the early 11th and early 12th centuries (Stuart 2014: 91). During this century, several other Great Houses, including Chetro Ketl, which lies very near Pueblo Bonito, were constructed (this Great House has at least 400 rooms). The size of Pueblo Bonito and other Great Houses such as Chetro Ketl suggests that hundreds of people might have occupied them during their height. However, many scholars have come to believe that the Great Houses did not house communities of commoners, farmers, and elite families but rather served solely as the residences of high-status elite families, each of which controlled a vast number of rooms. Thus, the population of the Pueblo Bonito Great House might have been far smaller than the number of rooms suggests (Lekson 2012). The roughly dozen Great House communities spread across the Chaco region (with up to several hundred Great House communities throughout the

FIGURE 4.7 a. Photo of Fajada Butte in Chaco Canyon (by S.R. Steadman); b. Artistic Rendering of the Butte and the "Sun Daggers"

Source: R. Jennison

Colorado Plateau and Four Corners region), may have held relatively few elite families in contrast to the hundreds, and likely thousands, of commoners occupying the many small communities interspersed between the Great Houses (Lekson 2012).

That elites occupied Pueblo Bonito, and probably other Great Houses, is demonstrated by the contents of some of Pueblo Bonito's rooms. A number of rooms were deliberately built to serve not as living spaces but for storage (Neitzel 2007); items kept in these rooms included food resources and trade items, many of them exotic imports such as effigy pots from the Mississippian culture (see Chapter 11), shells from the California coast, and copper bells and scarlet macaw feathers likely imported from Mexico (Kantner 2004; Toll 2004). Another major import was pottery, brought from all over the Four Corners region. In part, the beauty of the pottery and the fact that it came from afar may have been part of its appeal, but also the lack of wood at Chaco necessary for firing pottery might have created a need to acquire wares from regions that could more easily produce ceramics. The limited number of rich burials at Pueblo Bonito may suggest that only the most important (ancestral) elites were awarded burial there (Plog and Heitman 2010).

To reach Pueblo Bonito and other Great House settlements in Chaco, people traveled on a constructed roadway system leading to Chaco from all directions (Kantner 2004). The roads were created by removing the top layer of earth sometimes down to 50 centimeters deep and lining the roads with earthen berms or low stone walls; their widths sometimes reached 6–7 meters. Within Chaco, these roads connected the Great House communities. The longer roads led out of the canyon to the higher bluffs and to some Great House communities at greater distances away. Resting at the center of this roadway system was Pueblo Bonito.

Elites also needed to harness the labor necessary for building the Great Houses in which they lived and to transport building materials such as wood from some distance away. Built in several stages, possibly with ritual feasting involved at major building events (Stein and Lekson 1992; Stuart 2014; Wills 2001), there must have been dozens if not hundreds of laborers involved in constructing Great Houses such as Pueblo Bonito. That powerful elites occupied high-status positions in the ancient Chacoan system is not really debated. What is consistently discussed is how they gained, and maintained, their power and whether terms such as "kings" or only "chiefs" should be applied to Chacoan leaders.

Dispersed Leadership or Centralized Control?

If there was a leadership structure in Chaco Canyon, and most now agree that such did exist, was it centralized with one leader or leading family, or did power shift between the hands of several or numerous sets of elites who engaged in competition with one another? Most scholars favor the latter interpretation, though some have suggested that power was held in the hands of a very few elites living at Pueblo Bonito, who controlled trade, religion, and the ritual calendar and who conducted warfare to expand their holdings using a substantial warrior force (LeBlanc 1999; Wilcox 1999). What is not clear is how leaders gained and maintained their positions. Some suggest leading families derived their power from economic sources through control of trade and the distribution of critical food resources, while others assert that power was seated firmly in their religious roles. These sources of power are discussed in more detail in the next section. Further complicating the archaeological understanding of Chaco complexity is the possibility that Chaco residents may have come from different regions of the San Juan Basin and even from differing ethnic groups (Judge and Cordell 2006). This might have contributed to a competitive-cooperative relationship between Chaco Great Houses in that outlying communities may have developed loyalties to a particular Great House due to ethnic affiliations and may have helped maintain and enlarge "their" Great House and participate in grand rituals there. Sources of elite power that may have engendered such ties of loyalty with outlying communities are a bit more opaque.

Sources of Elite Power

A multitude of research projects have defined two critical areas in which elites may have exerted control, which in turn elevated their positions: economic activities and religion. The economic control may have revolved around two important areas of the economy: agricultural production and trade. Already described are the large storage rooms found within the Great Houses of Pueblo Bonito and elsewhere. Regarding the acquisition and distribution of food resources, some argue that a fairly open and flexible reciprocity system may have emerged in the Pueblo I stage, developing into a tool by which leaders could control the actions of the commoners by the Pueblo II and III stages (Sebastian 1992). Residents of Chaco were fortunate in that rainfall and water management systems could provide a reasonable crop yield each year. Even so, the dry climate may have necessitated the stockpiling of subsistence resources for distribution in more difficult times. Leading families may have stored the tithed donations from each outlying community, redistributing fairly freely and generously in a Pueblo I reciprocity-based system. As such a system became more ensconced in Chacoan society, and as leading families acquired larger storage areas (Great Houses) and growing power, what had been "generous giving" in the Pueblo I phase may have morphed into more of a "lending" redistributive system by the Pueblo II and III phases. Those who received additional foods from the elites, and this may have included many commoners, became indebted to those elites and thus subject to their will (Sebastian 1992). Economic relationships that bound together elites and commoners loyal to their Great House need not have been contentious or perceived as "unequal" by either group. Economic "debts" incurred by commoners may have been repaid by labor: building larger Great Houses, the incredible road system, and other projects that served elites and commoners alike.

A second avenue of economic power may have been elite control over the acquisition of some utilitarian and most prestige goods such as those described earlier. That the vast majority of long-distance trade items are found in Great Houses, great kivas, and elite burials suggests that such items came directly to the upper echelon of Chacoan society rather than through a "down-the-line" trade that included the participation of multiple commoners located both outside and within Chaco Canyon. In the case of valuable items such as turquoise, Chacoan elites may have developed specific ties with residents at the turquoise sources (to the west and south) or even established kin members as residents there to aid in the acquisition of this important material (Hull et al. 2013). Once the raw turquoise reached the Chaco region, it was then fashioned into beautiful ornaments and jewelry at small Chaco villages where tools and bits of turquoise have been found (Toll 2004). After completion, these goods ended up in the Great Houses or in elite burials. The craft-workers may have been family relations of Great House occupants or were in some fashion contracted to perform these labors for Chaco elite consumption. In return for their work, commoners and artisans may have received permission to attend important Chaco ceremonies at central places such as Pueblo Bonito or may have been awarded other benefits that enhanced their households or communities (Toll 2004). In this system, elites acquired desirable goods, and commoners obtained access to Chaco, recognition for contributions to "center place," and other perks for positive participation (Toll 2006). Elites desired these items for the symbolism they expressed, awarding power and prestige to their possessors. Some items may have also served in important ritual contexts and been prominently displayed at public ceremonies, which also demonstrated the powerful positions of those who possessed them.

It is from the religious realm, even more than the economic, that elites and leaders may have derived their greatest sources of power. Archaeological evidence suggests that there were shared cosmologies and similar ritual practices across the Chacoan world (Heitman 2015; Mills 2015). The ubiquitous kivas were an important part of social and ritual life. These circular semisubterranean structures were likely where important kin-based rituals took place. Interior furniture included hearths and storage areas, benches so that groups of people could take part in rituals and meetings, and wall niches that may have once held important items. The *sipapu*, a small hole in the floor, symbolized the mythological passageway through which the first Puebloans ascended from the world of spirits below to become humans on the earth. Smaller kivas interspersed between rooms in Great Houses may have belonged to individual family groups who carried out household rituals; the one or two kivas in smaller communities probably served all members of the community who were likely kin-related. The "great kivas" at Pueblo Bonito and other Great Houses were significantly larger and may have been used for more public rituals, perhaps serving all residents of the Great House, or used for visiting VIPs. The rituals carried out in the great kivas, perhaps to encourage rain or promote healthy crops, may have been important to all Chacoan residents, elites and commoners alike; those allowed to participate in the ceremony would have been deemed critical actors, responsible for the ultimate health and well-being of all Chaco residents. Controlling access to the great kivas and their vital ceremonies would have afforded significant power to Chacoan leaders.

Already discussed is the theory that only a few elite "caretaker" families resided at Chaco Great Houses. These elite families would have greeted people arriving for various pilgrimage cycles for which Chaco Canyon stood at "center place," perhaps with Pueblo Bonito serving as the ultimate destination in the canyon (Lekson 1999). Known as the "pilgrimage fair" model (Mills 2002: 78), this scenario satisfies much of the evidence thus far retrieved from Pueblo Bonito and other Great House sites including little evidence of habitation debris; exotic and prestige items such as carved wooden sticks (often referred to as "prayer sticks"); the road system with Chaco/Pueblo Bonito standing at the center; the enormous astronomical device at Fajada Butte; and the great kivas, some of which were more than 14 meters across and could therefore accommodate dozens of people for a major ceremony. Pilgrimages, possibly occurring several times a year (seasonally or at each equinox), enhanced the importance of the Great House elites who were charged with guarding the sacred places, organizing and conducting the ceremonies, and ensuring that all went flawlessly so that the supernatural world was satisfied and would grant the wishes of the humans residing within the cosmological universe. Attendance at the ceremonies also demonstrated the devotion of non-Chaco Canyon residents who may have traveled some distance at both personal risk (dangerous roads in times of warfare) and economic risk (leaving fields untended). Pilgrims likely came bearing offerings such as building materials (e.g., wood from the surrounding mountains) or other critical items necessary to the elites and their sacred architecture (Kantner and Vaughn 2012).

These pilgrimages could have been a type of "glue" binding the social fabric of a people living across a vast and difficult landscape. Commoners, upon arriving in Chaco, would have been reassured upon seeing their leaders (who may have also been kin) properly caring for the sacred spaces and conducting the proper rituals. Economic ties between Chaco residents and outlying communities could be renewed as promises of reciprocity and redistribution were (re)established at each meeting. The social hierarchy was reaffirmed with elites ensuring the economic success of commoners through ritual action and provision of resources and with commoners supplying labor for the building of Great Houses, roads, and other services. Elites maintained their leadership status through the control of space (the Chacoan center), religion, and the economic system. As long as life operated smoothly, crops came in, goods arrived, and warfare was kept at bay, commoners were satisfied with the social hierarchy as it existed. By the Pueblo III phase, however, when environmental and social circumstances had become untenable, commoners and elites in Chaco and beyond fled the region, bringing Chaco society effectively to an end.

The Complexity of Chaco

The issue of "complexity" has been at the core of southwestern archaeology, or (some would say) has plagued southwestern archaeology, for several decades (Lekson 2005, 2006; Neitzel 2010; Sebastian 2006). Throughout the 1960s to 1980s, much of the scholarly discussion about Chaco and other southwestern societies centered on "how complex were they," with arguments ranging from identifying them as largely egalitarian to gauging them as "tribal," or alternatively "chiefdoms" (e.g., chapters in Alt 2010a; Neitzel 1999). A few argued for a state-like system. By the 1980s, "increasingly heated debates about whether or not various Southwest cases were in fact complex" began to crowd out the actual archaeological investigations of the regions concerned (Neitzel 2010: 157). By the 1990s, however, new emphases on archaeological fieldwork and data acquisition allowed for new approaches to understanding the ancient southwestern communities. The question that began to be asked was not "how complex were they" but rather "how were they complex" (Mills 2012; Neitzel 2010). This led to research on economic strategies, the role religion played in these types of societies, and the investment of labor into major building projects such as those in Chaco Canyon. Such studies have resulted in a more closely defined analysis of the sociopolitical and economic strategies that were operational during the height of the ancient Puebloan societies of the southwest and thus a more nuanced description of their "complexity" in the Pueblo II–III Periods.

The discussion in Chapters 2 and 3 suggests that cultural institutions found in Chaco Canyon communities might best be described as existing within a chiefdom or regional polity framework. A reciprocity-redistribution system provisioning critical resources; an elite-based control of trade and distribution of prestige items; and control of major religious activities, including residence at the center of what may have been a very sacred landscape, all fit well with a description of complexity existing beyond the "tribal" level.

Stephen Lekson perhaps explains Chaco complexity with the greatest clarity (2006, 2009, 2010, 2015). While he does not argue that the Chacoan system was a state, at least like those found in Mesoamerica, he does maintain that they *wanted* to be. Lekson (2006: 37) suggests that Chaco elites imagined themselves royalty and their Great Houses as palaces; that Chaco "was a city among villages"; and that it was "the center of a complex polity, suffused with ritual and ceremony, but fundamentally politically hierarchical: a chiefdom, a petty kingdom" thereby identifying Chaco society as a chiefdom-like regional polity with dispersed leadership. Lekson goes on to ask: "Is it so unthinkable that, at Chaco, Southwestern people experimented with centralized political hierarchy?" (2006: 37). In other words, Lekson advocates a view of Chaco as a society striving to emulate, nay, to *be*, a state such as those found to the south in Mesoamerica: that Chaco elites aspired to kingship, that Great Houses were meant to be their palaces, their rich burials and full storage rooms to have stood as testament to their power. While it *operated* as a regional polity, at least some residents *thought it to be* a state. Lekson perhaps captures this situation best (2012: 598):

> Great Houses were elite residences, like Mesoamerican palaces—or, rather, they were *intended to be* palaces.... They housed high-status families who were something like princes and kings–or they *tried* to be kings.... They built a city–or something *like* a city ... from which they controlled a vast region–or *thought* they controlled a region.... Chaco, with several hundred elites and a thousand commoners, was trying to be a local version of a Postclassic Mesoamerican capital.... But they got it wrong: they built it in the wrong place, at the wrong time.

In his most recent work, Lekson notes that Chaco can perhaps best be defined as a North American "secondary state," a unique complex society in the region that defies placement in any preciously created anthropological category describing levels of complexity (Lekson 2015). A difficult landscape prone to climatic variation, a small and likely multi-ethnic population, and a staunch commitment to reciprocal and redistributive exchange models, prevented Chaco society from emerging as one of North America's pre-Columbian Mesoamerican-style states. These factors, and others, caused the relatively short-lived system to collapse by 1300, only regaining prominence as a subject of intense scholarly debate seven centuries later.

The Polynesian World: Chiefdoms and Emerging Archaic States

The following discussion presents two Polynesian cultures, both identified as "chiefdoms" in the archaeological literature. The Maori population of today's New Zealand is offered as an example of a "simple" chiefdom (Earle 1991a). The Hawaiian example rests at the other end of the "chiefdom" spectrum. It is often identified as a "complex chiefdom," and in more recent literature, pre-contact Hawaiian society has been described by some as an archaic state.

In the two case studies several markers of sociopolitical structure, discussed as elements of "civilization" in Chapter 2, will be reviewed as a basis for comparative analysis. The role of kinship in both political and social life will form part of the discussion, as will the level of ranking or class distinctions. Associated with this is whether a hierarchy of governance existed, extending from the chief (or king) downward to the commoner or lowest rank or class. The nature of the leader is also relevant: what role did leaders play in religion? What was their involvement in the socioeconomic structure and the trade network? It will be clear that though both cultures had Polynesian roots, their trajectories were somewhat different. The Maori remained strongly kin-based with minimal socioeconomic stratification but became heavily ranked particularly in the upper societal levels. Hawaii developed a deeply sophisticated sociopolitical system with significant socioeconomic differentiation prior to the arrival of the first European ships.

The Maori of New Zealand

Today, the Maori rightfully take tremendous pride in their culture, working to retain and regain aspects of their cultural heritage that were diminished or lost after colonization of the New Zealand islands in the late 18th and early 19th centuries.

Maori Origins

Approximately 1,000 years ago, the Maori first arrived to the islands (Figure 4.8) known to them as Aeotearoa (Land of the Long White Cloud). There is some controversy over their origins, but most agree that the first settlers came by sailing canoes from an eastern Polynesian homeland typically called "Hawaiiki" by both the Maori and other Polynesian cultures (Bellwood 2013; Davidson 1984; Kirch 2000, 2001). The location of Hawaiiki is still in dispute; many argue that it is to be found in the Society Islands, but recent DNA evidence suggests that the Maori origins may have been more complicated (Knapp et al. 2012). When the Maori arrived to Aeotearoa, they found an uninhabited landscape consisting of two large islands (now known as North Island and South Island) and many smaller islands, featuring plenty of food in both plant and animal form. They settled and established a partially mobile, foraging subsistence economy (Davidson 1984; Firth 1929). The problem, however, was that these islands had never been occupied by humans, and the introduction of this new species had a rapid and drastic effect on the ecological balance. Most Maori settled on the warmer North Island, around the fringes where they could practice both inland hunting and gathering as well as take advantage of marine resources.

Initially, the Maori built small hamlets with seasonal lodging as they practiced a seminomadic hunting-and-gathering lifestyle (Davidson 1984; Walter, Smith, and Jacomb 2006). As resources grew more scarce, people settled more permanently and developed horticulture to create staple crops including sweet potato, yam, and fern root. Several important meat resources, including the moa, a flightless bird distantly related to the emu of Australia, and fur seals became extinct or unavailable, likely through over-hunting, beginning in the 14th century (Barber 1996); furthermore, the need to clear land for horticultural activities had a detrimental effect on the landscape,

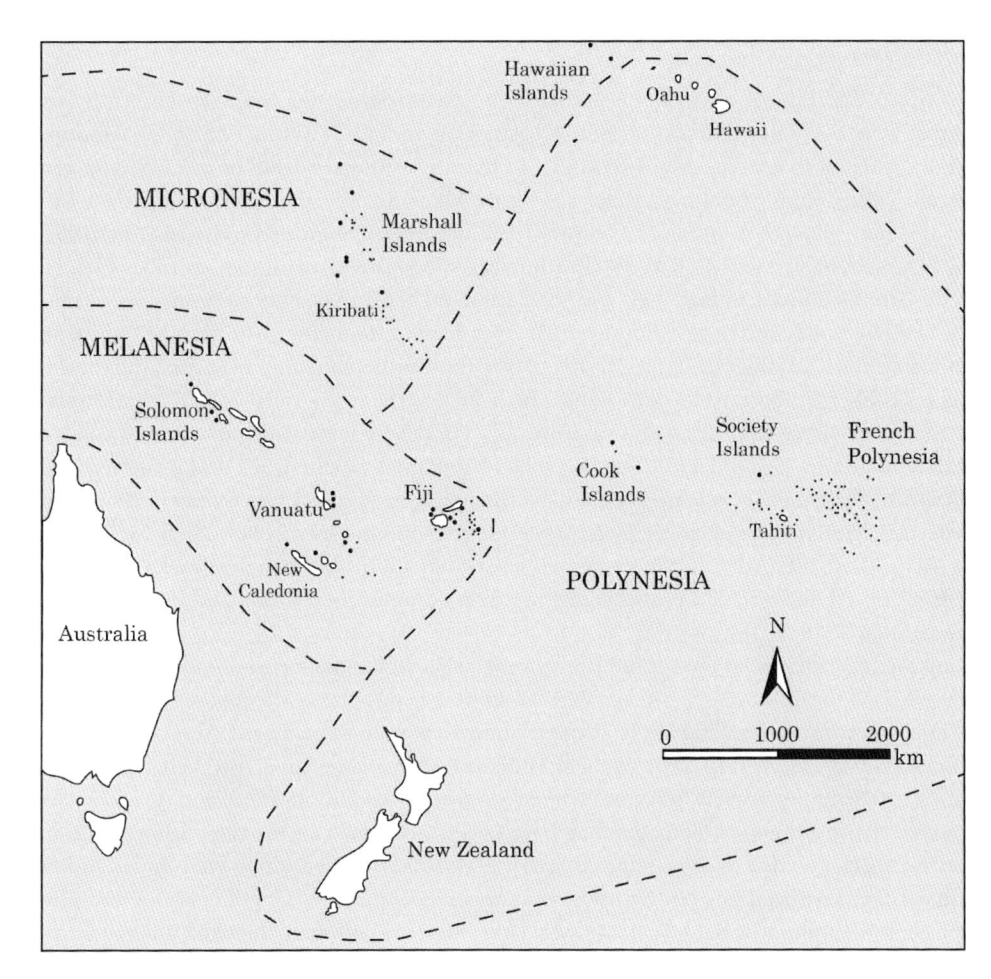

FIGURE 4.8 Map of Polynesia Including New Zealand and Hawaii

Source: S.R. Steadman

causing even more pressure on subsistence production (Sutton 1990). In addition to subsistence resources, other important items became harder to acquire, including the stone used in the production of agricultural tools such as adzes. It became increasingly important to control areas rich in subsistence-based resources.

After 1500, the Maori became wholly reliant on staple crops, and the population continued to grow. By 1770, when Europeans first arrived, the population was likely between 100,000 and 150,000 people, almost all of them on the North Island due to the ecological depletion of the colder South Island (Bellwood 1987; Walter, Smith, and Jacomb 2006). Between 1500 and 1770, Maori communities began to construct *paa*, which is the Maori word for palisaded fortified settlements, often located on hills and higher areas on the landscape (Allen 2006; Davidson 1987). Well over 5,000 paa have been identified, mostly on the North Island, with a few on the northern fringes of the South Island. Inside the paa were houses, storage facilities, and structures or areas devoted to ritual activities. Cultivated fields were outside the paa as were other hamlets and settlements; the fortified space may have been a place of refuge for all those in the region when they were under attack (Allen 2008; Davidson 1987; Fox 1976).

Maori Society and Leadership Structures

Right up to the time of contact, the Maori social organization was based on kinship relationships that were the "operative organizational basis of the society" (Sutton 1990: 683). Kinship was generally patrilineal, and the Maori considered themselves descendants of the first voyagers to the islands. Three units of kinship groups constitute Maori society: the extended family (*whānau*); the clan (*hapū*), which consisted of several whānau; and the tribal group (*iwi*), which in turn consisted of several hapū (van Meijl 1995). In some cases, a group of iwi might consider themselves related (forming a *waka*) in that their ancestors came on the same canoe to Aeotaeroa (Davidson 1984: 149). In some areas, a few houses made up a hamlet, probably consisting of two or more extended families. In other areas, large towns were the norm, consisting of several hundred people, all probably members of the same hapū. The hapū was the main social and economic unit and was probably the base of the political structure as well. Ethnographic accounts note the presence of elderly men who wore magnificent capes, had substantial facial tattoos, and possessed beautiful weapons; these men, considered "chiefs" by the colonists (and known as *ariki* in Maori), were probably the hapū lineage elders or perhaps the highest-ranking members in their iwi (Davidson 1984: 151). These men were highly respected and could advise and certainly make decisions for their hapū or iwi and wielded power across multiple communities within and beyond their territories (Allen 2008, 2016).

Ranking in Maori society was based largely on kinship affiliation and position within the family. Those who belonged only to whānau too small to be a hapū were at the lower end of the socioeconomic spectrum, controlling less land and trading on a more limited basis. Also on a more "junior" level may have been smaller or younger families within a large hapū; it is these people whom colonists may have considered "servants" when they first arrived in New Zealand (Davidson 1984: 151), since the more junior members may have performed much of the daily labor while more senior members attended to less strenuous activities. In Maori society there were larger and more prominent families (hapū or even iwi) whose lineage elders ("chiefs" or ariki) were more powerful and junior families that held far less power. Thus, there was substantial ranked differentiation in Maori society, with ariki and members of prominent hapū having far more privilege, bearing the symbols of class such as wearing cloaks and greenstone ornaments and notable tattooing to mark their position. That there were distinct differences in rank is also demonstrated by the burial goods found with some individuals; the presence of items such as large and well-made adzes and fine jewelry set some burials apart, likely identifying the occupant as a "chief" from that community (Walter, Smith, and Jacomb 2006). In pre-contact Maori society, members of prominent hapū and ariki stood out among the majority commoners.

Maori leaders did not seem to exert extensive control over trade activities. Maori material culture consists of tools necessary for fishing, hunting, and horticulture, household goods, personal items such as clothing, jewelry and hair decorations, and weapons. There was some trade across the islands mainly to distribute lithic resources including obsidian and the desired greenstone (nephrite) and other stone sources ideal for the production of adzes, a major wood-working and agricultural tool (Bellwood 1987: 141). Most regions had access to adequate stone resources suitable for normal tool production. The production of goods took place within the hamlet, town, or paa, perhaps by individual families, or in some cases in men's houses in the larger communities (Davidson 1984: 162). Evidence of community-wide workshops to make goods for large-scale distribution is lacking in Maori settlements.

The Maori were obviously capable of building monumental structures: the extensive paa with their palisades and internal structures are clear evidence of this. However, the Maori placed little emphasis on building formal religious structures and creating ritual spaces. There are no temples or even significant *marae* (the Polynesian word for ritual structures) across the islands. Open spaces inside a paa were sometimes marked with upright stones or wooden posts to signify a ritual space; small stone statues that likely represent Maori deities were probably placed in gardens to protect the crops (Davidson 1984: 171). The lack of monumental buildings and statuary does not mean that the Maori had no deep-seated beliefs. Quite the opposite. They had a very strong notion of *tapu* (from which the word "taboo" derives), which refers to items, people, or acts that are ritually restricted or forbidden. High-ranking people were tapu to those below them and thus had to be treated respectfully. In particular, a Maori's head was tapu because the spiritual essence (known as *mana*, stronger in higher-ranking Maori) rose to the highest point on a person, that being the hair. The Maori wore beautifully carved wooden and bone combs in their hair, which had to be ritually disposed of because they were tapu once they were no longer useful (such items have been found in hot spring swamps [Figure 4.9]). Obsidian found in swamps may have been used in cutting and dressing the hair (Davidson 1984: 172). Maori rock art displays elements of myth and ritual, and both oral tradition and archaeological evidence suggests that, prior to any building activity (house, canoe, paa), a ritual was performed, and a ritual deposit was made (Davidson 1984: 172).

The Maori are perhaps best known for their skill in the art of war. It is possible that, upon arrival to New Zealand a millennium ago, the Maori people were not disposed to war with one another, but as resources became scarce and population grew, conflict to protect lands and important resource-rich areas became increasingly important. The over 5,000 paa, employing significant labor to build such fortifications, testify to the importance of protecting people and property. The Maori short war clubs, called *patu*, were constructed of wood, bone, or stone; they were used in hand-to-hand fighting, and it is for their ferocity and skill in this that the Maori were famous

FIGURE 4.9 Example of Sacred Hot Spring and Swamp, Whakarewarewa Thermal Valley Near Rotorua, used by the Maori for Deposit of Sacred/Tapu Objects

Source: Photo by S.R. Steadman

among the initial colonists. Warriors consisted of the men in a hapū or iwi. In other words, there was no "standing army"; rather, when defense, or offense, was needed, the adult men of each extended family were gathered together for the task. Larger hapū could muster as many as a couple hundred men if necessary. Archaeological investigation does not yet allow for a full analysis of the level of warfare occurring among the Maori before the arrival of Western colonists and the advent of the Maori Wars (between the Maori and colonists) in the mid-19th century. Some pre-colonial paas were destroyed by fires, and burials contain individuals who died violent deaths (Allen 2006; Davidson 1984). Clearly, the Maori had opportunities to refine their fighting skills prior to the arrival of Western colonists, perhaps in inter-paa conflicts over land and other vital resources.

After the colonization of New Zealand, primarily by settlers from the United Kingdom, sociopolitical organization among the Maori shifted to promote singular individuals as representatives of a large group of people, i.e., to a system like what anthropologists today refer to as "chiefs" (Sutton 1990; van Meijl 1995), who carry individualized power. Colonists who wished to trade, acquire land, and enter negotiations with the Maori did not want to deal with a kin group (whānau) or an even larger group (hapū) and thus sought out the "elder" or ariki who seemed to garner the greatest respect in any given area. It is with those individuals that trade negotiations and land deals were then made. Ariki and leaders who once required kin-based consensus for major decisions began to make individualized determinations that affected land, trade, and other types of Maori-colonist interactions. Charismatic Maori leaders became even more important as hostilities grew between the Maori and increasing numbers of colonists in the early-to-mid-19th century; the gathering of warriors and mounting of defense, and attacks, fell to the Maori chiefs.

Complexity among the Maori

Prior to colonization, the Maori ariki served the role of "chiefs" for their people, but the differentiated ranking between them and the commoners, and the power they held, was far less substantial than is found on other Polynesian islands. Maori leaders were not "divine" nor did they serve as intermediaries between the people and their gods; they did not control the trade networks on any level, and they did not oversee a host of councilors and priests who might have served as conveyors of the chief's power among the people. In fact, Maori leaders did not "control" large land masses; rather their purview was usually the paa and the hamlets surrounding it. Maori leaders fought alongside their kinsmen in warfare but did not command professional warriors or a standing army. It was not until colonists arrived that individual leaders took on more prominence among the Maori, in part out of the need to deal with the encroachment of a new population unwilling to interact with large kin groups. But the power of Maori ariki was short-lived, existing only in the 19th century until Maori primacy in Aeotearoa was extinguished in the face of colonial advancement.

Pre-Contact Hawaii

The powerful kings and queens of Hawaii are well known due to historical records generated during the contact period. King Kamehameha I united the Hawaiian Islands during his reign in the second half of the 18th century. Queen Liliuokalani was the last monarch, and only queen, of Hawaii, ruling until 1893 when she was overthrown by the U.S. government. These were monarchs with significant power, ruling over a Hawaiian state-level society. Until recently, scholarship suggested that true "kingship" and state society were not present until the contact era, which commenced when Captain James Cook visited the islands in 1778. Scholars argued it was contact with the West, and the trade and political negotiations necessary for interaction, that catapulted Hawaiian leaders from chiefs to kings. The socioeconomic and political structures that existed on the islands prior to the contact era were generally described as complex chiefdoms (Earle 1978; Sahlins 1963). However, more recent studies suggest that pre-contact Hawaii is better described as an archaic state (Grinin 2011; Hommon 2013; Kirch 2010).

Hawaiian Origins

As was the case in New Zealand, human arrival on the Hawaiian Islands took place only about a millennium ago (Bellwood 2013). Unlike the Maori arrival on Aeotearoa, the ancient Hawaiians found a habitat very suitable to their subsistence needs; the subtropical climate and rich soils provided excellent opportunities to nurture the roots, tubers, and tree crops Hawaiians had brought in their canoes, probably launched from the Marquesas Islands to the southeast (Kirch 2000: 290–91). The total area of the Hawaiian Islands is larger than any other group of Polynesian islands, giving the first inhabitants plenty of space to occupy and develop. Again unlike the Maori, Hawaiians appear to have continued to interact with other island groups, exchanging material culture and perhaps ideologies. Initial settlements were in the form of small hamlets along the coast; evidence suggests that these residents kept cultivated gardens and had domesticated dogs, chickens, and possibly pigs (Kirch 2000: 293). By 1500 CE, the population of the Hawaiian Islands had expanded exponentially. Agricultural production intensified, with hillsides being terraced and the development of lowland irrigation systems; fish management systems (in the form of fish ponds) were created, and people began to live in more marginal areas due to their ability to produce food away from the optimal coasts. Land management became an important element in Hawaiian society.

Hawaiian Society

As population expanded and exploitation of less optimal regions intensified, the need to collect and store surpluses in case of temporary lower subsistence production became important. Community leaders advanced their political positions by organizing the construction of irrigation systems and associating themselves with important deities responsible for water and fertility (Kirch 2000: 295). It was not long before community leaders became territorial chiefs with substantial power, fielding warriors to defend and expand their territory, and constructing regionally important temple systems at which the chief conducted ceremonies critical to the well-being of the population. By approximately 1600 CE, a land tenure system known as *ahupua'a* had been created. Territorial units in this system consisted of land that extended from the mountains to the coast, thereby incorporating multiple ecological areas that produced a variety of crops and other resources (Kirch 2000: 296). It is the development of the ahupua'a system along with other factors in the Hawaiian social system that recently caused some scholars to define it as archaic state rather than complex chiefdom.

Unlike Maori culture, Hawaiian kinship structure did not define relationships or dictate land holdings. Descent groups and lineages were not at the forefront of social relationships; rather the Hawaiians saw themselves as differentiated by class distinctions (Kirch 2010; Sahlins 1985). Commoners, known as *maka'āinana* in Hawaiian, were utterly distinct from elites and the "chiefly class" and consisted of those who worked the land but did not own it; they were required to pay tribute to their overlords for the right to work the land (Kirch 2010). There was some differentiation among commoners based on their skill, but for the most part, they occupied the same stratum of Hawaiian society. Further, there was no movement out of the commoner class into the elite level; thus class society was endogamous or caste-like. A focus on lineage and descent groups was largely absent among the maka'āinana class. Ethnographic and historical reports note that commoners only reckoned ancestors back two generations (parents and grandparents) and kept track only of the two following generations (children and grandchildren). There is some evidence to suggest that this view of kinship was mandated by the elite class who made it *kapu* (forbidden) for commoners to trace kinship relationships into deep history (Hommon 2013: 11–17). Further, distinctions among various kin outside the nuclear family were largely absent. Though kin relationships were important on a day-to-day basis within the household, such ties did not define social identity or social positioning.

Below the commoner maka'āinana class was another class known as the *kauwā*, translated as "outcast" or "slave." Not much is known of this class and how it developed. Kauwā people were apparently marked in some fashion, probably by facial tattoos (Kirch 2010: 14). It is unclear what work they were assigned, and it may be that they lived apart from general Hawaiian society. Some accounts describe them as "low-born," but how they became differentiated from commoners isn't known. They may have had different origins or been war captives. One service the kauwā consistently supplied was to be the source of human sacrifices at Hawaiian temples (Hommon 2013: 11; Kirch 2010).

Hawaiian Leadership

At the pinnacle of Hawaiian society was the elite or *ali'i* class, which included a set of ranked chiefs, their families, and associated entourage. Members of the ali'i were the "kings, priests, governors, war leaders, landlords, and bureaucrats," occupying "virtually every administrative position of political, military, economic, and ritual power in ancient Hawai'i" (Hommon 2013: 17). Hawaiian ali'i derived their power from the land and the constituent commoners they controlled, their ability to acquire both subsistence and luxury goods through the labor of commoners, emphasis on their own ancestry, and their association with major religious practices and ritual purity (known as *mana*, similar to the belief found among the Maori). The ali'i class was ranked primarily on the basis of land ownership and ancestry, which in turn defined their level of possession of mana, wealth, societal position, and relationship to the king. Some studies have identified over ten chiefly ranks in the ali'i class with those at the top level (the king of course at the apex) being most godlike, i.e., divine, while those at the lowest level were generally one step above commoners. The two highest ranks, which included the king, required those in their presence to lie prostrate on the ground, those in the third highest rank may have required people to sit in their presence, and those in lower ranks required descending degrees of respectful treatment (Hommon 2013: 20–21).

Unlike the commoners, elites were quite concerned with kinship relationships since these, in part, defined their status. The ali'i needed to reckon ancestry back at least ten generations in order to legitimate their presence in the class. The more highly positioned the ancestors, the more highly ranked the family within the class. In fact, Hawaiian elite families are well known for interfamily marriage designed to keep the bloodline, and the mana, pure and powerful. Ultimate power and wealth was derived from one's position within the ahupua'a land management system. Lesser chiefs held territorial units (those running from coast to mountains), the size of which dictated their income; these lesser chiefs were beholden to more powerful or paramount chiefs who owned numerous territorial units. Lesser chiefs also owed tribute and services such as the provision of warriors to the paramount chiefs (Kirch 2000: 297–99). The "king" held all the ahupua'a units as his, with each descending chief owing tribute from the lands as well as necessary services to the king. Besides agricultural products from the lands, ahupua'a units may have held fish ponds, which could also provide a source of wealth. The ahupua'a were grouped into districts, some containing just a few units and other large ones containing dozens. By the time of contact in the 18th century, there were four Hawaiian kingdoms scattered across the islands, each containing at least 25 districts, some districts possessing as many as 70 ahupua'a (Hommon 2013: 21). Up-the-line tribute from this many units of land paid to the king would have created a tremendous revenue base for his economic power.

Besides their control of the lands, the ali'i had a firm hold on the production of desirable crafts, particularly those that symbolized power and wealth. Important crafts included helmets, feathered headdresses and capes (Figure 4.10), breastplates, woven mats, barkcloth, and wooden items (Kirch 2010: 42–46). Craft-workers who specialized in these goods had elite patrons and were often housed near or even within elite houses. Their labor was controlled by the chiefly class, and the goods were used exclusively by members of that class. The more highly placed and wealthy the ali'i family, the greater the number of craft-workers under their control. Most prized were the craft-makers who constructed canoes (Hommon 2013: 47). These were critical to the fishing industry but also to warcraft. Constructing a sea-worthy and properly designed canoe was necessary to demonstrate a chief's position in society. These craft-workers were from the commoner class but were more highly ranked than those who simply worked the land. At the top of the craft rank were the canoe-makers who were not far below the lowest level of the ali'i class. The ability of the ali'i to control the labor of commoners skilled in luxury crafts, and to prevent such items from ending up in the hands of commoners, was one more factor demonstrating that the economic system in place in ancient Hawaii was deeply sophisticated, verging on what is often seen in an archaic state society (see Chapter 3).

To protect and expand their lands, Hawaiian chiefs and kings could call on commoners who farmed their lands to serve as warriors; ali'i chiefs were often skilled in the art of war and served as commanders of the men (Hommon 2013). A number of historical records describe inter-island warfare between competing kings seeking to expand their holdings. Capturing new ahupua'a was a sure method to expand the wealth base of chiefs and kings. Besides the acquisition of the land, the commoners associated with it became part of the kingdom, as did any skilled craft-workers that had been attached to the ahupua'a. Intra- and inter-island conflicts appear to have been a consistent part of the emergence of the Hawaiian complex chiefdoms and incipient archaic state.

FIGURE 4.10 Example of a Hawaiian Feathered Cape, collected by Captain James Cook, and housed in the Australian Museum

Source: Licensed under Creative Commons Attribution-Share Alike 3.0 Unported license, via Wikimedia Commons

Hawaiian religion consisted of numerous gods and goddesses overseeing all elements of Hawaiian life. Of considerable importance was Lono, the god of clouds, wind, and rain, and Kane, the god of fresh water, each associated with successful agricultural production. The god of war was Kū and was critical to Hawaiian kings determined to enlarge, or protect, their kingdoms. There were lesser gods and goddesses who presided over other aspects of Hawaiian life including over various crafts, childbirth, fishing, and other activities. Commoner Hawaiians could build a shrine in their work areas or near their homes in order to worship these deities. Larger temples in ahupua'a and districts were usually built by the powerful chiefs of the region and were managed by priests dedicated to the god of the temple (Hommon 2013: 90–91). The most important temples were dedicated to the various gods of war, including Kū, and managed by the highest-ranking priests. It was at these temples that the king carried out ceremonies that included ritual human sacrifice likely of a member of the kauwā outcast class or of prisoners of war (Kolb and Dixon 2002).

In addition to the Hawaiian notion of mana, they had a strong belief in the concept of kapu (akin to "tapu" among the Maori). As noted, among the Hawaiians, there was a strong belief that mana flowed unequally; little was present in the bodies of commoners, but among the higher ranking Hawaiians, it was quite substantial: "in the more highly stratified societies the chiefs came to occupy particular roles as sources or vehicles of *mana* on which the society at large depended for its well-being" (Kirch 2010: 38). Kings and high chiefs were the most kapu, or sacred, and thus, strict prohibitions were associated with them. As noted, it was required to prostrate oneself in the presence of kings or high chiefs. Myriad prohibitions in the form of food preparation, clothing manufacture, and touching of their bodies were in place in order to preserve their purity and protect them from potentially polluting contacts (Kirch 2010: 39–40).

It was the belief of all Hawaiians that the mana present in their highest-ranking leaders was akin to divinity. They were, in fact, called *ali'i akua*, which translates to "god-kings" (Kirch 2010: 41). The king was not only the political and economic leader of his people but the ritual leader as well; due to his powerful mana and his deep ancestry, he was able to communicate with the Hawaiian deities and convey the people's needs. Thus, semidivine Hawaiian kings had ultimate power to ensure the health and well-being of their people; they had the power to require human sacrifice; they could command their men to take to land and canoes to pursue warfare; they could direct laborers to build massive temples to important Hawaiian deities (Kolb 1994). They were, in every way, supreme rulers of their people.

Hawaiian Complexity

Pre-contact Hawaiian society was deeply stratified with powerful rulers and elites who controlled lands, economic strategies, trade, and, to a large extent, religion. Warfare was waged in order to expand the power base of a king and his associated chiefs. A sophisticated craft production system and market economy was present throughout the Hawaiian Islands, and Hawaiian leaders organized the labor of the commoners to build elaborate temples at which human sacrifice took place on a regular basis. It is clear that the sociopolitical and economic structure of ancient Hawaii is qualitatively different from that which was present among the pre-contact Maori. Whether a highly complex chiefdom or an emergent archaic state, ancient Hawaii embodies many of the factors that scholarship deems necessary to identify a society as "state level."

Conclusion

The case studies in this chapter presented four examples of ancient cultures that, in comparative analysis, can be gauged as ranging from the less complex chiefdom structure of the Polynesian

Maori to the Hawaiian system that has recently been discussed as an emergent state. Sandwiched between these two is the less complex chiefdom found at ancient Great Zimbabwe and the far more economically and perhaps politically sophisticated Chacoan system in the American southwest. These case studies illustrated how the various human cultural institutions defined in Chapter 2, constituent in levels of complexity, play out in actual archaeological cultures that are not universally deemed (complex) ancient states. The remainder of this book, with the exception of Chapter 14, employs the same methodologies used here to define pre-state and emergent state societies to capture the intricacies of ancient civilizations across the continents and through time.

5

SOUTHWEST ASIA

Ancient Mesopotamia and Its Neighbors

Introduction

Mesopotamia and adjacent territories of the Near East (the modern Middle East; Figure 5.1) provide the earliest examples of complex societies in the ancient world, together with other "firsts"—first farming, first cities, and first writing—that supported and propelled that complexity. Over the span of several millennia, the Near Eastern world saw a range of political and social forms, from villages to city-states, to territorial states, to empires. Despite, or perhaps because of, environmental limitations, Mesopotamian and other Near Eastern societies developed political organizations that featured a deep intertwining of social, economic, military, and religious power. Political leadership required the support of the Mesopotamian gods and temples; it also relied heavily on high-yield agriculture that was the basis for each city's survival. As the first examples of complex societies in this book, ancient southwestern Asian states and empires provide a full range of types of political and economic organizations and social complexity.

Geography and Chronology

Geography and Ecological Setting

The vast geographic territory covered in this chapter has, at its core, the alluvial valleys of the Tigris and Euphrates Rivers and their tributaries in modern-day Iraq. These valleys provided the principal means of life for the ancient inhabitants—water and soil for crops, crafts, and building materials—and they became the focal point for most settlement. Beyond the valleys was the Fertile Crescent, a boundary zone of low hills extending from the Levant (Israel, Jordan, Syria, and Lebanon) through southeastern Turkey and along the modern border between Iraq and Iran. In all, the Middle East covers 5 million square kilometers.

This sizable territory encompasses a large range of local climate and vegetation zones. The Mesopotamian core has hot, dry summers, and cooler, moister winters, with an average annual rainfall of 250 millimeters. The shortage of rainfall meant that inhabitants of most areas of Mesopotamia practiced irrigation agriculture, while in many territories to the west, north, and east, they could grow crops using just the water provided by rainfall and snowmelt. These outer territories, many at higher elevations, experienced greater seasonal variability in temperatures and annual precipitation, which sometimes affected crop yields. Throughout southwest Asia, farming

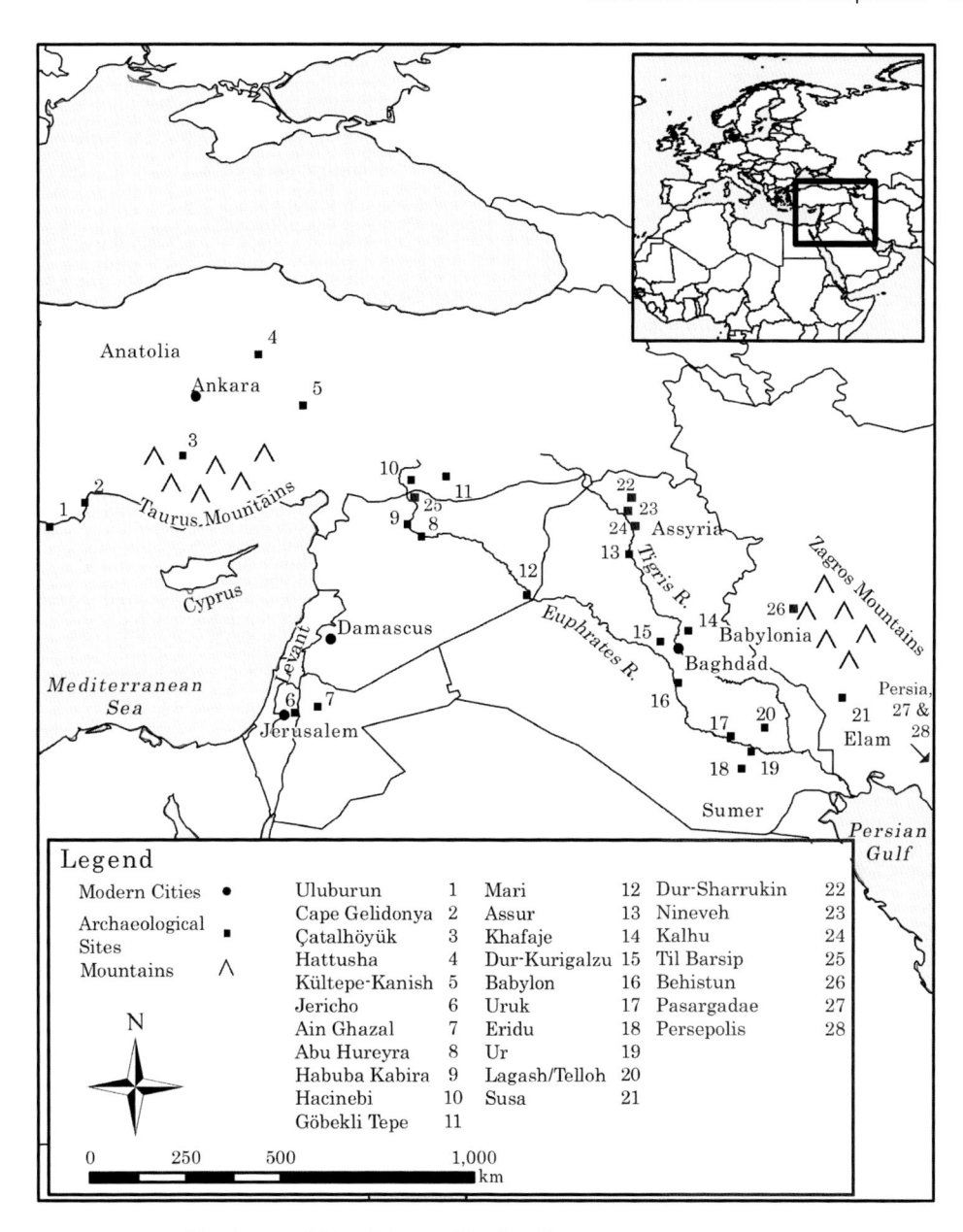

FIGURE 5.1 Map of Regions and Sites Discussed in the Chapter

Source: B. Spencer

was supplemented by herding domestic animals, maintained for meat, dairy products, wool and hair, and traction or transport.

Besides its rich soils and abundant water, southern Mesopotamia possessed few mineral resources before the discovery of oil. In the mountains and foothills beyond Mesopotamia, however, lie a variety of natural resources, including metals, stones, and other necessities. This disparity in the distribution of resources played an important role from the very beginning of settled life in southwest Asia in the development of economic, political, and social relationships between territories.

The Chronological Sequence

The timeline provided in this chapter (Table 5.1) covers the period from the beginnings of settled life in southwest Asia (around 12,000 BCE) to the rise and fall of empires in the 1st millennium BCE. In Neolithic farming villages (ca. 9600–6000 BCE), social and political differentiation and ritual behaviors developed. Subsequent Chalcolithic (ca. 6000–4200 BCE) settlements were established along the rivers of the Mesopotamian alluvium, and populations grew. To serve larger populations in towns, both occupational specialization and incipient forms of centralized government arose. Economic specialization and differentiation expanded in the period of urbanism and city-state development in Mesopotamia during the Uruk and Early Dynastic Periods (ca. 4200–2350 BCE) when populations collected in autonomous urban centers, each with a surrounding territory that provided for subsistence needs.

In the late 3rd and 2nd millennia, territorial states appeared, as charismatic rulers unified multiple urban centers under a single government. These leaders balanced military prowess with devotion to the gods of their home cities. The royal dynasties included the Akkadian, Ur III, Old Babylonian,

TABLE 5.1 Chronological Periods and Sites Discussed in Chapter 5

Dates	Period	Sites Discussed in Chapter	Cultural Horizons
ca. 20,000–9600 BCE	Epipaleolithic	Abu Hureyra	Sedentary communities; foraging
ca. 9600–6900 BCE	Pre-Pottery (Aceramic) Neolithic	Jericho, Ain Ghazal, Göbekli Tepe	Domestication of plants and animals; ritual and monumental architecture; mortuary behaviors
ca. 6900–6000 BCE	Pottery (Ceramic) Neolithic	Çatalhöyük	Ceramic production
ca. 6000–4200 BCE	Chalcolithic (Hassuna, Samarra, Halaf, Ubaid)	Eridu	Migration to southern Mesopotamia; formal temples; egalitarian society
4200–3000 BCE	Uruk Period	Uruk, Habuba Kabira	Urbanism; state organization; trade colonies; monumental art; kingship
3000–2350 BCE	Early Dynastic Period	Lagash, Khafaje, Ur	City-state organization; temples and palaces; dynastic rule
2350–1100 BCE	3rd- and 2nd-Millennium Territorial States (Akkadian, Neo-Sumerian, Old Babylonian, Kassite, Mitanni, Middle Assyrian)	Agade, Ur, Babylon, Mari, Assur, Kültepe-Kanish, Hattusha, Dur-Kurigalzu, Uluburun, Cape Gelidonya	Territorial states; standing armies; international trade and diplomacy
934–331 BCE	1st-Millennium Empires (Neo-Assyrian, Neo-Babylonian, Persian)	Kalhu (Nimrud), Dur-Sharrukin, Nineveh, Babylon, Pasargade, Persepolis	Empires; mass deportations and population movements; provincial governments

and Kassite states (ca. 2350–1150 BCE); this period is marked by more frequent warfare, as well as by trade and dynastic relationships with distant partners like Egypt and the Aegean. Territorial states comprised multiethnic and multilingual populations. Eventually, the 2nd millennium territorial states of Mesopotamia each fell to internal or external enemies, and their decline highlights the weakness of a large territory being administered by a single center. The empires that emerged in the 1st millennium BCE—the Neo-Assyrians (934–609 BCE), Neo-Babylonians (626–539 BCE), and Persians (539–331 BCE)—corrected for these earlier vulnerabilities by creating complex bureaucratic organizations that facilitated the administration of massive territories through a combination of militarism, religious devotion, and strategic economic management. Their infrastructure facilitated communication and trade at long distances, and their populations included a tremendous array of ethnicities, languages, and religious systems. Each empire was brought down by a combination of forces, culminating in the victory of Alexander the Great over the Persian king Darius III in 331 BCE.

Pre-State Cultures: Epipaleolithic and Neolithic Southwest Asia

Following the Last Glacial Maximum of 18,000 to 20,000 years ago, temperature and moisture levels across southwest Asia began to rise. In the Levant, this period of intensified climate change is known as the Epipaleolithic (ca. 20,000–9600 BCE). The warming period peaked around 10,800 BCE, and was followed by the Younger Dryas (ca. 10,800–9600 BCE), a brief phase marked by a spike of cold and dry weather that caused vegetation to contract (Bar-Yosef and Valla 1991). Early in the following Neolithic Period, the climate ameliorated once more, and warmer and wetter conditions prevailed.

Epipaleolithic

The term "Epipaleolithic" is applied mainly to the cultures of the Levant. During the Epipaleolithic, populations relied on hunting for subsistence, but plant foods played an increasingly important role in diets over time. By the end of the Epipaleolithic, people in the Levant had domesticated at least one cereal, whether intentionally or not, and at least one animal, the dog. They lived in sedentary communities, sometimes year-round, close to sources of fresh water and a variety of potential food sources (Simmons 2007: 61). Heavy groundstone tools attest to the processing (grinding) of seeds and/or nuts; they also suggest at least seasonal occupation of sites, as they would be impractical to move.

Toward the end of the Epipaleolithic, climate change intensified, and social change accelerated. Residents of the Levant continued to hunt and gather but relied increasingly on smaller territories around their sites, resulting in a more limited variety of food resources. At this time, a new focus on burials may indicate a concern for individual and group identities. Sites throughout the Levant include built structures, burials, and an increasingly diversified material culture. Abu Hureyra, on the Euphrates River in Syria, was a settlement of round, semisubterranean structures of perishable materials, each surrounded by smaller pits, housing 100–300 people, who hunted gazelles and other herd animals and collected 150 species of wild plants (Akkermans and Schwartz 2003: 29–30). Among the botanical remains of Epipaleolithic Abu Hureyra were seeds of domestic rye, a weed species that may have become domesticated as a by-product of selective harvesting and sowing of edible cereals that it grew near (Moore 1991).

Neolithic

The Neolithic Period (ca. 9600–6000 BCE) saw conditions of full domestication (eventually including herd and other animals) and full sedentism. Groups experienced significant social changes as well, including continued population growth, new levels of cooperative activities, and production of visual art. Technological change accompanied sedentism, with developments that facilitated farming, food processing, cooking, and storage. In fact, technology provides the division between the long Pre-Pottery (or Aceramic) Neolithic, ca. 9600–6900 BCE, and the Pottery (Ceramic) Neolithic, ca. 6900–6000 BCE.

Pre-Pottery (Aceramic) Neolithic (PPN)

The Pre-Pottery Neolithic (PPN) emerged out of the stark cold of the millennium-long Younger Dryas during which many sedentary Epipaleolithic communities may have turned toward more mobile subsistence strategies. After 9600 BCE, however, a new phase of higher temperatures and moisture favored sedentism, population growth, and renewed use of localized resources. Most early PPN sites were small, averaging 2,000–3,000 square meters (Barker 2006: 131), and their locations were near fresh water, alluvial soils, and forest (Bar-Yosef 1989). Sites yield evidence for the limited cultivation of domesticated cereals (emmer and einkorn wheat, barley) and pulses (lentil, pea, and bitter vetch), which did not yet make up the majority of plant foods consumed. Groups continued to hunt, though they focused on just a few species, gazelle in particular, that migrated seasonally.

Jericho, located in the Jordan Valley, is in some ways a typical early PPN site, with round to oval semisubterranean houses of sun-dried bricks. Burials in shallow pits were set in abandoned structures and spaces between houses; in a few cases, the skulls had been removed post-mortem and cached. A stone wall extended at least partly around the site and measured 3.6 meters high and 1.8 meters wide at the base; in the southwestern corner of the site, a round tower stood 8.2 meters high and 9 meters in diameter at the base. While scholars continue to debate the purpose of the wall, recent analysis suggests that Jericho faced no significant local enemies, so that the wall's function could be to protect animals from predators or to protect the town itself from potential floodwaters (Bar-Yosef 1986). Jericho's wall provides the earliest evidence for monumental architecture, requiring labor coordination and planning.

By the later PPN, some sites were larger, with areas up to 20 hectares, and with maximum population estimates of 2,000 people (Barker 2006: 137; Bar-Yosef and Meadow 1995). A number of these "megasites" were located at the boundaries between environmental zones (alluvium and forest, highlands and desert) (Simmons 2007: 176). Although most were short-lived, their size denotes population growth beyond natural processes; they attracted populations from surrounding areas.

Also by late PPN, the enclosure wall at Jericho went out of use. As earlier, skeletons between structures and in abandoned houses sometimes had their skulls removed; 12 of these skulls had features remodeled with plaster (Figure 5.2). More than 60 skulls found at sites throughout the Levant were manipulated in this way, used apparently in public events, perhaps representing a set of generalized "ancestors" for the people of the towns (Kuijt 2001, 2008). Other sites provide evidence of ritual as well. Ain Ghazal, on the eastern side of the Jordan Valley, possessed two caches of plaster anthropoid figurines, all about half life-sized, made on reed frames. The bodies of these figurines are curiously sexless, and the faces, with shell eyes and painted mouths, resemble the Jericho skulls in materials and lifelike appearance.

Overall, the Pre-Pottery Neolithic of the Levant provides evidence for momentous economic developments: the full adoption of an agricultural lifestyle, with domesticated plants and animals; long-distance trade for particular natural and mineral resources; and the development of technologies to aid subsistence. Villages increased in size, growing from family-based groupings to settlements of hundreds of people. While some cooperative labor was necessary for building, the organization of agricultural labor is unknown; families may have tended their own plots of land and herds independently, or villages may have worked communally to produce for everyone's

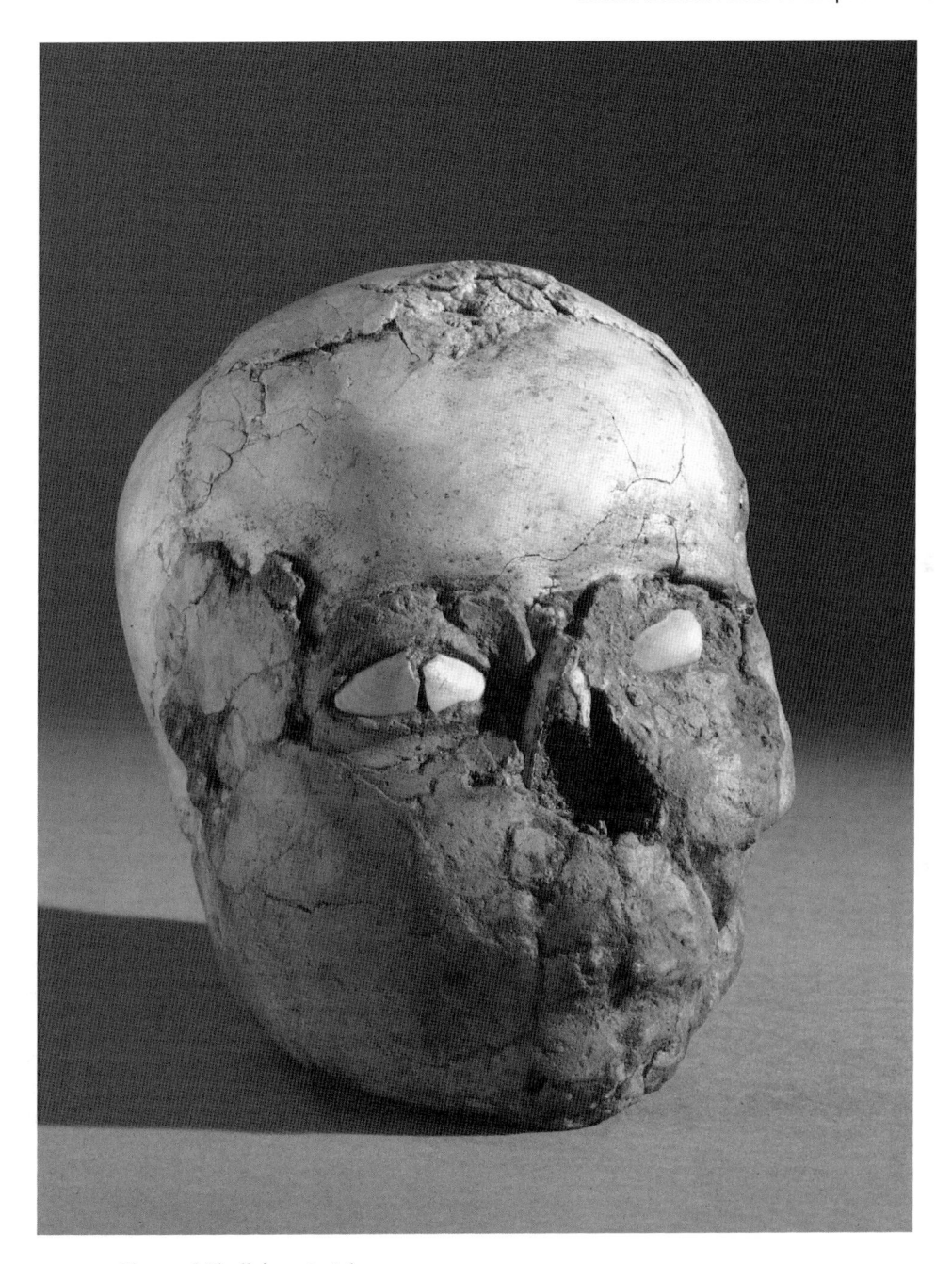

FIGURE 5.2 Plastered Skull from Jericho
Source: © Trustees of the British Museum; Photo Credit: Erich Lessing / Art Resource, NY

subsistence needs. Pre-Pottery Neolithic sites demonstrate the development of ritual processes and symbolism that may have eased tensions within growing communities, rituals that focused on bodies and burials (perhaps connecting a community to its past), special purpose structures that brought people together for common actions, and the creation of attention-focusing works of "art" like the Ain Ghazal plaster figurines and Jericho skulls (see Box 5.1).

BOX 5.1 NEAR EASTERN RELIGION

The site of Göbekli Tepe, in southeastern Turkey, profoundly demonstrates the significance of religion and the sophistication of symbolic manipulation at an early stage of societal complexity. All of the structures so far excavated were special purpose, all semisubterranean; each contained a number of monolithic stone columns (weighing up to 10 tons each) sculpted in relief with depictions of animals, including snakes, foxes, boars, felines, and birds (Peters and Schmidt 2004). Some of these animals were hunted in the Neolithic, but most were not, suggesting that the symbolic world in which these images participated focused more on their social meaning than dietary function. As Göbekli has neither domestic architecture nor evidence for food processing or consumption, its users must have come from outside the site; it functioned as an aggregation site for ritual activities conducted by surrounding mobile and/or sedentary groups.

By the 3rd millennium BCE, city temples for major gods had been established at major settlements across Mesopotamia. The names of these gods are attested on cuneiform tablets found in or near temples, and their representations are found in relief sculpture and seal iconography. Temples served a variety of functions in an Early Dynastic Period city. Smaller temples were integrated into neighborhoods, functioning as neighborhood places of worship, or locations for the worship of minor gods, while the oval temple precincts were state-supported and hosted major festivals.

Pottery (Ceramic) Neolithic (PN)

The Pottery Neolithic Period (PN; ca. 6900–6000 BCE) in the Levant is briefer than the Aceramic Neolithic, and the archaeological remains suggest something of a decline in population, with fewer sites overall and generally smaller settlement sizes. In the southern Levant, clay use for pottery and figurine production became widespread. Small farming villages, with a full range of domestic plants and animals, were the rule, with few if any public or special purpose sites or structures identifiable. Pottery production, for cooking, storage, and display purposes, developed first in Syria and spread quickly throughout the Levant.

The Precursors to Complexity in the Neolithic

The Neolithic Period therefore sets the stage for all subsequent political, economic, and social developments in southwest Asia. The establishment of sedentary communities, and their progressive reliance on food production over hunting and foraging, allowed for population growth and surplus production rooted in a reliable food supply. Missing from the archaeological evidence are conscious signifiers of social and economic differentiation. Most work and day-to-day decision-making appears to have taken place within the family or co-residential household. At the same time, larger-scale projects required communal action and perhaps temporary forms of labor command. Community activities focused on rituals may have served to reduce the tensions of life in larger settlements.

The shifts to sedentism and to food production were necessary precursors to further developments in complex society in southwest Asia. Village life provided the setting for changing attitudes and perceptions about human nature and community. Within villages, there developed concepts of privacy and private property, potential for conflict, and new ways of thinking about and organizing production and reproduction (Byrd 1994). Within the growing sedentary communities of the Chalcolithic, divisions and distinctions among individuals, and among groups, accelerated and became more finely articulated, eventually giving rise to urbanism and rulership in the Uruk Period of Mesopotamia.

Pre-State Cultures: Chalcolithic and Uruk Mesopotamia and the Rise of Urbanism

Two significant environmental factors contributed to the development of Chalcolithic and 4th-millennium societies of Mesopotamia. One was climate stabilization, resulting in the recession of the Persian Gulf to the present sea level (Huot 1989), which opened up significant areas for settlement and established the major rivers into fixed beds. The other was the introduction of irrigation agriculture, which allowed for long-term settlement in areas that received under 200 millimeters of rainfall per year on average. Irrigation also produced significantly higher yields than dry farming, meaning that larger populations could be sustained within a given area.

Chalcolithic

It is during the Chalcolithic (ca. 6000–4200 BCE) that the southern alluvial zone of Mesopotamia was settled, while in the 4th-millennium settlements there grew to city size and developed the main features of sociopolitical complexity. By the end of the Chalcolithic Period throughout southwest Asia, settlement size increased to nearly urban proportions, clear signs of social and economic differentiation emerged, long-distance trade relations intensified, and craft specialization developed in various technological realms. These processes culminated in the emergence of the city of Uruk and other urban centers toward the end of the 4th millennium, settlements with new and deliberate manifestations of belief and new positions of leadership.

Early Mesopotamian Chalcolithic cultures, the Hassuna (ca. 6000–5000 BCE) and Samarra (ca. 5750–5000 BCE), were based in northern Mesopotamia and relied on both dry farming and irrigation agriculture, as well as herding. Adults and infants were buried in and around houses (Matthews 2000). Residents engaged in long-distance trade for turquoise and rock crystal (both probably from Iran), obsidian from Anatolia, and shell from the Mediterranean or Red Sea (Roaf 1990). Samarran material culture included stone stamp seals with geometric designs and female clay figurines in seated or standing position, sometimes placed in graves.

The Halaf culture (ca. 5500–4500 BCE) succeeded the Hassuna in northern Iraq, but extended also into southeastern Turkey, Syria, and the Zagros foothills of Iran. Typical Halaf material culture included open form ceramic vessels, often intricately painted, sometimes with bichrome (red and black) and even polychrome (with the addition of white) designs. Architecture included both rectilinear structures and round *tholoi*—circular brick structures on stone foundations, ranging from 3 to 9 meters in diameter, with an adjacent rectangular room. Halaf sites sometimes feature clay female figurines with exaggerated sexual characteristics, found in domestic contexts.

The final Chalcolithic phase is the Ubaid, dated ca. 5500–4200 BCE. Unlike earlier Chalcolithic Periods, Ubaid pottery is dominated by simple decorative motifs; some vessels were made on the slow wheel, with some standardization and specialization in production. Ubaid cultural elements appeared in northern Iraq, outside its southern Mesopotamian core region, as well as in southwestern Iran, and in the Persian Gulf region. In the latter area, at least 50% of the pottery was made in southern Mesopotamia; Ubaid-Period residents probably explored this region, arriving on boats, and traded with its residents (Frifelt 1989; Oates 1983).

Ubaid architecture is distinctive; both domestic and public structures were built of mudbrick and shared a common tripartite form: three parallel sections, the central one running the full length of the building. On either side, smaller rooms housed a variety of activities; some served as staircases up to a flat roof. At Eridu, the principal architectural remains belonged to a long-lived temple, rebuilt and remodeled 15 times. It began as a single room with a raised altar inside, and grew to a complex tripartite structure atop a brick platform, with niched and buttressed elaboration (Roaf 1984). Fish remains found within the Ubaid-level temple are taken to be appropriate offerings to the god of fresh water, Enki. Eridu also had an extensive off-site cemetery during the Ubaid Period (Hole 1989). The burials suggest an egalitarian society: both sexes and all ages were represented, with most tombs containing jewelry and a couple of pots only.

Overall, the Ubaid Period provides evidence for significant development of social complexity. Eridu's temple attests to the appearance of formal religious practices in monumental, public settings. Different-sized Ubaid-Period houses indicated differences in wealth and social standing. But in general, identifiable physical evidence for elite objects of display is missing. Stein (1994) suggests that this absence means that Ubaid towns were the centers for chiefdoms based on agriculture, with elites dominating subsistence production through their control over land, water, and/or labor. Ubaid society may have experienced some social differentiation, but it may have been masked, as political leaders sought to provide stable economic backing to their supporters, sometimes using religion to bolster their positions.

Uruk Period

With the end of the Ubaid Period, Mesopotamia entered into a new and distinctive phase of development, the Uruk Period (ca. 4200–3000 BCE), in which patterns of social, economic, and political life underwent a set of intensely disruptive changes. While the reasons for change are unclear, by the start of the Late Uruk Period, around 3300 BCE, much of southern Mesopotamia's population lived in a city with a single ruler, and many were employed in areas other than agriculture. This urban pattern of settlement and political organization then dominated Mesopotamian society into at least the mid-1st millennium BCE.

Despite the enormity of these changes, Uruk culture shows great continuity from the Ubaid Period (Oates 1960). The core area of settlement continued to be in southern Mesopotamia. The public institutions of the central settlements were still religious in function, and even the expansionist tendencies of the Ubaid Period are reflected, and built on, by Uruk-Period centers (Nissen 1995). Yet the changes that took place, especially in the Late Uruk Period, were stark. Most notable, archaeologically, is the difference in site size: several Mesopotamian and Syrian sites of the 4th millennium grew to near 100 hectares in area, with abrupt changes in population numbers and the abandonment of rural settlement in some regions. Monumental administrative and religious buildings literally towered over residential areas. In the Late Uruk Period, the material culture changes also stand out: new, unpainted pottery forms, new types of administrative artifacts, and newly monumental art that focused on particular individuals and their roles.

The physical changes evident at Uruk Period sites signal two key sociopolitical developments: a shift to urban settlement and the development of state-level organization. New types of administrative leadership were required to organize and carry out subsistence production, manufacture, and long- and short-distance trade, including the establishment of settlements and trade outposts beyond the boundaries of the state.

Survey data indicate that between the Early Uruk Period, ca. 4000–3600 BCE, and the Middle Uruk Period, ca. 3600–3300 BCE, the number of sites in the area around Uruk jumped from 18 to over 100 (Adams 1969). Adams and Nissen (1972) attribute this rise to an influx of population from elsewhere, as this is not natural population growth; Pollock (1999) suggests that the Euphrates River itself changed course in this period, causing disruptions in settlement upstream. By the Late Uruk Period, ca. 3300–3000 BCE, site numbers in the south decreased, but the remaining sites were larger and aligned along water courses. Toward the very end of the period, a single very large center, the city of Uruk, remained.

The City of Uruk

Uruk was 50 to 75 hectares in area in the Middle Uruk, growing to 100 hectares or more (some estimates put it at 250 hectares) by late in the Late Uruk Period (Sweet 1997). Population estimates for the site also range, from 10,000 to 40,000 people (Nissen 2002). The city itself provides the best evidence for urban organization and state development. Uruk has revealed only a partial view of urban planning, as excavations focused largely on the monumental cult buildings in the city's center. Whether Uruk was fortified in the Late Uruk Period is still debated. Evidence for manufacturing is present in one area of the site, though it is not clear what was being made. Residential areas, however, are not yet attested; the Late Uruk neighborhoods must lie below significant deposits of later millennia. Two temple precincts dominated the central section of the city (see Box 5.2). Their contents included both religious and everyday items; especially significant were objects used in communication and administration of the city and its surrounding areas.

BOX 5.2 KEY SITE: URUK AND ITS TEMPLES

The southern Mesopotamian site of Uruk represents the earliest city attested archaeologically in the world. By 3300 BCE, population at this river-based center likely exceeded 10,000, though archaeological research in the 20th century focused on the two temple precincts in the middle of the settlement. The cultic areas of Uruk occupy the central 6 hectares of the site. Two temple areas, one traditionally identified as the temple of the sky god Anu, located in the west, the other dedicated to Inanna, goddess of sex and battle, in the east, rose above the rest of the city. In the Anu temple precinct, the White Temple (so named for its white plaster coating) stood atop a platform with a ramp (Figure 5.3 above). This tripartite structure measured over 22 by 17.5 meters and was decorated inside and out with patterns of niches and buttresses. To the east, the Eanna ("house of Heaven") precinct of Inanna (Figure 5.3 below) held a variety of structures within a 250 by 400 meter area. Over several archaeological levels, there were regular changes to the overall precinct plan. Many buildings had typical tripartite plans like the White Temple; others were more unusual in plan, including platforms topped with pillars, two structures with immense open central courts, and maze-like subterranean buildings. Missing from the Eanna complex is a single structure identifiable as a center for worship; several buildings had plans and features parallel to the White Temple.

The contents of these two temple precincts provide evidence that upholds and builds on the impression that the Late Uruk Period was one of profound social, political, and economic change. Most of the evidence comes from the Eanna precinct and includes religious, administrative, and economic objects. A number of images from Eanna depict religious practices and worshippers, signaling a major shift in artistic practices from previous periods. This includes one near life-sized head, in limestone, of the goddess Inanna, which was probably embellished with metal overlay and stone inlay and which would have been attached to a body (maybe of

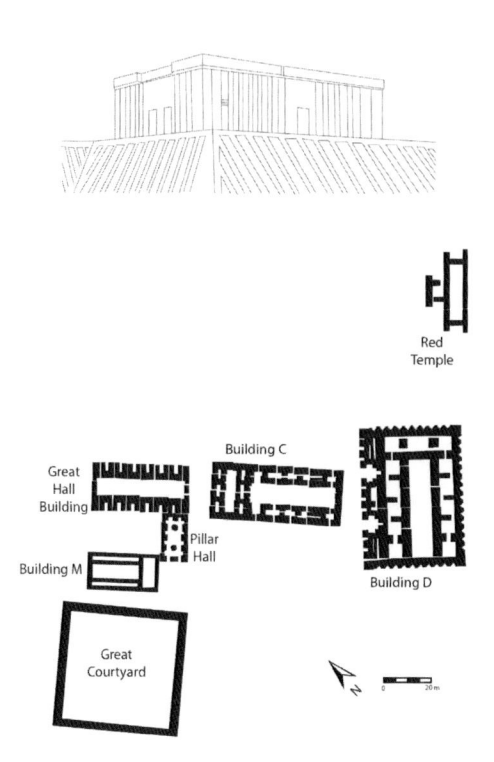

FIGURE 5.3 Above: Reconstruction of the White Temple at Uruk; Below: Plan of the Eanna Precinct at Uruk

Source: J.C. Ross

wood) and set in one of the structures. The Warka Vase, a 1-meter high alabaster vessel with religious carvings, depicts plants, animals, and a procession of nude males bearing vessels filled with food; this procession culminates, at the top, with two figures: a male in a headband and elaborate belted skirt facing a woman standing between two doorposts, with marvelous manufactured items (including two vessels shaped exactly like the Warka Vase itself) behind her. Most scholars see this set of images as a depiction of a religious ritual, perhaps an annual offering of thanksgiving to the city's patron goddess (or her priestess), led by its ruler (often dubbed "the man in the net skirt").

Most of Uruk's pottery was unpainted and utilitarian, used in cooking, serving, and storing foods and other items. Few decorative devices were applied; at most, jars might be slipped and incised with geometric patterns. While this is a significant change from earlier in the Chalcolithic, the trend toward simplification and standardization of pottery had begun in the Ubaid Period. The ultimate example of this is the beveled-rim bowl, a coarse clay vessel that was mass-produced in molds, creating a standard-sized pot. The thousands of these vessels found at Uruk-Period sites suggest that beveled-rim bowls were made by specialist potters, perhaps working full time for the temple institutions. The absence of elaborately decorated pottery suggests that clay vessels were no longer used in status display and public rituals. Stone vessels, like the Warka Vase, may have taken their place.

Quite abundant at Uruk are objects with economic and administrative functions. These indicate that the temple precincts possessed significant land holdings, flocks, and manufacturing interests; they also supported large numbers of employees. Some of the administrative and economic items are of types already known in earlier periods: clay tokens used for counting and simple transactions of goods (Schmandt-Besserat 1992) and seals, in stamp and new cylindrical form. The cylinder seals, carved with complicated scenes, had an advantage over stamps in that they could be rolled over larger clay surfaces and repeated endlessly. The larger surface area allowed for greater elaboration and the creation of more distinctive, individualized designs.

Cylinder seals were pressed on a variety of clay items, including object closures and door sealings. More important, though, is their use on a new class of administrative item, clay tablets, which appeared at Uruk and a number of other sites at this time. The 5,000 tablets from Uruk are the earliest written documents known to us; individual signs, each standing for an object, idea, or amount, were incised or pressed into wet clay in records of economic transactions. These records did not have a long use-life; the majority were used as architectural fill, providing leveling material for later building projects. The types of items recorded in Uruk's tablets offer a view into the temples' many economic and administrative responsibilities, including land, agricultural products, domestic animals and animal products, labor, textiles, and other manufactured items (Englund 1998; Nissen 1985). The labor force employed by the temple may have been paid, in part, in food rations, supplied to them in the ubiquitous vessel type found at nearly every Uruk-Period site, the beveled-rim bowl. This coarse, mass-produced vessel could have held 1 liter of barley, a standard ration size for Mesopotamian workers (Nissen 1985).

The Uruk Landscape: Social, Political, and Economic Structures

Other southern Mesopotamian sites show elements of the same sociocultural developments as at Uruk, albeit at a smaller scale and a slightly later date. These parallels suggest that a similar cultural and social system and language dominated the whole southern alluvium (Collins 2000). Material culture parallels included administrative artifacts like seals and sealings, tablets, and beveled-rim bowls; monumental architecture; and iconography, including representations of the man in the net skirt. While Uruk appears to have led the way in the development of complexity, the opportunities for cooperation and competition that other southern towns offered may have fueled the political and social advances of the Late Uruk Period. Evidence from both Iran and Syria indicates that urban development also took place during the 4th millennium outside Mesopotamia proper. In Syria, a sophisticated indigenous culture seems to have developed urbanism on its own, with sites growing to up to and over 100 hectares before contacts began with Late Uruk Mesopotamia (Dolce 2000; Ur 2002).

One feature of the Uruk Period that sets it apart from prior phases of Near Eastern prehistory was that southern Mesopotamians founded colonies distant from their homeland. Unlike earlier periods of extensive long-distance trade, Uruk-Period colonialism involved the movement of people to permanent settlements far from their homeland. This facilitated trade and the extraction of raw materials unavailable in the south, including metals, timber, stones, and bitumen. Southern Mesopotamian colonies are found in southeastern Turkey, northern Syria, and the highlands of western Iran, in all cases located near river and overland routes. Settlements took a variety of forms, from true colonies, with a completely southern Mesopotamian population and material culture, to small outposts attached to indigenous settlements (Stein 1999; Stein and Özbal 2007). Colonialism dates to the Middle to Late Uruk Period, peaking and then rapidly falling off in Late Uruk. Some settlements appear to have been occupied for over 100 years, while others were short-lived. Colonies are recognized largely on the basis of their intrusive material culture: architecture, pottery, and administrative items that would be at home in southern Mesopotamia but not among the local cultures of Syria, Anatolia, or western Iran.

Complexity in the Uruk Period

This overview of the evidence from the Uruk Period has pointed to a number of areas of significant change from the Chalcolithic cultures that preceded it: changes in art, artifacts and their production, spatial organization, and the extent and intensity of contacts with regions beyond southern Mesopotamia. These material changes suggest more profound societal changes, namely, the development of social complexity and political statehood. They indicate that a central administration was involved in economic management, both of trade and local agricultural and craft production. A set of elite artifacts signified status and roles in a more populous setting. These focus on a specific individual, the man in the net skirt, who played roles in the economy, religion, and military, merging in his person both religious and secular institutions. A similar set of circumstances prevailed, to some degree, in southwestern Iran and northern Syria.

What remains is to consider the reasons that the 4th millennium witnessed such sweeping changes. Initially, when the principal evidence for complexity consisted of Uruk's excavated remains and the changing settlement patterns in its vicinity, explanations focused on demographic change, seeing Uruk itself as a sort of vacuum that drew ever-larger populations into its orbit. More recent explanations have concentrated on the economic causes and benefits of the rise of the Uruk state, particularly since excavations in Syria and Turkey began revealing colony sites beginning in the 1970s.

Guillermo Algaze (2001, 2004, 2008) is the most ardent advocate of these economic viewpoints, postulating that state organization developed in the late 4th millennium in order to regulate trade at both the local and long-distance level. According to this reconstruction, Uruk, settled in the Late Ubaid Period, rapidly capitalized on the natural advantages of its position at the juncture of rich alluvial lands, marshy habitats, and both water and overland transport routes. Algaze believes that Uruk experienced an initial phase of natural population growth in the early 4th millennium, fueled by high agricultural yields made possible by irrigation. As this advantageous position became unmistakable, local hinterland populations moved there as well, introducing a larger pastoralist (and animal) population. With an increased population and a broad range of local resources, the city's leaders, drawn from the families that held the largest and/or most productive land holdings, coordinated the labor and subsistence distribution in ways that supported the larger numbers of people and likely benefited the elites as well. The redistribution system allowed some members of society to turn to pursuits other than farming and herding, including pottery and stone tool production and possibly intellectual pursuits as well.

In the Middle Uruk Period, by 3600 BCE, Uruk began to extend its economic reach and population into areas beyond the southern alluvium, founding colonies along the Euphrates River. It is likely that other southern towns began to grow and compete with Uruk for resources at this time. This competition may have fueled Uruk's final steps toward complexity: the development of institutionalized leadership, and the ideology that supported it, as well as the need to keep track of institutional resources. Full state organization began at Uruk and was then emulated by other Mesopotamian, and later Syrian and Iranian, centers.

While the precise details of Algaze's reconstruction are disputed, most scholars agree that the primary driver of statehood in Mesopotamia was the economy. Wright and Johnson (1975) focused on control of local economic production in the early urban centers of southwestern Iran, and Adams (2005) has stressed the central role of the state in offsetting year-to-year fluctuations in agricultural yield. But Uruk's material culture also focuses attention on the central role of the religious institutions in the early state, a concern that will re-emerge in subsequent sections. These too may have drawn populations to the center, enhancing the prestige of the settlement and propelling it toward urban organization.

City-States: Early Dynastic Mesopotamia

After a brief period when the cultural unity of the Uruk Period broke down into more regional cultures, Mesopotamia experienced a new phase of unity in the Early Dynastic (ED) Period (ca. 2900–2350 BCE). Over the next 500 years, political developments across Mesopotamia saw the land divided into politically autonomous city-states; during the final century of the ED Period, this autonomy broke down somewhat, as charismatic rulers sought to unify larger territories under their control. This latter trend ended with the advent of the Old Akkadian Dynasty, ca. 2350, whose founder created the first Mesopotamian territorial state.

Early Dynastic Period history and developments encompassed all of Mesopotamia, extending into Syria and into regions beyond the rivers. This common culture spanned a number of ethnolinguistic populations. Sumerian speakers, who may be traced back to the Ubaid Period, were the predominant southern population. In the course of the 3rd millennium, however, populations of Akkadian speakers moved into central and northern Mesopotamia, mixing with resident populations. Semitic speakers also dominated Syrian territory. Despite the variety of people from different places of origin, Mesopotamian cities seem to show no ethnic conflict.

Settlement form and political organization of the ED built on Uruk urban development; the majority of the population lived in cities, which were set along rivers and canals (Adams 1969). Each city controlled approximately 15 kilometers of land around it, including a variety of small settlements and production areas; at the city-state boundaries were buffer zones where cities competed with one another for territory and resources. Each city's ruler controlled agriculture, trade, and other economic activities within his territory. Each city-state had its own patron deity, who lived in the main temple of the city, often with his or her family, and whose temple, as in the Uruk Period, was the principal employer in the city.

Textual Evidence

The Early Dynastic Period is the first in Mesopotamia for which a significant amount of historical, as well as economic, information comes from texts. ED texts offer substantial data on politics and society. They reveal the workings of the city-states of Sumer, each with its own division and configuration of administrative powers; they demonstrate also that groups of city-states formed cooperative alliances, apparently for collective labor (and perhaps for military actions as well) (Leick 2001; Steinkeller 1993). At Lagash, the city-state best represented by textual and artistic evidence, each ruler was responsible for managing the two main temple institutions (Bauer 1998). While most ED sites have not yielded the number of tablets that would allow such fine-grained analysis, there is an overall sense that ED city-states experienced a delicate balance of secular and temple power, in the hands of a ruling family or sequence of rulers. Almost no evidence exists for the workings of private households, but it is likely that each town's or city-state's assembly provided a check on institutional powers.

Archaeological and Artistic Evidence

As was true for written documents, the archaeological and artistic evidence from the ED is widespread and varied, though unevenly distributed in space, time, and context of use. ED sites are found spaced along waterways across the whole of Mesopotamia; each city-state included one or more large town or city, as well as smaller villages and specialized sites. This particular settlement pattern is indicative of the irrigation-based subsistence economy that sustained all further activities. The central, largest city had administrative control over all the residents of the region and typically contained the main temple(s).

In general, the overall plans of ED settlements are poorly known; many of the sites were occupied in later periods of Mesopotamian history, making it difficult to reach 3rd millennium levels. ED architecture is often recognized on the basis of a common building material—the loaf-shaped, plano-convex brick, curved on top and laid in herringbone patterns. The best-known sites were in the Diyala River valley in northern Iraq. There, full ED-Period neighborhoods have been excavated in which multi-roomed houses arrayed on both sides of streets and alleys suggest that large populations were crowded into the city (Banning 1997). Houses had a larger central room, perhaps open to the sky, with smaller rooms on one or more sides. Variations in number of rooms and overall size may have correlated to family size or wealth. This "courtyard house" replaces the earlier tripartite plan for all subsequent phases of Mesopotamian history. House contents include areas and objects for cooking and work, storage, and other activities of daily life.

Better known than domestic architecture is the monumental architecture of the ED, projects that would have required a collective labor force and major supplies of tools and raw materials. Early Dynastic rulers took both credit and responsibility for a variety of public works, including those that are no longer extant, like irrigation canals. The fortification wall around Uruk was made famous in the later epic of Gilgamesh, a heroic account of the deeds of one of Uruk's Early Dynastic leaders. Public storage facilities were probably built at many major cities; water storage within city walls would also have been a necessity.

A number of ED sites contain palace buildings: monumental, non-temple structures that may have served administrative and residential purposes. These have a massive outer wall, with niches and buttresses; each comprised dozens of rooms, sometimes including large open courtyards that would have allowed circulation of light and foot traffic to surrounding rooms. Some may have had a second story. These early palaces were located on the peripheries of sites, rather than centrally, suggesting a concern for protection and maybe a need to control materials and people arriving at the city from the outside (Margueron 1982: 69).

ED sites have also yielded significant numbers of temples. A variety of temple plans exists for the Early Dynastic Period. Except for a stress on monumentality and visibility, the plans owe little to the Ubaid- and Uruk-Period tripartite type. The most impressive form is the "temple oval," attested at several sites. These consist of a walled-off, oval-shaped temple precinct comprising several city blocks. Excavations at Khafaje revealed that the soil underlying the precinct was specially prepared, with vast amounts of pure sand brought in before construction began. Within the precinct, a small temple sat atop a larger platform, reached by staircases. Other areas of the precinct were devoted to services such as food preparation, storage, administrative activities, and probably housing for priests and staff. The wall of the precinct, and the rounded form, marked this space off as special and holy; within the wall, the open spaces could have held hundreds of people, while the temple itself held only a few at a time. This difference suggests a hierarchy of access to the gods worshipped within and an emphasis on the visibility of those permitted to enter the presence of the gods.

Early Dynastic material culture took a variety of practical and ceremonial forms. Prestige goods highlighted the special functions and identities of the elite, while pottery and metal tools, found in domestic contexts, did not serve as signifiers of particular roles or status. Religious items from Early Dynastic sites indicate the centrality of the temple institution to ED city-states (Braun-Holzinger 1991). Among the most recognizable ED artifacts is the votive statue: 10–50 centimeter tall figurines, usually in stone, that represent worshippers standing before their gods (Figure 5.4). These would have been set on benches or on the floors of sanctuaries in front of the god's statue. Votive statuary goes back at least to the Uruk Period; what distinguishes the ED figures are their number and the identifying inscriptions on their shoulders and arms. The named individuals are both men and women and occupied a variety of offices in city-states. Of the over 500 ED votive statues known, under 20% (90) are inscribed, suggesting that people of all statuses could dedicate a statue. The statues' purpose of eternal communication and communion between donor and god is underlined by their durable material, solid pose, and wide-open eyes. In contrast, no cult statues of the period survive.

Other types of stone objects were also dedicated to the gods (Braun-Holzinger 1991). Usually, sculpted and inscribed pieces were dedicated by rulers; they include maceheads, vessels, and square plaques with central holes, which seem to have been affixed to temple walls. Relief scenes on these objects depicted banquets and combat between men and animals. Another category of temple

FIGURE 5.4 Early Dynastic Votive Figurine from Mari

Source: National Museum Damascus, Syria; Photo Credit: Alfredo Dagli Orti / The Art Archive at Art Resource, NY

dedications was the inscribed and sculpted stele, or carved stone block. The Stele of the Vultures was dedicated by Eannatum, governor of Lagash, to the warrior god Ningirsu to celebrate a military victory against a neighboring city-state (Winter 1985). While one side depicts the ruler and his troops defeating their enemies, who have already fallen, been stripped, and are being picked at by vultures, the other depicts the battle as divinely fought, with a large-scale image of Ningirsu holding the same enemies in a net. Eannatum set the stele within Ningirsu's temple as a commemoration of this victory by the god, achieved through the agency of his chosen representative. Like other artwork within ED temples, the dedication provided evidence, visible to people and the gods, of the ruler's special relationship with Ningirsu.

Tombs and cemeteries provide additional information on Early Dynastic society. Best-known is the Royal Cemetery at Ur, where 2,000 relatively simple tombs, each consisting of an inhumation in a pit with one or more pots and jewelry, dating from late in the ED into the Akkadian Period, surrounded a group of 16 or 17 "royal" tombs. The latter were distinct in their construction; grave goods (quality, type, and numbers); and the number of people within each grave. The royal tombs belong to the end of the ED and attest to the capacity of a few city residents to remove items of wealth from circulation and to dispose of the lives of remarkable numbers of people. The spectacle that attended these burials would have focused attention on both the dead and on those who furnished the tomb and oversaw the rituals of burial and commemoration (Moorey 1977; Pollock 1991; Woolley 1934).

What made these tombs so spectacular? The first factor is the sheer splendor and amounts of material that went into them. Besides clay vessels, objects were made from a huge variety of materials, many of them derived from distant sources: precious metals (gold, silver, and electrum) from Anatolia and Iran; lapis lazuli from Afghanistan; carnelian from Iran or further east; and a wide array of other colored stones that had to be obtained through trade. The forms into which these rich materials were worked also focused attention on the tombs' owners. In the graves of both men and women, jewelry covered all parts of the body but especially framed and encircled the face, neck, wrists, waist, and ankles. Weapons and tools were found in many of the royal tombs, but while the shapes may have been practical (daggers, tweezers, chisels), the precious materials from which they were made, and their ornament, were such that they would be impossible to use. The workmanship, including the use of filigree and granulation on such items as gold scabbards, and engraving on a gold helmet, had never previously been achieved.

A final group of objects, having particular artistic significance, may have been manufactured specifically for the funeral itself, or for the tomb's owner, intended to aid the owner's entry into the Netherworld or signify something about the tomb's occupant. A number of stringed instruments, both harps (with strings of different lengths) and lyres (with strings of the same length) were deposited in the Royal Tombs. A pair of rampant goats, sculpted from gold, lapis lazuli, and carnelian, lean against and feed from abstract trees. These intricate composites of gold, lapis lazuli, and shell have no discernible function; they may have had significance to their owner or a symbolic meaning relating to provisions for the afterlife. Finally, the Standard of Ur, a box measuring 21 by 50 centimeters, covered on two sides with stone inlay in three registers, came from Royal Tomb 779. The function is unclear, but the inlay scenes are familiar from seals and relief sculpture of the period: on one side, a peaceful banquet scene; on the other, preparations for war. On each side, the largest and central figure is clearly a ruler, surrounded by court and troops.

The identity of the tomb owners at Ur is uncertain. Many of the objects in the graves symbolize fertility and other divine forces; others clearly refer to warfare (Cohen 2005). Some scholars have suggested that these were the city's rulers; others prefer to see them as representatives of a temple household (Pollock 1991, 2007; Woolley 1934). These would not necessarily be different groups of people. What is clear is the tremendous power of the individuals buried in the Royal Tombs and those who buried them; not only did they remove immense quantities of precious goods from circulation, they also took the lives of other people. Typical of the Royal Tombs was human sacrifice: together with 1 queen were buried 9 men and 10 women, while the "Great Death Pit" contained 75 bodies. Leonard Woolley (1934), the excavator of the Royal Cemetery, noted the apparent willingness of these victims; he believed that each one drank poison from the numerous cups later stacked in the tombs, and all were dead before the earth was shoveled in.

Complexity in Early Dynastic Mesopotamia

Textual evidence indicates that Early Dynastic southern Mesopotamia was organized into a collection of autonomous city-states, in a state of constant competition and cooperation with one another.

A number of questions remain, including who the rulers of the city-states were. Baines and Yoffee (1998) believe that they were drawn from the largest landowners of each city, suggesting secular roots. But a complication derives from the variety of ruler titles provided in the texts, which imply a similar variety of potential sources of power. Early Dynastic rulers could be called by one of three possible titles: EN, ENSI, or LUGAL (the use of capital letters to designate these titles indicates their Sumerian reading). The title EN was used infrequently in the ED and had religious connotations. ENSI, translated as "governor," was the main title of the rulers of Lagash, while LUGAL (literally, "big man") came to be the main title used by kings for the rest of the millennium and in subsequent periods, especially as rulers extended their power over larger territories. There is a lack of consistency in the usage of the three titles and a fluidity in their precise meanings and connotations. To some degree, the preference for one title may have been one of location, or tradition, or specific historical circumstances. ED rulers did the same things: they conducted wars, dedicated objects, controlled land, and, ideally, provided stability and prosperity for the people of their city-states.

That ED society included a range of socioeconomic statuses below that of ruler is also made clear by the archaeological and textual data. Ur's Royal Cemetery graves reveal a continuum in number and types of goods. Even the people in the private graves at Ur must have been considered special in some way, as the cemetery could not accommodate the entire population of the city (Pollock 2007). The limited domestic architecture of the ED provides additional evidence for status distinctions in the size and layout of individual houses. Similarly, votive statues show that many different kinds of people were able to donate offerings to the gods. Textual evidence offers the clearest data on the variety of people who lived and worked in ED cities; these ranged from slaves and dependents of the temple institutions to the many officials who oversaw each city-state (Bauer 1998; Diakonoff 1969). Residents of ED cities must have had a variety of ways in which they recognized and negotiated their positions vis-à-vis others.

It is likely that internal conflicts existed within city-states, particularly among elites over the right to rule, but these are seldom apparent in sources. Some struggles took place between the growing power of the ruler and that of the principal economic institution, the temple. An underlying tension between these forces is typical of early state formations and may be masked by royal or elite ideologies that represent power as divinely bestowed. That ED rulers owed their position to the temples is not in doubt, but this debt did not prevent them from deriving personal enrichment from their position. Where private households stood in relationship to temple and state is unclear, but certainly many took part in this balancing act. The next-to-last ED ruler in Lagash enacted a set of reforms intended to return economic and political power to the temples and to counter the corruption of officials. This document, the Reforms of Uruinimgina, was a rebuke to his predecessors; at the same time, Uruinimgina consolidated his control over the main temple estates—a timeless example of political gamesmanship (van de Mieroop 2004: 45).

Much more evident in the sources are endemic external conflicts over land and resources. The Stele of the Vultures illustrates this type of warfare, a border conflict, from the viewpoint of the victor. The Stele also demonstrates that war between cities could be envisioned as a conflict among gods. The need for a regular army, with trained soldiers and state-supplied weaponry and food, may have been a major force in the rise of secular kingship (Baines and Yoffee 1998; van de Mieroop 2004: 44–45).

Territorial States of the 3rd and 2nd Millennia

Old Akkadian Period

Directly from the city-states of the Early Dynastic Period emerged the Old Akkadian Dynasty (2334–2150 BCE), the first territorial state in Mesopotamian history, uniting disparate regions and peoples under a single ruler. The Akkadian Dynasty originated under Sargon I, whose name, "True King," suggests just the opposite. Sargon was the cupbearer for an Early Dynastic city ruler; he usurped this king's throne then centralized control over all of Sumer and eventually territories beyond Sumer. The Old Akkadian Period provided a model for consolidation of power for later rulers; by melding administrative reforms with propaganda centered on the might of the king, its rulers set a strong precedent. At the same time, they built on forces of expansion that went back to the Uruk and ED Periods. At its peak, the dynasty controlled a territory reaching from the Persian Gulf to the Mediterranean and conducted trade with lands as far away as the Indus Valley.

What made this first period of unification so significant was the power of a centralized authority over a wide range of ethnolinguistic groups. One way of dealing with diversity—in language, background, and beliefs—was to demand a degree of standardization in administration. The Old Akkadian kings employed Akkadian as the language of administration, despite the range of languages spoken within their state. They also established a set of common administrative methods across their territory. At the same time, they appealed to local religious and material traditions.

To run a territorial state, Sargon and his successors introduced a number of reforms that reached into economic, social, and religious life as well as into political organization. To centralize his government, Sargon first moved the capital to Agade, a newly founded town in central Mesopotamia with no prior religious affiliations; this site has never been found. From here, Sargon reorganized the Mesopotamian city-states so that the local rulers answered to him; in many cases, he replaced local Sumerian governors with loyal Akkadians. Further from the Mesopotamian core, he established fortresses permanently staffed with officers and soldiers, who oversaw governance of distant territories and the movement of goods along trade routes (Larsen 1979). Much of this was achieved through deployment of a standing army.

In the economic realm, the Akkadian kings resolved the tension between palace and temple by appropriating nearly all temple lands (Diakonoff 1969). Royal land could be awarded to officials of all ranks in exchange for their service, but it could not be sold or handed down by those officials, so it reverted back to the state on completion of service. A sizable amount of private and community land also existed. Sargon and his successors made an effort to quell concerns about their commitment to traditional religion by rebuilding major temples across Sumer and by appointing their relatives to priestly positions.

Art and archaeology demonstrate the balance between tradition and innovation achieved by the Akkadian kings. One source comes from dedications to Mesopotamian gods, a traditional category of material, but one these kings exploited in new ways (Eppihimer 2010). Royal votive statues include a significant number found at the site of Susa in western Iran, where captured war booty was taken during the reign of a 2nd millennium Elamite king. The piety of Akkadian rulers and their families is also evident on several remarkable works attributed to Enheduanna, a daughter of Sargon, who was appointed high priestess to the moon god Nanna at Ur. A limestone disk, 25 centimeters in diameter, from that site has an inscribed dedication by Enheduanna on one side and an image of the priestess, offering a libation before a stepped altar or structure, on the other side. Even more noteworthy is a series of hymns professing devotion to the goddess Inanna and another set of verses extolling individual Mesopotamian temples and their gods, both composed by Enheduanna, making her the world's earliest named author (Westenholz 1989; Winter 1987).

Even more indicative of the messages they wished to convey were victory steles of Sargon and Naram-Sin, his grandson. These were taken as war booty to Iran; their original placement is unknown, but like the Stele of the Vultures, they were dedicated in a temple. On Naram-Sin's stele, the king is the main figure, large and central in the composition (Figure 5.5). Naram-Sin's stele violated the traditional structured arrangement of a stele in registers, bringing just a few figures into the scene so that the focus could be on the king. The stele is subdivided into left and right sections, with the king and his soldiers ascending a mountain on the left side, and their enemies,

FIGURE 5.5 Naram-Sin Stele

Source: J.C. Ross

a mountain people in Iran, falling away and down the slope along the right edge. In the center, an underdressed Naram-Sin, in horned helmet, necklace, belt, and short kilt, stands on top of two small, lifeless bodies and has apparently just dispatched a third with a spear, while a fourth pleads for his life. No fighting need take place on this work, as the king has already taken control of the situation. Unlike the Stele of the Vultures, this piece is not two-sided—its meaning could be conveyed and taken in from a single view. And unlike the earlier work, as well, the gods on Naram-Sin's stele take only a passive role in the battle, abstracted into star form and hovering above the king. Instead, Naram-Sin takes sole credit for victory, to such a degree that he wears the horned crown of a god; contemporary inscriptions also called him a god. Nearly everything about this work was new, from the single, complex scene, to the radical reconfiguration of the image of the king (Winter 1996).

The charisma and confidence of Naram-Sin was not sufficient to prolong the Akkadian Dynasty much beyond his death. His son led a series of successful campaigns against rebellious Sumerian cities, but the final decades of the 23rd century were a time of migration and environmental degradation, and the state eventually fell to a combination of internal upheaval and external enemies. The Akkadian Dynasty, however, introduced a number of innovations that were repeated by later state organizations: the establishment of a new capital, the creation of a standing army, and the reorganization of administrative functions that worked to counteract the inherently unstable Mesopotamian political landscape.

Neo-Sumerian Revival (The Ur III Dynasty)

As the Old Akkadian Dynasty declined and lost territory near the end of the 23rd century, the city-states of southern Sumer returned to their traditional order of small-scale political organization and religious piety. This return to "traditional values" is sometimes called the Neo-Sumerian revival (2200–2000 BCE), when Sumerian replaced Akkadian as the language of administration. The period culminated in the rise of another territorial state, centered at Ur (2112–2004 BCE), whose rulers, like those of the previous Akkadian Dynasty, established power over a sizable territory encompassing a diverse population.

Neo-Sumerian bureaucracies produced tens of thousands of tablets, largely economic, that allow for a fine-grained reconstruction of their history and organization. The texts focus almost exclusively on the public institutions of palace and temple, showing a highly centralized government where each city kept its own records but also reported to the capital. The founder, Ur-Nammu, conquered the local governor at Uruk while he governed Ur and spread his rule from there, establishing what is often called the Ur III Dynasty. Subsequent kings of Ur expanded the state north and east, while the kings at the end of the dynasty faced migrations and invasions from the northwest (the Amorites) and the east (the Elamites). As with the Akkadian Dynasty, the Ur III Dynasty collapsed under pressure from these outside groups and from internal economic crises.

While the early part of the Neo-Sumerian Period saw the reversion of politics to city-state organization, in the second half, under the Ur III kings, these city-states were again organized into provinces under the capital at Ur. Kings appointed governors to serve at provincial centers; beyond Mesopotamia, military leaders, with Mesopotamian troops, governed the territories (Larsen 1979). Ur-Nammu and his son, Shulgi, instituted a number of administrative reforms to make all of the territories easier to govern. These included several types of standardization, so that all territories under Ur III control used the same systems of writing and rhetoric, weights and measures, accounting, and calendar. Shulgi instituted a standing army and promulgated a code of laws ascribed to his father that covered a variety of criminal behaviors and penalties that would apply throughout the state. By his 20th regnal year, Shulgi declared himself a god, as Naram-Sin had before him; his successors followed him in this practice (Michalowski 2008; Steinkeller 1987).

Art and archaeology offer an additional window onto the strategies employed by Neo-Sumerian rulers to legitimize their power. At Ur, Ur-Nammu and his successors reorganized the temple precinct, walling it off and building structures that may have served to house the royal family and priests and a new temple type, a ziggurat. This structure of solid brick rose in a series of platforms, with stairs leading to a small temple at the top, where the moon god Nanna came down to dwell. In effect, the ziggurat replaced earlier temples on platforms; it served, also, as an artificial mountain, climbing to the heavens.

The focus on temple-building and religious piety was manifested also in the artwork of the Neo-Sumerian Period. Gudea, the governor of Lagash, created a number of stone votive statues, seated and standing, that attested to his devotion in their inscriptions and traditional poses (Winter 1989). Some of these were life-sized, a trend that Ur III kings did not follow, though a number of their votive statues also survive. Some of Gudea's statues and those of the Ur III kings refer, in their poses, specifically to building projects: Gudea holds the building plan for Ningirsu's temple on his lap in one statue, and the Ur III kings are sometimes depicted with a peg-shaped body and holding a basket on their heads, both referring to materials used in construction. Relief carvings also illustrate the dominant message of the king as the main human devotee of the gods. The Stele of Ur-Nammu, found in pieces at Ur, shows the king with construction tools in one register and offering libations to both Nanna and his wife Ningal in the upper registers (Canby 2001). The message to the Sumerian city-states was clearly one of proper piety, demonstrated by restoration of religious places and values.

Old Babylonian Period

After the fall of the Ur III Dynasty, centralized power over Mesopotamia was not re-established for a while. The next historical phase, the Old Babylonian Period (2000–1595 BCE) is typically divided into two subphases: the Isin-Larsa Period (2000–1763 BCE), when city-states vied with one another for control over more Sumerian territory, and the first Babylonian Dynasty (1763–1595 BCE), when Babylon conquered Mesopotamia and parts of Syria. During both phases, kings attempted to balance the militarism that dominated Old Akkadian Period rhetorical and visual strategies with the reverent attitude of Neo-Sumerian rulers; achieving such a balance was really a goal in every phase of Mesopotamian history.

While the first half of the Old Babylonian Period saw the rebuilding and consolidation of some of the Sumerian city-states, the territory held by each was relatively small, intermediate between the ED city-states and the Akkadian and Ur III territorial states in size. It was not until Hammurabi came to the throne in Babylon that one ruler brought all of the south under his power. Hammurabi spent the first three decades of his reign (1792–1750 BCE) expanding power outward, eventually conquering territories in Syria, northern Mesopotamia, and western Iran. His successors would maintain, but not extend, the borders of this state and eventually lost much of it. The development of new polities is reflected in sources of this time: a separate, small state centered on Assur in northern Mesopotamia; a new ethnolinguistic group, the Hurrians, in Syria; and in central Anatolia, an Indo-European-speaking group, the Hatti, who rapidly coalesced into the Hittite state. By 1595, this latter state was strong enough to march on and destroy Babylon, bringing the dynasty to an end.

Sources for the history of the Old Babylonian Period are rich and varied, as literacy spread from Mesopotamia into the Levant and Anatolia. In fact, the two largest tablet collections from the period are from outside Mesopotamia: over 20,000 tablets each from the palace at Mari, in Syria, and the Old Assyrian merchant colony at Kültepe-Kanesh, in modern Turkey. Both collections contain large numbers of letters on economic and political matters. Both public institutions and private households in Mesopotamia created and kept archives, which included receipts, contracts, letters, and other documents with legal content. Hammurabi created the most famous legal text of antiquity, his law code, attested in full on a stele found at Susa (another example of war booty) and in extracts at a number of sites (see Box 5.3).

BOX 5.3 KEY OBJECT: THE LAW CODE OF HAMMURABI

Among the achievements of the Mesopotamians was the establishment of the earliest law codes, somewhat systematic lists of crimes and their punishments. While Hammurabi's Law Code Stele is not the earliest such collection attested, it is justifiably the most famous. Hammurabi's code provides 282 individual laws relating to nearly all aspects of life: birth, adoption, marriage and divorce, inheritance, economic activities, and many types of criminal conduct. It describes a society that observed strict hierarchies of class and gender. Significantly, though the prologue indicates that Hammurabi intended his code to be consulted by anyone who felt unjustly treated, there is no evidence in the contemporary juridical documents that judges employed the code in their rulings. The justice system in practice was far more fluid in application than Hammurabi's Law Code suggests.

A highly structured hierarchy was expressed in the art of the Old Babylonian Period, on both items viewed publicly and on privately held objects. Images of kings serving the gods were put on display at temples throughout Mesopotamia. At the top of the 2 meter-tall Law Code Stele of Hammurabi is an image of the king standing, one hand before his mouth, before Shamash, the god of the sun and of justice (Figure 5.6). Shamash holds out to the king the "rod and the ring," traditional symbols of Mesopotamian kingship, transferring to Hammurabi the right and responsibility to uphold order in the land. This image of reverent king and generous god is borrowed from earlier rulers. The image of king before god was also held in private hands, as it was a favorite seal motif at the time, serving to remind private citizens and officials of the proper order of the universe.

FIGURE 5.6 Law Code Stele of Hammurabi; Diorite

Source: © RMN-Grand Palais / Art Resource, NY; photo: Hervé Lewandowki

Textual evidence indicates that both the government and private citizens embarked on extensive economic ventures; the Old Babylonian Period is the earliest for which so much is known about the economic activities of private citizens. The records of merchants from Assur who settled in a trading colony at Kültepe-Kanesh, just outside a town of indigenous Anatolians, show that the merchants were engaged in family-based private businesses; their families in Assur produced and obtained textiles and tin, which they transported in donkey caravans to Anatolia (Larsen 1987). In exchange, the merchants bought copper and silver to send back to Assur. Sons followed their fathers into business; wives managed the supplies of cloth at home in Assur. Similar circumstances are documented at Ur, where sea-going ventures could be funded by private or institutional donors, who expected a profit (Oppenheim 1954).

The Old Babylonian Period exhibits a wide array of architectural types. Palaces have been excavated at a number of sites. Temple precincts grew in complexity, as they housed a variety of officials. Best documented, however, are residential neighborhoods, particularly at sites in Sumer and Babylonia (Keith 2003; Stone 1987; Stone and Zimansky 2004). Though houses and services were densely packed into neighborhoods, private archives indicate that houses could be rebuilt, modified, and subdivided as families grew and fractured. Taken together, the texts and archaeology offer a view into the dynamic social and structural changes that could take place over even a generation or two.

The Late Bronze Age (1600–1100 BCE): Territorial States in an International Age

The Old Babylonian Period ended with the Hittite destruction of Babylon in 1595—an event neither anticipated by the Babylonians nor capitalized on by the Hittites. It was followed by a period of relative obscurity; in Mesopotamian terms, this means a phase when power was not centralized, though most people continued to live in cities. After 1500 BCE, a number of large territorial states emerged across the region. These eventually developed an unprecedented international system of diplomacy, trade, and rivalry. In Mesopotamia, the core states were the Kassites in the south; the Assyrians in the north; and the Mitanni, ruling a territory largely occupied by speakers of Hurrian, in Syria. Bordering on Mesopotamia were the Hittites in Anatolia and the Elamites in Iran; in Egypt, the powerful Eighteenth Dynasty of the New Kingdom rounds out the assortment of players in this International Age (see Chapter 6).

Evidence for international relations comes especially from the Amarna Letters, correspondence between the Egyptian court and its political partners found at the site of Tell el-Amarna (Akhetaten), a late Eighteenth Dynasty Egyptian capital (Moran 2000). Of the 380 letters, mostly in Akkadian (the diplomatic language of the time), just over 40 belong to the category of "international letters," written to or by Egyptian kings and exchanged with their counterparts in Babylonia, Assyria, Washukanni (the as-yet unlocated Mitanni capital), Arzawa (south-central Anatolia), Hattusha (the Hittite capital), and Cyprus. The principal topic of these letters is exchange—of gifts, messengers, princesses, advice, and threats—all among men who called one another "Brother" and were considered "Great Kings." These documents convey a sense of the tremendous wealth and sizable entourages that traveled between courts, an impression partly filled in with archaeological evidence. The textual record suggests a balance of state powers ruling territories with highly varied populations. By the end of the Late Bronze Age, this relative balance was disrupted, however, as the first moves were made toward imperialism, with one group (the Assyrians) expanding power at the expense of all the others. This trend eventually led into the series of empires that dominated the 1st millennium BCE Near East.

The Kassite State

During the 100 years or so of textual "silence" in Mesopotamia, following the Hittite raid on Babylon in 1595, a new ethnic group moved into the south, quickly filling the power vacuum caused by the fall of the dynasty at Babylon. The origins of the Kassites are obscure; some Old Babylonian Period documents have them located already in northeastern Mesopotamia (Reade 1978). By 1475, they had unified Babylonia. Once the dynasty was established, with a capital at the site of Dur-Kurigalzu, the Kassites had adopted a fully Mesopotamian identity: building temples to the traditional gods; writing in the Babylonian dialect; and promulgating Mesopotamian literature by copying old texts, translating Sumerian sources, and creating new literary compositions. The Kassites retained their native language only for their names and the names of their gods, who were adopted and assimilated into the traditional pantheon.

By the time of the 14th century Amarna Letters, Babylonian power under the Kassite kings was fully re-established. The kings requested gold from the Egyptian pharaoh in exchange for royal brides, horses, and chariots; with this gold, they said, they would ornament their palaces and temples. The 14th century was a period of royal construction in Babylonia, with a ziggurat and palace built by Kurigalzu I at Aqar Quf and a number of other temples rebuilt across the land. It is clear that the Kassite kings adopted traditional Mesopotamian expressions of legitimacy and power. Kassite rule went into decline in the late 13th century, as Assyria, to the north, grew in power. In 1154, the Assyrians and Elamites together overthrew the Kassites, and Assyria took over rule of Babylonia.

The Mitanni State

At the same time that the Kassites consolidated their rule in Babylonia, Mitanni rulers took over much of Syria, also capitalizing on the absence of centralized power there. The population of the region was ethnically Hurrian; the Mitanni were the elite class among the Hurrians, writing in Akkadian but with some Indo-European words in their language. Because their capital, Washukanni, has not been discovered, textual data on the Mitanni are limited, although archives at provincial centers provide some information, as do the Amarna Letters and contemporary Hittite and Assyrian texts. At one point, the Mitanni state stretched from southeastern Anatolia to east of the Tigris River, and Mitanni rulers considered themselves equals to the Hittite, Assyrian, and Egyptian kings. This state of affairs prevailed only for two centuries, after which the geographical position of Mitanni, in a buffer zone between Egypt, the Hittites, and Assyria, proved to be a disadvantage, and it lost territory first to the Hittites and then to Assyria (van de Mieroop 2004: 144).

Because its capital has not been found, little is known about the visual and architectural expressions of Mitanni royal power. The Mitanni introduced new glyptic styles; they mass-produced seals from faience or frit, using a cutting wheel and drill to create the designs on these and on seals of harder stone (Collon 1988: 61–65). Most Mitanni seals illustrate animals, sometimes caprids standing on either side of a "sacred tree," sometimes winged griffins and sphinxes. Very few were inscribed. The Amarna Letters suggest that the Mitanni kings patronized a thriving industry in prestige goods, especially metal vessels. While these did not survive archaeologically, some traces of Mitanni glass-working do, along with the related production of faience seals and vessels.

The Assyrian State

The Middle Assyrian state (14th–11th century) offers just a hint of the achievements of the subsequent Neo-Assyrian kings. It was built on the same foundation of dry-farming agriculture, military prowess, and control over major routes that the Old Assyrian kingdom had been and the Neo-Assyrian Empire would be. Middle Assyrian kings took advantage of periods of Kassite and

Mitanni weakness to gain territory and insert themselves into the international trade networks of the Late Bronze Age. One major activity of Middle Assyrian rulers was construction; three ziggurats and additional temples at their capital at Assur attest to their devotion to traditional royal values.

Complexity in the Late Bronze Age

This survey of the major powers of Late Bronze Age Mesopotamia has highlighted the distinct trajectory of each and the surviving evidence for its participation in the International Age (see Box 5.4). The collapse of this networked system was not due to any single factor but rather an assortment of circumstances that affected each partner individually and the system as a whole. The Assyrian military struck fatal blows against its neighbors, the Mitanni and Kassites; later, Assyrian hegemony in Syria was challenged by new city rulers, and its territory was reduced to its homeland. In Anatolia, the Hittites faced military challenges from a mountain tribe, the Kashka, who exploited a situation of internal conflict between rivals to the throne. Egyptian sources of the Nineteenth Dynasty speak of expansion into Syria and a truce with the Hittites, but Egypt also faced subsequent attacks by a coalition of enemies, some traditional (Libya) and others new (the "Peoples of the Sea"). As always, no single cause fully explains the decline of one state, and the decline of many requires an even more nuanced accounting.

BOX 5.4 LATE BRONZE AGE MARITIME TRADE

Further archaeological evidence for the sheer economic scope of International Age trade derives from a pair of shipwrecks off the Anatolian coast, at Uluburun and Cape Gelidonya, dating to the end of the 14th and the late 13th century, respectively. Though they carried somewhat different cargoes, both ships wrecked while transporting goods from one part of the Mediterranean to another and both, apparently, when traveling from east to west. In neither case is the national or ethnic identity of the ship's crew, or of their sponsor, obvious; personal items found at the Uluburun wreck suggest that its crew included Canaanites from the Levantine coast (Cline and Yasur-Landau 2007). The amount of cargo lost in each wreck, however, goes beyond what a private entrepreneur could have afforded; calculations of the Uluburun loss indicate that it was the equivalent of 1,000 years' worth of a worker's salary (Monroe 2010). Such a load could only have been subsidized by a royal sponsor.

The cargo on these wrecks belonged in part to the sphere of royal gift exchange as detailed in the Amarna Letters; by weight, however, the largest portion of the load was more mundane. Uluburun's wreck was dominated by copper: over 350 oxhide-shaped ingots, each weighing nearly 30 kilograms, and another 900 kilograms in ingots of other shapes. Tin ingots, weighing 1000 kilograms in total, together with the copper, would have enabled bronze production at their destination. Other raw materials on the Uluburun wreck included glass ingots and hippopotamus and elephant ivory, materials destined for palace workshops for the production of luxury goods. Clay storage vessels held a variety of fruits, olives, resin, and probably wine and oils. Manufactured goods were less common on both wrecks; only a gold chalice and silver bowl from Uluburun are of the type of royal gifts described in the Amarna Letters. The perishable materials on board, however, might also have included gifts exchanged between courts. These data provide a snapshot of the complicated networks of economic and social relationships that tied individual rulers to their subjects and rivals (Monroe 2009, 2010).

What is particularly clear is that, beginning in the mid-13th century, the ideology and material basis for the power of kings, and their single-handed control of extensive territory, was challenged and ultimately restructured. Disruptions in the international trading system caused by warfare, movements of people, and interruptions in the supply of raw materials were all significant factors. But the circumstances that brought new groups, like the Kassites and Mitanni, to power and set their elite class at the head of older societies may also have been challenged from within society, and coercive practices within territories broke down. For many, the removal of the ruling class may have freed them from taxes and labor obligations, but life itself may have gone on much the same as before.

Empires of the 1st Millennium

The Neo-Assyrian Empire

Out of this phase of collapse, which has left few textual or archaeological records, the Assyrians were the first to emerge, after about 100 years. Beginning in the late 10th century, Assyrian rulers began a series of campaigns of expansion, marking the start of the Neo-Assyrian Period (934–609 BCE). Ultimately, the Neo-Assyrian Empire, ruled by a succession of kings from three different families, covered most of the Near East, from the Mediterranean Sea to western Iran, and from Anatolia to Egypt. The empire also encompassed many different ethnolinguistic groups, eventually adopting Aramaic, written alphabetically, alongside the Assyrian dialect of Akkadian, as their principal languages. Sources for the history of the period are multiple, ranging from royal records to official correspondence, to literature and religious texts; written sources from the edges of Assyria, especially Egypt and Syria-Palestine (including the Hebrew scriptures), provide additional perspectives.

Assyrian expansion took place in two major phases, with periods of decline and retraction between and at the end of the period. Assyrian kings led their armies on campaign, and the success (or failure) of military endeavors was seen as directly correlated to a king's leadership. Neo-Assyrian kings of the 9th century, particularly Assurnasirpal II (883–859 BCE) and Shalmaneser III (858–823), extended Assyrian rule to the north and west, conquering Arameans and Neo-Hittites in Syria, Urartians, Lullubi, and Guti in northern Iran. While the early part of the 8th century saw a decline in Assyrian power, Tiglath-Pileser III (744–727), an army general, regained Syria, much of the southern Levant, and Babylonia. Subsequent kings of the Sargonid Dynasty—Sargon II (721–705), Sennacherib (705–681), Esarhaddon (681–669), and Assurbanipal (669–627)—expanded further into Anatolia, Egypt, and Iran. Assyrian power after Assurbanipal went into decline, as Babylonia and the Medes, a new power in Iran, eventually overthrew their overlords and divided the empire between them.

Although some scholars apply the term "empire" to earlier phases of Mesopotamian history such as the Old Akkadian Dynasty, consensus indicates that the Neo-Assyrians were the first to control a "true" empire. The definition of empire is disputed among scholars; perhaps the most distinctive elements of any empire are its size, the diversity of the people and the territories it controls, and the image it conveys (Eisenstadt 1979). Successful imperial rule is distinct from successful conquest; the integration of new territories into an empire requires economic, administrative, and ideological strategies that uphold the superior position of the "center" (in the case of Assyria, the king and his court, and the territorial center), while also assimilating new groups into it, reconfiguring their identities into the ordered whole that the king has engineered (Eisenstadt 1979; Liverani 1979).

Neo-Assyrian Sociopolitical and Economic Strategies

During the over-300-year history of the Neo-Assyrian Empire, a number of organizational strategies were deployed. From early on, conquered territories came under Assyrian rule as vassals, paying tribute (especially in resources specific to their territory) to the king in the capital. For the most part, conquered rulers who submitted were allowed to stay on their thrones; if they rebelled, however, they would be executed and replaced by Assyrians. The policy of deporting and resettling conquered people had been practiced in earlier periods (Gelb 1973), but the Neo-Assyrians took it to a new level; it has been estimated that up to 4.5 million people were deported during this period (van de Mieroop 2004: 219). One effect of deportations was to move labor forces to territories where they were needed, especially to underutilized agricultural lands. But the policy also had the effect of disrupting geography-based identities, mixing people of distinct origins, ethnicities, languages, and even beliefs, perhaps forcing them into a sort of homogenized condition in which they lost (or alternatively, clung to) those cultural elements that distinguished them.

Tiglath-Pileser III, in the mid-8th century, pushed through a number of reforms intended to strengthen the central Assyrian government. He redrew the borders of provinces, making each one smaller, thereby reducing the power of individual governors (van de Mieroop 2004: 233). Provinces paid taxes in silver and labor, to support public works, to work royal lands, or to serve in the Assyrian army. Officials of the empire were given lands as payment; these, and the offices themselves, were heritable, a move that also increased loyalty to the royal household (Jakobsen 1969). The army, which eventually campaigned year-round, was made up of paid officers, Assyrians serving full time or part time as part of their labor service, and foreign mercenaries. Depictions suggest a hierarchical, highly disciplined, and well-supplied force.

Other state income consisted of manufactured goods, sometimes provided through labor service but often supplied from booty or tribute from vassal states. Craftsmen deported from their native lands brought their skills and expertise to the Assyrian heartland, together with raw materials captured from their lands. Many would have worked to supply tools and weapons to government troops; still others would have created the luxury goods that ornamented palaces, temples, and elite residences. Assyrian expansion toward the Mediterranean coast was driven, in part, to exploit seagoing trade, much of which was conducted by Phoenician merchants.

Palaces and Artwork

A major means of ideological expression for an Assyrian king was the creation of a new palace, and, in a few cases, the construction and settlement of a new capital city. While the initial capital of the empire was Assur, which remained an important religious center throughout the period, Assurnasirpal built a new capital at Kalhu (modern Nimrud), located north of Assur on the Tigris, in 879 BCE; the "Banquet Stele" from his palace claims that he hosted a feast for 47,047 people from all ends of the empire when the new city was officially inaugurated (Harmanşah 2013). A subsidiary palace, called "Fort Shalmaneser" by archaeologists, served as palace and a military headquarters for Assurnasirpal's son, Shalmaneser III. When the empire went into decline in the 8th century, few new palaces were constructed, but Sargon founded a new capital at Dur-Sharrukin (Khorsabad) during a time of renewal. It is likely that this palace was never completed, as Sargon died in battle; his son and successor, Sennacherib, moved the capital once more to Nineveh, where he built his palace (which he called "The Palace without a Rival"). A final palace was constructed at Nineveh by Sennacherib's grandson Assurbanipal, whose artwork is found in both the Southwest Palace and his own North Palace. Each of these structures served as royal residence and administrative headquarters for the state, but each also served as the place where the king's achievements were displayed. Each was an individual expression of the "personality" of the ruler who built it (Reade 1979).

The Neo-Assyrian palaces included large open courtyards (at Fort Shalmaneser, the especially large courts may have seen assemblies and provisioning of troops) and formal areas for reception, including, in each, a throne room, suites of rooms for conducting the business of the state, and private areas for the royal family. While the buildings were of brick, the most important rooms were lined with gypsum orthostats, blocks carved with a variety of scenes with religious import and significance to the life of the king. Similar scenes were rendered in metal, on bronze strips that covered wooden doors, and in paint. But the reliefs from the palaces are particularly informative about royal power and rhetoric because of the distinctive combinations of text and image. From Assurnasirpal on, the palace walls were inscribed with sections of the royal annals, the year-by-year accounts of royal victories (see Box 5.5).

BOX 5.5 PALACES OF THE ASSYRIAN KINGS

Neo-Assyrian kings were especially savvy in their use of art and architecture to convey the intensity and extent of their political and religious power. From the time of Assurnasirpal II, each king with enough time and economic capacity built a new palace, sometimes in a new city, as a forum for broadcasting his achievements to his court and people and to foreign visitors. Artwork in the palace was accompanied by texts of various types. In some cases, the annals were juxtaposed with relief images, showing (some of) these deeds; in others, the inscriptions were reduced to name and title captions. In all cases, the match of visual and verbal rhetoric was inexact; different audiences were expected to "read" each kind of text (Winter 1997). A similar degree of attention was paid to the artistic layout of different sections of the palace, as different types of people would have had access to different areas.

In all art of the Neo-Assyrian Period, the king was the focus and principal actor. This is true even of works with religious content; winged "genius" figures and colossal *lamassu*, creatures combining the features and qualities of bulls, lions, and eagles, protected the king and sometimes even bore his face (Figure 5.7). These apotropaic figures stood at gates, doorways, and corners, entry points for both human and spiritual enemies. The only major god to appear in Assyrian art is Assur, patron god of the land and the royal household. Unlike most previous phases of Mesopotamian art, however, the Neo-Assyrian sculptors depicted their god at a miniature scale; he hovers in a winged disk, holding out the rod and ring, above the king. This conveyed the god's protection of and assistance in royal endeavors, while maintaining the focus on his approved agent, the king. In relief scenes of formal worship, such as in Assurnasirpal's throne room (twice), the king stands on either side of a stylized tree, finger pointing at the tree in a gesture of reverence, while Assur flies above. Direct interaction of god and king was replaced by more indirect means of expression of divine support, but text and image continued to convey the religious underpinnings of royal power.

Much of the other "public art" (that intended to be seen by more than just the royal family) in the Neo-Assyrian palaces was narrative in purpose: it told a story of sorts, in a sequence, about the king's achievements (Winter 1981). As in previous royal art, the idea of movement could be conveyed by having multiple representations of the king. Neo-Assyrian art reversed the traditional order in which registers were read; earlier events are placed above, their consequences below. So, in a scene of warfare, the battle is in the upper register, while the conquered people bring tribute in the lower one. The general principle, and even the major scene types—battles and hunts—remained the same; in this, Mesopotamian art, and its goals, had changed little over the space of three millennia.

In both hunt and battle, the king was depicted at the same size as his officials, soldiers, and enemies; sometimes he is set off at a slight distance from the others, and always he is a more active participant than the others. He is distinguished, also, by headgear and by the richness of his jewelry and clothing (Reade 1979). Beginning with Sennacherib, the use of registers became less common, although they never disappeared altogether; instead, entire rooms could be filled with the depiction of a single event or campaign, with movement and time conveyed by spreading the scene across the multiple walls. Details of foreign costume and belongings were rendered with greater specificity as territories further from the Assyrian core were conquered. A similar degree of specificity went into the rendering of exotic landscapes; plants and animals as well as people were transferred to the capital in physical and artistic form to serve as a visual reminder of Assyrian power. Scenes of battle and of the hunt and even depictions of the palace and gardens were intended to show the king, and by extension the Assyrian state, as master of the known world.

FIGURE 5.7 Colossal Winged Lion (*lamassu*) from the Northwest Palace of Assurnasirpal II at Nimrud (Kalhu)

Source: British Museum, London, United Kingdom (Album / Art Resource, NY)

Sculptural imagery was a major part of the experience of Assyrian domination, but the minor arts also instilled some of the same messages. Many items with smaller-scale imagery also come from Assyrian palaces and therefore were part of the localized expression of power. At Assurnasirpal's Northwest Palace and Fort Shalmaneser at Nimrud and at a provincial palace at Til Barsip in Syria, archaeologists have found hundreds of sculpted pieces that were fitted to furniture such as beds, couches, and tables, as well as other kinds of objects including vessels, horse equipment, and sculptures. They were the private belongings of palace residents, some made specifically for their use and others captured as war booty or made by captive craftsmen. The imagery is eclectic; many pieces adopt Egyptian motifs of sphinxes, winged disks, and even hieroglyphic inscriptions. Others depict Assyrian women, or supernatural winged figures. It is likely that most of these images were intended to entertain and protect the users of the furniture, but their styles and material would also be reminders of territories and peoples under Assyrian control. Similarly, a group of tombs of Assyrian queens found under the floors of the Northwest Palace contained gold and bronze vessels and gold jewelry like that worn by kings on royal reliefs; the figural decoration of animals, hunts, and winged figures replicated, in miniature, the projections of royal protection and might found on the relief images (Oates and Oates 2001: 80–88).

One category of representation not yet mentioned is statuary. Kings and prominent citizens commissioned votive statues for temples; these were much like statues of previous eras and also resembled the relief images of kings in reverent positions from palaces and on steles. Temples were also repositories, as in older periods, of victory monuments. One such object was the Black Obelisk, erected outside a building at Nimrud that was probably a temple, which depicted the king receiving tribute from a variety of peoples, including the king of Israel. It is likely that temples also received some of the war booty captured from enemy states, put on display so that both human and divine witnesses would be reminded of the king's accomplishments.

The Neo-Assyrian People

Because of excavation strategies applied at the Assyrian capitals, we have little evidence for the houses and belongings of typical residents of cities like Nimrud and Nineveh. One consistent find where houses have been excavated, however, is the deposit of apotropaic figurines, intended to ward off physical and emotional harm. Like the lamassus and geniuses in palaces, these are found (buried) at entrances and corners. They may take the form of fantastic creatures, mythical beings, or priests in their garb but could also be dog figurines, one (at least) famously inscribed "Bite!" Those from private houses were made from clay; the same objects, coming from public buildings, could be of bronze or stone. Of similar purpose are a number of bronze amulets with the heads and bodies of demons and inscriptions that clarify their use in healing: the demon represented was thought capable of causing, and removing, serious illnesses.

Neo-Assyrian seals survive in significant numbers; because of the introduction of Aramaic as a language for administration, written alphabetically in ink on papyrus and parchment, stamp seals reappeared in this period and were used to seal scrolls closed. Cylinder seals continued to be manufactured, and a few cylinders with stamps on the end survive. A typical seal design of the period, on both stamp and cylinder seals, shows the king fighting a lion, an abbreviated version of the palace hunt depictions. Other seals carry images of hunts, battles, banquets, and worship (Winter 2000). All Neo-Assyrian seals put the king foremost, so that his image was present in all sorts of agreements and transactions, guaranteeing their validity.

Although the artwork of the Neo-Assyrian Period almost exclusively focused on the charismatic persona of the king, the state itself was a complex institution based in the smooth interaction of coercive power and administration. Even more importantly, over the 300-plus years of the Neo-Assyrian Empire, its institutions and organizations were constantly readjusted and reanalyzed, because of the advent of a new king, arrival of new peoples, and addition of new landscapes. This dynamic is hard to unearth below the rhetoric of continuity and cultural superiority, but it was an important ingredient in the survival of the Neo-Assyrian state.

Neo-Babylonian Empire

Of the vast territories they conquered, the Neo-Assyrian kings experienced the greatest discomfort with the conquest of Babylonia. They recognized that the Babylonians shared their culture, history, and pantheon and that Babylonian history went back far beyond theirs in time. Babylon first came under Neo-Assyrian rule under Shalmaneser III, but when it rebelled in 689, Sennacherib destroyed the city and its temples, apparently taking the statue of Marduk back to Assyria to serve as a reminder and example to any potential rebels. After Sennacherib's death, his son Esarhaddon began restoring Babylon and set one of his sons on the throne there. Ultimately, Assyrian hesitation to do more harm to Babylon allowed a rival dynasty under Nabopolassar to be established in 626 BCE. Nabopolassar was a member of the Chaldean tribe, from far southern Mesopotamia, a group that had previously opposed Assyrian rule. After uniting Babylonia under his rule in 616, Nabopolassar allied with the Medes to defeat the Neo-Assyrians. His dynasty, the Neo-Babylonians (626–539 BCE), inherited most of Assyrian territory and ruled until 539.

The Neo-Babylonian rulers left a series of historical chronicles that describe their rule. Additional information derives from building inscriptions, especially as the rulers restored temples destroyed by the Assyrians. As they do for the Assyrians, books of the Hebrew scriptures provide additional insight; the Neo-Babylonians had similar expansionist goals as their predecessors and eventually conquered the southern Levant in 587–586, sacking Jerusalem and deporting the royal family of Judah.

A second "outsider" perspective on Neo-Babylonian rule in its final years comes from Cyrus, king of the Persians in western Iran and eventual conqueror of Babylon. The Cyrus Cylinder, found at Babylon, describes the disarray and decline of Babylon under the last ruler, Nabonidus, who was a devotee of the moon god Sin and eventually moved his court to the Arabian city of Teima so as to more easily practice his preferred religion. According to Cyrus, the Babylonians, in the absence of firm leadership, and fearful at this betrayal of their gods, voluntarily turned over the city and empire to him, whom Marduk had already selected, making the Persians the heirs to all imperial territory and power (Beaulieu 1989).

No state archives of the Neo-Babylonian Period survive, but archives of temple and private households reveal their roles in economic activities. Temples, as in previous periods, had significant land holdings and oversaw various business ventures. The private economy was especially active at this time; records suggest that privately held businesses could contract to do business for the state, the temples, or themselves (van de Mieroop 2004: 263). Such businesses included local and long-distance trade ventures.

Art from the Neo-Babylonian Period in Mesopotamia can be difficult to distinguish from that of the succeeding Persian Period, and the apparently peaceful transition to Persian rule has left no datable destruction layers. At Babylon, archaeologists have excavated a variety of Neo-Babylonian contexts belonging to the reconstruction of the city following the Assyrian destruction. The Neo-Babylonian kings reorganized the center of Babylon into a fortified space containing secular and religious buildings, including a ziggurat dedicated to Marduk, a number of other temples, the palace, and (supposedly) the famous "Hanging Gardens," probably a terraced structure near the palace. A branch of the Euphrates River flowed through the inner city. At least nine gates led into this sacred area from all directions, and through two sets of fortifications, both of baked brick. Most impressive among the gates was the Ishtar Gate, decorated in registers with molded brick relief images of the city's sacred animals: lion, bull, and dragon. Closest to the gate, one section of this brickwork was glazed, with multicolored animals and dazzling blue background, mirroring the nearby river.

Persian Empire

The triumphant, and peaceful, overthrow of Babylon by Cyrus in 539 BCE provides an appropriate entry point for the final ancient Near Eastern empire, that of the Persians (539–331 BCE). Founded by Cyrus at around 560, the Persian Empire (often called the Achaemenid Empire, after an ancestral local ruler) eventually encompassed an area stretching beyond the Near East into Europe (parts of eastern Greece and the Caucasus mountains), Central Asia, the Indus Valley, and Egypt. After a series of battles, Alexander the Great of Macedonia defeated the Persian army in 331, putting an end to Near Eastern self-rule (for a time) and bringing all of Persian territory under Hellenistic control (see Chapter 7).

When Cyrus became king in 559 BCE, the Persians were relative newcomers to southwestern Iran. Their earliest mention was in Assyrian records of the 9th century BCE, at which point they were a tribal group occupying parts of the Zagros Mountains (Root 1979). Like the Medes, they spoke an Indo-Iranian language and were part of the movement of Indo-Iranian groups that began in the late 2nd millennium. Cyrus was the grandson of the final Median king, Astyages; the route by which he became king is disputed, but once on the throne, he (and his successors) took pains to represent the Medes and Persians as a unified people.

This guise of unity was extended to all peoples of the empire; Persian royal rhetoric focused on peace, while acknowledging ethnic, historical, and linguistic differences among the people they ruled. While local and foreign documents of the period indicate that local rebellions against Persian rule were frequent and that court intrigues led to numerous usurpations of the throne, official images and inscriptions stressed harmony and good will, particularly an openness and tolerance for local traditions and religions (a central theme of the Cyrus Cylinder). Persian administrative strategies also allowed for significant variety in local languages: in the core region of western Iran, they employed Elamite, the traditional language and writing system, for administrative texts; in Mesopotamia, it was Akkadian; in Egypt, it was hieroglyphic and demotic. Other writing systems stretched across the full territory: Aramaic for administrative and economic records and Old Persian for royal inscriptions. Publicly visible inscriptions were sometimes trilingual—Persian, Elamite, and Akkadian—even when they could not have been legible to viewers, as with the cliff-face victory inscription of Darius I at Behistun. This diversity of languages is another sign of the multiethnic nature of Persian society.

While private enterprise seems to have dominated the economy during the Persian Period, the central and provincial governments were financed by taxes, which supported public works and maritime trade. Exchange and tax collection was greatly eased by the introduction of coinage, which meant that goods and services could be valued against a single metrical standard guaranteed by the government. Persian kings introduced a number of other reforms, reorganizing their territories into satrapies, each ruled by a Persian governor; the satrapies provided tribute in gold, silver, and labor (van de Mieroop 2004: 277). To ease communication, a network of roads and stations was constructed across the empire, and a system of messengers devised. Otherwise, Persian kings pursued a policy of what Nylander (1979: 346) termed "minimal interference" in the lives of their subjects.

This sense of non-interference is conveyed in Persian art and archaeology as well. Because they lacked a prior tradition in monumental architecture and public art, the Persian kings borrowed heavily, but selectively, from their neighbors, including Assyria and Babylonia. For the most part, their artwork depicts an empire in harmony. Public art focused on the king and his court and depicted Persians and Medes as distinct, but equal; it depicted also the diversity of the people of the empire as they all worked in its support.

Most of the surviving architecture and art of the period dates to the reigns of its earliest kings, Cyrus (559–530), Darius I (522–486), and Xerxes I (486–465). This is largely because these three were charged with founding the two major cities of Persia: Cyrus's capital at Pasargadae, and Darius's (and his successors') at Persepolis. At both sites stand monumental stone structures filled with columns, overlooking gardens and landscapes that epitomized the king's power (Stronach 1990).

Both sites also housed royal tombs: at Pasargadae, a stone chamber atop a stepped platform, and at Persepolis, a set of rock-cut tombs, each with reliefs and inscriptions identifying the owner.

Persian royal art portrayed the king and his court in harmony. At Persepolis, on Darius's audience hall, the Apadana, the exterior of the eastern side of the structure bears a remarkable image: representatives of all the lands of the empire, each identifiable by their clothing and the objects they carry, bring their tribute to the king, who sits in the center surrounded by officials, guards, and the crown prince. So popular was this image that it was reproduced on a second side of the building when the main entrance was moved. As people visited or worked in the capital, they would walk by this scene, perhaps reproducing its solemnity and its sense of the scope of Persian control. While Assyrian art had featured tribute scenes, none was as detailed, nor as harmonious, as this representation. A similar sense was conveyed by the tomb reliefs at Persepolis (at Naqshi-I Rustam), where the king is shown standing before a fire altar, with the Persian god Ahuramazda above in a winged disk; the podium on which the king stands is held up by men in varied costumes, again representing the lands of the empire (Root 1979: 73–74). The same harmonious cooperation and support is depicted on a statue of Darius, found at Susa but probably made in Egypt in an approximation of Egyptian style: on the base, men in a variety of costumes kneel atop oval rings that approximate fortifications that contain the names of their lands. They raise their hands in a gesture that suggests that, together, they support the statue of the king above (Roaf 1974).

A final image, also of Darius, conveys both the debt owed to Assyrian imagery and the ways in which the Persians reshaped the image type and its meaning. The victory monument at Behistun, with accompanying inscriptions in Old Persian, Elamite, and Akkadian, was carved high on a cliff face along a road through the Zagros Mountains. Erected soon after Darius's accession in 522 BCE, it depicts the armed king, larger than anyone else, standing atop one man, with another nine standing, bound, in front of him. Each wears a different costume, a strategy used in other Achaemenid reliefs to identify the nations of the empire, but each is also identified in a caption as a leader of a rebellion against Persian rule. Above the prisoners, Ahuramazda faces the king in his winged disk; the inscription gives the god credit for Darius's victory. The artists drew on various sources for this image: Assyrian steles show kings holding ropes attached to rings in captives' noses, while palace reliefs sometimes showed bound prisoners. But Darius's relief lacks the implied violence of such Assyrian scenes and the usual accompanying narrative depictions of combat. Instead, the Behistun relief is another example of the harmony provided by Persian rule, even while the inscription makes it clear that the rebel leaders were executed (Root 1979: 182–93).

The Persian Empire was the last of the successful Near Eastern 1st-millennium empires. Like its predecessors, it governed a vast multiethnic territory using a combination of diplomacy and coercion. All three empires faced, and eventually fell to, pressure from foreign powers. And all employed a combination of social, economic, and administrative strategies to even out territorial differences and to support a vast corps of military and official dependents.

Conclusion

The ancient Near East, the first state society to be considered in this book, presents a full range of sociopolitical forms: from sedentary foragers to village agriculturalists, to urbanism and the first city-states, to territorial states and empires. The over seven millennia discussed here show tremendous growth and consolidation of territory, the development of complex strategies of dominance, and a full range of rhetorical expressions that supported these strategies. At the same time, they witnessed remarkable instabilities, especially when the territorial extent exceeded the means of control. Cases within this chapter will be cited as examples elsewhere in this book where they illuminate comparable situations.

6
THE NILE VALLEY OF EGYPT

Introduction

The development of complex society in ancient Egypt contrasts sharply with Mesopotamia, its neighbor and contemporary, despite a similar reliance on river-fed agriculture and divinely appointed kings. Egypt is the earliest known territorial state, encompassing a large geographic area ruled by a king, a status it achieved at the same time as it developed urbanism. At its peak in the Middle and New Kingdoms, Egyptian material culture was dominated by monumental temples and funerary monuments; an ideology that focused on the deeds, death, and afterlife of its semidivine kings; and a visual culture that certified the continued prosperity of society by ensuring that the kings acted in accordance with the desires of the gods in perpetuity. Because most archaeological efforts in Egypt have focused on royal monuments and iconography, the discussion that follows in this chapter necessarily concentrates on political history; aspects of village life and social relationships will be noted where there is evidence for them.

Geography and Chronology

Geography and Ecological Setting

The ancient Greek historian Herodotus called Egypt "the gift of the Nile," and its ancient economic, political, and religious systems converged on the annual cycle of the Nile River (Figure 6.1). From its sources in Uganda and Ethiopia, the Nile flows north for 6,670 kilometers, 1,000 kilometers through Egypt, before separating into channels for its last 160 kilometers. For most of its route through Egypt, the Nile defined a narrow ribbon of rich alluvial land, where most people lived. This distinction between the narrow valley and the swampy delta region provided both a practical and ideological dividing line between Upper (southern) and Lower (northern) Egypt that dominated Egyptian thinking. On either side of the Nile Valley for much of its course were the Eastern and Western Deserts—rocky, mountainous regions containing a variety of mineral resources and crisscrossed by overland routes; these areas were by no means devoid of population, despite their aridity. This unique geography fostered a sense of isolation from its neighbors for much of Egyptian history, allowing its leaders to represent outsiders as enemies, distinctly different in appearance, beliefs, and culture from the people of Egypt.

The Nile was also responsible for the annual environmental cycle that regulated Egyptian life until the 20th century CE. Fed by spring monsoons from the Indian Ocean, the Nile overran its

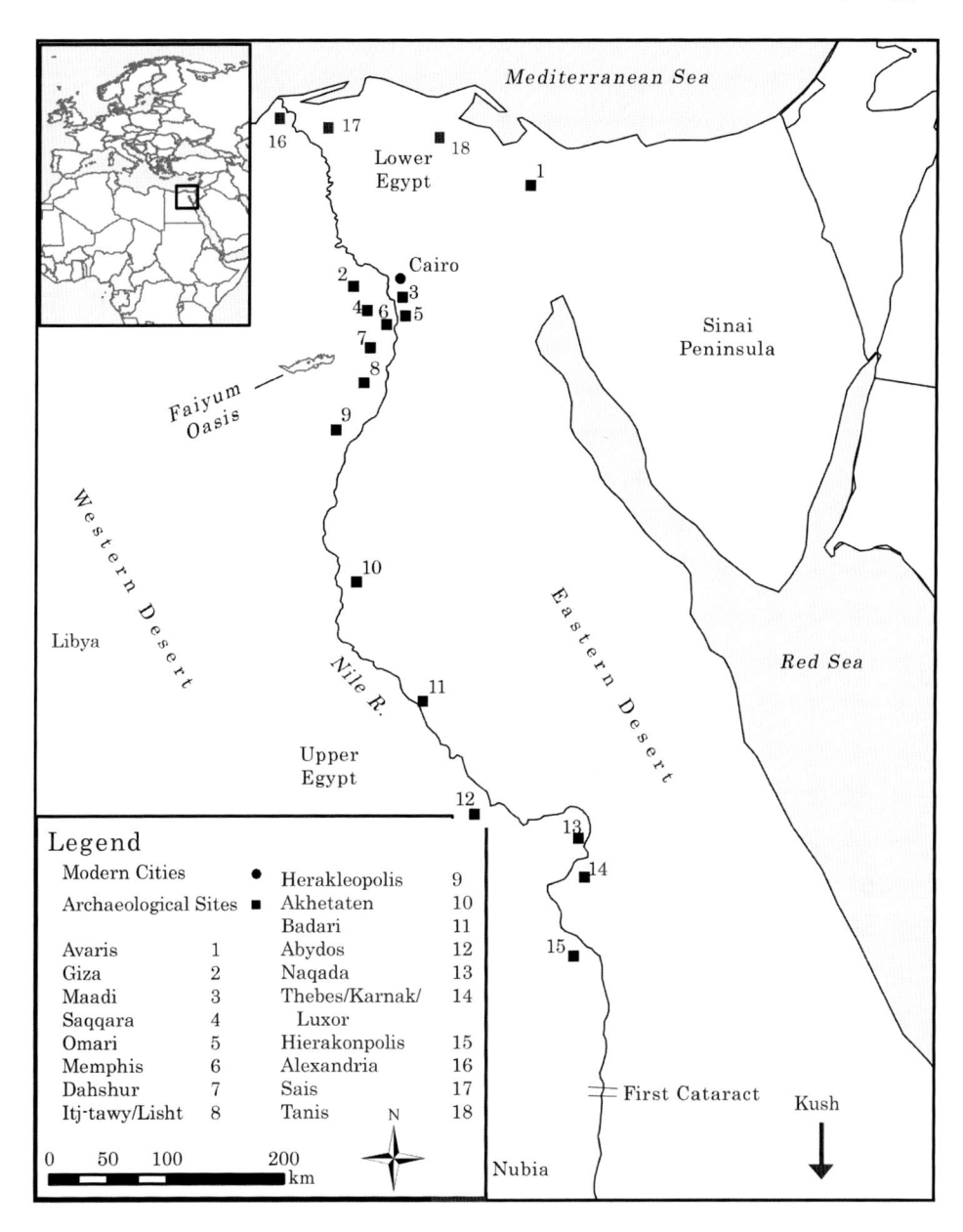

FIGURE 6.1 Map of Regions and Sites Discussed in the Chapter

Source: B. Spencer

banks in a yearly summer flood the ancient Egyptians called "The Inundation." For a period of weeks in August and September, water covered the fields; as it receded, farmers sowed their crops for an eventual spring harvest. The monsoons also brought a small amount of summer rainfall to Egypt itself, enough to renew pastureland in the desert regions (the "red land") beyond the alluvium (the "black land").

There is some evidence for climatic fluctuation in Egypt over time. During the Neolithic, the climate was generally wetter, and occupation in desert regions was possible. This seems to have come to an end before 3000 BCE. Egyptian documents also record periods when the flood was significantly lower than the expected 1 to 1.5 meters (Eyre 1995). When such conditions persisted for more than a couple of years, political and social disruption could ensue.

The Chronological Sequence

As with Mesopotamia, this chapter will outline a period of time (Table 6.1) that stretches from the advent of agriculture in Egypt in the Neolithic Period (ca. 10,000–4000 BCE), through the establishment of royal power and its ideological underpinnings in the Predynastic (ca. 4000–3000 BCE)

TABLE 6.1 Chronological Periods and Sites Discussed in Chapter 6

Dates	Period	Sites Discussed in Chapter	Cultural Horizons
ca. 10,000–4000 BCE	Neolithic	Nabta Playa; el-Badari; el-Omari	Mobile and semisedentary communities; domestication of cattle; adoption of domesticated plants and animals; ritual behaviors; emergent social stratification
ca. 4000–3000 BCE	Predynastic (Naqada I, II, III [Dynasty 0])	Hierakonpolis; Naqada; Abydos; Maadi	Emergence of elites; incipient urbanism and state development; first kings of unified Egypt; first writing; development of royal iconography
ca. 3000–2520 BCE	Early Dynastic (Dynasties 1–3)	Abydos; Memphis; Saqqara; Hierakonpolis	Monumental funerary architecture, with human sacrifice; early stages of administrative organization
2520–2100 BCE	Old Kingdom (Dynasties 4–8)	Saqqara; Giza; Memphis	Pyramids; provincial administrative organization; solar cult
2100–2010 BCE	First Intermediate Period (Dynasties 9–11)	Herakleopolis; Thebes	Dissolution of state organization; provincial government
2010–1660 BCE	Middle Kingdom (Dynasties 11–13)	Itj-tawy; Thebes; Deir el-Bahri	Reunification; militarization; literary development
1680–1549 BCE	Second Intermediate Period (Dynasties 14–17)	Avaris; Thebes	Hyksos rule; political fragmentation
1549–1073 BCE	New Kingdom (Dynasties 18–20)	Memphis; Thebes; Deir el-Medina; Akhetaten (Tell el-Amarna)	International Age; imperialism; religious reforms; eventual stagnation
1073–664 BCE	Third Intermediate Period (Dynasties 21–25)	Tanis; Sais	Libyan and Kushite kings of Egypt; imperialism
664–332 BCE	Late Period (Dynasties 26–31)	Memphis	Rule of Egypt from abroad; Neo-Assyrian and Persian kings
305–30 BCE	Ptolemaic Dynasty	Alexandria	Hellenistic rule

and Early Dynastic Periods (ca. 3000–2520 BCE), and then examine how initial ideas about power and governance evolved with changing conditions in the Old, Middle, and New Kingdoms. Throughout, three nested systems of timekeeping, deriving from different sources, will be used. At the finest level, events and lengths of the reigns of individual kings were recorded on contemporary documents, objects, and monuments. During the 3rd century BCE, Manetho, an Egyptian priest writing in Greek, compiled a list of kings and the length of their reigns that went back to Egypt's first rulers. For convenience, Manetho organized these hundreds of individuals into 30 dynasties or royal families, a concept that would have made sense in his time, the Hellenistic Age, but was not fully accurate, as not all kings in each of Manetho's dynasties were related by blood. Manetho's conceptualization of successive dynasties has required revision, given that there were several periods in which multiple dynasties ruled different parts of Egypt simultaneously.

The largest chronological divisions were devised when Egyptology began to develop as a discipline in the 19th century CE—the grouping of dynasties into periods called "kingdoms," during which Egyptian kings ruled over a unified and generally stable nation. The Old, Middle, and New Kingdoms are each followed by a phase of political instability and disunity, the "Intermediate Periods" (First, Second, and Third). While these long phases provide a useful shorthand for archaeological and historical generalizations, they would have meant little to an ancient Egyptian, whether court official or village-based farmer.

Pre-State Cultures: Neolithic and Predynastic Egypt

Neolithic

The Egyptian Neolithic began around 10,000 BCE, a period of higher temperatures and greater moisture in North Africa. While this early date might appear to indicate an earlier date for the advent of farming in Egypt than in southwest Asia, it really reflects a relative lack of precision in the reconstruction of Egyptian prehistory, due to a paucity of archaeological evidence. During the Neolithic (ca. 10,000–4000 BCE), population groups were able to occupy areas further into the Sahara and Egyptian deserts than today; the moister climate meant that grasslands extended into presently arid regions (Butzer 1995). A number of Neolithic sites are known along now-dry lakes and oases (Midant-Reynes 2000: 100–51).

The Neolithic saw two different geographic centers and two sets of domesticates, with both independent invention of domestication *and* adoption of domesticates and farming knowledge from elsewhere. This phenomenon reflects the distinct environmental niches available in Egypt. In Upper Egypt, sites and rock art imagery suggest that small groups of mobile hunters began to manage herds of wild cattle early in the Neolithic in the grasslands east and west of the Nile. Wild cattle were native to Egypt and Nubia to its south; bovine images and cattle bones in ritual contexts indicate that groups already venerated these wild beasts. By 7000 BCE, cattle were domesticated in these regions, and with desiccation late in the Neolithic (starting around 6000–5000 BCE), groups moved in an annual cycle between the Nile and desert pasture (Hassan 1998).

At around the same time, 7000 BCE, domesticated cereals, sheep, and goats made an appearance in the Delta region. These species had no wild progenitors in Egypt; they must have been brought from the Levant (Wengrow 2006: 25). Once Delta dwellers adopted agriculture, it quickly spread south. For most of the Neolithic, settlements throughout Egypt were ephemeral, and residents pursued flexible strategies of hunting, herding, fishing, and gathering to take advantage of the rich subsistence resources available. As climatic conditions became more demanding in the later Neolithic, domestication took firmer hold.

The evidence from sites in each region clarifies the cultural circumstances. Some of the oldest sites in Egypt come from the Western Desert area, particularly the Nabta Playa, where an ancient lake attracted humans and animals before desiccation set in. Between 10,000 and 6500 BCE, the Nabta Playa was home to a variety of temporary encampments of hunters and foragers. After 6500 BCE, incipient cattle domestication, large grinding stones, and pottery indicate a greater degree of permanence (Midant-Reynes 2000: 75). Still later, around 5000 BCE, at least one permanent village was founded, with round huts of perishable materials and at least 44 types of plants, including domesticated grain (Davies and Friedman 1998). Still, cattle dominated the material world of the residents of the Nabta Playa: immense mounds of stone covered, in some cases, the bones of young cattle apparently sacrificed in community ritual acts (Wendorf and Schild 1998). Other stone monuments in the area also required communal labor: a stone circle oriented toward the sunrise on June 21, traditionally the first day of summer rainfall, and a line of stones with possible calendrical significance. Residents and users of this Neolithic oasis were already dependent on the predictable natural cycle of the Nile but relied also on the single local domesticable animal species for sustenance and ceremonial acts.

In the Delta region, seasonal sites of the early Neolithic have yielded evidence of Levantine Epipaleolithic and Pre-Pottery Neolithic tools. These are found in association with domesticated grains (emmer wheat and barley) and animals (sheep and goat), indicating that the Delta-dwellers adopted both Near Eastern domesticates and technologies of farming. It is not known whether the population included migrants from the Levant. The earliest permanent sites in the Delta date to the later Neolithic, ca. 5100–4500 BCE (Koehler 2010). By this time, pottery technology had also diffused from the Levant. Residents pursued a flexible subsistence strategy that included wild plants, aquatic resources (fish and waterfowl), the Levantine domesticates, and domestic cattle. Burials in these villages were dug into abandoned buildings, with bodies wrapped in reed matting. A similar merging of traditions from the Western Desert and the Delta is found at the Faiyum Oasis, just beyond the Nile Valley. In all cases, people lived in small settlements with no indications of social differentiation.

Badarian Period (Late Neolithic)

The apparently slow development of sedentism and agriculture during most of the Neolithic Period in Egypt stands in stark contrast with the following millennia: rapid urbanization and state formation set in by the mid-to-late 4th millennium. Major developments began in the Badarian phase, the final phase of the Neolithic, dating ca. 4500–4000 BCE, at semisedentary settlements in Middle Egypt, particularly near the site of el-Badari. Settlement remains consisted of round structures of perishable materials, located at the edge of the floodplain. Residents herded cattle, sheep, and goats and farmed wheat and barley; they may have continued to move between pasture and field on a seasonal basis (Hoffman 1979).

While the settlements offer no traces of social differentiation, the graves of the Badarian Period do, suggesting that the roots of social ranking in ancient Egypt went back to this time. Hundreds of Badarian tombs have been excavated; most are simple pits and contain handmade pottery, with the deceased lying on his or her left side, head facing west (Midant-Reynes 2000: 153). But some tombs were larger, and contained more objects, including imported materials, such as jewelry made from ivory, copper, or ostrich eggshell, and siltstone palettes for grinding minerals into a powder or paste for cosmetics. Other special items, found in just a few tombs, were clay human and animal figurines, shells from the Red Sea, and clay boat models. This differentiation in death, particularly in items associated with bodily expression and display, shows an interest in marking an individual's social status or role (Wengrow 2006: 27). It is possible that these simply expressed personality, but special status objects continued to be important political symbols in the following periods.

In Lower Egypt, pottery and other material culture items suggest a distinct culture existed in the Delta region contemporary to the Badarian. Social stratification, though at a low level, is detectable in tombs here as well; one grave at el-Omari contained a wooden staff, akin to staffs of office in later Egyptian depictions and texts (Trigger 1983). In Upper Egypt, variability in flood levels between sites and even at a given village may have provided some members of society with a greater yield; they may have, in turn, deployed this surplus to enhance their own status.

Predynastic Egypt

In the subsequent Predynastic Periods (ca. 4000–3000 BCE), collectively known as Naqada I–III, this incipient social stratification grew, and signs of the consolidation of power in the hands of the elite occur in higher numbers. By the end of Naqada III, around 3000 BCE, all of Egypt was ruled by a single individual. The signs of unification are discernible in archaeological contexts, especially tombs, but also in the iconography of power. Many of the ideas and motifs of the Predynastic Period became standard elements of the representation of royal power in the Early Dynastic Period and Old Kingdom, and some survived intact throughout Egyptian history.

During the early part of the Predynastic Period, Naqada I (previously called "Amratian"), most of the major political developments took place in Upper Egypt, in the area around Hierakonpolis and Naqada. Naqada I seems to have grown out of Badarian material and political culture. Dating ca. 4000–3600 BCE, Naqada I sites show a full array of plant and animal domesticates (including pig), as well as the exploitation of aquatic resources (Hoffman 1979).

Signs of social stratification increased during Naqada I, as population grew and trade relationships expanded. Settlement evidence for the period is still limited, with the majority of evidence coming from tombs. At Hierakonpolis in Upper Egypt, excavation exposed a house containing a kiln, suggesting some craft specialization and investment in technologies (Midant-Reynes 2000: 184). In Lower Egypt, a number of settlements have yielded evidence of trade with the southern Levant (Faltings 2002). In turn, Egyptian pottery is found at a line of sites, probably way-stations for merchants and other travelers, across the northern Sinai Peninsula. The goal of early trade with the Levant may have been acquisition of copper, which made its way into some graves (Krzyzaniak 1979).

Graves provide the principal evidence for social and economic differentiation in this period. Many Upper Egyptian sites had adjacent cemeteries with up to several hundred individual graves. While each burial typically held a couple of clay vessels, within each cemetery were several tombs distinguished from the others by size, number of pots, and other gifts with special significance. Some items were made from imported materials, including ivory, copper tools, and ostrich eggshell beads (Wilkinson 1999: 29). Others were of significant forms: ivory and clay figurines, stone palettes in animal shape, or stone maceheads (Midant-Reynes 2000: 175–79). In general, these items are similar to those found in the richest Badarian graves. They denote a special status for the deceased. The use of grave goods to distinguish individuals was specific to Upper Egypt at this time, as few goods appeared in contemporary Lower Egyptian graves, most of which were located in the settlements rather than in separate cemeteries.

The other arena in which Naqada I society began to distinguish itself was in iconographic expressions of status and role, an area that expanded in the subsequent Predynastic phases, as themes of kingship and power were gradually elaborated. Figural art in Naqada I primarily appeared on pottery. While some vessels were undecorated and on others geometric patterns appeared in white paint on a darker background, some of these pots had figural designs depicting people hunting hippopotami and other wild animals, boats, and groups of people with distinctive feathered headgear (Hendrickx and Förster 2010; Wilkinson 2003: 64). These designs also appear in rock art of the Western and Eastern Desert regions, suggesting that a portion of Nile Valley residents continued to practice transhumance (Trigger 1983; Wilkinson 2003: 93). The designs are important also because they presage major motifs of Dynastic Egyptian art, where, for instance, depictions of the king spearing a hippopotamus were metaphorical expressions of his vigilance and triumph over chaos, and boats were needed for the journey to the afterlife. A final example of the early appearance of significant motifs on Naqada I pottery is a sherd from Naqada with a depiction of the Red Crown, traditionally the crown of Lower Egypt, in relief (Midant-Reynes 2000: 182). Whether this indicates that this headdress was worn by a ruling figure—a king or chieftain—at this early date is unknown.

By Naqada II, however, clearer signs of positions of power emerge from the archaeological evidence. Dating 3600–3200 BCE, Naqada II (formerly "Gerzean") developments were centered on Upper Egypt. Some of the population growth in the Nile Valley may be due to reduced transhumance and increased intensity of agriculture, but a reduction in overall settlement numbers also suggests convergence into certain population centers (Krzyzaniak 1979). It is difficult to call the Egyptian settlements "cities," as evidence is lacking for dense occupation by thousands of people; still, as in contemporary Uruk-Period Mesopotamia, this coalescence of population brought with it new economic, social, and political configurations. It is likely that the larger Egyptian towns of Naqada II were largely inhabited by elites and craft-workers, supported by nearby villages of farmers (Trigger 2003: 111).

Developments of the Naqada II Period are apparent in both settlement and cemetery contexts. At both Naqada and Hierakonpolis, the main centers in Upper Egypt, residents built mudbrick enclosure walls, although Hierakonpolis quickly outgrew the enclosed area (Wilkinson 1999: 38–39). This town had a walled oval precinct of 32 by 13 meters, the wall enclosing a courtyard that fronted an apparent shrine or ritual area, with a façade of large vertical timbers (Friedman 1996). Deposits within the enclosure included an array of animal bones from sacrifices, local and imported pottery, and debris from stone tool production. The precinct appears to have retained its importance as a location for ritual performances even after the shrine went out of use; Early Dynastic (Dynasty 1–2) objects indicate that the falcon god Horus was worshipped at Hierakonpolis in later centuries.

As important as Hierakonpolis's temple is for the history of Egyptian religion, its contemporary cemeteries furnish even more evidence for both the evolution of leadership and the history of art. Several hundred tombs at Hierakonpolis, in numerous cemetery areas, date to Naqada II. Most of these graves were small and simple, with a few grave goods, but several are larger, including that of a child who was buried with significant numbers of vessels and copper objects that denote a status he or she could not have gained through achievements but must have inherited (Adams 1996). Another, Tomb 100 (the "Decorated" or "Painted" Tomb) at Hierakonpolis, consisted of two mudbrick rooms; on one long wall was a painting whose motifs will be discussed later. The tomb itself exhibits two features found in nearly all Dynastic-period tombs to come: the provision of built spaces for offerings to the deceased, and decorative art. Many other Naqada II cemeteries across Upper Egypt show a similar set of distinctions in numbers and types of grave goods and in the location of tombs within cemeteries, indicating that elite classes at multiple sites were beginning to enjoy access to exotic and crafted items and to deploy these items in situations of public display, particularly in funerals (Bard 1994: 105; Wengrow 2006: 38–40).

Trade, particularly in crafted prestige goods, appears to have been a major factor in the growth of complexity and settlement at key locations during Naqada II. At Maadi, just outside Cairo, the layout and material culture was organized around the import of goods from the southern Levant and Upper Egypt, but little at that site indicates that its residents gained wealth or status from trade. Rather, the economic and social impact of trade was limited to southern centers like Naqada and

Hierakonpolis. Each of these sites benefited from a set of propitious economic circumstances: location on a stretch of especially productive agriculture land; access to nearby routes that led to key mineral and other resources (gold for Naqada, Nubian goods and gold for Hierakonpolis); and positions along the river that allowed them to control traffic (Wilkinson 1996: 89, 1999: 46). In each case, the local elites exploited these natural advantages for personal and political benefits.

The end result of these economic processes is materialized in the floruit of figural art in the Naqada II phase, art that focused on the ideology of power and rule. In the largest Naqada II tomb at Hierakonpolis, the Painted Tomb, the rich array of grave goods was complemented by a wall painting that combined Naqada I motifs (boats, dancing women, hunts) with new ones that directed attention to a single figure: a man between a pair of lions (a motif borrowed from Mesopotamia) and another wielding a mace over a group of seated prisoners. Hunts and battle scenes also dominated small-scale relief images on stone palettes and ivory knife handles, which at this time seem to have circulated in highly restricted elite circles. The images are better understood as metaphorical expressions of power and control over forces of nature than as depictions of actual events; the smiting motif and hunt both continued into Dynastic-period Egyptian art as representations of royal power (Davis 1992, 1993). They also signified the responsibility the king had to the gods to maintain order.

During Naqada II, then, positions of political power emerged in at least two southern centers, whose economic and religious interests coalesced in the hands of a small elite class. In Naqada III, this was taken a step further, with a single town, and single leader, consolidating power over all or nearly all of Egypt. This short period, 3200–3000 BCE, saw the political and cultural unification of Egypt. At its end, the First Dynasty of Egyptian kings took power, from which point historically attested rulers are documented in contemporary and later sources. But how Egypt came to be unified, overcoming what were geographically circumscribed power bases, is unclear. Because the names of some kings predating Dynasty 1 are known, Naqada III is often referred to as Dynasty 0.

To later Egyptians, a major feature of their land was its dual character, Upper and Lower; a significant duty of the king was maintaining the unity of these two lands. This was signified in two royal titles: the king's "Two Ladies Name," which symbolized his ability to placate the vulture goddess Nekhbet, of Upper Egypt, and the cobra goddess, Wadjet, of Lower Egypt, and the *nswt-bity* ("dual king") title, written with the hieroglyphs for sedge and bee, referring to the distinctive plant and animal symbols of south and north. Beginning in the middle of the First Dynasty, kings were depicted wearing the Double Crown, a headdress that combined the Red Crown of the north with the White Crown of the south. Historical sources attributed unification to the first king of Dynasty 1, Narmer (or his successor, Aha), suggesting that he brought troops from the south and defeated northern forces in battle. Narmer's artwork offers the same perspective. But archaeological and iconographic evidence indicates that unification was achieved by 3100 BCE, at least 100 years before Narmer.

The cultures of Lower and Upper Egypt were already merging in the centuries leading up to Naqada III, as seen at sites like Maadi. Southern ceramics displaced typical northern forms and wares, but northern types were also adopted in the south (Wilkinson 1996: 6). Mudbrick architecture, already present in Naqada II Hierakonpolis, also moved northward. But evidence for warfare and destruction at Delta sites is lacking; the iconography of violent conquest did not necessarily reflect real circumstances. It is likely that political unification occurred gradually, one or two towns at a time. Over the course of Naqada III, Hierakonpolis took over Naqada, then competed with the increasingly powerful town of Abydos for control of a larger territory.

No major disruption in occupation or in culture accompanied unification. But a rupture took place within Egyptian social structure, one that defined for the first time a visible distinction between ruler and ruled. What had previously appeared to be a general continuum of status and role differentiation, seen especially in tomb size and numbers of grave goods, in Naqada III gave way to a situation in which one individual stood out in mortuary treatment, while all others were relegated to a status of generalized equality. New kinds of representation applied to this person only and conveyed his particular status as king.

Some of the iconography and meaning of kingship derived from traditions of Naqada II art, and some was strikingly new. One innovation that appeared first in Naqada III was the explicit linking of the ruler with the gods, a focus that remained central to kingship for the rest of Egyptian history. The king's name was placed in a *serekh*—a frame with a niched palace façade depicted below the name and with the Horus falcon above it. Horus was the god of Hierakonpolis and a god of kingship, whom the king personified during his reign. The serekh first appeared in Naqada III, written in ink on jars and incised on seals, both denoting ownership of goods; in a number of instances, no king's name was written in the serekh, perhaps simply conveying royal possession (Bard 1992; Midant-Reynes 2000: 247). Objects with serekhs appear throughout Egypt during this period.

Other artwork of Naqada III points to royal powers and responsibilities. Cosmetic palettes and knife handles continued to bear scenes of hunting and fighting, but artists began to impose more rigid controls on the space, using horizontal registers and variations in scale to impart the relative status of individual figures. These representations conveyed royal responsibility for maintaining order in the land. The Scorpion Macehead belongs to another type of object with royal associations; found at Hierakonpolis, it depicts a king whose name was written with a scorpion glyph, wearing the White Crown of Upper Egypt and performing an agricultural chore with a pointed tool. In the register above is a line of standards carrying divine symbols, suggesting that the king is performing a ritual act that is witnessed by gods; the impression is supported further by the bull's tail he wears (Hendrickx and Förster 2010). Here, an early king is seen acting for the benefit of his people with the approval and oversight of the gods. Texts dating soon after this time suggest that the king was held responsible for the agricultural prosperity of the entire land of Egypt; as mediator between the people and the gods, his proper ritual performance conveyed his subjects' wishes for fertility and success.

From Naqada III on, artwork and writing in Egypt were linked, and writing was invented at this time as a tool of the new political organization. From its beginning, hieroglyphic writing played a dual role in administration and ideology in Egypt. Its use in Naqada III marked the ownership and origin of goods; although precise readings for individual glyphs are lacking, the objects marked with writing were commodities. Simultaneously, though, writing was a royal prerogative and could illustrate, in examples like the serekh, the source and content of the king's power (Baines 1983, 1988).

Objects with writing—jars and labels—are concentrated in the Naqada III royal tombs at Abydos, where at least three Predynastic kings of Egypt—Iry(-Hor), Scorpion, and Ka—were buried, as were their Dynasty 1 successors. Several other contemporary tombs were near theirs, but the names of the deceased in these have not been preserved on inscribed objects. Most notable is Tomb U-j, in Cemetery U at Abydos; it consisted of 12 subterranean rooms filled with goods. A number of scholars have suggested that this tomb, which dates to ca. 3150 BCE, belonged to the first king to unify Egypt. The layout and contents evoke a multi-roomed administrative building, even a palace (Figure 6.2). Tomb U-j contained an ivory scepter, a symbol of kingship; other objects denote the immense economic power of the deceased and the provision for his comfort in the afterlife. These include over 100 wine jars imported from the southern Levant, a bowl made of obsidian, probably from Ethiopia, and other luxury items of cedar and ivory (Wengrow 2006: 137). In addition, a collection of over 150 ivory and bone labels had been attached to other goods, probably perishable items like textiles; signs incised on them likely indicated their source or owner. Writing, imports, and crafted goods came together here to accompany this powerful individual into the afterlife.

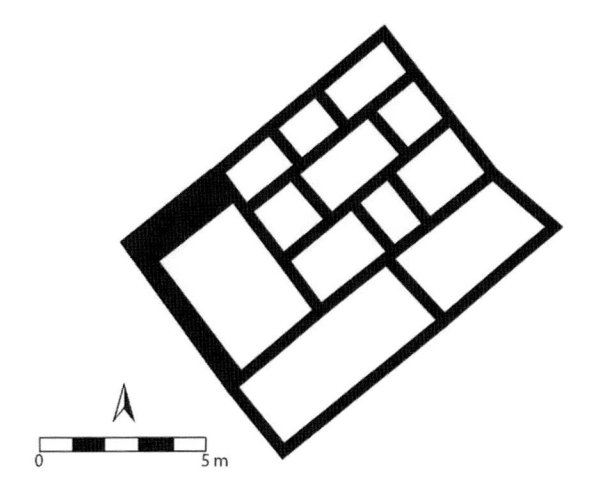

FIGURE 6.2 Plan of Tomb U-j at Abydos
Source: J.C. Ross

The Egyptian Territorial State (3000–1073 BCE)

The Early Dynastic Period

With Dynasty 1 (3000–2720 BCE), Egyptian history began in earnest, defined as a line of named kings holding the throne of Egypt as semidivine mediators between the gods and populace. As will be seen in the pages that follow, that generalization tells only part of the story. The earliest phase of Egyptian history is the Early Dynastic Period (ca. 3000–2520 BCE), comprising Dynasties 1 through 3. This was a transitional period leading up to the great pyramid- and temple-builders of the Old Kingdom, but what was achieved by these early kings of Upper and Lower Egypt, documented in king lists and inscriptions both in Egypt and beyond its borders, set important precedents for later rulers. Most significantly, they established their capital, and eventually their burial grounds, at Memphis, and they established standards for the monumental architectural and artistic expression of royal power.

The transitional nature of these early dynasties is especially true of the first two. Dynasty 1 comprises eight kings, attested by both contemporary materials (objects and inscriptions) and by the later king lists. The dynasty's founder at around 3000 was the aforementioned Narmer, called Menes in the king lists. The Narmer Palette (Figure 6.3) was long thought to represent this king's historic victory over Lower Egypt and unification of the two lands, but as already discussed, that unification took place 100 or more years before him. It is likely, however, that Narmer and his successors faced periodic rebellion, and the Palette may not be completely ahistorical. The term "commemorative" may convey this sense and also refers to the periodic ritual re-enactments of victory that kings performed (see Box 6.1). A similar statement of divinely appointed rule over the dual kingdom was made on the macehead of Narmer, from the same cultic context, which recorded the delivery of over 100,000 captives and nearly 2 million cattle to the king on a ritual occasion (Hendrickx and Förster 2010; Wengrow 2006: 211). Narmer's artwork established an iconography of exclusive royal power from which his successors borrowed liberally; at the same time, the physical forms his works took appropriated from the grave goods of earlier times and after him were never again used for royal display.

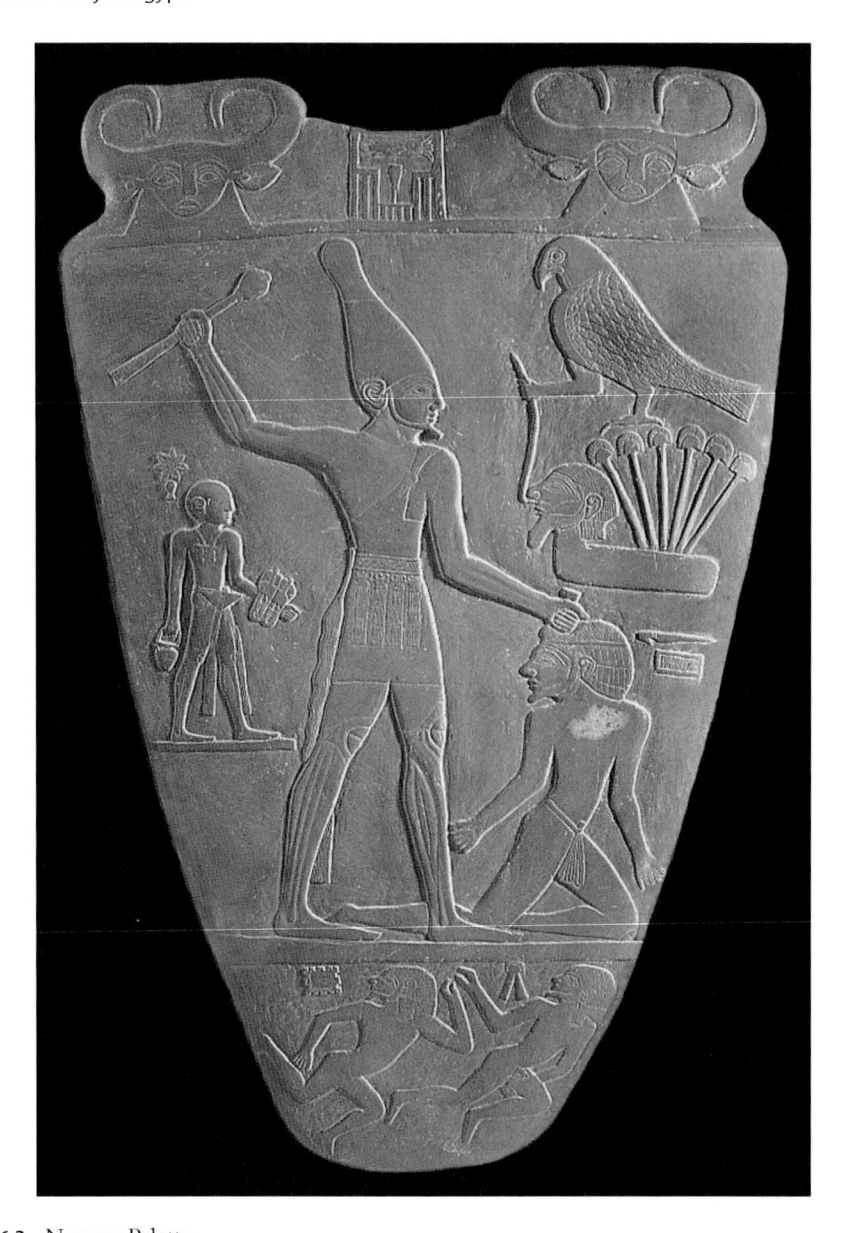

FIGURE 6.3 Narmer Palette

Source: Werner Forman / Art Resource, NY

BOX 6.1 KEY OBJECT: THE NARMER PALETTE

The Narmer Palette is one of the most recognizable artifacts from early Egypt. At 63 centimeters high, it replicates and reinterprets a practical object form from the Predynastic Period but on a large scale. On one side, the king wears the White Crown and smites an enemy; on the other, he

FIGURE 6.3 (Continued)

wears the Red Crown and reviews the battlefield dead. Gods watch over these actions, but the king also acts as a supernatural being, wearing a bull's tail. This ceremonial palette was dedicated at the temple of Horus at Hierakonpolis. It probably had a ritual use; its imagery, both familiar and innovative, would have required multiple viewings, but its message of royal power and divine approval would have been instantly apparent (Davis 1992: 161–85, 1993; O'Connor 2002).

Narmer's successors included several additional kings of Dynasty 1; three to nine more are attested for Dynasty 2, though contemporary records and later king lists do not agree on their names. Together, these rulers made significant political adjustments in order to rule so large a territory. Narmer founded the capital at Memphis, at the junction between the Delta and Upper Egypt. Strategically, this location made it easier to collect taxes paid in agricultural surplus, the bulk of which came from the fertile Delta region, where a significant number of Egyptian farmers lived. This surplus supported governmental functions but was also intended to supply offerings in perpetuity for the mortuary cult of the king (Wilkinson 1999: 112). Memphis's location was favorable for trade and communications as well: trade routes from both the Eastern and Western Deserts entered the Nile Valley at Memphis.

From Memphis, royal officials could also track and administer commodities coming into Egypt from the Levant through the Sinai Peninsula. During Dynasty 1, this trade became so important to Egypt's rulers that Egypt established direct administrative control over parts of the southern Levant, where Egyptian settlers used locally made pots in Egyptian forms, and oversaw the movement of copper, timber, olive oil, and other natural resources (de Miroschedji 2002). By Dynasty 2, however, Palestine had developed an urban culture and Egypt, perhaps to avoid conflict, abandoned its settlements there, establishing in their place a significant maritime trade relationship with Byblos in Lebanon. This ship-based trade allowed for import of larger items, like cedar logs, and higher quantities of goods. At the same time as overland trade with the Levant declined, Egyptian administrators were also extending political and economic control into Nubia.

Significant religious activities were conducted by Dynasty 1 kings, especially actions that underlined their relationship to the gods in public events. The Palermo Stone, which records major annual events during the reigns of Dynasty 1 through 5 kings, lists a number of rituals performed, cult images dedicated, and temples constructed by these kings (Wilkinson 1999: 64–65). Each ruler must have traveled regularly across Egypt to conduct economic and religious business; his visibility on these occasions was a major means of broadcasting and maintaining power. Royal expenditures and devotion were focused on Egypt's major gods—like Horus, Re, Osiris, and Hathor—who had significant cosmic roles and a special relationship with the king. Archaeological evidence suggests that many local gods were worshipped by everyday Egyptians in their own towns and even their own houses.

Spectacle and durability were also elements of the royal mortuary practices established at this time. Where Predynastic tombs, even of the early kings, were largely subterranean, the Early Dynastic kings commissioned above-ground monuments, with some parts made in stone to emphasize the enduring power of the king even after death (Smith 1998). Burials of family members and officials clustered around the royal tomb, replicating and making permanent the hierarchies experienced during life. At this early date, it is unclear whether anyone other than the king could earn a happy existence in the afterlife, but it seems that elites were required to continue to serve the king after death.

Royal burials of Dynasty 1 were in Abydos, while most Dynasty 2 kings chose burial near Memphis, at Saqqara. Over time, the royal burial complexes grew in size, with more chambers added for goods, more subsidiary burials (family and officials) nearby, and a tumulus, hidden within the superstructure, built above the burial itself. This last feature seems to have replicated the mythical primordial mound of creation and suggests the king's hope for rebirth. In time, the Dynasty 1 kings added a second structure to their mortuary complexes nearer the river: a funerary enclosure. These may have looked like palaces, with niched facades, and served as locales for rituals that sustained the king in the afterlife. Khasekhemwy, the last king of Dynasty 2, built one of these structures at Abydos and another at Hierakonpolis, suggesting that the king's cult could be celebrated in various locations (Wilkinson 1999: 246). Kings also exercised power over life and death, as at least two Dynasty 1 royal tombs at Abydos included individuals who were buried along with the king; as in Mesopotamia, human sacrifice in Egypt was a briefly practiced royal prerogative that may have provided a king with his court in the afterlife. It may also have eliminated possible rivals to the throne for the next monarch.

Royal tombs were often looted in antiquity. Only in rare instances, such as Aha's tomb at Abydos, were the contents recovered by archaeologists; these included rich materials such as copper, ivory, faience, and marble. Items of wealth and value have also been found in the dozens of graves that surrounded the royal tombs and in the tombs of Dynasty 1 and 2 officials at Saqqara, 500 kilometers from the royal burial ground (Kemp 1967). Because these private tombs contained objects with the king's name, probably donated by him, it was long thought that the Saqqara tombs were the true royal burials. But the earliest kings retained their ties to their ancestral home at Abydos, while officials could mark their connection to the capital city by being buried near it. The Saqqara tombs of officials took the form of *mastabas* (an Arabic word meaning "bench"), low solid brick structures, with a deep pit dug for the burial itself; like the royal funerary enclosures, they may have imitated, in appearance at least, a house (Wengrow 2006: 244). Even geographically separated from the king's burial, elite individuals may have hoped to partake at least to some degree in the sort of afterlife he had earned.

Dynasty 3

The Third Dynasty (2584–2520 BCE) marks yet another transitional period in Egyptian society; scholars are divided on whether to include it in the Early Dynastic Period or the Old Kingdom. Although the exact order and genealogical relationships of its five kings are unclear, during the Third Dynasty, Egypt experienced remarkable political stability, perhaps for the first time since unification. Its rulers therefore embarked on economic and religious ventures that set in motion and made possible the even more monumental achievements of the Dynasty 4 pharaohs.

By the close of Dynasty 3, the provincial system that subdivided the Delta region for purposes of taxation had been extended to Upper Egypt, with governors appointed to rule each region, so that the population could pay taxes to local establishments. Central storehouses were constructed at provincial centers to hold agricultural surpluses. The Egyptian crown also pursued a number of new mining ventures, both in Egypt and in the southern Sinai Peninsula. The main goal of the latter was to obtain copper, needed for tools to supply state workshops and support new building projects. Much of this work was overseen by the newly created office of the vizier, the highest official below the king, a position usually held by one of the king's sons at this early date (Wilkinson 1999: 137). It is likely that the writing system was adjusted to support these economic projects, but the absence of surviving papyrus documents from this time hinders interpretation; what is apparent is that writing was adapted in Dynasty 3 to better reflect speech, but evidence is limited to religious texts in tombs (Baines 1983, 1988).

The most visible remains of the Third Dynasty are precisely those monuments intended to demonstrate the political power and divine nature of the king: stone burial complexes designed to allow him to continue to exercise kingship in perpetuity. In Dynasty 3, the kings again decided to build their tombs near the capital, guaranteeing the largest possible viewership. They experimented with a new form for royal burial: a step pyramid (a series of ascending platforms, each smaller in area than the one below), which seems to have grown out of the Early Dynastic mastaba tomb. The earliest step pyramid was built by Djoser; his architect, Imhotep, earned such fame for the innovation that he was worshipped by later generations of Egyptians (see Box 6.2).

BOX 6.2 KEY MONUMENT: THE STEP PYRAMID OF DJOSER AT SAQQARA

Djoser's Step Pyramid at Saqqara comprised a complex of buildings, all contained within a wall enclosing an area of 545 by 277 meters (Baud 2010). It was the first Egyptian monument to be completely constructed in stone. Djoser rejected previous tomb types that featured palace-like layouts; instead, within the enclosure wall were spaces for mortuary ritual and offerings, burial, and for the continued performance, after death, of royal rituals like the Sed festival. In the Sed ritual, the king renewed his commitment to governing Upper and Lower Egypt and was himself renewed and rejuvenated by the gods. The burial place was originally designed as a mastaba but then enlarged and enhanced in stages, finally rising to a six-step pyramid over 60 meters high. It would have been visible from miles around, reminding those still living of the power of the deceased king. It is also a monument to the workers who created it; one estimate is that between 5,000 and 7,000 workmen took 20 years to complete the complex (Stadelman 1995). It is not surprising that new supplies of copper were necessary at this time, nor that no other Dynasty 3 king left such a monumental funerary monument.

Djoser's Step Pyramid complex encapsulated a number of religious developments of the Third Dynasty. The shift from low mastaba to pyramid form may be partly explained by a desire to make something more monumental, but it is likely that a new belief that the king ascended to the stars after burial developed at this time; the pyramid assisted this ascent. Along the north side of the pyramid was the mortuary temple for celebration of the king's cult, and the *serdab*, a chamber that contained Djoser's *ka* statue, which housed his spirit and was able to accept offerings. The northern orientation of these features may also reflect the growth of an astral religion, with special focus on the never-setting stars that circle the North Star. In later texts, these stars were said to be royal ancestors.

Djoser's limestone ka statue was nearly life-sized and painted. Two holes in the serdab's northern side allowed the ka to move in and out of the statue to see and smell offerings. A number of reliefs in the underground corridors of the complex depicted the king performing feats of endurance during the Sed festival, which he could celebrate in perpetuity in the courtyards (Friedman 1995). In other subterranean storage spaces, archaeologists have recovered over 40,000 stone vases with the names of Djoser's Dynasty 1 and 2 predecessors, effectively making them donors to his mortuary equipment.

While no other royal burials of Dynasty 3 are as well-preserved as Djoser's, significant numbers of official tombs clustered around his tomb and those of his successors; as previously, private citizens could link their afterlives to the king's by physical proximity. The mastaba tombs at Saqqara featured a space for offerings; frequently, a room recessed into the façade held a statue intended to receive the soul of the deceased (the ka) and carved or painted scenes of the owner with a table full of offerings, standing in permanently for the perishable goods left by relatives at the chapel. In private tombs, like royal ones, the use of stone increased. Writing also appears in these tombs, giving the names and titles of the deceased and sometimes lists of the offerings they received. Together, writing and stone provided a lasting witness to these lives and deaths.

The Old Kingdom

The Old Kingdom (2520–2100 BCE), comprising Dynasties 4 through 6, represents a period of tremendous royal power in Egypt, expressed especially in terms of the king's close relationship to the gods. In later phases of Egyptian history, long-ruling innovative and charismatic kings ruled over more territory, but the Old Kingdom is the main period during which kings had exclusive rights to power both during and after their reigns. Even before the end of the Old Kingdom, Egypt saw a decline in royal might and a reduction in the centralization of power. The high point of the period was the Fourth Dynasty (2520–2392 BCE), whose rulers built the pyramids at Giza (Figure 6.4), demonstrating their grip on power with both the scale of these undertakings and the hierarchies they built into the "city of the dead" that surrounded them.

The six rulers of the Fourth Dynasty expanded the ranks of officialdom, adding a second vizier position to oversee public works and tax collection in Upper Egypt, and allowing the levels and types of administrative positions to proliferate, to account for increased building activities and government functions (Baud 2010; Kanawati 1980; Leprohon 1995). Royal building projects, particularly tombs for kings and their relatives, expanded to an unprecedented level, and the expenses were handled through a combination of tax income, further agricultural surpluses, corvée labor, and military activity. This variety of activities is attested as early as the reign of Sneferu, the first king of the dynasty (Callender 1998: 101–102).

The most tangible result of this administrative expansion are the royal tombs, epitomized by the pyramids at Giza but located at a number of other sites as well. The shift to true pyramid form, which also occurred during Sneferu's reign, attests to a transformation in religious focus; the pyramid may replicate a ray of sunshine, by means of which the king could ascend to heaven to join his father, the sun god Re. There are other signs of the ascendancy of sun worship in the Fourth Dynasty. Egyptian religious belief saw the king as representative of all the gods; that one god received special focus at this time in no way detracted from the power of the others.

The three pyramids at Giza belonged to three mid-dynasty kings: Khufu, Khafre, and Menkaure. Khufu's is the largest, originally standing nearly 150 meters high; Stadelman (1995) estimates that

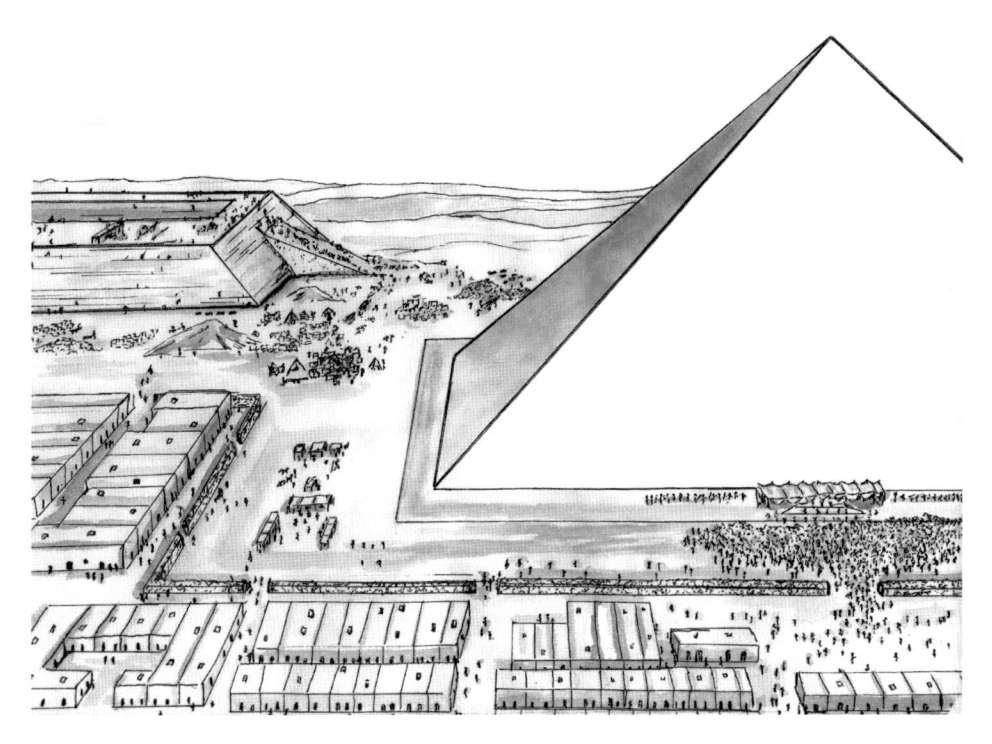

FIGURE 6.4 The Pyramids at Giza

Source: M.J. Hughes

20,000 to 25,000 laborers quarried, dragged, and positioned the stones over the course of Khufu's reign. Each pyramid had both a mortuary temple and a valley temple, with a long, covered causeway connecting them. The height of this elaboration is the Great Sphinx, which sat beside the valley temple of Khafre. At 73.5 meters long and 20 meters high, carved from the surrounding rock, it too may have made particular reference to the solar cult.

The first king to be buried at Giza, Khufu, laid out the cemetery surrounding his pyramid to reflect the hierarchy within his administration and to maintain those ties of loyalty and service in the afterlife. To the east of Khufu's complex stood three small pyramids belonging to his wives; beyond them were the large mastaba tombs of his children, many of whom held high office. West of the pyramid were the smaller mastabas of lower-ranking officials, many of them the king's more distant relatives and priests charged with the upkeep of his mortuary cult. Construction, decoration, and furnishing of all of these tombs were done at the king's expense; he also would have paid for the funerals and for continued offerings for the sustenance of his relatives and officials in the afterlife. A village built at Giza at first held artisans and laborers working on the kings' and others' tombs; later, the same houses were occupied by the priests who served the cults of the scores of deceased individuals.

Much of the artwork found in the private tombs of Dynasty 4 is finely made, probably by royal craft-workers. Life-sized statuary represented the tomb owner and his family, serving as their ka statues. Fourth Dynasty private tombs also featured relief carvings and paintings depicting an idealized daily life and an array of wooden furniture to serve the needs of the dead and provide a setting for a happy and well-endowed afterlife.

After this period of construction activity and administrative expansion, Dynasties 5 and 6 (2392–2117 BCE) in some ways represented a refocusing of royal attentions but also a decline in royal power. At least 15 kings ruled Egypt during this 275-year period, several for two decades or more. During Dynasties 5 and 6, Egypt experienced another expansion in the number of administrative positions available and in their ranking. This has been seen by scholars as evidence for a more professional bureaucracy, with office-holders recruited from outside the royal family (Baud 2010). A significant portion of Egypt's administration was still centered in Memphis, but provincial governments also grew in size and responsibility, perhaps with expanding populations or a need for more tax revenues (Callender 1998: 100). This suggests a balancing of local and centralized authority not previously found in Egyptian records. Royal inscriptions of the Sixth Dynasty record significant investments in provincial temples (Richards 2010). A sign that the king was losing some of his ideological authority is the growth of provincial cemeteries, especially during the Sixth Dynasty; rather than burial near the king, provincial officials chose to be buried in increasingly elaborate tombs near their own homes, with the tombs of their administrators clustered around them, a hierarchy familiar in previous generations at Giza and Saqqara but until this time limited to the royal tomb.

Still, royal authority and legitimacy in the late Old Kingdom was not questioned. The trend of sun worship that was evident in the pyramid form of Dynasty 4 tombs continued into the Fifth Dynasty. The Fifth Dynasty kings introduced a new temple type, the "sun temple," dedicated to Re; each king was apparently expected to build a sun temple, though only two have been identified with certainty. The excavated sun temples consist of a number of structures within an enclosure wall; the focus of cult activities appears, however, to be in the open: an altar in a courtyard for animal sacrifices and an obelisk representing and attracting the sun's rays (Murnane 2012: 165). Decoration within the sun temples depicted the sun's seasonal cycles. During Dynasty 6, kings also began to build at the cult center of Osiris, god of the dead, at Abydos (Richards 2010).

Meanwhile, the late Old Kingdom kings appear to have invested less in their own mortuary facilities. All of them built pyramids in the region of Saqqara. These pyramids were a fraction of the size of those at Giza, and in some cases had to be finished in mudbrick, but some were decorated with fine reliefs. In the Saqqara pyramid of Unis, the final king of Dynasty 5, are the earliest attested

Pyramid Texts, a collection of spells and prayers intended to protect and assist the king on his journey to the afterlife. These texts multiplied in Dynasty 6, even being found in at least one queen's tomb. They demonstrate that the king and his immediate family continued to be most closely associated with the gods and had earned a place beside them in perpetuity.

Following the long reign of Pepy II in the Sixth Dynasty, the dynastic succession broke down, with only briefly ruling kings to follow. The Sixth Dynasty was followed by two more at Memphis, the Seventh and Eighth, which controlled the capital region and, nominally, the rest of Egypt. The king lists provide a very confusing sense of these years, leaving the impression of rapid turnover and conflict over the throne; some scholars believe there was no Seventh Dynasty. The larger question of why decline occurred at this time is much discussed, but unresolved; some evidence survives to suggest environmental crises such as low Nile floods, famine, or warfare, but these problems do not appear to have affected the entire country. A crisis in kingship and overall leadership ensued, and the land fragmented into regional polities that formally recognized central authority but with only local loyalties (Willems 2010).

First Intermediate Period

The First Intermediate Period (ca. 2100–2010 BCE) comprises Dynasties 9, 10, and the early part of Dynasty 11, before Mentuhotep II reunified Egypt by force. While some scholars might include Dynasties 7 and 8 in the First Intermediate Period, those kings did, nominally, rule over all of Egypt, while their successors had a more limited geographic reach. The Dynasty 9 and 10 kings, who forcibly overthrew Dynasty 8, ruled from Herakleopolis, near the Faiyum Oasis, to as far south as Abydos. Dynasty 11 kings began their reign as the provincial governors of Thebes, contemporary to Dynasties 9 and 10. Thus, at least two sets of kings ruled simultaneously, though the king lists make them look consecutive.

There is limited historical and archaeological evidence from the First Intermediate Period. The burials of governors at their provincial capitals continued from late in the Old Kingdom, and some seem to have ruled more than one province. These officials appear to have governed independent of overarching authority, taking in local taxes to fund their own public works and armies (Hayes 1975b). The governors of the area around Hierakonpolis sent troops to aid the Herakleopolitan kings against Thebes (Dodson and Hilton 2004: 80). And Theban early Dynasty 11 rulers funded temple construction at several neighboring centers (Willems 2010).

The fragmentation apparent on the political stage is also evident in funerary art found at the provincial capitals. A number of inscriptions in private tombs describe the owner's military service, suggesting that local overlords felt the need for defensive as well as offensive action. Governors and officials under them built rock-cut tombs in Upper Egypt; in these tombs, artistic expression was typically limited to an offering stele, depicting the owner and his family. This traditional scene, though, looks strange: bodies and facial features are oddly proportioned, and at times, the stele is painted rather than carved. It seems that professional artists remained only in the Memphis area, where funerary art retained its high standards, while art in the provinces reflected the fragmentary, localized outlook that dominated politics during the First Intermediate Period. Despite the decline in centralized power, evidence about the lives of the majority of Egypt's citizens during the First Intermediate Period is still lacking.

Middle Kingdom

In mid-Dynasty 11, Mentuhotep II took the position of governor of Thebes and proceeded to expand his territory. In year 14 of his reign, he defeated the final king of the Tenth Dynasty, and unified Egypt under a single ruler for the first time in nearly 100 years. His successors in Dynasties

11, 12, and 13 belong to the Middle Kingdom (ca. 2010–1660 BCE); they re-established Egyptian might abroad and restored, in their administrative methods and iconography, the traditional belief in the king as divinely sanctioned ruler of the dual state, charged by the gods to uphold the order of the land and the cosmos. To re-establish this perspective was no trivial matter: early in the Middle Kingdom, provincial officials continued to hold significant power. To reassert a hierarchy they, and their subjects, had not recognized during their lifetimes required shrewd, coercive managerial and rhetorical skills.

One feature of Egyptian culture that expanded during the Middle Kingdom was the power of the written word; often, rulers of the time used their privileged access to writing to reassert and sustain their positions. New types of literary texts appeared in the Middle Kingdom, including legends and "instructions," wisdom literature formulated as advice from father to son (Enmarch 2010). Early manuscripts of popular stories, like the Legend of Sinuhe, come from Middle Kingdom contexts. This is indicative of a thriving intellectual class, serving rulers and officials in various capacities. The products of intellectuals—writers and artists—had a wider distribution across the population than before. The Pyramid Texts of Old Kingdom royal tombs were transferred and rewritten, becoming Coffin Texts, painted on the wooden sarcophagi of a wide range of Middle Kingdom Egyptians. Divine images are also found in contexts associated with all classes, particularly in the form of scarab seals, symbols of bodily transformation in death (Wegner 2010). This evidence suggests a widening of access to a better life and afterlife to more of the Egyptian populace, a circumstance that would have been theologically impossible during the Old Kingdom.

It is unquestionable that Mentuhotep II's takeover of Egypt required significant military action; the mass burial of young men with major injuries near his mortuary complex at Deir el-Bahri is usually taken as evidence for at least limited warfare (Hayes 1953). Throughout the Middle Kingdom, the military played an important role in expanding Egyptian territory; early in the Twelfth Dynasty, local rulers in Lower (northern) Nubia were deposed, and the land was annexed to Egypt. A series of fortresses was constructed along the river to maintain this control and facilitate the movement of trade goods and tribute northward (Kemp 1989). Kings of the late Eleventh Dynasty also restored trade routes through the Eastern Desert, reopening quarries and initiating trade via the Red Sea to coastal regions of East Africa. The Eleventh Dynasty also saw the renewal of trade with Byblos, bringing timber for construction and a variety of resources from the inland regions of the Near East (Watrous 1998).

During the Middle Kingdom, kings made changes to the political organization of the land that were designed to centralize control over all aspects of governance. The Eleventh Dynasty kings ruled Egypt from Thebes and appointed Theban natives to a number of governmental offices (Hayes 1975b). Amenemhet I, the first king of Dynasty 12, moved the capital back to the Memphis region, founding Itj-tawy near Lisht. By the mid-Twelfth Dynasty, new constraints were imposed on local governors, offering the central government greater control (Leprohon 1995). Several Dynasty 12 kings solidified the lines of succession by appointing an heir apparent to serve as co-regent (Murnane 1977). These policies consolidated royal power, producing stability and facilitating significant public works projects, including an irrigation system that brought the Faiyum basin under cultivation and fostering long-distance trade relationships that stretched into the Near East and to Crete.

Early rulers of the Middle Kingdom took pains to rebuild and revitalize the royal image with monumental tomb complexes and significant investment in art. The stages of construction of Mentuhotep II's tomb at Deir el-Bahri, across the river from Thebes, reflect his progress toward rule over all of Egypt. Its location was determined by the nearby tombs of his predecessors, but its scale and design, laid out in a series of terraces that rose toward a cliff face to the west, was unprecedented. It incorporated the burials of several of the king's wives, a possible "model" pyramid within a columned hall, and a progressive development of relief style that evolved over time from local First

Intermediate Period high relief to typical Middle Kingdom flat relief (Freed 2010). A deep shaft in the front court held an empty sarcophagus and an enthroned statue of the king, brightly painted but otherwise seemingly barely carved. Vividly painted art is found in contemporary private elite tombs; on painted coffins; and in the form of wooden models of private estates, complete with herds, granaries, gardens, and houses. Provision for burial of people of middle-class status is more visible in the Middle Kingdom than previous eras; many individuals and families were buried in mastaba-type tombs, with wooden coffins sometimes inscribed with Coffin Texts to aid the deceased in the afterlife.

While Mentuhotep II's tomb provided a new model for royal mortuary design, that model was not taken up again until the New Kingdom. Dynasty 12 kings, instead, chose to be buried near Itj-tawy, the new capital, which was also, not coincidentally, near their Old Kingdom predecessors. While they revived the pyramid form of Dynasties 4 through 6, most of the construction was in brick and stone rubble, substituting cheaper materials and greater speed and efficiency for the grandeur of Giza. A limestone casing covered the pyramids, giving the appearance of solidity and durability (Smith 1998). These kings and their families also added more passages beneath tombs for greater protection of their mummified remains against robbery (Dodson 2010). As at Giza, the cemeteries of family members and officials radiated out from the pyramids, in a reflection of the lived hierarchy.

Widespread temple construction projects offered an opportunity for the Middle Kingdom rulers to place their portraits in public view, creating a level of interaction with the king's image not seen in the Old Kingdom (Smith 1998). As in all periods of Egyptian history, few non-elite people would have had access to divine images in temple interiors, but they could leave offerings at royal statues in the outer areas of temple precincts so the king might convey their wishes to the gods. During the Middle Kingdom, this sort of encounter appears to have inspired experimentation and innovation in statue forms and styles. Colossal statues of a number of Dynasty 12 kings are spread across the country. Some are sphinxes, combining the king's face with a lion's body, invoking a form of the sun god; others show the king as Osiris, the god of the dead, wrapped tightly and holding the royal attributes of crook and flail. During the Twelfth Dynasty, there was a new conception in the art of kingship: instead of the ideal proportions and youthful faces of the Old Kingdom kings, Dynasty 12 kings have lined faces, heavy eyelids, and downturned mouths. Most Egyptologists agree that this change in style, which culminated in portraits of Senwosret III (Figure 6.5) and Amenemhet III, reflected a desire to convey the king's maturity and gravity, his concern for his people and duties. This change in style carried over to officials, who imitated the king's careworn look on their own portraits. Biographical texts in the tombs of officials also focused on individuals' service to the king, as well as their personal achievements (Willems 2010). By the mid-Twelfth Dynasty, administrative and religious life once again revolved around the king's dominant role in society.

In Dynasty 13, royal power again experienced a steep decline, as 60 kings ruled for 100 years (1760–1660 BCE). The rules of hereditary kingship that had held constant in the past (though not exclusively so) dissolved, with multiple family lines competing for the throne. By the end of the dynasty, Egypt had lost its hold on Lower Nubia, and large numbers of migrants from the Levant occupied the eastern Delta region. Much of this population appears to have been working for the crown, conducting trade with the Levant and Crete from an administrative center at Avaris (modern Tell el-Daba) (Bietak 1995). Excavations at Tell el-Daba have revealed a Thirteenth Dynasty palace or administrative building containing the graves of Levantine workers and soldiers, some buried with donkeys (Schneider 2010).

Despite these changes, much of the administrative structure and cultural system of Egypt persisted. During the reigns of longer-lived kings, military and quarrying expeditions kept raw materials flowing. Kings of Dynasty 13 continued to construct their tombs near Itj-tawy, at south Saqqara

FIGURE 6.5 Portrait of Senwosret III as a Sphinx

Source: The Metropolitan Museum of Art, New York, NY, USA. © The Metropolitan Museum of Art. Image source: Art Resource, NY. Gift of Edward S. Harkness, 1917 (17.9.2)

and Dahshur, but few of these appear to have been completed; on average, reigns were too short for workers to have made much progress on funerary monuments (Dodson and Hilton 2004: 100–102). The same is true for artwork; only about 40 royal statues of Dynasty 13 survive, and most were of longer-reigning kings (Freed 2010).

As had happened at the end of the Old Kingdom, the final decades of the Middle Kingdom saw a dissolution of royal power and an increase in private wealth. Private tombs located throughout Egypt present extensive official biographies, sometimes without giving the name of the king served. To some degree, this may be an indication of the unpredictability of rule: while an official's tomb was being prepared, he might serve several kings. But it also signifies a more general decline in regard for royal power (Quirke 1991), as the dynasty ended with little fanfare, perhaps withdrawing to the stability of Thebes under growing pressure from the Levantine populations of the Delta (Schneider 2010; Willems 2010).

Second Intermediate Period

Beginning in the later Thirteenth Dynasty, Egypt again underwent a period of political fragmentation, the Second Intermediate Period (1680–1549 BCE). During this time, Egypt was split between a northern capital (Avaris, in the northeast Delta), controlled by Dynasties 14 and 15, and a southern one (Thebes), under Dynasties 16 and 17. Dynasty 16 rulers may have been the heirs of Memphite

Dynasty 13, forced southward under pressure from growing Levantine populations in the Delta (Dodson and Hilton 2004: 116). The rulers of Dynasty 15 eventually spread their territorial control southward, ruling over nearly all of Egypt. The Second Intermediate Period is often referred to as the "Hyksos Period," *hyksos* being the Greek transcription of the Egyptian term for these rulers, *heqau-khasut*, or "rulers of foreign lands." New Kingdom kings looked back on this time as one of upheaval, due to the non-Egyptian background of the dynasties. In fact, the archaeological evidence bespeaks a degree of stability, with conflict erupting only at the end of the period.

The Fourteenth Dynasty is poorly understood; according to Manetho, 76 kings ruled for just 184 years (Hayes 1975a). They seem to have been rulers of the eastern Delta who asserted their independence as the Thirteenth Dynasty declined (Dodson and Hilton 2004: 114), occupying an older palace at Avaris. Mass graves at the site may indicate an epidemic or famine at the time. Similarly obscure are the rulers of the Sixteenth Dynasty at Thebes, only one of whom left a monument with his name.

Dynasty 15 represents a new group of rulers with Levantine background, who ousted Dynasty 14 from Avaris. These are the Hyksos proper, with roots in the urban Middle Bronze Age society of the southern Levant. They overthrew the Dynasty 16 kings at Thebes and ruled over most of Egypt until new rulers asserted themselves at Thebes as Dynasty 17. Despite their foreign origins and West Semitic names, the Hyksos kings ruled as Egyptians, adopting Egyptian material culture, dedicating monuments to Egyptian gods, claiming the throne at the traditional capital at Memphis, and adopting the full royal titulary (Hayes 1975b; Schneider 2010). At Avaris, buildings of this period were Levantine in design, including a typical "fortress" temple of Middle Bronze Age type, but the material culture includes significant amounts of Egyptian pottery, suggesting a mixed population (Bard 2008: 199). Hyksos art, often in the form of scarabs, is Egyptianizing as well, including representations of the king with a weapon in a raised hand; instead of a mace, he brandishes a branch-like object, more like a Syrian god than an Egyptian king (Morenz and Popko 2010). Hyksos scarabs are widespread in Egypt and the Levant, suggesting an extensive audience and an array of craftsmen.

The Dynasty 17 kings of Thebes asserted their independence from the Hyksos rulers and eventually mounted a military challenge, conquering territory as far north as Middle Egypt and south into Lower Nubia, setting the stage for the final expulsion of the Hyksos by Ahmose, the first king of Dynasty 18. Inscriptions from these kings are the only surviving sources about this conflict, though the mummy of Seqenenre Taa, the next-to-last king, also attests to a fatal battlefield injury (Bard 2008: 206). One pyramid has been identified for the time, indicating that these kings attempted to pursue the traditional rites and trappings of kingship (Bard 2008: 205).

New Kingdom

The lengthy process of driving out the Hyksos, taking place over at least three generations, culminated in the re-establishment of rule over a unified Egypt by Ahmose and the founding of the New Kingdom (1549–1073 BCE). In this chapter, it is not necessary to provide a full outline of the complicated history of the imperial New Kingdom (Dynasties 18 to 20), but it is useful to outline the major social, economic, and political developments that shaped this period of Egypt's greatest extent and highest expression of royal power. While the Old Kingdom pyramids may dominate our modern sense of Egyptian achievements, the labor and resources that went into New Kingdom temples and tombs were far greater.

The New Kingdom, and especially the Eighteenth Dynasty (1549–1291 BCE) was the period of the International Age (see Chapter 5), a time of economic and diplomatic exchange among Near Eastern kings, including the Egyptian pharaohs. Egypt reached its greatest geographic extent at this time, in the wake of the expulsion of the Hyksos expanding into the Levant, and retaking territories in Nubia that had been held by Middle Kingdom kings. Troops were garrisoned and governors installed in both the southern Levant and Nubia, and military-minded kings like Thutmose III of the Eighteenth Dynasty and Ramesses II of the Nineteenth Dynasty led their armies on multiple campaigns to extend Egypt's boundaries (Weinstein 1981). These campaigns brought in tremendous wealth in captured booty and prisoners; they guaranteed a continual flow of trade goods and Egyptian-controlled raw materials that could further enhance royal stature. A well-known image from Hatshepsut's mortuary temple at Deir el-Bahri shows Egyptian ships docked at a village in the African land of Punt, where royal officials traded with non-Egyptian-looking people. At the same time, the depiction of the king smiting Egypt's enemies—especially Asiatics, Libyans, and Nubians—became a favorite scene on the exterior walls of temples, where it showed that the king protected his people from outside harm and protected the gods from forces of disorder.

The letters exchanged between late Dynasty 18 kings and their vassals and officials in the Levant reveal (and sometimes open up to question) the scope of Egyptian military activity there. These, as well as dozens of "international letters" (described in Chapter 5), were found at the temporary Egyptian capital of Akhetaten (Tell el-Amarna) in Middle Egypt. The letters speak to a balance of power among the kings of the Near East and Mediterranean region, undergirded by family ties through marriage and a historical knowledge of one another's lands and resources. The gift exchange described in these letters is depicted in art in a number of tombs belonging to Egyptian royal officials, in which the tomb owner is shown overseeing the delivery of expensive and exotic goods— Aegean stone and metal vessels and textiles, African animals—by foreigners. Diplomacy could also follow military conflict, as the treaty between Ramesses II and the Hittite king, attested by sources deriving from both sides, indicates. Artists and scholars moved from court to court; a palace built under Thutmose III at Avaris was decorated with Minoan frescoes using Minoan techniques (see Chapter 7; Bietak, Marinatos, and Palivou 2007). Although the historical record suggests that these international relationships were more or less balanced, to an internal audience, Egyptian kings and artists depicted Egypt as the superior partner, always receiving more than it gave away.

Egypt's imperial rule had a major impact on royal rhetoric and iconography during the New Kingdom. The king's name and image were displayed in a wide array of contexts. With their establishment of political stability and increased economic resources coming in from provinces and trade partners, New Kingdom rulers embarked on a number of major building projects. These included fortresses in foreign territories and palaces and temples in Egypt, all of which served as monumental reminders of royal power. Temples also required "renewal" after the perceived disorder of the Second Intermediate Period (Bryan 2010). Images of military action, as noted earlier, are common on temple exteriors. Inside temples, peaceful images prevail—akin to the order within Egypt's borders—with depictions of rituals, of the king making offerings, and the gods reciprocating by granting him their favor. A number of New Kingdom palaces also survive; these served as places for the king to stay while he traveled through Egypt and as administrative centers for officials year-round.

During the New Kingdom, the identification of the king with the gods grew even stronger; the principal state god of these dynasties was Amun-Re, a composite form of the sun god, whose main center of worship was Thebes. As before, kings were believed to be sons of the sun god; but more than before, some represented themselves as his living manifestation. New Kingdom kings built or rebuilt temples to Amun throughout the country and incorporated open-air altars to the sun god within their own mortuary temples. At Karnak and Luxor, the principal cult centers for Amun at Thebes, construction began early in the Eighteenth Dynasty, but every king who had the time and resources added his own monuments and architectural elements to the precinct. At both locations, temples incorporated an axial approach to the god's inner sanctum that began in a series of well-lit courtyards and progressed toward dark inner rooms where the god's statue, and

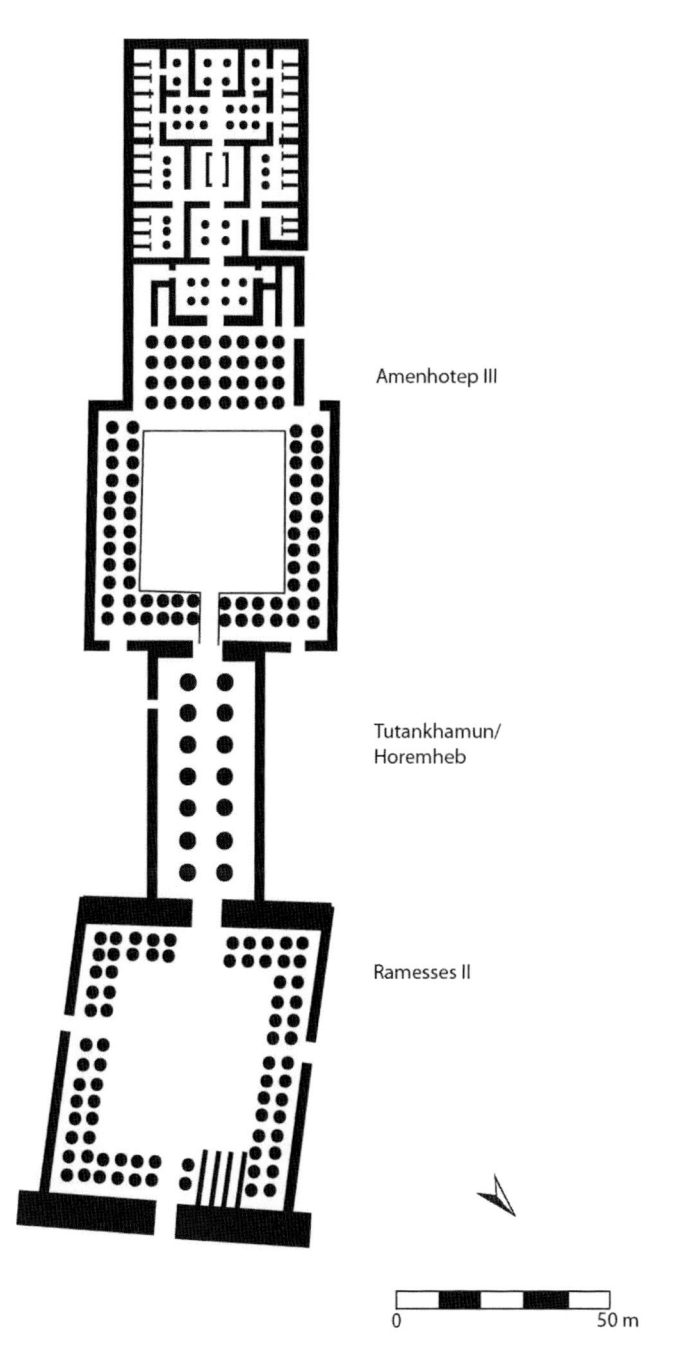

FIGURE 6.6 Plan of the Temple of Amun at Luxor, Showing Additions over Time

Source: J.C. Ross

the boat he rode through the sky and underworld, resided (Figure 6.6). Only the highest-ranking priests, the king chief among them, would have access to the image of the god. Other worshippers could, however, leave offerings at the feet of the royal statues that filled the courtyards and lined the outer walls of the temple precinct, knowing that the king would communicate their prayers and gifts to the god. Kings also filled the temples, Karnak in particular, with booty from their campaigns; these gifts of thanksgiving for the gods' help served as tangible evidence of the king's constant vigilance and service to *maat* ("order") on behalf of all Egyptians (Baines 1995; Morenz and Popko 2010). Another means of legitimizing and strengthening royal power was for a king to ally himself with the high priests of Amun, often through family ties; the priestly position of "God's Wife of Amun" was a new one in the New Kingdom and was usually filled by a king's wife, sister, or daughter.

These strong royal ties to Amun were broken just once during the New Kingdom: during the late Eighteenth Dynasty, when Akhenaten (formerly Amenhotep IV) shuttered the state temples of Egypt and instituted sole worship of Aten, the solar disk, who could be approached only through the royal family. The reasons for this religious revolution are unclear; it had major economic ramifications, cutting off income to temples, and could have derived from a wish to divert wealth and political power from Amun's priests. The same impetus may have stood behind Akhenaten's relocation of the capital to a newly built town in Middle Egypt, which he named Akhetaten (modern Tell el-Amarna, after which this "Amarna Age" is named) (see Box 6.3). But true religious feeling seems also to be present: Akhenaten's father, Amenhotep III, had intensified construction of sun god-related temples and may himself have been worshipped as Re (Dodson and Hilton 2004: 142). The "Hymn to Aten," purportedly composed by Akhenaten himself, praises the god as creator and cause of all things.

BOX 6.3   KEY SITE: AMARNA

The city of Akhetaten (Amarna) was built from scratch as a new capital by Akhenaten in the late Eighteenth Dynasty; it was located far from the traditional centers of Egyptian royal power, Memphis and Thebes. Most of the city was occupied for a total of 12 years only, with a population of 30,000 to 50,000, at all levels of economic and social status (Mumford 2010). While the central section of the city was ceremonial and formal in function, with palaces, temples, and an array of administrative buildings, the rest was more "organic" in form, conforming to the requirements of its residents and revealing their adaptability to changing economic and political circumstances (Lehner 2010). Archaeological evidence of house and neighborhood layout and domestic goods suggests that most residents of Akhetaten were independent of the state for their economic well-being, producing, storing, and preparing their own food. Despite the unusual circumstances of its foundation, Amarna may provide the best evidence for a functioning Egyptian city from antiquity.

Amarna was also a place where the king could advocate for new modes of artistic expression in support of his new religious system. New artistic subject matter is especially apparent in elite tombs at Amarna, set in the cliffs on the east side of the river, where the deceased appeared only in scenes of worship of the Aten disk; rather than the afterlife, the focus of tomb art was the royal family and the city (Bard 2008: 227; Dodson 2010).

Akhenaten's religious and political actions resulted also in a new artistic style, one whose main subject was the royal family: Akhenaten, his queen Nefertiti, and their daughters (Figure 6.7). In highly personal scenes, the family was shown interacting with each other and worshipping

FIGURE 6.7 Family Scene Depicting Akhenaten, Nefertiti, and Their Daughters

Source: Aegyptisches Museum, Staatliche Museen, Berlin, Germany (bpk, Berlin / Art Resource, NY)

the abstract Aten disk, from which rays descend that end in hands that bless them. These scenes were carved on relief blocks that adorned the temples, palace, private homes, and private tombs at Amarna. People's access to Aten then came through these images. There was also a radical change in artistic style in the art from Amarna; the king is shown with a sunken chest and distended belly, and his family members were depicted with unusually elongated skulls. Here, too, the causes for change are unknown: medical explanations that suggest Akhenaten suffered a disfiguring genetic syndrome do not account for the fact that the queen shared the same features in art; perhaps more convincing is a religious explanation that sees Aten's rays as illuminating what appears to be unnaturally exaggerated features.

Akhenaten's religious and political reforms did not last long; by Tutankhamun's fourth year, 15 years later, the new king moved the capital back to Memphis and the royal burial ground to Thebes. Later rulers depicted the Amarna Age in inscriptions as an era of corruption, remedied by the re-establishment of Amun worship and the onset of their own dynasties. Similarly, the reign of the mid-Eighteenth Dynasty pharaoh Hatshepsut was disparaged by a later king, but for different reasons. Hatshepsut was the daughter of king Thutmose I, wife of Thutmose II, and stepmother of Thutmose III. When her husband died, Thutmose III, his designated heir, was only a child; Hatshepsut stepped in and ruled in his stead, ostensibly as his regent but eventually as sole ruler, for 22 years until her death (see Box 6.4). Hatshepsut discharged all the traditionally required roles of a king: she carried out successful military campaigns, conducted long-distance trading expeditions, served as chief priest to Amun and other state gods, and built or added to a significant number of temples. Yet after her death, Thutmose III (who went on to be perhaps

Egypt's most successful military ruler) had her name erased from inscriptions and usurped many of her monuments, substituting his name for hers. Whether his motives were personal, deriving from resentment, or political, concerned with the long-term implications of a female ruler, are unknown.

BOX 6.4 ROYAL WOMEN IN ANCIENT EGYPT

Hatshepsut was not the first woman to rule Egypt as pharaoh, but based on her surviving monuments and records, she was the most successful one, at least until Egypt's final non-Roman ruler, Cleopatra VII. Hatshepsut came to power, and maintained it in her own hands, in a devious way, striking a nearly impossible balance between male and female standards of behavior and power. Hatshepsut's statuary is instantly recognizable, balancing her feminine features with royal attributes, and it survives in quantity despite Thutmose's actions. She was the first New Kingdom ruler to produce so much statuary, and the wide range of her statue types—Osirid, seated, kneeling, sphinx—attests to the high achievements and output of her royal workshops (Smith 1998).

The New Kingdom was an era of women, of sorts, during which royal women, in particular, played major roles in politics and religion, and women, more generally, became more visible in written and visual sources. Besides Hatshepsut, whose name and representations were found throughout Egypt, we find other royal wives featured prominently in art: Tiye, the wife of Amenhotep III and mother of Akhenaten; Nefertiti, Akhenaten's wife, who may have ruled briefly upon her husband's death; and Nefertari, one of Ramesses II's wives. As the exchange of royal brides was a major theme of International Age correspondence, this new standing for women may not be completely unexpected; it is, however, worth noting that all of the women named earlier were Egyptian, not foreign brides. One particularly visible role open to New Kingdom royal women was the priestly title "God's Wife of Amun." This title, held by queens and princesses, made the holder the second-most important figure at the Karnak temple of Amun. She officiated, together with male priests, at temple rituals and was permitted to enter the inner chambers where the god's statue was housed (Robins 1993: 152).

The most famous queen of Egypt was a non-Egyptian: Cleopatra VII (51–30 BCE), the final ruler of the Ptolemaic Dynasty, which was set in place after Alexander the Great conquered the Persian Empire and replaced the principal local rulers with Greeks. Unlike many of her predecessors, however, Cleopatra reputedly learned to read Egyptian hieroglyphs and observed the rituals and rules of Egyptian traditions. At the same time, she clearly had grander ambitions, having a child with Julius Caesar and aiming to set that child on the Egyptian throne. With her ally and purported lover, Mark Antony, she challenged the expansionist aims of the first Roman emperor Octavian (Augustus); she and Antony died in the aftermath of their defeat in the Battle of Actium (31 BCE). Because her reputation for unbridled sexuality and lust for power, spread by Roman propagandists, has dominated perceptions of Cleopatra's rule from antiquity to today, it is difficult to obtain a precise view of her achievements and her location within either Egyptian tradition or Hellenistic innovation. She remains an object of fascination without ever coming clearly into focus.

The monumentality of the state cult places during the New Kingdom stands in stark contrast with royal burial places, a reversal from previous periods. Unlike their Old Kingdom and Middle Kingdom predecessors, New Kingdom kings abandoned the pyramid form and opted for rock-cut tombs in the Valley of the Kings at Thebes, across the river from the temples to Amun. Near the river, however, they built immense mortuary temples, which served as locales for rituals relating to the king's mortuary cult, providing continual support for his afterlife. These structures were designed like state temples, with a progression toward inner sanctuaries that combined the royal cult with worship of other gods, especially Amun. The decoration of these buildings also replicates that of the state temples, with representations of the king with the gods and depictions of major achievements of the king's reign. Besides the trade expedition to Punt that Hatshepsut commissioned, other events of major historical importance find expression in reliefs at mortuary temples: Ramesses II's nearly single-handed "victory" against the Hittites, on the walls of the Ramesseum, and Ramesses III's defense of Egypt against attacks by the Sea Peoples, at Medinet Habu.

In contrast, the design and decoration of the royal burials, in the Valley of the Kings beyond the floodplain, were devoted not to royal achievements but to the king's transformation and rebirth in the afterlife. The tomb of Tutankhamun, excavated by Howard Carter in the 1920s and virtually undisturbed after the king's burial, is justly famous, but it is perhaps the least typical of royal tombs in the valley; smaller than most and largely undecorated, it was probably built for a high official but used for the king when he died unexpectedly (Bard 2008: 233). Most royal tombs consisted of a series of corridors and shafts leading back to the king's sarcophagus. This change in location and design of royal tombs seems largely due to a concern about, and familiarity with, contemporary tomb-robbing. In the end, it proved fruitless, and priests during the Twentieth Dynasty and later collected the remaining royal mummies into a pair of tombs that could be more easily monitored (see also Box 6.5) (Bard 2008: 244).

> **BOX 6.5 ANIMAL MUMMIES**
>
> While scholars and students have long been fascinated by the variety of methods and results of Egyptian mummification of kings and elites, the study of animal mummies is less well established. Excavations have produced thousands of mummies of mammals (especially cats and bulls), birds, and reptiles (including snakes) (Figure 6.8). The largest numbers of animal mummies come from the New Kingdom and later periods; they derive from both tombs and religious complexes. Like humans, animal bodies were first embalmed (and sometimes had their internal organs removed to prevent further decay), then treated with natron (a naturally occurring soda ash deriving from salt beds) to dry the corpse. Oils and resins were then applied, and the body wrapped in linen (Buckley, Clark, and Evershed 2004).
>
> Animals were mummified for a number of reasons. "Victual mummies" of birds and joints of beef have been found in some royal tombs of the New Kingdom, intended as a food source in the afterlife (Ikram 1995: 203). Mummified pets were also placed in the tombs of their owners. In temple contexts, animals that served as representations of certain gods were mummified and placed in the temple, as were animals that were sacrificed as votive offerings. The last category seems to be responsible for the majority of animal mummies; the large-scale production of animal mummies also seems to have led to abuses of the system, as "cheaper" animals, or animal parts, were mummified and wrapped to look like more expensive ones. Radiography has revealed large numbers of these fakes in recent years (Jackowski, Bolliger, and Thali 2008).

FIGURE 6.8 Cat Mummy from Abydos

Source: British Museum, London, United Kingdom (Album / Art Resource, NY)

Because of extensive robbing, only Tutankhamun's tomb contained the full array of objects that accompanied the king into his tomb. In Tutankhamun's case, many of these items seem also to have been used during his life. Better preserved from the tombs are the reliefs and paintings from the walls, scenes drawn from the Book of the Dead and other contemporary texts that described rituals for rebirth and instructions for safe travel to the netherworld. In each tomb, the selection of scenes and their combination and layout are unique. Altogether, they provide a very different sense of the obstacles an individual faced before he could achieve the afterlife than either Old Kingdom scenes or Middle Kingdom Coffin Texts, focusing more on reaching the afterlife than on what would happen once a king was established there (Dodson 2010).

Private tombs of the New Kingdom provide a similar perspective on life and death and of the expectations that people outside the royal family and bureaucracy had of the afterlife. A large number of private tombs near the royal necropolis belonged to artisans residing at Deir el-Medina, a state-constructed village for the builders and decorators of the royal tombs. The 400 tombs near the village span the entire New Kingdom. While those of the Eighteenth Dynasty featured typical "daily life" scenes such as agricultural activities and craft-working, a profession in which the deceased presumably planned to continue in the afterlife, those of the later New Kingdom were starkly different. These contained art much like that in the royal tombs, depicting rituals performed for the dead and scenes from the Book of the Dead (Meskell 1999). It seems that the pervading beliefs regarding the afterlife were finally shared between the king and his subjects. While the king, on reaching the afterlife, would merge with his father Amun, all of his subjects could also potentially enjoy the afterlife. But they had to pass a series of tests of character and perseverance first.

Deir el-Medina is one of a number of excavated New Kingdom cities and towns yielding evidence for the daily lives of Egypt's populace. It was, however, not a typical city; the state provided its residents with housing, food, and tools, and even a laundry service (Lehner 2010). The residents of its 68 houses enjoyed a high literacy rate, as was appropriate for their positions as court artisans. This, in turn, has resulted in the discovery of a significant number of written documents, including nearly 500 letters (some written by women), economic texts recording ration payments and barter transactions, court records, and even literary and medical texts (McDowell 1999). As demonstrated by their highly decorated tombs, Deir el-Medina's residents did not live ordinary lives, but their town illustrates one facet of the New Kingdom world.

After the stunning cultural accomplishments of the Eighteenth Dynasty, and the military and construction prowess of Ramesses II, the longest-reigning king of the New Kingdom, the late Nineteenth and Twentieth Dynasties saw Egypt undergo a steep decline. The most obvious loss was of territory; kings following Ramesses II, for the most part, did not lead campaigns to protect or expand Egypt's borders, and distant vassals in the Levant, sensing opportunity, broke away from Egypt. Merneptah, Ramesses II's immediate successor, faced attacks on Egypt's borders from a combined force of Libyans and the "People of the Sea." Ramesses III of Dynasty 20 fended off a series of attacks by the same foes. Egypt lost its grip on Nubian territory and in the Levant. Egypt was subject to many of the same upheavals, migrations, and incursions experienced across the eastern Mediterranean at the end of the Bronze Age.

Loss of territory meant a loss of supplies of exotic goods, raw materials, and labor for the state. Other signs of economic decline in the late New Kingdom include a falling off in the pace and scale of monumental construction, with the exception of Ramesses III's mortuary temple at Medinet Habu. Some of this reduction in royal building activity may also be due to a growing rivalry between the kings and the priesthood of Amun for political power, a competition that compromised, to some extent, the royal image and had the potential to split the country. Fewer and smaller royal statues were created following the extreme levels of production (and usurpation) under Ramesses II (Bryan 2010).

New Kingdom records also describe rampant tomb looting and worker strikes, as the state was unable to support its laborers, all signs of a crumbling infrastructure and decline in royal status, eventually leading into the Third Intermediate Period and the end of native rule of a unified Egyptian state. Significant numbers of foreigners lived in Egypt and worked for the government as laborers and soldiers during the New Kingdom, perhaps leading to a loss of the distinctive identity Egyptians had held to in past generations.

Egypt under Foreign Rule: Dynasties 21 through 31 and Beyond

The final millennium of Egyptian history (1073–31 BCE) is distinct from those that preceded it in that it featured a series of dynasties of non-Egyptian rulers. But it offers, in many ways, a reiteration of the long-term cycles of growth and contraction seen in the previous sections of this chapter. The Third Intermediate Period, Dynasties 21 through 25 (1073–664 BCE), saw political fragmentation and the decline of ideology, while the Late Period, Dynasties 26 through 31 (664–332 BCE), witnessed expansion and renewal, albeit under foreign rule. Finally, imperial forces from Greece and then Italy, across the Mediterranean, gained control of Egypt's vast trade network and agricultural wealth with their conquest of the great Near Eastern empires.

Third Intermediate Period

Dynasties 21 through 25, the Third Intermediate Period, saw a division of the land of Egypt again, but this time under the control of Egypt's long-time subjects and rivals from the west (Libya) and south (Nubia and Kush). The weakness of the central government at Thebes at the end of the New Kingdom had allowed significant integration of Libyans into the military and religious establishments of Egypt, first gaining a political foothold in the Delta region and then rising to the priesthood of Amun at Thebes. During Dynasties 21 (1073–945 BCE) and 22 (945–720 BCE), these new rulers established their capital at Tanis in the Delta. Expansionist policies, especially under Shoshenq I, the first king of the Twenty-Second Dynasty, meant that Egyptian power and material culture again spread to neighboring lands, as the king recorded conquests at various cities in the Levant (Wilkinson 2010: 384).

Unity under the Dynasty 22 kings was short-lived, however, as the priesthood at Thebes eventually broke away and ruled as Dynasty 23 (837–728 BCE). A new Libyan capital was established at Sais in Dynasty 24 (732–720 BCE), but these kings ruled for only two generations and were replaced by another Saite family in Dynasty 26.

More problematic for the Libyan dynasties of the Delta were rivals from the south, another area traditionally under Egyptian political and economic control. The kings of Kush, a land south of, but later incorporating, Nubia, extended their rule into Egypt, eventually ruling from the traditional capital at Memphis as Dynasty 25 (732–653 BCE). These kings, too, considered themselves heirs to the earlier kings of Egypt, adopting Amun as their chief god and taking on titles that had been part of Old Kingdom royal titulary (Wilkinson 2010: 402–3). Meanwhile, the Neo-Assyrian kings (see Chapter 5), as part of their expansion toward the Mediterranean and defeat of Israel, clashed with and eventually conquered the Egyptian military, claiming control first of the Delta and later of all of Egypt, under Assurbanipal. But the annual nature of Assyrian campaigning, and the spread of its forces across its empire, meant that its rule of Egypt was brief and without significant impact on Egyptian culture. For a number of decades, the Kushite kings and Assyrians competed for control of Egypt, with the kings of Kush withdrawing to their capitals at Napata and Meroe when the Assyrians were ascendant. When Assyrian power finally waned, in the second half of the 7th century, Dynasty 26 (Saite) (672–525 BCE) re-established control of Egypt from the Delta region.

The Late Period

Kings of Dynasties 26 through 31 ruled during Egypt's Late Period (672–332 BCE), marking the takeover of Egypt by foreign powers, ruling from outside the country. The Persian Empire, under Cambyses II, incorporated Egypt as its sixth satrapy in 525 BCE by defeating the last king of the Saite Dynasty. Persian expansion to Egypt may have been motivated by desire for economic gain, particularly for access to Egyptian trade relationship with the south (Manning 2013). Dynasties 28 to 30 represented successful secession from Persian rule, and the movement of the capital from Sais to Memphis, but Persia regained the country again in 343 BCE, establishing the short-lived Thirty-First Dynasty (343–332 BCE). In 332 BCE, finally, Alexander the Great took over the Persian Empire, including Egypt; his brief rule set up the rise of the Ptolemaic Dynasty (305–30 BCE), which ruled until the Battle of Actium and Cleopatra VII's death resulted in the Roman capture of Egypt.

Despite the instability of the dynasties who ruled Egypt during the Late Period (with the exception of the Ptolemies), the country experienced strong economic and demographic growth, reaching its peak in population under the Ptolemies. These kings, all named Ptolemy (I–XV, the last being Cleopatra's son by Julius Caesar), were the descendants of one of Alexander's generals, Ptolemy I Soter (305–282 BCE). Their tangled genealogy of brothers marrying sisters, and cousins succeeding cousins, does not seem to have stood in the way of tremendous military and political successes; during the Ptolemaic Period, Egypt again reached the same boundaries it had held in the New Kingdom, with control over Libya, Syria, and northern Nubia (Dodson and Hilton 2004: 264; Manning 2013). Egypt under the Ptolemies took on a new urban outlook, with the fastest-growing and most cosmopolitan cities those, such as Alexandria, that had been founded by Alexander and his successors. The population was diverse and multilingual (the royal family mostly spoke only Greek) and bore limited resemblance to Egyptians of millennia before. Yet the kings and elites continued to pay homage to the traditional gods of the land and took on the trappings of power of their predecessors, adding further to the sense that Egyptian culture was limitless and changeless.

Conclusions

What stayed constant through all of Egyptian history was its environmental setting, which provided predictability and productivity, bringing together two disparate territories and providing additional resources through expansion. Late kings also appropriated traditional representations of royal power, rooted in a special relationship with the gods of the land. They perpetuated this ideology, as had all kings before them, through monumental construction, sculpture, painting, and inscriptions that reinforced the mystical qualities of the royal image and through a focus on the tomb that would provide a permanent conduit by which a king, his gods, his land, and his people remained forever intertwined.

7

THE AEGEAN BRONZE AGE AND THE CLASSICAL WORLD

Introduction

This chapter examines the complex societies of the Aegean Sea region during the Bronze Age—the Minoans on the island of Crete and the Mycenaeans on the Greek mainland—and the Classical cultures of Greece and Roman Italy. The maritime environments of these peninsular lands presented particular challenges and opportunities that had significant bearing on the course of their development, fostering periods of isolation and of interconnection. The Bronze Age developments brought palatial government to Greece and nearby islands, although the structures of governance are still in question. Both democratic Athens and republican Rome were relatively short-lived products of specific economic, political, and social forces. Altogether, the cities and lands encompassed by these civilizations offer a high degree of variability in their organization and institutions and attest to the adaptability of social and political systems to a broad array of local circumstances.

Geography and Chronology

Geographic and Ecological Setting

The Aegean Sea is set between modern Greece and Turkey. There are three distinct adjacent land masses examined here: the Cycladic Islands, the island of Crete, and mainland Greece (Figure 7.1). The Cyclades, whose name derives from their arrangement in a circle around the holy island of Delos, are rocky, small islands, only a few dozen of which were suitable for habitation in antiquity. Others were sources for mineral resources—obsidian, marble, copper—beginning as early as the Mesolithic Period in the 9th millennium BCE. Crete is the largest island in the Aegean; long and narrow, it stretches 260 kilometers east-west. On mainland Greece, most of the areas inhabited during the Bronze Age were near the coast or along major land routes. On Crete, the best farmland is located in the south-central region, the broad Mesara Plain; on mainland Greece, it is in the northwest, in the regions of Thessaly and Macedonia. Greece's Mediterranean climate provides a long growing season with plentiful rainfall (300–1,200 millimeters annually), and topographic variation means that ancient occupants raised a variety of crops beyond grains, including olives and grapes, as well as herd animals. Environmental variation created conditions for localized agricultural specialization and for regional self-sufficiency.

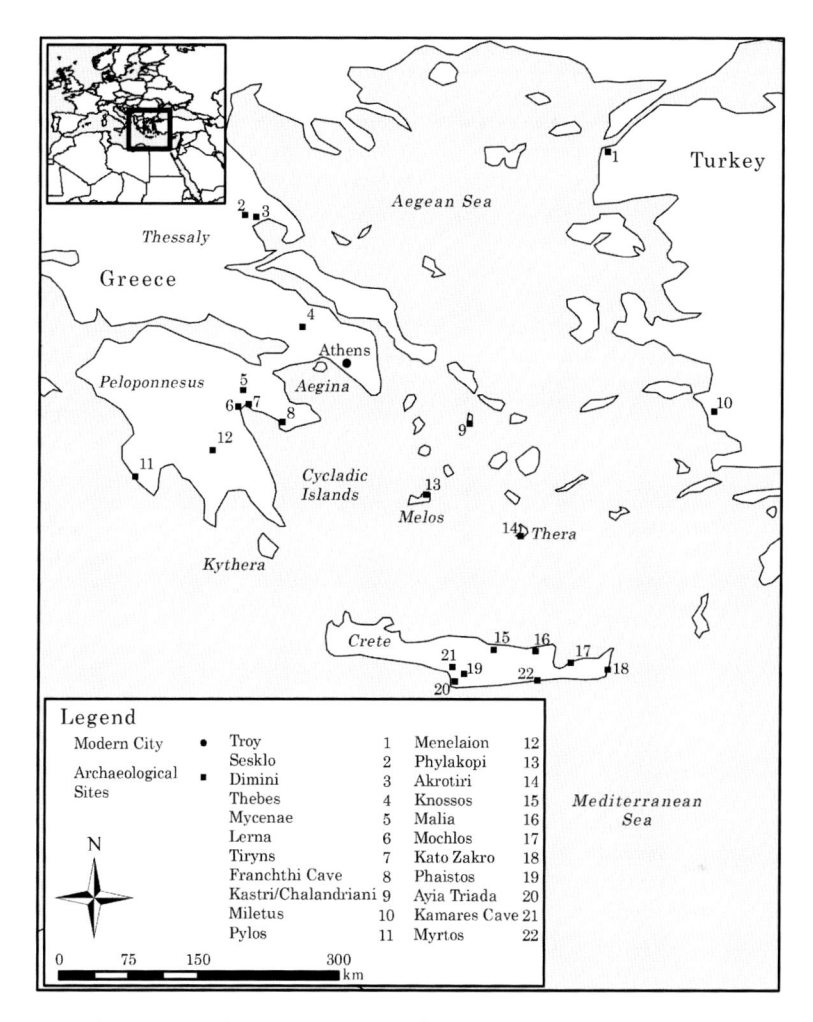

FIGURE 7.1 Map of Regions and Sites Discussed in the First Part of the Chapter

Source: B. Spencer

Coastal living made the Greeks expert sailors, and during the periods considered in this chapter, the sea opened up opportunities for trade, military domination, and political expansion. Greek colonizers headed to the Italian Peninsula, later controlled in total by the expansive near-coastal city of Rome. Much like Greece, Italy possesses a number of harbors and a mountainous interior and north. Italy's rivers, however, have shaped wide, flat floodplains conducive to intensive agriculture. The rivers are also navigable, facilitating communication and movement. With a mild Mediterranean climate, the societies of Italy also developed self-sufficient village-based societies. Copper sources and high-quality stone brought contacts with a variety of cultures.

The Chronological Sequence

This chapter will examine the archaeology of the Neolithic (ca. 7000–3000 BCE) and Bronze Age (ca. 3000–1100 BCE) periods of the Aegean, and the Greek and Italian Iron Ages and Classical Periods that followed (Table 7.1). While Aegean prehistorians follow a typical tripartite (Early, Middle,

TABLE 7.1 Chronological Periods and Sites Discussed in Chapter 7

Dates	Period	Sites Discussed in Chapter	Cultural Horizons
ca. 7000–3000 BCE	**Neolithic Period**	Franchthi Cave; Knossos; Sesklo; Dimini	Adoption of domesticated plants and animals; agricultural villages; cooperative construction projects; some craft specialization
ca. 3000–2000 BCE	**Early Bronze Age** (Early Cycladic, Early Minoan, Early Helladic)	Kastri/Chalandriani; Lerna; Myrtos Fournou Korifi; Mochlos	Emergence of elites; monumental construction of fortifications and tombs; formalized ritual activities; coordination of commodity movement
ca. 1900–1750 BCE	**Protopalatial Period** (Middle Minoan IB–IIIA)	Knossos; Malia; Phaistos	Urbanism; monumental palaces with ritual and administrative functions; rural cult; writing
1750–1500 BCE	**Neopalatial Period** (Middle Minoan IIIB–Late Minoan IB)	Knossos; Malia; Phaistos; Kato Zakro; Ayia Triada; Akrotiri	Centralized economic administration in palaces; secondary administrative centers (villas); urban cult; widespread international trade contacts
ca. 1550–1400 BCE	**Mycenaean Protopalatial Period** (Late Helladic I–II)	Mycenae; Menelaion	Emergence of mainland elite; funerary display and monumental tombs; international trade
1400–1200 BCE	**Mycenaean Palatial Period** (Late Helladic IIIA–B)	Mycenae; Pylos; Tiryns	Monumental palaces and fortifications; palace control of prestige good production and distribution
1200–1100 BCE	**Mycenaean Decline** (Late Helladic IIIC)	Troy; Mycenae; Tiryns	Ruralization and regionalization; migration
Classical Greece			
ca. 1100–700 BCE	**Dark Age/ Early Iron Age** (Submycenaean, Protogeometric, Geometric)	Lefkandi; Athens	Initial depopulation, decline in external contacts; then, return of monumental construction, wealth in burials; figural art and international contacts
ca. 700–479 BCE	**Archaic Period**	Athens; Olympia; Corinth	Colonization; reintroduction of writing, literary culture; emergence of *poleis*; pan-Hellenic contests and cults

Dates	Period	Sites Discussed in Chapter	Cultural Horizons
Classical Greece			
ca. 479–336 BCE	**Classical Period**	Athens; Sparta; Thebes	Athenian democracy; Persian and Peloponnesian Wars; theatrical, philosophical, and artistic achievements
336–146 BCE	**Hellenistic Age**	Vergina (Aegae), Pergamon; Alexandria	Kingship; imperial rule
Italy			
ca. 7000–900 BCE	**Italian Neolithic and Bronze Age**		Introduction of agriculture; cremation and inhumation burials
900–500 BCE	**Italian Iron Age** (Villanovan, Etruscan, Roman monarchy)	Veii, Vulci; Rome	Urn burials in Rome; tumuli in Etruria; urban development; contacts with Greek and Phoenician colonies
500–31 BCE	**Roman Republic**	Rome	Oligarchic rule; military expansion across the Italian Peninsula and overseas; class conflicts and Civil Wars
31 BCE–476 CE	**Roman Empire** (Principate and Dominate)	Rome	Imperial rule by a single (or several) ruler; spread of Christianity; eventual loss of territory and collapse

and Late) subdivision of the Bronze Age, additional chronological terminology must be introduced here, as developments are different for the various regions of the Aegean. Therefore, in the Cyclades, the chronological divisions will be Early, Middle, and Late Cycladic (EC, MC, and LC); in Crete, they are Minoan (EM, MM, and LM); and on the mainland, they are Helladic (EH, MH, and LH). Few absolute dates have been recovered for the Bronze Age; even the major linchpin of the eruption on Santorini is without a sure date.

The collapse of the Mycenaean palaces on mainland Greece in Late Helladic III was followed by a Dark Age (ca. 1100–750 BCE) without writing and with impoverished archaeological remains. During the subsequent Archaic Period (ca. 750–479 BCE), populations rose, and city-states began to emerge, increasing in complexity over time. The Classical Period of the 5th and 4th centuries was a phase of intermittent warfare, political development, and unrivalled cultural achievements. It culminated in the conquest of Greece and the Near East by Alexander the Great (336–323 BCE); Alexander's empire, ruled by his successors, belongs to the Hellenistic Age (336–31 BCE).

In Italy, a Neolithic Period (ca. 7000–2000 BCE) during which agriculture was introduced was followed by the development of regionally distinct Bronze Age (ca. 2000–900 BCE) cultures. During the Iron Age (ca. 900–500 BCE), a few of these began to show more centralized settlement patterns, a rise in population, and evidence for public ritual and monumental tombs and temples. Foremost among these groups were the Etruscans, located in northwestern Italy. Soon after, the city of Rome also began to grow. The early periods of Roman development are poorly attested archaeologically, but evidence from both contemporary texts and archaeology increases in the Roman Republic (ca. 500–31 BCE), when Rome expanded and consolidated its control over the entire Italian Peninsula and began to expand its power, first to coastal regions around the Mediterranean and then further inland. Meanwhile, economic and social conflicts in Rome itself revealed the inherent instability of the Republic's political organization and ultimately led to the rise of single rulership under Augustus, inaugurating the period of the Roman Empire (31 BCE–476 CE). When the Roman Empire "ended" is a matter of substantial debate; in this chapter, it will be traced through its division into Eastern and Western empires, and to the deposition of the last Roman emperor in 476 CE.

Pre-State Societies in the Aegean

The Neolithic Period: Agricultural Origins

At the beginning of the Neolithic Period (ca. 7000–3000 BCE), agriculture was introduced to the Aegean region from the east. Over the course of the Neolithic, people settled into permanent villages in all three regions of the Aegean. The highest populations and largest sites are found in northern Greece, particularly on the broad Thessalian plains, while geographic limitations may have inhibited settlement and growth in the Cycladic Islands. Fishing, crafts, and trade supplemented the subsistence activities of Neolithic inhabitants. By the end of the period, social ranking and economic differentiation emerged.

On the mainland, a significant focus of land use during the pre-Neolithic Mesolithic (8700–7000 BCE) was along the northeastern Peloponnesus. During the Mesolithic, mobile hunters and foragers used Franchthi Cave as a temporary shelter and burial place. They exploited the sea and coastline for mollusks and fish, and the nearby forests for red deer and wild pig. It is likely the cave was visited as part of an annual cycle of mobility; burials may indicate that the cave had territorial and ceremonial significance to a particular group (Demoule and Perlès 1993; Perlès 2001: 34).

Franchthi is the best-attested Aegean site with continuous use from the Mesolithic into the early Neolithic; it therefore provides evidence for the advent of farming. At the beginning of the Neolithic, ca. 7000 BCE, house structures were built for the first time outside the cave; with stone foundations, they suggest permanent residence. In addition, the subsistence base of the settlement was entirely transformed: domesticated emmer wheat and barley were introduced, together with domesticated sheep and goat. Franchthi became a fully agricultural settlement (Perlès 2001: 46–48; Runnels and Murray 2001: 48). Over time, new sites were founded in Greece; in Thessaly, where early Neolithic settlement was densest, at least 250 sites of the period have been identified in survey, each with a population of 100 to 300 (Perlès 2001: 178).

The sudden appearance of agriculture and rapid expansion of settlement in the early Neolithic present major problems to Aegean prehistory: who were these first farmers, and where did the domesticated plants and animals come from? The second question is easier to answer than the first: the wild progenitors of the domesticated species exploited in the Early Neolithic—cereals, legumes, sheep, goats, cattle, and pig—were not native to Greece. The Mesolithic populations at sites like Franchthi Cave were mobile and exploited a wide range of wild plants and animals. Domesticated plants and animals must have been introduced from elsewhere; their most likely sources were the Levant or Anatolia. Scholars continue to debate the method by which the species and the understanding of herding and farming were transferred to the Aegean. Given the sharp increase in population, the settlement of previously unused but fertile territories like Thessaly, and the wholesale

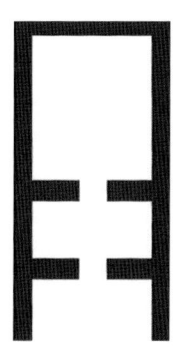

FIGURE 7.2 Standard Megaron Plan
Source: J.C. Ross

adoption of a full array of domesticates, a colonization model appears to be the best fit: a movement of people, plants, and animals, largely by boat, from the Near East into the Aegean region (Demoule and Perlès 1993; Perlès 2001: 96).

Before a decline in population in the Late Neolithic, some Thessalian sites reached populations in the thousands (Hansen 2008). At both Sesklo and Dimini, walls enclosed mounded sites; others had ditches around the settlement (Demoule and Perlès 1993). At Dimini, the enclosure wall system of concentric ovals created a labyrinthine path toward the center. Both Dimini and Sesklo had a larger structure at the center, with a distinctive plan: a narrow porch and vestibule leading into a larger back room, arranged axially and entered on one of the short sides of the building (Figure 7.2). This is a standard megaron plan, which would be revived in the Bronze Age for public buildings. All buildings at these sites were domestic in function, probably housing nuclear families; the megarons also served as residences.

The Early Bronze Age: Complexity without States

During the Early Bronze Age (ca. 3000–2000 BCE), regions across the Aegean show signs of increasing levels of complexity but without the political and economic coordination of states. A variety of cultural practices united groups at a regional level; this is especially apparent in the burial practices and grave goods (see Box 7.1). Some social and economic differentiation among individuals and households existed, but burial practices seem to have masked and smoothed out most differences. Some families could afford prestige goods for the burials of household members; made by specialists, these objects were also exchanged and imitated in distant territories. The mainland, in particular, yields evidence for bureaucratic intervention into economic lives, but this was a short-lived phase before a return to egalitarian agricultural villages.

BOX 7.1 EARLY BRONZE AGE SOCIETIES OF THE AEGEAN

The Early Bronze Age (3000–2000 BCE) was a time of continued small-scale settlement in the Aegean but with evidence for increasing population and political complexity. Despite widespread contacts across the Aegean, distinct regional cultures developed.

The Cycladic Islands: Early Cycladic

The Early Cycladic (EC) Period (ca. 3000–2000 BCE) is notable for the development of prestige goods and their deposit within fortified settlements and cemeteries, as well as their exchange and imitation on the mainland and Crete. Adjacent to most EC settlements were cemeteries; unfortunately, the regularity of this pattern, and the high modern market value of some of the grave goods, has resulted in widespread looting of tombs, with significant loss of archaeological context. Grave goods varied considerably within and between cemeteries. This suggests that a wide range of identities was recognized in death, including age, sex, individual achievement, and personality. Most object types buried with the dead are found also in settlements. In general, the dead received a small amount of pottery, originally containing food remains; other grave goods included stone vessels and figurines. Metal jewelry, tools and vessels marked status differences in a few EC II tombs (Broodbank 2000; Renfrew 1972: 374–5).

Some distinctive material culture items were made in the Cyclades. One is the folded-arm figurine, a marble female figurine, 10 to 150 centimeters in height (averaging 30 centimeters), nude, with arms folded across the stomach (Figure 7.3a). The carving is angular and schematic, with low modeled nose and breasts, incised arms, pubic triangle, and jewelry and, often, painted eyes and eyebrows, hair, jewelry, and other features (Hendrix 2003). When found in burials, they appear in only one or two graves per cemetery, suggesting that they were not appropriate gifts for everyone. Yet their function and meaning are unclear; with feet angled downward, they could not stand on their own, which suggests their natural position was either lying down or held in the hand. The added paint could have provided appropriate situational meaning (Hendrix 2003). Besides the 300 or so female figurines extant, three dozen males survive; they are marked by particular attributes (belt, weapon, musical instruments) and occur in more active poses than the female figurines.

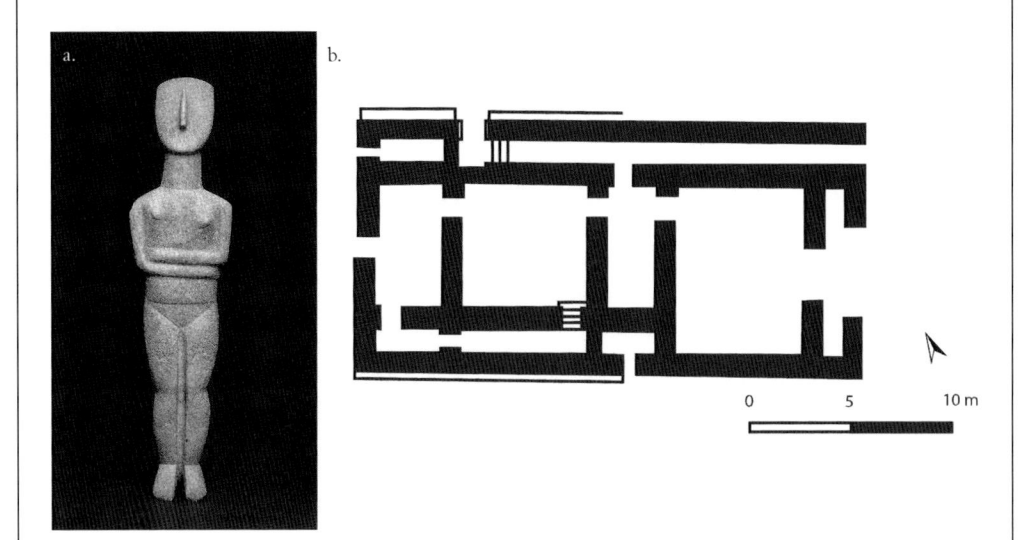

FIGURE 7.3 Early Bronze Age: Cycladic Folded-Arm Figurine; Plan of the House of the Tiles at Lerna

Source: © Trustees of the British Museum, Photo Credit: Erich Lessing / Art Resource, NY; J.C. Ross

The Mainland: Early Helladic (EH)

Early Helladic (ca. 3000–2000 BCE) settlement on the mainland was focused in central Greece, with large towns by 2500 BCE that controlled territories and smaller settlements within a 5 kilometer radius (Runnels and Murray 2001: 69; Weiberg and Finné 2013). In the towns of EH Greece, administrators coordinated the movement of some economic activities and commodities. The most thoroughly excavated EH site is Lerna, located in the eastern Peloponnesus. What distinguished Lerna and other urban EH centers from Cycladic fortified towns was their size and the existence of monumental buildings. Around 2300 BCE, the residents of Lerna built in succession a pair of "corridor houses": first Building BG, and then, partly covering the remains of BG, the "House of the Tiles" (Figure 7.3b). The latter structure derived its name from the baked clay and stone tiles that once covered its roof. The plan of this building consists of a pair of large, nearly square rooms, surrounded on all sides by narrower rooms. At least two of the corridor-like rooms at the edges were stairways leading to an upper story. On two sides, benches lined the long walls outside an entrance into the structure. At 25 by 12 meters in area, and 2 stories high, the House of the Tiles was by far the largest structure at Lerna. One of the square rooms was a space for gathering, with extra-wide doorways leading into it. Some scholars suggest that the corridor house plan is simply an elaborate megaron, with parallels to both earlier residential structures and Late Bronze Age mainland palaces.

It is not at all certain that the House of the Tiles served as a residence; the contents suggest that residents or workers at the House of the Tiles collected and disbursed some unknown type of goods. Clay seal impressions, 143 in number, mostly from a single room that could be entered only from the outside, had been attached to boxes, jars, and baskets, none of which were discovered in the room. Impressions were made by at least 70 different seals, indicating that no one person sealed many items (Pullen 2011). Objects being sent to the House of the Tiles must have come from a variety of different places—from the surrounding villages as taxes or commodities to sell, or from abroad, to be checked and then redistributed by Lerna's administrators. Pottery found in the room with the sealings included small serving dishes; if the contents of the sealed containers were food and drink items, the House of the Tiles might have hosted feasts (Pullen 2011).

Crete: Early Minoan (EM)

On Crete, the Early Minoan Period (ca. 3000–2000 BCE) saw steps toward state development—a progression that culminated in the first palaces in the early 2nd millennium. Agricultural practices may have expanded in the 3rd millennium to include olive exploitation and pastoral activities, and surpluses supported specialists in ceramics and metallurgy. While settlement evidence suggests an egalitarian social structure, a more complicated picture derives from funerary practices, including unequal access to prestige goods, especially imports. Monumentality in EM Crete took the form of funerary architecture. Burial practices varied by region; in most areas, tombs were communal and long-lasting, focusing on family and community identity rather than the individual. Two types, in particular—the house tombs of central and east Crete and *tholoi* in the south—were also remarkable for their visibility and monumentality. Tholoi are round structures, 4 to 13 meters in diameter, with a single entrance. Primary burials were set inside the round structure; when new bodies were added, bones of previous burials were selectively removed and redeposited in adjacent rectangular annexes. House tombs served a similar purpose, first built in central and eastern Crete in the mid-3rd millennium, and constructed through the early 2nd millennium. Tholos tombs also moved into the same regions in EM II. Like tholos tombs, the house tombs were used over long periods of time for primary burials of family or village members. But unlike the tholoi, at larger sites multiple contemporary house tombs were built; varying in size, these tombs may have become arenas for competitive display.

First States in the Aegean: Protopalatial Crete

After a brief Middle Minoan IA phase (ca. 2000–1900 BCE), the first palaces were constructed in eastern and central Crete, signaling the rise of a political system of multiple small states, each approximately equal in power. This Protopalatial Period lasted 150 years (ca. 1900–1750, MM IB–MM IIIA) before one or a series of pan-island earthquakes caused massive damage to the monumental structures. At least three palaces were built at this time; in each case, excavations have revealed that they replaced earlier structures on the same locations, which may have had similar administrative functions. The palaces served multiple functions in response to local economic and other needs.

Palace Layout and Functions

The palaces must have been built by local populations; construction materials were local (stone, brick, and wood), but some elements required additional effort to prepare (cut stone for exterior façades and lime plaster for interior walls). Although they have largely been covered by the palaces of the Neopalatial Period, a sketch of the physical plans may be attempted, and some features are shared among the palaces. Most notably, they are organized around a pair of large, open-air courtyards: a western court and a central court. The latter is within the building, and comprised a long rectangular space with the long axis oriented north-south. The western court, by contrast, stood outside the palace, forming an irregularly shaped buffer zone between the surrounding town and the palace. At Phaistos, the best-preserved of the early palaces, the western court spread across three levels, descending as one approached the main entrance to the palace. The space was paved, and raised walkways (causeways) delineate a path through it toward the entrance.

Also set in the western court were deep pits called *koulouras* (Greek for "rings") by the early excavators. These were recovered at Knossos and Phaistos. Knossos's were larger, at 5 to 6 meters in diameter and 3 meters deep. Scholars have long debated their function; when the first was excavated at Knossos, Arthur Evans asserted that it was a rubbish pit (Strasser 1997). Alternative explanations include long-term or short-term storage of staple goods. The idea that koulouras served as granaries for their settlements is attractive; those at Phaistos could have held enough grain to feed 300 people for a year, and Knossos's could feed 1,000 (Branigan 1988). Centralized storage of staples is often an indication of chiefly or royal capacity to collect and redistribute resources. Yet the koulouras were poorly suited to storing grain, being neither air- nor moisture-tight (Strasser 1997). Alternatively, they could have been used in public events of food delivery as part of a celebration of the harvest, after which materials could be collected and brought into the palace, a typical element in a redistributive economy (Hitchcock 2000; Marinatos 1987).

Besides pottery for storage, the Protopalatial Period palaces contained other objects that indicate their function. Fine painted pottery of a distinctive style—painted in red and white on a dark slip—came from palace contexts. Called Kamares Ware, its forms were typically those used to pour and drink liquids in commensal events that took place in the palaces and may have united and legitimized participants (Day and Wilson 1998). The palaces were the primary consumers of this specialized product; testing indicates that a single production center located in the Mesara Plain provided vessels found at both Knossos and Phaistos (Day, Relaki, and Faber 2006). Kamares Ware vessels were also traded to northern Syria and Egypt, as well as areas within the Aegean region. It is unlikely they were traded for their contents; often eggshell-thin, Kamares Ware vessels were too delicate to be moved long distances when full.

Writing and Administration

Other objects in the palaces yield evidence for administrative and economic activities. Most significantly, workers in the Minoan palaces adopted writing systems for administrative purposes during the Protopalatial Period. As in Mesopotamia and Egypt, Minoan writing was closely tied to seal use and commodity movement; from its start, signs could be inscribed on seals or incised on clay objects that were also impressed with one or more stamp seals.

In its first stages, Minoan writing served the needs of palaces in tracking goods. The first palaces had two different writing systems: Minoan hieroglyphs in the north (Knossos and Malia) and Linear A in the south (Phaistos). Neither system has been deciphered, although a significant number of Linear A signs can be "read," thanks to their pictographic appearance and resemblance to signs of a later Bronze Age writing system, Linear B. In neither case is it known what language was being recorded. Excavations of the first palaces have revealed only small numbers of inscribed documents, suggesting that the Protopalatial Period was a time of experiment with this new technology. In the Neopalatial Period, Linear A spread from Phaistos to the rest of the island, becoming the preferred communication system.

By contrast, seal use in the Protopalatial Period was ubiquitous in the palaces. Similar to the Early Helladic House of the Tiles at Lerna (see Box 7.1, earlier), Protopalatial palaces contained hundreds of clay seal impressions, most of them removed from containers. Writing, seals, and seal impressions indicate that the Protopalatial Period palaces played a role in the administration of goods. This is suggested also by their storage capacity, both outdoors (if the koulouras served as storage containers) and indoors. Palace administrators seem to have overseen the production of some goods, including fine pottery and perhaps textiles. Some of those products were traded to other regions of the island; others, like Kamares Ware pottery, were also exchanged internationally. The palaces may also have coordinated the import of international items, including stones and metals from the Levant, and stone vessels from Egypt.

Leadership

What the palaces may not have done was to serve as the residences of regional leaders. This may seem counterintuitive, given their name, but "palace" is a term provided by researchers; the Minoan name for these buildings is unknown. They functioned as administrative office buildings, where some people worked and others visited to do business. They served as gathering spots for religious and other community-centered rituals. The western and central courts, in particular, were designed to enhance visual effect, with sightlines, terracing, and walkways directing attention to ritual participants and actions.

While the palaces played a major role in coordinating community activities, evidence from nonpalatial contexts rounds out our view of Minoan society of the Protopalatial Period. At the site of Malia, about 40 kilometers east of Knossos, a palace was complemented by a number of other structures that also served public administrative and ceremonial functions and probably housed elite families. A neighborhood called Quartier Mu by its excavators included workshop areas for the production of seals, metal, and fine ceramics. Building A, the largest structure in the neighborhood, possessed a number of architectural elements that were later incorporated into all of the Neopalatial

Period palaces. These included a "Minoan hall" system: a suite of interconnected rooms, with a forecourt lit by an adjacent lightwell (a space open to the sky); a stone paved hall, which could be shut off from or opened to the forehall by a series of doors separated by columns (a "pier-and-door" arrangement); and an inner room containing an L-shaped "lustral basin," a sunken space, 2 meters deep, reached by stairs (Figure 7.4). The first excavator of Knossos, Arthur Evans, believed that lustral basins were bathing areas, as most are stone-lined, but they lacked drain systems, a feature found in other parts of the palaces. Their precise function is still debated, but the formalized layout, the fact that many have provisions for seeing into them from adjacent rooms, and their proximity to other ceremonial spaces suggest a ritual function.

Religion and Ideology

Another category of religious spaces was located far from the palace centers. Peak sanctuaries are open-air ritual spaces, located 2 to 3 hours by foot from a settlement, at or near the top of a hill or mountain. About 25 have been identified, based on collections of objects, including clay animal and human figurines and clay models of body parts, as well as pottery of Protopalatial date (Jones 1999: 5). Each one is visible from one or more towns, and those associated with the palaces were visible from the central court. They cluster, like palaces and towns, in eastern and central Crete. While it is tempting to attribute the foundation of peak sanctuaries to the rise of the first palaces, the sanctuaries may, in fact, be earlier; they also are not limited to locations near large settlements (Marinatos 1993: 116). The figurines deposited at the sanctuaries are modest in appearance and may represent the donor,

FIGURE 7.4 Lustral Basin in the Palace at Malia

Source: Photograph courtesy of Bernard Gagnon, licensed under GNU Free Documentation License via Wikimedia Commons

his or her hope for wealth, or a wish for health or healing. Nothing that could be identified as a cult statue has survived, nor is it clear that any stood in these locations. Rather, abstract forces of nature or benevolence may have been the focus of ritual and individual worship practices.

The Protopalatial peak sanctuaries served a geographically dispersed populace of seemingly humble means. A smaller number of cave sanctuaries also existed, including Kamares Cave, where the distinctive polychrome pottery of the time was first found. While caves were also visible from major palatial centers, deposits of ritual objects are sometimes found deep inside caves, including bronze tools and weapons but few figurines (Jones 1999: 8; Lupack 2010). It is possible that people worshipped different divinities within the caves than on the hilltops. Caves may have been considered entryways to the underworld, as some of the earliest burials on Crete were in caves.

Complexity in Protopalatial Crete

With the Protopalatial Period emerged a new level of sociopolitical integration and organization in the Aegean, unmatched by contemporary developments in the Cyclades or the mainland. Much of the population moved into urban centers, several of which held monumental palace structures, where people gathered for work and ritual events. Why the palaces arose at this time remains uncertain; Knossos, Phaistos, and Malia all were located on good agricultural land, and collection and storage were among the major activities at the palaces. While they had similar layouts, each palace was designed according to local needs, and each functioned independently of the others, at the center of its own local polity. Little evidence for complexity beyond the monumentalism and ritualism at the palaces comes from Middle Minoan Crete.

A number of scholars, citing the lack of political and economic institutions beyond the level of the village in the Early Bronze Age, have suggested that the palace system on Crete was inspired by contacts with such institutions in the Near East (Hitchcock 2010a). Third-millennium contacts through trade provided the background for secondary state development. First, elites emulated the trappings of power from a distant land; eventually competition among elite households on Crete may have led to the rise of one or a few families with power over the social storage of agricultural goods, ritual leadership, organization of international trade, and labor mobilization for building and producing prestige goods (Halstead 1981, 1997; Schoep 2006; Watrous 2004). The result was the rise of these enigmatic institutions, alongside more heterarchical ritual practices that bound communities together.

Full-Fledged States? The Neopalatial Period on Crete

The Protopalatial Period ended with a bang: one or a series of strong earthquakes leveled the palaces at the end of MM IIIA, around 1750 BCE. During the subsequent Neopalatial Period, MM IIIB–LM IB (ca. 1750–1500 BCE), all major palaces were rebuilt, and a number of additional ones arose across the island. This did not happen all at once; while repairs at Knossos began nearly immediately, Phaistos's palace lay in ruins for a while, and some new palaces were not completed until LM IA. This new phase brought considerable design changes: the palaces now all conformed to a regular layout, suggesting a single template and perhaps a single group of architects. The palace at Knossos was the first palace rebuilt but also was the largest and by far the most ornate. While other palaces and cities may not have been politically subordinate to Knossos, the city seems to have possessed religious and cultural significance beyond all others. Its Neopalatial re-emergence was accompanied by a number of other administrative, economic, and religious developments.

While palaces dominated the landscape, they were not the only monumental structures of the Neopalatial Period. New settlements were founded across Crete, and new types of buildings appeared. At least ten cities had palaces, while other towns had administrative and religious buildings that archaeologists call "villas," which possessed some palatial elements but lacked a central court. At least 20 of these date to the Neopalatial Period. The palace at Knossos was surrounded by villa-sized buildings that housed elites. Settlement patterns also included smaller agricultural villages within the territory controlled by each palace. Peak and cave sanctuaries continued to be used, with new building activities at some of the peaks, but the growth of palatial power seems to have resulted in a reduction in the number of outlying religious spaces.

Knossos

Evidence from Neopalatial Crete suggests a realignment of social and political hierarchies at this time, with Knossos as the "superordinate center"; elites elsewhere sought to emulate the appearance and features of Knossos (Soles 1995). Knossos may be representative of the architecture of the other palaces, but its decorative program was unique, perhaps because of its stature as the leading institution of the day but also because it employed the best artists on the island. The palace at Knossos (Figure 7.5) covers an area of 2 hectares, the size of some Early Bronze Age villages, and some

FIGURE 7.5 Knossos Palace Plan

Source: J.C. Ross

portions stood up to five stories high. While the western court still served as a paved gathering space, the Protopalatial koulouras had been filled in, and whatever function they had fulfilled was transferred into the palace or discontinued. The main entrance was on the western side. Similar courts and entrance systems are found at Malia and Phaistos.

From the western entrance at Knossos, a visitor meandered through a decorated corridor that finally led into the central court, another paved space 54 by 27 meters, oriented north-south. The courtyard at Malia was nearly the same size as Knossos's, at 48 by 23 meters, while that at Phaistos was elongated, at 63 by 22.5 meters; all have the same north-south orientation. From the courtyard, which was probably the principal destination for many visitors, one could enter a variety of functional areas. At all three of the major palaces, religious spaces occupied the ground floor west of the courtyard. The religious wing is best understood at Knossos: entered from the center of the western side of the central court, a vestibule led into a room with a pair of deep stone boxes cut into the floor. Among the finds in these rooms were incomplete faience figurines depicting women handling snakes. The larger of the two well-preserved figurines (a third was too fragmentary to reconstruct) stood 35 centimeters tall; whether goddess or priestess, these are images of supernatural force (see Box 7.2).

BOX 7.2 MINOAN FORGERIES

The excavation of the palace at Knossos by Arthur Evans in the early 20th century fueled a thirst for Minoan objects among wealthy collectors in Europe and the United States. In the early decades of the 1900s, antiquities laws did not yet govern the export of archaeological finds, and significant numbers of Minoan objects, especially small figurines made of ivory and faience, reached the hands of collectors and eventually the halls of museums. Some of them came from illicit excavations at Knossos and elsewhere predating Evans's work, but others arrived on the market while Evans was excavating, and some of these were even certified by Evans as genuine. In particular, suspicions about authenticity swirl around a group of "goddess" figurines made from ivory, with gold attributes like snakes and crowns. These stand in poses much like the faience figurines found in the palace at Knossos, with arms held above or away from the body, and in similar clothing. They were supplemented by stone goddesses in similar poses. As early as the 20th century, some figurines were recognized as forgeries, some even made by workers and artisans employed by Evans. But many, of uncertain provenience and authenticity, remain on display in museums worldwide (Lapatin 2002).

Just north of this suite, facing onto the central courtyard, was a "tripartite shrine": a niche divided into three parts, the central one higher, with a column in each portion. The religious nature of this shrine façade is indicated by the contemporary "Grandstand Fresco" found nearby. It illustrates an event attended by hundreds of men, with fewer but more prominent women, who sit to either side of just such a façade. The numbers of people depicted suggest a large open space, likely the central courtyard.

North of the tripartite shrine façade was a monumental staircase; beyond this was a final major ceremonial area: the throne room complex. Knossos is the only Minoan palace with an intact throne. Steps from the central court led through a columned opening down into a vestibule, then the throne room, where stone benches lined the walls other than the one occupied by a scallop-backed gypsum throne. Off the main room is a lustral basin. A north-south corridor separated the western ritual spaces from a suite of long and narrow storage magazines filled with *pithoi*, each of which held hundreds of liters of contents (Christakis 2011). A western storage space is common to Malia and Phaistos as well.

Other areas of the palace at Knossos can be dealt with more quickly. If the western portion of the palace's ground floor was largely devoted to ritual activities, the areas east of the court are more administrative in function, containing Linear A tablets and seal impressions. At the northern end of the central court is a large pillared room adjacent to a kitchen area and fine pottery storage; a set of steps led up to what was probably a second-story dining area. This may have been a gathering spot for commensal feasting, bringing palace officials and other elites together. Other upper story activities remain indefinite; residential facilities for a royal family or families are possible but unproven: the palaces may have continued to be spaces for ritual and politics, but not for domestic activities. While the palaces at Phaistos and Malia are about half the size of Knossos's, the same array of functions is common to them too.

Knossos is distinguished, however, by the extent of decoration in the palace. Wall and floor paintings were in true fresco technique, with paint applied to wet plaster surfaces. Throughout the palace were depictions of men and women, sometimes interacting and sometimes separate. Some individuals represented may be gods, based on their dress, attributes, and actions. The Minoans adopted the Egyptian conventions of red skin color for men, white for women; dress, hairstyle, and headgear were also different (Lee 2000). Some depictions, however, defied the rules; these may represent an alternative gender or some other social distinction (Alberti 2002). Landscapes and animals, sometimes fantastic ones like griffins, also appeared throughout the palace. The frescoes at Knossos do not depict anyone identifiable as a ruler (Davis 1995).

The motifs and scenes at Knossos are dominated by gatherings; they may depict typical ritual events inside and outside palace walls (Cameron 1987). In the corridor leading from the western entrance to the central court, the Procession Fresco depicts groups of people carrying objects such as visitors to Knossos might (Boulotis 1987). In the throne room, griffins protect both sides of the throne, marking the space as sacred. Large groups of people are gathered in a pair of miniature frescoes with very small human figures that fell from a room on the upper story in the northwest corner of the courtyard. These are the aforementioned Grandstand Fresco and the Sacred Grove Fresco, where women dance along paved causeways among trees, in front of a large gathering of male and female onlookers. Finally, a number of frescoes depict bulls (Hallager and Hallager 1995). These include at least five painted panels showing acrobats somersaulting over the backs of bulls, a dangerous sport that could have been a rite of passage for elite Minoan youths. The repetition of bull imagery at Knossos may indicate that the animals symbolized the power of royalty or a particular god worshipped at Knossos; both interpretations have parallels in the contemporary Near East (Hitchcock 2000).

Beyond Knossos

The near-absence of fresco decoration at Phaistos and Malia may, as noted earlier, indicate Knossos's dominance over these two similar-sized centers. The same is true of the other Neopalatial Period palaces identified on the island, which contained storage areas, cultic suites, Linear A archives, but little or no surviving visual imagery. An exceptional building is the palace at Kato Zakro on the far eastern end of Crete, which differed from the others in design and orientation. The structure was inserted into a thriving harbor town toward the end of the Neopalatial Period and may have been under the control of the political authorities at Knossos (Chrysoulaki and Platon 1987; Platon 2010). Because it had to fit into the existing space, the palace is small—one-fifth the size of the palace at Knossos—with a 29 by 12 meter central court oriented northeast-southwest (Preziosi and Hitchcock 1999: 106). It differs in other ways, lacking a spacious western court and placement of its main entrance on the northeast side, along a road coming from the harbor. This suggests that the Kato Zakro palace played a central role in commerce. It also had numerous workshop areas. Kato Zakro's palace played an important role in prestige goods production that enhanced the symbolic power of Knossos's elites and broadcast that power beyond the island.

The architectural and settlement patterns of the Neopalatial Period indicate the dominance of an elite class in the ritual, artistic, economic, and administrative organization of the island. Palaces spread to new parts of the island, and secondary administrative centers sprang up to fulfill many of the same functions as the palaces but lacked the spaces for ceremonial gatherings of townspeople or elite families. Knossos held the dominant position among the palaces in their ideological expression of power and in ritual activities, but it is likely that each palace center's functions were adapted to local administrative and religious needs.

Religion in Neopalatial Crete

The rebuilding of the palaces in the Neopalatial Period marked a decline in rural ritual, as palaces, villas, and towns appear to have brought religious activities into settlement areas. As seen earlier, palaces had several spaces reserved for worship. Symbols like double axes and horns of consecration marked these spaces as sacred (Lupack 2010); similar objects appear in villas and mansions. At the same time, separate spaces within towns may have been used by the rest of the populace for everyday or periodic acts of devotion; these locations are recognized by the presence of figurines, stands to hold double axes, and stone tables with depressions to receive libations. Some items, like votive figurines, may have been widely available, but most stone and metal objects were probably donated by elites (E. Adams 2004; Betancourt 1999, 2007: 95).

In contrast, peak sanctuaries experienced a marked decline in the Neopalatial Period, and this too seems to indicate the rising power of the Minoan ruling class. Of the 25 Protopalatial peak sanctuaries, only 8 or 9 continued in use in the subsequent period, and each of those can be associated with a nearby palace (Peatfield 1992). At the peak sanctuaries still in use, enclosure walls, altars, and structures for storage of cult paraphernalia were built, and expensive items like bronze and gold double axes, bronze votive statues, and inscribed objects were deposited (Lupack 2010). This suggests that elites became the principal sponsors of sanctuaries, and the ceremonies that took place there were more exclusive than previously.

How Minoans worshipped, and what, are difficult questions, despite over a century of excavation. Early archaeologists believed that the principal deity was a goddess of nature, a "mother goddess" responsible for animal and human fertility and for cosmological cycles. In fact, figurines and seals depict a number of different divinities, male and female, associated with mountains and weather, animals (real and fantastic), snakes and the underworld, birds, and double axes (Marinatos 1993: 139–58). Rituals depicted involved dance, song, offerings (especially of robes), and invocation at a rock or tree (Goodison 2009). Rites of passage and epiphanies, perhaps acted out by a priest or priestess, may have been particularly important.

Economic and Political Organization in the Neopalatial Period

The palaces played a role in local agricultural administration, collecting and allocating grain; they also operated workshops (ceramic, stone, and metallurgical) on their grounds (Betancourt 2007). Textile production was more dispersed, taking place in houses and villas, but it is likely to have been at least partially subsidized by palace authorities (Militello 2007). Although Linear A has not been deciphered, the tablets clearly record economic goods such as animals, olives and figs, wine, and human labor. Presumably, these were items collected by each administrative center as taxes from surrounding communities (Schoep 2002: 90). Linear A was also used on votive objects, where the inscription gave an offering formula, maybe with the name of the donor.

Linear A documents have been found at 13 sites on Crete, one on the mainland, and several in the Cyclades, as far as the island of Samothrace in the northern Aegean (Palaima 1987; Palmer 1995). This suggests active Minoan participation in long-distance trade and a degree of administrative control over trade. Minoan presence in various locations in the Aegean has fueled claims that the Minoans controlled a vast empire by means of their naval forces. The reality was probably less extreme: the Minoans of the Neopalatial Period took advantage of their long history of maritime trade to extend economic and political relationships to the Levantine coast and Egypt. But beyond a Protopalatial Period colony founded on Kythera near mainland Greece, it is not likely that Cretan palaces dominated any other territory.

It is in art and imagery that Minoan influence is most apparent, but it is doubtful that Minoan ideology was exported extensively. Several monumental buildings in the Levant have frescoes of Aegean style, possibly even made by Minoan artists. At Tel Kabri in northern Israel, a palatial structure had both a painted floor, akin to some at Knossos, and a miniature fresco with a ship scene (Niemeier 1991). Even more intriguing are the paintings from two palaces at the Eighteenth Dynasty center of Avaris (Tell el-Daba) in the Nile Delta region in Egypt. Here, Minoan-style frescoes on both wet and dry plaster had fallen from the mudbrick walls and were dumped outside the structures. One palace had a 4-meter long, 90-centimeter high frieze showing bull-leaping activities. The athletes are all male, with Minoan-style costumes and hair. At the same time, some elements are non-Minoan: the leapers are more solidly built than typical "wasp-waisted" Minoan men, the bulls turn their heads toward the viewer, and the skin color of some of the leapers is yellow rather than the usual red (Shaw 1995). But other than the body proportions, these are also non-Egyptian features; they could have resulted from the hiring of itinerant rather than palace-based artists or from a mix of Egyptian and Cretan designers. What is undeniable is that an Egyptian king of the 15th century commissioned an overtly Aegean-type decorative program for a pair of buildings; Bietak (2000) has suggested that the reason was the arrival of a Minoan princess to be his bride (no such marriage is noted in Egyptian records). Whatever the reason, the style was short-lived.

Minoan influence was even stronger within the Aegean region itself. A number of the Cycladic Islands participated in trade with Crete; Neopalatial impact on local material culture is clearest at the site of Akrotiri on Thera (modern Santorini), buried under more than 30 meters of ash following a volcanic eruption that may be dated to 1628 or 1627 BCE (Manning and Sewell 2002). Prior to the eruption, Akrotiri had been a prosperous harbor town, filled with two- and three-story houses (Doumas 1983). Most of the excavated structures combine domestic and ritual spaces; in a few cases, religious rooms may have been open to larger public gatherings. No administrative building has been identified at Akrotiri, and it is unlikely that the settlement required bureaucratic institutions to organize its economic activities.

Where Minoan contacts are especially apparent at Akrotiri is in the frescoes that adorned the houses (Chapin 2010). Specific motifs and themes are similar to those found at Knossos: landscapes, isolated plants and animals, humans in a variety of activities, and ritual scenes (Cameron 1978). There is even a possible narrative: a mythological or historical scene of shipwreck and land battle (Davis 1983; Säflund 1981). Rituals depicted may include a festival celebrated by ships sailing from island to island; a rite of passage ceremony for young women of marriageable age; and an offering of crocus flowers to a seated goddess, who is attended by a monkey and a griffin. The Akrotiri frescoes possess shocking preservation and vibrancy; they also supplement the more fragmentary paintings at Knossos. While it has been suggested that they were created by artists trained at Knossos, it is perhaps more likely that they were expressions of a widespread set of beliefs and practices, emanating from Knossos but adapted to local needs and representational traditions.

The Destruction of the Minoan Palaces

That the eruption of Thera's volcano had devastating consequence for the island's inhabitants and its archaeology is undeniable. Far less certain is the impact of the eruption on Crete, just 100 kilometers away. The eruption would have been visible from Crete, and in its wake, towns on the northern coast experienced some ash fall and may have suffered earthquakes and a tsunami, as well as receiving refugees (Driessen 2002). Harder to interpret are the long-term effects; significant disruptions, in the form of fire destructions and temporary abandonment of buildings and settlements, took place in late LM IA and early LM IB, near the time of Santorini's eruption. Of 54 LM IA settlements known on Crete, over one-third were abandoned by the end of LM IA; 32 continued to be occupied in LM IB, but by LM II, only ten survived (Driessen and Macdonald 1997). Even more significantly, every Neopalatial palace experienced a destruction by fire and then plundering. Only the palace at Knossos was rebuilt and reused in LM II, under profoundly changed political, economic, and social circumstances.

Although the eruption on Santorini could not have directly caused the destruction of the palaces at the end of the Neopalatial Period, it is likely that it contributed to the crisis on Crete. The crisis was, however, driven by people: destructions were selective, targeting palaces and their users or inhabitants and effectively removing or realigning the power structures across the island. In the wake of the natural disaster, population movements away from the coast to inland areas, as well as short-term suppression of crop growth, may have led to food shortages. As Thera was a major stopping point on trade routes through the Aegean, supplies of metals and other trade goods would have been disrupted (Driessen and Macdonald 1997: 80). In the end, an ideological crisis relating to religious beliefs and practices and to distrust of ruling powers seems to have led to attacks on all the palaces.

Most intriguing is the role of Knossos in these processes. The palace there also suffered destruction but was quickly rebuilt. Did interpolity warfare bring down the palaces, with Knossos arising as the winner after a period of conflict? Or were the elites at Knossos the best-equipped to deal with internal rebellion and therefore able to reassert control over the palace and then over the rest of the island? That residents of Knossos were not immune from the instability of the time is suggested by apparent child sacrifices and cannibalism found in an LM IB house west of the palace (Wall, Musgrave, and Warren 1986; Warren 1981); such practices were not a normal part of Minoan religion and may reflect a reaction to extreme crisis.

Knossos's palace was rebuilt and reoccupied from LM II to IIIB (ca. 1500–1350 BCE), while the rest of the island took a century or more to recover. By the Final Palatial Period (LM IIIA–B), Knossos itself may have been controlled from abroad (see later), while new economic and religious structures arose across the island (Hallager 2010). During LM II, Knossos was the only urban administrative center, and the population and territory it controlled may have provided a limited supply of food and other resources.

A Military-Industrial State: Mycenaean Greece (LH I–III)

While the Neopalatial Period was still in bloom on Crete, the stage was being set for the rise of Mycenaean city-states during the Late Helladic (LH) IIIA–B Period on the Greek mainland. The origins of these states are somewhat murky, as the Middle Helladic Period (ca. 2000–1550 BCE), contemporary with the Protopalatial and early Neopalatial Periods on Crete, shows a pattern of generally small, isolated agricultural settlements on the Peloponnesus and central Greece, with cemeteries of poorly endowed cist graves. An exception is the site of Kolonna on the island of Aegina, lying off the southern coast of Attica. There stood a fortified citadel with a monumental building, and a wealthy tomb with an array of gold jewelry of hybrid Minoan, Egyptian, and Levantine styles (Gauss 2010).

The Shaft Graves and Tholos Tombs of Mycenae

At 1600 BCE, additional mainland cemeteries began to display significant variations in wealth, expressed particularly in terms of the effort expended on tomb preparation and the materials deposited in graves. This happened first at the site of Mycenae, which was to lend its name to this final stage of Aegean proto-history, the Mycenaean Age. There, two concentrations of shaft graves (inhumations at the base of a deep rectangular shaft), inside precinct walls, contained the bodies of the town's wealthiest families. One cemetery, Grave Circle B, was located near the western foot of the citadel; burials there began in the Middle Helladic Period and continued into LH I. The other, Grave Circle A, opened slightly later (LH I) and was located on the citadel's edge; its placement and contents suggest that the family buried there came to be the founding dynasty of the Mycenaean state.

Grave Circle B, the earlier of the two, had ten shafts, with 24 skeletons. Most male burials included bronze weapons (Graziadio 1991). In Grave Circle A, burial practices were the same (shaft graves, with multiple extended bodies in each), but with 7 shafts containing 19 bodies. These were deeper than those in Circle B, up to 4 meters deep, and the quantities of goods, especially metal objects of fine workmanship, far exceeded those in Circle B. Each grave appears to have been marked by a stone marker, some with a sculpted scene of hunt or battle (Figure 7.6a) (Betancourt 2007: 142).

The shaft graves at Mycenae indicate a sudden increase in wealth on the Greek mainland, held in the hands of a small number of people. Gold is concentrated in Circle A, where it was shaped into elaborate jewelry and ornament sewn onto clothing, for a vessel in the shape of a lion's head, for ornament on bronze weapons, and for the sheet-hammered masks placed over the faces of several men and at least one child. No such concentration of gold is known from 2nd millennium Crete. The amounts of silver and bronze in the shaft graves are similarly high, though these two metals were not used for the highest-status items.

The styles and workmanship of materials from the shaft graves point to possible artists and influences from Crete. Minoan artistry was deployed for distinctly Mycenaean motifs of lion hunts and battles. A number of daggers also had inlaid scenes of gold, silver, and niello (a black copper, lead,

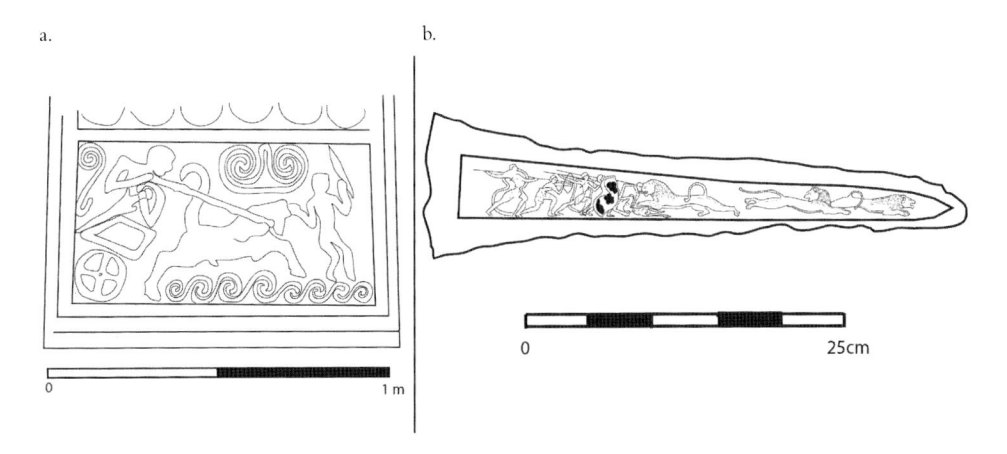

FIGURE 7.6 Shaft Graves at Mycenae: a. Drawing of Stele; b. Drawing of Dagger

Source: J.C. Ross

or silver sulfide paste) that portrayed floral and animal scenes and a hunt where four tiny-waisted, long-haired men (a fifth has fallen) confront an attacking lion while two other animals run away. This masterpiece of miniature art (Figure 7.6b) is a hybrid of Minoan design and execution in service to a Mycenaean patron.

But if the artists producing at least some of the shaft grave items were Minoan, who were their patrons? Some have suggested that the shaft graves were burials of Minoan rulers, who established new settlements on the mainland at the height of the Neopalatial Period. But the artistic themes do not support this view: while Minoans certainly hunted and waged war, they mostly avoided such themes in their art, stressing instead communal ritual and bull sports (Molloy 2012). Examination of the skeletal remains shows that men were taller and in better health than contemporaries buried elsewhere at Mycenae (Graziadio 1991). The burials included non-local women (based on bone chemistry analysis) and may have been an elite class with access to a better diet and living conditions than their townspeople (Nafplioti 2009). Their burials are also distinguished by access to trade items including gold and amber, both of which could have come from central Europe. The people buried in the grave circles had economic resources to enhance their social prestige, but no great political power, yet.

The rest of the mainland took time to catch up with Mycenae. In LH I to II (1550–1400 BCE), the numbers of settlements increased across the mainland, and sites that would later see monumental fortifications and palaces began to grow. The dead in the region of Messenia in southwestern Greece were buried in tholos tombs. As previously on Crete, these combined a round burial chamber with stone corbel-vaulted walls and an adjacent rectangular room. Unlike Minoan tholoi, mainland examples were intended to hold one or two burials, rather than the entire community. By LH II, tholos burial spread to Mycenae, where it replaced the earlier shaft graves of the elite. At Mycenae, nine tholoi were constructed in LH II–III; some of the remaining population was buried in family chamber tombs, a tomb type known from earlier, while graves are unknown for the rest of the population. Mycenae's tholoi are truly monumental: 8 to 15 meters in diameter, up to 15 meters high, with lintel blocks weighing up to 120 tons. The precise identities of their occupants are unknown. They were probably the successors of the shaft grave occupants (Mee and Cavanagh 1984).

Besides monumental tombs, another monumental building type developed in LH II: palaces. The best-preserved of four possible palaces of this date was built at a very different scale and different design from the early palaces on Crete. The Menelaion, located in the central Peloponnesus near Classical Sparta, stood isolated on a hilltop. Its plan of about a dozen rooms was centered on a megaron, the axial arrangement of porch, forehall, and hall that had its roots in the Greek Neolithic. The building occupied a total area of only 25 by 25 meters, about half the size of Knossos's central court (Catling 1976–77). It had limited storage or communal space. Because later Mycenaean palaces also shared its central megaron plan and its high placement, the Menelaion provides the first clue that Mycenaean political organization and administrative needs were far different from those embodied by the Minoan palaces.

The Late Helladic IIIA–B Palatial Age

By the beginning of the LH III Period, around 1400 BCE, elites in various parts of the mainland consolidated political control over surrounding populations and constructed monumental residences and administrative buildings capable of broadcasting their ambitions. Most of the main LH III palatial settlements were located near harbors and trade routes (Runnels and Murray 2001: 96); while control over agricultural production was important for supporting the ruling class and its dependents, the main focus of the Mycenaean political economy was trade. The palaces stored oil, wine, grain and other agricultural products for their own use; they also ran workshops where these products, as well as metals, timber, and wool, were transformed into valued prestige goods, used locally and traded great distances. Mycenaean goods are found archaeologically from Italy to the Levant and Egypt. There was no single Mycenaean state; like Crete during the Protopalatial Period, various polities competed with one another, each under the leadership of a king.

LH IIIA–B (ca. 1400–1200 BCE) palaces are known from at least 4 and as many as 11 sites (scholars differ in their willingness to call all monumental Mycenaean administrative buildings "palaces"). At Pylos, where the surviving remains date to LH IIIB (the 13th century), excavations have revealed a four-building complex atop a promontory (Figure 7.7). The complex was added to over its lifespan. At its heart was the "Main Building" (30 by 55 meters), entered through a guarded gateway. Once inside the gate, a visitor could move through a courtyard into the megaron. This housed the formal throne room, common to each palace; at Pylos, the back hall had a large, raised, central hearth (nearly 4 meters in diameter), surrounded by four columns. Against the right hand wall, a stone base supported a wooden throne. A fresco program ran from the forehall into this room, with a bull sacrifice and banquet with seated lyre player providing the entertainment on one side of the throne, a lion and a griffin providing protection on the other. Painted decoration also adorned the raised rim of the hearth (flame and spiral patterns) and the floor (a grid with geometric patterns in most squares) (McCallum 1987). This space was certainly used in cultic activities, overseen by the person occupying the throne. Interestingly, no one individual stands out in the fresco depiction as an officiant, priest, king, or god, leaving open the question of who sat on the throne.

At Pylos, the megaron was surrounded on three sides by rooms in which oil, wine, and vessels for serving were stored. The megaron and its adjoining courtyard could not have accommodated

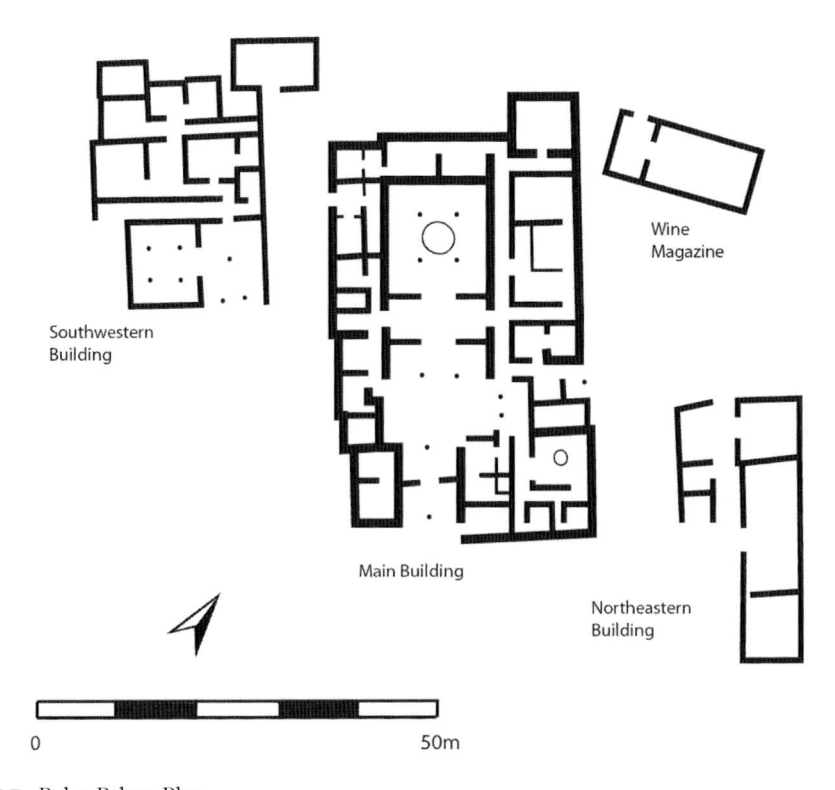

FIGURE 7.7 Pylos Palace Plan

Source: J.C. Ross

thousands of people for a feast (in contrast to Crete's palaces, with their vast open areas), but some large commensal events must have taken place given the numbers of ceramic cups. Also within the Main Building is a second, smaller megaron and a pair of rooms that contained several hundred tablets, recording commodities and people as they entered and left the palace. If residential areas existed here, they would have been on the second story.

Three additional buildings complete the palace complex at Pylos. West of the Main Building was the multi-roomed Southwest Building. It has been suggested that this was another area for feasting. On the other side of the Main Building, the Northeast Building held concentrations of bronze and flint arrowheads and debris from chipped stone production (Bendall 2003). Tablets in the building documented the distribution of grain, wine, textiles, and items of military equipment; this structure may have been used by military officials as an armory and workshop (Bendall 2003). Finally, the Wine Magazine held dozens of large storage jars for wine. The entrance to this building faced away from the other structures on the hill, suggesting collection and distribution activities, rather than consumption.

Pylos's palace offers evidence for formal ritual and state gatherings, economic activities, residence, storage, and coordination of military activity. Above all, it was a place for administering production and trade. At Knossos, the palace underwent a final series of internal modifications in LH IIIA–B, but the central court, storage areas, cult places, and Minoan hall systems remained intact. The gypsum throne may have been added to the throne room at this time, and a last set of frescoes created, including banquet scenes akin to those in the megaron at Pylos. Excavations at Knossos uncovered the largest number of Linear B texts known to date: over 3,000. These are the main indication that the palace may have been in Mycenaean hands; about one-third of the names preserved in the texts are Greek (Baumbach 1983). In line with the other Mycenaean sites, it is likely that a ruler now resided in Knossos's palace.

Aside from the palaces, monumental effort also went into the construction of fortification systems at Mycenaean centers. Citadel areas were especially well fortified and may have served as places of refuge for the population when a city was under attack, but the massive scale of their fortification systems also suggests that they stood to impress and intimidate visitors and their own people (Wright 1994). At Mycenae, the system was built and remodeled in three phases, eventually bringing the entire high mound and access to its water source within the walls. Walls stood up to 6 meters thick and could reach several stories in height. Fortification systems of LH IIIB were constructed from massive boulders, in a style known among archaeologists as Cyclopean; the boulders were roughly finished but carefully fitted, with small stones set into the spaces between the rough courses. The main entrance to the citadel at Mycenae was the Lion Gate, on the west side. Here, the gate was wide enough to admit wheeled vehicles. Above a lintel weighing 20 tons is a triangular relief sculpture with a pair of rampant lions standing alongside an altar-like podium topped with a column. The lions turn their heads toward a person entering the citadel; their heads were attached by dowels and lost in antiquity.

Economic Organization

Nowhere is Mycenaean bureaucracy more in evidence than in the Linear B tablet archives, found at the palaces at Knossos and Pylos and in small quantities at other palace sites. The Mycenaeans adapted Linear A, which they first encountered at Knossos, to write their own language, an early form of Greek (Palaima 2010). Linear B tablets record the movement of goods into and out of the hands of the extensive palace bureaucracy. While the Knossos tablets focused on sheep for textile production, those from Pylos are more wide-ranging, documenting the palace's intake of taxes in agricultural products, its land holdings, and its involvement in both industrial and religious activities.

The Pylos tablets offer especially detailed information on palace management of workshop production, especially of prestige goods intended for redistribution to palace officials, other Mycenaean centers, and trade abroad. Pylos focused on the creation of textiles, bronze military equipment, and olive oil, which was a valued commodity in the ancient world (Parkinson 1999). Much of the oil produced by Pylos's presses was packaged in clay storage and shipping containers for immediate use or distribution. But a significant portion was sent to workshops, together with a range of aromatic herbs and resins, to produce the scented oil that was used as a perfume across the eastern Mediterranean.

Crete also conducted an active trade in olive oil or wine, held in characteristic LM III large stirrup jars. These 40 to 50 centimeter high globular jars had a wide spout and two or three handles, configured like stirrups; those of distinctly Cretan fabric have been found at various Mycenaean cities, and in Italy, Egypt, Cyprus, and the Levant (Ben-Schlomo et al. 2011). Meanwhile, Mycenaean palaces imported prestige goods, including faience, ivory and bronze from the Levant, and scarabs and other inscribed objects from Egypt.

Mycenaean states also participated in the international trade represented by the shipwrecks at Uluburun and Cape Gelidonya, described in Chapter 5. Onboard the Uluburun wreck, excavators found 18 stirrup jars, together with Aegean-style weapons, tools, and seals (Bachhuber 2006). These may have been personal possessions of the crew or items exchanged as international gifts. Since the ship appears to have wrecked after leaving Cyprus with a full load of copper, it is likely that a port in the Aegean region was the next planned stop.

Social Organization

Evidence available on Mycenaean society is heavily weighted toward elites, as their monumental palaces and tombs have attracted excavation, and they are well attested in the Linear B records. The texts indicate also that a range of occupations and social classes existed in Late Helladic society, including slaves. Work groups were segregated by sex, as men and women held different types of jobs, overlapping in only a few roles including that of priest (Olsen 1998). A lack of social differentiation among most Mycenaeans is apparent in tomb and house contents.

At the top of the political hierarchy stood the *wanax*, translated as "king"; Pylos and Knossos each had a wanax. The word wanax survived until the time of Homer several centuries later; Homer used it as a title for the chief god Zeus, suggesting that by his time, it must have implied something like "traditional king" (Palaima 1995). In Homer, the Greek heroes like Agamemnon and Menelaus are called *basileus*, another term found in the Linear B archives, where it denoted a more localized power-holder ("district governor" or "mayor"). Also near the top of the hierarchy was the *lawagetas*, whose duties revolved around military matters. The texts rarely provide personal names for any of these office-holders; one wanax may be identified by name at Pylos but even that is unclear (Nakassis 2012).

Religion

Among the chief responsibilities of the wanax was to provision the gods and their priests. The palace funded offerings and organized festivals to honor the gods (Bendall 2001). The Linear B texts mention at least 30 gods by name, including a number known from Classical Greece: Zeus, Hera, Eileithyia, Poseidon, Apollo, and Dionysus. Athena may be attested in an early form as Potnia, "The Lady." Other divine names are not Greek; these may be survivals from a pre-Greek population (especially on Crete) or adopted from neighboring regions.

Temple buildings have been excavated at a number of sites. Surprisingly non-monumental, these buildings have house plans but with non-domestic features like platforms and benches, and they contained large numbers of terracotta figurines and sometimes frescoes. In no case is the name of the god worshipped in a particular building preserved, and archaeologists have been unable to assign any shrine to a particular god on the basis of finds. Outside the palaces and citadels, other places of worship have been identified, including rural shrines (Wright 1994). A class of very small terracotta female figurines in several different poses is found in Mycenaean houses and tombs; these could have been votive figurines used in domestic cult.

Sociopolitical Complexity in the Mycenaean Age

This review of LH IIIA–B art and architecture and Linear B documents has revealed both the debt Mycenaeans owed their Minoan predecessors and the innovative character of Mycenaean political structure. Mycenaean polities evolved as another case of secondary state formation, under the influence of Minoan Neopalatial economic and political contacts. But without extensive and productive agricultural territories, mainland political leaders instead monopolized production of prestige goods that could be traded both locally and abroad. The territory controlled by each palace was largely defined and delimited by geographical features; each wanax was roughly equal in economic and social power. Homer's texts give primacy to Mycenae as foremost among contemporary cities; while this may reflect a circumstance recognized across the mainland, archaeological support for it is lacking. It is likely that the elites at mainland centers were in a continual state of competition, both within the cities and among them, a situation that will be seen again in the rise of Classical Period Greek city-states.

The Trojan War and the Decline of Mycenaean Power

The final century of the Mycenaean polities, LH IIIB (ca. 1300–1200 BCE), saw both the most intensive expressions of their power—in terms of monumental construction and foreign trade—and the beginning of their decline. By 1150 BCE, every Mycenaean palace had been destroyed at least once, and all indications of elite hegemony had disappeared. The disappearance of Mycenaean power was part of an overall pattern of disruption and decline at power centers, major and minor, across the eastern Mediterranean and Near East at the end of the Bronze Age (see discussions in Chapters 5 and 6).

Homer and Hesiod, the great epic poets of Archaic Greece (the 8th–7th centuries BCE) regarded the end of the Bronze Age as a major turning point, signaling the start of a decline that lasted until their own time. While neither poet was an historian, their works describe conditions and events about which memories had been passed down orally for several centuries. It is no accident that the first official excavations conducted in the Aegean—by the German businessman Heinrich Schliemann—had as their goal the rediscovery of Troy, the setting of Homer's epic the *Iliad*. The Trojan War, with Achaean Greeks fighting Troy, a powerful city in Anatolia, and its allies, was an event recognized by ancient historians as pivotal to early Greek history.

The *Iliad* describes a period of a few days near the end of a ten-year war on Trojan soil. It depicts the Greeks at the height of their wealth and power and puts leadership in the hands of Agamemnon, the king of Mycenae. Each of the Greek leaders led his troops autonomously; Agamemnon was most powerful because his force was the largest and he had called for the alliance against Troy. Homer's description of the Greeks' political organization, their shared value system and material culture, is confirmed by the archaeological evidence reviewed earlier. During LH IIIA–B, Mycenaean economic and cultural contacts extended to the Anatolian coast and islands (Mee 1998) (see Box 7.3).

> **BOX 7.3 EVIDENCE FOR THE TROJAN WAR**
>
> While later Greek authors placed the Trojan War within the Anatolian Peninsula, Linear B documents do not, to date, mention locations in Anatolia, nor are the names of any individuals from Homer's epics preserved in them. By contrast, the Hittites, the contemporary rulers of central Anatolia, kept abundant records of their dealings with both foreign nations and neighboring and subject polities in Turkey. Over a period of about 100 years, the Hittite kings corresponded with kings of Ahhiyawa, whom they called "Great Kings" (Kelder 2005). Toward the end of the 14th century, Ahhiyawans were present at the city of Milawatta, identified by archaeologists as Miletus on the western coast of Turkey; later, the Hittites would challenge Ahhiyawa for political dominance at various locations along the coast, including Taruisa (Troy). Most scholars agree that the Ahhiyawans are Homer's Achaeans, i.e., Mycenaean Greeks. These two great powers struggled for control along the coast, for trade dominance and territorial rule. Troy was one of several points of contention (Cline 2008).
>
> Excavations at Troy have revealed not one but two destruction layers from late in the Bronze Age, each potentially identifiable with a Mycenaean siege and destruction of the city. Mycenaean pottery at the site dates as early as LH II, confirming Hittite records of Achaean presence on the coast (Mee 1998). Troy was one of many Anatolian sites destroyed in LH III, a pattern of violence that eventually included the fall of the Hittite Empire. Unfortunately, despite the details provided by Homer and other ancient writers, the destroyers left no telltale artifacts by which their identities could be confirmed.

In Homer's imaginative re-creation of the Bronze Age collapse, the Greek victors were met by betrayal and upheaval when they returned home, the order they had maintained in their individual polities breaking down during their ten-year absence. Archaeological evidence shows that the LH IIIB cities in Greece succumbed, one by one, to destruction by fire, including palace centers from Thessaly to Crete (Drews 1993: 21–29). A number of them had seen some disturbance earlier in LH IIIB, followed by rebuilding. Others were destroyed in late LH IIIB, then reoccupied in LH IIIC. Many smaller sites were simply abandoned.

Limited continuity and significant change mark the LH IIIC Period (ca. 1200–1100 BCE). Some cult places survived and continued to receive offerings (Cosmopoulos 2003), while all administrative and military monumental architecture was destroyed. Sites were resettled in some regions (Jung 2010). People continued to use chamber tombs, reusing old ones and building new; at the same time, new practices of cremation and single burial were introduced (Hitchcock 2010b; Mee and Cavanagh 1984). Even international trade did not fully disappear; LH IIIC vessels reached Italy, the Levant, and, especially, Cyprus.

But this recovery was short-lived (Shelton 2010). The loss of an elite class meant that economic resources to fuel a recovery were limited, and LH IIIC society seems to have existed at a subsistence level, with no need for monumental structures, writing, fresco painting, or any other signs of elite administration. By 1100 BCE mainland Greece, Crete, and the Cyclades entered a Dark Age (see later).

Theories explaining the collapse of Mycenaean civilization are varied, and like most collapses, it probably had multiple causes. Natural disasters like an earthquake or drought may have exacerbated a looming crisis, but the fact that the destructions played out over a period of several decades, and resulted in the lopping-off of the entire ruling class, speaks for human protagonists (Betancourt 2007: 156; Drews 1993: 89). The end of the Bronze Age was a time of migration, but an organized and armed invasion of Greece should have led to a replacement of leaders rather than the complete loss of leadership. If new groups moved through Greece at this time, they did not stay, and they uprooted much of the local population. The Sea Peoples and Dorians have both been proposed as invading forces, mentioned in the records of other lands or later accounts of the period. Neither group has left an archaeological signature—a characteristic material culture that could be identified with them with certainty. LH IIIC material culture is, instead, Mycenaean; it is an impoverished version of the architectural and ceramic repertoire that existed at the height of the Mycenaean palaces. It is possible that at least some part of the mainland population migrated to other regions; another part, perhaps including much of the elite, moved off the mainland to Cyprus.

Classical Greece

The Dark Age

Protogeometric Period: The Reappearance of Wealth

Following the Mycenaean collapse, and the subsistence-level existence of LH IIIC, signs of demographic and economic recovery emerged gradually in the Protogeometric Period (ca. 1100–900 BCE), so-called because of the geometric decoration on ceramics made in Athens and the surrounding territory of Attica (see Figure 7.8 for regions and sites dating to the Classical Period). Athens

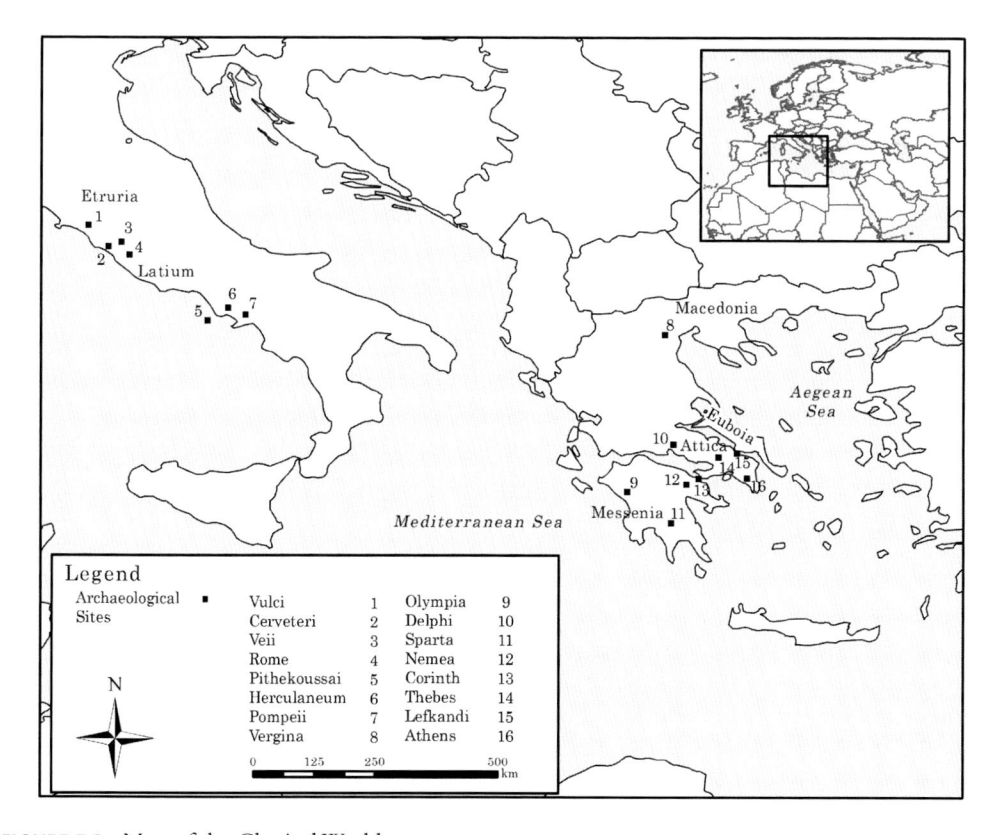

FIGURE 7.8 Map of the Classical World

Source: B. Spencer

in this period continued to consist of houses clustered into small villages, but new developments took place on the island of Euboia, off the Attic coast. There, the earliest monumental non-domestic architecture of the post-Mycenaean Age was built at Lefkandi: an apsidal structure of mudbrick on a stone base, measuring 45 by 10 meters, with wooden columns along the two sides and an additional row inside. Unusual in its plan and size, the structure also held a pair of wealthy cremation burials: a man, his bones set in a bronze vessel, with an iron sword and spear and a woman with numerous gold ornaments. In an adjoining cist were the bones of four horses. No contemporary burials in Greece are comparable in monumentality or wealth. In subsequent generations, additional wealthy tombs were set near the structure, suggesting that this was the tomb of the founder of an elite dynasty. The name archaeologists have given it, Heroön—applied in antiquity to the burials of heroes, which received offerings and care similar to temples—reflects this interpretation (Osborne 1996: 43). Besides the rich couple at Lefkandi, Protogeometric Period burials show limited expenditure of wealth, although the numbers of goods deposited within graves increased toward the end of the 10th century (Morris 1987: 18–20). As at Lefkandi, most adult burials of the time in Athens were cremations, another change from the previous period.

Geometric Period Greece: Literacy, Art, and the Emergence of the Polis

During the subsequent Geometric Period (ca. 900–700 BCE), the signs of recovery, seen already in places like Lefkandi, spread, and evidence for both wealth and the suppression of its overt expression emerged. Among the most significant changes of the time was the reintroduction of writing, an innovation that brought the Dark Age to its end around 750 BCE. Political and economic developments, new social organization, and a corpus of art and literature focusing on human concerns indicate that settlements began a transition to city-state (*polis*) organization at this time. Explanations for this phenomenon vary, but growing international contacts, culminating in Greece's first overseas colonies at the end of the period, were a factor.

As a first element in the rising prosperity in the Geometric Period, the 8th century saw a rise in settlement numbers and in overall population density across Greece (Osborne 1996: 70). Houses were rectilinear, multi-roomed, and probably occupied by nuclear families (Morris 1997). Temple buildings were constructed in mudbrick: long, narrow structures with columns around and through the center of the building. Offering the first evidence for formal religious practices in the post-Mycenaean period, these structures could be located in the middle of a town or at its edge, or even outside a settlement altogether. Temple buildings are attested on the Athenian Acropolis and other towns around Attica, in locations associated later with major gods of the Greek pantheon.

Altars and temples were more than places for prayer and adoration of the gods. Temple-building, and subsequent rituals, provided opportunities for constructing community based on a common core of beliefs and practices. A community's identification with its patron deity and his or her temple lasted into the Hellenistic Period. Because they served as gathering spots, sanctuaries could also host events of competitive display; during the Geometric Period, significant numbers of metal objects, especially figurines, were dedicated to the gods. It is assumed that these dedications were made by individuals and families to accompany a prayer or as thank-offerings after a wish was granted. Some Geometric Period sanctuaries received foreign goods, sometimes in significant numbers; items from Egypt, Cyprus, Anatolia, Phoenicia, and Italy are among those identified (Osborne 1996: 93). At Olympia, a rise in dedications coming from various parts of Greece may mark the advent of the pan-Hellenic Olympic Games, traditionally dated to 776 BCE.

The display and deposit of wealth in sanctuaries during the Geometric Period stands in stark contrast to the situation in cemeteries, where such displays apparently were suppressed. In Athens, a number of changes to burial strategies and practices took place in the 8th century, including a sharp increase in the number of burials and a shift back to inhumation. While the increase in burials was due in part to increased population, seen also in the settlement patterns of the time, Morris (1987: 125) regards it as evidence for an opening-up of Athenian cemeteries to a wider range of social personae than previously. At the same time (around 750 BCE), the number of grave goods deposited in Attic graves declined sharply (Osborne 1996: 82), another indication that social categories were being realigned. But not all people received the same kind of burial, which suggests continuing divisions in society.

Changes in social structure are articulated in other kinds of evidence. Artwork of the Geometric Period includes depictions on ceramic vessels, the most ornate of which must have been the work of specialists, and figurines of terracotta and bronze, found especially at sanctuaries. Figural decoration on pottery is found in Athens and beyond, with representations of humans increasing dramatically around 750 BCE (Coldstream 1991). Major motifs include men accompanying or riding horses, women dancing, men wrestling, and a variety of isolated animals. Depictions of shipwrecks may be early references to myths (de Polignac 1994). Peculiar to Athens was the depiction of funerary rituals: the laying out of the body, mourning by family members and companions, and the procession to the grave by wagon (Figure 7.9a). These scenes are appropriate to the usage of these vessels, as they marked the location of a grave. The "geometric" label is appropriate to all of these vessels; they are decorated with bands of repeated shapes, and even the natural elements are highly stylized and repetitive.

"Geometric" also applies to small three-dimensional works found in sanctuaries. These include numerous animal figurines, perhaps standing in as symbolic sacrifices (Figure 7.9b). Especially popular were bronze figurines of warriors, representing gods or, perhaps, wealthy donors (Stewart 1990). These too look as though they were conceived as a collection of shapes: a triangular head, triangular or rectangular torso, thin cylinders for legs, arms, and neck.

Some of the inspiration for this figural art may derive from increased international contacts in the course of the Geometric Period (Powell 1997a). A number of sanctuaries received Near Eastern goods. It is impossible to know how these objects arrived at a given sanctuary: were they dedicated by Greeks who had acquired them in the east? Or were they brought by Phoenicians from the Levantine coast who had contacts with the source areas?

By the 8th century, Greek cities were actively involved in trade, first perhaps through Phoenician middlemen, then independently. Greek pottery reached the Levantine coast as early as the

FIGURE 7.9 Geometric Period Art: a. Krater and b. Figurine

Source: Left: National Archaeological Museum, Athens, Greece, © Vanni Archive / Art Resource, NY; Right: Metropolitan Museum of Art, New York, USA

10th century; by the 8th century, a wide range of vessel types, largely associated with feasting, were imported (Hodos 2006: 39). In the other direction, Greek pottery began to appear in northern Italy early in the 8th century; this is usually interpreted as the result of Greek exploration for copper, but it inaugurated a long-term set of cultural interactions with Etruria that had a major impact on the development of Italian societies (see later) (Osborne 1996: 105).

In the second quarter of the 8th century, the age of Greek colonization began, with the founding of Pithekoussai on an island in the Gulf of Naples in southern Italy by a group of colonists from Euboia. For the most part, Greek colonies were established by individual city-states. The Euboians were soon joined in southern Italy and on Sicily by settlers from Corinth and Megara in Greece, and from Rhodes and Crete. On arrival, Greek colonists met Iron Age Italian inhabitants, who opposed or accommodated the newcomers, or both (Hodos 2006: 152–53). At the same time, Phoenicians from the Levant were establishing colonies in many of the same areas. A distinction between the types of settlement provides a view into the motivations behind colonization: while the Phoenicians settled harbor towns along the coast that would serve as ports of trade, Greek settlements pushed further inland and were founded near arable land and valued resources (Crielaard 1995). They provided land and opportunities that may not have been available at home. Described as "spear-won land," they were also places of competition and conflict (Cartledge 1998). The idea of the polis, a community defined by the unified self-interest of its citizens, had its origins in this aspect of the Geometric Period.

Prolonged contact with the Phoenicians brought a further innovation to Greek society in the 8th century: the reintroduction of writing. Objects with Phoenician alphabetic script appear in 9th century contexts in Greece (Osborne 1996: 107); by the early 8th century, the Greeks adopted the Phoenician system and added vowels to write their own language. The earliest known object with Greek writing comes from Gabii, near Rome, and has been dated to 775 BCE (Powell 1997b). The invention of the Greek alphabet must have taken place somewhere with repeated and prolonged Greek-Phoenician contacts; Euboia, Cyprus, and the Levant are most often suggested, but Italy is also possible (Hurwit 1993; Powell 1997b).

The Archaic Period: City-States in Development

During the Archaic Period (ca. 700–479 BCE), the fledgling political institutions of the Geometric Period took root, and Greek city-states (*poleis*, from the singular polis) began to develop their individualized characters. Although art historical and historical surveys often subdivide these two centuries into Orientalizing (ca. 700–600 BCE) and Archaic (ca. 600–479 BCE) subphases, it is just as appropriate to treat them as continuous in nature. Each polis underwent a unique set of transformations, but all were characterized by competition among classes and power struggles among elites. Competition broadened into conflict between city-states as well and became a component in pan-Hellenic identity, epitomized by the various intercity games that started at Olympia. Conflict and competition were celebrated in the literature of the Archaic Period and enshrined in colonial endeavors; they reached their peak of importance with the wars against Persia (490–479 BCE). The first written Greek laws to survive appear intended to allay and refocus the more violent consequences of competition. In Athens, the best-known and best-documented of the Archaic city-states, legislation intended to stave off violent clashes led ultimately to the establishment of democratic institutions in 508–507 BCE.

During the Archaic Period, settlement numbers and sizes continued to increase. In excavated towns and cities, agora areas—open spaces that housed a variety of public institutions, including meeting spaces, altars, and shops—were established at this time. Athens's original Agora was on the northeastern side of the Acropolis; late in the 6th century, the Classical Period Agora was drained and leveled to provide for the needs of new institutions of the city (Figure 7.10). Houses continued to follow a courtyard plan; despite a stated ideal that the sexes should be separate even at home, there is little physical evidence for spatial differentiation within excavated houses (Jameson 1990). The exceptions are spaces that were open to the street: privately owned shops and the *andron*, a distinctive space for male dining and leisure, characterized by couches along the walls and an open space for food and drink service in the center.

The numbers of temples increased again in the Archaic Period, especially during the 6th century. Structures previously made of wood and brick were transformed into buildings of stone. Even when these were replaced by even larger and more ornate structures in later periods, their foundations survive. Many scholars have attributed the inspiration for stone construction to Egypt, part of a package of influences on Greek life that also affected representations of the human figure but that mysteriously left no imprint on political or economic life. The basic Greek temple plan had two or three rooms and was entered from one of the short sides, like Bronze Age megarons (see Figure 7.2); it had a gabled roof with terracotta or stone roof tiles, supported by columns around the outside and on the inside. Painted scenes on flat square *metopes* (decorative elements right below the roof line in Classical architecture) depicted mythological characters and scenes (de Polignac 1994).

Hesiod's *Theogony*, written around 700 BCE, combines a genealogy of the Greek gods with snippets of myth; Homer's tales, dating about 50 years earlier, also provide various stories about the Olympian gods. Artworks of the Archaic Period—adorning the temples and painted on vases—complement

FIGURE 7.10 Plan of Classical Period Athens

Source: J.C. Ross

these written sources and indicate that many additional stories of gods and heroes circulated widely. During the Archaic Period, the technology and artistry of vase-painting developed, first at Corinth, where individuals in miniature scenes of myth were identified with captions (Figure 7.11a), and then in Attica, where events from the legends of Perseus and Odysseus were especially popular (Figure 7.11b). Corinthian and Attic pots fill museums but are rarely found in excavations. Most were dedicated in sanctuaries or went into graves; many, in fact, traveled to Italy—to Greek colonies and trade partners—and became part of funerary deposits there (Shanks 1999: 176). Images of gods and heroes were often appropriate to the vessels on which they were depicted: Dionysus, the god of wine, appears on a great many vessels for wine storage, mixing, and drinking, while Athena, patron goddess of Athens thanks to her gift of the olive tree to the city and goddess of competition, was depicted on thousands of oil-filled jars given to victors in Athens's Panathenaic games.

The major sanctuaries of Greece—Olympia, Athens, Delphi, and Nemea—were gathering spots for Greeks from around the Mediterranean and for visitors from foreign lands. At Delphi, people came to ask advice of the oracle of Apollo; the questions and answers often had political implications. Pan-Hellenic competitions were held at all four of these sanctuaries; games were on a regular schedule, and cities ceased fighting for a time to channel their hostilities into athletic competitions. Some sports favored aristocratic investment, such as chariot races, but many were open to all competitors (Kyle 1992). In Athens, part of the Panathenaic games was devoted to competition in musical events and recitation. These sanctuaries brought men together in a spirit of shared Greek identity, while still enflaming competitive feelings. In Athens, that competitiveness was also on view during the twice-annual festivals of Dionysus, when the god was celebrated in theatrical performances of tragic and comic plays, themselves a competition among playwrights.

FIGURE 7.11 Archaic Period Pottery: a. Corinthian Oenochoe, Showing Thetis Consoling Achilles; and b. Attic Black Figure Showing the Blinding of Polyphemus

Source: a. Musees Royaux d'Art et d'Histoire, Brussels, Belgium (SEF / Art Resource, NY); b. © Trustees of the British Museum

Economic and Sociopolitical Organization of the Archaic Period

Farming continued to provide the bulk of economic prosperity in the Archaic Period; the Greeks idealized the image of self-sufficient agricultural households. But neither land, nor the labor that went into it, were evenly distributed across society. Lin Foxhall (2007: 75) estimates that by the Classical Period, when the Athenian democratic ethos dominated the political system, a mere 10% of the citizen population held one-third or more of the land. The situation in other regions of Greece was even more uneven. Over the course of the Archaic Period, the Spartans subjugated the neighboring territory of Messenia and created a class of helots—a subordinate population who farmed their lands while citizen Spartans trained for war. Continued colonization in Italy and North Africa provided new income for Greek cities, as well as a supply of foreign-born slaves.

Besides farming (which included a diversified set of crops, including olive and grape), a number of occupational specialties developed. Most agricultural households likely produced most of the things they needed, and very few luxuries appear in the archaeological record. The exceptions are sculpture in stone and vase-painting. That these types of works were signed suggests that some degree of expertise in these fields was recognized, and particular architects, sculptors, potters, and painters were sought out. These specialists appear to have been independent; they fulfilled both private and public commissions, with architects and sculptors traveling to locations where their services were needed. Pottery workshops in Attica were hierarchically organized, with a "master potter" at the head and an array of assistants below him.

Archaic Period city-states experienced tremendous internal economic differentiation, and competition among elites was a major factor in persistent fighting within the city-states and periodic conflict with other poleis. While elite display moved from grave to sanctuary contexts in the Geometric Period, in the Archaic Period the movement went in the opposite direction: wealthy families set lavish sculptural monuments atop the graves of young men. These included *kouros* (literally, "young man") statues (Figure 7.12a): nude, painted marble, life-sized males depicted at the height of their beauty, with broad shoulders, narrow waists, and muscular builds (Carter and Steinberg 2010). It is unclear if these statues were portraits or if they epitomized the warrior and athletic ideal of the time (Osborne 1988; Stewart 1990: 109–10).

Kouros statues were also dedicated in sanctuaries, where they were joined by a clothed female counterpart, the *kore* ("maiden") (Figure 7.12b). Dedicatory inscriptions on the Athenian Acropolis suggest that many different kinds of people could afford these dedications; a number of men, in fact, dedicated kore statues, presumably representations of Athena in this context (Keesling 2003: 98). Other statue types, both large and small, were dedicated on the Acropolis, as were other objects. People from all walks of life, including a variety of occupations, could leave dedications in Athens and presumably other cities; this is a marked change from the Geometric Period pattern of elite dedications.

Elite competition was overt in the workings of city-state politics. Historical sources indicate that different city-states had different political organizations, juxtaposing royal powers with oligarchic control by senior males and more representative deliberative bodies (assemblies). Each government was the outcome of particular tensions within the city and of actions against neighboring polities. Sparta's subjugation of its neighbors has already been noted; it also had an unusual leadership structure with two simultaneous, hereditary kings from competing families, who maintained the city's vigilance with periodic military campaigns. Battles in the Archaic Period required masses of heavily armed hoplite warriors, expensive to arm and to maintain, an innovation that required the recruitment of more and more men.

In Athens, the 6th-century elite class broke into factions based on family ties and loyalties, resulting in periodic violence and seizure of political control by tyrants (single rulers). These high-born men relied on outside help from cities like Sparta (Osborne 1996: 215). Eventually, factions turned

FIGURE 7.12 a. Kouros From Volomandra, ca. 560 BCE; b. Peplos Kore, ca. 530 BCE. Acropolis Museum, Athens, Greece

Source: a. National Archaeological Museum, Athens, Greece (Universal Images Group / Art Resource, NY); b. Nimatallah / Art Resource, NY

to legislation to quell the violence and to prevent Athens from falling into enemy hands. A series of lawgivers, including the famous Solon, sought to redistribute power and wealth and to redefine rules of citizenship to build more ties between men and their city. Their reforms, requiring periodic renewal and revision due to rekindled violence, eventually inspired the constitution of Kleisthenes, in 508–507, establishing a democratic form of government.

The End of the Archaic and Transition to the Classical Age: Athenian Democracy and Struggles

The Classical Age (479–336 BCE) is the Golden Age of Athenian democracy (see Box 7.4), with new ideals of political engagement and identities that spread throughout the Greek world, though the effects of those ideas were highly variable. It was preceded by a period of 30 years, during which two major events set the stage for it: the democratic reforms of Kleisthenes in 508–507 and the Persian Wars (490–479). The reforms introduced to Athens in 508–507 BCE were intended to counteract power struggles among the elite that had inflicted significant violence in the city; in turn, they reorganized the political, economic, and social structure, bringing to Athenian citizens a broad new set of legal rights and political powers. Athenian democracy did not offer rights to the majority of its residents: women, foreign residents, and slaves were excluded from the rights of citizenship. Nor did it end conflict; struggles continued within Athens, and intermittent warfare against both Greek and non-Greek foes continued. Attempts by Athens to impose democracy on other Greek territories led to debates over how just the democratic system was. Historians, archaeologists, and literary scholars possess a rich array of sources on this period coming from Athens; considerably less information is available on other city-states, and much of what survives derives from the Athenian standpoint.

BOX 7.4 ATHENIAN AND ROMAN REPRESENTATIONAL GOVERNMENTS

Athenian Democracy

The reforms of Kleisthenes in Athens in 508 or 507 BCE expanded freedoms provided by 6th-century legislation. They reorganized the populace of Athens and its hinterlands into ten "tribes" that cross-cut lineages and topography to reduce family loyalties and geographic advantages. The tribes then became the basis for military organization and for the administrative and legislative bodies: the Council of 500 (50 men per tribe, chosen by lot) and the Assembly, consisting of all citizens over 18, which debated and enacted legislation forwarded to them by the Council. Few offices remained hereditary, further reducing the power and influence of the upper class. Even the position of *strategos*, responsible for military preparation and action and therefore the most powerful in the state, was shared by ten men at a time. No office in Athens afforded a single person lasting political power.

Roman Republicanism

Roman state offices were religious, economic, legal, and military in function. Most turned over each year; the exception was the "dictator," who was appointed in times of military emergency and was expected to surrender his powers at the end of the crisis. At a certain point during the Republic, some priesthoods became lifetime positions, including the Vestal Virgins, a group of aristocratic women who guarded the sacred fire of Rome, symbolic of the city's perpetual existence, and some of its most important documents. Other than priestly positions, the annual rotation of men in and out of office was intended to restrict any one person's ability to garner personal power and prestige, so that political service retained the sense of a moral duty to the community of Rome.

Athens was not the only city to expel its tyrants in the 6th or 5th century, and a number of city-states adopted similar democratic reforms in the decades that followed. Others, like Sparta, maintained their monarchies, although most advocated citizens' rights and responsibilities. Throughout Greece, to be a citizen was to participate in political decision-making and to fight for the polis;

this was the ideology behind Sparta's extraordinary system of military training (Cartledge 1998; Osborne 2000). The endemic warfare of the 5th century justified such a standpoint and may have encouraged the adoption of liberal definitions of citizenship in order to expand the rolls of eligible fighters.

Nearly all city-states of peninsular Greece were drawn into the Persian Wars of 490–479 BCE, beginning when the Greek cities of Ionia revolted against the overlordship of the Persian Empire. Athens sent help in 499 BCE, but the Persian forces maintained their foothold. Herodotus, the historian of these wars, indicates that the Persian kings then set their sights on control of Greece itself. Athens led the Greek resistance to the Persian invasions of 490 and 480–479, calling on all mainland cities to defend Greece and fostering a pan-Hellenic identity and ideology built on a common language, religion, and interests. Although Persian forces sacked Athens, the Greek defense held, and Greek victories on land and sea forced Persia to retreat.

The Classical Age: Athenian Highs and Lows

After victory in the Persian Wars, Greek unity swiftly fractured, and city-states revived long-standing rivalries. Athens parlayed its leadership against Persia into a new alliance, the Delian League; allies contributed ships or tribute in silver to guard against further Persian incursions. Many of the Cycladic Islands quickly joined up, so that the new alliance rivaled the Sparta-controlled Peloponnesian League. In practice, Athens supplied most of the naval power, manning its ships with lower-class men and slaves. When the Delian League treasury was transferred to Athens, the tribute payments funded public works in the city.

This growth of Athenian power and self-image did not go unchallenged. Athens began to speak of its allies as being under its "control," and some revolted (Cartledge 1998). It was clear that Athens used the threat of military force to create an empire; when it defeated a former ally, it appropriated land on which it established a colony (Morris 2008). Eventually, Sparta began hostilities against Athens in the two-phase Peloponnesian War, 431–421 and 412–404 BCE. As described by Thucydides and Xenophon, the course of the war was determined by a combination of charismatic personalities, intrigue, infighting, and disastrous decisions made by both sides. The war eventually extended to Sicily, where an Athenian loss left thousands of men stranded and subjected to forced labor. In the end, Athens surrendered, and Sparta imposed an oligarchic government on the city. This was swiftly overthrown, but Athens never regained the full force of its democratic institutions. The 4th century saw the rise of a monarchy ruling multiple poleis in Macedonia in the north. A delicate balance of power, with near-constant skirmishing, held until the second half of the 4th century.

The Archaeology of Complexity in Classical Athens

Though recorded in contemporary histories and plays, the great battles of the 5th and 4th centuries have left little mark on the archaeological record. Rather, Classical Age archaeology offers an image of tremendous prosperity, with strategic investment in public buildings for worship, governance, competition, and performance. This is especially the case for Athens, where much of the funding for construction derived from the city's allies. At Athens, the basic city layout changed little over the course of the Classical Period.

The greatest transformations in the years following the Persian Wars took place in the main public spaces of the city: the Agora and the Acropolis. Work took place first on the Agora, where structures were built for meetings (the Round Stoa), worship (the Sanctuary of Theseus), and educational purposes (the Painted Stoa) (Pedley 1998: 215–16). The open space of the Agora served as a meeting space for other deliberative bodies and for worship; it was adorned with sculptural dedications that reminded viewers of the sacrifices made for the sake of democracy (the statue of the Tyrannicides) and of the city's glorious present (portraits and anonymous athletes). While the assembly of all citizens originally met in the Agora, a dedicated space west of the Acropolis, the Pnyx, was created in the early 5th century for meetings of these 6,000 to 13,000 men.

After 450 BCE, construction shifted to the Acropolis, with a building program intended to celebrate the city's patron goddess Athena and other gods of the city. These buildings also symbolized Athenian history and its present position. The epitome of this expression was the Parthenon, a new temple to Athena, which also may have served as the city's treasury. Its pediment sculpture depicted major events in the life of the goddess (her birth and victory over Poseidon for patronage of the city); its metopes portrayed divine and heroic battles. The meaning of the frieze that wrapped around the entire structure has been fiercely debated; it depicts a religious procession of soldiers, citizens, and Athenian women, culminating in a scene where a garment is folded by a man and child in the presence of the Olympian gods. Whether this showed the yearly ritual in honor of Athena, or its mythical origin, is unclear (Connelly 2014; Neils 2001). Inside the temple stood a colossal statue of the goddess, gleaming with a layer of ivory and gold. The building and its ornament took 15 years to complete and brought the most famous architects and sculptors in the Greek world to Athens. It invited Athenians and visitors to contemplate the reasons for Athens's success—the steadfastness of its citizens and the favor of its gods—while underplaying or ignoring other possible local and recent histories.

The Parthenon was surrounded by other temple buildings and by an array of sculptural dedications. These increased after 450, then dropped again in the 4th century, after the Athenian defeat in the Peloponnesian War and the subsequent decline in democracy (Keesling 2003). The Theater of Dionysus, erected on the southern slope of the Acropolis in the early to mid-5th century and periodically expanded, was another location for the celebration of democracy. Attendance at tragic and comic performances was a part of religious festivals; plays were performed and judged by citizen males and funded by the polis and wealthy citizens. The theater setting was much like the law court and assembly where citizens judged the quality of performance and argument. Tragic playwrights—Aeschylus, Sophocles, and Euripides foremost among them—used myth and legend to confront the audience with the most important paradoxes of their age: the tension of loyalties to family and state, mother and father, personal achievement and service to the greater good of society. Comic plays often covered the same themes but with characters drawn from contemporary Athens. Other patriotic actions were incorporated into the same festivals of Dionysus: ritual acts by the ten elected generals, the display of annual tribute from the Delian League, and a parade of war orphans as part of their initiation, which committed the city and citizens to their continued support (Goldhill 1990).

The sculpture that adorned Athenian temples and open spaces is often considered the apex of Classical art. In many ways, it also characterized the ideals of citizenship, celebrating youth and beauty with perfectly proportioned bodies and an absence of facial expression. In Classical Period art, the only figures who express emotion are extremely young or extremely old men, and women—all people who were not considered citizens or who could no longer enjoy or contribute to the full responsibilities of citizenship. The same ideals, including the need to suppress emotion, were expressed in speeches, such as Pericles's funerary oration over Athenian dead soldiers, in 431 or 430, as reported by Thucydides. As democratic institutions broke down in the 4th century, there was a concomitant experimentation with emotion in sculpture.

Styles of vase-painting also evolved during the Classical Age, as domestic scenes in red figure became more popular than mythical ones, probably reflecting changing tastes and a different customer base. Vessels for wine-drinking featured symposium scenes of males dining, often in the company of female courtesans and musicians. But storage vessels and water jugs—vessel types that may have been given to brides as gifts—portrayed a variety of courtship, marriage, and daily life scenes in which women took active roles (Sutton 1992). After Athenian losses in the Peloponnesian War, the Attic ceramic industry went into decline, and the center for red figure production moved to southern Italy.

While Athens offers an array of architectural and artistic riches, most of them well dated, by which to trace the development of Greek sociopolitical institutions, other cities did not lag far behind. The sanctuaries of Apollo at Delphi and Zeus at Olympia underwent significant phases of construction and ornamentation in the Classical Period, by some of the same artists and architects who worked in Athens. Much of this work was funded by donations that came from participants in the pan-Hellenic games held at both sites and from visitors to their oracles. The wealthy Greek colonies in south Italy and Sicily also built imposing sanctuaries. While Athenian wealth meant that its value system survived in text and archaeology most prominently, the archaeological evidence suggests that a similar set of polis-centric values was held throughout Greece and its colonies in southern Italy.

Much has already been said about the economic systems of the Classical Period city-states and need not be repeated here. The Greek ideal of the self-sufficient farming household continued to be upheld, although many urban-dwellers lived far from their agricultural holdings. Much of the day-to-day work on the farms—from farm labor to tool manufacture and repair to wool production—would have been done by slaves. The Classical Period population of Athens, estimated at 250,000 to 500,000, included 30,000 to 100,000 slaves, or 10%–30% of the population, with perhaps 3 or 4 slaves per household (duBois 2009; Oakley 2000).

Even with its emphasis on farming, Athens imported a significant amount of grain, especially from North Africa, to feed its population; piracy, warfare, and bad seas had the potential to significantly disrupt the food supply. Athens was also celebrated for the rich variety of items that arrived through its port. While much of this external trade was in perishable goods and therefore archaeologically invisible, it is significant that Athenian domestic contexts were austere (Morris 1992: 120); egalitarian ideals discouraged individual spending and ideally funneled luxuries to the gods and the state.

The democratic reforms of 508–507 did not eliminate the importance of family and lineage to the social structure of Athenian society, though it did reduce disparities in the distribution of wealth and rights based on lineage. In fact, the constitutional reform placed new focus on legitimacy of birth as a means of access to citizenship. The effect was the imposition of new restrictions on women, whose supposed sexual appetites seem to have inspired (and horrified) writers from Hesiod to Aristophanes. Both written and iconographic sources stressed that women should remain secluded in the house, so that wives could focus on their proper role of bearing and raising legitimate heirs. Women performed public rituals and probably equally important but behind-the-scenes roles in family political and economic actions. Masculinist ideology was certainly not limited to Athens, but it played out differently in each polis. In Sparta, for instance, girls as well as boys were expected to undergo athletic training. But in no city-state could women vote or hold office.

The Hellenistic Age: The Re-Emergence of Monarchy

To say that these social, economic, and political conditions changed significantly in the Hellenistic Age (336–146 BCE) is nothing short of an understatement. This period saw Greek values and culture extend across the Near East and Egypt due to the spread of the empire won by Alexander of

Macedon (Alexander the Great). But the culture of Greece was much changed due to imperial organization. Most significantly, it had a single ruler at its head and a capital city with royal architecture and tombs. While cities survived and thrived, the organizing principles of citizenship and polis identity disappeared. This created new possibilities for social and economic mobility and revised attitudes toward women's activities, while political control rested firmly in the hands of royal families. Throughout the empire, mixed populations of Greek and local origin blended cultural features, with greater or less success. Alexander's empire then set the stage for Roman expansion into the same areas: first Greece, then Egypt and parts of the Near East.

Historical Background

The rise of the kingdom of Macedonia, in the far northeastern corner of Greece, was not a complete surprise to Greeks of the 4th century, but neither was it fully desirable. Macedonian kings had involved themselves in the affairs of their southern neighbors during the 5th century, most notably by playing both sides during the Peloponnesian War. Timber was a major Macedonian export, particularly important in the construction of Athenian ships. In its early days (the 6th and 5th centuries), the Macedonian state appears to have consisted of a confederacy of poleis, each self-sufficient, under the overarching control of a tax- and tribute-collecting ruler, who did not otherwise interfere in their affairs.

That situation changed in the mid-4th century, with the accession of Philip II (360–336 BCE) and his son Alexander III (the Great) (336–323 BCE). Philip rebuilt the Macedonian kingdom, using warfare and diplomacy in equal measure, and restructured the government in such a way that cities' democratic institutions survived but were under the authority of the king (Hatzopoulos 2011a, 2011b). Alexander expanded the Macedonian realm to include all of Greece, then conquered Egypt and Persia in succession, relying on a vast mercenary army and on the weakness of the central governments in both areas. With these conquests, the Macedonian Empire stretched nearly to India, over 5 million square kilometers.

After Alexander's death, his empire was subdivided among his three main assistants: Ptolemy I controlled Egypt, Seleucus I took Syria and the Near East, and Antigonus governed Macedonia. No single governmental structure took root, and some semiautonomous dynasties were established in the territories in between. Still, the Hellenistic Empire survived for 200 more years, largely because it offered a flexible enough system to be assimilated into local structures of governance. Eventually, the Romans added each of the Macedonian regions to their own growing empire, beginning with Macedonia (167 BCE) and Greece (146 BCE), then Asia Minor (133 BCE), and finally parts of Seleucia (starting 191 BCE) and Egypt (30 BCE).

Settlement and Cities

The Macedonian Empire grew and shrank over its time span of 200–300 years, with much of its organization embedded in local conditions and pre-existing political structures. With a population of 30 to 50 million people, very little could have bound the areas together. What Alexander created relied heavily on three features: the pre-existing system of Persian provincial governments (satrapies), which collected taxes and governed individual regions; a highly mobile army that was well armed, well paid, and supplied from the taxes paid into satrapal coffers; and a unifying appearance of Greek culture and values, spread by free movement around the Empire, but especially by the relocation of Greeks into urban centers in newly conquered lands. There, Greek became the language of choice for the elite educated class, temples and altars to the Olympian gods were built, and public spaces were filled with art in Greek artistic styles.

Archaeological Evidence of Hellenistic Power

The monarchical organization of the Hellenistic Period introduced the most significant changes to the Greek city-states and had, arguably, the greatest impact on the archaeological record of the time. The standing mercenary army, with its heavy reliance on cavalry, was capable of campaigning year-round. This allowed it to travel much longer distances at a time, with no need to turn back for agricultural or other seasonal duties. The army was paid in coinage and with land in Macedonia and elsewhere. The Classical ideal, which equated citizenship with readiness to fight on behalf of one's polis, became a thing of the past. The loyalty of a soldier was to his king, who led the army on campaign.

Democratic institutions in the Greek city-states were largely left intact after the Macedonian takeover (Hornblower 1983: 276). But decision-making power was reduced to questions of local management, while the king, his councilors, and provincial government systems stood above them. In Egypt and the Near East, where imperial rule was the norm, Macedonian control changed very little about government structures, other than the ethnicity of the king and the language of the bureaucracy.

The physical signs of kingship had a major impact on urban design, architecture, and art. New kinds of buildings appeared in Greece during the Hellenistic Period. Most obvious is the construction of palaces, best attested at Vergina (ancient Aegae) in Macedonia, where Philip built an impressive structure on a hillside, combining outward-facing stoas (as in an agora) with an inward-facing monumental courtyard "house" (Kottaridi 2011; Lane Fox 2011). The palace's interior courtyard included a surrounding colonnade, with rooms devoted to reception, dining, and worship opening off it. These rooms were lavishly decorated with mosaic floors, an artistic genre with its origins in Macedonia. It was a building intended for display and diplomacy, visible from all parts of the city.

Royal sponsorship of buildings and new cities and towns extended to all ends of the empire. In some cases, typical Greek building forms—stoas, peristyle temples, and theaters—appeared in new places. Greek learning and literature also spread, leading to the construction of libraries in places like Pergamon in Asia Minor and Alexandria in Egypt. Kings and governors facilitated trading activities by creating agoras and stoas, as well as through the introduction of a single coinage system. The combination of wealth and cosmopolitanism resulted in construction on a massive scale in the imperial capitals and in secondary centers.

This monumental scale also applied to artistic production in the Hellenistic Age, a complementary sphere of royal sponsorship. The spread of Hellenistic styles and artistic themes was a means of assimilation in newly conquered areas (Stephens 2009). Hellenistic sculptural style built on earlier Greek artistic ideals of youth and beauty but with a new emphasis on expression and emotion. Both mythological and historical scenes were represented in painting and sculpture. Some of the most stunning art comes from Pergamon in Asia Minor, where an open-air altar to Zeus included both local legend and the cosmological story of the battle between the Olympian gods and the Giants. Bodies twist, faces show pain, and the viewer feels the tension of the battle (Stewart 1983). Hellenistic art portrayed dramatic moments: the honorable death of a vanquished enemy (the Dying Gaul), the precarious balance of a goddess alighting on the prow of a ship (Nike of Samothrace), the kidnapping of Persephone (on the walls of a royal tomb at Vergina). Other artwork represented royal personages in such a way as to embody personality: the upward tilt of Alexander's head in portrait statues conveyed both vigor and thoughtfulness (Pedley 1998: 301–2). The exaggeration of movement and emotion may have been a means of communicating across cultural boundaries, perhaps more successfully than the earlier emotionless Classicizing styles had.

Hellenistic Economic and Social Organization

Tremendous wealth was deposited in the tombs of Hellenistic kings, a sharp break from Classical Age austerity and indicative of the imposing display that took place during royal funerary rituals (Whitley 2009). Royal tomb deposits also draw attention to the new levels of economic differentiation in the Hellenistic Age. Kings signified their power by founding new cities and establishing new temples, providing for the economic and religious needs of their subjects in all regions of the realm. These trends, though, were cross-cut by others that allowed for class mobility; with freer movement of goods and services came the capacity to enhance one's economic position. Members of the army, craftsmen, and merchants could gain wealth and status in this new, wider world. Greek economic institutions, especially a reliance on long-distance trade and on coinage, spread into territories with older traditions and were incorporated in new ways (Manning 2007).

As materials moved across the Hellenistic kingdoms, so did ideas and even gods. Temples to the Olympian gods sprang up across the empire; some gods were easily syncretized to local divinities. The exchange went both ways, as the Anatolian Mother Goddess Cybele became increasingly popular in Greece, and Egyptian gods attained standing there also (Roller 1999). Local Hellenistic rulers sponsored temple-building in their lands as well (Manning 2007).

Kingship itself required new forms of ritual. Living Hellenistic kings received divine honors; in Egypt, this represented no change to regular practice, whereas Greek city-states were unaccustomed to such worship. Rituals were intended to integrate populations into the Hellenistic system, creating new community identities that overcame prior political and social commitments.

As noted earlier, the loss of emphasis on citizenship allowed for greater economic and social mobility. It also loosened many of the restrictions on women's activities, as legitimacy of children became less of a concern. Judging from art and literature, Hellenistic women were more visible than their Classical Period predecessors (Lefkowitz 1983). With the spread of Greek values and language, the strength of older ethnic and linguistic identities declined.

The Roman World

Bronze Age Italy

The Roman Empire was the eventual beneficiary of the Hellenistic state. Unlike Greece, where the Bronze Age cultures provided precedents for later cultural developments, Bronze Age (ca. 2000–900 BCE) occupation in Italy was limited to village settlements throughout the peninsula. The majority of the Bronze Age villages were located in the central mountainous zone of the peninsula; their economy combined pastoralism and farming. In the Late Bronze Age (ca. 1200–900 BCE), site numbers and population increased, settlement spread into the foothills and river valleys, and people practiced cremation burial.

Early Iron Age: The Development of Regional Cultures

Late Bronze Age developments set the stage for the emergence of distinct regional culture groups in the Early Iron Age (900–700 BCE). The main archaeological distinction among groups was their burial practices: while cremation dominated in the northern half of Italy, groups in the south practiced inhumation. Further regional subdivisions likely reflect the geographical isolation of culture groups, each of which probably spoke a distinct language or dialect and developed different economic, social, and religious systems. In the late 8th century, the southern groups began to have periodic and then more intensive contacts with Greek and Phoenician traders and colonists. Some retreated from the area of the coast, while others absorbed or were absorbed by the new settlements.

Differences among the northern cultures were largely manifested in the array of items buried with the dead. It is the southernmost of the groups, called the Villanovan Culture, that is most relevant to subsequent developments. Villanovan practices originated in the area of modern Bologna, but the culture extended as far south as Rome. In tombs across the area, cremation urns were set at the base of burial shafts, together with bronze and iron tools and weapons, jewelry, and pottery (Cornell 1995: 35–36). Around Rome, the urns took the form of one-roomed houses, called "hut-urns." Cemeteries combined a few cremation burials of high-ranking males, buried with miniature vessels and weapons, with inhumation burials of both men and women. This arrangement is suggestive of social organization: prominent male lineage heads, surrounded by descendants and subordinates (Cornell 1995: 51–53). Each village probably consisted of one or more lineage groups, linked by economic and marital ties. Villages were economically self-sufficient with little production beyond the household level.

Evidence at Rome suggests that population there grew in the 8th century, and villages coalesced into larger settlement areas. This prosperity seems based on expanded agriculture and the cultivation of olives and grapes. Enough surplus was produced to allow for some specialization in ceramic production; the growing towns provided markets for producers of foods and wares. The arrival of Greek and Phoenician settlers and merchants in the south, traveling north in search of metals, other resources, and markets, also sparked the development of complexity in central Italy (Cornell 1995).

Urbanism and the Establishment of City-States

Traditionally, archaeologists have turned to Etruria, north of Rome, to examine the origins of urbanism and early states in Italy. More recent excavations suggest that Rome experienced many of the same changes at the same time. But the Etruscans deserve an extended discussion of their own, as their political and economic organization exhibits similarities with Greek city-states, and contrasts to some degree with later Roman developments.

The Etruscans emerged as a distinct cultural and linguistic group in the early 7th century, located in the modern regions of Umbria and Tuscany in northern Italy. They seem to have derived from the prior Villanovan residents of the area, but early contacts with Greek colonists and merchants left a lasting mark on their material culture. As early as the 7th century, Etruscan inscriptions appear, written in an alphabetic script adapted from Greek. Etruscan inscriptions tend to be short, consisting of names and a few other words, hindering translation efforts. Later Roman sources indicate that Etruria was divided into a number of city-states that coexisted in a state of continual competition, alliance, and hostility. Etruscan inscriptions of 6th and 5th century date suggest there were significant numbers of Etruscans in southern Italy as well, with mixed Etruscan-Italian towns coexisting with Greek and Phoenician settlements (Cornell 1995: 154).

Archaeology at Etruscan sites long focused on the extensive cemetery remains, but plenty of information on settlements also exists. In particular, several sites in the southern part of Etruria, closest to Rome, grew in the 7th and 6th centuries. This growth is attributed to economic prosperity derived from trade relations with Greeks and Phoenicians (Peña 2011). The Etruscans possessed rich copper resources. Major settlements combined agricultural and mineral resources with beneficial locations near the coast or on a north-south communications route. Each grew to city-state size, controlling the local territory, in the early 7th century (Redhouse and Stoddart 2011). Elite residents appear to have sponsored building projects in a move to enhance status (Murray 2011).

Relatively little survives of Etruscan houses, which must have been constructed mainly of perishable materials. Houses with a large central space and rooms opening off it are inferred from tomb plans. What does last are painted terracotta panels, which served as decoration for houses. Terracotta is also the main surviving element of Etruscan temples; while the structures themselves were of wood and mud, ceramic roof tiles and sculpture adorned the exteriors. Temple plans are distinct from Greek structures, with a focus on frontality: steps led up to a line of columns along just one side of a rectangular structure. Beyond the columned entrance, a porch led into one or more rooms, each dedicated to the worship of a different god. The temple itself was set on a podium, focusing attention on the building, its decoration, and the people going inside. The structures stood within a walled precinct, marking off the space as holy. The process of enclosing the sanctuary and building up the temple was a way to draw attention to the devotional efforts of elite sponsors (Izzet 2001; Murray 2011).

In the cemeteries of Etruria, this same monumentalizing drive highlighted the economic, political, and social distinction of the elite class. Etruscan cemeteries were located along the roads and pathways outside towns. At Veii and other locations, cemetery use began in the 10th century with Villanovan-type cremations in urns. Over time, though, there was a shift to inhumation burials, and tomb forms became variable. While most people continued to be buried in individual rock-cut cists, a type of multigenerational family tomb emerged, consisting of one or more chambers, also rock-cut, surmounted by an immense mound of earth. These tumulus graves were introduced in the 7th century; at Cerveteri, they reached up to 50 meters in diameter, and 12 to 15 meters high, representing a significant expenditure on labor (Izzet 1996). Inside the tombs, rooms were furnished with furniture and architectural ornament, some carved directly from the rock, thought to imitate the furnishings of elite houses. Bodies were laid on couches as though they were dining in the afterlife. This action was reiterated in the paintings on tomb walls, where men and women were often portrayed in precisely the same attitude (Figure 7.13). Although the Etruscan necropoli

FIGURE 7.13 Etruscan Mural: Detail of a Banqueting Scene, Tomb of the Leopards, Tarquinia, 480–470 BCE
Source: Scala / Art Resource, NY

were robbed extensively in the 19th century, enough has been preserved to know that each tomb held the remains of a number of people, probably multiple generations of a family, as well as a wide range of food, drink, and personal items such as jewelry, weapons, clothing, and mirrors. People retained their identities, and their wealth, in death.

The tombs and their contents suggest that families could occupy a range of economic and social positions within Etruscan society. They provide additional economic information as well: namely, the extent of Etruscan relations with the Greeks, a set of relationships that may have been a major source of wealth for individual cities and families, as well as an important impetus to political and cultural developments. Some of the painted designs in tombs depict scenes drawn from Greek legend, especially the Trojan War cycle. Even more impressive are the hundreds of Greek vessels, especially those made in Attica with black- and red-figure decoration. Vessels were imported over a long period, especially 550–400 BCE. Because Greek vases are found in houses across Etruria, they appear to have had a primarily domestic use, especially in drinking contexts, and then were placed in graves as part of the property of the deceased (Reusser 2002). Attic painters produced some iconography found only in Etruria: women taking part as equal members in of a symposium party, or clothed athletes. They clearly had a particular market in mind (Osborne 2001). Another type of vessel is unexpected: Panathenaic vases, awarded to victors in the games in Athens. Etruscans, as non-Greeks, could not have competed in the games; they must have acquired the vessels, perhaps still filled with the prize oil, through trade (Bentz 1998).

Greek influence in Etruria extended to religious depictions, if not to ritual practice itself. It is unclear what divinities the Etruscans worshipped before contact with the Greeks; after contact, however, some native deities were syncretized with Greek ones, and some Greek gods may have been adopted in full. Life-sized terracotta statues of gods survive from Etruscan sanctuaries, including a statue of Apollo that stood atop the roof of the temple at Veii (Izzet 2001). The striding pose of the god recalls contemporary Greek sculpture, but the figure is fully draped, in Etruscan style.

The paintings from Etruscan tombs expressed an idealized social structure, as did the terracotta sarcophagi that appeared around 520 BCE. In both media, the focus is on the married couple as partners in life and in death, reclining at banquets or dancing (Rowland 2008). While this apparent equality may be more ideal than real, it reiterates the family focus of the burial chamber, with its multiple generations of Etruscan dead.

Etruscan cities appear to have been self-governing, with no overarching federal structure to unite them. Independence was maintained until the Romans began to conquer Etruscan towns in the late 6th century. And even after that time, most Etruscan cities were permitted to remain autonomous, until most of Italy was incorporated into Roman territory and all Italian men became Roman citizens, in the 4th and 3rd centuries BCE.

Early Rome: Origins and Early Institutional Development

From the standpoint of Roman historians of the Late Republic and Empire, the trajectory of Roman institutional development was determined early on, and yet it was constantly teetering on the brink of disaster, brought back by the heroism and self-sacrifice of its best residents (both men and women). Supposedly founded by Romulus, the son of a god, in the 8th century, the city was ruled by a series of increasingly despotic kings until the people of Rome replaced monarchy in the 6th century with rule by the oligarchic Senate, a circumstance that continued until the Civil Wars of the 2nd and 1st centuries BCE. The agony of the Civil Wars, and the size of the territory ruled by Rome, then forced the populace to put their trust and political power in the hands of Octavian

Caesar, awarding him the title Augustus (27 BCE) and permanent rule. The earliest surviving histories of these events were written in the 3rd and 2nd centuries BCE, and their outlines may now be checked against and corrected by additional archaeological evidence.

Rome was inhabited by 1000 BCE, with houses atop several of its hills and cemeteries in the valleys between them. Its location on the Tiber River gave it access to routes to the sea and put it at the intersection of several different ecological zones and near the metal resources of Etruria. Rome had additional resources—timber, stone, and clay—in its vicinity (Woolf 2012: 35–36). At the same time as Etruscan towns grew, in the 8th century, Rome also coalesced into a town.

The period when Greek contacts with Italy increased, 730–500 BCE, brought further developments to Rome. According to traditional chronology, this was the time of the monarchy, with cultural and political domination by the Etruscans. The archaeological record, however, provides little evidence for Etruscan dominance. During this time, the architectural design of Rome changed, and it took on features characteristic of its later urban form (Figure 7.14). Most important, a number of public buildings and spaces took shape. Activities included the earliest leveling and drainage of the Forum, located at the base of the Palatine and Capitoline Hills, a space that would house the major political and religious structures of the Republican Period. This denotes a major investment of materials and labor and indicates some organizational coordination in the rapidly urbanizing town.

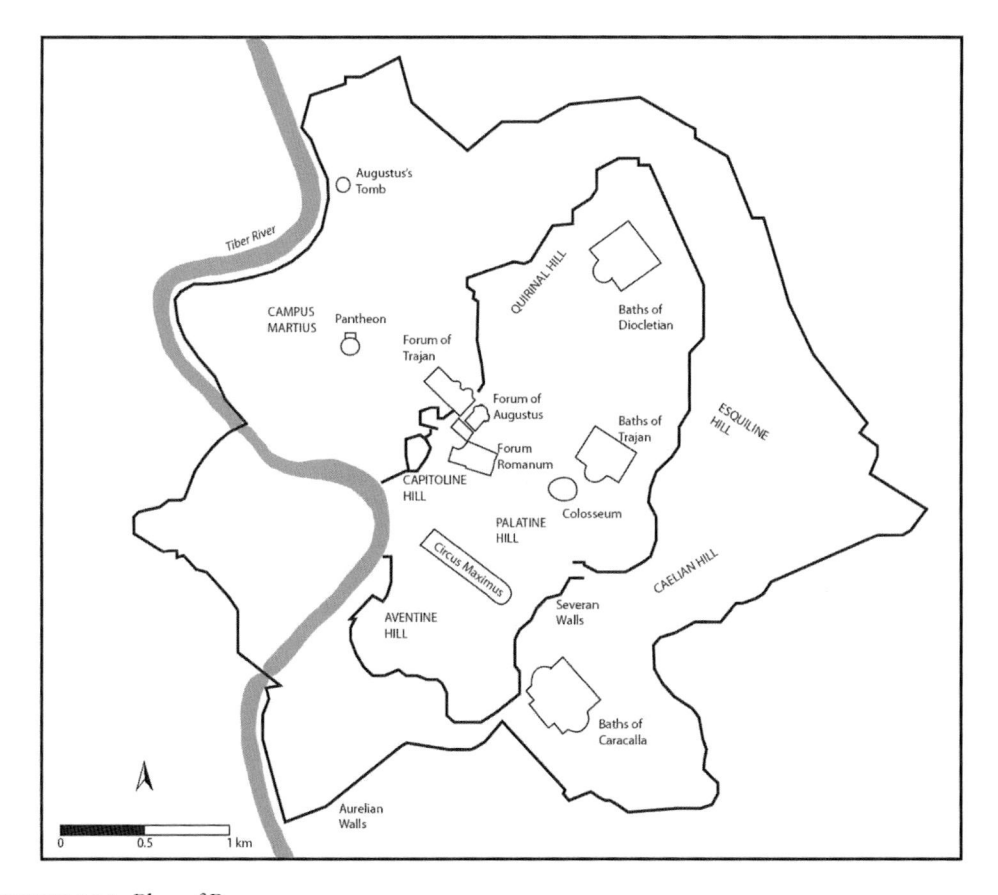

FIGURE 7.14 Plan of Rome

Source: J.C. Ross

Monumental structures, including possible palatial complexes and sanctuaries, were built on or near the Forum during the 6th century.

As was true in the Villanovan Period, graves in Rome offer a view of early Republic social and economic structures. During the 7th century, clustered graves suggest that family and lineage continued to exert a strong influence on funerary practices. As in Etruria, the wealthiest graves received an array of precious metal jewelry, tools and weapons, imported pottery, and chariots, which occur in both men's and women's graves (Cornell 1995: 82–84). But, in a change reminiscent of contemporary Greece, elaborate burials declined around 600 BCE, just as investment in public buildings and more permanent and standardized residential structures arose. This suggests a shift in elite priorities from the dead to the living, taking advantage of new public spaces and a rising population to assert their authority and status in the city.

The Roman Republic: Oligarchy and Empire

The traditional date for the expulsion of Rome's early kings is 509 BCE, offering a striking (and probably purposeful) parallel to Athenian democratic reforms of 508–507 BCE. The period that followed in Rome was not, however, a democracy in which all citizens were equal under the law. Rather, the Romans instituted a republican form of government in which all citizens were represented by deliberative bodies, but those institutions had unequal power (see Box 7.4). Ultimately, this complicated system, with a hierarchy of officials possessing a broad array of powers that encompassed administrative, economic, military, and religious functions, annexed the entire Italian Peninsula and began conquest of regions around the Mediterranean Sea. The system broke down only during the Civil War Period of the 2nd and 1st centuries BCE.

Over the long period of the Republic, which can be formally dated 509–31 BCE, Rome went from being a city-state surrounded by others of similar strength, to a territorial state encompassing the entire Italian Peninsula (in the 3rd century), to an empire, with victories over Carthage (by 146 BCE), Macedonia and the rest of Greece (also by 146 BCE), and Seleucia (starting in 192 BCE) (see Figure 7.15 for a map of Hellenistic and Roman territories). Roman values and citizenship were selectively spread into new territories—in some regions, replacing earlier Greek-based systems, and in others, being assimilated to local traditions. This growth is documented in later histories by both Greek and Roman writers, in legislation and other epigraphic materials, and, to a degree, in archaeology. The historical sources agree that the early stages of expansion, in the 5th and 4th centuries, were often undertaken in defense of Rome's territory. Later expansion, however, was more clearly focused on gaining land, labor, tribute, and plunder from conquered territories. These economic gains fueled further growth in what may have seemed an inexorable and violent cycle.

Rome's territorial expansion had a major impact on both the city itself and subject regions. In the city, the individual hilltop areas were surrounded by walls at an early stage, as each had its origin as a distinct village. Not until after a sack by Gallic tribes around 380 BCE was the entire city surrounded by a stone fortification wall, over 11 kilometers in circumference, surrounding an area of 427 hectares (Cornell 1995: 200). At this time, fewer than 30,000 people lived in the city. Expansion in the Italian Peninsula brought in money from plunder, which funded major construction projects, especially temples, as well as infrastructural improvements like roads, drainage, and a supply of fresh water. By the early 3rd century, the city's population neared 100,000, a number that could not be fed by the produce of local fields but for whom grain was imported (Cornell 1995: 385). By the mid-3rd century also, as most of Italy came under Roman control, the full extent of Roman territory was nearly 27,000 square kilometers, with a population of nearly

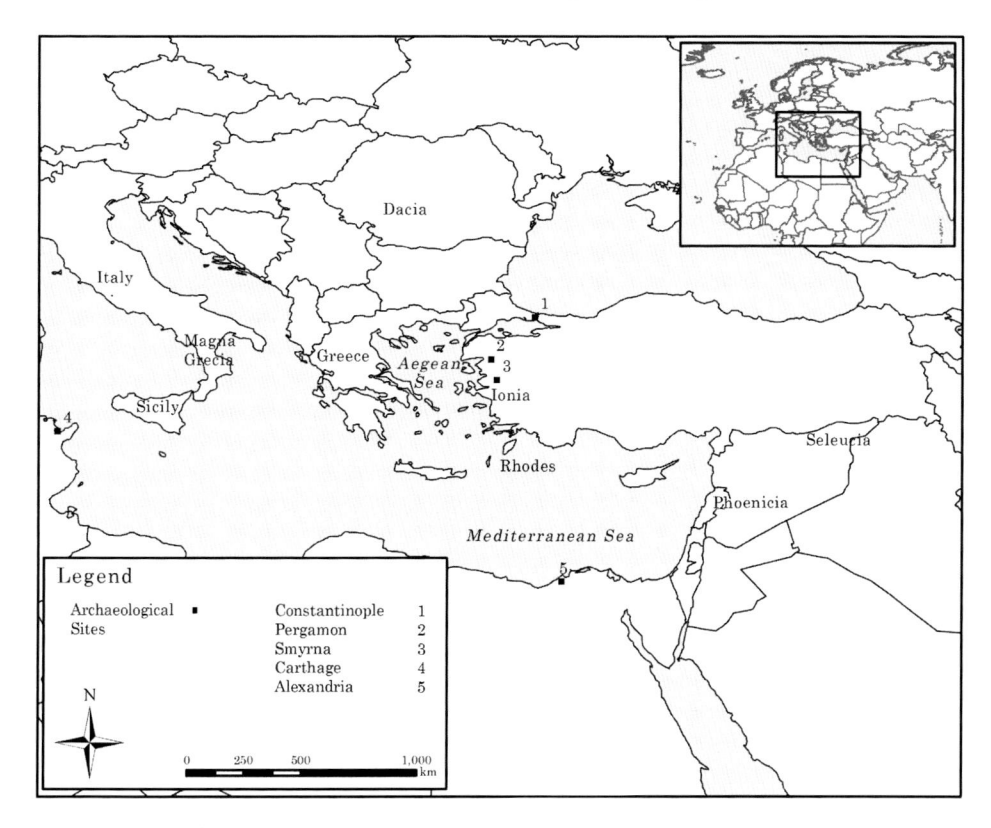

FIGURE 7.15 Map of the Hellenistic and Roman Empires

Source: B. Spencer

1 million (Cornell 1995: 380). Cities throughout Italy took on a Roman appearance, with marble temples, bathhouses, theaters, and formal meeting spaces. These signs of Roman identity spread to foreign lands as well (Purcell 2010). At its greatest extent during the Republic, the Roman Empire stretched a little under 5 million square kilometers, with an estimated 50 million people. Yet even into the Late Empire Period, the empire retained its sense of having a physical and cultural core in Rome itself.

The Republic: Political Organization

With the end of monarchy in the late 6th century BCE, Rome turned to an aristocratic system of rule, with a complex hierarchy of administrative positions. The patrician class, drawn from the heads of the wealthiest families, seems to have already played an advisory role during the monarchy (Cornell 1995: 247). Now they held the major decision-making powers, although the populace annually elected the two consuls who served as heads of the military and state. The patrician Senate may have come into being only when the lower classes, the *plebs*, asserted oppositional force by developing their own governing institutions. Eventually the two sides came to a sort of power-sharing agreement, before the social wars of the last century BCE sapped all representative power.

The physical and political center of Rome was the Forum, a rectangular space where altars and a speaker's podium allowed for public worship and pronouncements, merchants sold wares, and statues of great men of the past reminded passersby of their own responsibility to guarantee the glorious future of the city. The Senate met in the Curia, at one end of the Forum; basilicas were constructed for courts, and various temples in the Forum made it clear that Roman greatness was the product of both men and gods. The basic shape and function of the Forum was replicated across Italy and the rest of the empire, in cities founded and conquered by Rome, indicating the adoption of a common system of Roman institutions and values. The Senate appointed governors from its ranks to serve short terms in the provinces, collecting tribute and taxes and leading troops in defense of Rome's borders.

The hierarchy inherent in the political institutions of the Roman Republic was also built into its economic and social systems. The Romans idealized the citizen-farmer, but land distribution in the area of Rome was far from even. The "conflict of the orders," an occasionally violent confrontation between patricians and plebs, had land at its root: while most male citizens owned some land, for most the yield was just enough to feed their families. Any disruption to the growing season—such as shortfalls in rain, flooding, or enemies marching on Rome—could send the poorest families into debt. Arrangements could be made with patricians to feed a poor family, but defaulting on a loan led to debt-bondage, in which a debtor was forced to work off his debt (Cornell 1995: 282–83). Legislation enacted in the 5th and 4th centuries was aimed at reducing the problems of debt bondage, but the most successful solution was the seizure of land in conquered territories, and the resettlement of poor Romans on it.

Conquest alleviated the problems of the poorest Romans, but it also removed a source of very cheap labor from the patricians. The solution to this problem also derived from conquest, which brought into Rome large numbers of slaves: captive men, women, and children. Patricians sent some slaves to work their estates outside Rome, retaining others to serve in their households. Slaves were legally able to purchase their freedom or could be manumitted in a will. Significant numbers of such freedmen owned property, manufacturing businesses, and shops, even employing slaves of their own.

Expansion also benefited members of the army financially, as war veterans were paid wages in coinage and were awarded land for their service. Conquered lands paid an annual indemnity, which funded further expansion. They also served Rome by providing troops; as the empire's border pushed outward during the Late Republic, non-Italian troops became more important to its success (Woolf 2012: 75).

Rome's economy was largely market-driven, and given limits on agricultural land, many citizens turned to manufacturing. Roman cities and towns were filled with workshops producing metals, ceramics, and textiles. Raw materials came from all parts of the empire. Businesses appear to have been largely privately owned and ranged from shops to bakeries, to oil presses, to schools and brothels (Kehoe 2007). Certain merchants and manufacturers probably did much of their business with the government, but were free to pursue private ventures as well. The non-agricultural economy created a sizeable middle class (some even born as slaves) with political ambitions of their own.

Physical evidence for social organization is detectable in both public and private spaces of Roman cities (see Box 7.5). Roman houses varied in size, decoration, and quality of construction, depending on socioeconomic status, but most had a similar ground plan that allowed for a combination of private and public functions (Clarke 1991). Guests entered into an open atrium space with a pool for catching rainwater. From there, friends might be led to private internal quarters, while business partners and clients met with the *paterfamilias* in a reception room, the *tablinium*. Public and private quarters could be decorated with statuary, paintings, and mosaics; these are well illustrated in the rich array of housing uncovered at Pompeii and Herculaneum.

> **BOX 7.5 THE ROMAN FAMILY**
>
> Hierarchical structures were part of the Roman social systems of the Republic. The Roman family was a multigenerational group with its own ruler: the paterfamilias, the oldest male member. Under him were his wife and children, the family's dependents and slaves, and a set of clients—men who had bound themselves to the family through economic, social, and political obligations. Within the household, the paterfamilias ruled as a monarch, with ultimate authority over money, marriages, and even life and death. Even adult sons, though legally considered citizens, could not vote while their father was alive; only after his death did the original family dissolve, and each son became paterfamilias in his own family (Cantarella 2003).
>
> Within such a hierarchical system, Roman women went without political representation like Greek women, but they had more legal and economic rights. While the principal function of marriage was the procreation of Roman citizens, Rome's looser definition of citizenship meant that there were fewer restrictions on women's movements or controls over their sexuality than in Athens (Cantarella 2002). Still, as in Athens, marriage meant the transfer of control of a woman from one man to another. Patrician families used their daughters to build alliances with other wealthy families, even inducing women to divorce one husband so an alliance could be created through a new marriage. Also as in Athens, Roman women were central to performance of ritual and cult, at home and in public (Hammer 2000). In the Republic, women were an important economic force, as they had access to their dowries and could own, inherit, and bequeath land and other property.

The Roman family and state shared the value of *pietas*, best translated as "duty" rather than "piety." Pietas refers to an individual's duty to his family, the gods, and the state. Service to the gods, whether through worship, offerings, or sponsorship of temples or cults, benefited a man's family and the Roman community as a whole (Orlin 2002: 4–5). At the same time, spending private money on a temple's construction and adornment was a means of garnering personal prestige; the same was true for the construction of temporary spaces for and sponsorship of public spectacles: games, theatrical events, and gladiatorial contests, all with their roots in religious festivals (Beacham 1999; Purcell 2010). Roman values were perpetuated through performance and public artworks—statues of men who served the state, relief scenes from myth and history. Styles were borrowed from Greece, but such artwork served a particularly Roman purpose.

Civil War

Rome's political institutions during the Republic were constantly changing. Social upheavals by and demands for reform on behalf of the lower classes were sometimes successful, even when the status quo remained in place. But in its last century, Republican systems of governance and social organization faltered, during the period called the Civil Wars (133–31 BCE). A series of men including Sulla, Pompey, and Julius Caesar used their positions as dictator, with the backing of the army, to seize sole (or nearly so) power over Rome. In some ways, this was an inevitable conflict; Rome's expansion into an empire had been accompanied by no major adjustments to its political system, and abuses of power by men appointed to positions at the edges of the empire had long been sources of instability. Later historians saw the struggles of the time as a moral failure, when men abandoned pietas for their own individual gain. The conflict led to significant loss of life among the senatorial class and left the political system forever changed, in anticipation of the sole rule that would arise under Octavian Caesar.

The Civil Wars left a significant mark on the art and archaeology of the Roman world. The internal struggle for power allowed some conquered regions to break away or be taken by opportunistic enemies, although these losses were soon reversed. At the same time, the military dictators gained the trust of their troops by resettling veterans in frontier areas, increasing Roman presence at the boundaries of the empire (Purcell 2010). Rules of propriety and humility prevented the generals from erecting monuments to their victories in Rome itself, so they placed them in distant lands instead (Mackay 2000; Rose 2010). Julius Caesar was the first man to issue coinage with his own portrait (Rawson 2010). Art of this period built on Republican traditions of public portraits but shifted focus from Rome's great past to its present.

The Empire

Given the upheaval and loss of life of the Civil War Period, it is no surprise that Augustus, Rome's first emperor, organized his government and Roman territories with a view to the more distant past. Augustus came to power as Octavian Caesar, nephew and adopted heir of Julius, in the final stages of the Civil Wars. The act that established his position as monarch was victory in the Battle of Actium against Mark Antony and Cleopatra VII in 31 BCE, a victory that also finally brought down the remaining Hellenistic kingdom in Egypt. Augustus's reign established (or re-established) the principle of single rule over Rome and its territory, the period typically called the Empire (ca. 31 BCE–476 CE). This label may be misleading, for two reasons: first, Rome already had ruled an empire for over 200 years before Augustus came to the throne, and second, the title *imperator* (emperor) had existed since Republican times to denote a victorious general; eventually it became part of the standard titulary of the ruler.

The period of imperial rule stretched from the awarding of the title Augustus ("venerable") to Octavian in 27 BCE, to 476 CE, the date of the fall of Rome to invaders. Typically, it is divided into two halves: the Principate (31 BCE–284 CE) and the Dominate (284–476 CE). While both periods saw central rule, their division exposes the differences in the organization of power. Emperors during the Principate retained the Republican institution of the Senate, but in name only. During the Dominate, which followed the period known as the "Third-Century Crisis," power was more clearly in the hands of the emperor, although emperors in this period experimented with governance structures in order to cope with the vast stretch of empire. By the 5th century, as Rome fell under more frequent barbarian attacks, the empire split into western and eastern halves. The eastern empire, centered on Constantinople, survived into the Middle Ages, while the western empire fell when the final emperor in Rome was deposed by Odoacer, an invader from the north, in 476 CE.

Augustus

Augustus (r. 31 BCE–14 CE) introduced many of the features of the Principate, and later emperors modeled themselves on him. His rise to power owed much to his association with Julius Caesar, his uncle and adoptive father. After Julius's assassination in 44 BCE, Octavian vowed revenge on the assassins. Having defeated his main rival, Mark Antony, Octavian assumed single rule in Rome, consolidating his power in a series of steps, including the Senatorial decrees that awarded him the title of Augustus (27 BCE) and gave him provincial command (23 BCE). By the 20s BCE, there could be no doubt in Rome that Augustus planned to remain in power—there would be no return to the power-sharing of the Republic. He did, however, retain the Senate as a consultative body, capable of passing the legislation that he proposed. His preferred title was *princeps*, "first man," implying shared responsibility among the political institutions; the Principate label for the first half of the imperial period derives from this term. As ruler, Augustus had tremendous military success, extending the borders of the empire and bringing the "Roman Peace" (*pax Romana*) to all territories in Roman hands. Another significant element of his success was an enormous propaganda machine, abetted by his sponsorship of artistic and literary production of all types.

The most remarkable expression of Augustus's self-promotion was the *Res Gestae* ("Deeds"), written by the emperor toward the end of his life and listing his actions on behalf of Rome. This text was intended to be copied and sent out across the empire for public display and consultation. While Augustus, in the text, focused on military accomplishments and setting the Roman state back on its feet, he also drew attention to his public works and to the physical rebuilding of Rome. The building and artistic programs that Augustus inaugurated demonstrate his savviness when it came to the public display and perception of power (see Box 7.6).

BOX 7.6 THE ARTWORK OF AUGUSTUS

Augustus's artwork focused on his family as the model Roman family, the bulwark of Republican Rome, and he manipulated their image to portray his rule as a return to the central values that had made Rome great. He also used his own portrait as a means to convey his obedience and service to the gods. The emperor employed public art as another means of conveying his accomplishments and values. His statuary contrasts with the self-aggrandizing styles of the generals before him, who pictured themselves in the guise of gods. Augustus chose more modest poses, though they were no less celebratory of the emperor's deeds. Best known is the Prima Porta statue (Figure 7.16), the surviving marble replica of a probable bronze original: Augustus, garbed as a general, seems to be addressing his troops. Youthful and poised, he wears a breastplate that illustrates the recovery of the legionary eagles from the Parthians (Persians) in 20 BCE, thus reversing two of the most psychologically devastating Roman losses of the previous decades (Zanker 1988: 189). Diplomacy was here recast as victory, overseen and approved by an array of gods. Similarly self-effacing is the depiction of a robed Augustus as *pontifex maximus* (chief priest) of Rome. On the Ara Pacis, with senatorial participants depicted in sacred procession on one side of the altar and the imperial family on the other, the sculptors suggested a balance of powers in line with Republican ideals—not reality, but representational propaganda (Ramage and Ramage 1996: 116).

FIGURE 7.16 Prima Porta statue
Source: Alinari / Art Resource, NY

Augustus's munificence in the first half of his reign centered on the army and public celebration of its successes, especially those that brought him to the throne. He reorganized the funding for the army so that the emperor became its sole financier, taking over that responsibility from the Senate. At the same time, the imposition of peace allowed him to reduce its size, cutting the number of legions in half (Bang 2013). In his public building projects, Augustus celebrated the death of his rivals as revenge for Julius's assassination and subsequent Roman losses, but nowhere did he express explicitly the fact that he fought Romans. In a new forum adjacent to the Republican Forum and one begun by Julius (which Augustus completed), he built a temple to Mars Ultor ("The Avenger"), with sanctuary areas for Mars, Venus, and Julius. The temple was paid for with plunder from Augustus's conquests (Kellum 1996). Augustus's dedications of a number of temples in Rome and elsewhere demonstrate his commitment to serving the gods, embodying the traditional value of pietas (Zanker 1988: 102–103). It is hard to deny Augustus's claim, reported by Suetonius, that he "found Rome a city of bricks and left it a city of marble."

During the second half of his reign, Augustus turned to the third element of pietas—duty to family—as he presented his household as the model Roman family and tried to rebuild through legislation the ranks of the upper classes. Augustus enacted legislation in 18 BCE that penalized young men and women who were unmarried and rewarded them for having children, as well as punishing adulterers (including members of his own family). The Ara Pacis (Altar of Peace), set in the Campus Martius, made a similar statement about morality and the centrality of the family to Rome's past, present, and future by showing the emperor surrounded by his family, and senators with theirs (Kleiner 1978).

Beyond the Italian Peninsula, the establishment of Augustus's rule had a different manifestation. In many areas, particularly in the Greek east, the tradition of monarchy was of long standing. The portrait of the emperor was put up in cities across the empire, often in Hellenistic styles that suggested divine status (Zanker 1988: 299). As early as 30 BCE, before Octavian even received his honorary title of Augustus, an Eastern cult to the emperor arose; he was worshipped at various Anatolian cult centers. A similar message is conveyed by the Gemma Augustea, an onyx gem from the time of Tiberius, Augustus's successor. On this piece of private art, the sculptor used imagery that could not have appeared in public in Rome: Augustus sits, draped like Jupiter, with the personification of his city, the goddess Roma. Beside them, Tiberius celebrates a military victory, earning his right to follow his stepfather on the throne (Pollini 1993).

Later emperors would not be so circumspect about their image, but Augustus was aware of the sensitivity of Romans to the dangers of an individual's drive for power. Not only the art and architecture of his reign, but also the poets and historians he patronized stressed the emperor's humility, making monarchy more palatable. In Virgil's epic, the *Aeneid*, the poet imitated Homeric style and story-telling, but for a literate audience, one capable of comparing the work and story to its distinguished predecessors. Aeneas, a survivor of the Greek destruction of Troy, travels to Italy with family, gods, and people, making possible the eventual foundation of Rome. At several points in the epic, Augustus's reign is foretold as a new Golden Age after years of violence and pain. Virgil's is not a straightforward praise poem, however; success—for Aeneas and Augustus both—would be achieved only after great personal loss.

The Principate after Augustus

Following Augustus's death in 14 CE, there was little doubt that the new monarchy under a princeps would continue. Augustus's focus on his own family's image included several potential successors. In the end, the throne went to his stepson Tiberius; in the following decades, it stayed within Augustus's extended family, the Julio-Claudians. Even with a number of later dynastic changes, the basic structure of power, with the emperor nominally sharing power with the Senate, was preserved; the Principate survived until the "Third-Century Crisis." Both before and after the crisis, the emperor was the central focus of the empire; his image traveled with him and was embodied in his statues erected across the empire (Woolf 2012: 178). Despite profound changes in the empire over this period, the emperor was recognized as divine or nearly divine during his lifetime; more than half of the emperors into the 4th century underwent *apotheosis* (transformation into a god) at the end of their funerals (Price 1987). This process was aided by the fact that emperors continued to be cremated, even as the rest of their subjects turned to inhumation burial, under the influence of the Greek east. An eagle released while the emperor's body was burned atop a six-story pyre symbolized his translation to divine form (Price 1987).

During the Principate, the borders of the empire remained stable, with few major gains after Augustus's death. Rome's 50 million subjects were spread from Spain to Britain to the Near East and North Africa. A significant percentage of this population lived in cities, a trend that began in the east in the Hellenistic Period but was relatively new to territories in the west like Britain, Germany, and Spain. Cities replicated Roman institutions and buildings, with forums, temples, theaters, bathhouses, and public inscriptions in Latin, all part of an effort to produce citizens by means of the physical experience of Romanness (Revell 2009).

With the emperor as head of state and principal commander of the army, the Senate and elected officials lost most of their traditional powers; as the emperor made most official appointments, the populace itself lost the capacity to make its voice heard in traditional ways. A vote of the Senate was necessary to confirm each emperor's accession to the throne; this was, presumably, a formality. An emperor could not afford to ignore his subjects, however; many authors of the imperial period, Juvenal foremost among them, made note of the "bread and circuses" provided by the emperor to appease the populace and keep them distracted. The phrase refers to government-funded grain distributions and public spectacles like games and blood sports. While these practices went back to the Late Republic, the construction of the Colosseum in Rome under Vespasian, in 70–80 CE, provided a venue that held over 50,000 spectators and was the first permanent space for contests in Rome (Ramage and Ramage 1996: 136–38).

As the power of the emperor rose, and the Senate's declined, there were additional changes in Roman bureaucracy. Membership in the Senate turned over regularly, as patrician families died out and wealthy citizens from the provinces became eligible for service. Most of the imperial appointments to office in Rome came from the wealthy "middle" class of equestrians, preventing patricians from wielding too much power (Bang 2013). In the provinces, most local elites retained power, ruling as governors or serving as local officials and providing most of the income and support for the empire's 350,000 troops (Noreña 2010; Woolf 2012: 210).

The art of the Principate had two major themes: the emperor and the frontiers. These two elements were frequently combined in scenes of warfare and imperial triumph, as a reminder of the emperor's singular power. Perhaps the best example of this is the art of Trajan (98–117 CE), who erected a number of victory monuments after his defeat of the Dacians (residents of modern Romania) in 101–2 CE. The works declared the might and virtue of the emperor and, by extension, of his troops, as they extended Roman force by means of battle, justice, and mercy (Ferris 2000; Hannestad 1979). The Column of Trajan stood in the emperor's new forum in Rome, whose library and markets were funded by the spoils of war. On it, the artists carefully contrasted Roman discipline with Dacian violence and frenzy, a trope that goes back to the literature of Augustus's time. These images were repeated on monuments and statues in Italy and Romania and even on widely circulating coins of Trajan. The repetition of the imagery speaks to its use in self-conscious construction of Roman identity from the emperor on down (Hopkins 2008). Later emperors of the Principate used similar imagery, but the battles are shown as harsher, the barbarian enemies more humiliated.

The relative peace of the Principate generated growth in population and in the economic wealth of the Roman state. Agricultural production must have increased to feed the over 50 million people in Roman territory; significant amounts of grain were shipped to various parts of the empire. Rome itself imported grain, wine, and olive oil from a variety of production areas. Wealthy citizens invested in land and capitalized on the demand for cash crops; on villas in Italy and elsewhere, slaves provided the majority of the labor. The state itself seems to have interfered in economic activities very little, beyond its need to pay its troops; for the most part, exchange took place on a private basis (Kehoe 2007).

Third-Century Crisis

A number of factors contributed to Rome's Third-Century Crisis, a half-century that began in 235 and ended with the crowning of Diocletian in 284 CE, with no single cause alone pushing the empire to near-collapse. Rather, political (civil war, rebellion, and territorial loss); economic (agricultural shortfalls); and demographic (plague and population movements) failures coalesced. A situation of near-anarchy afflicted Rome itself, with swift turnover on the throne. By 284 CE, the population of the empire was depleted, with an accompanying trend of ruralization, as people moved out of urban areas, where the upheavals may have been felt most acutely and disease (probably smallpox) spread fastest (Giardina 2007; Woolf 2012: 191).

The Dominate: Recovery and Transformation

The most important change to the Roman Empire as it recovered from the turmoil of the 3rd century was its decentralized nature. With the loss of cities as administrative and economic centers, the empire also lost its communication and social hubs, the places where people learned how to be Roman. Instead, pronounced regional cultures arose, subject to local conditions, resources, economic and legal constructs, and religious trends.

The emperors who followed the crisis, beginning in the late 3rd century, responded to decentralization in a variety of ways. Diocletian (284–305 CE) introduced a new division of rule, with two senior and two junior emperors, each ruling his own group of provinces from a different capital city. The tetrarchy ("rule of four") structure acknowledged the challenges of the huge territory of the empire; no man could rule it alone. It also recognized that Rome was no longer the most important city in the empire; several cities, even in Italy, had high populations and could claim similar status. The four-part division of rule did not survive long after Diocletian's death, but other experiments in divided rule were attempted down to the time of Constantine. For the most part, the soldier emperors of the late 3rd and 4th centuries had to maintain mobile courts and armies to regain and retain territory. The empire no longer enjoyed the same degree of long-distance movement of goods as in the previous period; localized economies supported the smaller and more dispersed populations of the Late Empire.

The imagery of the Late Empire continued to focus on the emperor's victorious status; these emperors imitated earlier imagery that emphasized the difference between Romans and barbarians (Ferris 2000). Under Diocletian, an acknowledgment of shared imperial power appeared in art; the statue of the tetrarchs, now in Venice, shows the four rulers in interlocked pose, with identical features (Rees 1993). Constantine was particularly inclined to borrowing imagery, even actual sculpture, made by his predecessors; the Arch of Constantine, erected in Rome near the Colosseum in 315 CE, incorporated reliefs carved under Trajan and Marcus Aurelius, as well as images depicting Constantine's victories. In this way, the later emperors evoked the accomplishments of the Principate, presenting themselves as worthy successors to powerful earlier emperors.

The major religious change from the time of the Principate was the emergence of Christianity and its elevation from a cause for persecution to the empire's official religion. Christians had been seen as a danger to the traditional Roman value system, which was built on service to the state and family; Christians advocated breaking down hierarchies and severance of family ties in the interest of personal salvation (Sivan 2010). Though Christians made no attempts to overthrow Roman political institutions, their commitment to religion was a threat to the emperors of the 3rd and 4th centuries, and they proved convenient scapegoats for the Third-Century Crisis (Woolf 2012: 262). The persecution of Christians ended when Constantine I (306–337 CE) converted to Christianity, opening up a tolerant attitude previously impossible to imagine. Following Constantine, nearly every emperor was Christian, and the Roman Empire became a Christian one (Woolf 2012: 266).

Collapse of the Roman Empire

The course and causes of the Roman Empire's collapse have been a matter of considerable debate for centuries. Even the date for the collapse is controversial, with suggestions ranging from 395 CE (the death of Theodosius I and final division of the empire into eastern and western halves) to 800 (the coronation of Charlemagne as emperor, in Rome) (Lim 2010). A number of attacks on Rome and losses of territory in the 4th and 5th centuries, including Spain and North Africa, make this a pivotal period of decline. In 476, a Goth won the throne in Rome; he took Roman imperial titles and ruled over a core area of Italy and southern France (Woolf 2012: 276).

An alternative perspective, however, suggests that the Roman Empire never fully collapsed but underwent processes of readjustment and realignment that were made possible by precisely the same reforms instituted by previous emperors (Bowersock 1988; Woolf 2012: 278–85). Regional divisions of power during the Dominate meant that provincial power and self-sufficiency developed, reliant on local troops and factional support. Elites abandoned cities, which no longer provided economic or social services to support them; the clientage system that dominated the Republic and early Principate disappeared completely (Woolf 2012: 281). In the end, only the eastern empire survived, as a city-state centered on Constantinople.

Conclusions

This chapter has reviewed very different examples of complexity: Protopalatial Crete, Neopalatial Crete, Mycenaean Greece, and Classical Greece and Italy. This variety demonstrates how contingent the development of complexity can be: within a circumscribed geographical territory, and within a few millennia, very different systems developed due to a combination of prior sociopolitical institutions and economic configurations. The Protopalatial Period on Crete followed a phase of egalitarian public ceremonial performance at monumental tombs; public ritual then shifted to rural sanctuaries and urban palaces, the latter apparently also taking charge of surplus agricultural yields. In the Neopalatial Period, the palaces became more exclusive, but economic redistribution took place in multiple locales. Craft production and exchange took on a larger role in the palaces, and ritual dispersed to a variety of urban locations. Finally, the Mycenaean polities, adapted to mainland ecology, arose out of exclusive control of particular raw materials and the production of prestige goods for trade. In all of the Bronze Age cases, the role of a single ruler was underemphasized in imagery and text, a situation in stark contrast to contemporary Near Eastern and Egyptian civilizations but providing a noteworthy precedent for Classical Greece.

Because of the wealth of textual and archaeological evidence they boast, the Classical civilizations of Greece and Rome offer a rich field in which to examine the components of complexity in detail. Rather than presenting static, long-lasting political entities, these civilizations exhibited striking variety and flexibility. Many political actors, exercising a variety of political strategies, gained and lost power over time, while core value systems and identities remained intact.

8

THE INDUS VALLEY CIVILIZATION

Introduction

The ancient Indus Valley civilization, also known as the Harappan civilization, is, to quote Winston Churchill, a riddle, wrapped in a mystery, inside an enigma. At the time of the Mature Harappan civilization (ca. 2500–1900 BCE), arts and crafts were traded far and wide, a sophisticated writing system was fully developed, and vast cities were surrounded by towns and villages. And yet other major traits usually associated with complexity appear missing from the Harappan world, including a standing army, major palaces and temples, celebrations of individual rulers and their accomplishments, and significant social stratification. Recent scholarship, however, defends the designation of "archaic state" for the ancient Harappan world but with a caveat: it may have been a state-level society but with elements peculiar to south Asia. This chapter examines current evidence that helps to reveal the emergence and structure of the ancient Harappan state.

Geography and Chronology

The Harappan civilization was spread over two modern countries: eastern Pakistan and western India. The Indus River itself serves as the major divide between the two.

Geography and Ecological Setting

The Indus River rises in the Himalayas and flows from the mountains southward through fairly arid desert regions, finally emptying into the Arabian Sea. The Indus River joins five other major rivers that rise in the Himalayas, merging at the Panjnad (Figure 8.1), which serves as the dividing point between the upper and lower Indus River. Below the Panjnad, the Indus becomes a mighty river, subject to flooding, which was a major aid to, and concern of, the ancient Harappan people. The Indus basin is bordered by a variety of ecozones: the vast Himalayas in the north, the arid Iranian desert to the west, another desert to the northeast, the tropics to the southeast, and finally the Arabian Sea to the south. After rising in the Himalayas, the five rivers, Jhelum, Chenab, Ravi, Beas, and Sutlej, flow through the Punjab (the area encompassing the five rivers) and Cholistan regions, which form the northern reaches of the Harappan civilization.

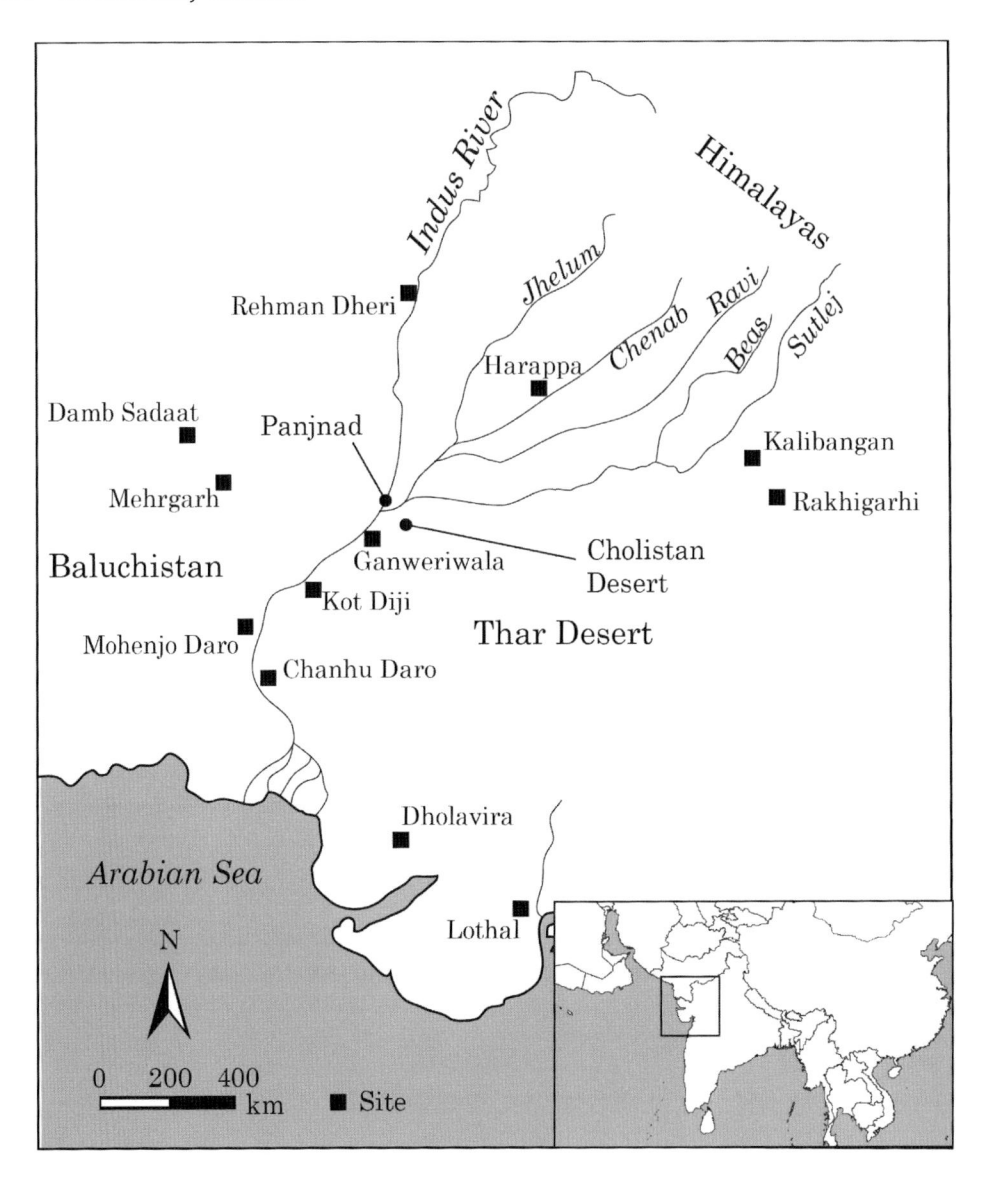

FIGURE 8.1 Map of Regions and Sites Discussed in the Text

Below the Panjnad the then larger Indus flows past the Thar Desert; to the west is the region of Baluchistan and the Iranian Plateau. East of the Indus another mighty river, the Saraswati, once flowed; it may have rivaled or even surpassed the power of the Indus. Today, only small seasonal rivers flow here, but in Harappan times, settlements were spread along this ancient river. Environmental change and possible tectonic activity may have altered the Saraswati's course in antiquity, eventually causing it to split into smaller, seasonal streams.

Though much of the ancient Harappan homeland is composed of arid landscapes, monsoon rains occur annually causing the rivers to flood. The land below the Panjnad is relatively flat, allowing the rivers, including the Indus, to migrate over the millennia and create a rich alluvial plain. Riverine movement also created "sand bars" or elevated plateaus that remain unaffected by the annual floods. It is upon these that most Harappan cities and smaller settlements were situated. From the Panjnad, the Indus flows 800 kilometers to the Arabian Sea as a single river, but during Harappan times, it may have had several channels between which Harappans settled (Wright 2010: 36). The Harappan agricultural cycles flourished in this semi-arid climate, watered by spring melt, summer monsoons, and some winter rainstorms. While the inhabitants had to weather floods and other environmental risks, it was a region well equipped to support a vast civilization.

The Chronological Sequence

Up until approximately 7000 BCE, the Indus River Valley and the regions surrounding it were inhabited by hunter-gatherers (Table 8.1). Beginning in the later 5th millennium, the Indus experienced an era of "regionalization" (ca. 4300–3200 BCE) in which differentiated cultural traditions developed to the west in Baluchistan, to the northeast in the Punjab, and to the southeast in a region today known as Gujarat. Along the ancient Saraswati River, survey has revealed settlements whose inhabitants practiced a variety of socioeconomic strategies including pastoralism and settled agriculture.

Harappa, the type site for the Indus River Valley civilization, was occupied at least by 3300 BCE, slightly pre-dating the Early Harappan Period (also known as the Early Indus Period; ca. 3200–2600 BCE). It is during the Early Indus Period that a significant craft industry developed, and evidence suggests that precursors to the later Harappan writing system were in use. Residents of the different regions of the Indus River Valley engaged in trade with one another and with more distant regions such as Baluchistan. At approximately 2600 BCE, many of these Early Indus sites were abandoned; roughly a century later, beginning ca. 2500 BCE, the Mature Harappan Period (ca. 2500–1900 BCE) crystalized in the emergence of large cities with satellite settlements surrounding them.

TABLE 8.1 Chronological Periods and Sites Discussed in Chapter 8

Dates	Period	Sites Discussed in Chapter	Cultural Horizons
ca. 7000–4300 BCE	**Neolithic**	Mehrgarh	Domestication of plants and animals; small agricultural villages
ca. 4300–3200 BCE	**Food Producing Neolithic**	Mehrgarh	Increased craft production and trade; larger settlements and growing population; highly decorated ceramics and terracotta figurines
ca. 3200–2600 BCE	**Early Harappan Period (Regionalization)**	Amri-Nal sites; Dholavira; Kot Diji sites; Damp Sadaat; Sothi-Siswal sites; Kalibangan	Development of regional ceramic decoration; some evidence of defensive architecture
ca. 2600–2500 BCE	**Transitional Period**		Early Harappan sites are largely abandoned and some razed; new sites are rebuilt
ca. 2500–1900 BCE	**Mature Harappan Period**	Mohenjo Daro; Dholavira; Lothal; Harappa	Rise of the state; complex craft production; long-distance trade; writing; state-sponsored religion(?)
ca. 1900–1800 BCE	**Harappan Demise**		Large-scale abandonment of settlements

The Harappan civilization consisted of at least five large cities, including Mohenjo Daro, Harappa lying north in the Punjab, Rakhigari to the east, Ganweriwala on the Saraswati, and Dholavira in Gujarat; it stretched from the foothills of the Himalayas to the deltaic drainage into the Arabian Sea and from Baluchistan in the west across the river valleys to Gujarat in the southeast. In the early second millennium, however, the Harappan civilization entered a steep decline.

Pre-State Cultures: The (Neolithic) Food Producing Period

The pre-Indus Valley phase, termed "Neolithic" by some and "Food Producing Period" by others (see discussion in Coningham and Young 2015: 26–27), has not been as extensively explored as have similar periods in the Near East and China. This is, in part, due to difficult conditions in the region (alluvial deposit overlying sites, political unrest limiting work). Nonetheless, excavations and surveys offer some indications of the cultural trajectories from pre-agricultural India to the eve of the Indus civilization.

Cultivation and animal domestication was underway by the 8th millennium BCE, demonstrated by the excavations at Mehrgarh in Baluchistan (Jarrige and Jarrige 2006). This settlement supported both agriculturalists and pastoralists from ca. 6500 to 2500 BCE. How and when agriculture first came to the region and to Mehrgarh itself is still a point of discussion among scholars. Knowledge of cultivation, particularly of wheat, likely spread to south Asia from the Near East where grains were first domesticated in earlier millennia (see Chapter 5), indicates south Asians were experimenting with local crops including cotton (Fuller and Murphy 2014; Moulherat et al. 2002). Cultivation brought changes to the south Asian diets and, therefore, their cultural patterns (see Box 8.1).

BOX 8.1 NEOLITHIC DENTISTRY AT MEHRGARH

In the excavations at Neolithic Mehrgarh, human remains dating to the 8th millennium BCE were retrieved that showed evidence of early dentistry (Coppa et al. 2006). Eleven teeth from nine individuals show evidence of drilling but not for decorative purposes since the holes were in teeth located too far back in the mouth to be visible. Flint drills, normally used to drill holes in beads, are thought to be the tools used to drill the holes in the teeth. While the reasons for the drillings were not apparent due, in part, to lack of adequate preservation, the archaeologists and scientists studying these remains suggest that, rather than for religious or decorative purposes, the goal of the work on the teeth was likely to do with dentistry and health maintenance.

Animal domestication was also underway in this era. From the earliest levels at Mehrgarh, faunal evidence indicates that goats were present, found even in burials, suggesting that goats were undergoing domestication at the site (Meadow 1984). By ca. 5000 BCE, cattle and sheep (the latter possibly imported from the Near East) were part of the socioeconomy of Mehrgarh and were of increasing importance, even outnumbering wild game; cattle, especially the South Asian zebu type, were probably domesticated locally (Possehl 2002: 27).

Three occupational phases at Mehrgarh (I: 6500–4800 BCE, IIA: 4800–4300 BCE, and IIB: 4300–4000 BCE) reveal a settlement that increased subsistence productivity and regional connections over time. Phase I dwellings, when the site was approximately 3 hectares in size, were typically four-roomed and built of wood, baked mud, and animal skins (Jarrige, Jarrige, and Quivron 2005). One building type was compartmented, consisting of up to a dozen rooms too small for habitation, leading archaeologists to believe they were communal storage buildings (Jarrige, Jarrige, and Quivron 2005). By the close of Phase I, Mehrgarh residents were producing handmade, chaff-tempered ceramics and fashioning human figurines; woodworking and leather production were also carried out (Possehl 2002: 30; Wright 2010: 61). By Phase II, the site had grown to 12 hectares; structures were similar in size and nature but more numerous. Burials indicate that there was no significant social stratification present at early Mehrgarh though men and women received different goods likely related to their predominant activities (men had stone tools, and women had textile production items). Mehrgarh residents engaged in trade to obtain some raw resources.

Mehrgarh Phases IIB–III (ca. 4300–3600 BCE), along with other sites to the west and north in Baluchistan, to the east in Cholistan and Thar Desert, and to the southeast in Gujarat, saw larger and more economically diverse settlements with people engaging in significant craft production activities. Mehrgarh increased in size up to 100 hectares during this time, and a wider variety of domesticates was farmed including oats and several types of wheat.

The house plans remained essentially the same in these phases, but thicker walls suggest that Mehrgarh residents had begun to build second stories (Wright 2010: 65). Burials indicate that some differentiation among individuals was present in Phase III Mehrgarh: some individuals had no grave goods; some had a typical set of jewelry and tools; and some had additional items such as pottery, baskets, and semiprecious stones (Wright 2010: 66). Male and female burials continued to show differentiation in goods present, and in fact, it was more common for females to receive exceptional grave goods than for males. An important sociotechnological development during at this time was the invention of the wheel; pottery of superior quality, finely decorated with images of animals and geometric figures, appeared. Other workshops at Mehrgarh show evidence of bead and jewelry production, which, in addition to fine ceramics, became important products in later Harappan times; production of terracotta items such as figurines and clay jewelry also began. The increase in craft production at Mehrgarh marks an important change in the Indus region; previously, Mehrgarh residents had acquired these finished products from elsewhere, but at this time, raw resources were acquired so that goods could be produced in the local workshops (Kenoyer 1994).

At other contemporary sites in Baluchistan, Cholistan, and the Punjab, terracotta figurine production, ceramics in differing regional styles, textile and jewelry production indicate that the entire region was engaged in economic development and interregional trade. As early as 3500 BCE, the site of Harappa was settled. Certainly by 3300 BCE, domestic architecture, storage pits, and the accessories associated with the craft production activities noted earlier were present at Harappa. Also discovered there were several sherds inscribed with designs that may represent early stages of the Indus script. The settlements found throughout the Indus region show signs of agricultural intensification commensurate with an increasing population, a growing reliance on animal husbandry, a quickly developing craft industry, and new technological innovations especially regarding ceramic production and steatite production. Local and regional trade not only brought raw resources to settlements but served as a way to distribute goods, particularly differing styles of pottery, from region to region.

State Origins: The Early Harappan (Early Indus) Period

The Early Harappan stage (ca. 3200–2600 BCE) saw a great expansion in the number of settlements along the upper and lower Indus River and increasing technological and agricultural development. These regions, which were well watered and thus lush, provided excellent fishing and hunting resources to residents but also presented dangers such as tigers, poisonous snakes, and tropical diseases. A growing population and expanding economy made it necessary for Early Harappan peoples to develop technologies to not only survive but thrive in these regions.

The Early Harappan Phase: An Era of Regionalization

Archaeologists have divided the Early Harappan Period into several phases that are generally simultaneous and correspond more to regionality then to temporality (Possehl 2002: 40), some of which are outlined here. The Amri-Nal phase sites are found in southern Baluchistan, the Sindh region, and part of Gujarat. The small (3.5–4 hectares) Amri-Nal sites are identified by their fine red or buff pottery, with decorative motifs that include geometric patterns and sometimes animal decorations (particularly fish). The houses at Amri-Nal sites did not differ significantly from those found at Mehrgarh. Some settlements had walls surrounding them, which may have served as fortifications (Possehl 2002: 43). One Amri-Nal site, Dholavira in Gujarat, was one of the larger settlements in this phase, at about 60 hectares; this site became one of the five major Harappan sites in the Mature Period.

The Kot Diji phase has sites in Baluchistan, Cholistan, and in the Punjab. While Amri-Nal houses were generally built of mudbrick, Kot Diji houses were often constructed of clay slabs cut from riverbeds. Sometimes considered part of the Kot Dijian phase is the Sothi-Siswal material culture that includes the site of Kalibangan, an important Mature Harappan settlement. The Sothi-Siswal pottery does not differ significantly from the Kot Diji type, which is similar to that of Amri-Nal but distinct enough for differentiation; the base ware is red or buff and painted decoration is dark bands, wavy lines, or fish scale patterns. Another Kot Dijian site is Rehman Dheri; both it and Kalibangan had revetment walls surrounding the settlements. The purpose of these walls, whether to defend against attack or flooding or for some other reason, is as yet unknown. Some organization of labor was required for the building of these reinforced walls. Also notable is that both were planned settlements (Coningham and Young 2015: 163–65), a feature found in the later Mature Harappan settlements as well.

The site of Damb Sadaat gives its name to the third regional phase. Damb Sadaat sites are mainly in northern Baluchistan and include Mehrgarh. The major defining characteristic of Damb Sadaat sites is the plant and animal decoration on their ceramics and the distinctly gray color of the pottery (achieved through oxidization).

While there are hundreds of sites dating to the Early Harappan Period in these various phases, they do not constitute Harappan "civilization" or "state-level society." They do, however, presage what would come in the Mature Harappan Period a century or so later. A diverse socioeconomy based on agriculture and animal pastoralism was well established by the Early Harappan Period, and the presence of differing ceramic types along with other products indicates a robust craft industry existed across the region. The occurrence of regional ceramic types at settlements some distance from their source is evidence of a trade network that also carried marine shells northward from the Arabian Sea and saw the movement of other raw resources such as lapis lazuli and carnelian, as well as copper ore, across the regions. In spite of what appears to have been a sound socioeconomy, burial data, household contents, and other evidence suggest that social differentiation in Early Harappan sites was minimal (Possehl 2002: 46). Relatively small site sizes indicate that full-fledged cities had not yet developed. Barring disruption, the region seemed on the brink of developing a state-level society, but a disruption did occur, delaying the emergence of the Harappan state.

Beginning around 2600 BCE, something happened in the regions outlined earlier, particularly in the Indus River basin, that caused a massive abandonment of sites; some estimate that three out of five, or even three-quarters of the sites, were totally abandoned between 2600 and 2500 BCE. At Kalibangan, apparent displacement led some scholars to believe that an earthquake may have been at least partially responsible for the site abandonment there (Lal 1979). The most common trauma to occur at the abandoned sites was widespread fire. In fact, many were completely razed.

Besides earthquake, other natural events such as regional flooding or environmental disaster have been suggested as causative. The burning episodes have led to the positing of abandonment due to attack resulting either from interregional sources or from external invaders. However aside from the fires, there is little evidence of mass destruction; weaponry and other accoutrements of war were at a minimum, and the sites that survived do not appear to have weathered a battle.

Failing natural and violent explanations, many scholars have turned to one that might seem surprising, but perhaps not in the unique Harappan realm: intentional destruction by the Harappan peoples themselves. This explanation derives from the nature of the rebuilt settlements, many of them on virgin soil and sometimes near where a previous settlement had been razed (Possehl 1998). By 2500 BCE, these rebuilt settlements employed strategies that gave them remarkable similarities across the breadth of the Indus Valley. The architectural plans of Harappan cities and towns are described in more detail later. What astonishes scholars is the planning that must have gone into the building of these settlements in a relatively short period of time. These and other factors add up to the conclusion that the intentional razing of settlements starting around 2600 BCE was accomplished by the Harappan peoples themselves; in the place of old settlements were new, well-planned towns and cities with streets, water management systems, large-scale storage systems, flood protection systems, and craft production areas. It would almost appear that a central governing agency organized the building of these settlements although no such entity was detected during the Early Harappan Period. Nonetheless, whether by a centralized power, a cooperative effort among regional polities, or from outside influence, the towns and cities of the Harappan civilization emerged during this century-long transitional period.

The Indus Valley Civilization in the Mature Harappan Period

During the Mature Harappan Period (ca. 2500–1900 BCE), major centers were located near the Indus and the Saraswati Rivers, but the over 1,500 cities, towns, and villages that are identified as "Harappan" are spread over a vast region extending southeast and far to the east in the region of the Thar Desert and of Gujarat, to Baluchistan in the west, and from the foothills of the Himalayas to the Indus delta at the Arabian Sea (Gangal, Vahia, and Adhikari 2010; Mallah, Shaikh, and Veesar 2002). Some settlements such as Harappa date back to the Early Harappan Period or even earlier, though many of the Mature Harappan settlements were newly founded in the mid-3rd millennium BCE based on the standardized "city plan" for streets, houses, and water management noted earlier. Among the hundreds of settlements dating to the Mature Harappan Period, only five are considered major cities, discussed in more detail later.

The Harappan culture was mainly agrarian (see Box 8.2) with animal husbandry being another important part of the subsistence pattern. Wheat and barley were staple crops across the breadth of the Harappan region, with additional cultivation of lentil and chickpea in most places. Millet, a crop that flourishes in more arid climates, became common in the 3rd millennium as well. During the 2nd millennium, rice cultivation began in the more eastern, wetter areas of the Harappan civilization. These staple grains were accompanied by a few other crops including grapes, sesame, linseed, and a variety of pulses. Animal husbandry was an important part of the Harappan economy; large animals such as cattle were used not only for secondary products (milk, cheese) but also for agricultural work. Various types of cattle were found at Harappan settlements including the humped zebu, water buffalo, and the standard *Bos taurus* (Kenoyer 1998). Pastoralist groups also moved across the Harappan region. The presence of pastoralists, and also what may have been hunter-gatherer groups, explains why Harappans relied most heavily on bovines for milk and for labor; sheep, goat, and wild meat (such as deer) resources may have been readily available from these mobile groups. The Harappans also had domesticated dogs, demonstrated by both the faunal record and figurines of dogs, as well as a south Asian cat species. They may have also made use of the Bactrian camel, though this is less certain, and elephants were hunted for their bones, ivory, and meat. It is possible that some elephants were essentially domesticated, but there is no firm evidence of this as yet. Finally, riverine resources were an important part of Harappan subsistence; Harappan sites have produced extensive faunal evidence of fish exploitation and thus served as an important source of protein in the ancient Harappan diet.

BOX 8.2 HARAPPAN MULTICROPPING

Work at the site of Harappa itself has revealed a sophisticated use of seasonal climates to produce a variety of crops (Weber 1999, 2003). During the south Asian winter, Harappans used the natural rainfall to water crops such as barley, wheat, and legumes, which were staples in the Harappan diet. In the summer, the monsoon rains arrive. At this time, the ancient Harappans grew crops less suitable for subsistence but perhaps intended more directly for trade relations with regional pastoralists (Weber 1999). These crops included cotton and dates, as well as foods that may have been used to feed the animals and people, including millet and rice, though the latter was something of a risky crop in the Harappan landscape (Weber 1999).

Mohenjo Daro: A Harappan Capital

Mohenjo Daro is the most extensively excavated of the Harappan cities and has offered a great deal of insight into how the ancient Harappans organized their social, political, and economic lives. Most believe Mohenjo Daro, which literally means "mound of the dead," was built relatively quickly beginning in the Early Harappan phase, but the high water table here may be hiding earlier occupational levels (Lawler 2013). As is the case with most Harappan settlements, Mohenjo Daro is elevated above the floodplain, built on mudbrick platforms and surrounded by walls that prevent flood waters from entering the city. Like many Harappan cities and towns, Mohenjo Daro has a "citadel" that sits higher on the plain than the rest of the settlement (Figure 8.2).

Situated on the citadel are several non-residential structures, each presenting opportunities for multiple interpretations as to their functions. Perhaps best known is the "Great Bath," which is a rectangular bathing pool; most agree that this water installation was related to Harappan ritual belief and practice (Figure 8.3). North of the Great Bath, in an area called "Block 6," were bathing rooms that may have been contemporary with the Great Bath (allowing people to cleanse themselves prior to entering the sacred pool), or they may have been built late in the Harappan Period to replace the Great Bath. West of the Great Bath is a large structure, originally built of wood, that was initially identified as a granary but has since been alternatively described either as a warehouse for the storage of trade goods or as possibly a public assembly hall (Fentress 1984; Kenoyer 1998; Possehl 2002). East of the Great Bath is a multi-roomed structure called "The College of Priests" by early excavators, thought to be where religious personnel were housed. Most agree this structure was probably residential in nature, and there is some consensus that it may indeed have housed those connected to Harappan religious practices. Finally, just north of the College is an open area identified as the "Great Courtyard," which may have hosted public assemblies for ritual or secular events. The southern part of the citadel held a structure called the "Pillared Hall," which may have

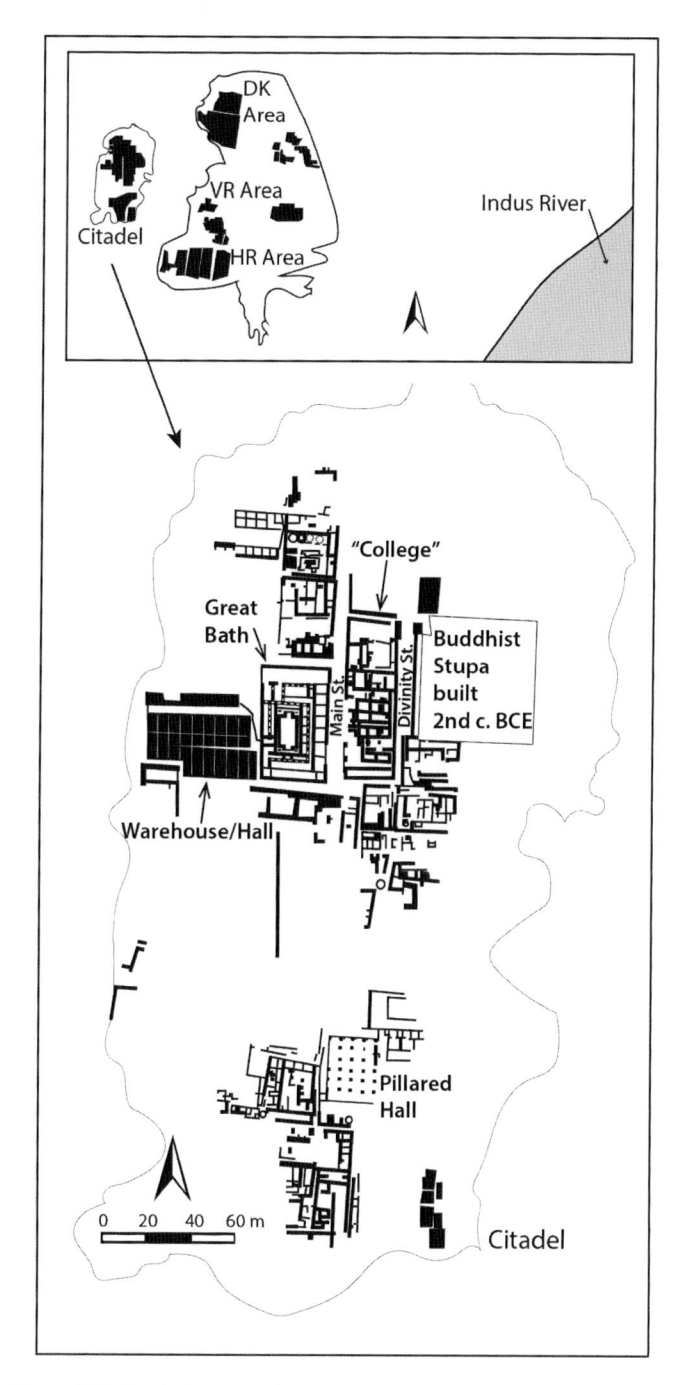

FIGURE 8.2 Top: Plan of Mohenjo Daro settlement; Bottom: Close-up of Structures on the Citadel

Source: Top: After Possehl (2002: 186, figure 11.1); Bottom: After Possehl (2002: 188, figure 11.3)

also been used for public assembly; also located here were craft workshops and residential structures possibly belonging to city elites.

The majority of the Mohenjo Daro population resided in the Lower Town. The entire area was bisected by planned streets (Figure 8.4) built on a grid pattern aligned with the cardinal points.

FIGURE 8.3 Photo of the Great Bath at Mohenjo Daro

Source: Copyright J.M. Kenoyer/Harappa.com, Courtesy Dept. of Archaeology and Museums, Govt. of Pakistan

Smaller streets and alleys separated neighborhoods and blocks of houses. Craft workshops and houses are described in more detail later, but it can be said here that, with only a few exceptions, houses had similar architectural footprints and were generally two-storied with rooms arranged around a central courtyard. A sophisticated water management system snaked throughout the city, allowing for gray water from residences and even workshop areas to be transported either to buried cesspits or through drains leading outside the city walls. Not surprisingly, earlier excavators labeled larger structures in the Lower Town as either temples or palaces, assuming that a major Harappan center must have had such institutions. For instance, the structure known as House I in the DK-G excavation area was identified as a "palace" by an early excavator (Mackay 1938). Houses XXX and L in the HR-B area were also designated as either temples or palaces based primarily on their size. More recent interpretations offer alternative suggestions for some of these buildings; the houses in the HR-B area may have been "a kind of Mohenjo Daro motel" (Possehl 2002: 204), serving as temporary housing for those visiting the city. While some of these structures may have indeed functioned as temples, several scholars assert that they were residences belonging to Harappan elite families (Vidale 2010).

In addition to craft workshops in the Lower Town, market stalls may have existed in the city's open areas, but it is likely that they were most numerous at the city's main gates. Mohenjo Daro as a "type city" lacks only the "fire altars" found at other Harappan settlements (see later under "Harappan Religion"), but these may exist in as yet unexcavated areas.

The Harappan Cityscape and Hinterlands

In part, the Harappan civilization is so intriguing to, and poses such an enigma for, archaeologists because of its remarkable cities and towns, all of which would seem to confirm the presence

FIGURE 8.4 Photo of Typical Street at Mohenjo Daro
Source: Photo courtesy of Saqib Qayyum, 2014

of a central authority that organized the labor, engineers, and architects who designed and built them. Yet there is a paucity of evidence indicating the presence of any major central governmental instrument. Five major cities may have served as the regional centers or capitals of their "states," responsible for administrative, religious, and economic matters: Harappa (ca. 150 hectares) is in the Punjab to the north, Mohenjo Daro (ca. 200 hectares) in Sindh on the Indus River itself, Rakhigari is to the east, Ganweriwala lies in the middle region of the Saraswati (see Box 8.3), and Dholavira (ca. 100 hectares) is in Gujarat. Of these only Harappa, Mohenjo Daro, and Dholavira have been extensively excavated. By far the largest of these centers, Mohenjo Daro may have served as the Harappan "capital city," but this is at present only speculative. The populations of these centers are very difficult to estimate since most of the lower towns remain unexcavated; it is safe to say that the largest cities such as Mohenjo Daro and Harappa harbored populations of upwards of 40,000 people, a number of whom may have been migrants from other south Asian regions (Kenoyer 2005; Valentine et al. 2015).

BOX 8.3 GANWERIWALA AND RAKHIGARI

Neither Ganweriwala, in the Cholistan desert and resting on the ancient Saraswati River, nor Rakhigari in the far eastern reaches of the Harappan area, has been extensively excavated. Survey at Rakhigari suggests it was at least 100 hectares in size. As is the case at other Harappan cities (see later), the city was built on a set of an artificially constructed mudbrick platforms, resulting in at least five mounds enclosed by a revetment wall (Coningham and Young 2015: 192). Ganweriwala was somewhat smaller, roughly 80 hectares in size, and consisted of at least two mounds (Mughal 1990). Both settlements appear to have been built in the Mature Harappan Period, or perhaps just prior to it, and both may have functioned as regional centers.

Most larger Harappan settlements were built on mudbrick "platforms," raised sand bars that served to elevate them above the floodplain. The construction of the mounds is an example of "city planning" by a central authority in that these platforms were necessarily built before the structures were placed upon them. Also remarkable was the uniformity of the brick sizes used at Harappan sites, suggesting that a centrally organized brick-making operation, perhaps even a "class" of brick-makers, masons, and even architects was responsible for building the major and minor centers (Jansen 2010; Kenoyer 1998: 56). In the case of smaller towns, a single wall surrounded the entire settlement, but in the large urban centers, there were often several walls surrounding the separate mounds created by the platforms. Rather than for defense, recent scholarship suggests they were more likely built for practical and possibly symbolic reasons. On a practical level, they were ideal bars to the floodwaters that rose annually from the rivers; they also may have been used to regulate traffic in and out of the settlements, especially with regard to traders and marketeers. In fact, some of the main gateways have small rooms flanking the doorways, which may have housed gatekeepers or tax collectors. Kenoyer suggests that another function of these massive and impressive walls may have been symbolic: those approaching the city—visitors, travelers, traders—saw a majestic scene of great walls enclosing a well-ordered and thriving populace (1998: 56).

Most Harappan cities and towns were arranged in grid patterns with streets and buildings generally oriented to the cardinal points. Architects using astronomical methods may have been responsible for these precise layouts (Kenoyer 1998: 52) (see Box 8.4). Smaller streets and alleys separated neighborhoods. In some cases, the grid pattern became a bit jumbled with additions and reorganizations; not all small streets and buildings were on the cardinal points, but even these neighborhoods were well built (Kenoyer 1997a).

BOX 8.4 DHOLAVIRA OBSERVATORY

The large Harappan city of Dholavira is located on the Tropic of Cancer. An area known as "the Bailey" features a structure containing 13 rooms that are mostly square or rectangular, but 2 are circular in shape (Vahia and Menon 2013). Some of the rectangular rooms contained bathing facilities while the circular structures were too small for residential use. This structure would have once sat quite high on the citadel mound. Inside one of the circular rooms is a long bench-like structure that faces due north (Figure 8.5). Researchers have determined that

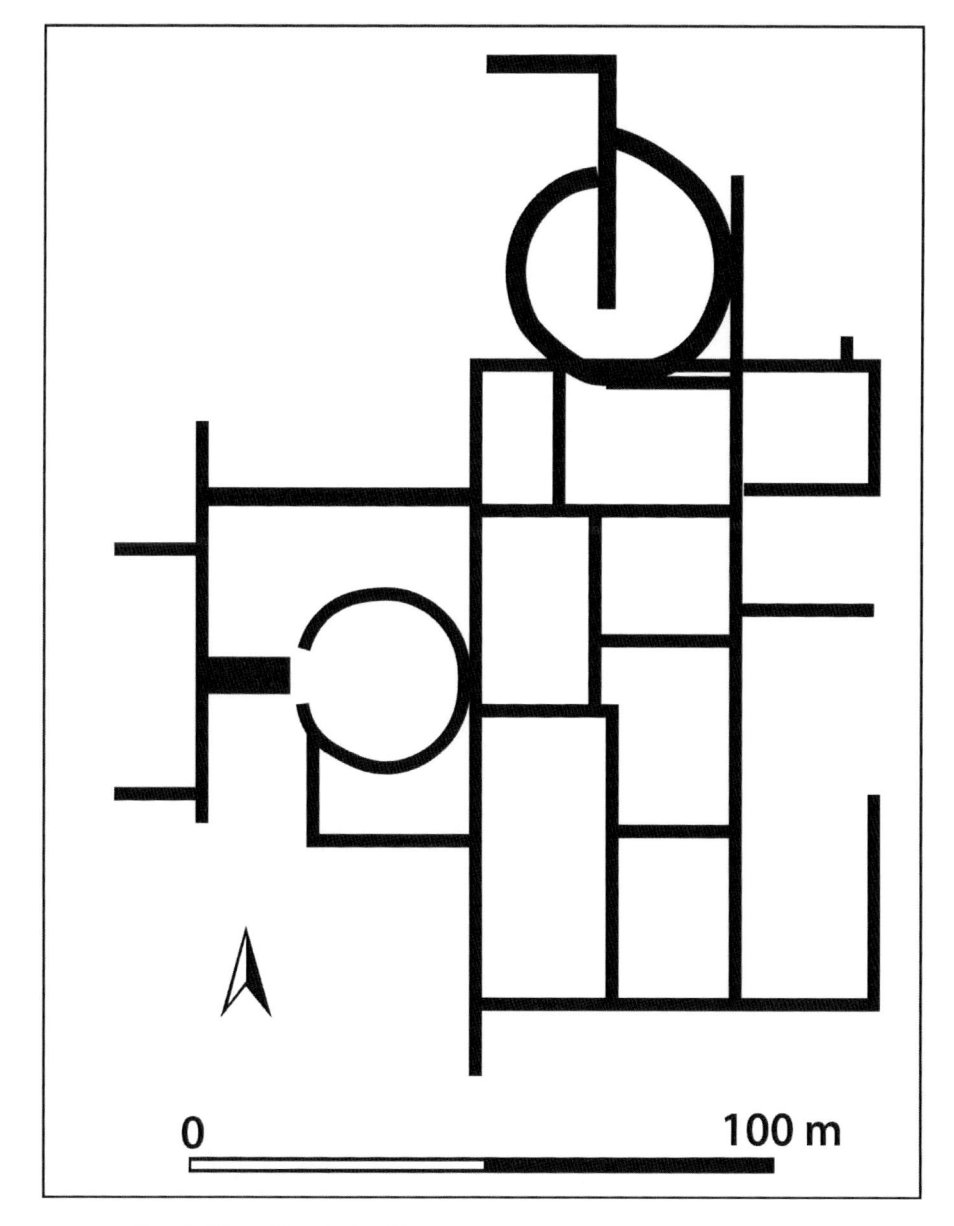

FIGURE 8.5 Sketch Plan of Dholavira Observatory

Source: After Vahia and Menon (2013: 3, fig. 4) (not to scale)

holes cut into the roofs of the two circular buildings offer the opportunity to track the arrival of the summer and winter solstices at noon and at sunset (Vahia and Menon 2013). In the room with the "bench," the light will shine at one end of the bench at noon on the summer solstice, and at the other end, at noon on the winter solstice. In the empty circular room, the light shines one side at sunset during the summer solstice and directly across on the other side at the winter solstice sunset. The changing seasons could be tracked in these unusual rooms at Dholavira. This would have been vitally important to an agricultural society such as the ancient Indus civilization.

Among the utterly remarkable features of the ancient Harappan settlements are the drainage and sewage systems that run through the neighborhoods, to the streets, and then under the outer walls to the floodplains beyond. Again, these are evidence of considerable planning as they had to be built prior to, or contemporary to, the streets and buildings. Drains either ran underground or were covered with brick corbelled arches and paralleled the streets. They carried water from the bathrooms and latrines in houses (see later) to outside the city, ensuring the luxury of clean houses and public areas for most residents.

Most Harappan houses were built on a similar layout, though there was some variation in internal detail; a recent study suggests that different internal plans and some size differentiation reflect family structures and perhaps class status (Cork 2011). Houses were built with rooms arrayed around an interior courtyard, and most houses were two- and sometimes three-storied. Household activities took place in the inner courtyard, and doors and windows had wooden shutters that were probably latticed to allow light and air in even when closed (Kenoyer 1998: 58). Harappan houses may have had one room dedicated to worship at a household shrine. Hearths are curiously few in number, leading archaeologists to speculate that cooking areas were on the second floor rather than at ground level. Based on the more extensive excavations at Mohenjo Daro, it can be said that most Harappan houses had a well or at least had access to a neighborhood well (Figure 8.6); Harappa had fewer household wells, but a large central reservoir may have replaced the need for individual house wells. At Dholavira, stone-lined cisterns, logical given the far more extensive rains that fall in Gujarat, replaced individual wells. Whatever the system, each Harappan settlement ensured easy access to clean water for its residents.

The desire for purity in residences is clearly seen in the presence of bathrooms and latrines in most Harappan houses. The bathrooms had sloped baked brick floors that allowed the water to drain, through gutters or holes in the floor, into the city sewage system or into underground cesspits (Jansen 1989; Possehl 2005). Latrines were separate from the bathrooms and had a large jar or sump pot built into the floor; a small hole allowed the waste to drain into the sewage system. Kenoyer suggests the pots were regularly cleaned, perhaps by a special class of laborers dedicated to this task (1998: 60).

Most houses were sufficient for housing nuclear families (Sarcina 1979). A few dwellings were larger, sometimes located on the highest citadels, and consisted of the standard house surrounded by smaller units and courtyards. A common interpretation for these structures is that they may have belonged to the wealthy elite in Harappan society, or perhaps to leaders (either secular or religious), or that they reflect extended family structures with several (related) nuclear families co-habitating.

Public architecture in Harappan settlements is comparatively rare, quite a reversal from the description of the many palaces and temples found in Mesopotamian, Mesoamerican, or southeast Asian civilizations. Religious structures are singularly lacking with only a few exceptions described

FIGURE 8.6 Example of a Private Well at Mohenjo Daro
Source: Photo courtesy of Usman Ghani, 2014

in more complete detail later. Other public areas and buildings include open courts, halls likely meant for public assemblies, and warehouses. A final class of structures in Harappan cities and towns can be defined as dedicated to craft production and industry and possibly to business activities.

Craft Production and the Harappan Trade Network

Although the Harappan civilization was primarily an agrarian one, it had a thriving craft production industry and traded its goods far and wide. Given the wealth of resources available in the Indus and Saraswati river valleys and surrounding regions, it is not surprising that a great variety of Harappan crafts was produced throughout the region. Utilitarian goods included household ceramics, usually unpainted, metal or flint agricultural and fishing tools, baskets and mats, and likely leather goods. Also found in Harappan houses were terracotta figurines, many of animals and even replicas of ox-carts and the cows/oxen that pulled them, as well as human figurines. The latter are discussed in greater detail later; the former may have been used in religious ritual, as "toys," or replicas used for teaching. Cotton textile production, as well as possibly flax production, was also likely a typical household craft. Simple furniture, some made of wood, was also produced for the home.

Crafts produced for trade or for elite consumption included beautifully painted ceramics (usually black paint on a red slip with floral or geometric designs), fine jewelry made of carnelian, lapis lazuli, agate beads and semiprecious or precious metals, copper/bronze, shell, and ivory objects (including inlay in wood furniture), and perfumes. Indus craft-makers were also skilled in the production of faience items (rock quartz mixed with colored minerals to produce a glassy material) including amulets and pendants, small containers for unguents or oils, and ornaments (Kenoyer 1998: 156).

A remarkable technology invented by Indus artisans was the production of the black, gray, and red stoneware bangles and rings that were made specifically for the elites. These earliest examples of extremely highly fired ceramics were inscribed with what were likely the names of their bearers; stoneware bangle production seems to have been a tightly controlled state craft, kept so secret that the technique was lost when the Indus civilization fell (Kenoyer 1998: 75; Vidale 2000: 92). Another controlled product was steatite seals. Soft soapstone was carved into square stamp seal shapes inscribed with symbols and writing; the soapstone was then fired resulting in the much harder material known as glazed steatite. Recent evidence suggests that Harappan artisans may have also produced textiles made of silk (Good, Kenoyer, and Meadow 2009), making this region the only one outside of China involved in silk production at this early stage. Besides the craft-making professions, there must have been other specialists such as architects and masons, well-digging engineers, and street and sewer cleaners.

The raw resources for these industries were either located in the Harappan heartland or attainable through regional trade. For instance, clay was abundant in the numerous river valleys that crisscrossed the entire area, and flint could be obtained from the hills to the west and north. Timber was acquired from Gujarat and likely from the north in Punjab (Ratnagar 2004: 133), and marine shells came from the settlements located on the southern coastline. Carnelian and agate were available in Gujarat, and lapis lazuli likely came from a source in Afghanistan though another potential source has also been located in Baluchistan (Asthana 1993). Copper was available in the adjacent regions of Rajasthan and the Deccan plain (just east of the Harappan region), and an added bonus was the presence of arsenic in the copper ore from these regions, producing a natural bronze, which is a more durable metal than plain copper. Gold can still be found in the upper Indus River sediments, and electrum (gold with silver content) was available from south India (Agrawal and Kharakwal 2003: 79; Asthana 1993). Silver likely came from Rajasthan, east of the Harappan region, as well as Afghanistan and Iran (Asthana 1993). Given that the Harappans fashioned jewelry, vessels, amulets, and other items from all these materials, it is clear that they engaged in significant trade with the regions surrounding their civilization.

Where high-end crafts and trade goods were produced has been of great interest to archaeologists for the potential information this might provide regarding governmental control of the Harappan economy (e.g., Kenoyer 1992, 1997b; Miller 2007; Vidale 2000). Workshops for these types of crafts were located in various settings. Many Harappan houses had a workshop incorporated into the dwelling itself, indicating some members of the household engaged in craft production as a "family business," which might produce smaller but still valuable items such as beads, steatite objects, shell inlays, and jewelry (Coningham and Young 2015: 188).

In the cities and larger towns, there were often complexes of workshops, usually in rows along a street, where craft-makers specialized in the manufacture of specific products; artifactual analysis suggests that the craft-makers lived in houses in the same vicinity as the workshops, creating a "craftmakers' neighborhood" (Kenoyer 1998: 130). Most often, the crafts were located in the lower town residential neighborhoods, but a few were up on citadels. It is possible that the products that were of particular concern to the state, such as the stoneware bangles, weights and measures, and steatite seals, were produced in locations that were more tightly controlled on the citadels or in workshop neighborhoods that could be peopled by those designated by Harappan leaders; an entire workshop area dedicated to the production of stoneware bangles, walled off from the surrounding neighborhoods, was identified at Mohenjo Daro (Wright 2010: 160). At Harappa, a workshop dedicated to the production of high-end products made of semiprecious beads, gold, and other costly items was located near the city gate; some interpret this as evidence that city authorities could better control goods production if the workshops were in this more public area (Kenoyer 1997b; Vidale 2000: 138), while others suggest the location was chosen by craftspeople for its strategic proximity to the market and marketeers near the gate (Miller 2007).

While production of the items used specifically by elites may have been controlled at some level, there is nothing to suggest that Harappan craft-makers did not choose where they worked and what they produced. At Harappa, the production of ceramics and metals, requiring pyrotechnical equipment and producing noxious fumes, was located in the heart of residential neighborhoods (in many ancient civilizations, such crafts were located outside the town walls), suggesting that craft-makers chose to live and work in the neighborhood where the entire craft, from raw clay and ore to finished elite product, was fashioned (Miller 2007). There is also evidence that craft-makers lived in the same neighborhoods where they worked, suggesting to a number of archaeologists that the Harappan craft industry was organized along the lines of a "guild structure" or based on kin relations wherein craft-making techniques passed down through the generations and techniques could be closely guarded. While the structure of state control over artisans is unclear, the standardization of weights and even seal designs suggests a central authority was involved on some level (see Box 8.5).

BOX 8.5 HARAPPAN WEIGHTS

The volume of both raw resources and finished products moving in and out of Harappan cities and towns required a strong administrative system. An elaborate weight system consisting of cubical weights made of stone was used in Harappan cities and towns. They were standardized ensuring similar measurements across the breadth of the civilization (Kenoyer 2010). Weights were often found near main gateways demonstrating that goods were checked, measured, and probably recorded, as they entered the settlement. The small rooms on either side of major Harappan city gateways may have housed people who counted and weighed incoming goods and perhaps collected taxes from merchants who wished to conduct business in the city (Kenoyer 1998: 128). If goods arrived by boat, there was likely a similar system in place at the riverside dock.

Harappans made substantial use of their rivers to move goods from one region to another, attested to by the images of flat-bottomed boats found on Harappan artifacts Goods were also transported using human labor and ox-drawn carts. Some settlements in strategic locations seem to have been specifically devoted to the acquisition of raw resources. For instance, a settlement called Manda, located far to the north, was responsible for the procurement and subsequent movement of timber from the foothills of the Himalayas; Lothal, in Gujarat, collected many of the resources from that region including carnelian and agate for distribution to the rest of the Harappan region (Coningham and Young 2015: 219–20). The substantial amount of craft production that took place at Lothal, including bead, copper, shell, and ivory production, speaks to its important location as a resource procurement center as well as an industrial town (Rao 1973). An examination of raw resources used to make crafts at three Harappan cities—Mohenjo Daro, Kalibangan, and Lothal—suggests these resources came from the same origin, attesting to a well-organized trade and distribution system between the Harappan settlements (Chakrabarti 2004).

Besides the movement of goods within the Indus and Saraswati regions, Harappan crafts are found in locations far beyond the boundaries of the civilization. Harappans traded with south India and to the northwest with regions in Afghanistan and Iran. Harappans also engaged in a lively trade with cultures far to the west, including the Sumerians of Mesopotamia (see Chapter 5) and residents on the gulf coast such as ancient Magan (Oman) and Dilmun (likely Bahrain). To enable this trade, particularly with the gulf coast, several settlements were established on the Makran coast (today located in western Pakistan), an inhospitable location; the settlements of Sutkagen-Dor and Sotka Koh were established to facilitate the movement of shiploads of goods between gulf coast settlements and the Harappan heartland (Ratnagar 2004: 82–84). At sites in Magan and Dilmun archaeologists have discovered Harappan ceramics, jewelry, and ivory goods (Ratnagar 1981); Harappans likely gained products such as shells and leather, and possibly turtles, from these gulf settlements. There is substantial evidence of Harappan trade with southern Mesopotamia. The presence of carnelian jewelry in the Royal Cemetery of Ur (ca. 2600–2450 BCE, see Chapter 5) speaks to interaction with Harappa even at this early stage; archaeologists have launched studies on burials in the Ur cemetery to determine if actual Harappans might be buried there (Kenoyer et al. 2013). In their texts, the Sumerians referred to Harappa as "Meluhha" and records from the court of Sargon of Akkad, ruling in the late 24th century BCE, note that Meluhhan ships docked at his city on the middle Euphrates during his reign. Besides Harappan jewelry (made of gold, agate, carnelian, and lapis lazuli), Meluhha provided Mesopotamia with timber, ivory, ceramics (and likely their contents), metal objects, animals and possibly pearls (Ratnagar 2004). It is unclear what Harappans brought home from Mesopotamia, though woolen textiles, perfumes, and other liquids have been suggested as likely imports.

The thriving exchange network in which the Harappans engaged must be highlighted as one of the important elements that catapulted it to become a powerful ancient civilization. It may be here, in the organization and control of the trade in raw resources and finished products, that leaders and elites exercised the majority of their seemingly lightly expressed control over the Harappan population.

The Indus Script

With the extensive trade and administrative activities in the Harappan civilization, some record-keeping method was necessary and indeed the Harappans did have a writing system. Unfortunately, in spite of tremendous efforts, the Harappan script has not yet been deciphered. There are several factors hindering the attempt at decipherment. The first is that the vast majority of examples of Harappan script come from the small steatite seals (Figure 8.7) that probably list only names or offices rather than full sentences of any kind. Another is the lack of a bilingual inscription, for instance, one translating Sumerian words into Harappan ones, or vice versa. Finally, Harappan script consists of approximately 400 symbols, which are likely logosyllabic: one character represents a syllable (morpheme), resulting in a variety of combinations with no consistent patterning that might lead to decipherment. What is known is that Harappans were etching symbols (some identical to later Harappan script) onto pottery and other objects as early as the late 4th millennium BCE, making their experiments with writing roughly contemporary with those in southern Mesopotamia (Kenoyer 2005).

Harappan seals usually feature an image, often an animal, and a short line of writing that most likely provides either the seal owner's name or administrative position in the city. The animals on Harappan seals vary, though the most common is the "unicorn," which combines a cow with an antelope-like horn (Figure 8.8); zebu bulls are also common, and less often, other Asian animals are found on the seals. Other objects bearing Harappan writing include miniature tablets from cities such as Harappa, Dholavira, Lothal, and Mohenjo Daro. These are very small clay tablets that, like seals, feature a short line of writing and sometimes a picture. The function of these miniature tablets is uncertain; they may have served as accounting tokens for goods or perhaps to record offerings or represent prayers to the deities. Stoneware bangles and other small personal objects also have short inscriptions. At Dholavira, a large-scale inscription may have hung above a main gateway proclaiming the name of the city or perhaps of the gate. If Harappan cities, gates, and perhaps even

FIGURE 8.7 Harappan Script on Seals

Source: R. Jennison

neighborhoods were sign-posted, this raises an interesting question about the level of literacy in the Harappan population. Perhaps it was not only leaders and scribes who could read the signs and seals but also merchants, craft-makers, and even farmers.

Given that the Harappans had a well-developed script and clearly wished to account for the movement of goods, it would seem likely that extensive records were kept of the substantial Harappan economic activities. However, such records must have been kept on perishable materials, which may have been made of wood, cloth, or even bark or leaves. There is a variety of organic materials that would have been quite useful for short-term record keeping (for months or even years) but would not last in the archaeological record.

The Harappan People

Without written evidence, it is quite difficult to delve deeply into the social organization of a given society, particularly in the ancient world. Nonetheless, a few clues to Harappan status, kinship, marriage, and gender relations can be gleaned from data derived from figurines, burials, and the spatial organization of Harappan settlements.

That status differentiation existed within ancient Harappan society is almost a given, though the data demonstrating it is quite minimal. As already noted, there is a surprising lack of differentiation

FIGURE 8.8 Example of Harappan Seal With Unicorn

Source: Copyright Harappa Archaeological Research Project/Harappa.com, Courtesy Dept. of Archaeology and Museums, Govt. of Pakistan

in the size and decoration of Harappan houses. There are a few remarkable dwellings that may have housed secular or religious elites, though other explanations for these are also offered in this chapter. Beyond these, however, the lesser elites may have lived in houses that were not much different from those occupied by craft-makers and perhaps even farmers. One possible indicator of status is a preponderance of metal cooking vessels, which may have been used by elites, while lower classes used ceramics of varying quality depending on economic circumstances (Kenoyer 1998: 158). Otherwise, the superior construction of houses and their well-stocked contents suggest that most Harappans had a very good standard of living, regardless of their profession.

That most Harappans lived relatively well is borne out by biological anthropology. Harappan skeletons do not show vast differentiation in access to a balanced diet or exposure to disease or hard labor. Evidence suggests that many Harappans, whether wealthy or not, suffered from dental caries (tooth decay), which is typical in ancient populations. Another threat to Harappan health was malaria, and some Harappans showed evidence of stress on their necks from carrying heavy loads on their heads (Possehl 2002: 174–75). Thus, the architectural and biological data from Harappan settlements suggests that, while social differentiation most likely existed throughout the region, the gap between wealthy and "poor" was not a dramatic one when it came to living circumstances and health issues.

The evidence for kin relationships is also drawn from spatial and biological data. As described earlier, crafts were produced either within individual households or in craft production neighborhoods where the artisans also likely lived. While crafts produced in these areas sometimes changed, for instance, from shell-working to ivory-carving, this change took place only after a number of generations of making the original craft. At Harappa, a pottery production area, including two kilns to fire the finished products, existed for several centuries (Wright 1991, 2010: 187). Inhabitants of the craft production neighborhoods were related socially or perhaps more likely through kinship (see Wright 2010: 182–89 for discussion). Added to this are what appear to be residential neighborhoods consisting of nuclear family homes clustered together. This may reflect kin members living in proximity to one another. Biological anthropology also contributes to this picture. Genetic trait analysis of skeletal remains at Harappa show that males were only distantly related to one another while females had close genetic ties (Kenoyer 1998: 133). This would suggest a matrilocal residential practice (males moving to live with their new wives in the bride's ancestral home), possibly making the kinship ties based on matrilineal, female-centered relationships.

The position of women vis-à-vis men is quite difficult to ascertain with the evidence currently available. There was a higher incidence of dental caries in women than in men. Whether this is indicative of a better and more balanced diet for men is unclear. Another possible indicator of women's secondary status to men is found in the numerous female figurines found at Harappan sites. While many portray individual females, there are a fair number of females with infants or small children in their arms, figurines possibly used in rituals related to motherhood and fertility. What is notable is that where the sex of the infant or child is recognizable, they are almost always male, possibly indicating a preference for male children (Kenoyer 1998: 132).

On the other hand, there is plenty of evidence to suggest that women, at least in the elite classes but perhaps in the craft-making classes as well, held important positions in society. Burial evidence does not demonstrate strong differentiation between social status groups, nor does it distinguish substantially between males and females. Grave goods are found in fairly equal numbers in the graves of both sexes. As noted earlier, evidence suggests a matrilocal residence pattern following marriage; though not always the case, in many societies, matrilocal residence, often paired with matrilineal kinship systems, also means that property (land and goods) passes through the female line. A correlation to this are the many crafts manufactured in Harappan settings. Crafts were fashioned not just in the "craft-making neighborhoods" but also in individual homes. There is no reason to believe that it was only the males who made the crafts in the household; in fact, it might be more logical to infer that, while men were farming or carrying out other activities away from the residence, women were taking care of household tasks, which might have included craft production. Furthermore, in a detailed study of pottery production in a Harappan neighborhood, Wright (1991) found that women might have been engaged in this craft production industry. Finally, there may have been considerable female influence or power in Harappan religion. Discussed in much more detail in the next section, evidence suggests that, at the very least, there were important female deities in the ancient pantheon.

A last characteristic defining Harappan peoples was their attention to their appearance. Seen in the figurines and statuary, and representations on seals and tablets, it is clear that the proper clothing, jewelry, and hairstyle, for both men and women, were important to ancient Harappans. Social status may have been most prominently represented in Harappan dress and adornment. The number and type of bangles worn by Harappans may have been a very clear indicator of status: terracotta bangles for non-elites and the beautiful stoneware bangles for those at the upper echelon. Other ornaments such as shell bangles, faience rings, and various types of pendants and anklets may all have signaled societal position to the Harappans. The same may be said of hairstyles. Figurines and statuary show a variety of elaborate hairstyles that may have also clearly signaled a person's status and provided other information as well, including perhaps kinship group, marriage status, or even ethnic identity. Human figurines found at Harappa show evidence of painted-on clothing demonstrating a great concern for the sporting of stylish textiles (Kenoyer 2005) by the ancient Harappans.

The Harappan Religion

The ancient Harappan religion is perhaps the only subject that incites more scholarly speculation than the Harappan script or leadership structure. In most other chapters in this book, a reader will find that the building of temples, worship of deities, and some form of ritual obedience to usually a combination of secular and supernatural leaders was part and parcel of an ancient civilization. While the ancient Harappans clearly had deep religious beliefs, they were not expressed in fabulous temples or by lavish offerings. Harappan myth and ritual appears to be focused on the health, fertility, and success of the society as a whole. The majority of religious practice may have taken place in individual Harappan households.

Some of the architectural features most closely associated with Harappan religion have already been mentioned. Chief among these is the Great Bath on the citadel at Mohenjo Daro (Figure 8.9). The Great Bath, measuring 12 by 7 meters with steps leading into the pool at either end, was constructed so that it was watertight and allowed water to drain into the city sewage system; nearby bathing facilities, if contemporary, allowed for purification prior to entering the pool. Across the street is the "College of the Priests," which may have housed religious personnel but may have also been a secular residence. Though no "great baths" have been discovered at other Harappan settlements, some evidence for bathing platforms at sites such as Lothal and non-domestic water facilities on the citadel at Dholavira suggest that water and ritual purity were very important parts of Harappan religious ideology (Possehl 2005). The elaborate household bathing facilities and waste water management in Harappan settlements is further testament to this. Though no temples dot Harappan landscapes, there may have been altars present. Plastered mudbrick structures, set into the ground on Harappan citadels or in lower towns at sites such as Kalibangan, Lothal, Rakhigarhi, and elsewhere, may have functioned as "fire altars" providing for public sacrifice or some type of worship (recently some of these have been relabeled as hearths); at Kalibangan, some fire altars were installed within private residences (Bala 2004). Ashy remains in these structures, which include animal bones, are further signs of possible sacrificial rituals at these fire installations. Fire and water, central to modern Indian Hinduism, may have been sacred elements in south Asian religion as much as 4,000 years ago (see Steadman 2009 for discussion). If fire and water were central to Harappan beliefs, there is no overwhelming evidence that access to these elements was limited or controlled by the state.

In addition to these clearly non-domestic structures, some buildings in the residential areas of Mohenjo Daro and elsewhere may have had religious significance. Chief among these is "House 1" in the HR-A area of Mohenjo Daro. The structure contained no well nor other normal domestic items; inside were many seals, ceramics, and jewelry, and in the courtyard was a brick ring, which may have once held a sacred pipal tree (see later). Interpretations of this structure have identified it as a priest's house or a neighborhood temple (Ratnagar 2001), though the presence of the seals puts one in mind of administrative storage as well.

Among the Harappan artifacts touted as religious in nature, none are more often discussed in this context than the terracotta figurines. Many of the figurines are female, fewer are male, and a substantial number cannot be identified as to sex (Clark 2003). Figurines often have elaborate hairstyles

FIGURE 8.9 Artistic Reconstruction of the Great Bath

Source: M.J. Hughes

and headdresses, bangles and necklaces and may have been painted red (Figure 8.10). Some show evidence of soot stains suggesting they were used in or near fire, perhaps even as lamps. Though early interpretations suggested the figurines represented a strong female goddess or mother earth cult, the find spots of the figurines are not conducive to this proposal. Most were found broken and in what appear to be "trash" contexts in street debris and elsewhere (Ratnagar 2001). Recent scholarship suggests that these terracotta figurines were indeed likely used in ritual but only once. A figurine may have been quickly fashioned and adorned appropriately, perhaps adding clothing

FIGURE 8.10 Example of Harappan Female Figurine

Source: Copyright J.M. Kenoyer/Harappa.com, Courtesy Dept. of Archaeology and Museums, Govt. of Pakistan

or markings to evoke the appropriate deity, then used in the household or public ritual, and finally intentionally broken and discarded. After its religious use, it may have even become a plaything for the children; similar interpretations for the many animal figurines have also been offered. While female figurines holding infants and children might be safely interpreted as pertaining to fertility or successful childbirth, the adorned but childless figurines (both male and female) present more of an enigma. One may speculate that they simply represented the god or goddess to whom the prayer was offered (perhaps for a bountiful harvest, safe passage in a long journey, or recovery from an illness) or were perhaps self-representations of Harappan individuals making the offering. The presence of these figurines in streets and alleys around the Harappan settlements suggests they may have often been used in domestic contexts, attesting to household worship and ritual.

A far less frequent occurrence is Harappan stone statuary. Most examples depict males, but at least one, a head found in a colonnaded hall near the Great Bath, may be of a woman. If male statues

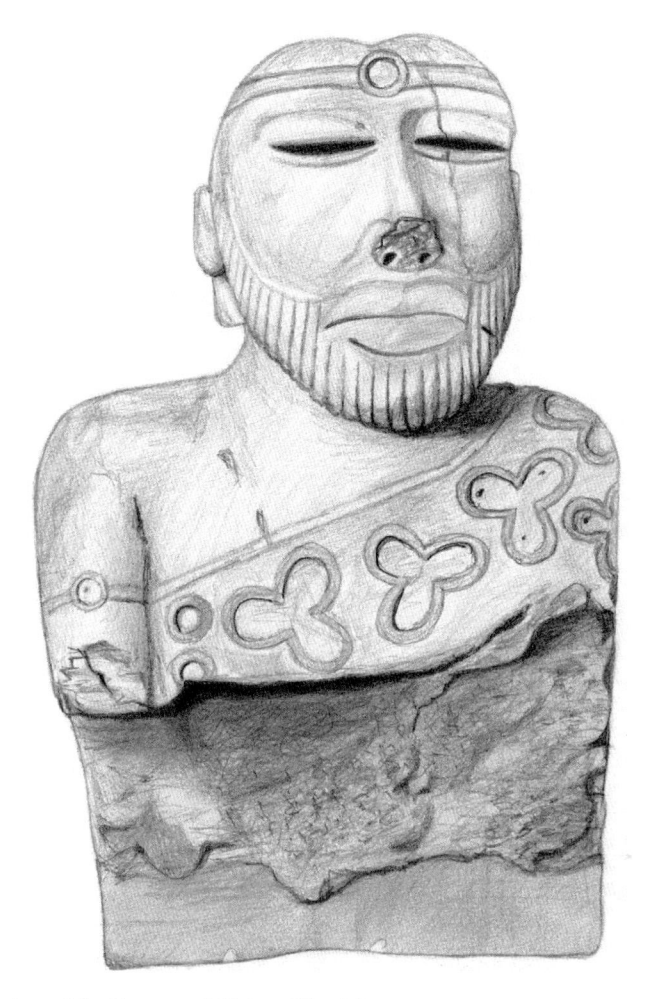

FIGURE 8.11 Drawing of the So-named "Priest-King" Statue

Source: R. Jennison

are clothed, they usually wear a robe that covers only the right shoulder; the most famous example of this is the beautifully wrought statue known as the "Priest-King" though there is no evidence to suggest he was either priest or king (Figure 8.11). His robe displays trefoil designs, perhaps embroidered, and on his forehead, he wears a cord holding a circle, possibly a stoneware bangle. Who was depicted in these stone statues—priests and priestesses, secular leaders, or a combination of these—is not known.

Some of the best insights into Harappan religion come from the seals depicting animals and what appear to be deities and sacred images. One or two representations are suggestive of the importation of myths from trade partners in Mesopotamia such as the possible "Gilgamesh" scene on two Harappan seals (Agrawal 2007; Parpola 1984), but the vast majority of seals depict purely Harappan themes. The human figures on seals typically wear bangles on their arms and horned crowns. Some are seated in a yogic pose (Figure 8.12) and appear to feature three faces (a fourth being assumed to face the back of the seal), and many are associated with a plant thought to be a pipal tree (*Ficus religiosa*), which is a sacred tree in modern India (Figure 8.13). Most scholars believe the anthropomorphic figures on these seals depict deities, both male and female. In some cases, the

FIGURE 8.12 Drawing of the "Proto-Shiva" Seal

Source: R. Jennison

FIGURE 8.13 Photo of a Pipal Tree (*Ficus religious*) and Its Heart-shaped Leaves

Source: Photo by S.R. Steadman

figure seems to be receiving offerings; in others, they are associated with animals, especially the bull; and in several, the plant/tree is prominent, portrayed either enveloping the figure or in one case growing out of the vagina. From their earliest discovery, there have been vigorous arguments identifying the male figure in the seals as a "proto-Shiva," referring to one of the most important gods in modern Hinduism, and the female figure as Shakti/Durga, who is Shiva's consort (Chakrabarti 2001; Possehl 2002; Ratnagar 2001). While there are certainly detractors to this argument (Hiltebeitel 1978; Srinivasan 1984), the majority of scholars believe there is reasonable evidence to suggest this ancient Harappan worship of deities and plants later became prominent elements in the Hindu religion. The depiction of both male and female deities on these seals (which may have belonged to religious personnel) might suggest that both female and male principles were important in ancient Harrapan belief and that that females may have served in some religious capacity.

The presence of animals, particularly the bull, and plants, especially the pipal tree, suggests these also played a role in Harappan beliefs. Bull imagery is found on seals, small tablets, ceramics, and even on small clay masks that might have adorned wooden statues or perhaps puppets. That the bull was a tremendously important animal in the Harappan economy, assisting both in the movement of trade goods and in the agricultural sphere, is undeniable. It is not surprising that some ritual or cult involving this and perhaps other animals was present in the Harappan religion. The pipal tree, featuring heart-shaped leaves, is easily recognizable and may have functioned as a center of worship in Harappan settlements (Kenoyer 1998: 106). Brick rings at Mohenjo Daro may signal where the sacred pipal tree grew, offering a place of worship for residents.

While some elements of Harappan religion appear to have been restricted to leaders and/or elites, such as the Great Bath on the Mohenjo Daro citadel and the possession of seals depicting apparently religious images, other aspects seem to have been freely available to the Harappan people. Chief among this was their access to ritual purity in their own homes. In addition, the ubiquitous fashioning of figurines, ostensibly for ritual use, the presence of open areas for public (religious?) gatherings, the access to pipal trees, and the publicly accessed fire altars all speak to a religion that was not used to control the population but rather to unify it and promote a well-ordered community.

Clues to the Harappan Sociopolitical Structure

This chapter began with a quote by Winston Churchill. Another quote, this one by a well-known scholar of the ancient Indus culture, expresses the same sentiment:

> Ever since the discovery of the Indus Valley civilization, archaeologists have been looking for objects that would help to identify the rulers and political leaders of the cities. . . . What they have found is quite unexpected, because it does not follow the general pattern seen in other early urban societies.
>
> *(Kenoyer 1998: 81)*

Kenoyer goes on to explain that what we have come to expect in complex societies, including large monuments built to signal power and control, elaborate religious centers, palaces and residences occupied by rulers and elites, and a standing army, are all largely missing from Harappan cities and towns or at least are not present in the forms we might expect. There is a remarkable lack of evidence that Harappans ever engaged in warfare; though metal tools abound, metal weapons of war are conspicuously lacking (Agrawal and Kharakwal 2003: 81). Several groups of dead Harappans, initially described as "massacred victims" of an attack (Wheeler 1968), have more recently been interpreted as victims of a contagious disease such as cholera; the dead were found buried in an abandoned house perhaps in an effort to stop the spread of the illness. On neither the "massacred" dead nor on any of those discovered in cemeteries has clear evidence of battle wounds been found. The title of a book by McIntosh, *A Peaceful Realm* (2002), appears to be a largely accurate description. While the clues to understanding the Harappan sociopolitical structure are quite elusive and can be interpreted in a variety of ways, they still provide some insight and are explored here.

That there was some sort of authority present in ancient Harappan cities and towns is at the very least attested to by the architecture of these settlements. The streets and buildings laid out on cardinal points, the water and sewage systems, and the city and neighborhood walls, all underpinned by substantial mudbrick platforms, point to the ability of some entity to not only plan out the settlements but to mobilize the labor to build them. At both Mohenjo Daro and Harappa, large buildings identified by the original excavators as granaries were probably not used as such given the lack of storage vessels and charred grains (Kenoyer 1998: 64–65). It is more likely they were public assembly halls where leaders might receive visitors and propitiates.

Since excavations began at Harappan sites in the early 20th century, some buildings were identified as elite houses. Already discussed are several large buildings in the residential quarter of Mohenjo Daro, one considered a "motel" for visiting merchants or officials, thereby explaining their multiple bathing facilities and larger size. A recent study of residential complexes at Mohenjo Daro (Vidale 2010) suggests that early identifications of some residential compounds as belonging to elites should be considered an accurate designation. The so-called "palace" in area HR may have had a monumental gate and limestone pillars (Vidale 2010), certainly speaking to significant labor investment and thus likely housing residents possessing the wealth and status to command such a structure (Steadman 2015). That elites and leaders must have existed at major Harappan cities and towns is largely indisputable. More technologically advanced archaeological techniques may yield new evidence that there was more visual differentiation between Harappan (possibly kin-based) residential complexes than is at present observable and that social stratification and economic competition was alive and well in the ancient Indus civilization.

Another area where a central authority must have been involved in Harappan life was in the extensive trade system. Not only were raw resources effectively transported within Harappan regions, but Harappan goods were traded from south India to Mesopotamia and to regions north and further east. This smooth and well-organized system almost certainly could not have resulted from independent merchants and traders working individually across the Harappan state but rather from some type of government regulation that organized, facilitated, and probably controlled the movement of goods and possibly peoples. A further clue to this control comes in the form of the standardized weights identical across cities and towns, which must have required a centralized system established by an authority overseeing Harappan trade.

While production of many crafts may have been at the household cottage industry level, there is evidence to suggest some crafts, especially those resulting in valuable trade goods, were controlled by a central authority. For instance, the workshop situated near the city gate at Harappa may have been located there because it could be more easily monitored than if it was nestled within a residential neighborhood. At the site of Gola Dharo in Gujarat, archaeologists discovered bead-making workshops in an unwalled area of the settlement; however, the materials needed to supply the bead-makers were stored in a building on the citadel (Bhan et al. 2005) suggesting a central authority oversaw the production process of this high-end craft.

Powerful clues reside in the presence of Harappan stoneware bangles bearing inscriptions worn by Harappan elites. The production of these items was more tightly controlled than even high-value trade items, and as already noted, the production technique was held in such secrecy, presumably by the central authority and designated craft-makers, that the art was lost after the collapse of the Harappan civilization.

Harappan seals were also markers of important positions in Harappan society. Seals were used to stamp wet clay that marked packages or closed jars. This clearly shows that the seals were used to demonstrate ownership (by individuals or the state) of goods and were important to the vast Harappan economic system. The depicted animals, the "unicorns," zebu cattle, and other animals such as rhinos and elephants, have been variously identified as kinship totems, city identifiers, or representations of occupational groups. What seems certain is that the animals on the seals were an easily recognized symbol of whatever position the bearer held in Harappan society; those who were non-literate or even those in other places, such as Mesopotamia, could immediately identify who, or at least what group or office, had "stamped" goods based on the seal image. McIntosh suggests that animals represented the "field of operation" of the bearer (2008: 258–59). Unicorns might have represented those in the state bureaucracy while bulls denoted traders and/or merchants. Seals with some of the more unusual imagery might logically then have belonged to those in the religious realm.

Transitions: De-Urbanization and New Regionalization

The Harappan culture's demise is shrouded in great mystery. Initially attributed to the arriving Indo-Aryans, horse-riders originally from the Russian steppes who brought Hindi and a major portion of Indian Hinduism to the subcontinent, archaeology finds no evidence of violence or even the arrival of a new population in the early centuries of the 2nd millennium BCE. Attributing the decline of a major civilization to just one factor is no longer a tenable option in today's archaeology, and like the rise of any civilization, its collapse is quite complicated. By 1900 BCE, the Saraswati River had shifted course and was in the process of drying up, severely affecting the agricultural and trade abilities of the Harappans living in Gujarat and nearby regions. People from these regions may have migrated to other Harappan cities and towns, possibly causing overcrowding and creating a strain on resources, which may have led to civic disorder (Kenoyer 2005). Maintenance of the significant water management systems may have placed stress on the governing councils, and in fact, the appearance of groups of dead bodies, sealed up in abandoned houses in the later phases of the Harappan state, speaks to the possibility that diseases such as cholera may have affected the society. While additional environmental evidence must be gathered, overuse of farmlands, a significant problem in contemporary Mesopotamia, may have also contributed to the abandonment of Harappan cities and towns between 1900 and 1800 BCE. By 1500 BCE, many Harappan sites were abandoned (Gangal, Vahia, and Adhikari 2010).

Some Conclusions: The Harappan Archaic State?

The title of this final section ends in a question mark because this is a question that many scholars have debated. The problem is that the ancient Harappan world seems to have lacked many things archaeologists have typically associated with archaic states like Mesopotamia and Egypt. This led some earlier scholars to speculate that ancient Harappa had reached only "chiefdom" status before its ultimate demise in the early 2nd millennium (Fairservis 1961, 1967; Malik 1979).

In the last several decades, however, many scholars, most of whom have excavated major Harappan sites, have argued that the ancient Indus civilization was indeed a state-level society, just not one that Western scholars are accustomed to recognizing (Kenoyer 1994, 1997a, 2008; Possehl 1990, 1998, 2002; Shaffer 1993). The lack of spectacular monuments and trappings of leadership are outweighed by the other elements that clearly speak to the existence of a state structure, including the thriving trade network and associated craft industry, the extraordinary city and town water management systems, and the well-established administration of the movement of goods employing a standardized weight system and stamp seals for identification. What continues to stymie archaeologists is the question "What kind of state was it?" Was there a central authority, a king, a religious leader, or was some other system of governance in place? In particular, how was order kept, control of the economy maintained, public secular and religious ceremonies organized, and a peaceful and successful society sustained?

As has been noted several times earlier, there is a growing consensus that the Harappan system was organized into at least five "polities" each with a central city offering leadership in the various social, political, and economic spheres. A very good case has been made that ancient Harappa was organized in a series of city-states, conforming to these five (or more) "polities" (Kenoyer 1997a). United by a common writing system, religion, market economy, and connected by an interlocking trade network, these city-states may have engaged in some competition with each other, but the majority of their interaction was essentially peaceful, ensuring the movement of raw resources and finished products to their final destinations both within and beyond the territory of the states. While different city-states may have emphasized different aspects of the religion—ritual bathing at Mohenjo Daro and fire altars at Kalibangan—the focus on ritual purity, animals, certain deities, and the sacred tree appear to be widespread throughout the Harappan lands. The question remains, even if we accept the notion of large Harappan city-states, who ruled them and how?

Present data does not allow for the identification of a Harappan king, queen, or council. Possehl calls ancient Harappa a "faceless" society (1998) given the lack of statuary proclaiming the power of individuals. Kenoyer (1997a, 2008) notes that while there were clearly elites living in ancient Harappan cities, evidence for royalty is conspicuously absent and that this might suggest that Harappan city-states were governed by non-hereditary councils, chosen from possibly competing elite families, who were entrusted with ensuring economic and political equanimity and success (one possible exception comes from the city of Dholavira, where a hereditary "ruling class" may have been in place). A non-hereditary process of leadership selection would explain the lack of a palace or centralized residential structure since a council would have had members who lived all over the city. Meetings might have taken place in the public assembly halls. But how might a leadership council control such a vast population, economy, and religion?

It is clear that Harappan society had a uniquely south Asian sociopolitical structure. The caste system, well defined in pre-modern and modern India, is quite ancient though its origins are not clear. The modern caste system is hierarchical with those engaged in professions related to religion, warfare, and land-ownership enjoying the higher echelons of Indian society, with those involved in the market economy, service industry, or (non-landowning) farming and herding filling out the lower levels of society. Kenoyer and others (Kenoyer 1989, 1997a; McIntosh 2008; Steadman 2009) suggest that the caste system may have had its roots in the ancient Harappan society. People in Harappan cities, towns, and villages practiced their professions as craft-makers, farmers, or traders just as did their parents and grandparents because of a caste-based societal construct that bound people to their professions. Where ancient Harappa and pre-modern India may have differed was in the application of a strict hierarchy in the caste system in which there is a significant divide between the lives of those in the "upper" castes and those further down. In ancient Harappa, might all professions, and their practitioners, have been deemed important? Farmers and herders fed the population, craft-makers ensured the provision of important material culture items, merchants enriched the economy, and of course religious personnel oversaw peace and well-being. The warrior class appears to have been altogether missing. Most Harappan residents had decent houses full of utilitarian goods, access to bathing for ritual purity, storage facilities for food; in essence, except for the few structures that may have belonged to elites, most inhabitants wanted for relatively little. In general, when a population is satisfied with their lot in life, heavy-handed social control is not necessary.

There is one last element that may have ensured the success of Harappan society. The focus on ritual purity and the power of fire, and the existence of the possible Shiva/Shakti deities, have caused some to suggest that other elements of Indian Hinduism may have been present in ancient Harappan society. Texts from a 1st millennium BCE Indian state note that the governing body was responsible for, among other things (Kenoyer 1997a: 65),

dharma ... fostering a feeling of piety and religiousness
artha ... [gaining] wealth, through the encouragement of trade, industry, and agriculture
kama ... to be able to enjoy the good life ... through peace and order.

If Harappan leaders held these principles as central to their governance of Harappan society, and if they were successful at instilling these throughout the society, then this would explain the well-ordered settlements, the high standard of living enjoyed by their residents, the almost total lack of violent engagement between Harappan settlements, the seamless movement of goods and resources, and the focus on individual access to religious practice. Though the Harappan state was unlike any other described in this book, an archaic state it was. If the suggestions here are valid, the regulation of crafts and trade, and the organization of labor for building projects, must have rested in the hands of city leaders; however, the philosophy guiding authority and management was not intended to allow a few to attain increasing levels of power and control but rather to adhere to spiritual and cultural principles deeply embedded in Harappan societal structure. After the Harappan civilization collapsed, its like was not again seen in south Asia or elsewhere in the world.

9
ANCIENT CHINESE CIVILIZATIONS

Introduction

The Shang Dynasty and the states that preceded it in China were as powerful as any found in the Middle East or Mesoamerica and South America. Royal power over the daily lives, and deaths, of the Shang people stemmed from a variety of factors, but none was as important as the royal and elite control of religious ritual and ceremony. A critical element in the religious organization was the role kinship played in ancient Chinese society; the more important the individual in ancient Shang culture, the more critical that family's ancestors were to the health and well-being of, not only the lineage itself, but all Shang peoples. Kin relations and religious mandates continued to be important elements in the Zhou state that followed the Shang. The compelling combination of family and religion were at the base of these Chinese states and can be found even in the Neolithic Period several millennia before.

Geography and Chronology

The national boundaries of the present-day People's Republic of China (PRC), the second largest nation in the world (after Russia), far exceed the area occupied by the ancient Chinese states under discussion here. Nonetheless, the areas controlled by the ancient Shang Dynasty and later states were quite enormous in their day, covering about half of the area of modern China and encompassing a region known as "inner China" today (Thorp 2006: 1–3).

Geography and Ecological Setting

The heartland region of China (Figure 9.1) in which the majority of ancient cultures flourished is divided into three geographical zones and climatic zones (Liu and Chen 2012: 25–26). The northern geographical zone, North China, includes the Huang He (Yellow) River, which rises on the Tibetan Plateau and then runs generally eastward, arching north through the Ordos Desert region, and then descends into the lower region of inner China emptying into the Yellow Sea. The Huang He traverses the Loess Plateau both before and after it passes through the Ordos Desert; the Loess Plateau features fertile soil with a yellowish cast, which lends its color to the Huang He waters. The high silt content, which made parts of the Huang He unnavigable, also raised the level of the

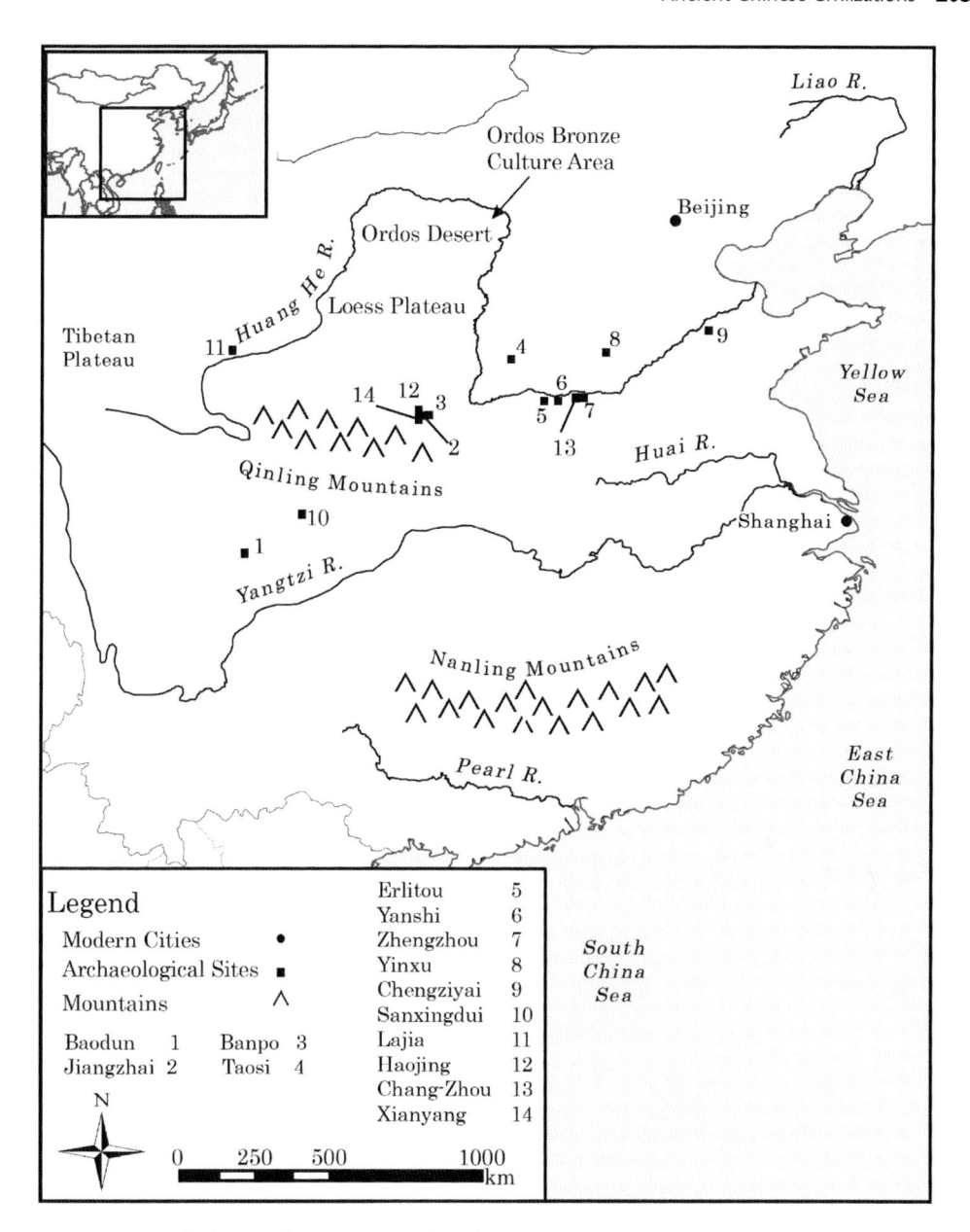

FIGURE 9.1 Map of China and Sites Discussed in the Text

riverbeds, facilitating the river's wanderings and allowing spring floods to have potentially devastating effects through the millennia (Liu and Chen 2012: 28).

South of the Huang He River and its fertile plains are the Qinling Mountains and the Huai River, which demarcate the division between northern and central inner China. The Qinling Mountains run east-west and reach a height of over 3700 meters, providing some of the highest peaks of inner China. The Huai River, far smaller than the Huang He or the Yangzi to its south, was still an important source of irrigation water for the farmlands of the ancient Chinese civilizations. Finally, south of these topographic features is the mighty Yangzi River, which also rises on the Tibetan Plateau and, in near mirror fashion to the Huang He, follows a southern loop before continuing eastward to empty into the East China Sea. The modern "Three Gorges Dam" was built on this river since three other significant rivers flow into the Yangzi from the south. The Yangzi also flows through fertile lands, and it is in this region that the earliest cultivation of rice took place (see later). Given the somewhat lower silt content in the Yangzi, the river is more navigable and served as a major trade route in ancient China.

The three climatic zones in these regions range from tropical, in the south, to arid, in the north. The Nanling Mountain range south of the Yangzi River basin runs east-west and forms an ecological and physical boundary between central and southern China. Rising to 2,100 meters, these mountains are sufficient to prevent cold air from traveling southward, making south China a tropical zone. North of the Qinling Mountains and Huai River is a more temperate climate, becoming increasingly arid and susceptible to harsh winters as one moves northward. In the region of the Huang He River the near arid climate, combined with the broad alluvial plains of inner China, provide ideal conditions for agriculture and cross-country travel. It is in the Huang He River valley that the earliest state cultures arose in China.

The Chronological Sequence

In the Huang He River region, the Neolithic Period in China begins ca. 10,000 BCE, ending with the Longshan culture in ca. 2000 BCE (Table 9.1). The middle Neolithic Yangshao culture reveals a more egalitarian, kinship-based society, and it is in the later Neolithic Longshan culture that the hallmarks of the earliest Chinese state begin to emerge.

TABLE 9.1 Chronological Periods and Sites Discussed in Chapter 9

Dates	Period	Sites Discussed in Chapter	Cultural Horizons
ca. 5000–3000 BCE	**Middle Neolithic** (Early Yangshao Culture)	Banpo; Jiangzhai	Domestication of plants/animals; ceramic production
ca. 3000–2000 BCE	**Late Neolithic** (Late Yangshao Longshan/ Dawenkou Baodun, Qijia)	Chengziyai; Taosi; Lajia	Increased craft production and trade; bronze metallurgy; warfare; religion and social stratification; development of regional polities
ca. 1900–1520 BCE	**(Early) Bronze Age** (Sanxingdui Culture Erlitou Phases I–IV)	Sanxingdui; Erlitou	Development of state center; increased social stratification; walled elite precinct; elite control of craft production
ca. 1600–1400 BCE	**(Middle) Bronze Age** (Erligang–Early Shang)	Yanshi; Zhengzhou	Extensive fortifications; elaborate burials; increase in bronze production
ca. 1400–1300 BCE	**(Middle) Bronze Age** (Middle Shang)		Early Shang sites abandoned and decentralization occurs

Dates	Period	Sites Discussed in Chapter	Cultural Horizons
ca. 1300–1046/1026 BCE	(Late) Bronze Age (Late Shang)	Yinxu	Emergence of major Shang Dynastic center; extensive human sacrifice; elite burials; extensive ritual cycle
ca. 1046–771 BCE & 741–221 BCE	Western Zhou Eastern Zhou Warring States	Haojing; Chang-Zhou	Dynastic Chinese rulership; divine right of rule; feudal-style land management system; age of philosophers (Confucius)
ca. 221–206 BCE	Qin Dynasty		Imperial China; building of Great Wall begins; "Legalism" system of rule
ca. 202 BCE–220 CE	Han Dynasty		Expansion of Great Wall against nomadic incursions; reintroduction of Confucianism; emergence of Silk Road

Source: Based on Liu (2009a)

The Bronze Age sees the emergence of the first state, known as "Erlitou" after the city of the same name (ca. 1900–1520 BCE). The last stages of the Erlitou state overlap with the beginning of the Erligang culture (ca. 1600–1400 BCE), which heralds the first phases of the Shang Dynasty. After a short period of abandonment (ca. 1400–1300 BCE), the Late Shang Dynasty (ca. 1300–1046 BCE) emerged at Yinxu (today known as Anyang). The Zhou state defeated the Shang in 1046 BCE and reigned in inner China until the late 1st millennium. By 221 BCE, the Qin Empire arose and shortly after the great Han Empire ruled for four centuries (ca. 206 BCE–220 CE).

Pre-State Cultures: Neolithic China

The Neolithic Period hunter-gatherers of inner China lived primarily along the major and more minor river valleys. By the Early Holocene era (ca. 9000–7000 BCE), when the Pleistocene Ice Age had ended and environmental conditions were changing to a warmer and more temperate climate, several sites near the modern city of Beijing, in northern China, demonstrate that Neolithic hunter-gatherers were constructing ceramic containers and burying their dead in vertical pits with intentionally placed burial goods (Liu and Chen 2012: 52). Recent work in western China and into the Tibetan plateau demonstrates there was significant Neolithic occupation of this region (Dong et al. 2013). To the south along the Yangzi River, some groups were living somewhat more sedentary lives, as demonstrated by the labor invested in house construction and storage pits.

It was not long after this shift to greater sedentism that the earliest cultivation of grains commenced. China is a primary region of plant cultivation, meaning that grains such as rice and millet were domesticated in eastern Asia and then the knowledge and techniques for cultivation spread to other areas (such as southeast Asia). Most scholars now agree that rice was the earliest domesticate in eastern Asia, primarily along the Yangzi River (Bellwood 2005; Crawford 2006; Zhao 2010). At present, the strongest data suggest that rice was fully domesticated on the middle and lower Yangzi and Huang He Rivers between 7000 and 6000 BCE (Crawford 2006). Following quickly on the widespread cultivation of rice were two species of millet between 6000 and 5000 BCE. Though millet did form part of the human diet, it was mainly a critical resource for feeding the newly domesticated animals. Following rice and millet, a whole host of other grains, tubers, and soybeans were domesticated over the succeeding millennia, making possible the rise of the earliest states in eastern Asia.

The earliest domesticated animal in China was the dog as early as ca. 8000 BCE. The burial of dogs at some sites suggests they may have had a role in village life, perhaps as hunting assistants; at other sites, there is strong evidence of the use of dog as a food source (Liu and Chen 2012: 97–98). Pigs were domesticated quite early in China (ca. 5000–4000 BCE) and quickly became a critical part of the Asian economy, ritual practice, and the demonstration of wealth (Kim 1994). Another extremely important species, cattle, was also domesticated in the Neolithic Period, by the late 3rd millennium BCE. Commensurate with, or shortly following, the domestication of cattle was the appearance of domesticated of sheep, goat (possibly from the Near East), and chicken. Water buffalo and horse (the latter likely coming from central Asia) were domesticated in succeeding millennia generally prior to the rise of the Erlitou and Erligang states (see later). With the relative economic stability provided by domesticated plants and animals, residents began to settle into permanent communities, develop craft specialties, and engage in regional and long-distance trade.

The Middle Neolithic Yangshao Cultural Complex

During the Middle Neolithic Early Yangshao cultural complex (ca. 5000–4000 BCE) in the Huang He River Valley, egalitarian foraging societies transitioned to sedentary communities with more complex socioeconomic organizational strategies. Domesticated rice and millet, and dog and pig, were present, and ceramic production was an important craft as were hemp and leather production (Underhill 2002; Underhill and Habu 2006). Two sites, Banpo and Jiangzhai, offer good evidence of Yangshao life in the Middle Neolithic.

Banpo, on a tributary south of the Huang He, dates to the earlier Yangshao Period (ca. 4800–4000 BCE). Banpo residents cultivated millet, mustard, and cabbage and had domesticated pigs and dogs and later cattle and chickens (Zhongpei 2005). Craft production of stone, wooden, and bone tools was well developed, and it appears that ceramic production at Banpo was technologically advanced with the early use of the wheel and the kiln (Zhongpei 2005). There is also evidence of metal manufacture at Banpo and other Yangshao Period sites. Banpo village was roughly oval in shape with about 100 semisubterranean houses (46 were excavated) in the center and work areas, including pottery kilns, in the eastern area (Chang 1986: 116). The earliest Banpo houses were generally circular in shape, but after ca. 4300 BCE, some houses were square or rectangular with rounded corners. A large rectangular building in the village center, with an open area in front, may have been for public (ceremonial/religious) use. In the cemetery north of the village, over 100 adult burials demonstrated that the norm was singular extended burial with a few burial goods included (usually ceramics); infants and children were more often buried in ceramic urns in the village area (Chang 1986: 116). Burial goods demonstrate gendered differentiation, but little other significant social stratification existed at Banpo.

Jiangzhai, not far from Banpo, has more than 100 structures arranged in a roughly circular plan around a central plaza (Figure 9.2) and grouped in five neighborhood (likely kinship-based) clusters; each group featured one large and multiple smaller and medium-sized houses (Gao and Lee 1993; Peterson and Shelach 2012; Zhongpei 2005). As at Banpo, houses were either circular or rectangular in plan. Households within each cluster selected several productive activities (such as hunting, agriculture, leather-working, or ceramic production) to form the bulk of their labor output; therefore, some households held significant numbers of farming implements and storage capacity, while others had strong evidence of engagement in craft production activities (Lee 2007; Peterson and Shelach 2012). Ceramic vessels were decorated with geometric and animal or human

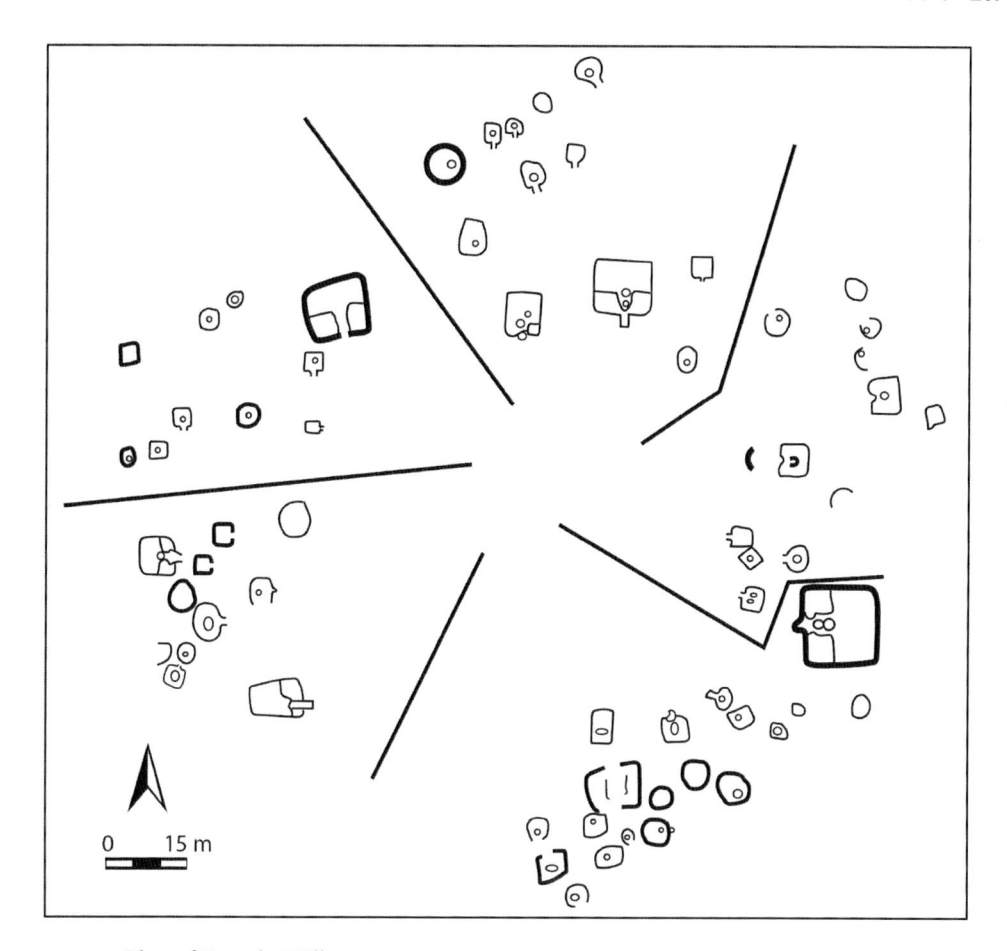

FIGURE 9.2 Plan of Jiangzhai Village

Source: After Peterson and Shelach (2012: 272, fig. 3)

designs; burial evidence in which certain individual graves contained paraphernalia associated with ceramic production suggests this art may have been kin-based (Yanping 2013).

Burials and associated burial goods, located outside the settlement, suggest a minimum of social differentiation between individuals or households (Lee 2007). Individual households engaged in significant exchange allowing each to acquire necessary subsistence and craft goods, demonstrating a reliance on kin, or kin-like co-residents, for risk management purposes. The Neolithic in the Huang He River Valley, in the early Yangshao phase, therefore, suggests a strong reliance on kinship ties for both social identity and economic solvency and a significantly burgeoning craft industry, particularly in the area of ceramic production and leather-working.

By the Middle and Late Yangshao phases (ca. 4000–2800 BCE), population had expanded, so settlements were larger and arranged in a hierarchy of larger to smaller, with larger communities functioning as central places (Underhill and Habu 2006). Burials were differentiated by labor investment and grave goods with some including items made of jade, ivory, and other precious materials. Ceramic production had become a mainstay of the Late Yangshao culture with specialized production centers and well-established trade networks (Underhill 2002). In addition to these socioeconomic developments, communities had begun constructing rammed-earth fortifications, suggesting that conflict and boundary definition was a growing concern late in the Neolithic Yangshao Period (Lee 2004).

The Late Neolithic Longshan and Qijia Cultural Complexes

The socioeconomic and political trajectories of the Late Yangshao phase continued into the Neolithic Longshan and Dawenkou cultures (2600–2000 BCE) that flourished on the middle Huang He River (see Box 9.1). Settlement nucleation and population growth, and increased fortification of settlements, an increase in projectile points, human skeletal remains showing evidence of violence, and the rammed earth walls are good indicators that regional polities were engaged in offensive and defensive tactics (Barnes 1993; Chang 1986; Liu 1996; Underhill 2002). Research has indicated that agricultural production increased through improved tools and methods (such as more efficient plows and irrigation systems), which helped to support an increasing population engaged in more diversified activities. Referred to as "city-states" by some (Sit and Xue 2010; Wangping 2000, 2005), settlements were arrayed into a tiered hierarchy of village–regional center–capital by the later Longshan/Dawenkou Period. Ample evidence of increased wood, jade, and ceramic craft production is found in household-based workshops; both locally produced and trade items appear in burials at Longshan sites. Ceramic data provide evidence of an entrenched and dynamic exchange system that extended southward to the Yangzi River region and eastward to the coastal region. Walls identified as defensive may have also served to demarcate important ritual areas at ceremonial centers, demonstrating a growing centralization of religious practice during the Late Neolithic, particularly with regard to rituals dedicated to ancestor veneration (Liu and Chen 2003; von Falkenhausen 2008).

BOX 9.1 THE BAODUN CULTURAL COMPLEX

The Baodun (ca. 2700–1750 BCE) is a Middle-Late Neolithic culture located on the Chengdu Plain in Sichuan Province along the Yangzi River in southwestern China. The type site of Baodun has an earthen wall enclosing the settlement and a second, larger rammed-earth wall enclosing a broader area that may have included agricultural fields or additional residences (Flad 2013). Other Baodun culture sites also have rammed-earth enclosures surrounding the settlements. The purpose of these walls may have been defensive, but other functions include serving as flood barriers (Flad 2013). What the walls demonstrate is that sociopolitical organization within the Baodun culture was sufficient for the organization of significant labor to build these substantial walls around Baodun settlements. As a farming culture, the Baodun people engaged in significant lithic production and also had a thriving ceramic production system that included both fine and utilitarian wares. Recent investigation has demonstrated that the earliest evidence of domesticated rice and foxtail millet in this southwestern region of China occurs at Baodun sites (Guedes et al. 2013). The Baodun culture gave way to the Bronze Age Sanxingdui culture discussed in more detail later.

Two sites on the Huang He, Chengziyai near the coast and Taosi farther east, demonstrate all of these elements. Chengziyai, approximately 20 hectares in size, and Taosi, roughly 300 hectares in size, represent the differing scales of Longshan settlements; in each case, smaller towns and villages surround the site, some as small as 3 hectares in size. Some archaeologists identify Taosi as a type of "capital" city, which was surrounded by "secondary centers," medium-sized and small towns, and finally very small hamlets (Nu 2013: 259). Chengziyai would fit into the lower tier of medium-to-small sized towns. Both settlements, rimmed by rammed-earth walls, featured a range of fine craft goods such as jade, eggshell-thin ceramics, and bronzes, and both have evidence of increased elements of conflict and rising levels of social stratification (Chang 1986; Liu and Chen 2012; Thorp

2006). At Chengziyai, a wide variety of burial types suggests a range of social classes spanning elite to commoner; the most elaborate burials consisted of painted wooden lacquered coffins and dozens of grave goods. At Taosi, elites inhabited large homes surrounded by walls, while non-elite homes were far smaller semisubterranean rammed-earth structures; recent work at the site has located an area in the center of the city where a palace may have been located (Nu 2013).

Three classes of the over 700 known tombs demonstrate a wide gap in wealth among Taosi residents. Large tombs (1% of the total) contained wooden coffins and as many as 200 burial goods of jade, stone, wood, ritual materials, musical instruments, and fine ceramic wares. Medium tombs (12% of all tombs) also had wooden coffins and held up to 20 burial items; the small tombs (87% of all tombs) were simple pits containing the deceased (sometimes wrapped in a reed mat) with few or no burial goods (Wangping 2005). The presence of an apparent observatory at Taosi may have given elites special religious standing if they controlled access to this important guide to the agricultural cycle (Liu 2009a; Nu 2013).

Further north, over 300 sites belonging to the Qijia culture are located on the Loess Plateau in the Gansu and neighboring provinces. The Qijia culture flourished in a region that offered difficult conditions and occasional natural disasters (see Box 9.2). This complex arose near the end of the Longshan phase and continued into the early Bronze Age (ca. 2000–1700 BCE). The Qijia culture had a rich agricultural economy, producing drought-resistant millet in this arid climate and in the loose yellow soil on the plateau; residents also kept livestock such as cattle, sheep, chicken, and horses, with pigs being the most important (Wang 1987). Small settlements consisted of square or rectangular single-roomed houses that were semisubterranean (Honghai 2013). A number of burials contained a male and female couple, apparently interred at the same time; evidence that some of the females were buried while bound suggests that they may have been sacrificial victims at the time of the male burial. It is possible that these women were the spouses of the deceased males, or they may have been slaves or servants belonging to a different ethnic group (Honghai 2013).

BOX 9.2 THE LAJIA CULTURE

Some of the best data for the Neolithic Period was recovered from the site of Lajia due to its destruction by the dual events of a flood from the Huang He River and a simultaneous earthquake (Yang, Xia, and Ye 2003). Because of the catastrophic destruction of the site, many "everyday" scenes were captured in the mud. In addition to the metal objects noted earlier, painted pottery, kilns, inscribed bones (see Box 9.3), and other goods describe a rich pre-Bronze Age culture. One of the best-known discoveries was that of millet noodles found in an overturned bowl (Lü et al. 2014), documenting this staple in east Asian cuisine existing at least 4,000 years ago.

Though bronze metallurgy was certainly present throughout the Longshan Period, it began to flourish in the Qijia culture. Both bronze and copper items, mostly tools such as fishhooks, awls, knives, ornaments and even spears and mirrors, have been recovered (Allen 2007; Zhimin 1992). Similarities in metallurgical methods and designs found in later Shang contexts suggest this Bronze Age culture may have acquired some of its metallurgical expertise from the earlier Qijia culture. Qijia settlements featured a rich ritual life as well. Evidence of animal sacrifice and the presence of divination bones (see Box 9.3) suggest funeral rituals may have been common (Honghai 2013). The culture's relationship to the roughly contemporary Longshan culture continues to be investigated by archaeologists.

BOX 9.3 KEY OBJECT: ORACLE BONES

Oracle bones (Figure 9.3), first appearing in the Longshan Period, continued to be used in the Erlitou and Erligang Periods. Diviners developed their techniques in the Bronze Age, including pre-treating bones by smoothing, polishing, and drilling or chiseling them prior to ritual ceremonies (Flad 2008). Diviners interpreted heat-generated cracks on turtle carapaces and animal bones and then inscribed their readings on the bones. It is from these inscriptions, which bear some of the earliest forms of Chinese writing, that much of the information about the Late Shang state derives. The role of oracle bones in Shang religion will be discussed in detail later.

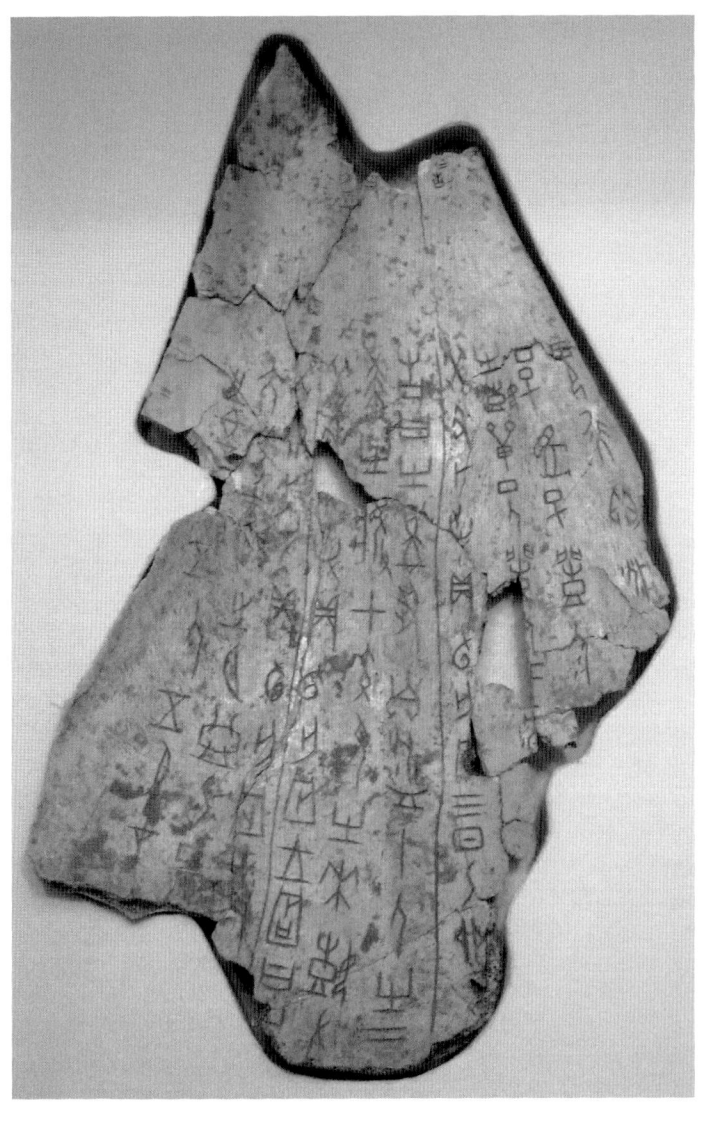

FIGURE 9.3 Example of an Oracle Bone From the Shang Dynasty

Source: Photo courtesy of BabelStone, licensed under CC BY-SA 3.0 via Wikimedia Commons

Ancestor veneration was firmly ensconced in ancient Chinese religious beliefs and practices, with solid evidence of its emergence at least in the Neolithic Period if not earlier. Divination using animal bones ("oracle bones") may have been performed by itinerant diviners traveling to settlements, likely responding to elite requests for their services (Flad 2008). Longshan and Dawenkou burials offer evidence of feasting at the mortuary rituals (Fung 2000; Underhill 2000). In the later Neolithic Periods, there was a growing differentiation in social status in communities and a commensurate emphasis on the attention paid to ancestors of high status lineages (Chang 2005; Liu 2000). During the earlier Yangshao Period, ancestor veneration and feasting rituals took place on a community-wide basis; village cemeteries featured ash pits containing remnants of food, ceramics, tools, and other items that may have been both dedicatory and part of a feast ritual (Liu 2000). By the Longshan Period, however, at sites such as Changziyai and Taosi, significant shifts in burial locations and grave good assignment had taken place, clearly showing socioeconomic differentiation in individual status. Lineage members conducted individual feasting rituals at family tombs rather than recognizing community-wide ancestors. Not only were the descendants of elite ancestors involved in mortuary and veneration rituals, but non-kin community members may also have contributed to these ceremonies, though whether they did so willingly is unclear. Ancestor veneration during Neolithic China developed from the collective recognition of ancestral groups to a more individualized practice; this change corresponds to the "overall development of social organization from egalitarian to stratified" society over the course of the Chinese Neolithic (Liu 2000: 156). As living community members gained higher levels of status, wealth, and power, so did their ancestors. This heralds the later development of a Shang religion in which all Shang peoples had to recognize, and worship, the ancestors of leaders and elites to ensure the health and well-being of all.

Bronze Age China: The Earliest Chinese States

The early 3rd millennium BCE sees the origin of the "three dynasties" period of pre-imperial China: the Xia, the Shang, and the Zhou (ca. 2000–221 BCE). These three cultures grew to prominence in the middle Huang He River Valley where the Longshan and, before it, the Yangshao Neolithic cultures had flourished. However, more modern scholarship has shown that the "Xia" Dynasty had a more complicated sociopolitical structure than previously thought, composed of various and competing city-states that did not recognize a single leader. Nonetheless, it is in the early 2nd millennium in the middle Huang He and on the Yangzi River that we see increasing sociopolitical complexity and the earliest states in ancient China.

Growing Complexity in Sichuan: The Sanxingdui Culture

The Sanxingdui culture, named after the type site, is located on the Chengdu Plain in the Sichuan Basin of southwestern China. The Yangzi River flows through this region creating a fertile plain suitable for extensive agricultural pursuits. Rising out of the earlier Baodun culture (see Box 9.1), the Sanxingdui culture (ca. 1750–1200 BCE) overlaps with the emergence of the Shang Dynasty to the north (see later). Like earlier Baodun sites, Sanxingdui was surrounded by a rammed-earth wall surrounding a community bisected by the Mamu River (Figure 9.4). Occupation at Sanxingdui is divided into an earlier phase (1750–1400 BCE) and later phase (1400–1200 BCE); it is during the earlier phase that the wall was constructed. During the later phase, residents began to produce extraordinary items of bronze and jade.

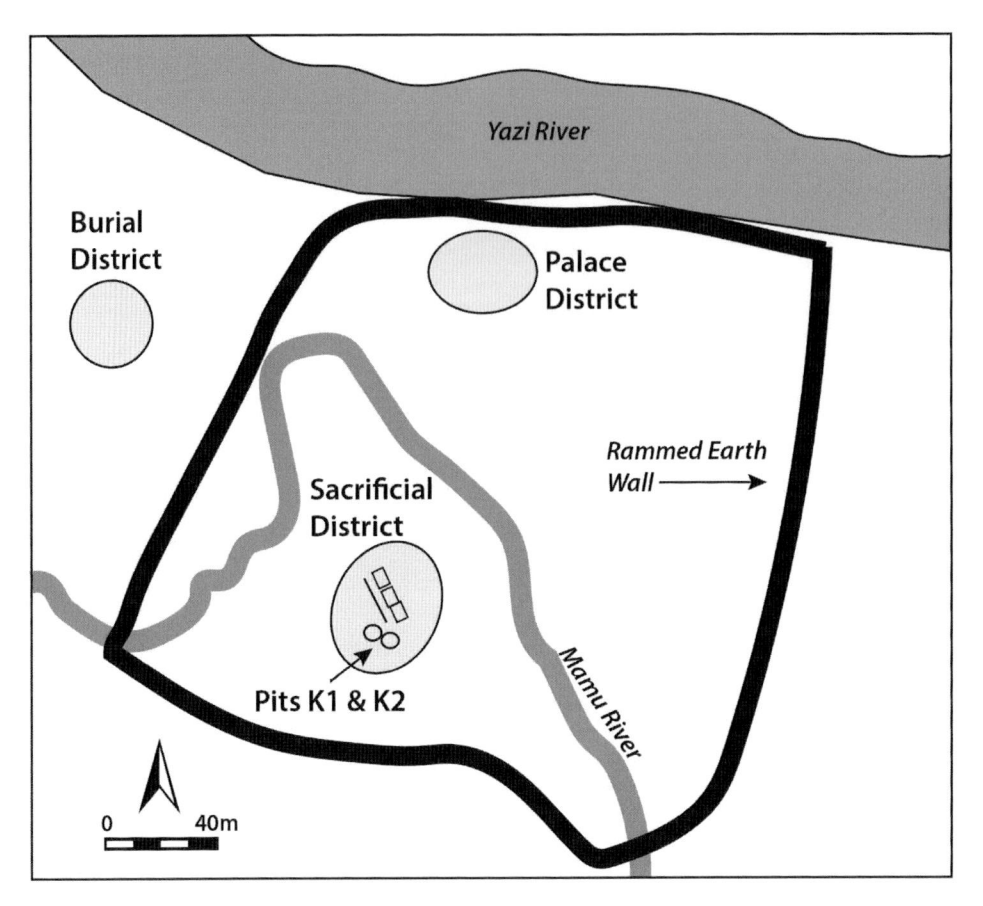

FIGURE 9.4 Plan of Sanxingdui Settlement
Source: After Hua (2013: 151, fig 8.2)

The surrounding wall is approximately 40 meters wide at the base, tapering to 20 meters at the top, and it encloses an area roughly 3.5 km^2; occupation outside the wall suggests the city was several times larger (Xu 2006). The area north of the Mamu is slightly elevated, and it is here that several large structures, described as "palatial," have been discovered (Hua 2013). Surrounding these were houses of the non-elites, constructed of wattle and daub, rectangular in shape, and ranging in size between 15 and 30 square meters, though some are a bit larger. Such houses are also found in the southern area of the settlement. Also present in the southern portion of the site are areas likely devoted to ritual activities. Jade was a specialty art at Sanxingdui, used for tool-making, in jewelry, and particularly for ritual objects.

One of the most remarkable discoveries at Sanxingdui were two large pits, designated K1 and K2, located in the southern area of the site. The pits were located atop earthen mounds created by the residents; the pits were filled with items made of bronze, jade, and other materials, and these objects have been interpreted as possessing deep religious significance. Both pits are rectangular, range between 12 and 15 square meters in size and are approximately 1.6 meters deep; a ramp leads up to the edge of K1, and a building once stood next to K2. Archaeologists discovered 420 objects in K1 and 1,300 in K2, though it is possible that a number of wooden objects may have once rested in K1; some objects had been burned, but others were pristine (Hua 2013).

The pits were constructed and filled with their objects in the later phase at Sanxingdui, and it is at this time that bronze metallurgy arose at the site, and jade-based craft production became more pronounced. The K1 pit contained several scepters or staffs, one made of gold, and others with animal images such as lions or dragons; also present in K1 were jade blades or images of birds and human heads made of bronze. The K2 pit appears to have been primarily meant for bronze objects though there were a number of jade axes as well. Bronze objects included human and animal faces, "sun wheels," trees, eyes, and human-animal figures that may represent deities. The function of these pits is deemed to be "sacrificial," in that people deposited important items during sacrificial rites. This is further supported by the fact that some of the items were burned, perhaps in a pre-deposition ritual. The fact that the objects were buried in the two pits is somewhat curious; it is possible that the objects were taken from various locales and deposited in K1 and K2 at a time of difficulty, possibly internal strife or external attack, near the end of the Sanxingdui Period (Hua 2013).

The objects in these pits reveal information about the people of Sanxingdui (see Box 9.4) and their religion. The scepters may have once been part of a leader's regalia, and the gold scepter suggests someone of significant standing made this offering. The "sun wheels" may indicate that the sun figured prominently in Sanxingdui belief, not surprising in a culture that depended heavily on agricultural production. The bronze trees are also indicators of sun worship. In Chinese mythology, the sun is pulled from the earth and across the sky by dragons; trees are a vital component in aiding the dragons in hoisting the sun from the earth at dawn. Finally, birds seem to have formed an important element in Sanxingdui religion. They rest on the branches of the bronze trees; bronze figurines combine elements of humans and birds, perhaps representing deities. Given that birds dwell in trees and the sky, it is quite possible that the bird imagery is related to Sanxingdui sun worship (Hua 2013).

BOX 9.4 THE SANXINGDUI PEOPLE

The many Sanxingdui representations of humans (Figure 9.5) offer archaeologists a good look at how people of this Bronze Age culture dressed and adorned themselves. One common trait was the braiding of hair down the back (called *bianfa* style), whether one was from the elite or commoner class. However, the braided treatment of the hair did vary depending on societal position. A few other hairstyles are also represented, one with a loose and unbraided style, and others with hair tied back or piled on the head (called *jifa* style). By far the bianfa is the most common, and the jifa the second most commonly seen (Hua 2013). The "loose" style is found on only one figure whose face exhibits obtruding eyes, a set of clenched teeth, and an unusual set of clothing; it is possible this figurine represents someone from another culture or community with whom the Sanxingdui were having problems. Those wearing the bianfa style can be divided into the elites and commoners; elites wear nice clothing and sometimes hats, while the commoners are represented as naked with hands bound behind their backs. The figurines with the jifa style may represent elites who had religious responsibilities in the communities; these figures tend to wear fine clothing and have bird or sun motifs associated with their clothing or head (Hua 2013). These images made from stone and bronze offer a relatively clear image of the secular and religious elites of Sanxingdui and also of those they ruled.

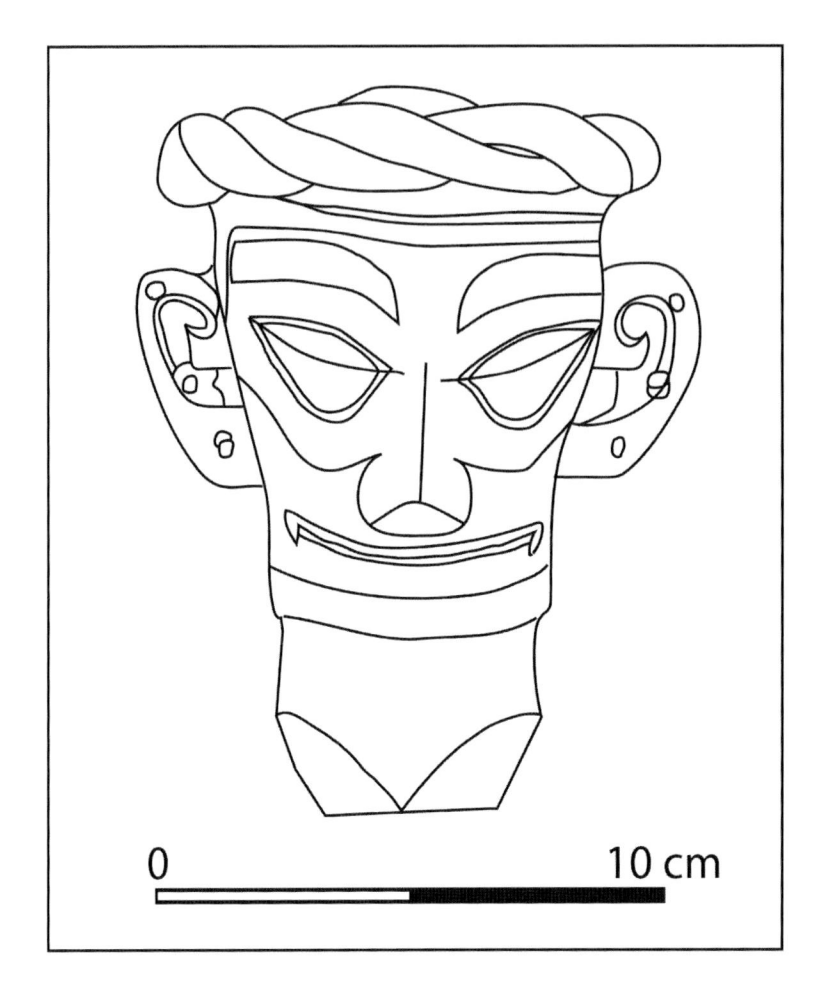

FIGURE 9.5 Example of Sanxingdui *Bianfa* Style Hair Braid on a Figurine
Source: After von Falkenhausen (2006: 194, fig 2.8)

How did the Sanxingdui culture develop such a rich bronze and jade craft production system? This is a subject of scholarly debate, with assertions suggesting that bronze technology flowed from the eastern Shang culture (see later) and alternatively that the Shang may have borrowed some know-how from the Sanxingdui (von Falkenhausen 2006). What is clear is that the Chengdu Plain saw the rise of a rich and vibrant culture that shared technology and belief systems with the better-known dynasties to the east.

The Erlitou State

One of the earliest and most impressive cultural complexes of Bronze Age China is the Erlitou culture, named after the type site on the middle Huang He River. Erlitou had been considered a capital city of the Xia Dynasty, but recent analysis of the city and its surroundings suggests it was a cultural complex in its own right and that the Xia Dynasty may not have existed as a pre-Shang complex society in any significant form (Allen 1984; Liu 2009b; Liu and Xu 2007; Thorp 2006).

The Erlitou culture, and the Erligang that follows it, will be discussed here as free-standing cultural complexes ushering in the first state-level societies in China.

Erlitou itself was occupied in both the Yangshao and Longshan Periods, and after an abandonment (ca. 2600–2000 BCE), a new population arrived, commencing the Erlitou culture in approximately 1900 BCE. Erlitou is located at the intersection of the Luo and Yi Rivers, just south of the Huang He. It sits, therefore, at the intersection of major riverine trade routes as well as heavily used land routes passing through the region. This provided Erlitou residents with access to resources from coastal China as well as the Yangzi River region (Liu and Chen 2003). Although there are many elements that contributed to the rise of the Erlitou state, the most prominent factors appear to be a rapid and robust development of a stratified society with a powerful elite class, the emergence of elite control over a significant craft industry, and the consolidation of ritual into elite hands.

The Erlitou occupation is divided into four phases, the last merging into the Erligang state (discussed in the next section). Phases I and II are quite short (1900–1800 BCE); Phase III represents the height of the Erlitou state (ca. 1800–1600 BCE). During Phase I, Erlitou was about 100 hectares and likely functioned as a regional center with a thriving craft industry in materials such as bronze, bone, and pottery. By Phase II, the site had expanded to 300 hectares, and the population had increased as had agricultural production (indicated by an increase in agricultural tools across the settlement) (Liu and Chen 2012: 268). Artifacts such as jade and "white pottery," typically used in elite contexts (Liu and Xu 2007), indicate a significant trade network was in place (Liu 2003). Recovered architecture clearly displays a significantly stratified society. The central area of the city was dedicated to palatial structures (described more fully later) built of rammed earth and enclosed by major roads many meters wide; rich burials in the courtyards contained several hundred grave goods. One grave of a 30–35 year-old male had, besides numerous other goods, a dragon-shaped cover made of over 2,000 pieces of jade and turquoise (Liu and Xu 2007). Evidence of human sacrifice was also found in these courtyard burials (Lee 2004). Other areas of the city were devoted to workshops producing crafts in great quantities, some of which were likely placed in the elite burials. Other large houses had floor plans similar to the palaces but without protective walls and spacious courtyards; smaller houses had only two rooms (Lee 2004). Commoner houses, sometimes located quite close to the workshops, were small and semisubterranean consisting of single rooms only a few square meters in area.

Phase III Erlitou shows the city at its height with an even larger population, a more robust craft industry, and additions to the palatial quarter in the southeast. The several dozen structures in this quarter were built atop rammed-earth foundations up to 3 meters thick. Two buildings, "Palace 1" and "Palace 2," were built of wattle and daub with spacious courtyards in front of the structures. A 2-meter wide rammed-earth wall surrounded the palatial quarter, perhaps limiting access by the more common classes. Layers of small pebbles included in the rammed-earth foundations were obtained from the mountainous areas to the east through trade (Liu and Chen 2003: 58). The person-hours necessary to build these massive rammed-earth foundations is remarkable. For instance, the foundation of Palace 1 contained approximately 20,000 cubic meters of earth, which would require tens of thousands of hours of labor (Liu and Chen 2003: 59). Sacrificial burials discovered in the rammed-earth palace foundations yielded evidence that victims were tied with ropes and partially dismembered; elsewhere on the site, as many as 40 other examples of possible human sacrifices were also discovered (Lee 2004). Those living in and/or controlling the construction of the Erlitou "palatial quarter" had the ability to command labor from city residents to import materials and construct the elaborate foundations and large structures atop them. They also were in a position to demand the ultimate sacrifice, the lives either of Erlitou residents or perhaps of prisoners of war.

Craft production in the Phase III Period increased substantially, with elites supporting full-time craft-workers to serve elite needs (Lee 2004). A bronze foundry located south of the palatial quarter

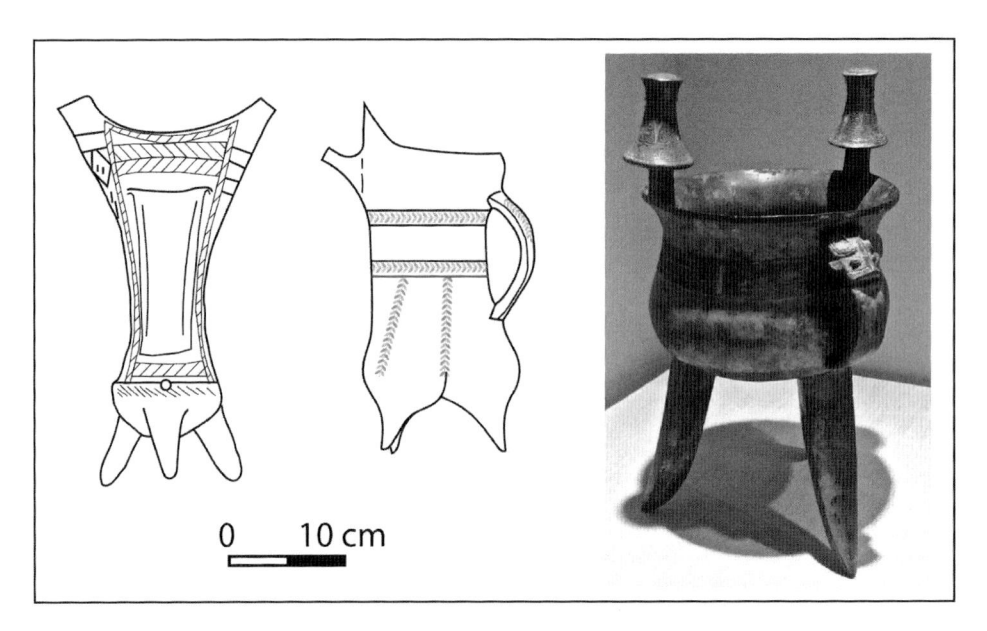

FIGURE 9.6 Examples of the *Jia, Jua,* and *He* Decorative Vessels: Left: Drawings of *Jua* Vessels; Right: Photo of *Jia* Vessel

Source: Left: After Thorp (2006: 56, fig. 1.17); Right: Photo courtesy of ellenm1, licensed under CC BY-SA 2.0 via Wikimedia Commons

made bronze tools, weapons, and ritual items (Liu and Chen 2003), the latter consisting of large, medium, and small vessels with decorative motifs (most notably *jia, jua,* and *he* [Figure 9.6], which were ritual drinking vessels). Other workshops north and east of the palace area were dedicated to the creation of bone, jade, and turquoise objects. The "white pottery," made of kaolin (a component of the porcelain so prominent in later periods) appeared in elite tombs and in the palatial buildings; kaolinite does not naturally occur near Erlitou, and thus, either this material or the vessels themselves arrived at the city through trade (Liu 2003). By Phase III, the bronze ritual vessels are found exclusively in elite burials (Liu and Chen 2003: 63), suggesting a fairly significant level of elite control over the distribution of goods produced in the Erlitou workshops. Some workshops at Erlitou became solely dedicated to the production of turquoise objects (Liu and Xu 2007), which also appear regularly in elite Erlitou tombs.

Elite ancestor veneration was well established at Phase III Erlitou. The bronze *jia, jua,* and *he* ritual vessels mentioned earlier are well known from later Shang Dynasty contexts as important items in ancestor veneration rituals in which food and drink were offered to ancestors. These vessels bore early versions of decorations that appear on bronze vessels in later Shang tombs. One motif, known as *taotie*, consists of two eyes combined with either an animal (including a dragon) or a human figure (Allen 2007). The meaning of these motifs in Shang culture is debated. Their presence on bronze vessels in Erlitou burials ties this Shang symbolism to the earlier Erlitou culture. Evidence suggests that by Phase III at Erlitou elites had commandeered the lead in practicing ancestral veneration rituals (Allen 2007), perhaps intimating to the rest of the Erlitou population that elite ancestors were more important for the health and well-being of the entire community. Since these "more important" ancestors were those of elites, it then fell to those same elites to conduct rituals and therefore take charge of important ceremonies and both private and public events that centered on ancestral veneration.

Regional surveys indicate that outlying settlements were economically and politically engaged with Erlitou. Larger settlements (20–60 hectares) close to Erlitou may have supplied important resources to the Erlitou center. Outlying settlements as much as 100 kilometers away demonstrate Erlitou cultural material and are described as having been "colonized" by the Erlitou state through the establishment of "outposts" (Liu and Chen 2003: 69–74, 2012: 273). Whether the Erlitou cultural presence manifested itself through colonization efforts or through other processes such as emulation, there is no doubt that these settlements, located both north of the Huang He River and even as far south as the Yangzi River region, were engaged in trade and exchange with Erlitou and its surrounding settlements, providing natural resources such as metals and other materials. What Erlitou may have provided in return is not clear, though its role may have been to serve as the political and ceremonial center, the real and ideological nexus of power and ritual manifested in grand buildings, life-sacrificing rituals, and lavish burials of important elites (Lee 2004). For this "service," Erlitou received raw resources and finished goods, basic subsistence items, and the loyalty of the hinterland around it.

The Erligang Culture (The Early and Middle Shang Dynasty)

The Shang Dynasty, according to tradition, rose after the Xia Dynasty. While this presents a tidy succession of the "three dynasties" of Bronze Age Chinese (the third being the Zhou discussed later), the archaeological record presents a somewhat more complicated process of transition from what was the Erlitou state to what became known as the Shang Dynasty (Liancheng and Wenming 2005). Archaeologically, the first stages of the Shang Dynasty may have had their roots in the Erligang cultural phase, which is partly contemporary with the final, fourth phase of the Erlitou occupation.

The Erligang Culture at Yanshi: The Early Shang

Though the Phase IV occupation at Erlitou (ca. 1560–1520 BCE) continued Phase III trends, just a few short decades later, Erlitou had been reduced to a far smaller settlement only 10% of its former size (Liu and Chen 2012: 269). Residents lived in small houses in a setting that must have looked much more like an outlying village than the center of a powerful state.

During the Erlitou IV phase, late in the 16th century, a new settlement, Yanshi, was established less than 10 kilometers from Erlitou. Like Erlitou, Yanshi, at least 200 hectares in size, boasted palatial buildings, impressive fortifications, and centers of craft production. Yanshi represents the Erligang phase of occupation in this region and is also called the "Early Shang" phase. Roughly simultaneous with the rise of Yanshi was another center, Zhengzhou, about 85 kilometers to the east, which later grew to become a major Shang center. Archaeological work at Zhengzhou finds evidence of major production of bronze items including the types of ritual vessels previously produced at Erlitou. It is possible that, as Yanshi rose to prominence so near Erlitou, craft producers, elites, and other residents moved out of the immediate Yanshi orbit to a new location where they could continue their livelihoods (Liu and Chen 2012: 270).

Three layers of rammed-earthen walls encircle the Yanshi settlement (Figure 9.7). Early in the Yanshi occupation the innermost walls were built to enclose a series of at least six palaces built in the same fashion as was found at Erlitou; at least two ponds were also constructed near the palaces. At the center was an area where both human and animal skeletal remains and ancient plant remains were found, suggesting the practice of sacrificial rituals at the center of the palatial district (Liu and Chen 2012: 280). Shortly after this, a second wall was built to encircle an area of roughly 80 hectares, which seems to offer a defense of the inner town. A bronze workshop was located outside

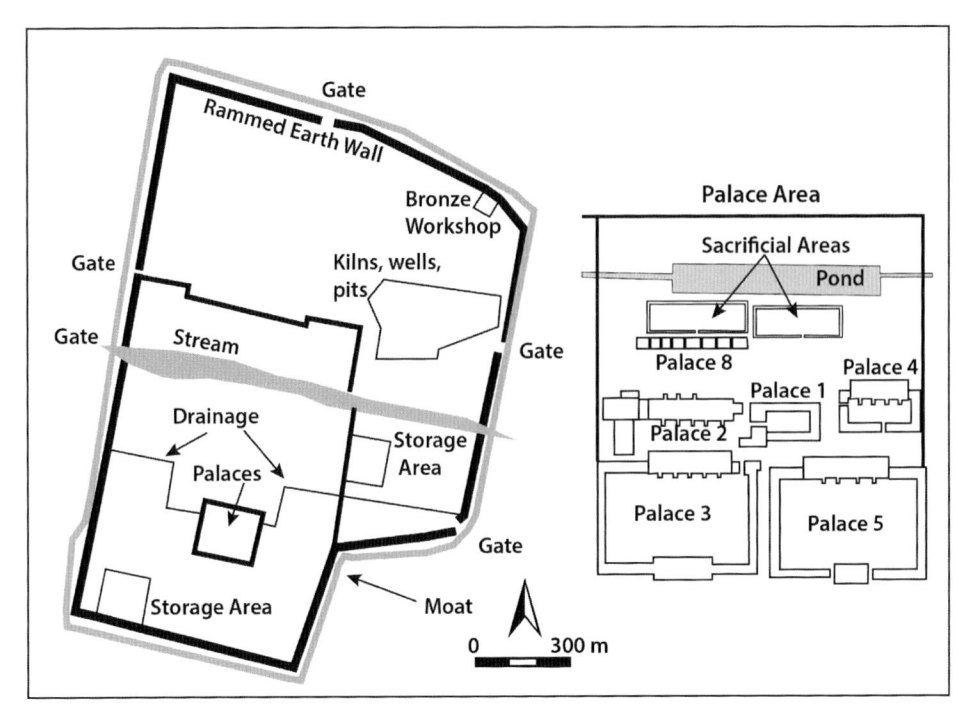

FIGURE 9.7 Plan of Yanshi City and Close-up of Palace Area (on right)
Source: After Liu and Chen (2012: 280, fig. 8.8)

the inner city wall and ceramic assemblages include vessels of Erlitou type, but also other forms that become known as Erligang/Early Shang types (see Box 9.5). Whether this suggests the arrival of a new population carrying the Erligang/Shang culture, as many Chinese archaeologists suggest (see Liu and Chen 2003: 89–91) or only a shift in styles is still a subject of debate. Somewhat later, a third, far larger, outer wall was constructed at Yanshi, expanding the town size to its full 200 hectares. Surrounding this outer wall was a moat; five narrow gates offered entry into the settlement. Soon after, the palace area was expanded and new palaces/buildings were constructed. Yanshi was abandoned by the late 16th century, and Zhengzhou rose to prominence in this area of the Huang He. Most suggest that Yanshi had a military purpose, perhaps meant to protect the inhabitants of Erlitou and surrounding regions. That defense was needed is demonstrated by the greater numbers of arrowheads at Erlitou in its Phase IV occupation and the discovery of dismembered human skeletons (Liu and Chen 2003: 92).

BOX 9.5 THE ORDOS BRONZE CULTURE

Far to the north of most of the cultures discussed in this chapter was the Zhukaigou culture on the Ordos Plateau in central southern Inner Mongolia. More than 40 sites have been discovered as belonging to this culture, which spans the first half of the 2nd millennium (ca. 2100–1400 BCE). The people of this culture were mainly farmers (relying on millet) and kept domestic animals including sheep, pigs, and cattle (Di Cosmo 1999). One of the remarkable things about the Zhukaigou culture is that bronze metallurgy begins very early here. Initially, in the early 2nd millennium, residents produced small pins and personal ornaments (possibly derived from the Qijia culture [Liu and Chen 2012: 321], see earlier) (Honeychurch 2015: 188). By approximately 1500 BCE, which corresponds with the Erligang/Early Shang Period, more elaborate bronzes including daggers, knives, and jewelry were produced. Items are found in both domestic contexts and also in the several hundred burials found at both the Zhukaigou type site as well as at other contemporary sites. Some of the designs on these bronze objects appear to be representations of snakes along with a flower design, both of which become common on the tools and weapons of later nomadic cultures in the region (Di Cosmo 1999). Of particular note are several Shang Dynasty bronze ritual vessels found in burials. The presence of these vessels at Zhukaigou sites suggests a strong connection with the Shang culture to the south. Several archaeologists believe that ethnic Shang people may have been living at Zhukaigou, perhaps helping facilitate trade between the Shang culture and the outlying regions to the north of the Ordos Plateau (Liu and Chen 2012: 320). The presence of oracle bones at Zhukaigou sites further suggests a strong connection with Shang culture. Whether the Zhukaigou region served as an "outpost" of the Shang cultures or was in a mutually beneficial relationship with this powerful Huang He River valley center will require additional archaeological investigation in the Ordos Plateau.

Zhengzhou: Middle Shang Period

Though far larger, less is known about the Erligang settlement at Zhengzhou because it rests under the modern city of the same name. The Zhengzhou occupation (ca. 1600–1400 BCE) corresponds to the Middle Shang Dynasty Period. The city is considered by some to be the first Shang Dynasty capital, known as Ao, but this remains a matter of contention. The inner rammed-earth wall, measuring 20–30 meters at its base, encircled an area of 300 hectares while the outer settlement expanded Zhengzhou's size to a massive 1,300 hectares; the city may have had a population as high as 100,000 (Liu and Chen 2012: 282; Thorp 2006: 64). The palace area in the northwestern part of the inner city contained several dozen structures, some as large as 2,000 square meters in area, that were likely both palatial residences and temples. Human and animal remains speak to sacrificial rituals, and the presence of 100 human partial skulls, bearing saw marks, is further evidence of human sacrifice within the palace area (Liu and Chen 2003: 95). Outside the inner city but still within the area of Zhengzhou were two bronze foundries producing tools, weapons, and ritual bronze vessels, in both Erlitou (e.g., *jia* and *jua* three-legged vessels) and Erligang (early Shang) styles, the latter consisting of heavily decorated *fangding* four-legged vessels. As they did at Erlitou, elites at Zhengzhou continued to wield strict control over the production and distribution of bronze ritual objects. At least 50% of the bones that were unworked or partially worked in this area came from humans.

The elite burials recovered from Erligang settlements feature differences in grave size and burial goods consistent with developed social stratification. The more elaborate graves consist of rectangular pits that once held wooden coffins; a ledge around the coffin pit held burial offerings and often a smaller pit containing an animal (usually a dog) or even human sacrifice (Thorp 2006: 102–104). The practice of elaborate burial and graveside ritual evident in the Erlitou phase is well documented as having continued into the Erligang/Early and Middle Shang cultural sphere.

Again like Erlitou before it, the Erligang state relied on outlying settlements to supply raw resources such as ores, kaolinite, and semiprecious stones to centers such as Zhengzhou. In fact, many of the outposts or "colonies" identified as being part of the Erlitou state were taken over in the Erligang phase with fortifications erected to protect Erligang interests. Raw resources were taken to the workshops at Zhengzhou and other centers to be crafted into beautiful and highly valued prestige goods, which were then distributed to elites. One undeniably important resource was salt, used in food preservation among other things (Flad 2007). Evidence suggests that the acquisition and distribution of salt resources was controlled by Erligang centers and presumably their resident elites.

Around 1400 BCE, many Erligang settlements, including Zhengzhou, were abandoned. While the cause of this depopulation is not at all certain, many archaeologists believe that internal sociopolitical turmoil and outright conflict may have been a major factor. One hint comes from the discovery of three hoards of bronze items, mostly ritual vessels, buried in wells and storage pits at Zhengzhou (Liu and Chen 2003: 96). This total of 28 objects, including bronze ritual cauldrons weighing 50 kilograms or more, might have been hidden by fleeing elite families in hopes that they could one day return to retrieve their buried treasures. Following the Erligang abandonment, the Late Shang Period emerges in the latter half of the 2nd millennium BCE.

The Late Shang Period

The Shang state is best known for its Late Phase (ca. 1300–1026 BCE) during which a full-scale and indisputable Chinese state arose. The best-known capital during the Late Shang phase is at the modern city of Anyang, which has been undergoing excavation since the 1920s. Because of these extensive excavations and due to the development of writing by the Late Shang Period (see Box 9.6), we know a great deal about the last capital at Anyang and the Shang culture that thrived there. The state-building trends observed in the earlier Erlitou and Erligang cultures were the foundations of this earliest Chinese state.

BOX 9.6 ORIGINS OF CHINESE WRITING

The origins of Chinese writing can be traced back to cultures of the 4th and 3rd millennia BCE (Keightley 2014: 229). The earliest forms of the script were found on pots, often recovered from burials, and may have served to mark vessels for social reasons such as kinship affiliation, station, or occupation. These images were either naturalistic, depicting recognizable images such as animals, or schematic in that they represented images that required interpretation (Figure 9.8). These images emerged as pictographs that carried meaning but were not yet "writing" as they may not have represented words. In the Bronze Age Erlitou Period, these images continued to appear on vessels and on oracle bones (see Box 9.3); these signs were certainly meant to convey meaning to those who saw them but were not yet a clear system of writing (Keightley 2014: 234). By the Late Shang Period, the signs had developed into logographic characters that corresponded to words. The number of characters inscribed on oracle bones has offered scholars a vast range of characters to identify (between 40,000 and 50,000 oracle bones bear inscriptions) that are syntactically organized and can be considered a fully developed writing system. It is likely that the pictographs of the late 4th millennium slowly transitioned to characters with standardized meaning by the early or mid-2nd millennium BCE (Keightley 2014: 234). By the Late Shang Period, Chinese diviners and scholars were adept at reading and writing; as the centuries progressed, the copious records kept by Chinese scholars and historians have been an enormous aid to archaeologists and historians seeking to reconstruct the complex ancient Chinese cultures, states, and empires of the last 4,000 years.

FIGURE 9.8 Examples of Naturalistic and Stylistic Early Chinese Pictographs: Left Image Could Refer to Sun and Fire or Mountain; Top Right Could Be an Axe; Bottom Right an Adze

Source: After Keightley (2014: 231, fig. 9.1b)

The historical name of Anyang is Yinxu, meaning "the ruins of Yin," Yin being the name of the ancient Late Shang capital city. It is located on the Huan River, with a mountain range visible to the west and the Huang He River to the east. Ancient Yin was a massive center, perhaps as large as 30 square kilometers. Inside this enormous Shang city were palaces and temples, a royal cemetery, workshops and residential areas and a clear indication that residential clusters were organized according to kin-based lineages.

Scholars have been able to establish a fairly reliable list of pre-dynastic and dynastic kings who ruled from various locations, using the written records compiled in later dynasties and checking them against Shang oracle bone inscriptions. The first known Late Shang ruler was named Pan Geng, who may have ruled for half a century (r. 1300–1251 BCE) and been responsible for establishing the Shang capital at Yinxu (Chang 1980; see Thorp 2006: 24 for regnal dates). One of the best-known Shang kings was named Wu Ding (r. 1250–1192 BCE) who carried out extensive military campaigns to enlarge the Shang state and who buried one of his wives, Fu Hao, in a tomb within the palace precinct (see next section). Little more than the names survive of the approximately five succeeding Late Shang kings who ruled a vast and powerful state that lasted until the mid-11th century BCE.

Shang control of surrounding regions was less extensive in the Late Shang Period following the Middle Shang abandonment. Nonetheless, Shang influence and control spanned several hundred kilometers in nearly every direction, reaching coastal China to the east, more arid areas to the north, and south to the Huai River and near the Yangzi. The interactions Shang kings had with these near and outlying polities, including diplomatic and economic interactions as well as outright war, are recorded on the thousands of oracle bones recovered from Yinxu and elsewhere.

The Late Shang Capital at Yinxu

The palace and ceremonial complex at Yinxu, located next to the Huan River, which runs through the city, was approximately 70 hectares in size and contained rammed-earth foundations for over 50 buildings (Liu and Chen 2012: 356). This area was surrounded by an enormous ditch, likely a moat, that was dug to a depth of 5 meters and varied in width from 10 to 20 meters; traces of materials that may be the remains of bridges were found (Liancheng and Wenming 2005; Thorp 2006: 135–36). It is possible that this ditch formed a real, or at least a symbolic, boundary to this ritual and elite center. The buildings that once stood on the rammed-earth foundations are gone, but excavations have determined that religion and ritual were central to the use of many of the structures. Other structures may have been royal or elite palatial residences, and possibly some were devoted to workshops producing crafts used solely by elites in religious activities.

This ceremonial precinct also contained elite burials and human and animal sacrifices. In some cases, skeletal remains, mainly of humans, were found in the rammed-earth foundations of buildings in what is known as Section B within this precinct. Archaeologists believe Section B was likely the area where the royal temples were located, while Section A was devoted to residences and Section C to ceremonial events (possibly both religious and secular) (Chang 1986: 322–24; Liancheng and Wenming 2005). A Section D has recently been located, but its function is still under investigation. Section B burials were likely ritual sacrifices carried out prior to or during the building of the royal temples. Well over 100 pits contained a variety of sacrifices including humans, sheep, and dogs, and burial items. Most pits contained three adult victims (usually decapitated, lying face down), but some pits had many more, and a few contained children; five pits contained chariots, complete with horses (Figure 9.9) (Thorp 2006: 187–88). Evidence suggests that each pit was dug, received its deposit, and then covered, indicating that multiple victims were sacrificed at the corresponding burial ceremony. Shang elites also conducted feasts at the graveside, and bronze vessels and eating utensils were included in graves for continued feasting for those moving beyond the Shang world (Nelson 2003).

One of the best-known tombs from this elite precinct is that of Fu Hao ("Lady Hao") whose name is known from the many inscribed grave goods buried with her; Fu Hao was one of Wu Ding's royal consorts (according to many oracle bone inscriptions), and she also served as a military leader and may have produced several royal progeny. Fu Hao's tomb was in a ca. 5.5 by 4 meter pit with two layers. The upper layer contained her lacquered coffin and roughly 2,000 burial gifts such as jade, bone, and bronze objects (some imported from the north) and ritual vessels, including a bronze cooking stove (Nelson 2003), and other items of pottery, stone, and ivory. Several thousand cowry shells were also buried with her (these may have functioned as a type of currency in the Shang world). Underneath Fu Hao's tomb was another layer containing the remains of sacrificial victims including dogs and humans. The tomb of Fu Hao, which was only moderately sized compared to those found in the royal cemetery (see later), demonstrates the incredible wealth possessed by the Shang rulers and elites; all other tombs at Yinxu had been robbed in antiquity.

There was a thriving jade, bone, ceramic, and bronze craft production industry at Yinxu. Some of these production centers were located in the elite precinct and were likely under the direct control of the elites there. Excavations have discovered six bronze foundries that produced weapons and tools in addition to ritual vessels; at least two of these foundries may have been controlled by the Yinxu royal elites (Liu and Chen 2012: 358). Houses near the bronze foundries contained casting molds and other paraphernalia associated with the bronze-working craft (Thorp 2006: 142), suggesting that artisans involved in a particular craft lived near the city's workshops devoted to these activities.

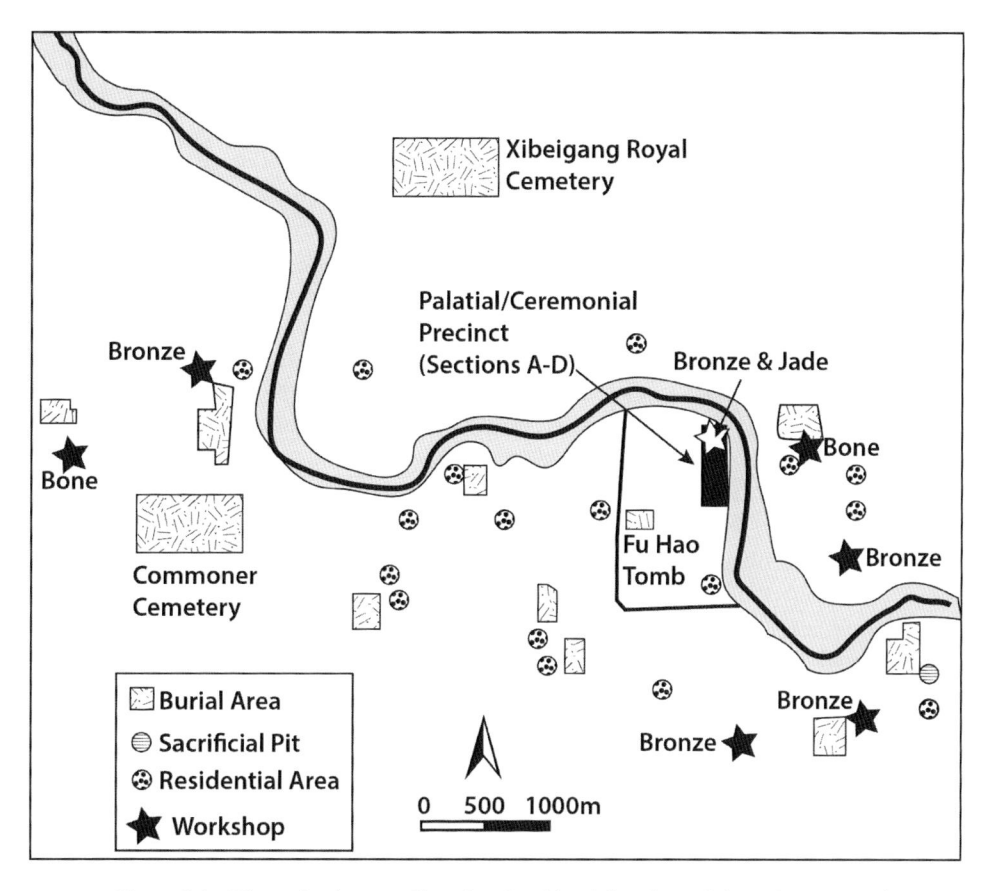

FIGURE 9.9 Plan of the Yinxu Settlement Showing Residential and Workshop Areas, Royal Cemetery, and Palatial/Ceremonial Precinct

Source: After Liangcheng and Wenming (2005: 157, fig. 6.19)

Sociopolitical Organization in Shang Society

It is through the oracle bones that much of the Late Shang social, political, and religious organization is understood. The Shang king was referred to by at least two names: *wang*, which means "king," and *yiren*, which essentially means "the first person" and designates him as the leader of the royal lineage and thus of the entire society (Liangchen and Wenming 2005). Members of the *Zi* lineage (the royal clan), or closely related lineages, held high positions in the royal court, overseeing political, legal, and religious affairs. Those in positions associated with Shang religion, especially "diviners" (interpreters of the oracle bones), were particularly powerful, as is explained in more detail later.

Shang kings controlled neighboring polities through a variety of means including diplomacy, trade, gift exchange, marriage alliances, and, when necessary, warfare. An important component of the Late Shang Dynasty was the maintenance of a standing army and defensive and offensive tactics in warfare. Under the Late Shang rulers, the army may have contained as many as 60,000 men, consisting primarily of those from the lower classes (agricultural workers and craftsmen) who went about their daily lives until called for military service (Liangchen and Wenming 2005). An upper echelon in the army consisted of horse-drawn chariot soldiers; examples of their gear were found in

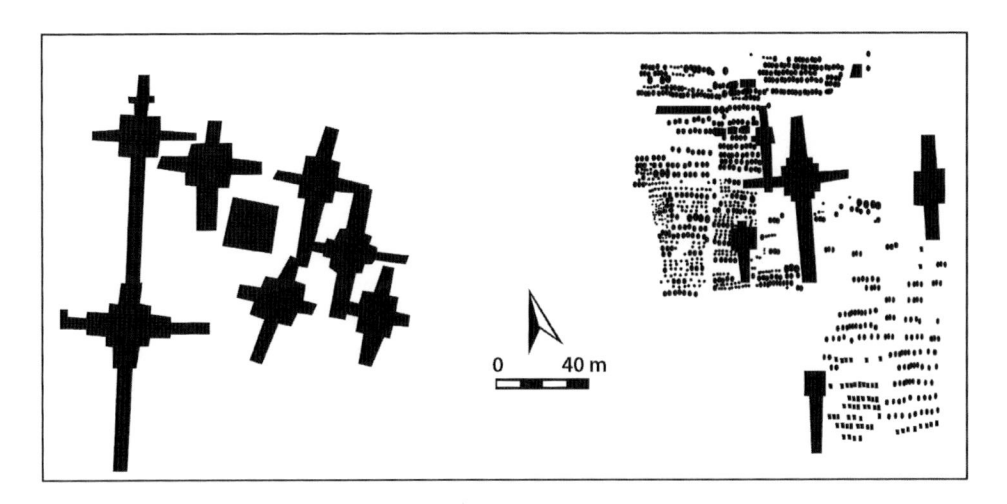

FIGURE 9.10 Plan of the Xibeigang Royal Cemetery at Yinxu

Source: After Liangcheng and Wenming (2005: 159, fig. 6.21)

the elite precinct tombs. The oracle bones record evidence of Shang wars with neighboring states, particularly during the reign of Wu Ding; prisoners of war acquired during these wars were essential to the elaborate ritual cycle that included human sacrifice.

That kinship was a central organizational principle in the ancient Shang Dynasty is clearly illustrated by the Yinxu settlement itself. Archaeologists have determined that the residential areas were organized in clusters, called *yi*, which can be roughly translated as "district." Within these districts were pit houses, storage areas for both food and water, and burials (Figure 9.9). These residential clusters corresponded to lineage groups who lived in their own *yi* and cooperated in subsistence production and consumption activities. There was a significant social stratification system at Yinxu with at least six socioeconomic classes, based on evidence derived from over 4,000 tombs and from house size, location, and contents (Liancheng and Wenming 2005). The highest elites resided in the precinct area and were buried either there or in the royal tombs area (see next section). The commoners lived in other areas across the vast expanse of Yinxu, including near the workshops where they toiled; they were buried in cemeteries within their *yi* in simple pit tombs.

Kin relationships were central components in Shang culture, and they were critical factors in the elite power structure, demonstrated in Shang religion and ritual, described later. The Shang social hierarchy is perhaps best characterized by Chang:

> [W]e see that the king was at the apex of a markedly stratified social order. The king, his family and his high officials enjoyed the highest quality of life at the time—above-ground houses, objects of bronze and other valuable materials, lavish feasts and banquets.... At the other end of the ladder, there were those whose whole life-needs were served by an underground pit-house a few metres in diameter, in which we find only the remains of a few pottery cooking and serving vessels.
>
> *(1974: 6)*

One's position in society was determined by birth, a system that had evolved in the later stages of the Neolithic only to grow stronger and more structured in the Bronze Age (Chang 2005).

The Xibeingang Royal Cemetery at Yinxu

Some of the best evidence of elite power during the Late Shang Period comes from the royal tombs in the Xibeigang cemetery at Yinxu (Figure 9.10). Over the decades of excavation, 11 of the most elaborate tombs (likely belonging to the 11 known kings of Yinxu, including Wu Ding) have been excavated in the royal cemetery. Other, less elaborate tombs, probably the resting places of members of the royal house, wives and consorts of the kings, or important officials, have also been investigated (Liancheng and Wenming 2005). Tombs in the Xibeigang area were looted in antiquity so it is only the labor that went into their building, and the associated sacrificial victims, that demonstrate their importance. The largest tombs were square or oblong, entered by long ramps into a tomb shaft that is up to 10 meters deep; the best-known of these tombs, Tomb 1001, measures 19 meters long and 14 meters wide (Chang 1986: 327). A wooden chamber was built in the tomb pit where the ruler's coffin rested, and the deceased was once surrounded by burial goods of jade, stone, bronze, ceramics, bone, and other materials (mostly looted in antiquity). The finds from Fu Hao's tomb give an idea of the richness of these royal tombs. The excavator of Tomb 1001 estimated that the labor involved in digging the pit for this tomb required 7,000 working days, and this was probably the average for all of the most elaborate Xibeigang tombs (Chang 1986: 327).

In addition to the extraordinary labor and elaborate burial goods, human and animal sacrifices accompanied elites into death. Archaeologists estimate that approximately 10,000 human sacrificial victims are buried in the Xibeigang cemetery, with several hundred being offered at a single burial. While it is likely that the majority of these were war captives (Campbell 2009), some may have been trusted servants or other favorite members of the royal courts. Human remains in sacrificial pits, and in the royal tombs themselves, are sometimes complete but more often headless, limbless, or represented simply by their skulls. When skeletal remains were complete, they were regularly accompanied by animals such as dogs, hawks, and even an elephant, and in a few instances, women and children were also sacrificed. Ritual life during the Late Shang Dynasty was dynamic and clearly concentrated in the hands of the elites.

Shang Religion: Divination, Oracle Bones, and Ancestors

Tracking the development of Shang divination and ritual activity offers a clear view of the consolidation of power into the hands of the elites and especially the royal court by the Late Shang Period. Two aspects of Shang rituals will be described here in more detail. The first is Shang divination and the ubiquitous use of oracle bones, which functioned as much to predict the future as to legitimate royal actions. Second, the rituals associated with worship of supernatural beings and ancestors illustrate the power Shang elites, especially the royal court, held over all members of the state.

Roughly 160,000 oracle bones have been recovered from excavations at Yinxu, which may represent less than 10% of those made in the Late Shang Period (Keightley 1978a). In the Late Shang Period, turtle carapaces became the primary vehicle for divination activities; turtle pens at Yinxu and turtle "tributes" from outlying polities demonstrate the importance of this animal to Shang religious practices (Flad 2008). By the Late Shang Period, written and archaeological records suggest that the ritual cycle was nearly constant (see later).

In general, oracle bones were used to answer questions (e.g., "Should we begin the harvest now?") or to seek divine approval for elite actions ("Attacking city X will bring us great bounty") or to entreat the ancestors for good will, protection, and success (Keightley 1988, 2000; Thorp 2006). Scholars describe the oracle bone divination process as one that included "pyromancy," that is, divination that employs fire. Written records have provided the names of over 100 Shang diviners, many of whom served King Wu Ding. While the vast majority of divination was carried out on behalf of the royal court and the elites, there is evidence that commoners also made use of diviners (Flad 2008). These were probably costly endeavors for the poorest members of the Shang culture and undertaken only when there was great need. Archaeological examination shows that oracle bones from elite contexts were of the highest quality—smoothed, polished, and carefully prepared with pre-fire inscriptions—while those found in commoner contexts had only minor preparation and ad hoc pre-fire treatment (Flad 2008).

The divination process began with the professional diviner preparing the bone, which, for the elite and royal ceremonies, included smoothing and thinning it, polishing it, and making sure the surface was ready to receive an inscription; then holes and indentations were drilled and chiseled onto the back or underside of the bone or carapace. The question or prediction was then addressed to the oracle bone, at which point the pyromancy—application of the heated bronze poker to the drilled and chiseled marks on the bone—took place (Figure 9.3). The cracks resulting from the applied heat were then read by the diviner, or in the case of a royal divination, by the king; the question or prediction was inscribed on the bone as was the answer (Keightley 1988).

Shang Period divinations had several purposes, depending on who was the intended client. Though records are minimal, it is likely that commoners who engaged a diviner truly wished to know the proper path for the future, couched in terms that were meant to yield good news ("My harvest will be good," "my son will survive his illness," "I will survive the coming war"), to which answers might be as simple as "yes" or more complicated such as "today there will be no death." Besides insights into the future, divinations, when carried out by the royal court, were meant to verify predictions by the king or to attest that his intended (or past) actions were the proper ones. Since it was the king himself, or perhaps a diviner in his employ, who read the pyromancy marks on the oracle bones, the king was rarely wrong.

In Shang religion, devotional ceremonies were dedicated to three different entities: a major god known as Shang Di; spirits of the natural world (water, wind, earth, clouds, sun, etc.); and ancestors. However, by the Late Shang, Shang Di had become the supreme being controlling all elements of the world, thereby also representing the spirits of these elements (Liangchen and Wenming 2005). Ceremonies honoring the ancestors were of two types: one was held at the temple (*miaoji*) and the other at tombs (*muji*); individual rituals for ancestors lasted approximately ten days, and by the Late Shang dynastic period, so many ancestors required worship that it took an entire year to properly recognize every ancestor (Liangchen and Wenming 2005; Thorp 2006).

The most critical ancestors to honor were those of the royal Zi lineage because it was they who could affect the future and the fortunes of the Shang people. The Zi ancestors, who included dead kings and queens, were able to intercede with Shang Di to ensure successful harvests and outcomes of war, bring desirable weather, keep illness and pestilence at bay, and so forth (Liu 1999). Thus, it was crucial that Zi ancestors be propitiated, and the only one able to do this properly and successfully was the Shang king and perhaps some members of the royal court and selected elites (Keightley 1978b). The ancestors required offerings to keep up their strength and to provide protection to the Shang people. Offerings included food and flesh of both animals and humans. Depending on the power and importance of the ancestor, hundreds of animals and humans (usually prisoners of war) might be sacrificed at a single ceremony (Keightley 1978b). The need to provide human sacrificial victims to the ancestors was a major component in legitimizing the king's war machine. The king, as the singular conduit to these critical ancestors, possessed immeasurable power over every aspect of Shang life. The king had to be obeyed, propitiated, and honored, so that he would carry out the life-giving, and conversely life-taking, rituals for his ancestors on behalf of all of his subjects.

The final component of all-consuming royal power was the claiming of Shang Di as part of the Zi ancestral line. This made all of the king's ancestors, and the king himself, a descendant of Shang Di, the all-powerful deity, and in fact, in the latter part of the Late Shang Dynasty, the king was known as the "son" of Shang Di (Liangchen and Wenming 2005). Worship of the dead king was therefore incumbent upon his successor. The incorporation of Shang Di into the King's Zi dynastic lineage ensured that the living king, and his deceased forebearers, remained the chief advocates for the Shang people and legitimized the ritual cycle that included food, animal, and human offerings and precious commodities. Social, economic, and political power flowed into the hands of the king and the royal court and attending elites, through the body of Shang religious belief.

The End of the Shang Dynasty: The Rise of the Zhou

As already noted, traditionally, pre-Imperial China consisted of three dynasties: the Xia, the Shang, and, finally, the Zhou. While the nature of the Xia dynastic state is still conjectured, this chapter has outlined the enormous amount of data available regarding the Shang. Similarly, a great deal is known about the third and final pre-Imperial dynasty, the Zhou, which is divided into two phases known as the Western Zhou (1046–771 BCE) and the later Eastern Zhou (741–221 BCE), the former considered a more peaceful and stable period. While the Xia Dynasty, if it existed in any recognizable form, seems to have segued into the Shang, the transition between Shang and Zhou was far more abrupt. Archaeological and written records identify a Zhou monarch, King Wen, whose reign overlapped with the last Shang dynast. King Wen was a benevolent and stable monarch, and many turned to him for leadership as the Shang king had become erratic and untrustworthy. By approximately 1050 BCE, the Shang rulership was disintegrating and many segments of Shang society, including the elites, were electing to follow King Wen. He encouraged the Zhou people to emulate the Shang culture, including their religion, and thus archaeologically, it is difficult to differentiate between the two in many cases. The majority of our information about the earlier Western Zhou at this time period derives from royal and local archives.

King Wen died in approximately 1050 BCE, and the Zhou throne went to his son, King Wu, who ruled from the city of Haojing (present-day Xi'an) in Shaanxi Province, hundreds of kilometers west of the Yinxu Shang capital. In approximately 1046 BCE, King Wu attacked and conquered Yinxu, once and for all bringing down the Shang dynastic line. Shang culture did not perish, as much of Western Zhou culture either mimicked or built upon Shang practices and material culture. King Wu and his successors then set about bringing the former Shang regions under Zhou control. One action that aided the Zhou was their claiming of the "Mandate of Heaven." This mandate was said to award rulership to a just and righteous clan or dynasty. The Zhou rulers argued that the Shang kings, especially the last one, had forfeited the mandate because his rule had become unjust and violent. The Zhou claimed they were the rightful rulers, receiving the "mandate" from heaven.

After the death of King Wu (ca. 1043 BCE), the throne was to pass to King Wu's son, but he was still a child; accordingly one of King Wu's brothers, known to historians as the "Duke of Zhou," stepped forward to act as regent for the boy. Other Zhou relatives, especially those to the east ruling the former Shang lands, believed the Duke meant to usurp the throne and mounted a rebellion. It took three years, but by 1040 BCE, the Duke of Zhou vanquished his detractors and re-established his position as regent for the young king, coming away with control of the Zhou lands, including Shang lands to the east. He built a second capital, Chang-Zhou (at present-day Luoyang), in traditional Shang territory to help control this growing empire. Shortly after putting down the rebellion and consolidating the lands, King Wu's son reached his majority, and the Duke of Zhou turned over the throne to the "rightful heir." This act in effect convinced the people of the Zhou lands that the Mandate of Heaven was indeed legitimately awarded to the Zhou Dynasty.

Zhou Society and Land Management

The Zhou are known for designing what can be called a "feudal" system to control the landscape within their empire, though it was quite different from the later European Medieval feudal model (Feng 2003). Zhou dynasts dispatched members of their family, mainly brothers, uncles, and male

FIGURE 9.11 Photo of Eastern Zhou Dynasty Bronze Cauldron Known as a "Ding"

Source: Los Angeles County Museum of Art, © Museum Associates / LACMA. Licensed by Art Resource, NY

cousins, to various regions of the former Shang lands where they were given land grants, which might be termed districts, or provinces. They ruled their regions on behalf of the Zhou king, employing royal Zhou edicts and ensuring loyalty to the Zhou Dynasty (Feng 2003). Rule of the provinces was hereditary, though non-Zhou were also given smaller land grants and in effect were then "adopted" into the Zhou family.

Archaeological excavation of cemeteries has allowed for a better understanding of the Zhou ranking system among the elite classes, both through the excavation of burial goods and the inscriptions placed on Zhou bronze vessels. In the Jin district, located in Shanxi Province, the excavation of a cemetery revealed Zhou rulers were buried with their spouses and consorts, often accompanied by their court; in the case of one cemetery, six chariots accompanied the Zhou ruler into his next life (Xu 1996). Tombs were built as shafts with long ramps, sometimes as much as 18 meters, leading down to the tomb shaft; in the chamber, the deceased rested in wooden coffins, surrounded by burial goods of great wealth. Zhou elites were supplied with items of bronze, jade, gold, fine ceramics, and often chariots. The larger bronzes and ceramics usually surrounded the coffins, while the smaller and more precious items of gold and jade were inside the coffins (Cook 1997). A similar set of burial goods and elaborate tombs is found in a cemetery located in the Yan region, near modern Beijing. Here, burials suggest that several different ranks of Western Zhou elites are represented, which may include the ruler, who was a military leader, and his court. The leader's tomb included lacquer shields inlaid with bronze and bronze weapons as well as evidence for 19 chariots and over 50 horses (Jaffee 2013). Lower-ranking Zhou elites had descending numbers of burial goods ranging from items made of bronze and jade to ceramic food vessels; the lowest-ranking individuals had very few goods and no bronze vessels, and the presence of weapons suggests they may have been soldiers serving the ruler (Jaffee 2013). Western Zhou burials are clear indicators of the wealth and power held by the king and his various subsidiary rulers dispatched to outlying states to implement Zhou political authority.

Zhou Bronze Vessels

One of the activities that assisted Western Zhou solidarity and the authority of the rulers was their practice of gift-giving between elites. Gifts included the types of jades described earlier, as well as beads and beaded ornaments and cowrie shells, the latter possibly considered imbued with magical properties (Cook 1997; Hommel and Sax 2014; Yung-ti 2006). The most notable, and valuable, of the gifts were bronze vessels in the form of cauldrons, elaborate pots and jars, and bowls elaborately decorated and often carrying inscriptions (Figure 9.11).

Bronze vessels, mostly recovered from Zhou cemeteries, were only constructed after permission was given by the ruler for the elite to do so (Cook 1997). The permission from the king was tacit recognition of the elite's powerful position within the Zhou state and was a signal that the elite had the support of the king and therefore power over those whom he ruled in his designated district. The inscriptions offered vital information such as the origin of the vessel and the explicit granting of the land to the elite, thereby establishing his authority (see Box 9.7). These vessels and other bronze items were exchanged at ritual feasts as well as at funerals and sometimes at marriages, especially when a woman of one lineage was marrying into another. Vessels received from the Western Zhou court were displayed in the outlying regions and districts as a visual reminder of the power invested in the local ruler (Sun 2003).

BOX 9.7 THE NINE CAULDRONS

The nine ritual cauldrons possessed by the Western Zhou court were considered the root of their power in many ways. The cauldrons were said to have been cast in more ancient times, made of metals given as gifts by the nine provinces of the Xia state. This was a representation of the ruling elite's authority over metal and metallurgy, one of the very important economic concerns of ancient Chinese empires (Chang 1983). These tripod cauldrons were used at rituals where sacrifices were made. They were enormous, and later records claimed that only Heaven was capable of moving them. When the Western Zhou rulers fled the throne, they apparently left behind the cauldrons. They eventually disappeared during the period of the Warring States.

Even though the Western Zhou state was stable, by the early 8th century, trouble began brewing. There were some rebellions against Western Zhou authority within the state, as well as external attacks, including from nomadic tribes who would plague Chinese states for many future centuries (Di Cosmo 1999). Some sources suggest that the Western Zhou rulers had become avaricious and had therefore lost the right to the Mandate of Heaven. In 771 BCE, the king was overthrown, and the capital city was destroyed by raids from the nomadic tribes. One of the sons of the king was able to escape and fled eastward to the auxiliary capital, Cheng-Zhou, established by the Duke of Zhou. He re-established Zhou authority and the Eastern Zhou state arose.

The Eastern Zhou and the Warring States Period

The Eastern Zhou state was not the robust and stable system found in its previous Western Zhou incarnation. In part, this change in structure was due to the distribution of power. When the Western Zhou king's son fled eastward, he was aided by the provincial rulers who controlled the lands in these regions. These elites saw a chance to increase their authority, and thus, the Eastern Zhou state was ruled not by a single king, but by a collection of ministers who guided, and some might say controlled, the king. This period is known as the "Spring and Autumn" Period in Chinese texts, the "spring" referring to the period between 771 and 476 BCE, and the "autumn," to the Warring States Period from 476 to 221 BCE (see later). Because there was no central authority but rather a system of dispersed power, there was much more instability during the Eastern Zhou Period. Provinces vied for control of additional territories, and each provincial ruler built an army for protection as well as for expansionary gains. Several districts, including the Han, which later became a powerful Chinese dynasty (see next section), effectively broke away from the Eastern Zhou and became independent.

The instability of the Eastern Zhou state ushered in the age of philosophy. Elites consulted scholars who could guide them in the proper pathways to not only gain territory but to establish peace. One of these philosophers was Confucius, whose views on civility and morality and the proper structure of social relationships would shape Chinese thought for the next two millennia (Barrett 2013). Even though Confucius and his fellow philosophers attempted to help bring stability to the "Spring Period" of the Eastern Zhou state, this was not to last.

Beginning in the early 5th century BCE, by many accounts in 476, the Eastern Zhou Dynasty fell into disarray, and the period known as the "Warring States" (Autumn Period) commenced (Lianchang 2005). During this period, which lasted until 221 BCE, at least seven differing states competed for control of what was still nominally the Eastern Zhou Empire. Shifting alliances between the states and multiple attacks ushered in a 250-year period of instability. The Eastern Zhou king was unable to retain control of these rebellious states, and the king, though nominally still the highest regent, was permanently defeated by the ruler of the Qin state in 256 BCE. The Qin king and his successors then set about conquering the other warring states and firmly established the Qin Empire in 221 BCE.

Imperial China: The Qin and Han Dynasties

With the establishment of the Qin Dynasty, the world saw the rise of Imperial China; though the dynasties changed, the Chinese imperial structure lasted into the 20th century CE. After the chaos of the Warring States Period, the Qin Dynasty, though short-lived (221–206 BCE), brought stability to eastern Asia and made its mark on Chinese history. The very name "China" derives from the Qin Dynasty, which was responsible for re-establishing centralized political control in the hands of the leader, now termed "emperor." The first Qin Dynasty ruler was Ying Zheng who became the "Shi Huangti" or "first emperor" in 221 BCE.

The Qin emperor did not want to make the same mistakes of the Eastern Zhou and allow his empire to fall into the chaos that ensued during the Warring States Period. He invited a scholar named Shang Yang to his court to help him devise a system of rule that would return all power into the hands of the ruler (Tanner 2010: 84). Shang Yang suggested a system of government that has come to be known as "Legalism," which allowed the Qin emperor to remove power from regional aristocrats and consolidate it into his own hands. For instance, the farmers who had served landowners for decades, or centuries, in the Chinese-style feudal system established during the Western Zhou Period, were freed by Shi Huangti. This disrupted the power of the aristocrats who owned the land but could no longer effectively farm it using peasants bound to the land. A strict system of taxation was also

FIGURE 9.12 Photo of the Great Wall of China at Badaling

Source: Photo courtesy of Samxli, licensed under CC BY-SA 2.0 Generic via Wikimedia Commons

established, based on the productivity of each household; this policy generated substantial wealth, all of which was funneled back to the ruling dynasty (Loewe 2007). Further, each person within the Qin Empire had a responsibility to act correctly, and to report anyone who did not conform. Families were collectivized into groups of ten and were required to observe one another and report on any mis-doings. The breaking of laws, which could be reported by any member of the empire, was subject to harsh punishment (Lewis 2007). The age of the philosophers and scholars ended with the Qin Empire: knowledge and study were suppressed, allowing the Qin emperor greater control over his people; an infamous "burning of books" in 212 BCE is illustrative of this policy.

The political policies undertaken by Emperor Shi Huangti allowed for the building of a powerful army and the creation of subjects who were fanatical about following the law. During the Qin Dynasty China's economic system was stabilized. Currency was introduced as was a standardized system of weights and measures, allowing for long-distance trade as the Silk Road, a system of trade networks that eventually stretched from China to the Mediterranean Sea, began to emerge (Loewe

2007). It is during the Qin Dynasty that Chinese writing became standardized as well. The Qin Dynasty is perhaps most famous for its building projects, which included the Great Wall of China (see Box 9.8), meant to prevent the northern nomadic tribes, in part responsible for the downfall of the Western Zhou, from attacking the Qin Empire.

BOX 9.8 KEY MONUMENT: THE GREAT WALL

The Great Wall of China (Figure 9.12) is a stone, brick, and rammed-earth wall that runs roughly east-west and consists of many portions built during different dynasties. During the Warring States Period, some walls running north to southeast divided lands between enemies. However, beginning with the Qin Dynasty, the walls were built with the primary goal of keeping northern invaders, nomadic warriors from the steppe lands of Mongolia, from attacking Chinese states in inner China along the Huang He River. The main portion of the Great Wall was built during the Han Dynasty when emperors dealt with repeated, and often successful, incursions from the north. The walls were reconstituted and lengthened through succeeding dynasties; most of the visible wall today is due to rebuilding and enhancements during the Ming Dynasty (ca. 1368–1644 CE). The entire wall stretches over 20,000 kilometers and took an untold number of hands to build it over the millennia. During its building, it is likely that tens of thousands, perhaps hundreds of thousands, of workers died and were buried next to or even within the wall. The Great Wall often ends up on most lists of the "greatest wonders" of the world.

Though followed, Legalism was not favored by the people. Emperor Shi Huangti began to fear for his life, and in fact, he died in 210 BCE from unknown causes. Prior to his death, he constructed an elaborate tomb, which was discovered when peasants near Xi'an, the capital of the Qin Empire, attempted to dig a well and instead found Emperor Shi Huangti's tomb. The tomb is enormous, standing at a height of 43 meters (with an additional 30 meters of earthen mound over the actual tomb) and is spread over an area of 9 kilometers. The tomb is a virtual city (Wood 2007), including a palace, storehouses, and stables; an earthen tomb marks the emperor's burial place, which has yet to be excavated. Within this vast tomb complex are approximately 8,000 terracotta soldiers (Figure 9.13), accompanied by weapons, chariots, and horses. Each soldier has a unique visage and may have been modeled on an actual Qin soldier living over 2,000 years ago. This vast army was clearly meant to protect the emperor in his afterlife. It is estimated that as many as 700,000 workers were needed to build the tomb and create the army.

After the death of Emperor Shi Huangti, his son Hu Hai took the throne, but he did not wield power effectively, and those oppressed under the Qin Legalism policies began to consider revolt as a viable option. Former aristocrats and others within the Qin realm began to form alliances, and it was not long before the Qin Dynasty ended. In 206 BCE, those seeking the end of the Qin imperial order attacked the capital city, Xianyang, and killed the emperor. After several years of warfare and claims to the throne, a leader of the Han Dynasty emerged as the new ruler in 202 BCE.

Unlike the short-lived Qin, the Han Dynasty lasted four centuries (202 BCE–220 CE). It was established by Liu Bang, local ruler of the Han state. After defeating others vying for the now vacated Qin throne, he assumed the imperial throne and became known as Emperor Gaozu. Like the earlier Zhou, the Han Dynasty is divided into the Western Han (ca. 206 BCE–9 CE) and the

FIGURE 9.13 Photo of Terracotta Soldiers in Qin Emperor Shi Huangti's Tomb
Source: Photo courtesy of Nee, licensed under CC BY-SA 3.0 via Wikimedia Commons

Eastern Han (25–220 CE). By 206 BCE, the Western Han Empire consisted of 13 districts, each with its own regional leader who was required to remain loyal to the Han emperor. To the east were five more kingdoms that remained semiautonomous (having sided against the victorious Liu Bang in favor of one of his rivals). Over the first 50 years of the dynasty, Han rulers replaced the existing kings in the 13 Han states with relatives to ensure the loyalty of regional rulers. The power of these local kings was also limited, allowing the emperor to control important decisions, turning the kings into wealthy figureheads (Lewis 2007).

In 5 CE, Emperor Ping died, leaving no apparent heir. A regent, Wang Mang, was appointed to rule and he eventually assumed the throne. During his reign, the power of the Western Han was damaged by both inadvisable political decisions (failed reforms) and natural disasters. Silting of the Huang He resulted in major flooding, damaging crops and destroying settlements. Those opposed to land reforms and other political decisions instigated by Wang Mang teamed up with peasants who were incensed by the loss of their lands and homes. A revolt overturned Wang Mang's rule in 23 CE. Two years later, a new Han emperor emerged, re-establishing control of territories lost during Wang Mang's rule. A second period of relative stability was gained during the Eastern Han Period.

Just as the Qin gave its name to the modern nation, the Han Dynasty gave its name to the present day ethnic group. The term "Han Chinese" is used to refer to the majority and dominant ethnic population of the modern People's Republic of China. Under Han leadership, China gained economic and political stability. In part, this stability was achieved by the re-emergence of Confucian thought in the face of external threats.

Incursions into Han territory by nomadic steppe peoples to the north led to a substantial expansion of the Great Wall for defense (see Box 9.8). Most problematic for the Han were the Xiongnu who triumphed over the Han in a number of battles. The Han's long-reigning Emperor Wu (r. 141–87 BCE) was tired of Xiongnu and other attacks, and he went on the offensive. He substantially increased the size of the Han Empire; by the end of his reign, it stretched from what is today's Korea to the borders of modern Kyrgyzstan in central Asia (Di Cosmo 2009). The Great Wall was also strengthened and extended, forming a more substantial boundary against enemies to the north and east. In the face of these foreign threats, Emperor Wu determined that the Han people needed to be more unified. Philosophical thought, which had been de-emphasized during the Qin Empire, re-emerged with Confucian ideals as a unifying force (Barrett 2013). Han people were to be comforted by the notion that the head of state served as the head of the Han family and was also the link between them and heaven, through the Mandate of Heaven. Furthermore, all Han were linked to each other, to nature, and to the universe. Obedience and devotion to these principles resulted in a stable Han state and a powerful ruling class.

Another major development during the Han Dynasty was the full emergence of the Silk Road. The Silk Road stretched from the Chinese coastal region, followed the Huang He into eastern China, across central Asia, and eventually ended in Constantinople (today's Istanbul in Turkey); it stretched roughly 10,000 kilometers across the Asian continent. The creation of the full Silk Road, which was actually a network of roads with tendrils stretching down into India, the Arabian Peninsula, and eventually Africa, is attributed to the Han Dynasty. It derives its name from the Chinese production of silk, which was a major export along this trade route. Besides the many types of goods that were traded across the vast network, the Silk Road saw the exchange of peoples, including slaves, and ideologies. Travelers, explorers, and envoys were sent along this route to develop new trade links and to gather information on potential allies and enemies. This route remained the international highway linking Europe, Africa, and Asia until the advent of maritime trade in the 14th and 15th centuries CE.

By the late 2nd century CE, the Eastern Han had fallen into economic chaos. The sitting emperor failed to heed the needs of his people, and various populations within the Han Empire began to rebel against imperial edicts and, in essence, imperial rule. However, the past stability of the Han Empire was not to be regained. By 220 CE, the Han Empire was at an end.

Conclusion

Ancient China has long been known for its incredible crafts that speak of detail, patience, and skill. Museums across the world proudly display Chinese silks, bronzes, jade items, wood-working, and many other material objects that derive from centuries, actually millennia, of spectacular craft-working. It was in the acquisition of raw resources and the control and patronage of craft-workers and workshops that ancient Chinese society began its trajectory toward complexity. Beginning in the Neolithic Late Yangshao culture and continuing into the Early Bronze Age Erlitou phases, trade and the production of both utilitarian but especially prestige goods were critical to the development of social stratification and the emergence of elites in Chinese centers. Burials and fortification systems speak to the ability of high elites to command labor and garner extreme wealth during life and into death.

As social stratification and elite classes developed, so did the importance of their lineages and subsequently their ancestors. The importance of ancestor veneration and the recognition of the importance of elite lineages by commoners continued to be a prominent element of Chinese society in the later Erlitou and into the Early Shang Periods. Shang kings became utterly intertwined with state religion, and the role of diviners, many of them attached to the royal house, was paramount in the lives of most Shang inhabitants. By the Late Shang Period, not only were royal lineages of critical importance in general, but royal ancestors could intercede with the supreme god to ensure the health and welfare of the people. Religion and power were firmly and inextricably linked in ancient Shang complex society. Absolute rule emerged in the imperial systems of the Qin and the Han, with power and ideology extending from the throne downward, with the expectation that all peoples would adhere to the edicts issued by the emperor. This worked well until it didn't, and rebellion or internal collapse resulted in the emergence of a new dynasty. Such imperial systems were the norm until the rise of the People's Republic in the early 20th century.

10

EMPIRES IN SOUTHEAST ASIA

Introduction

The empires in southeast Asia, particularly the last and greatest, the Khmer, were all founded within the last 2,000 years. The Khmer Empire was contemporary with Great Zimbabwe (Chapter 4), but the method of governance practiced in these two cultures was starkly different, though both relied heavily on the use of religion as an element of retaining leadership and control.

Though the Khmer Empire is relatively recent, we know comparatively little about it due to poor preservation of non-monumental architectural remains and the total lack of any Khmer records other than building inscriptions. Nonetheless, it is clear that Khmer kings held powerful authority over a vast region of the southeast Asian mainland. Their power lay in control of a complicated bureaucracy that ensured the provision of goods and services to the king and in the Khmer king's representation of himself to his people as divine while on earth and as an agent of the powerful Hindu gods. Obeying and pleasing the king was tantamount to showing devotion to the state's main gods. The Khmer Empire, then, is an ideal example of the inextricable tie between power and religion found in many of the world's ancient archaic states.

Geography and Chronology

The southeast Asian mainland, today occupied by the countries of Vietnam, Laos, Cambodia, and Thailand, is one rich in flora and fauna and criss-crossed by numerous rivers, the most substantial of which is the mighty Mekong. The topography, though friendly to successful habitation, makes archaeological research a challenge.

Geography and Ecological Setting

The boundaries of the southeast Asian empires of the last two millennia are largely defined by three major rivers: the Red River in northern Vietnam, the Chao Phraya in Thailand to the southwest, and the Mekong River, which rises in Tibet and runs through the heart of the entire region (Figure 10.1). In northern Vietnam, from modern Hanoi northward to the Chinese border, the climate is defined as subtropical; winters can be cold and rainy, and rice agriculture is more difficult. The rest of southeast Asia has a tropical climate; temperatures rarely dip below 70 degrees

238 Empires in Southeast Asia

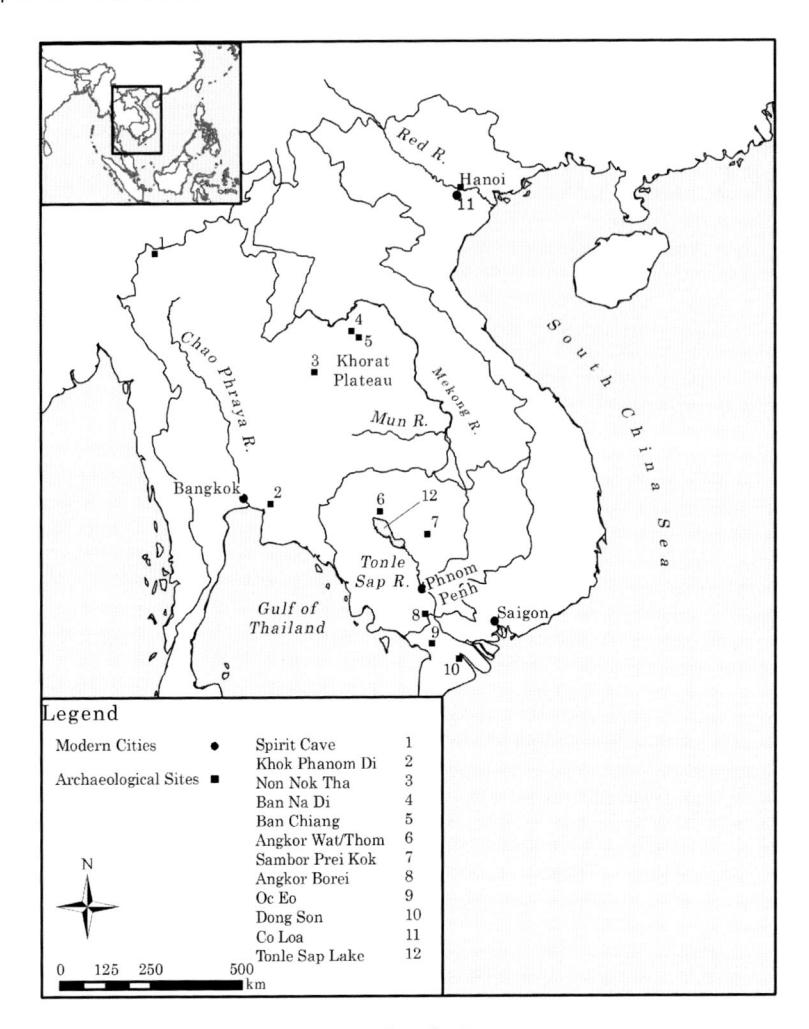

FIGURE 10.1 Map of Regions and Sites Discussed in the Text
Source: B. Spencer

Fahrenheit, and they range up to the 90s or higher with a high level of humidity for most of the year. In the north central part of the region lies the Khorat Plateau, home to some of the earliest settlements in the region. South of the Khorat Plateau lies the Cambodian Basin, which constitutes the majority of today's Kingdom of Cambodia. It is here that the heart of the Khmer Empire rested. A vital resource in Cambodia is Tonle Sap ("Freshwater") Lake, which is the largest on the southeast Asian mainland and has provided sustenance for millennia. The Tonle Sap River rises from the lake and flows southward to meet the Mekong before it empties into the South China Sea.

The climate of the entire peninsula is defined by the monsoon seasons. During the summer monsoon, rains feed the rivers and lakes, turning the landscape into a well-watered and sometimes flooded world. In fact, the rainy season so affects the region that the Tonle Sap River actually reverses its flow during the summer months, flowing back *into* the lake and thus causing the lake to expand its considerable boundaries. For this reason, modern residents on the Tonle Sap Lake reside in houses built on very high stilts (Figure 10.2) ensuring that their homes remain dry for the six-month rainy season. In general, annual rainfall fluctuated between ca. 140 and 240 centimeters

FIGURE 10.2 Photo of Cambodian House on Stilts at Kampong Phluk Village Near Tonle Sap Lake
Source: Photo by S.R. Steadman

each year. No matter where one lives in southeast Asia, however, the seasonal rainfall affects the agricultural cycle, the settlement patterns, and daily activities.

The Chronological Sequence

Humans have occupied the rich tropical environments of southeast Asia for thousands of years. Neolithic hunter-gatherers lived in both cave and open-air sites from at least ca. 9000 BCE. Beginning around 2500 BCE, rice cultivation and more settled communities began appearing throughout the mainland (Table 10.1). It is during this time that bronze metallurgy emerged, commencing the Bronze Age (ca. 1600–500 BCE). These millennia are a time of population expansion, the development of trade networks, and the emergence of more significant social stratification in communities.

In the earlier Iron Age (ca. 500 BCE–200 CE), some dramatic changes came to the region. Trade with south Asia brought in two new religions, Hinduism and Buddhism. Larger settlements began to appear, likely the seats of petty chiefdoms. Defensive architecture in the form of moats, extensive earthworks, and forts made their appearance, and territorial competition became the norm in the region. During what is technically the later Iron Age but is more commonly called the "Early Kingdoms" Period, ca. 200–802 CE, there is indisputable evidence for the emergence of true complex chiefdoms or actual kingdoms. The earliest and best known of these is the Funan Kingdom (ca. 245–6th century CE), which was followed by the Chenla Empire (550–802 CE). These were not the only kingdoms in southeast Asia during these centuries, but they were likely the most powerful.

TABLE 10.1 Chronological Periods and Sites Discussed in Chapter 10 and List of Khmer Kings

Dates	Period	Sites Discussed in Chapter	Cultural Horizons	Khmer Kings
ca. 8000–1600 BCE	Neolithic	Spirit Cave; Lang Kamnan Cave; Khok Phanom Di	Emergence of farming; pottery production; regional trade	
ca. 1600–500 BCE	Bronze Age	Ban Chiang; Ban Na Di; Non Nok Tha	Emergence of bronze metallurgy; evidence of emerging social differentiation; building of moated mounds	
ca. 500 BCE–200 CE	Early Iron Age	Dong Son; Co Loa; Noen U-Loke	Hinduism and Buddhism arrive; iron working develops; emergence of chiefdoms; long-distance trade	
ca. 200–802 CE	Early Empires Period (later Iron Age) (Funan; Chenla)	Angkor Borei; Oc Eo; Chenla Sambor Prei Kuk	Funan and Chenla Kingdoms; capital cities; significant social stratification; temple economy; major temples; god-kings	
802–1431 CE	Khmer Empire Period	Angkor Wat; Angkor Thom	Deified kings (Shiva/Vishnu); stone temples/mausoleums; defensive systems; extensive bureaucratic system	Jayavarman II (770–834 CE) Jayavarman III (834–870 CE) Indravarman I (877–889 CE) Yasovarman I (889–910/912 CE) Rajendravarman II (944–968 CE) Jayavarman V (868–1000 CE) Suryavarman I (1002–1050 CE) Suryavarman II (1113–1150 CE) Jayavarman VII (1181–1218 CE) Jayavarman VIII (1243–1295 CE) Indravarman III (1295–1308) Thommo-Soccorach/Dharmasoka (1429–1431)

In 802 CE, Jayavarman II gained the throne of the Khmer kingdom, which became a vast and powerful empire. It ruled most of southeast Asia from the early 9th century until its demise in the 15th century and left an indelible mark on the landscape and in the minds of the people who occupy it even today.

Pre-State Cultures: Neolithic Foragers and Bronze Age Farmers

Archaeologists are fortunate in that quite a few prehistoric sites in southeast Asia have been carefully excavated allowing for the documentation of the transition from hunting and gathering in the Neolithic to subsistence farming in the Bronze Age (Higham 1994). While the vast majority of data comes from cemeteries, other types of reconnaissance such as ground and satellite survey have revealed much about changes in settlement patterns and settlement types during the periods just prior to, and during, the early southeast Asian empires.

The Southeast Asian Neolithic

Approximately 10,000 years ago, in the Late Pleistocene/Early Holocene Period, southeast Asia was occupied by hunter-gatherers who dwelled in rock shelters, caves, and open-air sites. Sometimes called the Hoabinhian phase, it is clear that the region was occupied not by one but many different cultures (Bellwood 2004). Some of the best information for this period comes from sites in northern Thailand such as Spirit Cave and Lang Kamnan Cave (Higham 2002a; Shoocongdej 2010). Occupants of these and other sites had an extensive stone toolkit to exploit the land and riverine resources and fashioned earthenware pottery (Stark 2004). These foragers were fairly mobile, perhaps sheltering in caves during the rainy season but also occupying lakeshores and other open-air sites during other climatic periods (Higham 2004; Rabett and Barker 2010). The rich tropical landscape ensured a steady subsistence diet as the climate stabilized in the Early Holocene.

Several thousand years later, some groups continued to practice a hunting-gathering economy while others settled into a farming-based subsistence strategy. The site of Khok Phanom Di (ca. 2000–1500 BCE), near the Gulf of Thailand, demonstrates that residents were fashioning pottery, heavily exploiting the freshwater and brackish estuaries and possibly experimenting with early rice cultivation (Higham 2004). Numerous burials suggest residents at Khok Phanom Di lived in kinship-based groupings, retaining these ties after death through interment in kin-based clusters. Burial goods differentiated men from women, with the latter receiving tools related to pottery production, suggesting women were the primary potters at this Neolithic site.

Though rice was domesticated in east Asia over 9,000 years ago, its cultivation did not begin in the southeast until about 5,000 years ago (Bellwood 2006). By the mid-3rd millennium, rice cultivation was fairly widespread throughout northern Thailand in the Khorat Plateau and the Chao Phraya river basin (Higham 2002a). Residents of settlements here were likely a mixture of indigenous peoples and migrants from China (who may have brought the art of rice cultivation with them); the combination of people created the Austroasiatic and Austronesian language families spoken all over southeast Asia today (Bellwood 2005; Higham 2002b). With the domestication of rice and more permanent settlement, residents of the region began experimenting with metallurgy and quickly learned the art of bronze metalworking. This ushered in the Bronze Age of southeast Asia.

Bronze Age Farmers and the Beginnings of Metalcraft

Knowledge of bronze casting in southeast Asia was likely acquired through trade contacts with China where it had been practiced for a millennium (see Chapter 9), though the technology appears to only have been adopted in southeast Asia in the mid-2nd millennium (Higham et al. 2011). The Bronze Age (ca. 1600–500 BCE) lasted roughly a thousand years before yielding to the Iron Age early kingdoms. Archaeologists have excavated several important Bronze Age sites in northern Thailand, and for now, they must serve as exemplars for life across the region as archaeological data for this period in Cambodia and Laos are rare.

On the Khorat Plateau sites such as Ban Chiang, Ban Na Di, and Non Nok Tha offer some insights into Bronze Age life, though mainly through the recovery of materials from cemeteries. Graves consisted of simple inhumations placed in shallow pits or possibly on the ground with earth mounded over them. It is possible that cemeteries existed below houses as some post-holes were discovered at Non Nok Tha (Higham 1989: 101), though these might also correspond to mortuary structures built over the graves. Many burials, including those of children, were accompanied by whole pots, which may have contained food (a number did in fact contain fish bones), possibly used in a mortuary ritual or provided for a presumed afterlife. Ceramics in the earlier phases of the Bronze Age mainly consisted of handmade corded ware styles, but by the later stages, particularly at Ban Chiang, vessels decorated with red paint, incised and often pedestaled, began to appear. During the earlier phases of the Bronze Age, grave goods made of bronze were comparatively rare, but in later stages, bronze jewelry, tools, and other items became more common. Faunal remains in some burials indicate food or animal offerings were included; entire pigs, portions of cattle, chickens, and also dog remains have been found in Non Nok Tha burials. A few burials exhibited shells, which must have come from coastal regions, but in general, grave goods do not reflect an extensive trade network in this earlier stage of the Bronze Age.

At Ban Na Di, as was the case at the other two sites, the majority of finds were retrieved from the cemetery, but there was also greater preservation of the living site. In particular, a clay-lined furnace, stone mold fragments, and broken crucibles along with bronze fragments were recovered, all attesting to the production of bronze items at the site (Higham 1989: 115). The cemetery revealed the same types of burial goods found at other sites. At all sites, grave goods are indicative of some social differentiation; some individuals were buried with a variety of goods in numerous quantities, while others had nothing more than a few complete ceramic vessels. While both men and women, and sometimes children, received significant numbers of grave offerings, there was a consistent gendered difference in burial orientation for men and women, with the former buried with the head to the south and women's heads to the north. There were likely symbolic and possibly religious reasons for this gendered burial orientation, but these are lost to modern archaeologists.

Bronze Age inhabitants were rice cultivators who had domesticated pigs, cattle/water buffalo, dog, and probably chicken; fish and shellfish were also important subsistence items. In addition to domesticated species, village residents also hunted animals to provide a more diverse diet. It is likely residents exploited plant species found in the surrounding forests such as wild yam, mushrooms, bamboo, fruits, and other foods (Higham 1989: 138).

Evidence from various sites and from moated mounds (see Box 10.1), particularly from associated cemeteries, suggests that populations in Bronze Age southeast Asia were increasingly socially differentiated as to wealth and likely social standing; burials indicate both males and females held high status in Bronze Age society. Power and wealth may have been held by certain lineages (possibly matrilineal), making some families prominent members in Bronze Age settlements (Bacus 2004; Higham and Thosarat 2004). As iron metallurgy made its appearance in the region, so did the earliest recognizable power centers.

BOX 10.1 BRONZE AGE MOATED MOUNDS

Over 200 sites known as "moated mounds" have been found in the Khorat Plateau and in areas of Cambodia as well. These are a series of circular or rectangular areas surrounded by mounded earth that date to the Bronze Age or perhaps even the Neolithic Period (E. Moore

1988, 1997; Stark 2004). Because of the poor preservation of organic remains, the houses that may have once stood inside these embankments have been erased. In general, there is a single opening in the embankment allowing ingress to the interior habitation area; surrounding the interior mound was a channel, which may have been water-filled, thus a "moat," leaving an interior raised platform upon which residents could build their homes. When first discovered in the early 20th century, these earthen structures were determined to be defensive in nature, which may be an accurate assessment of their function. However, they may have also served other practical purposes such as to keep animals penned in at night or to keep wild animals at bay (Stark 2004). Given that rivers flood during the rainy season, the mounds may have helped with water management. If they were built, in part or in whole, for defensive purposes, they are an excellent harbinger of the highly competitive chiefdoms that emerged in the Iron Age.

The (Early) Iron Age: The Emergence of Chiefdoms

Between 500 and 300 BCE, iron technology developed in mainland southeast Asia, and it is during these centuries and just after that first Hinduism, and then Buddhism, arrived from south Asia. Like bronze technology, knowledge of iron smelting may have come from China where it was likely in use by the 6th century BCE. Hinduism and Buddhism, which would become the major religions of southeast Asia in the coming centuries, arrived from India via the maritime and overland Silk Road trade routes, carried by traders and missionaries who brought ideologies as well as trade items to the small chiefdoms that had developed across southeast Asia. Hinduism was, at this time, the more ancient and fully developed religion, possessing a pantheon of many deities headed by gods such as Shiva, Vishnu, and Brahma. Hindu gods were relatively easily incorporated into existing indigenous southeast Asian beliefs, becoming part of the local religion; alternatively, if Hinduism was adopted as the main religion in a region, it incorporated local spirits and deities into its pantheon (Snellgrove 2004). Buddhism may have arrived soon after Hinduism in the late 1st millennium BCE (Trainor 2001), but it was not prominent until the establishment of the Funan Empire in the 3rd century CE (see next section).

The Emergence of Chiefdoms

Whatever the social and political structure of Bronze Age settlements, by the late 1st millennium BCE, they had, in many areas, coalesced into larger unified polities that can be termed early chiefdoms (ca. 500 BCE–200 CE). The most extensively excavated and thus best understood culture is known as the Dong Son (ca. 600 BCE–200 CE), located in the Red River valley in northern Vietnam. Many sites along the Red River and its tributaries, including the type site Dong Son and the larger Co Loa, have produced strong evidence of extensive trade contacts, bronze and iron production, and attention to significant defensive architecture. Once again, the majority of information about the Dong Son culture comes from burial data as centuries of monsoon seasons and rather acidic soils have destroyed most material remains on the surface. The Iron Age burials demonstrate strong social differentiation featuring exceedingly rich burials with the deceased interred in wooden coffins shaped like boats. These contained bronze weapons and other items such as vessels, drums, iron objects such as spades resembling Chinese forms, wooden lacquered vessels, fabrics, jewelry, and even Chinese coins (minted 9–23 CE) (Higham 2002a: 171–74). The latter objects show clear interaction with Chinese dynasties to the north, and in fact, the Dong Son culture is mentioned in Han Chinese documents.

Co Loa, located in the Red River floodplain and near the modern city of Hanoi, was a far larger settlement, spanning an area at least 600 hectares in size. The settlement was constructed in a series of three concentric embankments, or ramparts, with the outer two combined with moats and the innermost possibly encircling the settlement (Higham 2002a: 172). Co Loa likely functioned as a center or even a capital of the Dong Son chiefdom and is cited in Chinese texts as an important city. Chinese records report that a man known as Thuc Phan overthrew an existing ruler around 258 BCE and established the Au Lac Kingdom, making Co Loa his capital (Kim, Toi and Hiep 2010). The Dong Son culture is traditionally considered to have come to an end by approximately 200 CE.

It was in the periods just before the Dong Son and during it that bronze metallurgy flourished, even influencing bronze craft in China (Yao 2010). In the Dong Son Period, a class of bronze objects, including vessels, drums, and daggers, became symbols of the culture's elites (Higham 2002a: 172–78). Bronze daggers were finely made, with human figures serving as the hilts. The dress, hairstyle, and elegance of the dagger hilts (Figure 10.3) offer a visual image of how Dong Son elites might have appeared walking the streets of Co Loa 2,000 years ago. Bronze drums and vessels, and other objects, which were used in mortuary rituals as well as possibly for other religious ceremonies, were decorated with daily life scenes including rice farming, the conducting of warfare on land and from boats, musicians, animals cavorting, and finely dressed humans including males with daggers at their waists. Though belonging to the Iron Age, and iron technology was indeed present, bronze was the preferred metal for ritual and elite items.

Further to the south and west, in the Mun River Valley of Cambodia and just north in the Khorat Plateau, another Iron Age chiefdom featured similarly large settlements and fine material goods. Large settlements surrounded by moats are the norm in this region, some situated so as to control important resources such as salt and lead, used not only locally but also exported as important trade items (Higham 1994, 2010). The site of Noen U-Loke (ca. 800/700 BCE–400/500 CE), on the Mun River, offered an extensive cemetery that testified to the wealth and social stratification of residents in this region. The excavator of Noen U-Loke, Charles Higham, notes, "The excavations at Noen U-Loke suggest a vigorous and innovative community, adept at manufacture and the expansion of agricultural production" (2001: 21). Burials occurred in clusters that might reflect kin relationships. Interestingly, goods suggest specific life status of those interred in various burial clusters; for instance, one cluster held most of the carnelian jewelry found at the site while another cluster had the majority of clay-lined coffins (Higham 2010). Such division of grave goods may represent the particular levels of status these families held in life or perhaps their association with particular crafts and activities. In several of the clusters, a single male had significantly richer grave goods. It is possible that the males in these richest burials were high elites or even chiefs in the Mun River/Khorat Plateau chiefdoms.

Long-distance trade with India across the Bay of Bengal aided the growth of sites and possibly competitive chiefdoms on the southeast Asian mainland (Glover 1996, 1998). Beads of carnelian and glass, jade objects, fabrics, and bronze bowls seem to have been at the center of the trade between southeast Asian sites and India (Bellina and Glover 2004). The bronze bowls are particularly illustrative of contact; vessels in both locations sport incised designs featuring people, animals, domestic scenes, and geometric motifs that are virtually identical in both locations (Higham 2010). The evidence from numerous sites indicates that regional centers, perhaps the seats of small chiefdoms, were heavily engaged in long-distance trade and were likely controlling the acquisition and distribution of imported goods as well as engaging in craft production activities. These goods made their way not only to elites living at these coastal sites but were traded inland to locations such as Noen U-Loke as well.

Though architectural data and other types of material culture are largely absent from these Iron Age sites, burial evidence does offer some hints as to why these chiefdoms surged to prominence at

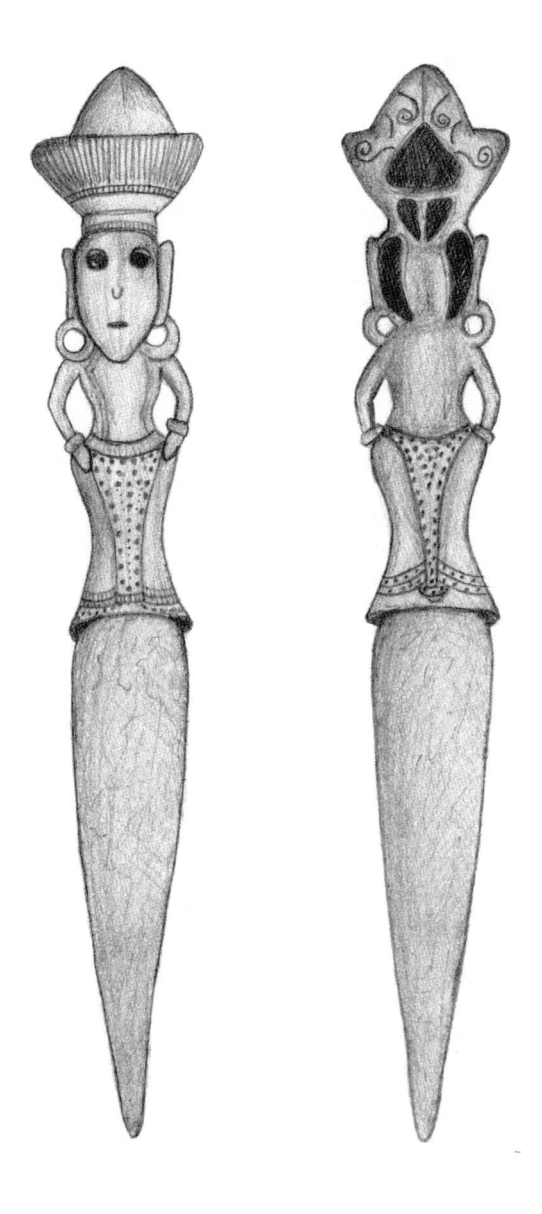

FIGURE 10.3 Example of Dong Son Bronze Dagger With Elegant Hilt

Source: R. Jennison

this time. The development of iron technology was a critical factor. Though bronze was preferred for adornment and ritual, iron was recognized as vital to agricultural life, used for plows, spades, and other farming-related equipment. The emergence of iron for agricultural activities enabled increased productivity, which in turn allowed the population to expand; commensurate with these was a growing differentiation in wealth and the status that came with it. Those who controlled greater areas of productive land likely held the upper hand in their communities. The presence of rice in many burials attests to the recognition of its importance in Iron Age cultures. The regular occurrence of moated settlements encircled by ramparts, and the increase of weaponry in burials, clearly indicates that conflict became more common during the Iron Age. This would seem to go hand-in-hand with the commandeering of larger tracts of land for agricultural production and the need to house, and protect, larger communities. Finally, the engagement in long-distance trade, the control of maritime trade routes, and the acquisition and distribution of luxury goods from abroad were also likely critical factors in the establishment of powerful elites during the Iron Age. The role of religion at this early stage of growing complexity is entirely unknown at present, but the connection between secular and religious leadership became central to the concentration of power into elite hands and eventually into those of the king, in just a few centuries.

The (Later) Iron Age: The Early Empires

It is during the 1st millennium CE that the trends begun in the Bronze and earlier Iron Ages coalesced into the earliest complex societies of southeast Asia (ca. 200–802 CE). The 1st-millennium Funan and subsequent Chenla cultures have been termed "kingdoms" as well as "city-states" (Manguin 2004); both are appropriate descriptors. City-states is applicable given that, though only the Funan and Chenla kingdoms are described here as the most prominent kingdoms, archaeology and documentary evidence from China describe a 1st-millennium southeast Asian world filled with competing polities and rival leaders.

The Funan Empire

The first known southeast Asian empire is the Funan (245–6th century CE), which arose in the Mekong Delta region of Vietnam and Cambodia; legend suggests it was founded by an Indian man who conquered a small "Fu Nan" chiefdom headed by a woman, whom he married (Jessup 2010). Funan was large enough in the 3rd century CE to be recognized by the Chinese Han Dynasty, whose Emperor Wu sent two ambassadors to the Mekong Delta on an exploratory mission; they reported back on the Funan Empire, which, they said, had defended settlements, fine material goods of gold and jewels, a writing system, and a legal code (Higham 2001: 24). Other Chinese documents describe a Funan society in which many secular and religious behaviors show a blending of Hindu and indigenous beliefs; it is certain that, by the emergence of the Funan Empire, many elements of Indian/Hindu traditions had made their way to the southeast Asian mainland.

The Funan capital appears to have been Angkor Borei, located slightly inland, but connected to the Gulf of Siam by canals leading to the port city of Oc Eo (see Box 10.2). Its inland location is somewhat puzzling given the importance of maritime trade to the Funan, but Angkor Borei is located in a region ideal for rice cultivation, which may explain its placement. Over the last two decades, archaeological work at Angkor Borei, mostly obscured by a modern city covering the ancient one, has begun to document some of the remains of this large Funan center (Stark 1998, 2003; Stark et al. 1999). Ancient Angkor Borei stretched across roughly 300 hectares and was encircled by a substantial masonry wall; the city housed as many as 20,000 inhabitants (Stark 2006). Inside the wall, archaeological work identified nearly three dozen brick masonry mounds that probably corresponded to architectural platforms or buildings, a series of moats and water reservoirs, and a series of burials with associated burial goods (Stark 2003).

BOX 10.2 KEY SITE: OC EO

Excavations at the port city of Oc Eo in the 1940s demonstrated that this was a very important Funan trading center; its location in a swampy lowland suggests it was not founded for its agricultural productivity. Furthermore, its distance from Angkor Borei (70 kilometers) makes it likely it was not the only, or even the main, port city (Miksic 2003). If Oc Eo was one of several, or even many, trading ports, the richness of goods at Oc Eo is indicative of the importance of trade to the Funan culture. Ceramics from India, well-documented exchanges with China, and the extensive canal system enabling the movement of goods on boats offer solid evidence of a young empire heavily engaged in trade. Archaeological investigation at Oc Eo revealed a large town (ca. 450 hectares), enclosed by the now familiar earthen ramparts topped by a palisaded wall. Canals criss-crossed the settlement, allowing for boat transport of goods and people within the city. Workshops produced jewelry of varying materials including gold, carnelian, agate, jade, and other semiprecious stones, as well as gold plaques depicting images that appear to represent Roman rulers perhaps based on Roman coinage, which Funan traders may have encountered. Roman coins found at southeast Asian sites, including one struck in 152 CE and representing Emperor Antoninus Pius and another representing Emperor Victorinus (268–70 CE) suggest exchange between the Mediterranean, through India, to southeast Asia (Bellina and Glover 2004; Higham 2001: 27; Miksic 2003). Also produced at Oc Eo were seals, usually of carnelian, portraying Hindu, Buddhist, and somewhat surprisingly, Mediterranean-style images and some bearing Sanskrit inscriptions. The latter were perhaps imports from India (Miksic 2003).

In addition to Angkor Borei and its port city Oc Eo, archaeological survey has identified roughly a dozen other urban centers and many smaller settlements that likely belonged to the Funan Empire; as many as 200 kilometers of canals connected these settlements (Khai 2003; Stark 2003). Archaeology and Chinese documentary information suggest that there were at least three social classes: the rulers and elites at the top; a middle group, which may have comprised landowners; and a lower class, which some have identified as "slaves" but which may have constituted the majority of the society, including farmers, artisans, religious personnel, and merchants (Stark 2003). Though the brick masonry structures at Angkor Borei remain largely uninvestigated, there are some hints as to Funan religion. Hinduism and Buddhism, already present on the southeast Asian mainland in the early centuries of the Funan Empire, clearly intertwined with the indigenous belief system. The recovery of various types of relics, including lingas (see Box 10.3) and stupas (common in Buddhism) attest to how well ensconced these religions were by the early 1st millennium CE. Near the end of the Funan, in the 6th century, both Hindu and Buddhist statuary became far more common.

BOX 10.3 HINDU LINGAM

The lingam stone (Figure 10.4) is found in many Hindu temples dedicated to Shiva, an exceedingly important Hindu god. Shiva, "The Destroyer," is responsible for the renewal and creation of life. The lingam represents energy and vitality, necessary for the process of renewal. Some

248 Empires in Southeast Asia

have suggested the lingam also represents a phallic shape, pertaining to Shiva's role in the re-creation of energy. Dedications to Shiva are made at the lingam, which usually stands at the center of the temple. The lingam inside a Hindu temple dedicated to this god is often called the "Shiva-linga."

FIGURE 10.4 Photo of a Lingam Stone in a Hindu Temple (in India) Dedicated to Shiva; Lingam in Southeast Asian Temples Were of Similar Form

Source: Photo by S.R. Steadman

Textual evidence is particularly critical in explaining the role of religion in Funan culture. A major aspect of the Funan economy was run through, or by, the temple. Inscriptions describe the types of offerings made to the temple by wealthy elites, which included not only a variety of goods and property (such as coconut trees and rice fields) and animals but also people such as slaves, dancers and singers, and laborers (Stark 2003). These offerings were made to gods, both indigenous and Hindu, as well as to the temple itself. An inextricable tie between economy and religion was already established as part of early southeast Asian states by the early 1st millennium CE.

The combined evidence from Angkor Borei, Oc Eo, and the dozens of other Funan settlements inspires Stark (2003: 90–91) to note that the Mekong Delta and ancient Funan culture

> was the center of the first cultural system with trappings of statehood: (1) high populations and urban centers; (2) the production of surplus food through intensive rice cultivation; (3) sociopolitical stratification legitimated by Indic religious ideologies; (4) a system of writing by the end of the early historic period; and (5) a vigorous network of long distance trade.

The Funan Empire came to an end in the 6th century CE when a new empire, the Chenla, arose in its place.

The Chenla Empire

While the transition from the Funan to the Chenla Empire (ca. 550–802 CE) is not fully understood, it may have consisted more of a transition from one set of rulers to another than violent overthrow. The Chenla were Khmer-speaking, the same language as the later Khmer Empire and the national language of Cambodia today. Inscriptions found on Chenla monuments, particularly temples, provide some information about rulership, descent, and the power structure in the ancient Chenla Empire. A stela erected at one temple describes the kings that an elite family served, beginning with a Funan king (Rudravarman, ca. 514–50 CE) and ending with a Chenla king, Jayavarman I (ca. 635–80 CE) (Higham 2001: 37). The Chenla rulers established their court and capital in a different location from Angkor Borei, likely at a site known as Sambor Prei Kuk not far from Tonle Sap Lake in Cambodia. This effectively placed the imperial center away from the Mekong Delta region, where the Funan was located, further up the river in the Cambodian heartland.

Sambor Prei Kuk is thought to be Ishanapura, which, according Chinese documentarians, was the name of the Chenla capital. The Chenla built their architectural structures of brick and thus some remnants have survived the centuries though they are in exceedingly poor condition. Sambor Prei Kuk (ca. 400 hectares) was surrounded by a massive moat, inside of which as many as 200 major and minor structures may have stood (Stark 2004). Only a fraction of these have been investigated archaeologically, but they reveal the nature of Chenla temples, which were built upon brick platforms to elevate them above the ground. The brick walls were decorated with reliefs and inscriptions identifying the temple founders and often give some vital information about donations and family relationships to the temples. Each temple housed an altar to whichever deity it was dedicated; many of the altars appear to have featured a pedestaled lingam dedicated to Shiva. Temples were also dedicated to other Hindu deities and to some who must have been indigenous gods and goddesses. Archaeological and inscriptional evidence suggests that religious beliefs in southeast Asian polities focused on Hindu gods such as Vishnu or Shiva or on Buddhist beliefs and practices (O'Reilly 2007: 113–14). However, underlying all was a persistence of indigenous practices including ancestor veneration and likely a tendency to acknowledge indigenous deities along with those transported to southeast Asia from India (Stark 2006). The architecture from this period reflects these various beliefs, often offering a blend of Hindu and Buddhist decorative motifs but with inscriptions that also acknowledge ancestors and local deities who were known as *vrah* (male) and *kpon* (female) (Vickery 1998).

Given the lack of domestic architecture and other residential material culture, our understanding of daily life including marriage, kinship, and gender relations is somewhat limited. Inscriptions and the ever helpful Chinese documents do provide some insights into these areas. Scholars are fairly certain that the Chenla kinship system operated on a matrilineal basis, with property and title passing from male to male through the female side (Vickery 1998: 260–270). This meant that inheritance was transmitted from a man to his maternal nephew. Whether the practice of matrilineal kinship elevated the position of women in Chenla society is not as yet clear. However, women's names appear frequently in foundation inscriptions on temples, which may reflect their ability to sponsor the building and the donation of goods and workers from their own personal holdings. Further, many temples were dedicated to female deities (kpon), demonstrating a female prominence in the indigenous religion. Female ancestors appear to have also been important and may have been a major part of the household or local religious beliefs in ancestor veneration practices.

Women appear to have been active in the craft industry as well; lists of workers associated with, or dedicated to, temples included many names of women engaged in all manner of activities including the production of baskets, metalcrafts, ceramics, and cloth (Higham 2001: 44). Some elite women appear to have held the title of *tan*, which carried some official status, perhaps indicating the control of lands and resources. Finally, records suggest that a woman actually ruled the Chenla Empire from roughly 681 to 705 CE. Jayadevi succeeded her father Jayavarman I (ca. 655–681 CE), a powerful leader who elevated himself to divine status during his reign (see later). That Jayadevi was able to advance to the throne and retain her position for over two decades indicates that the people of Chenla were perhaps not unfamiliar with the presence of powerful and wealthy women in their midst.

As demonstrated by the title *tan* held by some women, inscriptions reveal a variety of titles that identified important positions in Chenla society; the titles *mratan* and *pon*, the latter an inherited position, marked men who might have ruled territories, held political positions in the king's court, or served society in a religious capacity. Thus, mratan and pon could acquire significant individual wealth. Temples could also be wealthy institutions since they possessed lands, field laborers, and even artisans (Snellgrove 2004: 24–25). Both the temple and the pon in charge of the territory that included the temple and its lands benefitted from surplus production from temple lands and workers. These surpluses could be traded for necessary and luxury goods and to stockpile for future lean times; pon and temples could also use surplus to acquire additional lands and add to their holdings. Thus, early in the Chenla Empire, and probably in the Funan before it, there was a substantially decentralized dispersal of authority that stockpiled resources across the region, with mratan and pon capable of amassing significant wealth and power over a region and temples capable of controlling the production and distribution of food and luxury items. While Chenla kings also controlled territories and peoples, they must have had some concerns over the ability of individuals from rival families to potentially challenge a sitting king for the throne.

During the Chenla Period, Chenla kings began to take steps to consolidate power, wealth, and authority more firmly in their hands. One problem faced by the kings was the matrilineal inheritance pattern, which prevented one's direct descendant from receiving both title and property; these passed to a maternal nephew. Quite early, Chenla kings decreed that inheritance in the royal family should follow that practiced by the deities: direct descent from father to son. This allowed Chenla kings to retain the supreme royal position and to keep their amassed wealth within the nuclear family, passing both from father to son. A second move by Chenla kings was critical to their ability to centralize power into royal hands. Even in the Funan Empire, kings took names with the suffix *-varman* meaning, in Sanskrit, "protected by" a god. In addition, several early kings of the Chenla Empire took the designation *vrah kamraten an* (Khmer for "royal and divine") upon their deaths, suggesting that at the time of death they became divine and thus resided with the gods. However, Jayavarman I took on this title *during* his reign, as did his daughter Jayadevi, thereby elevating himself to divine status while he ruled as king. He and succeeding rulers then used this status to supersede the control of regional pons, decreeing that surpluses from lands, workers, and temples belonged to the divine king, essentially usurping the power, wealth, and authority of any potential rivals across the Chenla lands. These new political and economic strategies were well in place by the time the founder of the Khmer Empire ascended the throne in 802 CE.

The Khmer Empire

The Khmer Empire was founded by Jayavarman II in 802 CE when he ascended the throne; from this point on, the region was called Kambuja, yielding its modern name of Cambodia (Jessup 2010). Jayavarman II consolidated various small kingdoms into a single Khmer Empire that eventually encompassed most of northern Thailand, Cambodia, Laos, and part of Vietnam. Jayavarman II, according to a stele inscription in southeastern Thailand, first established his throne at a site known as Indrapura, perhaps located in southern Cambodia near the modern capital of Phnom Penh, and then launched a military campaign that established his vast empire. He moved his capital city several times during his reign, probably to ensure it remained in a strategic and defendable location inside his increasingly large empire. He eventually settled at a site known as Hariharalaya, which is likely located north of Tonle Sap Lake in the northern area of Cambodia. By the time of the demise of the Khmer Empire beginning in the 15th century, the dynasty had seen nearly three dozen rulers, an empire that extended across nearly the breadth of the southeast Asian mainland, and the building of hundreds of stone temples and monuments. It was, without a doubt, the largest empire the southeast Asian mainland has ever produced.

The marshaling of people and resources to construct this massive and powerful empire was significantly aided by several actions undertaken by its founder, Jayavarman II (802–834 CE). His acquisition of neighboring polities, through military means, was an initial critical factor in establishing the empire. Jayavarman II took another important step in securing power and obedience to the Khmer kings: the installation ceremony. By the time Jayavarman II came to power, Hinduism, and to a large extent Buddhism, were well ensconced in southeast Asian religious practices. Jayavarman II had his royal coronation at a site known as Phnom Kulen just northeast of Tonle Sap Lake. Phnom Kulen is a sacred mountain that is considered the home of Indra, a powerful Hindu deity. It was here that Jayavarman II became king in two simultaneous ceremonies. The first was likely the more standard one used by previous kings in which a Brahmin (Hindu) priest declared Jayavarman the *chakravartin* or "universal monarch" (or alternatively, "king of kings") thereby identifying him as ultimate ruler of all Kambuja. This, of course, established Jayavarman II as the ruler of the Khmer people. The second ceremony was the *Devarâja*, a Sanskrit word that translates to "god-king" (in the Khmer language it is more literally stated as *kamraten jagat ta raja* or "Lord of the World who is King") (Snellgrove 2004: 48–51). This second ceremony was carried out by Jayavarman II's *purohita*, the chief priest who served the Khmer king. This ceremony linked Jayavarman II with the Shiva-linga in the temple, and with the god himself. The Devarâja and associated Shiva-linga were the imperial symbol of the Khmer reign and were meant to keep the empire prosperous and safe from attack, ensuring that the supreme Hindu gods would protect the king and his empire. The dual ceremonies inextricably linked the Khmer kings, beginning with Jayavarman II, with the powerful Hindu pantheon and particularly Shiva. The Devarâja ceremony made the king the Hindu pantheon's representative to the people, certifying the king's presence among the gods even while he ruled (Jacques and Lafond 2007: 19). From this point forward, the Devarâja constituted the Khmer state religion, with the divine king as its chief representative.

Following Jayavarman II is a long succession of Khmer kings (see Table 10.1), not all of the same family, who are known to scholars mainly through inscriptions on temples and from Chinese records. A few who contributed greatly to the Khmer Empire are described here. After Jayavarman II, his two sons took the throne, followed by seven more kings including Jayavarman V (968–1000 CE) who, though he was a Buddhist, allowed Hinduism to remain the state religion. All of these kings built spectacular stone temples to the Hindu gods and deified ancestors, along with *barays* (see later), palaces, and other structures (note that palaces, though large and opulent, were often constructed of wood and thus do not remain today). After the death of Jayavarman V in 1000, there was a two-year period of civil war and struggle for the throne. From this emerged Suryavarman I (1002–1050 CE) who not only expanded the kingdom's boundaries through military exploits, but also launched a massive building campaign at Angkor, constructing a huge royal palace and an enormous 8 by 2.2 kilometer reservoir known as the West Baray.

Suryavarman II (1113–1150 CE) was perhaps the greatest of the Khmer kings. He is known for defeating two enemies intent on bring down the Khmer Empire including the powerful Champa kingdom to the southeast (in today's southern Vietnam). During his long reign, he also established diplomatic and economic relations with China and ruled a Khmer kingdom that was at its height in power and wealth. He built numerous temples and complexes including Angkor Wat, described in more detail later.

The next Khmer king of note was Jayavarman VII (1181–1218 CE), who was a devout Buddhist. Just prior to his reign, the Chams (from the Champa Kingdom) had marched on Angkor in 1177 and sacked it. Jayavarman VII took the city back, ousted the Chams, and even took over their lands. Like Suryavarman II, Jayavarman VII built many structures; his most famous achievement is the building of Angkor Thom, described later. After Jayavarman VII, the Khmer kingdom began a slow and then fairly rapid decline until its collapse in 1431.

The Khmer Landscape

The tropical climate in southeast Asia, with its six-month monsoon season, lends itself to a rice-based economy practiced across the breadth of the region. Rice was, and is, grown in bunded paddies (small earthen dykes that surround rice fields) that can hold water. During the rainy monsoon season, a major rice crop is grown across the region. When the monsoon season ceases, farmers store water in bunded paddies and release it into other paddies that can then produce rice during the dryer season. Water management, not just for agriculture, but for the transport of goods through canals and for moated defensive systems, was a critical aspect of state control during the Khmer Empire. Settlement layout across the landscape featured urban centers surrounded by rural farming communities that were likely responsible for supplying the centers (Stark 2006). Many of these settlements had reservoirs or other systems for retaining water, possibly for agricultural production; these may have been managed by the state.

Peasants in these farming communities lived in wood and thatch homes, often built on stilts to avoid inundation during the annual rainy season (Jacques and Lafond 2007: 31). Archaeology can tell us little of what these villages looked like as preservation of them is almost non-existent. However, most scholars believe that the houses that dot the Cambodian landscape today (see Figure 10.2) are not dissimilar to those occupied by farmers under Khmer rule.

The political and religious centers are far easier to find given that the major structures were built of brick or stone and many still stand today. After Jayavarman II's capital city at Hariharalaya, Khmer kings moved their capital several times, building major temples and other constructions in each new location. In addition to those built at the capital city, other temples were built, dedicated to Hindu deities or Buddhist worship, often intended to recognize an important royal family member or the king himself. In 1181 CE, Jayavarman VII came to power (1181–1218 CE); he completed the building of Angkor Thom, the largest religious complex in the world, as well as many other stone monuments and temples, bridges, hospitals, and roads. After Jayavarman VII, the Khmer Empire began to experience intense difficulties, but by then, the landscape featured hundreds of brick and stone structures that had been constructed and maintained by the builders, artisans, and commoners who dwelled within the kingdom.

The king and high elites controlled the lands outside the urban centers. Inscriptions on rural temples and other records indicate that the king could award lands to a trusted elite, usually a mratan, who would then build a temple (usually dedicated to a Hindu deity) and be awarded the products of the farmers and craft-makers who lived in the villages associated with those lands (Higham 2001: 65–67). A good example of this is the beautiful temple of Banteay Srei, not far from Phnom Kulen. This temple, consecrated in 967 CE, was built by the grandson of a former Khmer king; it was dedicated to Shiva in the first year of Jayavarman V's reign (968–1000 CE). The temple (Figure 10.5) is built of reddish sandstone featuring intricate carvings displaying Hindu gods and stories from Hindu mythology. Three outer stone-built enclosures surround the central shrine that houses the Shiva-linga. The inscription associated with Banteay Srei notes the boundaries of the lands belonging to Yajnavarsha and what products from those lands belonged to the temple. Given that mratan overseeing these lands had often been given them by the king, or were beholden to the king for other types of support, any surpluses belonging to each mratan's temple were considered essentially the property of the state; certainly records show that a mratan paid taxes to the state, which surely came from the labors of the people living on his lands. In this complicated bureaucratic system, the products issuing from the work of the people, whether food or craft, as well as their labor to build temples and other state projects (such as reservoirs and canals), were possessed directly by the king or by the local mratan who was loyal to the king.

Also scattered across the Khmer landscape were a series of barays or artificial water systems consisting of reservoirs and canals; these were found at the major centers such as Angkor, but also at smaller centers and temples. The function of these water management systems is still disputed by archaeologists, but the building and maintaining of them demonstrates central organization by the state. One interpretation of the barays is that they could provide water for rice cultivation during the drier season (Higham 2001: 156–60). The other interpretation of the barays suggests that they instead provided water for the canals and moats around the sacred precincts at Khmer centers and temples (Higham 2001: 160–62). As is described in more detail later, the major temples represented the mountain on which the gods dwelled, and from which human civilization emerged. In Hindu/Khmer mythology, the mountain, known as Mt. Meru, was surrounded by the primordial ocean from which it arose. The vast reservoirs that surrounded these sacred buildings may have been meant to symbolically represent the waters of the ocean, and the canals served not only to regulate the waters within them, but perhaps also as transportation systems as well. Whether the barays were meant for agriculturally based water management or served a far more symbolic role in ancient Khmer society, they represent major construction projects undertaken by the Khmer state and reflect either the economic, or religious, power wielded by that state.

Religion and Empire

As has been noted, religious practice in southeast Asia a millennium ago was a varied one. Travelers and ideologies arrived via the Silk Road bringing a rich Hindu mythology and a number of deities, of whom Shiva (the "destroyer"), Vishnu (the "preserver"), and Rama (a Hindu god representing

FIGURE 10.5 Photo of One Heavily Carved Tower Inside the Banteay Srei Temple in Cambodia
Source: Photo by S.R. Steadman

virtue and chivalry) were most enthusiastically incorporated into the already existing indigenous belief system. Buddhist missionaries brought their religion, evidenced by the presence of stupas (sacred Buddhist structures) and statues of Buddha that appeared in southeast Asia by the 5th century CE; likely the basics of Buddhism were practiced by the 1st or 2nd century.

Hinduism became the main "state" religion during the Chenla Empire and remained so in the Khmer Empire until the 12th century when Jayavarman VII (1181–1218 CE), a devout Buddhist, came to power. Even prior to Jayavarman VII, temple iconography depicted a blending of Hindu and Buddhist images, but during and after his reign, Buddhist imagery and practice were far more common. It was in fact after Jayavarman VII that the Khmer Empire began its decline until it was eventually overrun by a neighboring Thai state in 1431 CE; the shift to Buddhism as the state religion may have been one of many factors that eventually weakened the Khmer state. In addition to the state religion, Chenla and Khmer people continued to practice their indigenous beliefs, though these temples, located in rural communities, were likely built of wood or organic materials and are lost to archaeological investigation. Residents also continued the practice of ancestor veneration, called *Neak Ta* in Khmer, probably in their houses and in local shrines just as they do today (Jacques and Lafond 2007: 19). While commoner and even elite Khmers may have been devoted to their ancestors and local deities, it was vital that they be publicly devout practitioners of the state religion (usually Hinduism).

Major and smaller temples were built to honor the Hindu deities (and later, Buddha) whom the state promoted as critical to the health and well-being of the Khmer people. In addition to building brick and stone temples dedicated to Shiva, Vishnu, or Rama, temples were built to deified royal ancestors considered to live among the gods on Mt. Meru. The rural temples served as the collection centers for surplus from agricultural and other production-related activities, much of which was sent to the capital. The rest remained in the hands of the mratan elites in charge of the lands and temple.

Most of Khmer kings (prior to and including Jayavarman VII) launched building campaigns once they ascended the throne, including commissioning a temple dedicated to their own protector-deity (usually Shiva or Vishnu), which would probably also serve as their mausoleum upon their death. These temples were not meant for major ceremonies but rather as "houses" for the chief god, which was represented by statues and linga. Thus, temple buildings were not large, usually built of stone or brick, but they were spectacularly decorated and often had satellite buildings such as other temples to lesser deities or buildings known as "libraries" associated with them. The intertwining of temple to the state god with the king's final resting place served to remind the populace of the king's deified status both before and after death. Stark (2004: 107) succinctly describes the position of king vis-à-vis gods:

> At the top of the cosmic order were the gods and their human emissary, the king, who, by virtue of his position, was associated with divine power. The prosperity of the kingdom was bound up with the welfare of the royal *lingam*, a phallic-shaped stone that was the physical manifestation of the Hindu god Siva and also of the royal lineage.

The temple/mausoleum symbolized the Khmer creation myth, drawn from Hindu mythology, in which the sacred Mt. Meru (the temple) emerged from the surrounding ocean (the moats and barays) to then be the home of the gods, whence humans were created.

The most spectacular temples and royal complexes were found at the urban centers, especially at Angkor, which became the new Khmer capital during the reign of Yashovarman I (889/890–910/912 CE) after a short period of civil war. After Yashovarman I several of his successors, including his two sons, reigned from Angkor; Jayavarman IV (928–941 CE) moved the capital to another location, but after his death, Angkor became the capital again and remained so until the collapse of the Khmer Empire. Between the reigns of Rajendravarman II (from ca. 944) to the enthronement of Suryavarman II (1113–1150 CE), various temples and barays were constructed at Angkor, each dedicated to a Hindu deity or associated in some way with the state religion. Suryavarman II

FIGURE 10.6 Photo of the Five Towers, the Central One Representing Mt. Meru, at Angkor Wat in Cambodia

Source: Photo by S.R. Steadman

began the construction of Angkor Wat, the most famous of the Khmer temples. Angkor Wat, surrounded by a 200 meter-wide moat, rests on an "island" inside this moat (Figure 10.6). Laid out on a square plan, the buildings at Angkor Wat are located inside several stone enclosures displaying Hindu sacred stories as well as records of Suryavarman II's military exploits carved into the stone (see Box 10.4). The central shrine has five heavily carved stone towers, the highest central tower representing Mt. Meru with the four surrounding towers representing other peaks. Angkor Wat was dedicated to Vishnu to whom Suryavarman II was devoted; the temple also served as Suryavarman II's tomb.

BOX 10.4 HINDU APSARA

Among the most common decorations at Angkor Wat are the carvings of Apsara (from Sanskrit), a female supernatural being seen in Hindu art and mythology. Apsaras are young and beautiful, and are usually shown in a dance pose, which represents, in part, their role as dancers in the court of the powerful Hindu god Indra. They were considered wives of the *Gandharvas* who were the court musicians and singers in Indra's court. There are 26 named Apsara beings; they are thought to be associated with gambling and so might bring luck if acknowledged properly. Many Apsaras decorate the Angkor Wat temple (Figure 10.7).

FIGURE 10.7 Photo of Two Apsara Dancers Carved in Stone at Angkor Wat

Source: Photo by S.R. Steadman

FIGURE 10.8 Photo of Bayon (Three of Four Faces) at Angkor Thom, Cambodia

Source: Photo by S.R. Steadman

The other famous Khmer complex is the nearby Angkor Thom. It represents what is known as "Bayon art and architecture," which features a blending of Buddhist and Hindu art with a predominance of serene faces looking out from the stone-carved buildings (Figure 10.8). Angkor Thom was built by Jayavarman VII who ascended the throne in 1181 CE. Angkor Thom is 3 by 3 kilometers in size surrounded by a moat and stone wall. Inside is a huge religious complex known as "The Bayon," which features images of Hindu deities but also recognizes Buddhism as the state religion. At the center of the complex is the face of a serene and smiling Buddha (likely meant to be a blended image of Jayavarman VII as well) looking out in all four directions. Another impressive aspect at Angkor Thom are the bas-relief carvings showing Khmer people engaged in everyday activities (Figure 10.9a–b). It is from these that much of our information about non-elite Khmer life is derived. The labor that went into the building of these and other state projects is simply beyond account. That it was accomplished mainly by the Khmer common people is indisputable; masons, stone carvers, artisans, cooks (to feed the workers), and many others must have dedicated vast portions of their work lives to build these monuments. That they did this because their kings were not only royal and powerful but gods as well is very likely. Whether they accomplished this work joyfully with adequate compensation from their leaders or through coercion and ill-treatment is harder to discern.

FIGURE 10.9 Stone Carvings at Angkor Thom: a. Khmer People Roasting Food at a Picnic; b. Khmer People Roasting a Pig

Source: Photo by S.R. Steadman

Khmer Socioeconomic and Political Structure

There is no doubt that the Khmer imperial infrastructure relied on successful rice farming. One study suggests that during the seven centuries of Khmer rule as many as 50 million rice paddies were cultivated using a variety of cultivation methods and a sophisticated water management system (Van Liere 1980). Tight administrative controls executed by the Angkor kings and their emissaries ensured that the products from land and craft shops made their way to the capital and the king's court. It is doubtless that the Khmer Empire kept assiduous records of all its vast economic dealings, but these must have been written on organic materials that are now lost to modern archaeologists. Most of the information about the socioeconomic and political system derives from inscriptions on monumental buildings and in part from the observations of the 13th-century Chinese visitor Zhou Daguan, a resident of the Shanghai area, who visited Angkor in 1296 CE (Zhou 2007).

There was a very complicated hierarchy of officials charged with various duties ensuring the smooth running of the empire. At the royal court, a cadre of high administrators served the king in several capacities; some of these came from his family, and others were selected as trusted advisors. Each of these administrators had a particular title and a set of responsibilities that may have been religious, judicial, economic, or administrative in nature. Many served as liaisons to the provincial administrators described later. Also attached to the royal court were retainers charged with entertainment (dancing, etc.), those who were dedicated to the comfort of the king and the royal family, such as fan bearers and house servants, and a group who were tasked with medical care (Higham 2001: 84–85). Royal inscriptions also list architects and artisans such as stone carvers who worked for the king and who were likely sent out to oversee the labors associated with the many royal building projects.

In addition to this vast retinue at the court, there were even more officials out in the Khmer provinces, all charged with service to the royal court. The hinterland of the Khmer Empire was divided into territorial districts called *praman* or *visaya* (Higham 2001: 86). Within these were villages (*sruk*); depending on the size of the visaya, there may have been just a few sruk, several hundred, or perhaps over a thousand. Officials called *khlon visaya* were in charge of these territorial districts and were responsible for keeping track of who farmed which lands, overseeing land transfers and the collection of taxes, and ensuring that surplus products left their provinces for the capital. Though sruk had village elders, the recognized "village chiefs" were the *khlon sruk*, who, like the khlon visaya, were appointed by the court and were essentially royal representatives in the provinces. Village elders may have carried out duties associated with marriages and other social activities, but politically they had little power. In addition to the khlon visaya, inscriptions identify other provincial administrators who had specific duties such as to muster laborers for royal/state projects and for military service, to keep records, and to oversee judiciary functions. A final group of officials were known as *tamrvac*, again appointed by the royal court, who were government representatives charged with ensuring that royal edicts were carried out properly. The tamrvac were not assigned to particular provinces but moved throughout the lands apparently checking on all aspects of how the countryside was faring and whether the royal court's concerns were being attended to.

This vast bureaucracy ensured that the majority of the products of the land and its people went to the royal court, its temples, and its administrators. A great deal of this came to the king through taxes assessed on everything from land to products of the forest (Jacques 1986). Another area of control over the people and their lands may have been the water management system. In the provinces, the construction of reservoirs and canals in various visaya and sruk was most likely for agricultural use (Stark 2004). The state-appointed officials in the provinces may have been responsible not only for the collection of waters during the rainy season, but also the release of them in the dry season, allowing Khmer farmers to grow at least two rice crops per year. While the majority of that crop was destined for mouths beyond the farmer's household, what did remain in-house was essential for survival. Obeying local and state laws and customs regarding the payment of taxes, temple donations, and other acts of devotion and obedience likely helped farmers ensure a consistent water supply and a healthy dry-season crop.

The Khmer Empire had a sophisticated legal system composed of judicial officials in both secular and religious capacities that functioned at every level from the royal court to the sruk. Most of the inscriptions and texts describing infractions and punishments relate to land holdings (Higham 2001: 87) as these were more permanently inscribed on buildings, but Zhou also offers some accounts of punishments he witnessed. A court case could involve witnesses and testimony, and eventually, a verdict was rendered by the official. Punishments ranged from simple fines, to the amputation of body parts including hands and nose, to death by live burial and stoning (Zhou 2007). There was clearly a tight judiciary control over the actions of the people, and while the accused were sometimes found innocent (Higham 2001: 88), a conviction possibly carried a heavy price.

Finally, the Khmer Empire must have been heavily engaged in trade with neighboring regions, and Zhou explains that China was a vital trade partner. Chinese merchants resided at Angkor, facilitating trade between the Khmer capital and the giant empire to the north (Higham 2001; Zhou 2007). Zhou offers a detailed description of items obtained from China, which includes precious metals, silks, paper, and other items; the Khmer Empire sent items such as elephant tusks and rhinoceros horns northward. The Khmer king's coffers were filled with riches derived both from his lands and likely from long-distance trade contacts from all over east and southeast Asia.

Khmer Daily Life

Some of the best evidence of Khmer life derives from documentation by Zhou Daguan (Zhou 2007). This, in combination with the scenes of daily life carved on the walls of Angkor Thom and data retrieved from recent archaeological reconnaissance, is all that allows for a reconstruction of Khmer social structure.

As already noted, the Khmer people were divided into social classes consisting of elites, commoners, and slaves (Stark 2004). Besides royal families, elite classes included government bureaucrats, large-scale landowners (the mratan), and those in religious service such as the purohita (the king's chief priest). Commoners were far less powerful; some may have been small land-holders (essentially farmers), as well as artisans, those involved in the markets and trading, and lower-ranking religious personnel (Stark 2004). Slaves were apparently common and were associated with temples, but they also served elites; they were listed in inscriptions as *khnyum* (Khmer for "slave") (Jacques and Lafond 2007: 28). One might become a slave through several avenues including being sold into slavery by a family member as payment of a debt or due to capture through military exercises. Zhou (2007) describes the life of slaves, who were primarily prisoners of war, as one of real and lifelong servitude. The military was constituted by three main groups: a local standing army (and also a navy), including the *anak sanjak* who protected the king; mercenaries from foreign lands; and conscripts from the Khmer commoner population.

Women could hold important positions in Khmer society; even commoner women had important work outside the home including in the markets, in the performing arts, and even in the military (Stark 2004). We know little about marriage practices though, according to Zhou, women could "discard" their husbands suggesting a fair amount of social equality, at least in the area of marriage. Kinship may have remained matrilineal, at least among commoners, as it had been in previous centuries.

The ancient Khmers tended to wear kilts or skirts, leaving the upper body unclothed, not surprising in the hot and humid southeast Asian climate. The only people shown with upper-body clothing are kings and sometimes soldiers where it may represent armor rather than clothing. Women wore their hair up, and those engaged in the performing arts often sported elaborate headdresses, as did female deities, Apsaras, and other women who may have been royals or elites. Most Khmers, whether elites or commoners, appear to have worn jewelry on their arms, and some had necklaces, anklets, and earrings as well.

How much the average Khmer resident believed in Hindu deities or Buddhist tenets and thus gladly gave to the temple, and how much their donations came simply from the desire to be considered devout by those in power, is impossible to ascertain. In reality, it is unclear whether Khmer commoners lived comfortable and enjoyable lives or were more constantly in fear of military conscription, increased taxation, or being forced into debt slavery. Certainly the images of daily life sculpted onto the walls at Angkor Thom show a variety of activities that suggest the Khmer people worked hard but could also engage in various entertaining activities such as watching dances or other performances, participating in sports or cock fights, and having what appear to be outdoor picnics with barbequed meat (see Figure 10.9a–b). Zhou reports that dysentery was a serious problem, not surprising in a water-filled land, and Jayavarman VII built hospitals for his people suggesting the state was, on some level, concerned for the overall health of its people. All in all, life for the Khmer people was probably much the same as for any other residents in a centralized and powerful ancient empire.

Khmer Power and Its Collapse

The roots of the Khmer rise to power were founded in the royal control of the domestic economy and the religion. One without the other would likely have relegated the Khmer Empire to history books as simply another small-scale kingdom or even just a chiefdom, among many others in southeast Asia. Instead, after establishing a secure power-base militarily, the first Khmer king used a pattern first established in the Chenla Empire: deification. Several Chenla kings became *vrah kamraten*, "royal and divine," at their deaths, but Jayavarman I took this designation during his lifetime, establishing the notion of a divine king ruling his people. Jayavarman II, in 802 CE, took a page from this book but went even further, claiming divinity but *also* linking himself with the chief state god Shiva through the Devarâja ceremony. From Jayavarman II onward, until Indravarman III (1295–1308 CE), who made Buddhism the state religion, the Khmer kings were essentially one-in-the-same with the state god (usually Shiva, sometimes Vishnu) and thus wielded tremendous power; while a king's role was to keep his people safe and prosperous, he could also punish them for disobedience. A divine king who has the ear of the state god to whom hundreds of temples are dedicated is indeed a powerful monarch.

Combined with his divine status, the Khmer king's complicated bureaucratic apparatus also served to keep power bundled tightly in the royal court. A generous reward system of land grants, administrative titles, and even riches, kept provinces carefully monitored by khlons, tamrvacs, mratans, and others charged with keeping close tabs on all economic transactions and with collecting the taxes owed to the royal court and the donations required by the temple (and thus essentially also destined for the royal court and its retinue). A strict judicial system helped to ensure capitulation to royal and administrative requirements. Perhaps the royal rule in the ancient Khmer Empire should be described as a "benevolent dictatorship" in which things ran smoothly and people fared well as long as they played by the rules set by the king and his subsidiaries.

Even in a utopia, which the Khmer Empire almost certainly was not, there are those who long for change. After the reign of Jayavarman VII, Khmer power began to slip; the reasons for this decline are numerous and debated. Prior to the reign of Jayavarman VII but certainly after him, outlying portions of the Khmer kingdom, regions conquered by one Khmer king or another, attempted rebellion and had to be subdued. Additionally, threats to Khmer power began to increase from outside with a growing threat from the Champa Empire to the east (which sacked Angkor in 1177), Thai armies to the north and west, and Viet powers to the northeast. It was an attack by Thai neighbors in 1431 that eventually brought a weakened Khmer Empire to its knees and thence caused it to disappear for good.

Many scholars argue that it was not only external attack but internal infrastructural problems that contributed heavily to the Khmer demise. Jayavarman VII's extensive building campaign (at least ten temples, plus hospitals, bridges, and other structures) may have resulted in overuse of the taxation system and the need for corvée labor from the people. Even the full coffers of the Khmer royal court may have been exhausted, not only by Jayavarman VII's building campaigns, but also by the need to maintain the resulting structures. Further, the extensive barays and canals, located in the capital and provinces, required maintenance (dredging, for instance) to keep them functional. A poorer and weakened state may have been less diligent in maintaining the water management system, which could have had a devastating effect on the production of surplus rice supplies.

Finally, another possible nail in the Khmer coffin was a shift in the state religion. Jayavarman VII was a devout Buddhist but left Hinduism and Shiva in place as the state religion and god. However, a successor, Indravarman III (1295–1308 CE), established Buddhism as the state religion. This shift had several ramifications. First, there was no longer a powerful Hindu god with whom the Khmer monarch was associated; secondly Buddhism is, by its very nature, more egalitarian and does not lend itself to "rule of the people" in the way that a Hindu-based state religion did (Stark 2004). During Indravarman III's reign and afterwards, the king became more accessible to the people, holding public audiences and shifting away from the building of major monuments and the military-based expansionist strategies (and thereby no longer routinely conscripting commoners for the army or to build royal projects) of his predecessors. In fact, after Buddhism became the state religion, there is no record of any more major royal construction projects (Stark 2004).

It isn't accurate to say that the Khmer Empire arose and declined based on the use of religion to rule its people, but certainly, the powerful combination of religion and economy were at the core of Khmer power. When skillfully combined and managed, as they were by 9th–12th century Khmer kings, an empire equal to any of its time flourished across the southeast Asian peninsula. Today, the magnificent stone temples built by these kings are nearly all that remain testament to that power.

Conclusion

Religion was a critical component in the rise of the Khmer Empire and a very effective tool that allowed Khmer kings to maintain ultimate power over their lands and people. While the bureaucratic system for land management was complicated, it worked well in part due to the system of rewards available to landowners and managers for their devotion to king and gods. The king and Khmer elites fostered a vast agricultural system through the sophisticated water management system, in part maintained by those who were the subsistence producers. Work on barays, canals, or temples was all in service to the king and therefore to the important Hindu deity that the king represented. The Khmer kingdom, and the Funan and Chenla before it, were powerful economic entities engaging in long-distance trade and enjoying the goods resulting from the work of skilled craft producers. However, while a robust economy was certainly critical to the growth and eventual emergence of empires in southeast Asia, the linchpin that allowed these societies and their elites to achieve the levels of power and complexity was the unified belief system supported and promoted by elites and commoners alike.

11

THE MISSISSIPPIAN SYSTEM IN THE AMERICAN BOTTOM

Introduction

The Mississippian cultural complex, located in the midcontinental region of the United States, emerged approximately 1,000 years ago and was essentially gone before the first European explorers arrived to the American shores. One of the controversies surrounding the Mississippian system is whether it should be characterized as a complex chiefdom or a state. In many ways, the Mississippian system is a "test case" of how archaeologists recognize complexity, a subject addressed in some detail in Chapters 2 and 3.

Prior to the appearance of the Mississippian system, the vast cultural systems of the Adena and Hopewell, located north and east of the Mississippian, laid the groundwork for a focus on trade and a religious ideology that included the construction of immense and remarkable earthworks. Though Mississippian elites derived considerable power from their involvement in long-distance trade and the acquisition of important resources, it was in the realm of religion that both their ultimate power, and eventual downfall, lay. By the 12th century, major religious practices had been consolidated into the hands of the elites and leaders at Mississippian temple centers, including Cahokia. Commoners and elites alike participated in the belief that the ceremonies held at these centers, and the ancestors buried in the major earthworks in the city center, would protect them from ills and ensure a stable subsistence base. Such promises, however, appeared to have been broken as the Mississippian system failed and was completely gone in the American Bottom region by the 14th century.

Geography and Chronology

The midcontinental cultures that form the most extensive discussion in this chapter are found in the regions that are today occupied by the states of Illinois and Ohio. These cultures are primarily found throughout the major river systems that span the center of the continent, and elements of these cultures can also be found in the American south and as far as southeast Florida. Some of the earliest mound-building cultures are located to the south in Louisiana. This chapter will focus primarily on cultures found in the Mississippi River region and specifically in the American Bottom in the state of Illinois and nearby regions.

Geography and Ecological Setting

The Mississippi River rises in Minnesota and extends over 3,700 kilometers southward to empty into the Gulf of Mexico just south of New Orleans in Louisiana (Figure 11.1). The first major rivers to join the Mississippi are the Missouri from the west and the Illinois from the east; above this point, the region is known as the Upper Mississippi River Valley. From the point where the Missouri River joins just north of the city of St. Louis, to the point where the Ohio and Tennessee Rivers converge, is the Middle Mississippi River Valley. It is in this area that the Mississippian culture, with its center at Cahokia, emerged. Below this point, the Mississippi River is known as the Lower Mississippi River Valley.

The Mississippi River emerged after the Laurentide Glacier receded at the end of the Pleistocene Epoch (ca. 8000 BCE). This largely flat landscape provided a perfect venue for melting waters to build channels that eventually became the vast drainage system of the North American continent. Due to the relatively flat area through which the Mississippi flows, it has altered its course through the millennia. The shifting of the river has created alluvial plains with rich sedimental deposits ideal for agriculture. The entire valley region provided lush plant life and was a favorite habitat of riverine animals such as fish, turtles and migratory birds (Bowne 2013: 7–8). Land species such as whitetail deer, fox, opossum, rabbit, and other smaller animals provided ample meat-based resources. The region has been inhabited by indigenous peoples for thousands of years due to the wealth of resources available to hunter-gatherer and, later, agricultural communities.

The Ohio River today forms the southern boundaries of Ohio, Indiana, and Illinois, joining the Mississippi River at the city of Cairo, Illinois. This river rises in Pennsylvania and flows westward

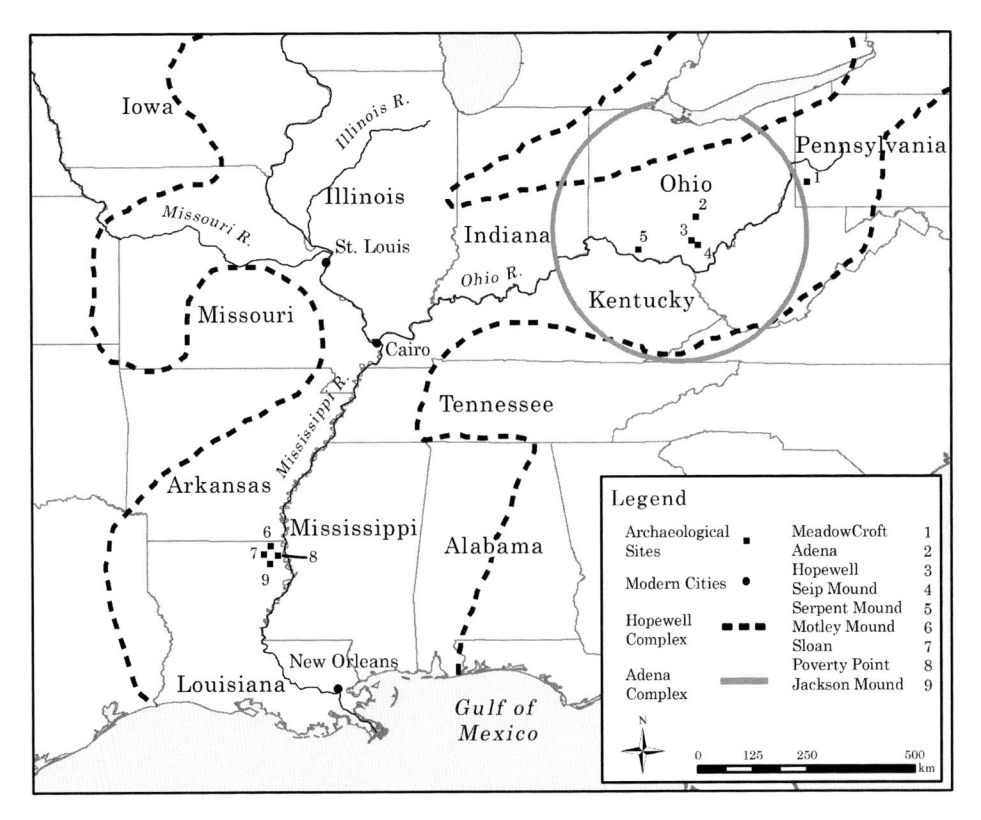

FIGURE 11.1 Map of Regions and Major Paleoindian, Archaic, and Woodland Period Sites Discussed in the Text

Source: B. Spencer

through alternating landscapes (today in southern Ohio, Indiana, and Tennessee) that include hills and forests interspersed with open prairies that serve as ideal farmland. As the Ohio approaches the Mississippi River, it flows through a somewhat more rugged region in southern Illinois where some limestone cliff faces rise over 200 meters from the forested lowlands. Though farming was possible here, it was likely a more successful undertaking in areas to the east or just to the west and south in the American Bottom region.

The "American Bottom" is a floodplain in the Middle Mississippian River Valley and lies east of the river in southern Illinois (Figure 11.2). Areas associated with the American Bottom also include the region on the west where modern St. Louis sits. In prehistoric times, this was a rich agricultural region but was also subject to flooding in the spring. Bordering the American Bottom on the east are limestone bluffs that rise a couple hundred meters above the floodplain effectively defining this middle river region. Just to the east, beyond St. Louis and Cahokia, additional escarpments that rise 30 meters or more form the western boundary of the American Bottom (Pauketat 1994: 4–46). The American Bottom featured prairies and forest land with oak, hickory and cedar trees and plentiful animal life including migratory birds.

This landscape emerged following the end of the Pleistocene when glaciers receded, taking with them the megafauna such as mammoths and mastodons. The Ohio and Mississippi River Valleys evolved into the alternating forest and prairie and lush river valley lowlands landscapes described earlier (Jeffries 2008). Except for a period of climatic variation in the Late Archaic Period roughly 3,000 years ago (Kidder 2006), the climate and landscape remained relatively stable until a slight warming trend, known as the "Medieval Warm Period," occurred. At this time, temperatures rose

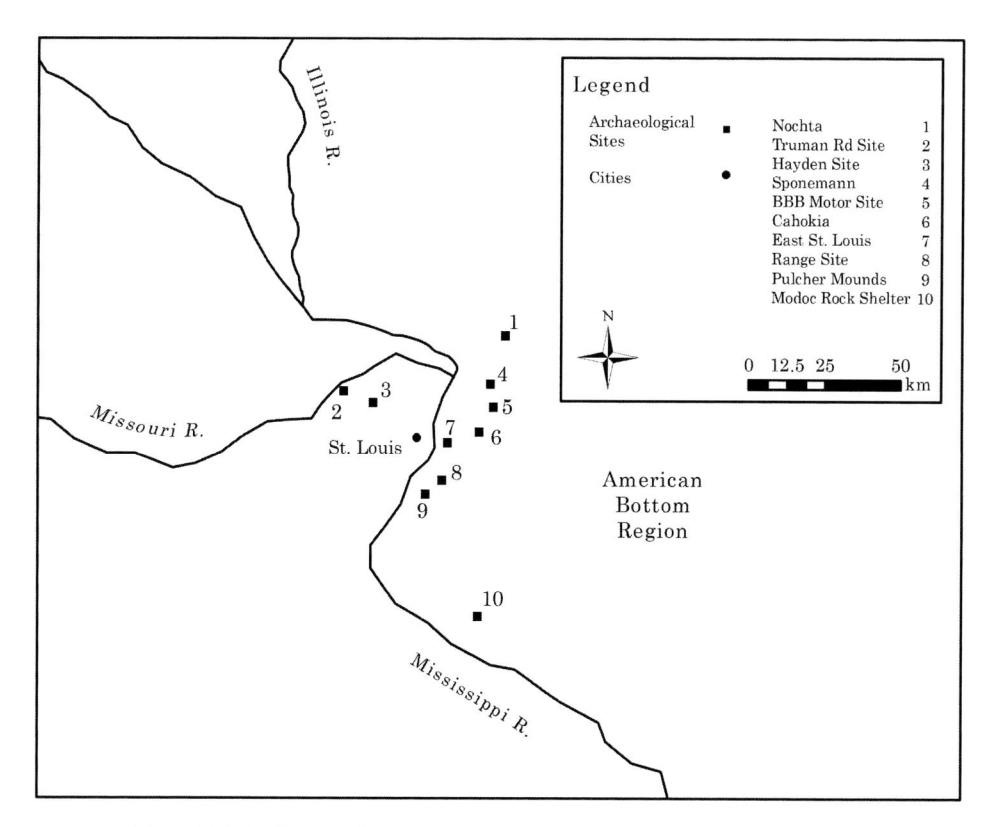

FIGURE 11.2 Map of Major Sites in the American Bottom Region Discussed in the Text

Source: B. Spencer

and some areas that might have been less viable for farming became far more suitable. The dates for this warming period are disputed but generally fall between 950 and 1300 CE; average temperatures warmed by approximately 1 degree Fahrenheit (Foster 2012; Mann et al. 2009). It is during this period that the Mississippian culture and Cahokia emerged as a major power in the Middle Mississippi River Valley (Foster 2012: 31; Pauketat 2004). Somewhat later, at approximately 1400 CE, another climatic change known as the "Little Ice Age" reduced average temperatures by as much as 2 degrees Fahrenheit (Mann et al. 2009). This negatively affected crop production in areas across the northern hemisphere (Benson, Pauketat and Cook 2009; Foster 2012). The Little Ice Age lasted for several hundred years into the 18th century, though some suggest it lingered to just a century ago. It is during the "Little Ice Age" that the Mississippian culture, and contemporary chiefdoms to the south and east, began to fade in power and prominence.

The Chronological Sequence

Significant debates regarding the first arrivals in North America abound. The earliest chronological period is known as the "Paleoindian" phase (Table 11.1), which begins between 18,000 and 16,000 years ago with the arrival of modern *Homo sapiens* in the Americas and closes in 8000 BCE (Goebel, Waters, and O'Rourke 2008). One of the earliest sites in the eastern region of North America is the Meadowcroft Rock Shelter in Pennsylvania, which was likely occupied by about 12,000 BCE (Adovasio, Donahue, and Stuckenrath 1990). More secure occupational dates begin with the Clovis Culture (ca. 13,500–11,000 BCE) in the west, the name based on a type of stone

TABLE 11.1 Chronological Periods and Sites Discussed in Chapter 11

Dates	Period	Sites Discussed in Chapter	Cultural Horizons
ca. 16,000–8000 BCE	**Paleoindian** Clovis Culture	Meadowcroft Rock Shelter; Clovis	First human occupation; hunting and gathering
ca. 8000–900 BCE	**Archaic Period** Early & Middle (8000–3000 BCE) Late (3000–900 BCE)	Strong Site; Truman Road Site; Hayden Site; Poverty Point	Advancement in stone tool technology; domestication of plants; cemeteries and social stratification emerges; celestial observations/ritual
ca. 900 BCE–1050 CE	**Woodland Phase** Early (900 BCE–100 BCE) Middle (100 BCE–350 CE) Late (350–1050 CE)	Adena Complex; Hopewell Tradition; Mound City; Seip Mound	Agriculture; mound building including burial mounds; mortuary ritual; long-distance trade; prestige object craft production; polity leaders/elites
ca. 1050–1400 CE	**Mississippian** Lohmann Stirling Moorehead Sand Prairie	BBB Motor; Sponemann; Cahokia; East St. Louis	Major mortuary ritual and presence of charnel houses; significant social stratification; fortifications; centralized religious practice; centralized leadership

tool technology first found at a site of the same name. During the Paleoindian Period, inhabitants across North American engaged in big game hunting and also relied on smaller animals, the latter a necessity as the climate transitioned from the colder Pleistocene to the more moderate Holocene and numbers of big game decreased. In addition to game, aquatic resources and gathered plants were an important part of subsistence.

In the Early Archaic (ca. 8000–6000 BCE), inhabitants continued to hunt, gather, and fish; game had changed almost entirely from the large mammals of previous times to the smaller and quicker animals of the Holocene. The development of smaller projectile points, as opposed to the large spearheads of previous times, demonstrates a change in hunting strategies and tool technology. Fishing, evidenced by an increase in the number of net sinkers, became more prominent. These trends continued into the Middle Archaic (ca. 6000–3000 BCE); growing quantities of plant processing equipment, such as mortars and pestles, suggest a greater reliance on plant resources. In the Late Archaic Period (ca. 3000–900 BCE), substantial changes to subsistence strategies and sociocultural structures took place. Residents began to cultivate plants such as gourds, sunflowers, and starchy seed plants like goosefoot and built structures that could shelter them for several seasons rather than just a few weeks or a couple of months.

In the midwest and northeast, the next phase is known as the "Woodland" Period and is divided into Early (ca. 900 BCE–1 CE), Middle (ca. 1–500 CE) and Late (ca. 500–1000 CE) phases. In the Woodland Period, large-scale and widespread mound-building began, primarily in the midcontinental region. The Adena Complex, in the Ohio River Valley, saw the development of long-distance trade in non-subsistence goods. Mound-building, including burial mounds, and long-distance trade connections continued into the Middle Woodland Period, represented by cultural complexes such as the Hopewell, centered in Ohio. The Late Woodland Period saw the end of the Hopewell and the rise of settlements possibly inhabited by a different culture group (Pauketat 1994: 50).

The final period discussed here is the Mississippian (ca. 1050–1400 CE) with its center at Cahokia. The Mississippian Period is divided into four phases, the first two of which, the Lohmann and Stirling, span 1050–1200 CE, encompassing the rise of the Mississippian polity. The Moorehead Phase (ca. 1200–1300 CE) sees the apogee of the system and its subsequent decline; the Sand Prairie Phase (ca. 1300–1400 CE) sees the final demise of this culture.

Pre-State Cultures: The Archaic and Woodland Periods

Archaeologists are still seeking to fill many gaps in the Early and Middle Archaic (ca. 8000–3000 BCE) culture history of the American Bottom region in the Mississippi River Valley. Cultural resource management work prior to the building of a major highway (FAI 270) in the early 1970s revealed a number of sites dating to these periods that began to shed light on the cultural occupation of the region (Fortier, Emerson and McElrath 2006; McElrath et al. 1984). While several sites such as the Modoc Rock Shelter and the Sloan site (Ahler 1998; Morse 1997) have offered important information on stone tool types used by the highly mobile hunter-gatherer cultures of the region, the Early Archaic in the region requires further intensive investigation. By the Middle Archaic Period, evidence for a greater number of sites and more extensive material culture has allowed for the creation of cultural phases. The earliest, the Dennis Hollow phase with the Strong site being the most prominent in this period (ca. 5700–5450 BCE), is primarily represented by over 60 shallow pits, which contained stone tool debris and food remains such as walnut and acorn (Walz et al. 1998). The Nochta site and phase (ca. 5450–5100 BCE) is also characterized by shallow pits filled with human-produced debris and offers the first evidence of a possible Middle Archaic structure in the American Bottom, as well as burials (McElrath et al. 2009). The overall material culture, however, suggests that inhabitants during this phase remained highly mobile. The remainder of this period in the American Bottom remains largely unknown due to a dearth of sites. It is in the Late Archaic that material culture and excavated sites provide a fuller picture of the occupation of this region.

The Late Archaic

The Late Archaic (3000–900 BCE) is divided into four phases. The earliest, Falling Springs (ca. 3400–2900 BCE), is largely a continuation of the Middle Archaic lifestyle with mobile hunter-gatherers occupying the region. Though living in bluff sites, inhabitants exploited resources from the lower regions, including fish and waterfowl (McElrath et al. 2009). At the Truman Road site in Missouri, a burial featured three adults and a child, all missing their heads, arms, and parts of their legs. The child had a projectile point inserted in its cervical column and examination confirmed the child was likely a victim of intentional killing (Harl 2009). The missing limbs from the other burials suggest this may have been their fate as well. Also present at Truman Road were very large limestone slabs that may have been used to mark celestial/seasonal changes (Harl 2009). Residents may have stayed at Truman Road for several seasons, at least through the winter. The burials speak of some level of violent interaction, either between settlements or within the Truman Road community. Non-local plant remains, suggesting trade with locations as far away as the Ozark Mountains, may have been served at ceremonies.

In the Titterington phase (ca. 2800–2500 BCE) there were significant changes in socioeconomy and habitation (Fortier 1983). Sites were still located on the bluff tops and residents exploited food resources from these upland regions more regularly. Waterfowl and fish became less prominent in the diet, replaced by deer and turkey; climatic variations in this period may have made the floodplain resources far less reliable (Kidder 2006; McElrath et al. 2009). Burials are found in this phase, in "cemeteries" near the sites, and grave goods were placed with the dead, suggesting the development of some social stratification (Charles and Buikstra 2009). At the Hayden site in Missouri, a wide variety of activities is represented by the material culture, including wood-, bone-, and hide-working; tool manufacture; and the wearing of personal adornments such as stone pendants and gorgets (neck and chest decorations) (Harl 2009). Hayden residents may have built a low mound near an important chert outcrop to mark their territory (Harl 2009). It is possible that the change in the climate caused American Bottom cultures to be more concerned about resource extraction and protection. This may have had an effect on social group interaction and the development of inequality as some (kin?) groups acquired control of desirable areas and others were relegated to more marginal resource areas.

That a microclimate change affected the region is further suggested in the Labras Lake phase (1750–1400 BCE) when there was a significant depopulation in the American Bottom. Inhabitants returned by 1400, and population grew significantly in the final Late Archaic Period during the Prairie Lake phase (ca. 1400–900 BCE). A number of sites in this last phase indicate that social changes had taken place in the cultural groups occupying the American Bottom region. Prairie Lake phase inhabitants were practicing incipient horticulture in small gardens in which they grew native seeds and grasses, providing a subsistence base that supplemented limited hunting and gathering practices. Settlements, now located on the floodplains, were larger and more permanent, perhaps occupied year-around, with habitation remains arranged in clusters, which may suggest cooperative kin groups working together as related nuclear families or in extended family structures (McElrath et al. 2009). Besides extensive evidence of food processing items, there were body ornaments such as stone beads and gorgets scattered across the settlements. In addition, pipes, associated with shamanistic activities, have been found at Prairie Lake phase sites. During the Late Archaic, cultures in the American Bottom were well on the road to domesticated agricultural practices and permanent settlement and likely were engaging in short-range and possibly long-distance trade. However, the period ended with a drastic depopulation, which seemed to disrupt these trends toward increasing complexity.

BOX 11.1 WATSON BRAKE

Though Poverty Point is more famous, it turns out that it isn't the earliest mound site in North America. The Watson Brake mounds in northern Louisiana (Figure 11.3) date to as early as 3500 BCE, nearly 2,000 years before the main mounds at Poverty Point. The people at Watson Brake built 11 mounds, connected by ridges, creating an oval with a diameter of over 300 meters. These mounds were constructed over several hundred years in bursts of activity until approximately 2800 BCE when the site was abandoned (Saunders 2010). Archaeological remains such as lithics, fire-cracked rock, and faunal and botanical remains suggest people inhabited the site, though the enclosure area was kept relatively clear of trash. It is possible that the interior area within the mound circle was reserved for ritual functions. Archaeological investigation has discovered a correlation between the major building activities at Watson Brake and climatic instability as a result of El Niño and other weather-related events (Saunders et al. 2005). Watson Brake residents may have been attempting to appease an unpredictable natural world through their monumental building efforts.

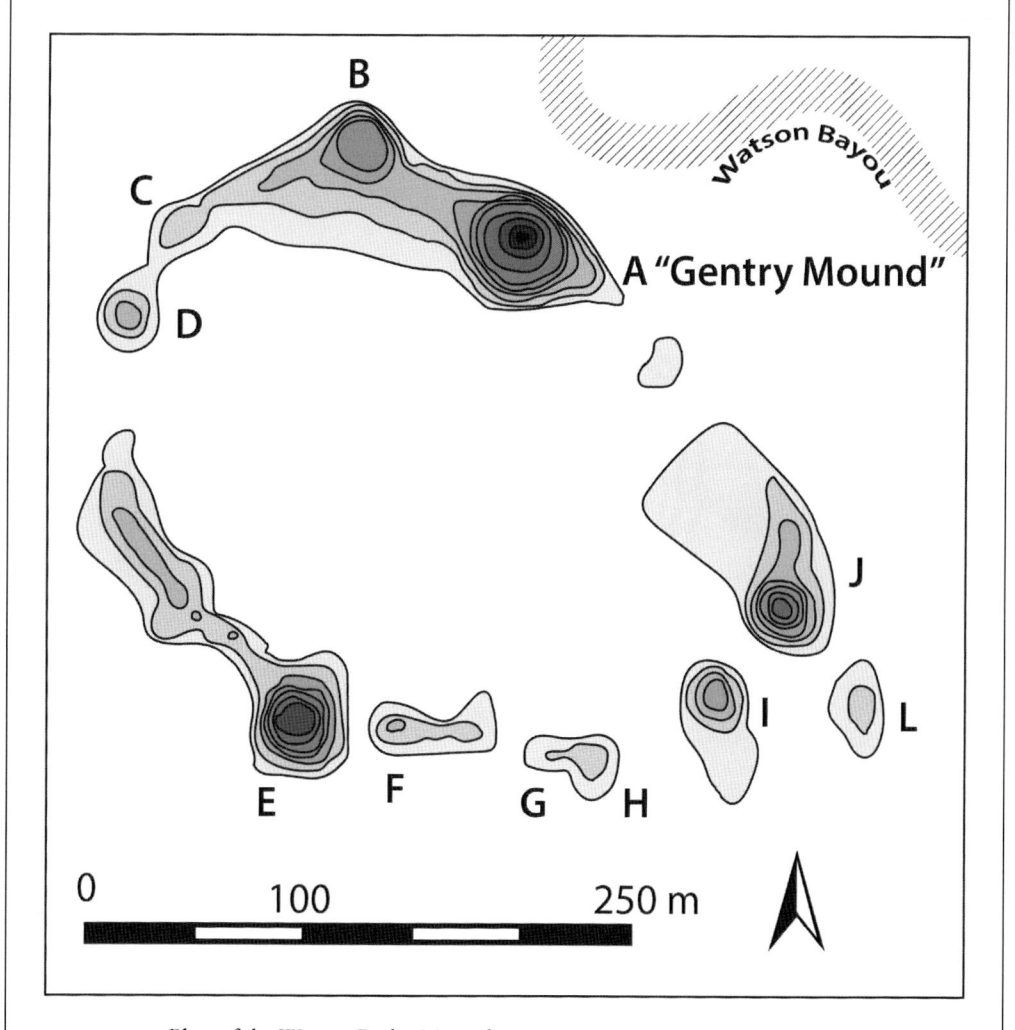

FIGURE 11.3 Plan of the Watson Brake Mounds

Source: After Saunders et al. (2005: 634, fig. 2)

272 The Mississippian System

Although far from the American Bottom region that is the focus of the discussion in this chapter, the site of Poverty Point on the lower Mississippi River in Louisiana bears some mention (see Box 11.1). Poverty Point was a community of people relying on a foraging-based economy, and

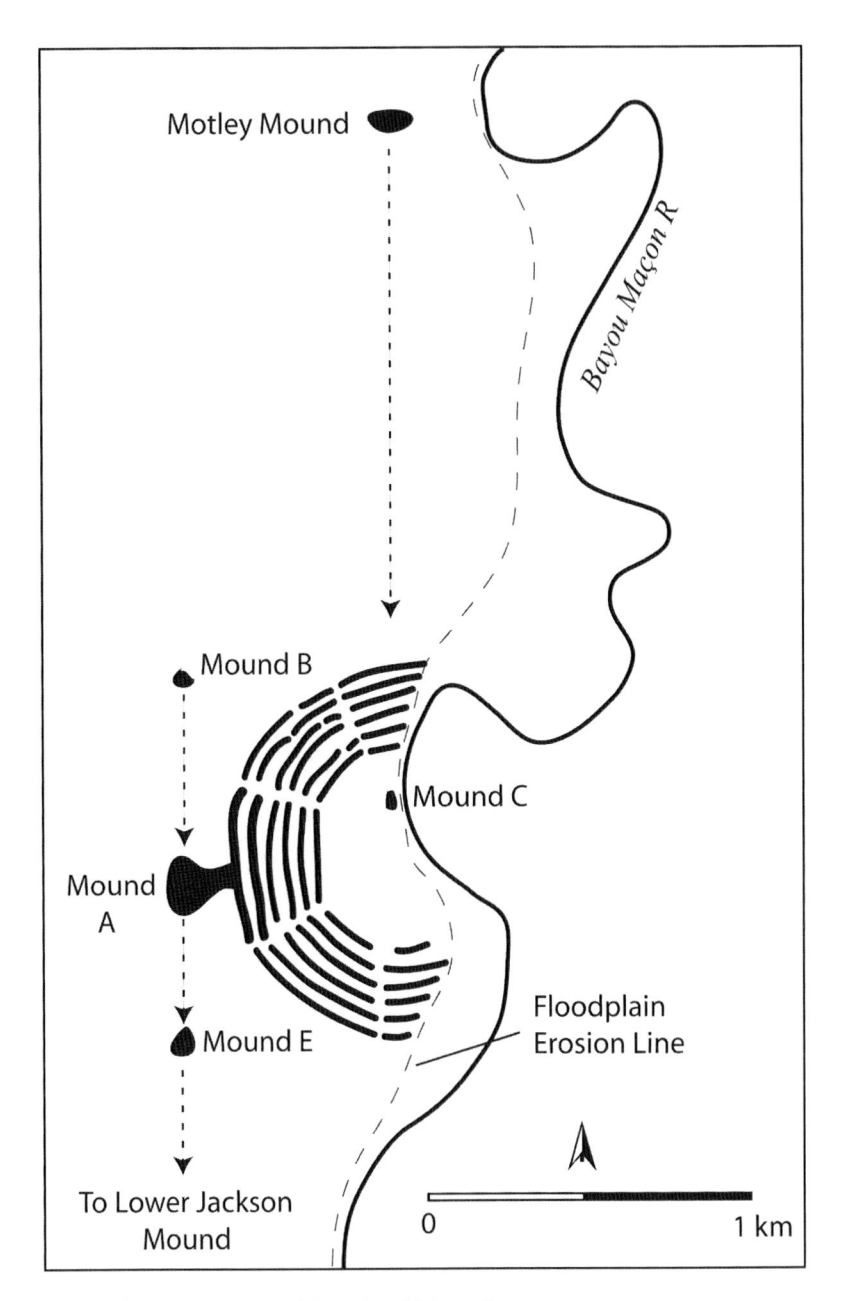

FIGURE 11.4 Plan of Poverty Point and Associated Mounds

Source: After Sassaman (2005: 339, fig. 1)

yet, they lived in a semisedentary location, atop the mounds and ridges they had created at this site. Mound construction began by 1600 BCE and continued for several hundred years (Sassaman 2005). It is possible that Poverty Point residents chose to construct their settlement there due to the presence of even more ancient mounds, built as much as two millennia earlier at Watson Brake (see Box 11.1) and elsewhere (Saunders et al. 2001). Upon their completion, however, the Poverty Point mounds were the largest complex yet built in North America. The majority of the mounds consist of sets of semicircular concentric ridges; these are broken at intervals. Remains of hearths, postholes, and domestic materials suggest that at least some Poverty Point residents lived atop the mounds (Gibson 2000). There are circular mounds, one roughly "attached" to the concentric mounds and others scattered on either side of the sets of the main earthwork construction (Figure 11.4). Standing atop Mound A, one may observe the sun rising over the river and the ridged mounds at the vernal and autumnal equinoxes. To the south, several kilometers away, lies Lower Jackson Mound, and several kilometers to the north is Motley Mound; Lower Jackson Mound dates to as many as 1,000 years before Poverty Point was inhabited, and Motley Mound may predate the site as well (Saunders et al. 2001).

Interestingly, the mounds near Poverty Point were built to create a direct north-south line with these two more distant mounds. Mounds A, B, and E, just outside and west of the concentric mounds, line up with the Lower Jackson Mound, and Mound C inside and east of the concentric mounds lines up with Motley Mound. It is possible that Poverty Point served as a focal point, almost a "religious center" for regional communities to come together for important astronomical and other ceremonial occurrences as well as for trade; many objects found at Poverty Point were made of stone derived from substantial distances (Gibson 2010; Sassaman 2005) (see Box 11.2). The mounds at Poverty Point stand as one example of the early precursors to the major mound-building efforts that commenced in the Woodland Period.

BOX 11.2 POVERTY POINT ARTIFACTS

In addition to the fascinating mound constructions at Poverty Point, over 70,000 artifacts were recovered (Figure 11.5). One set of artifacts consists of baked clay balls often decorated with carvings or made into various shapes (such as "melon" or biconical forms). The purpose of these clay balls is not entirely clear, though they may have functioned as "hot rocks" used to heat food in the cooking process (Webb 1968). The effort put into making the clay balls instead of just using actual rocks suggests they may have had some purpose, ritual or otherwise, in the cooking process. Human figurines made of clay, particularly the heads, were also recovered at Poverty Point. It appears that the majority of these figurines represent females, and some feature decorated heads (with puncture or groove marks). Residents at Poverty Point also engaged in the production of stone (usually red jasper) beads and ornaments sometimes representing animals and others in geometric shapes. One common occurrence is beads in the shape of locusts (Webb 1971), which are known for the tremendously loud male courtship calls. The combination of the mound construction and the presence of these items at Poverty Point highlight its ritual importance over 3,000 years ago (Gibson 2010).

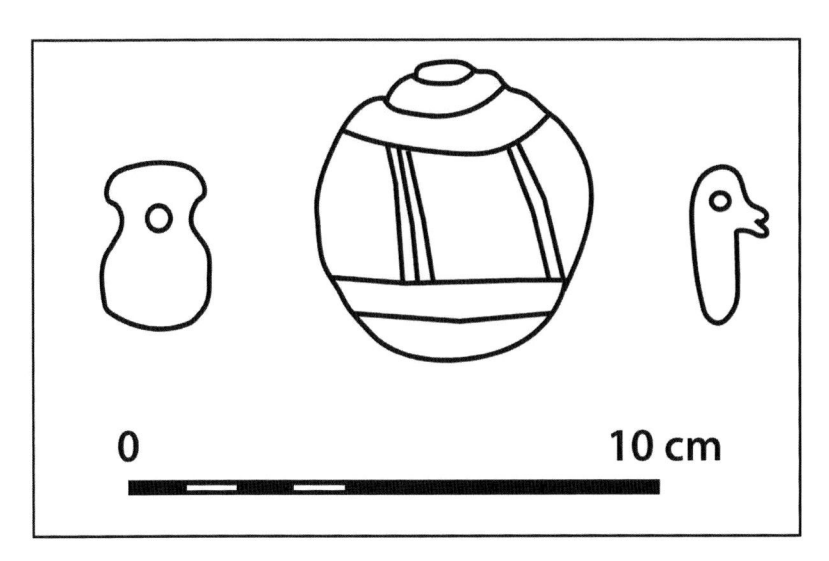

FIGURE 11.5 Examples of Poverty Point Artifacts
Source: After Webb (1968: 309, fig. 2, 316, fig. 7)

The Early Woodland Period

Following the Late Archaic depopulation, the Woodland Period (900 BCE–1050 CE) experienced a slow but steady re-emergence of different population centers and cultural frameworks (Emerson and McElrath 2001). There is significant debate surrounding the cause of the site abandonments of roughly 3,000 years ago, a phenomenon that occurred throughout the eastern United States. The most commonly cited explanation is that of climate alteration (Fiedel 2001; Kidder 2006; Thomas and Sanger 2010), which may have caused flooding, damaged subsistence resources and habitations, and affected navigability of the rivers (and therefore trade networks). Sassaman notes that the dispersal of people to the uplands caused new social relations to develop and new techniques for subsistence and survival to emerge (2010: 210): "The major changes we observe . . . after ca. 3200 cal BP, whether or not they were precipitated by natural forces (e.g., floods), entailed the realignment of social collectives and the alliances that connected them." Out of these early centuries of "realignment" came new and even more complex cultures that built extensive trade relations and elaborate ritual systems.

The American Bottom Region

The depopulation and habitation disruption at the beginning of the Early Woodland complicates the assignment of "cultural phases" in unpopulated regions. In the American Bottom, there are at least four different cultural phases, perhaps corresponding to varying ethnic groups occupying the region during this period. Two of these are briefly described here. The Carr Creek Culture (also termed the "Marion" culture), largely gone by ca. 400 BCE, features ceramics with cord decoration and a lithic toolkit with distinctive points (Fortier, Emerson, and McElrath 2006; Kelly 2002). At this time, Carr Creek sites are found both in the floodplain regions and the uplands. At approximately 400 BCE, the material culture of the American Bottom sites alters, and the Florence Culture emerged, again offering new ceramic styles, often featuring fabric impression as decoration, along with differing lithic tool types and styles. These changes may have been a result of importation, but equally likely is the arrival of new populations (Emerson and Fortier 1986; Kelly 2002). The movement of peoples during the Early Woodland Period may have been related to the development of the Adena cultural complex to the east.

The Adena

A set of interrelated cultures in the Ohio Valley commonly called the "Adena Complex" rose by 800 BCE and lasted a thousand years until the emergence of the Hopewell in the 1st century CE. The Adena is characterized by a dramatic increase in ritualized behavior, burial mounds, and domesticated cultigens. The Adena diet included squash, a variety of grasses, sunflowers, and other plants, grown in gardens near Adena villages; it was supplemented by hunted game and wild plant species. The term "Adena" encompasses several cultures spread across Ohio, Kentucky, West Virginia, and Indiana and even as far east as western New York and Pennsylvania. These peoples shared elements of material culture such as ceramic styles and stone toolkits. They engaged in extensive long-distance trade to acquire copper from the Great Lakes region, shells from the southern coast, and mica from the Carolinas.

The Adena cultural complex has been described as tribal in sociopolitical and economic structure (Abrams and Freter 2005; Mainfort 1989). Extensive trade aided in the development of Adena elites and their political structure though Adena communities may have been quite small. Adena people built structures that were likely circular or oval, though a few may have been rectangular in shape and were built of paired posts that connected walls and roofing material; initially thought to be houses, they may have been more often devoted to ritual functions (Baby 1971; Clay 2009). Structures ranged in size from 8 to 29 meters in diameter, with 11–12 meters being the average (Webb and Snow 1974: 53); the largest structures were likely unroofed and may have functioned as public or ceremonial areas. The majority of Adena structures have been recovered due to their preservation by Adena burial mounds. Perhaps initially used as houses, some Adena structures became tombs or charnel houses. Burial mounds were then constructed over these buildings.

It is the Adena burial mounds that have captured the greatest interest, in part because they are the most recognizable trait in the Adena cultural complex. Hundreds of Adena mounds are scattered across the Ohio River Valley and beyond. They are typically described as "conical" and range in size from approximately 6 meters to as much as 90 meters in diameter. In height, they can range from as low as the height of a human to well over 20 meters. Some mounds occur in clusters, even found inside earthen enclosures, and others are single mounds on the landscape (Hays 2010; Milner 2004). These differing configurations may have corresponded to the locations of Adena communities, to Adena perceptions of sacred nodes on the landscape, or to a variety of other factors still to be discovered.

Adena mounds contained burials of varying types. The most elaborate were tombs built of logs in which a few individuals were placed in extended positions; these graves usually contained the most elaborate goods including copper bracelets and breastplates, marine shell beads, items made of mica, stone gorgets, limestone tablets, and stone platform pipes (McCord and Cochran 2008). The stone platform pipes, perhaps precursors to the more elaborate platform pipes from the Hopewell tradition (discussed later), may have been used in ceremonial practices by elites or religious specialists (see Box 11.3); while they may have served a variety of purposes, sooting and carbonized residue on these items indicate that smoking was a primary use (Rafferty 2008). Many mounds contained multiple burials, likely placed there over time, even generations, resulting in large mounds holding dozens and sometimes over 100 burials. Possibly, each lineage constructed their own burial mound, and these earthen structures served as territorial markers for powerful and wealthy Adena elites. Other burial types included cremations or simple inhumations laid upon earthen platforms; occasionally, in place of a log tomb, some were covered with bark. While some mounds feature fairly consistent burial methods and grave goods, others have a variety of burial types and differing goods placed with the dead. The mounds with differing burial types may represent changes in kin groups using the mounds, changing ritual requirements, or contact with more distant peoples with varying death rituals (Hays 2010).

BOX 11.3 TOBACCO

Tobacco has long been a part of religious ritual among Native peoples of North America, Mesoamerica, and South America. For many cultures, tobacco serves as a gift to the gods or spirits within that culture's belief system. It could be offered to the supernatural world either through gifts of dry tobacco or by means of the smoke resulting from pipe-smoking. Besides serving as a gift, in many cultures, it was believed that prayers could be carried to the supernatural world by the smoke as it rose into the sky. Tobacco also served as a typical offering to honored guests arriving into a Native American community. Tobacco was also important in medicinal uses. It could be mixed with other native plants and then used as a pain reliever or to treat other ailments such as a cough or breathing problems such as asthma. Tobacco was likely first domesticated in South America several thousand years ago and slowly made its way northward. There is evidence to suggest that domesticated tobacco was in use at sites in the American Bottom and elsewhere in North America between 1,500 and 2,000 years ago (Rafferty 2006; Simon and Parker 2006). The presence of pipes at Late Archaic sites suggests that tobacco was in use far earlier, perhaps in its wild manifestation; future work may find that tobacco was being cultivated even earlier than the Early and Middle Woodland Periods in North America.

A final aspect of Adena mounds was what might have been a type of "renewal" ritual associated with some, but not all, mounds. In many of the mounds, Adena peoples placed a layer of earth over a set of burials, smoothing the soil to make an even mounded surface; into this, they then (or later) interred additional burials. Some mounds featured several of these layers that essentially separated one set of burials from the next. Whether these represent generational change, use of the mound by a new lineage, or other social factors requiring this treatment of the mounds remains undetermined.

The Adena cultural complex introduces extensive long-distance trade and the acquisition of non-utilitarian materials and goods to the midcontinental socioeconomy, including marine shells, mica, and copper. The fashioning of these materials into body ornaments and items such as pipes is indicative of two other important factors in Adena culture: the development of elites and the importance of religion and ritual. As noted earlier, the Adena cultural complex has been described has having a tribal political structure, perhaps based on lineage elders. The burial mounds themselves, the construction of buildings meant to (eventually) become houses of the dead, and the artifacts such as platform pipes, demonstrate the profound importance of religion and ritual in Adena social structures.

The Middle Woodland Period

The various cultural institutions described earlier grew in importance in the Middle Woodland phase (ca. 100 BCE–350 CE) and the Hopewell cultural complex.

The Hopewell Tradition

The Hopewell Tradition (ca. 1st century to 400 CE) is, in many respects, a continuation of the Adena cultural complex but larger in size and scope, though recent archaeological work has suggested that the Adena continued alongside the Hopewell for a century or more. Like Adena, Hopewell is named after a site in Ohio. The Hopewell material culture subsequently spread throughout the Ohio and Mississippi River valleys, encompassing Missouri to Ohio, north to Wisconsin and Michigan and south to Mississippi, Alabama, Georgia, and Tennessee (Abrams 2009). Also like the use of the cultural term "Adena," Hopewell no longer refers to a single culture or region but rather to a complex of cultures that were interlocked in trade and ritual actions during a specific period of time but that are likely quite disparate with regard to cultural traits, customs, and practices (Abrams 2009; Greber 2005; Mainfort 2005). In other words, both Hopewell and Adena have come to be "period" names rather than "culture" names.

Hopewell structures are either circular or rectangular with rounded corners (Baby 1971) and are built in the dual post format described earlier for Adena houses. Hopewell communities are best described as "hamlets" and were widely dispersed, consisting of two to four households (Dancey and Pacheco 1997). Residents were largely sedentary, growing local varieties of grasses and seed plants such as sunflower and squash and supplementing this garden-based diet with hunting and gathering. Although maize was present in some Hopewell sites, particularly in burials, it did not yet serve as a main subsistence item. Hamlets were dispersed across the landscape, but they were interconnected through trade and ritual practice. There is some evidence to suggest that hamlets with varying resource catchments may have traded subsistence goods (Ruby, Carr, and Charles 2005). Residents of these dispersed hamlets came together to create large-scale earthworks and to participate together in ritual and ceremonial events on what was likely a regular basis (Ruby, Carr, and Charles 2005).

The Hopewell Period is perhaps best known for massive mortuary mounds. The elaborate non-utilitarian goods placed in Hopewell mound burials demonstrate the long-distance trade relations that connected the different cultures constituting the Hopewell Tradition. Copper, from the Great Lakes region, was sometimes beaten flat and then fashioned into ornaments displaying silhouettes of animals, such as birds and bird claws, and of human heads or hands (Figure 11.6). Mica, from the Appalachians, was also used, in thin sheets, to fashion similar images and to create discs and chest coverings; copper was also made into body decorations such as breastplates, ear spools, and other items of jewelry. Marine shells and fresh water pearls from the Florida coast were found in abundance in some graves, perhaps sewn onto clothing. Exceedingly large chert and obsidian biface tools, some as long as nearly 25 centimeters, were also placed in graves, sometimes in vast numbers; several mounds in Ohio contained bifaces numbering in the thousands. The quantity of non-local goods found in some mound tombs is impressive; archaeologists have suggested that, rather than waiting for enough down-the-line trade to deliver sufficient materials for grave deposition, Hopewellians themselves may have traveled to the sources and acquired enough copper, obsidian, or mica to prepare for a major burial ceremony (Milner 2004). This would suggest fairly free movement across the landscape and a clear understanding of where various types of materials were to be found. Another artifact type found in burials are platform pipes, also interred with Adena Period people. The Hopewell pipes, however, are more elaborate, featuring animals "standing" on the platforms. These beautiful smoking pipes are discussed in more detail later.

Hopewell earthen mounds tend to occur in clusters, though there are individual earthworks as well. At Hopewell itself, 38 mounds were clustered inside a rectangular enclosure. The Hopewell built circular, rectangular, and occasionally octagonal enclosures of mounded earth and stone, some of which are connected by causeways (Figure 11.7) and may cover areas up to several kilometers.

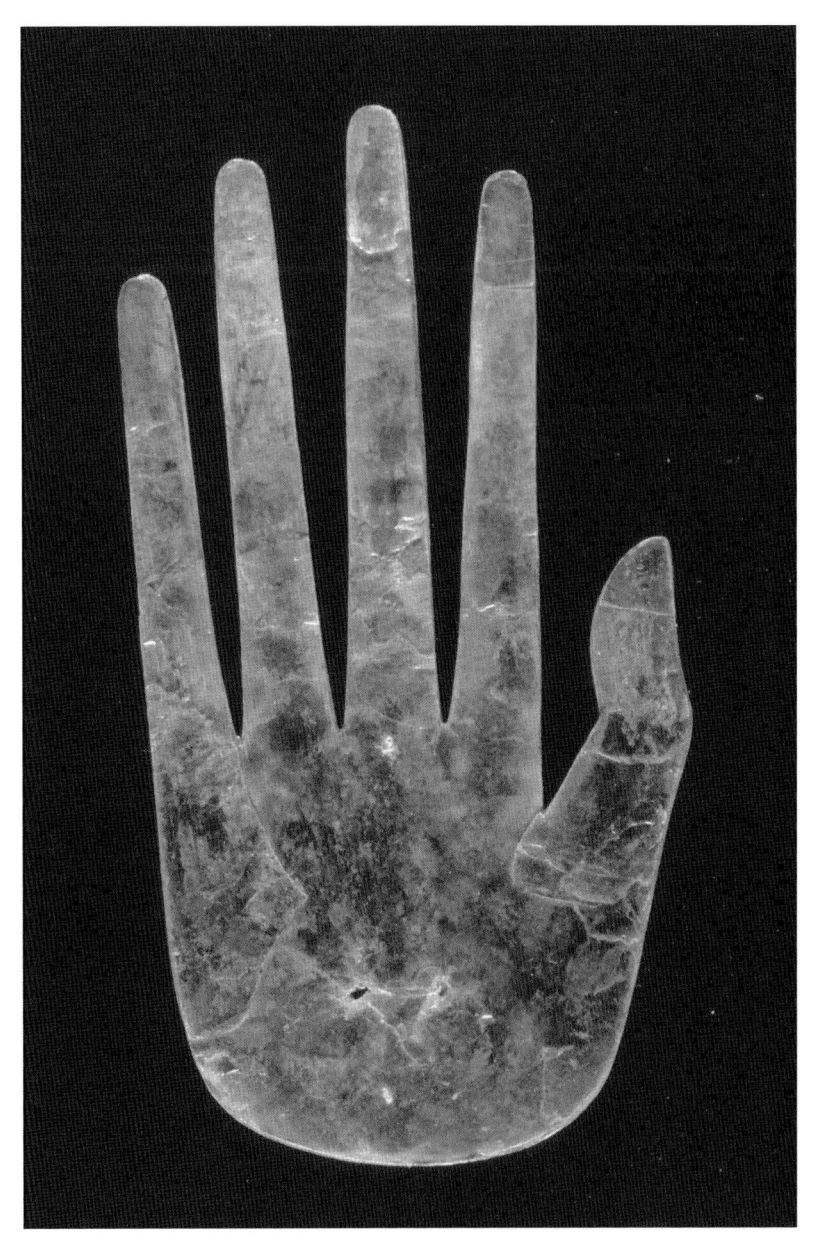

FIGURE 11.6 Example of Hopewell Period Effigy of a Flat Human Hand Cut From a Sheet of Mica, Excavated From the Hopewell Mound Group

Source: Photo courtesy of Ohio History Connection

The Hopewell enclosures were built to rather precise and possibly standardized measurements; circular enclosures found hundreds of kilometers distant from one another are of nearly the same size and proportions (Romain 2000, 2004). When standing at one end of these earthen structures, one can observe the rising and setting of the moon in accordance with the lunar calendar and observe the setting of the winter solstice sun (Hively and Horn 1984; Romain 2000). Therefore, the role of the enclosures, and perhaps the mounds held within them, may have extended beyond that of

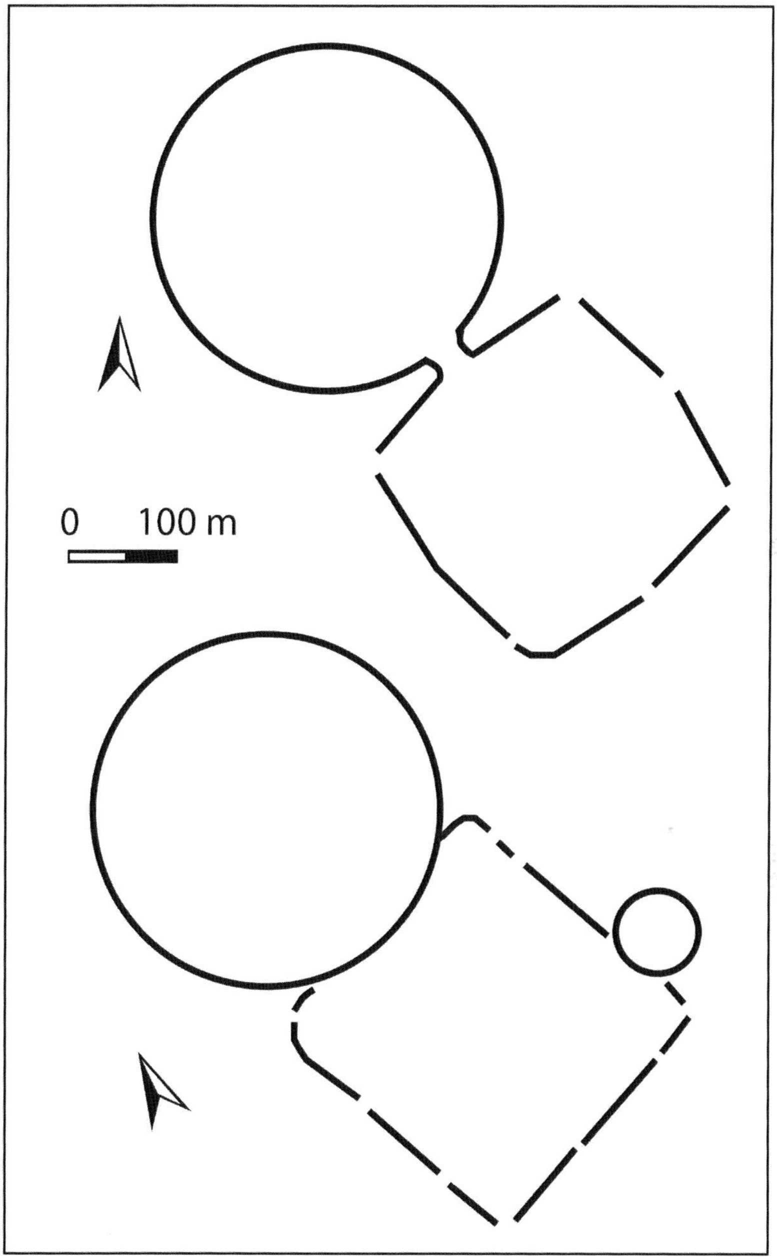

FIGURE 11.7 Sketch of Two Causewayed Enclosure Hopewell Sites: Top: "High Bank Works"; Bottom: "Hopeton Earthworks"; Both Located in the Hopewell Culture National Historical Park in Central Ohio

Source: After Squier and Davis (1848: plates XVI and XVII)

sacred burial ground into one of astronomical observational posts for important seasonal markers. At Seip Mound in Ohio, at least seven large, non-domestic rectangular wooden structures were built near and within enclosures and were perhaps associated with ceremonies conducted at the mounds (Baby and Langlois 1979; Burks and Greber 2009; Greber 2009). Analysis of the mounds suggests that they were built over generations (Greber 1997) with labor possibly contributed by people cooperating in Hopewellian "polities" discussed in more detail later.

Like the Adena, the Hopewell people built charnel houses for the dead. The majority of Hopewellians were cremated prior to placement in mounds, but some were laid in rectangular wooden charnel houses and cremated when the house was burned and then covered by an earthen mound. Burial mounds with non-cremation interments tended to occur on bluff tops. While a few skeletons were articulated, most were not, indicating they may have been placed in the tomb after the flesh had decayed or perhaps were pushed aside when a new burial was placed within a tomb. The burial goods in these constructed crypts tended to be the richest among Hopewell burials, and it is likely that they held community leaders. The burial complex was eventually enclosed by earthen mounds that stood as high as 9 meters.

Burial goods included the types of objects described earlier. The "Great Mica Grave," at Mound City, lined with mica and including a number of grave goods, contained four cremations; the grave held additional pieces of mica and other burial goods (Milner 2004: 64–66). One of the most notable artifact types found in Hopewell tombs were effigy pipes, which had the addition of an animal or other figure sitting atop the flat pipe (Figure 11.8). It is likely that these pipes were used by religious leaders who smoked the tobacco to achieve a trance state in order to enter the spiritual realm (Brown 1997). Less plentiful were human figurines depicting a human (male or female) who appears to wear the skin of an animal such as a bear or other ritual garb (Milner 2004; Keller and Carr 2005; Koldehoff 2006). Other burial artifacts also may have carried ritual significance, including the beaten copper images of human faces, hands, and animal parts such as claws from birds of prey. Crystals, colorful cherts, and mineralized rocks, found particularly

FIGURE 11.8 Example of Stone Hopewell Effigy Pipe

Source: R. Jennison

in American Bottom Hopewell mounds, may have also been ritually significant (Fortier 2008). Many other goods such as copper chest plates, jewelry, beads, stone tools, and pottery may have marked important leaders who held status positions that were not connected to a religious role in the community.

Ethnographic data suggests that Hopewell peoples may have equated circles with winter, rectangles with summer, and octagons with other seasons or that these shapes represented a multilayered universe (DeBoer 1997; Romain 2000; see Steadman 2009: 112–16). Animal imagery may represent the spiritual realm or be connected with shamanistic activity; the figurines depicting humans with animal "costumes" may support such interpretations. While Hopewell beliefs remain largely beyond the realm of interpretation at present, it is likely that various Hopewell communities came together for important ceremonies, perhaps conducted by acknowledged leaders.

What type of sociopolitical structure best describes the Hopewell cultural complex has been a matter of intense debate (e.g., Carr and Case 2005; Coon 2009; Ruby, Carr and Charles 2005; Seeman 1979). Most agree that the earthworks and long-distance trade are indicative of an organized political structure. Archaeologists are reluctant to use the terms "tribal" or "chiefdom" for Hopewell political structures because it is likely that neither is a good fit. Rather, it seemed to consist of a set of regional polities in which leaders, or a council of leaders, worked together and interacted with sets of leaders from other polities. Such leaders made important economic, religious, and social decisions for their communities and kin groups (Greber 2006; Pacheco and Dancey 2006). Members of the various communities allied in the polity would come together to create one or multiple major earthworks present in their region, especially for the burial of an important community/lineage leader.

The presence of "trophy skulls" leads some to suggest that leaders were skilled warriors, but most evidence indicates that the Hopewell Period was largely peaceful (Carr and Case 2005; Seeman 1988). Burial goods suggest that leaders may have held both religious and secular status roles, depending on their position within the lineage. Some people destined to be leaders (either chosen by their lineage or selected through some other means such as birth order) may have served as a shaman/healer prior to assuming their later prominent position (Carr and Case 2005). Burial goods such as the effigy pipes would be significant indicators of those who had held religious roles in their communities prior to death. Other leaders may have had other qualities that elevated them to their positions; non-religious burial goods such as metal breastplates and tools might be indicative of their secular but prominent societal positions (Carr and Case 2005).

Archaeological investigation suggests that, beginning in the 3rd century CE, the building of Hopewell Period earthworks tailed off, and at the same time, long-distance trade in non-local materials and exotic forms was discontinued. By the 4th century CE, the settlement system had begun to change in the Ohio Valley and beyond. The small dispersed hamlets, built in the polity-structure described earlier and centered on one or more ceremonial and earthworks sites and mounds, were largely abandoned. Rather, people moved to larger communities in different areas that were more defensible; in fact, some of these larger communities existed inside enclosure walls that may well have had a defensive function (Abrams 2009). Rather than a "collapse" of Hopewell cultural traditions, there seems to have instead been a significant shift in focus. What was once an open, largely peaceful, and wide-ranging set of polities and traditions in relatively constant contact with one another became a more insulated, protected, and even isolated set of larger communities. Residents shifted their priorities away from the acquisition of long-distance exotic goods and massive earthworks projects to more localized activities, perhaps in response to social or ecological changes in the early centuries of the common era. Certainly by ca. 400 CE the Hopewell Tradition had waned and the Late Woodland Period commenced in which more robust agricultural practices emerged (see Box 11.4).

BOX 11.4 EFFIGY MOUNDS AND SERPENT MOUND

After the impressive Hopewell mounds, it would seem that mound-building could become no more spectacular in the midcontinental region, but in fact, it did. The Late Woodland Period sees the emergence of "effigy mounds," mounds built in the shape of animals or other entities. These mounds are very hard to date and were originally thought to belong to the Adena or Hopewell Periods, but more recent research suggests many are Late Woodland in date. The mounds continued to be locations for burials, both inhumations and cremations, but the extensive grave goods found in Hopewell burials are absent in the effigy mounds. Mounds were also built in the shape of birds, panthers, bears, and turtles, among other animals. Effigy mounds are found spread across regions of Wisconsin, Iowa, Illinois, and Minnesota. Unlike the Hopewell mounds, which were constructed over time, the effigy mounds seem to have been built more consistently in one or a few events (Milner 2004). Those buried in them may still have been community leaders, but the importance of signaling wealth through the placement of burial goods had become less important. It is possible that the symbolism of the mound shapes had replaced the burial goods as markers of status and importance. Remnants of pottery, bone, and other material culture near these mounds suggest ceremonial and feasting events, perhaps at the time of building or burial. It is possible these mounds were also built to mark territories of kin or other cooperative groups (Milner 2004).

Although not considered one of the standard effigy mounds, one of the more spectacular mound constructions is "Serpent Mound" in Ohio (Figure 11.9). Serpent Mound has no burials

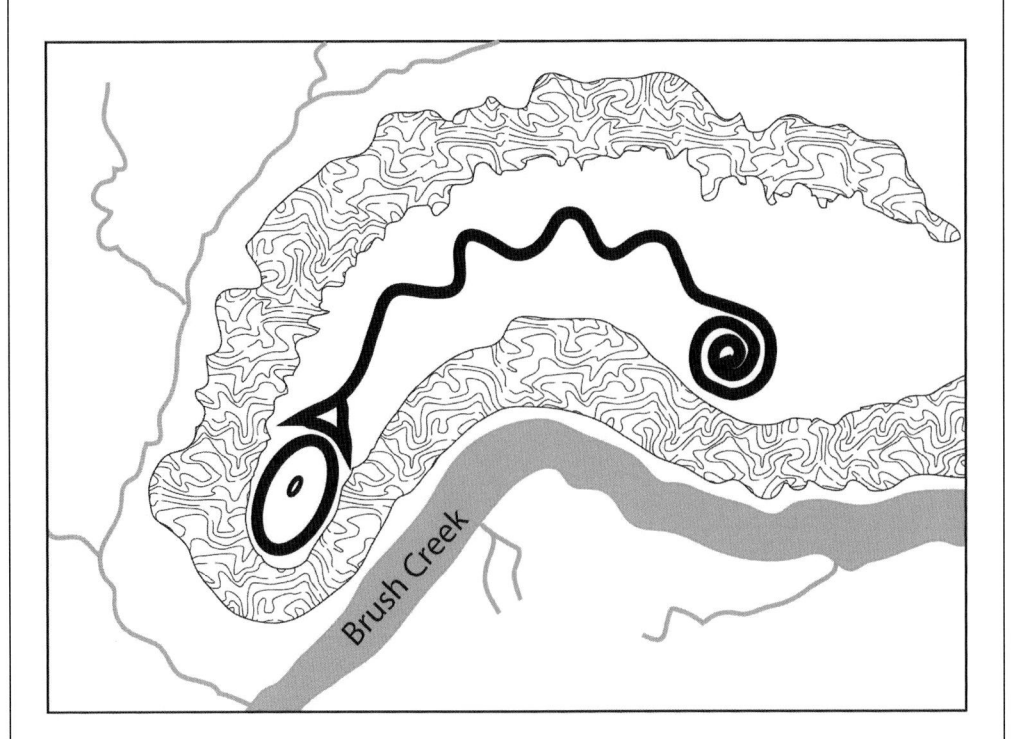

FIGURE 11.9 Sketch of Serpent Mound in Ohio

Source: S.R. Steadman

or burial goods, making its construction very difficult to date. Recent evidence suggests it was built during Adena times (Hermann et al. 2014), but earlier radiocarbon analysis also dates it to Mississippian times (see later). The effort put into building Serpent Mound, featuring a partially coiled snake appearing to consume an object that resembles an egg, suggests that it was a ritually important site for whomever constructed this fascinating landscape feature.

The Late Woodland Period

Contemporary with the Hopewell Tradition, the Middle Woodland Period in the American Bottom saw new ceramic and lithic forms emerge, and crops such as sunflower and squash were being cultivated at this time (Fortier 2001; Simon and Parker 2006). Residents continued to occupy the American Bottom in the Late Woodland Period (ca. 350–1050 CE) as the Hopewell tradition faded in influence. Archaeologists debate the causes for the demise of Hopewell ways, speculating on the role climate, warfare, migration, or other factors may have played. Whatever the causes, and they were likely varied, they resulted in a breakdown in the long-distance trade network and a change in the burial rituals that had defined the Hopewell cultural complex for several centuries. During the Late Woodland Period, inhabitants in the Ohio, Mississippi, and other river valleys of the midcontinent began farming more intensively and building larger and more permanent settlements. However, during the first 50 years or so of the Late Woodland, the American Bottom region appears rather empty of occupation, a circumstance perhaps related to the collapse of the Hopewell Tradition. After 400 CE, people begin to re-establish themselves in the region. Hamlets established in the earlier phases of the Late Woodland avoided the American Bottom floodplains and instead were located on the bluffs, perhaps due to a higher water table and potential flooding of lowland settlements (McElrath and Fortier 2000). In the Late Woodland Patrick phase (ca. 650–900 CE), there is a noticeable change in settlement practices and material culture concomitant with a lowering of the water table and expansion of occupation into the floodplains of the American Bottom.

Larger communities and greater numbers of inhabitants constructed new material culture that includes a hunting technology that made regular use of the bow and arrow and new pottery forms and styles (Fortier, Emerson, and McElrath 2006; Fortier and Jackson 2000). Patrick phase residents were employing slash-and-burn cultivation techniques to grow seed plants and grasses but were not yet reliant on maize as a domesticate (Simon 2014; Simon and Parker 2006).

Some scholars suggest that migrants moved into the region during the Patrick phase, settling both in the American Bottom floodplains and on the uplands and bringing this new material culture (Koldehoff and Galloy 2006).

Changes in architectural patterns also appear in the Patrick phase. Communities consisted of small groups of houses that were either rectangular or built in an unusual keyhole-shape. The ramps leading to the interior created the "keyhole" architectural footprint; the ramps were likely covered, and it is possible that these structures were mainly occupied in the winter (Fortier and Jackson 2000). Some houses had numerous pits in their proximity while others had only a few. At the Range site, one of the largest Late Woodland sites in the American Bottom, a number of houses were arrayed around a central square (Kelly 1990, 2002). There were two interesting aspects to the houses. First, the two largest faced one another across the central square; second, most of the oval keyhole houses were found in one half of the village, while the other half featured the more rectilinear structures (Kelly 2002). It is possible that the two largest houses were occupied by village leaders, engaged in a cooperative and/or competitive relationship. The different house structures may have reflected kinship and lineage affiliation, ethnic differentiation, religious symbolism, or a combination of these.

Skeletal analysis indicates humans were killed by arrow and club strikes, suggesting that strife between communities or regions was more commonplace in the Late Woodland (Milner 1999). This circumstance may have influenced the choice to live in larger communities in the last decades of the 1st millennium CE. The earlier Middle Woodland landscape that had been strewn with small hamlets and villages spread out along river valleys and floodplains transformed into one with larger towns with satellite villages around them, located both in the floodplains and in the uplands (Kelly 2002; Koldehoff and Galloy 2006). This meant that cultivation of staple crops, including an increasing reliance on maize, became the norm.

Political structures in the Terminal Late Woodland Period (ca. 800–1050 CE) have been described as "nascent chiefdoms" (Milner 2004: 120), acknowledging the importance of the elite burials, the central plazas, and the growing population. Other scholars have described the leadership structure as one of "big men" in which leadership positions were "fluid and not ascribed" (Kelly 2002: 156). Leadership was likely based on kinship relationships and settlement patterns (patrilocal, matrilocal, or a mixture of both). The Terminal Late Woodland segues into the early Mississippian phase, a period during which the purported Late Woodland "big men" transitioned into chiefs and even kings.

The Rise of the Mississippian Tradition and Cahokia

Without doubt, the Mississippian tradition (1050–1400 CE) was a highly complex society that saw elites gain substantial power over land and people through their control of the socioeconomic and the religious belief systems that formed the bedrock of their society. Though the Mississippian complex was spread across a significant region, this section will concentrate on the sites in the American Bottom and the largest of the Mississippian centers, Cahokia.

The American Bottom and Cahokia Mississippian complex is divided into four main archaeological phases with the Lohmann and Stirling (ca. 1050–1200 CE) seeing the main building of mounds, temple centers, and other significant architecture at Cahokia and the Moorehead and Sand Prairie phases (ca. 1200–1400 CE) seeing the apogee of the complex and its decline.

By the Mississippian early Stirling phase, a hierarchy of community types had emerged. In more rural settings, further from ceremonial centers such as Cahokia, certain houses in Stirling phase villages became significantly larger, with an expansive associated courtyard capable of accommodating numerous individuals. These "homesteads" were not situated alongside the rest of the houses but were located a short distance away; open plazas were no longer present in some of these villages, and it appears that gatherings took place in the homestead courtyards (Mehrer 1995). Residents of this nodal-type homestead, who may have been the wealthiest members of the community, seem to have acquired the ability to control the timing and location of public gatherings, many of which were likely of a religious nature.

Closer to the major centers larger settlements such as the BBB Motor and the Sponemann sites, both near Cahokia, appear to be "temple-mortuary nodes" (Emerson 1997a) featuring large buildings containing ceremonial items, storage and cooking facilities, structures that may have been sweathouses or purification buildings, and possible residences near the temples. At the smaller BBB Motor site, over 20 burials suggest that mortuary ceremonies may have been at the center of the ritual activity; at the Sponemann site, the discovery of many items signifying fertility, including figurines, leads scholars to believe that the rituals at this site were devoted to agricultural fertility rites (Emerson 1997a). Rural residents may well have traveled to the temples such as BBB Motor or Sponemann for important ceremonies, especially if they were barred from attending "state" events at the Cahokian center.

The organization of religious practice, defining when and where ceremonies were to take place and who was allowed to take part in those ceremonies, was taking place on a large scale at the Cahokian center. There was also a focus on the art of warfare, both in terms of defense and aggression; Cahokian elites were able to command enormous labor to build extensive defense systems, sending the message that they could protect all that was most valuable to Mississippian peoples. Finally, Cahokian elites and leaders were engaged in extensive long-distance trade, acquiring valuable raw materials that were then manufactured into spectacular objects that made their way into elite burials. It is these three elements—religion, warfare, and economy—that form a triad that allowed Mississippian elites to build a sophisticated society, centered at Cahokia.

Creating Cahokia

Cahokia first drew residents around 900 CE, growing into a major center by 1100 CE. By 1400, it was abandoned. The causes of the abandonment may have been multiple, including climate change and regional conflict. The main site rests on the eastern side of the Mississippi River, across from the modern city of St. Louis. Situated in the American Bottom, the site's location offered plentiful water for agriculture but was far enough from the river to avoid major flooding problems. Much of the Cahokian center was built during the Lohmann and Stirling phases. In the Cahokia vicinity were two other precincts including the East St. Louis site and, on the opposite side of the river, the St. Louis precinct (Emerson 2002; Pauketat 1998, 2004). These three ceremonial precincts may have been part of a large Cahokian city, and while the East St. Louis and St. Louis areas may have been subsidiary to Cahokia, they demonstrate the centralization of elites, religious practice, and socioeconomic activity and the drawing of labor forces to these centers from the countryside (Kelly 1997). Identifying all three precincts as part of a Cahokian city would make Cahokia's size comparable to any of the other major centers featured in other chapters in this volume.

The Cahokian center itself, the region one of its excavators termed "downtown" (Fowler 1974) due to the palisade that surrounds it, is an area of approximately 80 hectares. Construction of this area of Cahokia required extensive labor. First, the enormous plaza upon which the central "Monks Mound" sits had to be leveled, a feat as great as the creation of the numerous mounds in the region. As many as 120 mounds dot the Cahokian landscape. They take three primary forms: platform mounds upon which structures were built are the most common, conical mounds that sometimes served as burial locations, and ridge mounds that contain burials but may have also served as boundary markers or delineated important spatial nodes (Bowne 2013; Young and Fowler 2000). The platform and conical mounds often occur in pairs both inside the Cahokian center as well as across the landscape (Demel and Hall 1998). The central earthen structure at Cahokia is called Monks Mound (Figure 11.10), built in four levels and standing approximately 30 meters in height (Fowler 1997). A log-built staircase led to each of the levels; the first level is a large rectangular platform mound that supports three more platforms of successively smaller size, built over time. On the highest level stood a large wooden building surrounded by a wooden palisade. This structure may have served as a place of worship, an elite residence, or both. The position of Monks Mound at the center of Cahokia inside a defensive wall (see later) suggests that the religious or secular activities that took place on this central mound were attended only by Cahokian elites who ostensibly carried out rituals as proxies for the commoners beyond the city center. The building of Monks Mound was a monumental task, requiring approximately 730,000 cubic meters of earth. Some estimate that it took as much as a century to construct the four levels, but a recent study suggests that charismatic elites capable of organizing labor on a grand scale may have arranged construction of the largest earthworks in North America in as little as two decades (Schilling 2013).

FIGURE 11.10 Artistic Rendering of Monks Mound and Cahokian Center
Source: M.J. Hughes

An enormous open plaza sits in front of Monks Mound, which is surrounded by what may be three more plazas, all oriented to the four cardinal directions. Across the front Grand Plaza are two mounds known as Fox Mound and Round Top, the first a platform mound that may have held a charnel or mortuary house and the second a burial mound perhaps meant to receive those who resided atop Fox Mound after death. Surrounding this complex and the area around it was an extensive wooden palisade roughly 3 kilometers in length. The palisade consisted of thousands of wooden poles with guard towers stationed at intervals along the wall; the wooden poles were replaced on a regular basis and maintenance of this palisade must have required extensive labor (Milner 1998). Also present within the Cahokian center are enigmatic woodhenges. These are circles of wooden poles erected in quantities based on 12; five such structures, termed "sun circles" by some (Bowne 2013), have been discovered. It is likely that these structures are meant to track change in seasons; central poles within the circles may have served to mark the arrival of the summer and winter solstices.

Another mound worth mention is "Mound 72," which was excavated in the 1960s by Melvin Fowler. It is one of the ridge-top mounds and is generally in alignment with one edge of Monks Mound; initially a woodhenge stood where Mound 72 was later built. Excavations revealed nearly 300 human burials in Mound 72; some of these appear to have been Cahokian elites, and others may have been sacrificial victims killed and interred with the elites. Significant quantities of grave goods were buried with the elites. One of these, known as the "beaded burial," had roughly 20,000 shell beads arranged in the form of a bird, perhaps a falcon, under the male in the grave. In the same mound, one pit held 50 young women laid in rows and stacked on top of one another, and another held four young men who had been beheaded and behanded (Fowler 1991). Other pits also held groups of young people, mainly women, all buried simultaneously, suggesting sacrificial rites rather than mass death from other causes. Whether the sacrificial victims were from Cahokia or captured through warfare, sold for this purpose, or acquired by other means, their presence in Mound 72 demonstrates the ability of Cahokian elites to control the life and death of humans.

Residences are found across Cahokia, both in the center upon the platform mounds and radiating out from the center's edges outside the palisade and mound area. Structures atop the platform mounds may have been residences belonging to the elite class. Sometimes structures were circular, and in other cases, they were rectangular; the higher the platform mound, the greater may have been the status of its resident (Emerson 1997a, 1997b). Outside the Cahokian center, more mounds dotted the landscape; lesser elites who did not rate residences at the center may have lived atop these and buried their dead in adjacent conical mounds. Beyond these were the non-elite residences at the city's margins, extending as much as 8 kilometers away from the center (Kelly 1997). Estimates of Cahokia's population range widely, but most believe that 10,000 individuals or more may have occupied the settlement at its height; if one includes East St. Louis and other outlying areas, the population may have been as high as 40,000. It is likely that those living beyond the center were engaged in farming pursuits and also provided the extensive labor necessary for building the Cahokia earthworks.

Mississippian Peoples and Communities

A number of archaeologists have noted that Cahokia and other temple centers virtually exploded onto the scene around 1050 CE, a time many refer to as the "Big Bang" of Mississippian emergence (Alt 2010b; Milner 2004; Pauketat 1994, 2004). Most archaeologists believe that the sudden rise in population must have resulted from immigration to the centers not just from within the American Bottom region but from elsewhere as well (e.g., Emerson and Hargrave 2000). Not only was there likely insufficient population in the American Bottom to create these vast cities and towns, but varying mortuary practices also suggest ethnic diversity in the Mississippian population. While the cause of this sudden concentration of population is still far from understood, recent work has partially solved the riddle of where the inhabitants came from: they were from everywhere. For whatever reasons, and they may have been varied, in the late 10th and the early 11th centuries, hundreds, even thousands, of people began to converge on centers such as Cahokia, coming from all over the American Bottom region and beyond, including from southern Missouri, Illinois, Indiana, and from even farther afield (Emerson and Hedman 2015; Slater et al. 2014). While some of those moving to the centers may have had kin there, those from further away were "outsiders" likely with no kin connections in their new cities; their arrival brought ethnic and cultural diversity to the Mississippian centers and outlying regions. These newcomers may have aided in the trade connections developing between Mississippian centers and far-flung sources of desirable materials. The "outsiders" may have facilitated trade relations, thereby ensuring their welcome to and presence in the American Bottom. While the Mississippian "melting pot" seems to have worked for a couple of centuries, some suggest the arrival of social unrest by the 13th century may have had some of its roots in that very ethnic diversity in the Mississippian polity (Emerson 2007; Emerson and Hedman 2015; Pauketat et al. 2013).

The houses occupied by the majority of Mississippians were built of bundles of thatch intertwined with branches and supported by wooden posts or by wattle-and-daub construction. House floors were of pounded earth, and often the interior of the house had packed earth against the base of the walls (perhaps to protect against water seepage). Thus, even after the superstructure had decayed, the house footprints were visible. Unfortunately, many of the houses built outside the city centers were in prime agricultural lands, and the majority of them have been plowed away over the last three centuries.

Each house or group of houses had storage facilities, sometimes sub-ground pits and in other cases above-ground granaries. Houses were detached, and in larger towns, they sometimes surrounded or were near a large plaza that was likely meant for public gatherings. In the smaller settlements, homesteads were more distant from one another; people lived near their fields rather than in "town." Some communities had "sweat lodges" where heated rocks or hearths created a type of sauna; such structures could hold only a few people and may have served as a meeting place for ritual or political purposes. Other structures making up Mississippian towns and communities were T- and L-shaped buildings that could have been residential but may also have served more ritual purposes (Alt 2006; Emerson 1997a; Mehrer 1995). These structures are often found on flat-topped mounds or in prime residential areas. Ethnographic and archaeological work suggest that they may have been lodges reserved for high-status community members or visitors and that important religious items, used during public ceremonies, may have been kept in these specialized structures (Alt 2006).

While the commoner population may have in part consisted of immigrants and disparate groups, kin relationships were at the heart of the Mississippian social structure. Ethnographic work in the region suggests that unilineal descent systems (patrilineal or matrilineal) were the norm in Mississippian culture. In such systems, marriage relationships and post-marriage living arrangements are very important. Evidence suggests that the Mississippian residence pattern may have been "matrilocal" in that after marriage the groom left his own house to dwell in the house of his wife (which would therefore be the house of the wife's mother as well) (Muller 1997: 191–92). Such a residence pattern would keep ownership of wealth, property, and more ideological concerns, such as status and reputation, within the household throughout the generations. Societies in which social positioning and reputation of a kin group is of critical importance take great care in making marriage decisions. Marrying a son or daughter to someone outside the extended family or clan might open the door to a loss of wealth or social positioning to another family. On the other hand, a shrewd marriage alliance might ally two powerful families who could then cooperate in competitions to raise the status levels of their kin leaders in the Mississippian system. Who you were in Mississippian society was defined by who your family was and its position within the societal ranks.

Kin-related peoples formed corporate groups who worked together for the good of all and for the elevation of their kin leaders to increasingly higher levels of Mississippian society. Family members may not have all lived in the same community. For instance, each of the settlements near Cahokia, such as East St. Louis, perhaps part of a vast Cahokian center, was home to several thousand people (Emerson 2002; Pauketat 1998). Also nearby were the BBB Motor and Sponemann sites, and within 24 kilometers of Cahokia were other mound groups, such as the Mitchell Mounds and the Pulcher Mounds, each with at least ten mounds within the community (Bowne 2013). All of these may have been part of an extended Cahokia center. Kin groups possibly lived in these surrounding communities, helping to facilitate trade in raw resources, finished products, and subsistence goods. Kin-based cooperative groups engaged in agricultural endeavors outside the city centers and in surrounding communities may have contributed to a lineage leader's storehouse, not only supporting the leader and his or her bid to compete with other elites, but also to ensure the leader's ability to support the corporate kin group if food shortages were incurred (Milner 2004: 155).

Cahokia seems to have been a center of trade, with the majority of valuable raw resources directed into the hands of elites and leaders. These resources were then probably distributed to kin members who could turn them into valuable crafts and return them to lineage leaders for display and eventual inclusion in burial. Smaller amounts of these materials and crafts remained in the lower echelons of the corporate kin groups, used for the same purposes. Thus, the more highly placed the lineage leader, the greater the number of valuable craft items possessed by the corporate kin group. The same can be said for the distribution of food; the larger, more successful, and higher-ranking kin groups likely hosted more feasting events, which not only served to redistribute resources within the corporate group but also served to signal success of that group to the community and to competitive leaders. Skeletal analysis of both commoners and elites suggests that access to subsistence resources was not delineated by rank; elites buried in the city mounds and commoners in the most basic graves had similar access to maize and other foods and similar levels of disease and failings of health. This would suggest that the type of redistributive system described earlier worked well for all members of a corporate kin group.

Social ranking is illustrated by the size and location of houses and their contents and by manner of burial. Spectacular mound burials with substantial mortuary offerings and rituals belonged to elites. Mound burials with fewer goods and less labor invested in the interment may have been members of the same kin group but of lower-ranking status. The vast majority of Mississippians were buried in cemeteries or individual graves near their houses or settlements, often with no or only a very few burial goods such as ceramics or utilitarian tools. Occasionally, more exotic items such as marine shell beads, items of mica or crystal, or other materials were found in cemetery burials. These individuals may have been local leaders or perhaps the artisans who crafted these goods, keeping some as payment for their work (Milner 2004: 158). A recent study offered insight into Mississippian considerations of "personhood"; children younger than eight years of age sometimes received a few shell beads or pendants or antler bracelets in their burials (Strezewski 2009). Older children and adults received the types of goods noted earlier. It is possible that, around age eight, children advanced from "child" to "young adult" status, perhaps in a rite of passage recognized by the community (Strezewski 2009). The gifts buried with the young children may have had special significance as protective devices for the non-initiated in the afterlife.

Warfare and Defense

It is clear that Cahokia did not head up a "military state" as there is little evidence for a standing army or vast war machine. In fact, some argue that the defense of the Cahokian center was not a priority for Mississippian leaders. Certainly the city's suburbs, as well as the many villages and towns scattered across the American Bottom, would have been at tremendous risk if constant warfare was a significant factor in the Mississippian system. Nonetheless, some evidence does point to at least a modicum of effort dedicated to defense systems and the presence of conflict.

One piece of evidence is the substantial palisade that surrounded the city center (the palisade surrounded three sides and a steep riverbank delineated the fourth side). As noted earlier, an enormous labor force was necessary to construct and then maintain it. Thus, those responsible for its creation must have felt there was a critical need for such a wall, complete with guard towers. Though the vast majority of Cahokians lived outside the palisade walls, the large open plazas surrounding Monks Mound might have served as a refuge for residents from the countryside during times of attack. However, if the threat was internal, such as civil unrest, then inviting the non-elites in might not have been the norm. An alternative to the use for defensive purposes is that the wall might have been built to keep non-elite Cahokians out of the city center, especially during important rituals and other ceremonies.

A second possible indicator of conflict comes from the nearby East St. Louis site, possibly a part of a larger Cahokian center. The East St. Louis site began to grow in 1050 CE in the Stirling-Lohmann phases contemporaneously with Cahokia. East St. Louis eventually encompassed at least 50 mounds, a central plaza, many public and residential buildings, and possible "sun circles" (Galloy 2011). In the late 12th century, however, much of the East St. Louis site was burned to the ground (Pauketat et al. 2013); it is at this time that the Cahokian palisade was completed. Whether the building of the wall and the razing of East St. Louis are evidence of increasing warfare or civil unrest is unclear, but the timing of the two events is suggestive. Cahokia is not the only Mississippian site that was fortified. Excavations have revealed that other small and medium-sized settlements also featured wooden palisades surrounding a substantial portion of the settlement (Brennan 2010; Emerson 2007; Iseminger 2010; Milner 1999, 2004). The overall evidence suggests that Mississippian residents perceived either external or internal threat (the latter perhaps resulting from the varied ethnic mix of the Mississippian polity) and leaders took protective action.

Burials in Mound 72 as well as elsewhere may point to conflict as an integral aspect of ancient Mississippian society. The sacrificial victims described earlier may have been residents of Cahokia or outlying communities or acquired through regional conflict. The males, perhaps prisoners of war, and women, perhaps taken from homes vanquished, may have endured a final fate as sacrificial offerings. A particular set of interments in Mound 72 is worth noting. In one pit, nearly 40 individuals, both men and women, appear to have met a violent end. Some were partially or fully beheaded, some had arrows embedded in their bodies, and a few appear to have been buried alive though perhaps in a wounded state (Young and Fowler 2000). To many, this burial points more to an internal uprising than to external attack. Conflicts would have provided Cahokian and Mississippian elites the justification for managing civil behavior, controlling access to critical areas, and maintaining a significant defensive system. Thus, while constant warfare may not have been a paramount concern of ancient Mississippians, preparation for even minimally violent incursions may have provided a platform for an increased concentration of social, political, and economic control into the hands of the elites and leaders.

Trade and Economy

Mississippians participated in a vast trade network akin to that of the Hopewell and Adena from centuries before. Marine shells from both the Gulf of Mexico and Atlantic sources appeared in mortuary offerings. Copper, mainly from Michigan, was used for ornaments and jewelry; sheets of mica from beyond the American Bottom region were used to create images of human heads, hands, and other forms; cherts from Illinois were used to make various types of tools and weapons, while other types of stones such as quartz crystals and galena were acquired for various purposes and a variety of ceramics may have held contents desirable to the Cahokians (Milner 1991). Another important trade item was salt, coming from various places within and surrounding the American Bottom center (Muller 1997: 308–32). Evidence suggests that these items, either as finished products or raw resources, arrived first at Cahokia, which served as a "gateway" city for the trade of these items in the American Bottom region (Kelly 1991). The majority of these goods, especially the finer exotic materials, were concentrated in the hands of the elites to be used in their homes and in mortuary contexts.

This trade and exchange pattern—raw resources transported to a center where they were fashioned into luxury goods and sometimes into utilitarian items—has led some to speculate that the Mississippian complex should be viewed as a "world system" (King and Freer 1995; Peregrine 1992, 1995). In a world system, an economically powerful core dominates a weak periphery and extracts desirable raw resources; the periphery becomes dependent on the core for the provision of crucial goods, protection, and leadership. In a world system structure, the elites in the cores hold significant power over the economy and the distribution of goods. Some of the civilizations in other chapters in this book, such as the ancient Uruk system of Mesopotamia, the Mesoamerican Aztec system, and ancient Egypt, have been described as vast world systems by a number of scholars.

Rather than comfortably fitting into a world systems model, the exchange system in the ancient Mississippian world is more frequently described as "down-the-line" (Milner 1991; Muller 1997), suggesting there was more of an equal exchange between those existing at each end of the trade route. A majority of items in Cahokian contexts were made from local goods, including specialized items such as stone pipes and figurines (Emerson et al. 2003; Emerson and Hughes 2000; Pauketat and Emerson 1997). Goods may simply have been transported from settlement to settlement, with each taking quantities according to need and supplying local products of interest to those moving the goods. Nonetheless, non-local and regionally derived goods arrived at Cahokia and were immediately delivered into the control of elites for distribution to designated recipients and craft-workers.

Understanding how crafts were produced in Cahokia and the other centers has been one of the significant challenges of archaeological efforts at these sites. Craft production does not appear to have been centralized, nor located in a craft quarter within the communities. Households were largely self-sufficient regarding the production of subsistence goods (Muller 1997; Pauketat 2004). Outside the city center, people lived near their fields and produced sufficient quantities of food to support the household as well as a surplus that was traded to the elites living in the city centers. The production of specialized crafts may have functioned on a similar pattern.

Mississippian communities were likely organized in corporate groups consisting of kin-related households. At the head of a corporate kin group was an elite or leader; the status of that individual or small group/family may have dictated access to incoming supplies of raw resources of desirable materials. Various households within the corporate group may have then been tasked with producing various crafts, some kept within the household and others, perhaps most, returned to the corporate leaders (Pauketat 1997, 2013; Wilson, Marcoux, and Koldehoff 2006). This craft organization system allowed corporate groups, and their leaders, to engage in competition for status positions and greater levels of power in the Mississippian system.

As population and demand for non-utilitarian items increased, there was a greater specialization in the most prestigious crafts (Wilson, Marcoux and Koldehoff 2006; Yerkes 1989). Mica and copper objects, and the shell beads and disks found in so many burials, may have been produced in specific kin-related households who were supported by their Cahokia kin-based elites but located in outlying communities (Kelly 2006). After 1200 CE, there was even greater production of specialized crafts for the highest-ranking elites (Trubitt 2000). By this time, craft production of specialized luxury crafts may have transitioned from wide-scale production at many households of differing statuses to increasingly fewer households likely serving higher-status households. This would suggest an increase in elite control of both acquisition and distribution of desirable raw resources within the Mississippian system, though the production of subsistence items in the countryside was still largely in the hands of the Mississippian commoners. Thus, the Mississippian political economic structure was not the single linchpin in the elite and leadership power structure.

Mississippian Religion

It is in religion where the main source of elite power lay in Mississippian culture. The mound building and mortuary activities were only one part of what was clearly a vast and deeply embedded cosmology that was found not only in the construction of earthworks, but in the very houses in which Mississippians lived and the objects they used every day. While major rituals and ceremonies were likely carried out at the temple centers, religion and ritual was certainly alive and well in the more outlying communities as well. The numerous T- and L-shaped buildings found in Mississippian towns and villages may have been the seat from which Mississippian religious elites conducted local ceremonies on a regular basis (Emerson 1997a, 1997b). These religious practitioners may have been local or may have been sent from the Mississippian centers to officiate, and thus effectively control, religious practice among the commoners (Emerson, Alt and Pauketat 2008; Emerson and Pauketat 2008). Mississippian leaders would have had two avenues for maintaining religious unity and, by extension, control of the larger population: through scheduling important ceremonies at the larger temple centers and through the dispersion of sanctioned religious elites to conduct local ceremonies according to the auspices of the center. Through these, the entire Mississippian population was unified in a religious belief system within which leaders, likely located at Cahokia, sat at the helm (Alt 2010b).

Cahokia appears to have been constructed with Mississippian cosmology in mind. Evidence suggests that Mississippians believed in a four-sided and four-quartered universe that was simultaneously vertically layered with an upper and lower level (Emerson 1997b). The four-sided, or four-cornered, aspect of the cosmology, likely based on the cardinal directions, was represented by massive monuments such as Monks Mound and the platform mounds upon which residences rested. The quadripartite aspect on the horizontal axis was delineated by tracing lines from one ridge-topped mound to another, creating east-west and north-south axes that intersect at critical human-made features at Cahokia such as Monks Mound and Mound 72. The multilayered cosmos may have been physically represented using the mounds as well. The Cahokian residences on the platform mounds may have represented the upper layer of the universe and those living at ground level the lower layer (Emerson 1997a; Kelly 1997). An even lower level may have been represented by those in the countryside, in the American Bottom lands, where farming allowed them to deal with the earth and that which lay beneath. The cosmology was therefore represented visually and physically, not only at the Cahokian center with its platform mounds, but across the countryside where commoners farmed their lands and smaller religious centers duplicated the vertical and horizontal cosmological planes (Emerson, Alt and Pauketat 2008; Emerson and Pauketat 2008; Pauketat 2013).

Agriculture and fertility were likely at the center of Mississippian ritual practice. With the development of the smaller and larger temple centers by 1050 CE, ritual practice, which may have largely centered on fertility rites, had been removed from the countryside and centered at temples where religious practitioners, perhaps consisting of Mississippian elites, could carry out the critical ceremonies for the benefit of all people. Several categories of material culture demonstrate that agricultural fertility was of critical importance to Mississippians. Most notable are the figurines that have been recovered from various sites around Cahokia. These figurines typically feature a female engaged in agricultural work or associated with agricultural symbols (Figure 11.11). The majority of provenienced figurines have been found at the ritual centers at the BBB Motor and Sponemann ceremonial sites not far from Cahokia, and recently, a figurine was recovered at the East St. Louis site (Emerson and Boles 2010). The prevailing opinion is that the figurines represent a female deity or deities associated with the agricultural cycle or possibly represent the shamans responsible for healing and ritual activities (Emerson 1997a, 2003). The associated imagery, including plants coiling around the figures, agricultural tools grasped in their hands, snakes (deeply associated with fertility in Native American religions), grinding implements placed before them, and other themes found in these stone figurines, adds to the interpretation that they are related to agricultural productivity. Some of this same imagery is found on specialized Mississippian ceramics also found at the BBB Motor and Sponemann ceremonial centers. These ceramics may have featured in important rituals, conducted by elites on behalf of both elite and commoner, as "rites of intensification" to ensure agricultural fertility and successful harvests (Pauketat and Emerson 1991) (see Box 11.5). The Cahokian carved pipes may have been another item used by shamans in religious practice (see Box 11.3), serving as a critical element in shamanic paraphernalia that allowed them to carry out their critical duties (Emerson 2003).

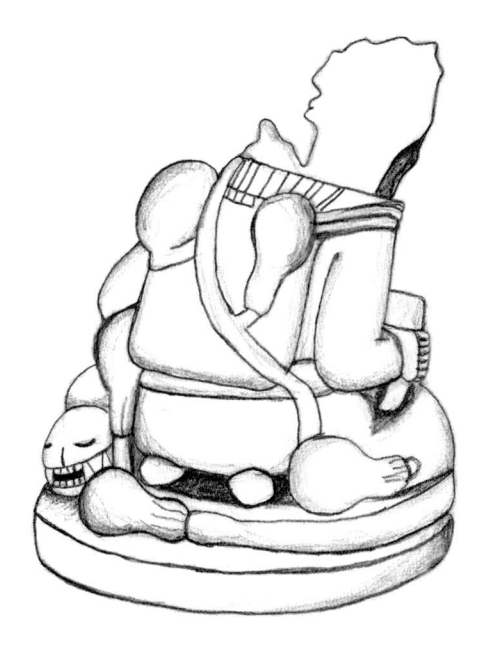

FIGURE 11.11 Example of the Type of Cahokian Figurines That Show Female Figure and Agricultural Symbols; This Example, Known as the "Birger Figurine," Shows a Woman Kneeling on a Serpent and Using a Hoe

Source: R. Jennison

BOX 11.5 RITUAL BLACK DRINK AT CAHOKIA

Recent studies of organic residue from ceramic beakers found at Cahokia have revealed that residents in the city center and surrounding regions consumed a drink made from a species of holly, creating a caffeinated beverage that archaeologists have dubbed "Black Drink" (Crown et al. 2012). Black Drink is made by parching holly leaves and then boiling them into a caffeinated froth, which is then consumed. Ethnographic accounts of more recent Native American cultures in the southern region of the U.S. describe this drink as typically consumed by men undertaking ritual activities or engaging in political councils and negotiations; it was consumed prior to the commencement of war-related activities. The holly leaves necessary for the making of Black Drink at Cahokia were imported from sources in the southeastern U.S. At Cahokia, where we have the earliest occurrence of Black Drink, it was likely consumed during important ritual events.

Mississippian mortuary cult may have included the element of ancestor veneration. The numerous burials in Mississippian mounds, some with grave goods and many without, suggest that a belief in the afterlife was prominent in this society. Evidence of feasting in the Cahokian city center (Pauketat et al. 2002) indicates that important rituals, including interment in the mounds (or perhaps in the charnel houses), were accompanied by the ritual consumption, and deposition, of food. The "beaded burial" in Mound 72 may have been meant to associate the individual with a possible

Mississippian deity usually shown on pottery as a human figure wearing falcon-like garb and carrying items associated with warfare (Brown 2007). Possibly the leader interred in the "beaded burial" tomb was meant to join this deity in the next realm and aid in the protection of the Mississippian peoples remaining on the human plane. The female sacrifices accompanying the Mound 72 burials may not have been related to war but rather to associate those interred with a female deity such as those depicted by the figurines noted earlier (Pauketat 2013: 103–104). Most Mississippians were not buried in earthen mounds; this labor-intensive burial method was reserved for those of higher status (Emerson, Hargrave and Hedman 2003) or those who had gained prominence in Mississippian society (perhaps as artisans or warriors). Evidence suggests that ancestors, especially from the elite lineages, were considered critical liaisons with the supernatural world and were tasked with continued protection of, and assistance to, the Mississippian elites and commoners who celebrated them.

Prior to the rise of Cahokia and the Mississippian centers, religion and ritual seem to have been primarily in the hands of individual homesteaders; household rites that were meant to ensure successful hunts and harvests and to honor the ancestors may have been at the center of such rituals. As temple towns and ceremonial centers emerged, daily ritual was first moved to "nodal households" in smaller settlements and eventually centralized in the larger temple towns and at Cahokia itself. Religious specialists charged with healing or leading rituals may have resided in the nodal households and likely could be found in the Cahokian center (Emerson 2003). Agricultural fertility ritual may have become the "state cult," with important ceremonies carried out at regional ceremonial centers by elites and leaders as proxies for the commoners who traveled to participate. Powerful ancestors of the elites, buried in the easily visible mounds, may have played a crucial role in these ceremonies, negotiating the intricacies of the dual-layered, quadrilateral cosmos and directing the attention of Mississippian deities to the agricultural cycle. It is in the religious realm that Mississippian elites and leaders likely held the greatest concentration of power in this North American system.

Mississippian Sociopolitical Structure

The Mississippian system has been described as a "complex chiefdom" (Beck 2006; Cobb 2003; Emerson 1997a; Milner 1998; Payne 2006), having exploded onto the scene with a rapid increase in population roughly 1,000 years ago. A "simple chiefdom" has one paramount leader while a complex chiefdom has several levels of leadership and also "at least an incipient form of class structure" (Cobb 2003: 66). The foregoing discussion elevates the Mississippian system, at the very least, to the level of a very complex chiefdom. Some employ the term "paramount" chiefdom (Hudson et al. 1985) to capture the utter complexity of the Mississippian system. The struggle regarding just how to describe, some might say "pigeon-hole," the Mississippian system, stems from the fact that it is not easily categorized. Was it a complex or paramount chiefdom, was it a state, was it both, or neither?

Recently, Stephen Lekson addressed the issue of the "complexity factor" of ancient Mississippian polities, as well as the system that existed roughly contemporaneously in the American southwest at Chaco Canyon (see Chapter 4). He argues that North American archaeologists wrestle with interpreting these complex systems as "states" because "We know, as a bedrock certainty, that nothing like a state ever happened north of Mexico, so it's pointless to think about it," and thus, "We can't even *pretend* they were states"; he goes on to note, however, that "perhaps *they* thought about it: those ambitious pretenders at Chaco" and at Cahokia (2010: 179). In other words, it is not the Mississippian system and its moveable parts that prevent the word "state" from being applied to this complex polity, but the archaeologists themselves who cannot bring themselves to apply it. Robert Chapman, who wrote an entire book on "complexity" (2003), does not work on midcontinental systems as a specialty. He notes, "The consensus (as far as an outsider can perceive) seems to be that

Cahokia was at the 'complex' end of a chiefdom society, just short of, or perhaps in the process of evolving into, a state," and he goes on to note, as have others (e.g., Pauketat 2004), that had such monumental earthworks, trade systems, centralized religion, and other Mississippian characteristics been discovered in Egypt, the Middle East, or east Asia, applying the word "state" would have been far less problematic (Chapman 2010: 205–6). Finally, Norman Yoffee, also well known for his work on the subject of "complexity" (e.g., Yoffee 1997, 2005, 2010), notes, along with colleagues, that "If you can argue whether a society is a state or isn't, then it isn't" (Yoffee, Fish, and Milner 1999: 262). They do not insist that the Mississippian system, and others like it, *wasn't* a state, but rather that archaeologists should not get caught up in trying to "type" ancient systems and rather should just explain how they worked (Yoffee 2010); this is a view also expressed by Pauketat (2007). Nonetheless, the archaeological nature is to "categorize" and thus the effort to do so, including by the two archaeologists writing this book, continues!

Contrary to the views expressed by Lekson, there are some archaeologists who have confidently labeled the Mississippian system as a type of state-level society based on elements at Cahokia and the surrounding region (Fowler 1975; Kehoe 1998; O'Brien 1989, 1991). The clear ability to control labor, the building of monumental structures, the construction of impressive defense systems, and a significant religious complex and ritual cycle are all elements that led to the description of Cahokia as the leading city in a midcontinental state system, even a world system (King and Freer 1995; Peregrine 1992, 1995).

Finally, some scholars have described the Mississippian polity, with the main center at Cahokia but also with outlying centers such as East St. Louis, as a "theater state" (Dalan et al. 2003; Holt 2009; Kehoe 2002; and see Brown 2006). A theater state, as described by Clifford Geertz (1980), is one in which elites and leaders organize spectacular events that serve not only to demonstrate their wealth and importance, but also to essentially "entertain" the populace and create a unity of community. Events such as the erection of the palisade walls, rituals at Monks Mound, and certainly the burials, along with human sacrifice at locations such as Mound 72, may have been public spectacles that drew people in and made them feel a "part of the system," even proud of their elites who could command such power and carry out such feats. The populace must have had a profound belief in the ideology expounded by the elites for them to not only attend these ceremonies but also participate in endeavors such as the construction of Monks Mound or the erection of palisade or woodhenge monuments.

So was Cahokia at the center of a state, a chiefdom, both, neither, or something else? The answer, according to some of the major voices in the field, may be the last one. In a number of publications, Thomas Emerson and Timothy Pauketat (e.g., Emerson 1997a; Pauketat 1994, 1997, 2002, 2004) have argued that the Mississippian polity was both state and complex chiefdom, shifting in and out of these "categories" both in terms of vacillations in elite power and also in the sheer complexity, or lack thereof, in the elements that define "stateness." At times, Cahokia was the center of a state, with elites controlling trade and craft production, organizing labor for major building projects, leading major rituals and ceremonies, protecting against real or imagined attack, and competing with each other for access to higher-status positions. Pauketat describes the meteoric rise of Cahokia as follows (2000: 120):

> The pre-Mississippian village-level chiefdoms gave way, within a span of no more than a few decades (and perhaps considerably less), to a hypercentralized and regionally integrated Cahokian polity within the eleventh century. The political, social, and demographic changes evident in the archaeological record are so pronounced as to make unlikely anything but an abrupt and radical consolidation of the regional population under the aegis of a Cahokian capital.

At other times, however, the "hypercentralization" was not in strong operation, and "stateness" was ephemeral. Craft production was accomplished at the household level, defense was of little concern, building projects were at a standstill, and elites went about their private business in their large houses, making no impression on anyone but themselves. At such times, authority lay in the hands of lineage elders, some of whom may have been Mississippian elites, but the daily operations of the Mississippian system at these times fit far better into the category of "chiefdom" than "state." The attempt to define the nature of the Mississippian system will go on, but at present, it is clear that this polity was incredibly complex and that Mississippians themselves *wanted* their system to succeed, to operate for the benefit of themselves and their leaders (Pauketat 1994, 2004), and to continue on as long as possible.

The End of Cahokia

After the end of the Stirling phase (ca. 1200) and into the Moorehead and then the Sand Prairie phases (1200–1400 CE), there were substantial changes at Cahokia and in the countryside. Construction of the earthen mounds at Cahokia and elsewhere tailed off as did the construction of the T- and L-shaped structures at both the centers and in the countryside. Also decreasing was the presence of raw and finished goods coming from great distances, suggesting trade connections were diminishing. The temple centers, including Cahokia, began to empty out; Cahokia was essentially abandoned by the mid-1300s. In general, many believe that by the beginning of the 14th century, the Mississippian system was all but gone in the American Bottom. Other mound centers to the south were still a going concern, and in fact, much of what archaeologists consider "Mississippian culture" shifted to the southeastern region of the continent. Here the Southern Ceremonial Complex emerged by ca. 1200 CE and was still to be found in major centers such as Moundville in Alabama and Etowah in Georgia upon Spanish arrival four centuries later. Ideologies, and perhaps populations, from the Mississippian system may have traveled east and south from their midcontinental homelands.

Explaining the Cahokian collapse is as difficult as defining whether the system was a chiefdom or a state. It was likely a combination of factors that coalesced at once. Sometime after 1200, mound construction ceased at Cahokia, and people began to leave residential areas as well. Cahokia may have become more of a "ritual center" than a functioning city in the 13th century, a destination place to celebrate major and perhaps minor events (Iseminger 2010). Also, the fire at East St. Louis and the strengthening of palisades around Cahokia and elsewhere at this time may signal increasingly violent interaction or internal social unrest within the region.

Dissatisfaction with Cahokian leadership may have stemmed from problems with subsistence supplies resulting from climate change and even natural disasters. During the decades in which the "Big Bang" occurred around 1050 CE, the American Bottom region experienced an extremely wet period, which likely aided agricultural production. However, by 1150 CE, the region was experiencing a series of droughts, with one of the worst taking place between 1150 and 1200 CE (Benson, Pauketat, and Cook 2009). Adding insult to injury, recent evidence suggests that the American Bottom experienced massive flooding around 1200 CE that may have heavily damaged Cahokia and the surrounding countryside (Munoz et al. 2014). If Mississippians depended on their leaders to ritually ensure bountiful harvests and stable livelihoods, then faith in those leaders must have eroded as the droughts began in the 12th century. The flood may have been the last straw. Residents possibly insisted on new leadership; perhaps different ethnic or lineage groups sought to take over so that agricultural stability could be regained. This may well have created social unrest, giving outside hostile forces the opportunity to attack. However, even the new leaders, if they were installed, seemed unable to right the listing ship of Cahokia, and the city became a ghost town by the mid-14th century.

In many ways, the collapse of the Mississippian system with its center at Cahokia may be laid at the doors of its own leadership system; as elites gathered religious and ritual power into their own hands, carrying out ceremonies on behalf of the people, they inherently guaranteed the health, well-being, and success of those people. Agricultural surplus, successful trade, peace, and stability were the responsibility of the leaders and their ancestors, buried with such pomp and circumstance in major mounds constructed by, likely, the very commoners who expected their lives to be prosperous and stable. As this religious "contract" began to collapse, so did the people's belief in the power of their leaders. People began to abandon the city and ceased to support the leadership, breaking out on their own to seek more stable subsistence strategies for their own families. The Mississippian system in the American Bottom had come to an end.

Conclusion

The Mississippian system is interesting for a number of reasons, not least of which is that it is one of the first complex societies in pre-colonial North America. Of even greater import, perhaps, is that it, in many ways, defies the norms of what archaeologists often consider critical elements of "state"-level society. Mississippian leaders did have significant control over trade and economic pursuits and may have emplaced themselves at the helm of a state cult. However, these are only two of the many facets that are embedded in the types of state-level societies discussed in other chapters of this book. The Mississippians, perhaps like the Harappan civilization (Chapter 8), serve as reminders to archaeologists that there is no simple way to explain "complexity" in the ancient world.

12
ANCIENT MESOAMERICAN CULTURES

Introduction

Mesoamerica encompasses the modern nations belonging to Central America and Mexico. Over several millennia, the region saw a variety of sequential and simultaneous social and political organizations, from mobile foragers and village agriculturalists to an empire. Cycles of centralization and fragmentation suggest that periods of political integration were somewhat short-lived and fragile (Nichols and Pool 2012). Yet a remarkable shared cosmology united these varied political entities over time and space; each translated that cosmology onto its landscape, and into its political institutions, in different ways.

Geography and Chronology

The whole of Mesoamerica (Figure 12.1) covers over 2.5 million square kilometers. The modern nation of Mexico, at nearly 2 million square kilometers, comprises the majority of this territory. As a land bridge between North and South America, Mesoamerica participated in economic and cultural relationships with both territories at various points in its history, as both a provider and recipient of trade goods and influences. No less important were interactions among the various environmental and political zones within Mesoamerica, which served to carry ideas, materials, and knowledge across cultural boundaries.

Geography and Ecological Setting

Within such a vast territory is a huge diversity of environments. The central spine of Mesoamerica contains volcanic highlands, while coastal areas are dominated by tropical lowlands, many densely forested. The region lacks the major rivers and alluvial basins that dominated and produced many of the Old World cultures presented in this book, though inland valleys and lakes were important centers of settlement. While the Mesoamerican landscape tends to isolate regions from one another, producing distinctive culture areas, all of Mesoamerica shared certain cultural features, including calendrical and symbolic systems; cosmology and particular divinities; architectural types such as ballcourts, platform mounds, and pyramids; and a reliance on maize for subsistence. The main regions to be examined in this chapter are the tropical lowlands of Mexico and adjacent Central America, the Gulf Coast region, the central highlands, and the Oaxaca Valley of southwestern Mexico.

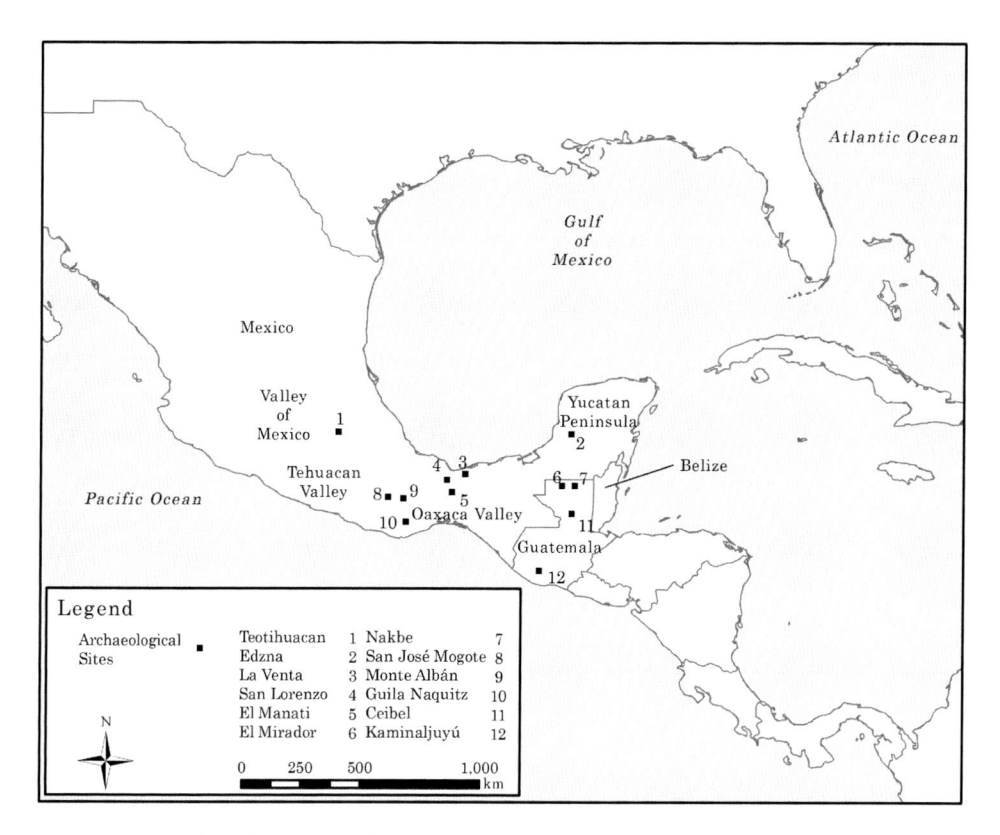

FIGURE 12.1 Map of Preclassic and Classic Period Regions and Sites Discussed in the Chapter

Source: B. Spencer

The Chronological Sequence

The first archaeological investigations of Mesoamerica explored remains of the Maya civilization of southern Mexico and its neighbors; since that time, Maya and contemporary cultures of central Mexico and the Oaxaca Valley have been considered the "Classic" civilizations of Mesoamerica (250–900 CE) (Table 12.1). By extension, the period predating the Classic Period is the Preclassic (2000 BCE–250 CE); some archaeologists prefer the term "Formative" for this period, to draw attention to the rise of social and political differentiation among the Gulf Coast Olmec, the early Maya, and the villages of the Oaxaca Valley. Before the development of large centers, however, residents in the Archaic Period (ca. 10,000–2000 BCE) in Mesoamerica introduced agriculture in sedentary villages. Postdating the Classic Period is the Postclassic (900–1521 CE); at its conclusion, the Aztec Empire was defeated by the Spanish army and its local allies.

Archaic Mesoamerica: Sedentism and Introduction of Maize Agriculture

Recent decades have seen progress in the discovery and analysis of sites and developments predating the Preclassic; this period, between migration and colonization, after 10,000 BCE, and the origins of ranked societies at around 2000 BCE, is the Archaic Period. Foraging groups roamed Central America and Mexico until around 8000 BCE, at which point, temperatures began to rise and new

TABLE 12.1 Chronological Periods and Sites Discussed in Chapter 12

Dates	Period	Sites Discussed in Chapter	Cultural Horizons
ca. 10,000–2000 BCE	**Archaic Period**	Guila Naquitz	Foraging groups; domestication of maize and other plant species
ca. 2000 BCE–250 CE	**Preclassic/Formative Period** (Olmecs; Oaxaca Valley sites)	San Lorenzo, La Venta, El Manatí; San José Mogote, Monte Albán; Nakbe, Ceibal, Kaminaljuyú, Edzna, El Mirador	Emergence of ranked society; monumental construction of platforms and pyramids; formalized ritual activities; colossal artwork
ca. 250–900 CE	**Classic Period** (Zapotecs; Teotihuacan; Maya)	Monte Albán; Teotihuacan; Yaxchilan; Bonampak; Tikal; Copan; Palenque	Urbanism; monumental buildings with ritual and administrative functions; writing; variety of political organizational forms
ca. 900–1521 CE	**Postclassic Period** (Postclassic Maya; Toltecs; Aztecs)	Uxmal, Cobá; Chichen Itza, Mayapan; Tula; Tenochtitlan	Territorial states; empire

plant species arose (Acosta Ochoa 2012; Flannery and Marcus 2012: 139). Evidence for human adaptation to these circumstances comes from several cave sites in central and southwestern Mexico. At Guila Naquitz in the Oaxaca region, groundstone tools dating around 9000 BCE indicate that people were processing seeds and/or nuts regularly.

The earliest domesticates in Mexico were gourds, apparently used for containers rather than food; in the Oaxaca Valley, these date to 8000 BCE (Piperno and Smith 2012). A number of sites dating 7000 to 5000 BCE yield evidence for domesticated plants, including squash, avocado, cotton, chili, and amaranth (Barker 2006: 251). It is important to note that none of these are cereals or high in carbohydrates, in contrast to the early domesticates in much of the rest of the world. In the Tehuacan Valley, the pollen of wild maize (*teosinte*) has been recognized in archaeological contexts; in its wild form, a maize cob is quite small, and the individual seeds (kernels) are difficult to remove from the cob. The second stage of domestication in Mexico, after 5000 BCE, was the hybridization of maize to produce a domesticated form with larger cobs and kernels, and the domestication of beans and edible squash; these were introduced from the tropical lowlands of southwestern Mexico. Early experiments and experience with agriculture also brought new ritual behaviors, intended to enhance fertility (Flannery and Marcus 2012: 138, 141). From 4000 to 2000 BCE, maize agriculture spread, allowing for the establishment of sedentary villages in various regions of Mesoamerica; this set the stage for the growth of complexity in the Preclassic Period (Evans 2012).

Pre-State Cultures: Preclassic Mesoamerica and the Rise of Ranking

The Preclassic or Formative Period (2000 BCE–250 CE) was the period of the first Mesoamerican chiefly or ranked societies, where political leaders emerged, their powers based on ranking within and between lineages. The earliest differentiation known archaeologically took place among the Olmecs of the Gulf Coast region of Mexico, reaching to the Tuxtla Mountains. The ancient name and language of the Olmec are unknown; they are characterized by widespread small settlements and some large regional centers. Monumental architecture and artwork at major and minor sites focused attention onto leaders and their special relationships to the gods. At the same time, signs of incipient social differentiation also arose in the Oaxaca Valley in the southwest of Mexico.

Olmecs

Two stages of Olmec culture are illustrated by the two largest centers: San Lorenzo (1500–1000 BCE) and La Venta (1000–400 BCE), belonging to the Early and Middle Preclassic Period, respectively. It is unlikely that either site was the center of a regional state; most Olmec sites were small, with at most a single monumental building (Manzanilla 2001). During the San Lorenzo phase, sites were concentrated in the wetlands, while the later La Venta phase saw movement inland for better agricultural productivity, especially for maize (Arnold 2012). Both San Lorenzo and La Venta stood at the head of a three- or four-level settlement size hierarchy, suggesting some degree of political integration and economic coordination as early as the 2nd millennium BCE (Pool 2012).

At 700 hectares, San Lorenzo covers an enormous area for such an early settlement. The wetland area it occupied had to be raised—a large-scale expenditure of labor—with artificial mounds and platforms, in order to be occupied; nearby hillsides were farmed. In this environment, water control (both drainage and provision of drinking water) required constant attention and maintenance. The central part of the site includes a complex of 13 mounds arranged around an interior plaza; the tallest mound was over 6 meters in height and 25 meters long (de la Fuente 1981). This monumental construction was accompanied by massive sculpture that depicted powerful individuals.

Five hundred years after San Lorenzo was built, La Venta arose in a more inland location. Its central area was more extensive than San Lorenzo's, with several plazas arrayed in a row, containing 80 monuments, and more "complexes" beyond them along the same central ridge (Figure 12.2a). At the northern end, Complex A contains two courtyards with long platforms surrounding them.

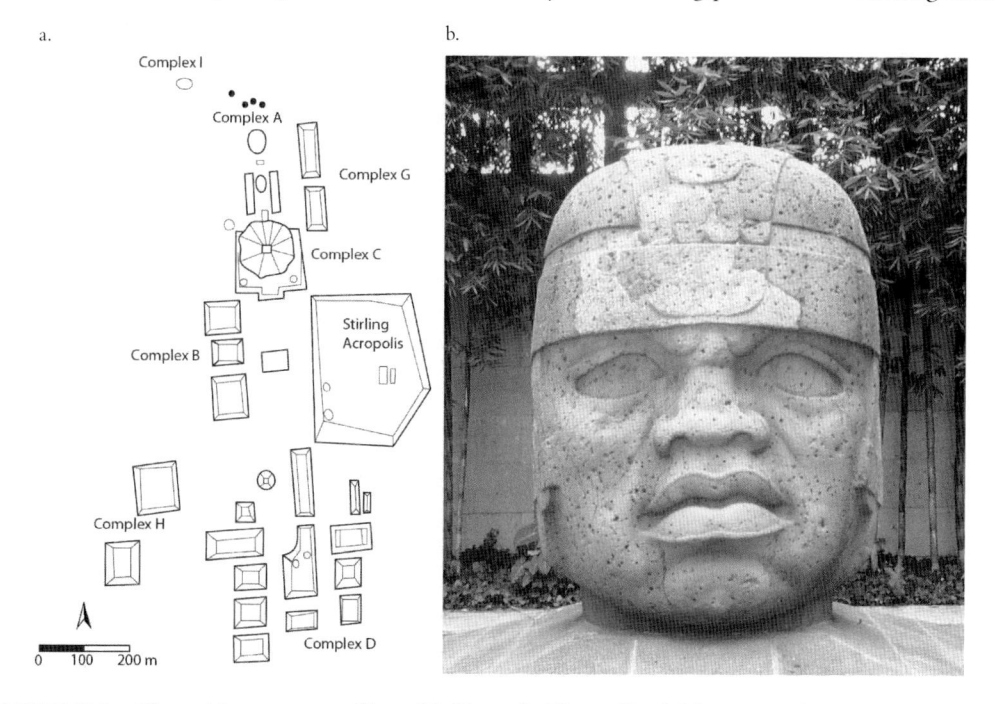

FIGURE 12.2 Olmec Monuments: a. Plan of La Venta; b. Olmec Head: Monument 1 From San Lorenzo, ca. 1250–900 BCE Anthropology Museum, Veracruz University, Mexico

Source: a. J.C. Ross; b. Anthropology Museum, Veracruz University, Mexico (Werner Forman / Art Resource, NY)

A series of underground pavements made up of serpentine blocks depicts anthropoid masks; the total weight of the serpentine is estimated at over 100 tons for each mask (Grove and Gillespie 1992). More than 50 caches of figurines and other objects were arranged on and around the masks. A burial with a frame of basalt columns and an empty sandstone sarcophagus was located within the complex (Flannery and Marcus 2012: 330); the amount of labor expended on the burial, as well as its location, suggest that the occupant was of high rank. Complex C, just south of A, contained a pyramid with a round base, perhaps imitating a mountain, while Complex B, further south again, had nine smaller mounds. The elaboration of the architecture at the site, and its sheer monumentality, indicate significant labor expenditure, joined to ritual expression and landscape modification (Diehl 1981).

Monumental architecture at the two Olmec centers was accompanied by similarly colossal artwork. A major feature of Olmec art was the production of huge stone (basalt) male heads, each made from a block 20 to 25 tons in weight (Figure 12.2b). No two were alike in expression or headgear. Ten of these stood at San Lorenzo, and four at La Venta. Other Olmec sites supply an additional three examples. In some cases, the heads were intentionally laid horizontally, damaged, and buried. Also found in the main Olmec centers were basalt "altars": rectangular slabs that depict a kneeling figure emerging from a cave, sometimes holding a baby, or attached to other figures by ropes. The dimensions and placement of these objects have prompted the suggestion that they functioned as thrones; the depictions therefore referred to the ruler and his connection to divine and ancestral forces. The basalt used for the heads and thrones came from a source 60 kilometers from San Lorenzo and 120 kilometers from La Venta (Grove and Gillespie 1992). They may have been floated on rafts downriver and through the wetlands.

The non-local stones and monumentalism of these works suggest that a centralized authority commissioned them. The individualized headgear on the colossal heads may indicate particular roles that these men filled (Gillespie 1999). On the thrones, the representations portray and embody a connection between the ruler and the gods, with prisoners presumably captured in war (Coe 1989). Other Olmec statuary depicts a range of divinities and mythological actions (Grove 1999). At a smaller scale, rulers were also represented as ballplayers, a precedent for later Mesoamerican societies (Bradley 2001) (see Box 12.1). The colossal artwork, found at both San Lorenzo and La Venta and at secondary population centers, underwent a "decommissioning" process, defaced or destroyed in various ways. Portrait heads were largely buried, while thrones were badly mutilated, perhaps at the death of the leader or user (Grove 1981). In such cases, the destruction might also imply the end of a particular dynasty's rule, as the thrones sometimes celebrated ancestral connections.

BOX 12.1 THE MESOAMERICAN BALLGAME

Like many other cultures of the world, Mesoamerican societies played games; in Mesoamerica, the predominant sport was a game played with a rubber ball. The rules, techniques of play, facilities, and meanings of the Mesoamerican ballgame varied from region to region. In the Gulf Coast region, among the Olmecs and Maya, the ballgame is attested in the form of figurines and depictions of elite men and women dressed in padded costumes, rubber balls, and narrow I-shaped courts with steeply banked sides for spectators. The Olmecs and Maya both appear to have associated the game with death and resurrection, and victory had both political and religious implications (Bradley 2001). Their version of the game was played in teams, using the feet and hips to guide the ball toward a goal, somewhat like modern soccer. By contrast, the Aztecs used just the knees and buttocks in their version (Day 2001).

> At Teotihuacan, the largest and most ethnically diverse of ancient Mesoamerican sites, no ballcourt has been discovered. Instead, scholars have suggested that teams played on the main north-south street. At the Aztec capital of Tenochtitlan, a large ballcourt occupied a space near the main temple. Offerings buried in the ballcourt included rubber balls, vessels, and musical instruments, as well as evidence for the sacrifice of the losing team: human skull fragments and a flint knife (Matos Moctezuma 2001). It is likely that the ballcourt was another locale for the performance of ritual sacrifice, where the king deployed and legitimized his divine right to take human life.
>
> As a form of competition, the ballgame may have served to train future warriors and to foster community spirit. Gambling on the game appears to have been a significant side-sport, one that may have enhanced wealth and prestige of non-players. The game spread together with other items of Mesoamerican exchange; one version eventually showed up at Hohokam culture sites in the southwestern region of the United States about 1,000 years ago (Wilcox 1991).

While Olmec monumental building projects and art are most often cited in the archaeological literature, other evidence for economic and religious organization exists. The Olmec economy was mainly built on fishing and farming; the earliest sites, belonging to the Early Preclassic Period, were located in the wetlands and relied on fish and other lowland products (turtles, waterfowl, and aquatic plants) for subsistence (Cyphers and Zurita-Noguera 2012; VanDerwarker 2006). Many of the wetland sites were artificially raised and may have belonged to families and lineage groups, part of a subsistence system that continued to be largely foraging-based (Cyphers and Zurita-Noguera 2012). In the Middle Preclassic, the shift of settlement toward the uplands signals a shift in subsistence toward domesticated plants, especially maize. A commitment to agriculture turned people to a more sedentary lifestyle than previously, with self-sufficient households farming their own plots and relatively little competition or ranking beyond the political leaders (VanDerwarker 2006: 195). In the largest centers, the elites may have controlled long-distance trade relationships, which brought in exotic stone (Cyphers 1999) and which spread Olmec influence (especially artistic styles and apparent religious imagery and beliefs) as far away as the Oaxaca Valley and the Pacific coast.

A number of ritual objects and sites have been identified in Olmec territory. The site of El Manatí comprises several phases of offerings at a natural spring; this coincides with a focus on natural features on the landscape found at other Olmec religious sites. Between 1700 and 1200 BCE, three phases of offerings there included rubber balls (perhaps relating to the Mesoamerican ballgame and its life-renewing aspects) in the earliest level and wooden statues, together with infant burials and other items, in the final phase (Ortíz and Rodríguez 1999). The statues depict bald figures (perhaps babies also) with closed eyes and frowning mouths, in characteristic Olmec style. Similar in style are widespread ceramic figurines depicting babies (Blomster 2002). These have been found at some of the larger Olmec sites, especially in elite houses; their lack of sexual marking has suggested to some researchers that they symbolized and embodied spiritual forces.

Despite its widespread contacts and shared material culture elements, it is unlikely that Olmec society had a state-level political system. Signs of social ranking and political leadership are clear, but the Olmec lacked a centralized and large-scale political center or any means of integration beyond a shared belief system (Earle 1990). The similarity of the colossal heads and thrones found at La Venta, San Lorenzo, and elsewhere indicates that each was an independent center serving a small area for a limited time, probably in competition with one another. Each site had its own ruler; the basis for his power is uncertain, although trade in exotic materials may have been under his control (Pool 2012).

Only late in the Olmec Preclassic Period did writing emerge in very isolated occurrences; the script and language are as yet unknown (Houston 2004). Partly because the Olmec political system did not coordinate food production or extensive economic interactions, writing never developed into a significant administrative device.

While the two major early Olmec centers—San Lorenzo and La Venta—both declined to village size at the end of a period of dominance, the same cannot be said of Olmec culture in general. Material cultural and architectural styles in Late Preclassic centers indicate cultural continuity, which combined with the political "cycling" that defined most Mesoamerican political centers, in which cities and states regularly consolidated, expanded, and dissolved and power passed to a neighboring city or region. The possible causes of such cycling are various and include the presence of competing centers, political factionalism within a polity, and external forces like environmental change or warfare. Hierarchical Olmec political society did not collapse but adapted to new political and economic landscapes with the rise of lowland Maya polities nearby (Pool 2009).

Oaxaca Valley

Also during the Preclassic Period, another ranked society emerged in the Oaxaca Valley in southwestern Mexico. The Oaxaca Valley is a region of 2,500 square kilometers where three valleys, surrounded by hills, converge. Similar to the Gulf Coast, the earliest sedentary villages in the region were settled around 2000 BCE; during the Preclassic Period, by ca. 1200 BCE, some socioeconomic ranking had emerged, and the number of settlements began to rise. By the Middle Preclassic, ca. 700–300 BCE, contemporary to Olmec La Venta, signs of military conflict and political complexity suggest that the Oaxaca Valley was emerging as a regional polity. This process continued into the Late Preclassic, which saw a state organization develop, centered at Monte Albán (Blanton et al. 1999).

Within the Oaxaca Valley, the first major settlement to develop was San José Mogote, which was settled before the Preclassic Period; by 700 BCE, the end of the Early Preclassic, it was 70 hectares in area and yielded evidence for social differentiation, as well as for political, religious, and economic centralization and integration. Excavated houses at San José Mogote differed in the quality of their construction, the types of craft production pursued, and the kinds and numbers of goods (Flannery 1976; Flannery and Marcus 2005). Some houses contained larger numbers of imported and prestige goods, including a variety of animal bones (turtle and deer) and animal products (macaw feathers and stingray spines), indicating that their inhabitants had access to special foods and exotic items that marked status and position (Flannery and Marcus 2005: 6–11). Subfloor burials also varied in contents; mirrors, jade, and decorated pottery were found in the wealthiest ones. Elite male burials sometimes contained pots decorated with symbols of lightening or earthquake, which may have connected the owner to cosmological forces that elites could evoke in rituals. A 2-meter high platform mound held a structure of special prominence; it has been identified as a men's house, for gender-exclusive ritual, meeting, and dining events (Marcus 1999). Carved stones with feline and bird imagery may mark the space as sacred (Blanton et al. 1999: 38–40).

Over time, San José Mogote's prominence was challenged by other settlements in the Oaxaca Valley. In 700–500 BCE, evidence of conflict appeared: the ritual building at San José Mogote was burned and rebuilt as an elite residence, and images at the site depict the sacrifice of captives (Blanton et al. 1999: 44). The number of settlements in the valley grew to 85, some of them with the potential to attract population and economic resources away from San José Mogote. These new centers competed for prominence, and by 400 BCE, new construction at San José Mogote ended. Its rapid rise and decline are typical of the cyclical patterns of political dominance experienced repeatedly in Mesoamerica.

The Classic Period: The Rise of State Organization

While at least two regions of Mesoamerica attained the status of regional polity during the Preclassic Period—the Olmecs of the Gulf Coast and the Oaxaca Valley under San José Mogote—it was not until the Classic Period that the first states emerged. One of these, Monte Albán, is considered a successor state to San José Mogote, developing out of the conflicts in the Oaxaca Valley during the 6th century BCE; its foundation marked the beginning of Zapotec civilization. Another, the Classic Maya state, developed in a new and diverse environment. A third state emerged in central Mexico: Teotihuacan grew to be the most populous pre-Columbian polity, and its history and monuments inspired the later Aztecs.

Oaxaca Valley: Monte Albán

The site of Monte Albán was first settled around 550 BCE and quickly grew to dominate the three arms of the Oaxaca Valley. Some have postulated that the founders were the leaders of San José Mogote, who moved their site and population altogether when competition among their near neighbors grew too fierce (Flannery and Marcus 2012: 368). Despite (or perhaps because of) its location on agriculturally unproductive land, Monte Albán grew to urban proportions and quickly developed from a regional center into a state by 100 BCE. Between 100 BCE and 500 CE, it dominated the Oaxaca Valley, seeing periodic building projects at its core and contacts with central Mexico. Despite its prominence, the political structure and basis for leadership at Monte Albán remain uncertain.

Settlement patterns indicate the degree to which Monte Albán served as the focal point for settlement in the Oaxaca Valley and its function in integrating social and economic activities there. The initial settlement at the site, at 550 to 500 BCE, covered an immense area. The site itself occupies a hilltop overlooking the valley; the first occupation covered the 69 hectares at the top and spread down the slopes (adding another 225 hectares). By 100 BCE, it is estimated that the original 5,000 settlers had grown to a population of 17,000, occupying nearly 450 hectares (Blanton et al. 1999: 53). Yet the settlement was located 4 kilometers from fresh water and good agricultural land; a system of political subcenters and agricultural villages would have been required to support Monte Albán's population (Redmond and Spencer 2012). The area of the site with monumental public buildings, at the summit, did not include large storage facilities for collection and redistribution of food; instead, the population must have either fed itself or engaged in market exchange for staple goods (Blanton et al. 1999: 51). From 500 to 100 BCE, the number of settlements in the Oaxaca Valley increased from 72 to 643, indicating both the need for a central integrative core and the potential for rival political centers to emerge (Blanton et al. 1999: 54). In subsequent periods, after Monte Albán's pre-eminence was established, the site's size decreased, as population was probably relocated to areas with better agricultural yields.

The site layout at Monte Albán was also designed to focus attention and resources on the actions of regional leaders, their connections to the gods, and their military prowess. The site's mountaintop location had both a defensive function and a ritual dimension, tying activities on the summit to the gods who ruled the sky and weather (Elson 2012). From the earliest settlement phase at the site, this central area was planned with an open plaza at the center, 300 by 150 meters in area, and structures atop platforms on all four sides (Figure 12.3a). Several of these buildings seem to have had public, ceremonial, or commemorative functions, while elite housing and burials were concentrated near the northern platform (Joyce 2000). Two structures near the southern end focused, in contrast, on warfare and its consequences: both the Danzantes building (Building L), atop a 7-meter-tall platform, and later Building J had stone relief decoration that (probably) depicted sacrificed

FIGURE 12.3 Monte Albán: a. View b. Drawing of Danzante

Source: a. Photograph courtesy of Matt Saunders, licensed under GNU Free Documentation License via Wikimedia Commons; b. J.C. Ross

victims. The over 300 Danzante slabs, so-called because of the distorted "dancing" poses depicted (Figure 12.3b), show maimed or dismembered people. While there are glyphs on some of the slabs, none include a geographical designation, suggesting that the victims were local. As one of the earliest structures on the site, Building L's decoration may evoke the processes of site and state formation out of a collection of rival local polities. In contrast, the disembodied heads pictured on Building J's "conquest slabs" are marked with place names, some as far as 150 kilometers from Monte Albán; these places and peoples may mark the limits of state territory (Marcus 1992: 394–95).

Scholars view the layout of Monte Albán as a means of expressing deeply held beliefs about the universe and about the hierarchy of humankind. Specifically, the leaders and residents at Monte Albán were integrated into a worldview held across Mesoamerica (and parts of North America; see Chapter 11) that saw the universe as layered, with heaven, the gods, and ancestral spirits above, the earth and the underworld (the land of the dead) below. At the site level, then, the makers and users of the structures raised atop platforms on Monte Albán's peak sought access and connection to divine powers. The non-elite residences on the terraced slopes below occupied the earthly realm. The Mesoamerican cosmological structure also worked on the horizontal plane, with temples and elites associated with the northern end of the site, more earthly and violent concerns in the south (like the depictions of military victory implied by the Danzante slabs). These conceptions were present from the very foundation of Monte Albán and were inculcated in the process of construction, carried out under the command of the site's leaders (Joyce and Winter 1996).

Monte Albán's political leaders thus connected themselves to the culture's religious ideals. The centralized nature of their rule was made clear by the concentration of population at this new site, while the sociopolitical hierarchy was epitomized by the site's physical layout. That much of their power was embodied in military prowess and command was illustrated on the sculpted slabs, though the choice to depict the victim rather than victor consciously de-emphasized individual achievements. Early writing at Monte Albán also focused on defining the geographic limits of control as an adjunct to the depictions of conquest.

Monte Albán continued to be occupied until the time of the Spanish Conquest in Oaxaca, although major construction there ended at the close of the Classic Period (Blanton et al. 1979). During the latter part of the Classic Period, the valley experienced several phases of population movement, as leaders at Monte Albán and other towns competed for economic and political power. In the Postclassic Period, especially, the valley was subdivided into a number of small political units, with Monte Albán itself no longer dominating all rivals.

Teotihuacan

At Teotihuacan in central Mexico, the early state leaders pursued a similar ideological strategy to those of Monte Albán: underemphasizing individual leaders and their accomplishments while simultaneously concentrating on their cosmological ties as fundamental to their capacity to integrate a large and diverse territory. Teotihuacan grew to be the largest city in the pre-Columbian New World, stretching 20 square kilometers and with a population of up to 125,000 at its peak (Millon 1970). It controlled a surrounding territory of 25,000 square kilometers, spread across the Basin of Mexico. Teotihuacan's population included a mix of ethnic groups, and its economic and political contacts reached north, east to Maya territory, and west to the Oaxaca Valley (Millon 1988). In several of these regions, political leaders imitated Teotihuacano styles of architecture and material culture to enhance their own prestige locally.

For nearly 1,000 years, Teotihuacan dominated parts of central Mexico. It was founded during the Preclassic Period, between 500 and 150 BCE, as an agricultural village with access to important resources: water, clay, and obsidian (Cowgill 1992b; Heyden 1981). By the later Preclassic Period, 150 BCE to 150 CE, Teotihuacan grew in spurts, apparently due to periods of immigration. People from various parts of central Mexico settled in the city as it became a refuge for groups displaced by volcanic eruptions and other crises (Manzanilla 2001). By 150 CE, it had reached its full extent of 20 square kilometers, with a population of 80,000. The central part of the city housed a vast ceremonial complex of pyramids, temples, and plazas along the north-south running "Avenue of the Dead" (a name given by the Aztecs). In the following Classic Period, the population at Teotihuacan continued to grow; the city coped with its population influx first by the construction of an administrative complex, the Ciudadela, and later with expansions of the ceremonial buildings and a reorganization of the residential quarters at the site. By the Middle Classic Period, 400 to 550 CE, Teotihuacan was at the height of its economic and political power, and the rest of the Basin of Mexico was largely depopulated (Cowgill 1992b; Millon 1988). But soon after this, at around 550 CE, the city was partially destroyed and largely abandoned, as new groups moved into the region and the political cycle began again in new locations (Parsons and Sugiura 2012; Soler-Arechalde et al. 2006).

A closer analysis of the layout of Teotihuacan's central district (Figure 12.4a) offers a view into the organizational principles that brought together such a large and diverse population and into the ideologies that integrated them into Teotihuacan's political system. The city was surrounded on three sides by mountains, a landscape that framed and provided a model for its design. Like Monte

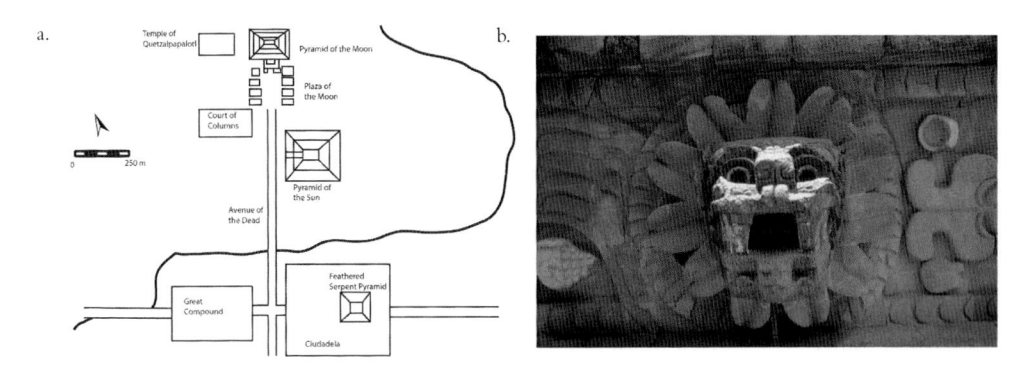

FIGURE 12.4 Teotihuacan: a. Plan; b. Photo of Feathered Serpent Head, Feathered Serpent Pyramid
Source: a. J.C. Ross; b. Danielle Gustafson / Art Resource, NY

Albán, Teotihuacan was laid out in accordance with the Mesoamerican cosmological template, tracing the movements of the sun and moon across the sky and distinguishing between the northern space of the city, reserved for religious display and actions, and the south, a space devoted to administration and to death.

The north-south street at the center of Teotihuacan, the Avenue of the Dead, ran over 5 kilometers; it pointed north to Cerro Gordo, one of the volcanoes that delimited the Basin of Mexico (Cowgill 2007). At its northern end was the Pyramid of the Moon, a stone and earthen structure measuring 130 by 156 meters at its base and 43 meters tall and fronted by a large plaza and over a dozen temples atop stepped platforms. While the Pyramid of the Moon, like other structures at Teotihuacan, was built and enlarged in several stages, its original construction between 1 and 150 CE was accompanied by a ritual deposit of 50 animals, most of them predatory, and at least one human burial (Sugiyama 2012). Further south along the Avenue was the Pyramid of the Sun complex: a pyramid 215 meters to a side and 63 meters tall, oriented toward another mountain peak. Built at the same time as the Moon Pyramid, it incorporated a smaller plaza, several temple platforms, and an underground quarry that provided stone for construction (Chávez et al. 2001; Manzanilla et al. 1994; Sugiyama 2012). A number of burials and caches in the quarry, now plundered, held obsidian arrowheads and a greenstone mask.

The builders of Teotihuacan's central precinct channeled the San Juan River so that it ran east-west below the Avenue of the Dead; it divided the religious precincts of the north from the administrative area of the southern end of the street. The Ciudadela was set on the eastern side of the street just south of the river; like the "Great Compound" across the street, the full range of its functions are unclear, but it is likely to have housed the political leaders of the city (Cowgill 1992a). In addition, the "Feathered Serpent Pyramid" and other temples sat within the precinct, though walls around them seem to have restricted access to ceremonies more than at the two larger pyramid complexes. The Feathered Serpent Pyramid featured depictions of the rain god (probably equivalent to Aztec Tlaloc), a snake with its neck encircled by feathers (Figure 12.4b); implying weather, fertility, and probably rebirth, this contrasts with the cosmic concerns of the two northerly complexes (Manzanilla 2001). As the pyramid was built, between 150 and 250 CE, over 250 burials were placed inside. Most are in groups, probably representing kin and occupational groups (both male and female) at court (Cowgill 1992a). It is likely that all the burials took place at once, perhaps on the death of a particular ruler, such as the occupant in Grave 13 in the center of the pyramid, who held a wooden staff in the shape of a serpent (Cowgill 1992b; Headrick 2007: 24). Among the other groups buried were warriors, who wore necklaces of human jawbones and teeth.

The planners and builders of the central core at Teotihuacan clearly held dominant power, commanding the labor of their subjects for construction and military endeavors and controlling life and death within the court. At the same time, their power and identities were masked; the artwork found at Teotihuacan features no representations of individuals who stand out from the rest of the populace (Blanton et al. 1996). Instead, murals in residential contexts (sculpture is largely absent) depict either abstract symbols and animals, myths, or processions of people, who may be distinguished by headgear, costume, attributes, or glyphs but not by scale, action, or isolation (Cowgill 1992a, 1992b; Headrick 2007: 27). The only exceptions are depictions of gods, who are at the endpoints of processions and who combine human features with natural and animal attributes (branches, leaves, feathers, water) (Headrick 2007: 29). The art seems to record ritual events and celebrate corporate activities and identities, rather than individual achievements or unique events (Feinman 2001).

While neglecting individual portraiture, Teotihuacan's art may not, however, have ignored the power of the ruler and ruling class. The central religious spaces of the city—the Sun and Moon Pyramid complexes and the Feathered Serpent Pyramid—were locales of ritual activities that were enacted by the city's political leaders in the sight of thousands of people. The ruler's presence is also implied by the decoration on the façade of the Feathered Serpent Pyramid, the single largest collection of sculpture at the city (Ringle 2014). On the face of each step of the pyramid, a frontal serpent's head emerges from a feathered "ruff"; on the body of the serpent, sculpted in relief, is the goggled headdress of Cipactli, the first day of the calendar (López Austin, López Luján, and Sugiyama 1991; Ringle 2014; Sugiyama 1993). This decoration, in some interpretations, symbolized kingship in Teotihuacan; the ruler's actions in rituals atop the pyramid cemented his unique position vis-à-vis the gods and people of his city. It may be significant, in connection to this, that Teotihuacan—uniquely among Classic-Period political centers—had no ballcourt (Taladoire 2001). This does not, however, mean that the game, which for much of the Mesoamerican world legitimized political power, played no role at the region's largest center. Rather, with people from across Mexico gathered at the site, many different versions of the game could be played, perhaps along the Avenue of the Dead (Uriarte 2006).

While the rulers of Teotihuacan must have mustered labor and resources for the construction of the city's ceremonial core and its residential areas, their presence is unmarked in the latter areas of the site, beyond standardized planning and construction. Most of the city's residents at Teotihuacan's height lived in its 2,000 apartment complexes: walled-off city blocks each containing multiple residences in an area up to 60 by 60 meters (Cowgill 2003). Each residence included one or more domestic rooms, work rooms, a kitchen, storage spaces, and a ritual patio; within some blocks was also a shared plaza space with an altar and temple on a podium (Millon 1981). While social and economic differentiation might be expected at Teotihuacan, given its size and complexity, it is difficult to discern this in the residences. Within a given compound might be residences of different sizes, often one substantially larger than the others, but all have similar contents (Manzanilla 2009). And while burials beneath the floors of the patios varied by type, elaboration, and grave goods, the main distinctions seem to be on the basis of sex and ethnicity (Manzanilla 2002). In fact, rich burials have been found within smaller houses, and poor burials in wealthier ones (Cowgill 1992a).

Residential compounds appear to have been organized along family lines, with some differentiation within the residential groups. Other than the ruling class, who lived in compounds along the Avenue of the Dead, little seems to have differentiated Teotihuacan's residents from one another in wealth or status. The majority of the population farmed the land around the city, growing maize, beans, squash, chile, cotton, and reeds (Millon 1981). The turkey was domesticated, as were dogs and rabbits, but hunting of small mammals and birds, and fishing, supplemented the diet (Manzanilla 1996). The absence of large storage facilities within the city suggests that residents were self-sufficient and that they paid taxes to their leaders in a form other than staples: perhaps in craft goods and labor (Smyth 1996). Evidence suggests craft production (pottery and stone tools) within residential compounds was largely for household use (Hirth 2010). One enclave of Oaxaca natives has been uncovered; these may have been merchants, bringing trade goods long distances to sell at markets in exchange for local staple goods, resources, and crafts (Hirth 1998, 2009). In other areas of the site lived people from the Gulf Coast region and other parts of the central highlands (Manzanilla 2009: 35). There is little indication of governmental intervention in the economic lives of Teotihuacan's residents. This may be another way in which a corporate governance strategy, stressing common identities and needs, proved to be the best way to hold together Teotihuacan's vast population.

Decline and Collapse at Teotihuacan

At the same time as Teotihuacan was at its peak in terms of population and geographical extent, signs of decline began to appear. Most stark was the increase in depictions of military personages and themes in artwork of the early 6th century; this suggests a new level of concern with order and conquest. Finally, around 550 CE, many of the major structures at the site were destroyed by fire, sculptures were damaged or destroyed, and the city was largely abandoned (Soler-Arechalde et al. 2006). Scholars disagree over the reasons for destruction and even the extent of abandonment; there is little sign of interpersonal violence. By the Postclassic Period, when the Aztecs arrived in central Mexico and regarded Teotihuacan as a place of mythical origins, the city's plan was still intact. It is possible that internal decline, perhaps environmentally driven, led Teotihuacan's residents and subjects to rebel against its rulers. The Late Classic was also a time of new arrivals, with immigrant groups settling in central Mexico; a rival polity may have arisen to challenge and upend Teotihuacan's hegemony.

The Classic Period Maya

The area covered by the prehispanic Maya culture is the largest in Mesoamerica, spreading over 250,000 square kilometers at its peak in the Late Classic Period (600–900 CE). This territory included extensive lowland areas of the Yucatan Peninsula of Mexico, northern Guatemala, Belize, and northern Honduras; it stretched also into the highlands of Guatemala, where some of the most important obsidian resources of Mesoamerica are located. The dense forest over much of the region, and the extensive wetlands near the coasts, present particular challenges to archaeologists but provided abundant and varied biotic and aquatic resources to the ancient Maya. The environment also contributed in significant ways to the political system; despite numerous attempts, Maya rulers were unable to unite more than two or three cities under their command, and both alliances and populations shifted too often to allow any ruler to create a territorial state or empire during the Classic Period. Populations could disappear into the rainforest if they were under pressure, and the generally poor soils could not support substantial populations over the long term. Despite their shared culture, language, and belief systems, the Maya of the Classic Period maintained city-states akin to those of the Classical Greeks.

Preclassic Maya Antecedents

For many decades, scholars believed that significant occupation of Maya territory and the establishment of political complexity there began in the Early Classic Period (250–600 CE), with only foraging groups and simple village agriculturalists in the territory before that point. In this scenario, the Olmec were the inspiration for, and even the source of, political complexity. Expanded programs of archaeological survey and excavation since the 1960s have put these views to rest. Sedentary occupation in southern Mexico and the adjacent Guatemalan highlands is contemporary to that in Olmec territory; both belong to the Early Preclassic Period (1500–900 BCE). And while the Maya and Olmec clearly shared beliefs and practices, and were likely in contact via trade (the Olmecs received obsidian from Guatemalan sources [Grove and Gillespie 1992]), the two civilizations arose and evolved independently. By the Middle Preclassic (900–600 BCE), social and economic differentiation in burials and monumental architecture may mark the development of ranked society in Maya territory. Also at this time, recognizably Maya cultural features began to appear in art and architecture (Chase and Chase 2012). By the Late Preclassic (600 BCE–100 CE), signs of centralization, hierarchy, and conflict signal incipient city-state organization; soon after this, a phase of decline and population movement marks the end of the Preclassic Period (Foias 2013: 11).

A number of Middle Preclassic sites in the Maya lowlands offer evidence of social differentiation and some degree of political authority. Already at this time, inhabitants were building platform mounds atop which houses were constructed. At some lowland sites, the variable sizes of these platforms suggest uneven degrees of wealth (Foias 2013: 9). Public architecture in the form of stepped pyramids also originates at this time, at sites such as Nakbe and Ceibal (Inomata et al. 2013). City leaders at these centers extracted labor from residents for construction of these monuments. At Nakbe, a paved causeway connected two pyramids that, based on later Maya practices, were likely the bases for religious buildings.

During the succeeding Late Preclassic Period, further differentiation and centralization are in evidence. At Kaminaljuyú, in the highlands, over 200 buildings were constructed atop platforms. The concentration of population, probably over 1,000 people here, may have been encouraged by the site's location alongside trade routes running inland from the coast. Kaminaljuyú's leaders may have gained status from special access to such exotic goods as obsidian, jade, cotton, and cacao (Arroyo 2012). Possession of such items allowed them to bolster their own prestige within the city, provide feasts and desirable items to supporters, and develop relationships outside the city through further trade in other exotic goods to which they had access.

Lowland sites like Edzna and El Mirador also participated in this highland-lowland trade system and built significant public architecture in the Late Preclassic (Matheny 1986). At Edzna, special effort was put into the water supply system, with canals built around and through the settlement to supply it with fresh water and in the surrounding fields to drain excess moisture from crops. El Mirador, located within the tropical rainforest zone, put even more effort toward public works, including causeways that linked it to other sites and monumental architecture that anticipated Classic Maya linkages of king and ritual. El Mirador succeeded nearby Nakbe in importance, growing to over 16 square kilometers and a population of 50,000 between 400 BCE and 100 CE (Foias 2013: 9). It had several clusters of buildings atop monumental platforms, but two especially important ones: the Tigre Pyramid, 55 meters high and 126 by 135 meters at its base, and the Danta Pyramid, at 72 meters high, 2 kilometers away. Between them, a plaza and acropolis area included a palace structure whose exterior façade was decorated with stucco relief masks depicting gods or supernatural forces (Matheny 1986). Rulers at El Mirador thus claimed a special relationship with the gods; their command over labor and ritual at an increasingly populous urban center suggests that they achieved incipient state organization. Other Preclassic Maya centers continue to emerge in archaeological excavations and will likely add to the evidence for the ritual basis for early political power in Mesoamerica.

Classic Maya

Classic Maya civilization, lasting more than 600 years (250–900 CE), is one of the most famous and enigmatic societies of antiquity. At its core was a mosaic of city-states led by charismatic rulers with ritual and diplomatic roles, who were surrounded by elites (see Figure 12.5 for a map of the sites and regions discussed in the latter half of this chapter). From its Preclassic origins, Maya culture grew in its monumental expression in the Early Classic Period (250–600 CE) but reached its peak in the Late Classic (600–900 CE), a phase of high settlement numbers, high population, and rampant conflict. Though Maya cities were united by a common economic base, belief system, political organization, and physical expression of these principles in architectural and iconographic form, no single kingdom rose to pre-eminence to lead all the city-states in a Maya "empire." The final years of the Late Classic may be interpreted as a collapse or a revival, depending on one's point of view.

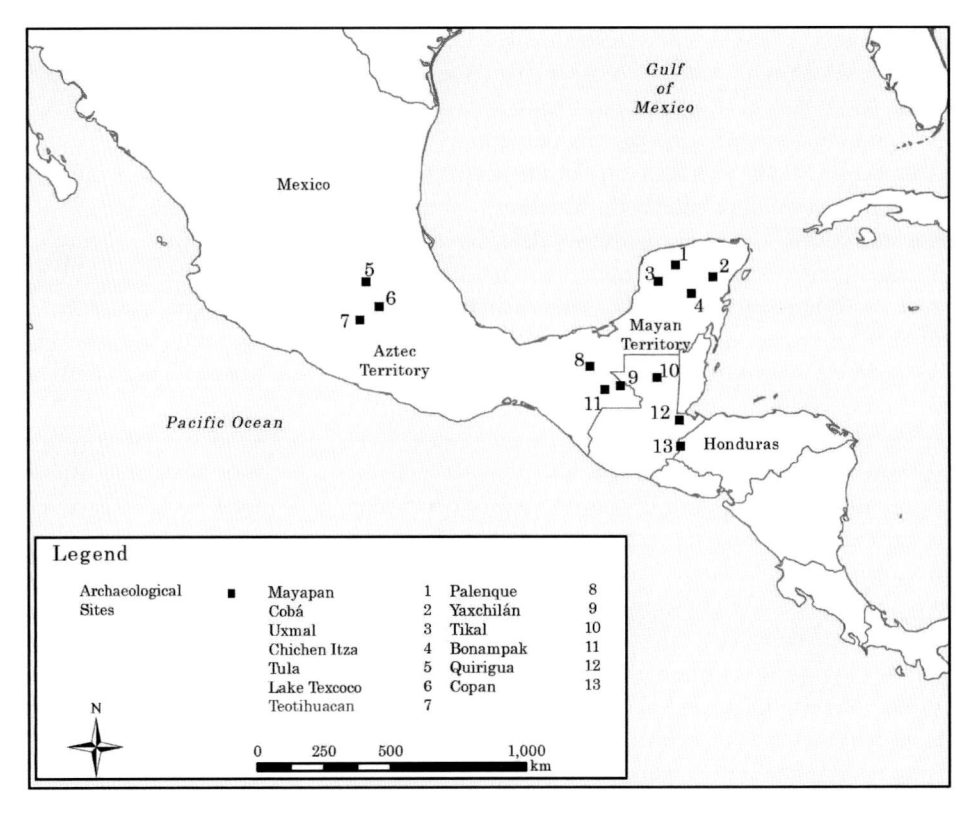

FIGURE 12.5 Map of Classic Period Maya and Postclassic Period Sites and Regions Discussed in the Chapter

Source: B. Spencer

Maya Economy

As with nearly all of the societies examined in this book, Maya society was built on an agricultural subsistence base, which supported a multilevel settlement hierarchy of major city-states, subsidiary administrative centers, towns, villages, and farming hamlets (Rice 1987). An early viewpoint, based on limited regional survey and showing the problems of detecting sites and their extents in the heavily forested Maya core, suggested that very few people actually lived in Maya cities, which served instead as nearly empty administrative and ritual locales. According to this view, the cities housed only the highest-level administrators and a permanent priesthood, while the rest of the population was spread across the countryside. Regional surveys and better recognition of sites and house platforms have now allowed archaeologists to "see" the high population levels of cities, as well as their diversity. With populations reaching the tens of thousands, Maya cities required an enormous subsistence base and infrastructure.

The Maya farmed a variety of crops; maize is most prominent in the iconography, as its lifecycle provided a profound metaphor for human life and death, but beans and squash, manioc, and gathered fruit and nuts were significant to the diet as well, with major regional variability (Atwood 2009; Trigger 2003: 300–303). Depending on local environment and needs, the Maya practiced dry (rainfall) farming, slash-and-burn cultivation, canal irrigation, raised bed cultivation, and terraced farming (Rice 1993). Like other Mesoamerican groups, the Maya lacked domesticated animals and supplemented their diet with hunting and fishing. Because of the high but seasonal rainfall and high water table, water management was an important aspect of the agricultural regime, as well as a major element in the ritual cycle and ideology (Fash 2005). Canals to supply settlements and fields, and reservoirs to catch drinkable water, are found as early as the Preclassic Period; deep reservoirs (*cenotes*) were the focus of rituals even into the Postclassic Period. Water management seems to have been the responsibility of residential groups at the neighborhood or lineage level (Fash 2005). Control of such a vital resource was unequal, sometimes traced back to individual ancestors and conveying prestige and wealth to their closest living relatives (Isaac 1996).

Other local resources were available to Maya settlements for their own use or for local or long-distance trade. Salt, obsidian, and volcanic stones for grinding equipment were all derived from highland sources; these were traded to lowland centers and outside groups (Rathje, Gregory and Wiseman 1978). Maya trade also included chert, jade, and slate; copper and shell; and such organic goods and processed products as ceramics, cotton, honey, cacao, copal (a resin used for incense), and stingray spines (used in bloodletting rituals) (Shaw 2012). In general, these items were not prestige goods with restricted consumer bases but moved freely across Maya territory in the hands of merchants, who sold them at markets. It is likely that higher-value goods that moved long distances were under the control of kings and elites who used their special access to such items to heighten their own prestige (Trigger 2003: 348).

Besides farming and trade, Maya residents pursued a variety of crafts. Some items, including textiles and ceramics, were produced for household use. Other decorated or high-value ceramic types were produced in workshops by full-time potters, and distributed through market-based mechanisms (Beaudry 1984). Other specialized occupations, with variability in the status of producers, included obsidian and flint-knapping, wood-working, and construction (Becker 1973, 1983). Prestige goods like ceramics with painted scenes of courtiers and kings, jade jewelry, and engraved shell ornaments were likely commissioned by elite consumers from attached or independent craft specialists. Scribes occupied an elevated status; the products of scribes were ideologically charged, and scribes were permanent, probably elite, members of court.

As seen in previous chapters, a major feature of the political economy of many complex societies was the collection of massive quantities of staple goods as taxes from citizens of their territory to support the activities of the ruling class. Maya society, too, engaged in the collection of staples and other items; artistic representations of "tribute presentations" to kings are frequent, although the items being presented are almost always prestige goods (elaborate textiles and high-value foods like cacao; see Box 12.2). However, the central areas of cities, where the principal elite residences and temples were, lack storage facilities for the collection and bulk redistribution of goods. It may be that, as at Teotihuacan, the administrators of palaces retained only small amounts of food and converted the rest of the tribute into other necessary items at markets (Smyth 1996). Similarly, Maya writing refers very seldom to the economic workings of society; such concerns were not part of court protocol.

BOX 12.2 MAYA CHOCOLATE-DRINKING

When Spanish explorers and conquerors arrived in Mexico, they discovered people who consumed a drink derived from cacao beans: chocolate. Vessels that hold a frothy drink are depicted on a number of Maya polychrome vessels, especially shown next to a seated ruler. Cacao could be grown in the Maya lowlands but probably had a limited distribution, making control of its movement the prerogative of royalty (McAnany et al. 2002).

Residue analysis on the interior of ceramic vessels now shows that chocolate-drinking began in the Preclassic Period among the Maya. Special spouted vessels were used in the Preclassic

> Period to create the froth on top of the drink by pouring from a height. By the Classic Period, the main form for drinking was a tall, cylindrical vessel, similar to the one depicted on Maya painted pots and similar in form to those pots themselves (Powis et al. 2002). Like ballcourts, cacao and its typical drinking-vessel form seem to have spread to the American southwest, appearing in Chaco Canyon by 1000 CE (Crown, Hurst, and Smith 2009).

Maya Social Organization

As archaeologists began to better recognize the presence of buildings made from perishable materials across the Maya landscape, they also came to understand how many people lived in the cities and their hinterlands. Earthen and stone platforms held the remains of house complexes of various sizes, often comprising multiple buildings sharing a common courtyard or patio. Within these patio groups, houses varied in size, number of rooms, and contents, suggesting social, economic, and/or functional differentiation. Nearly every house, though, included a cooking area, rooms for sitting and sleeping, and storage (Sanders and Webster 1988). Ritual activities are suggested by finds of figurines and ceramics of special form (Hendon 1991). Burials are frequently found below patio or house floors, and these also vary in wealth and effort expended. Food preparation took place within and outside houses; residences were also locations for various kinds of ritual actions (Foias 2013: 211; Hendon 2010). It is assumed that clusters of houses sharing a patio were extended family residences, with ranking of families based on their relative closeness in descent to the lineage head (Schele and Freidel 1990: 84). These same hierarchical principles applied throughout the political structure; barring conquest or usurpation, dynastic succession passed from father—the man considered closest in line to the dynasty's founder—to son.

Household organization was highly patriarchal as well, with patrilineal inheritance and patrilocal residence (McAnany and Plank 2001). Women's daily work focused on food preparation and child-rearing; women must also have been involved with agriculture and household craft production. At the upper levels of society, elite women could play major roles at court; they were sought after as wives and could affect succession. Maya rulers practiced polygyny, and it is likely that high-ranking elites did as well. Consequently, the rulers' palatial compounds must have housed large numbers of women and children. Some of the highest-ranking women were featured in inscriptions and artwork in which they are the main participants in ritual actions that supported the king. As the rulers' families grew in the Late Classic Period, and more people could claim blood relationships with the kings, the royal genealogy, including the high standing of the mother's line, became an even greater focus of art and texts.

Economic and social differentiation, visible in the house remains mentioned earlier, have been the topic of intensive debate among archaeologists. When Spanish chroniclers documented surviving Maya groups in the 16th and 17th centuries, they detected only two classes: elite and commoner (Chase 1992). Whether this dichotomy also applied to the Classic Period is unclear, nor is it certain that the Spaniards would have recognized, or even seen, persons of an intermediate social and economic status. Elites are relatively easy to detect in Classic Maya texts, iconography, and archaeology: they are depicted in the artwork, with status indicated by costume, attributes, actions, and their proximity to the king. Archaeologically, their residential complexes are the largest after the king's, as are their burials, but not all elites lived or were buried at the center of the city. As overall population increased during the Late Classic Period, gradations in status also increased among elites and commoners, and an argument can be made for a middle class of non-hereditary elites (chosen for their positions by the king), merchants, and some craft specialists (Chase 1992). Meanwhile, the elites held to the distinctness of their position, especially by maintaining an origin story that made their creation different from the creation of commoners (Foias 2013: 169).

Maya Political Organization

As mentioned already, no single Maya city or state dominated all, or even much, of the territory. Rather, a shifting collection of city-states, each ruled by a king, was engaged in a constant and dynamic set of alliances, conflicts, and conquests (Marcus 1998). By the 8th century, 60 city-states coexisted in this tense condition; the territory under the control of each ranged from 80 to over 11,000 square kilometers (Foias 2013: 105; Schele and Freidel 1990: 59).

Each city-state was ruled by a king, called *ahau* or *ajaw*. (The transliteration of Maya hieroglyphs is being constantly refined, and so the reading of this sign varies from scholar to scholar.) Certain kings had the additional designation of *k'uhul*, "holy"; literally, *k'uhul ahau* meant "holy shouter." The shouting may refer to one of the king's principal roles, as mediator between his people and the gods and as presider over religious rituals. All Maya kings were expected to play this role; the addition of "holy" then may be an indication of higher rank accorded to the kings of particularly powerful city-states. Besides straightforward worship, the king had responsibilities in diplomacy, feasting, warfare, and sacrifice, all contributing to maintaining the balance of the cosmos, the region, and his own city-state. Artwork and inscriptions of the Early Classic Period centered on the king's ritual duties; later, the taking of captives in war and their subsequent sacrifice grew in importance as a matter of artistic depiction (Foias 2013: 11).

The setting for the king's activities in each city-state was the monumental complex at the urban center, typically comprising a large open plaza in which a significant number of people might sit or stand, one or more stone stepped pyramids with a temple at their top, and an extensive palace compound in which the business of state was conducted (see Box 12.3). Some ritual actions also took place in the palace, including bloodletting, vision quests, and the display of captives. Palaces also served as the residences for the king and royal family. They are distinguished, typically, by their immense size, location, and the number of buildings in the complex, devoted to a variety of different functions (see Box 12.4) (Inomata 2001). Palaces were places of spectacle that reinforced the legitimacy of the king and his trusted inner circle in the eyes of the court, city, the gods, and visitors from other Maya cities and other regions (Inomata 2006).

BOX 12.3 KEY SITE: TIKAL

The site of Tikal, in the northern lowlands of Guatemala, was one of the largest and longest-lived of Classic Maya cities. Founded around 600 BCE as a successor to nearby El Mirador, Tikal grew to over 16 square kilometers, with a central core of monumental temples, palaces, and tombs and thousands of residential compounds stretching into the forests (Harrison 1986). Tikal best illustrates the additive nature of Maya cities: the 40-plus buildings on the Central Acropolis were the products of over 500 years of construction activity; the same is true of other parts of the central precinct. At each stage in its history, the rulers of the city added major structures and monuments to mark specific events and achievements. Only in the 9th century CE did Tikal's architectural layout reach the extent seen today (Figure 12.6a). Tikal's history also provides perspective on Maya warfare and conquest, and even on the interference of a distant power—Teotihuacan—in local politics.

Excavations from the 1950s through the 1980s at Tikal revealed the architectural succession as well as a variety of iconographic and epigraphic monuments detailing the city-state's history. A small village was established at the site in the Middle Preclassic; by the Late Preclassic, as El Mirador went into decline, the population at Tikal began to grow. Major structures

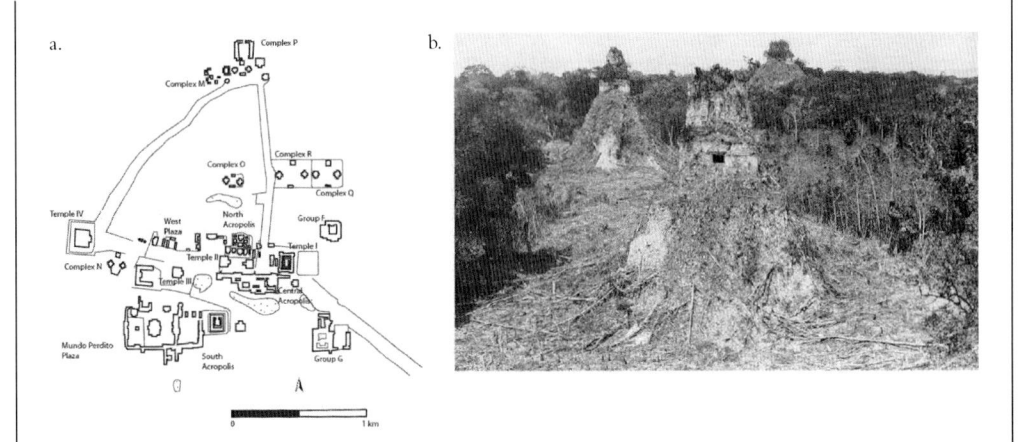

FIGURE 12.6 Tikal: a. Plan of Central Area; b. Photo of Temples I and II in 1882

Source: a. J.C. Ross; b. Photograph by Alfred Maudslay (https://commons.wikimedia.org/wiki/File:Tikal1882.jpeg)

were built on the Central Acropolis beginning in the 1st century BCE. A list of Tikal's 39 rulers goes back to the early 3rd century CE, a time of significant monumental construction. A series of wars in the 4th century against Uaxactun (25 kilometers away) ended with the "arrival" of Siyaj K'ak', a mysterious figure who came, apparently, from Teotihuacan and installed new rulers at both sites; for a time, Tikal's artwork featured characteristic Teotihuacano elements like "goggles" over the eyes of the king (representing the rain god, Tlaloc) and spearthrowers as part of the royal arsenal of weapons (Martin 2003). The Late Classic Period saw a revival in construction at Tikal but also a return of conflict, this time against Caracol, Dos Pilas, and Calakmul. Construction accelerated in the late 7th and 8th centuries; it halted after that, and Tikal was abandoned in 850 CE (Schele and Freidel 1990: 140, 195).

This long history produced a range of monuments in the center of the city, while residential compounds on low platforms throughout the settlement featured standard arrays of houses, kitchens, storerooms, shrines, and open spaces (Haviland 2003). The central core of the city comprises a number of monumental complexes, including several raised acropolis areas that held numerous buildings: these were connected by causeways that run a kilometer or more. In its earliest stages, Tikal's building projects focused on the North Acropolis and the Mundo Perdido complex to the south, with an open plaza between them. The Mundo Perdido complex included temples and a pyramid, while the North Acropolis became a funerary complex for the founding dynasty of the Early Classic Period. Their tombs were under platforms that also held buildings and monuments completed by later rulers. They differ from other Early Classic burials found across the residential precincts of the city in their size and the effort expended in their construction, in elaboration, and in the quantity and quality of objects buried with the dead. Some included human sacrifices, while the principal burials were of people of larger stature than was typical at Tikal (Haviland 1967). Paintings within the tombs may represent the tomb owner; at least one depicts a woman, who may be a rare female ruler among the Maya. The grave goods include fine pottery, jade and *Spondylus* shell beads, and stingray spines. The tombs attest to the wealth and distinction of the Early Classic rulers; continued monument-building on the North Acropolis in the Late Classic suggests veneration of and connection to these royal ancestors by later kings (Haviland and Moholy-Nagy 1992).

Over time, new structures filled parts of the central plaza at Tikal, south of the North Acropolis. The Central Acropolis held royal residences of the Late Classic kings. The best-known Late Classic ruler, Ah Cacaw, built a pair of pyramids between these two acropolis areas; Temples I and II are the tallest buildings at the site, rising 47 and 38 meters above the plaza, respectively (Figure 12.6b). They may have contained the tombs of Ah Cacaw and his wife; the temples at their tops are decorated in distinctive Tikal style, with substantial stone ridges atop the roof that serve to further emphasize their verticality (Harrison 1986). Also set between the palace compound and the North Acropolis was a small ballcourt, apparently reserved for royal-sponsored events with limited numbers of spectators (Ashmore 1992; Harrison 1986).

BOX 12.4 KEY SITE: PALENQUE

Another Maya city to be examined here is Palenque, located in Mexico. As at Tikal and Copan, genealogy and legitimacy were the major foci of art and architecture at this site, but their depiction is mainly focused on one ruler of the Late Classic Period. At its peak, Palenque was much smaller than Tikal or Copan, yet this 300-hectare city ruled a territory of 450 square kilometers (Liendo Stuardo 2007).

Several extant king lists from Palenque cover the Early and Late Classic Periods, 387 to 799 CE. Several buildings at the site were first built in the Early Classic Period, though they were periodically renewed during the Late Classic. Temples XVIII and XVIIIa comprised a pair of pyramid structures built in the early 8th century, but temple XVIIIA covered the burial of at least one Early Classic king, which included a room containing human sacrificial victims (Schele 1986), Early Classic ceramics, and various jade ornaments.

The majority of the buildings found in the core area at Palenque date to the reign of K'inich Janaab Pakal (henceforth Pakal), who ruled Palenque from 615 to 683 CE, and to his successors. Pakal is responsible also for most of the preserved king lists, which trace the ruling dynasty's history. He appears to have been especially concerned to establish his own legitimacy, placing king lists in the temple that topped his tomb, the Temple of the Inscriptions, as well as on the walls of the tomb and on his sarcophagus (Schele and Freidel 1990: 217–53). Pakal's concern may derive from the unusual circumstances of his succession: he came to the throne following his mother, the daughter of the previous king, who handed him the reins of power during her lifetime. This is depicted on the "Oval Palace Tablet," a slab carved in relief that showed Pakal facing his mother, who hands him the crown. Public display of this piece in the palace compound indicates that there was no embarrassment or need to hide the exchange; indeed, Pakal's grandmother also ruled Palenque (Schele and Freidel 1990: 221).

Pakal's tomb, built into the eight-stepped pyramid that supported the Temple of the Inscriptions, hearkens back to the design of the Early Classic burial described earlier, with a room containing five sacrificial victims, and a tube that connected the tomb with the temple above (a "psychoduct"), presumably so that the deceased king could be raised in vision-invoking ceremonies (Schele 1986). Pakal's burial equipment included a stunning jade mosaic mask and several jade heads, as well as a life-sized stucco portrait bust of the king.

Beyond and beside the king, a large number of elite administrators, and more humble workers, saw to the political business of a Maya city-state. Many administrative titles are attested in the texts, although their precise functions may have differed from place to place (Foias 2013: 111–62; Jackson 2013). Some offices were reserved for relatives of a king, others were passed down through families, and still others could be held by people new to administrative power. Elites conducted some state business and rituals within their own houses and could have their own employees. Those of highest status had biographical inscriptions within their homes, a privilege not open to all Maya residents. Besides elite officials (occasionally including women), many other individuals contributed to the smooth functioning of the court but have left little, if any, trace in the archaeological record.

Maya Religion and Ritual

For a society that emphasized iconography and valued ritual performance as much as the Maya, it is surprising how little information is available about their gods and belief system. One reason for this is the relatively recent decipherment—in the 1950s through the 1970s—of Maya hieroglyphs; another is that most Maya gods represented somewhat abstract concepts. Depictions of the gods were not consistent and often combined human, animal, and natural features. One exception to the problem of anonymous gods is the Maize God, whose Maya name, like those of most of the pantheon, is not yet clear. His story is one of the main myths of the *Popol Vuh*, the only surviving document of Maya mythology, represented by a manuscript of the early 18th century CE. In the *Popol Vuh*, he and his brother were killed by the gods of death after losing to them in a ballgame; he was decapitated. Yet the Maize God's head retained some life; he spits on a young woman, who becomes pregnant and gives birth to his sons, the Hero Twins. These avenge their father's death in a ballgame against the underworld gods and facilitate their father's rebirth. The Maize God's life, death, and rebirth exemplify the yearly agricultural cycle; like other vegetation gods worldwide, his life also provided a model and inspiration for human rebirth after death.

This story from the *Popol Vuh* has a number of archaeological correlates. The Maize God makes frequent appearances in Maya art, usually with his hair pulled back on top of his sloping head, like corn silk on a cob. His depiction is most common in tomb contexts: on painted ceramics left as offerings; on statuary and amulets; and also simply suggested by objects of jade, the color of which calls to mind fresh, growing maize plants. He was invoked during funerary rituals, and jade clothing (masks, pectorals, and jewelry) aided the deceased in the effort of rebirth (Miller and Samayoa 1998).

The Maize God's story also helps scholars understand the importance of the ballgame to Maya life. Though ballgames may have been (and still are) played on a casual basis across Mesoamerica, the Maya evidence suggests that it was a deadly serious contest. The ballcourt, like the tomb, could be a place of transition between life and death (Miller 2001). As in many societies, play simulated warfare; it is clear from Maya art that the rulers of rival city-states played to the death. (What is unclear is whether this was a re-creation of a battle that had already been fought and lost.) As a liminal place, the ballcourt also was the space of the Maize God's rebirth, a victory over death itself (Schele and Miller 1986: 266). The public location of ballcourts in most Maya sites indicates the ritual importance of the game to Maya political leaders.

Besides ballcourts, the Maya religious system shared additional features with other ancient Mesoamerican cultures. The Maya conceived of the world as layered (with heaven, earth, and watery underworld), as seen already at Teotihuacan, and modeled their cities to imitate the natural world and cosmos, with mountainous pyramids, and doorways that stood for entrances into caves (Schele and Freidel 1990: 67). Each king was a conduit for communication between his people and divine forces, particularly in his position as "world tree," the central point that anchored and connected the three layers of the cosmos and four cardinal directions (see Box 12.5 for an example). During rituals, many of them performed in front of much of the city's populace, and others in more private, enclosed spaces, the king used his shamanic, transformative power to communicate with the supernatural world, renewing the cosmic cycles that kept the world running (Freidel 1992; Schele and Freidel 1990). His powers might be enhanced, in some instances, by the shedding of his own, or others', blood, which fell onto bark paper that was then burned; the resulting smoke rose to the heavens and drew forth a divine vision, sometimes an ancestor (Schele and Freidel 1990: 89). Bloodletting rituals could be conducted by elites and members of the royal family as well. At Yaxchilan, the focus of a number of relief images was one or more bloodletting rituals led by a principal queen, Lady Xok, for the sake of her husband and stepson (Figure 12.7) (Schele and Miller 1986: 211). Most effective in provoking a vision was letting blood from the tongue (as Lady Xok is pictured doing), ears, and penis. Depictions of these events provide a sense of their intimacy and efficacy.

FIGURE 12.7 Lintel Relief (Lintel 25) Showing Bloodletting Ritual From Yaxchilan, Mexico

Source: British Museum, London, United Kingdom (HIP / Art Resource, NY)

320 Ancient Mesoamerican Cultures

BOX 12.5 KEY OBJECT: THE SARCOPHAGUS LID OF PAKAL

At Palenque, it is Pakal's immense sarcophagus that makes the most explicit statement about the king's rightful place during his life and for eternity. The sides of the 5-ton limestone sarcophagus depict Pakal's "ancestors"—ten kings who preceded him on Palenque's throne—while his parents are represented on both ends. Meanwhile, Pakal is not depicted on the sides, among these rulers. Instead, he is the central figure on the lid (Figure 12.8); his passage from

FIGURE 12.8 Sarcophagus Lid of Pakal

Source: J.C. Ross

life to death included the placement of his body in the box, to be received among his forbears, pictured beneath. The lid also marks his liminal status: the king, with hair styled like the Maize God's, lies between the gaping mouth of the underworld and the band of heaven. Falling or rising, his body overlays the vertical axis of the world tree; a celestial bird overlooks the scene. The depiction on Pakal's sarcophagus lid suggests that death cannot hold the king; his intercession for his family and his people would continue forever.

Even warfare had ritual significance to the Maya. Until late in the Classic Period, most warfare took the form of raids to gain captives or to destroy morale in a conquered city; these were not large-scale wars of conquest. One indication of this is the absence of fortifications or other defenses at Maya cities (Freidel 1986). Even in cases of conquest, the victorious king rarely imposed his own rule over the losers. Rather, he subjected the current ruler, or a new one set in his place, to tribute payments and a symbolic subjugation, depicted in art and probably in ritual. Warfare among the Maya was "scheduled," in a sense; it took place at particular points in the ruler's lifecycle: his accession, the birth of an heir, and on his death (Freidel 1986). A set of murals found at the site of Bonampak in Mexico illustrates this principle: in a three-room complex, two rooms appear to be devoted to the acknowledgment and accession of a child ruler, who is celebrated with music, dancing, and bloodletting rituals. The central room of the complex, then, should also relate to the same set of events; in this room is illustrated a single battle, spread out across three walls, with the torture and sacrifice of prisoners most prominently located in the center of the wall across from the doorway (Miller 2001). Prisoners were captured, tortured publicly, and sacrificed to legitimize the king's, or future king's, right to rule and right to divinity (Schele and Miller 1986: 216). Elites also had the ability to enhance their status by capturing prisoners and property in war (Pohl and Pohl 1994).

A final component of Maya religion and ritual was the calendar. Like other Mesoamerican groups, the Maya used two calendrical systems: a 260-day ritual calendar that combines 13 day numbers with 20 day names, and a 360-day solar calendar of 18 twenty-day months, which ended with 5 additional days to round out the solar year. Dated monuments in the Maya lowlands go back to 292 CE; most monumental inscriptions were dated. The calendar marked and reinforced the sense that time was both sacred and cyclical; individual days were propitious or unlucky, to the point that kings might shift their official birthdates to correspond to especially lucky days. The two calendars could be combined in the Calendar Round, which repeated the combined dates every 52 years. When documentation of dates or lengths of time over 52 years was necessary, the Maya developed the Long Count Calendar, which counted the days since a mythical creation date of August 11, 3114 BCE (Marcus 1992: 132–42).

Maya Collapse

But nothing lasts forever, and the high point of Maya culture in the 8th century CE quickly came to an end. The rapid demise of the Maya Classic Period city-states has long been recognized, and many archaeologists have endeavored to provide an explanation. Popular early explanations centered on warfare and disease. Perspectives since the 1970s have added environmental variables to the mix, citing evidence that the collapse took place over a longer period than previously suspected. The 9th century was clearly a period of social and political disruption and of population movements.

It is important to point out that, since the Maya cities were never united as a single state, this is not an issue of the overthrow of a king or government or of a single political collapse (Cowgill

1988). Yet the phenomenon resulted in the dissolution of political systems across the southern lowlands, the decline of dynastic power, and a permanent set of changes in the representation of political power, if not its practice. Evidence for Maya collapse highlights the disappearance of political structures: major construction at Maya centers slowed or stopped by the mid-9th century, effort and expenditure on tombs declined, and no dated inscriptions were carved after 830 (Culbert 1988). Major settlements were partially or fully abandoned; rural sites show less evidence of depopulation (Freter 1994). Evidence for kings and elites disappeared by the late 9th century. And skeletal analysis from 8th and 9th century burials suggests that significant numbers of people were suffering from nutritional stress (Rice 1993: 42).

As noted earlier, warfare and disease have been suggested as possible causes of the Maya collapse, but neither would explain the far-reaching and long-term abandonment of so many population centers. More compelling are theories that take into account evidence for environmental degradation caused by certain Maya agricultural techniques (including swidden agriculture and multicropping), which would have become necessary as populations grew, by climate change that brought declining rainfall totals, and by subsistence stress. It appears that, as major Maya cities increased their agricultural output to feed more people, the land itself could not or did not provide for those needs. One response to food shortages may have been movement from cities to less populated rural areas; another would have been intra- and intercity conflict. In the long run, the entire southern lowland region lost more than two-thirds of its population (Aimers 2007). While the crisis may not have been politically caused, it had immense and long-term social, economic, and political consequences.

The Postclassic Period: Territorial States

The Postclassic Maya: A Northern Revival

After the depopulation of the southern lowlands, Maya culture did not disappear—a phenomenon that adds weight to theories that suggest that environmental and social crises were at the root of the Classic Period decline. Instead, Maya cultural traits spread northward; the Postclassic Maya (900–1200 CE) territorial core was in the Yucatan Peninsula of southeast Mexico. This too was a lowland region, but with easier coastal and inland access. It is likely that the population of this area in the Postclassic Period included both long-time inhabitants, with a localized culture and institutions, and a large immigrant population from the south.

The resulting culture had many of the characteristic features of the Classic Maya: temples atop pyramidal substructures, intricate artistic representations of humans and gods, a concern for water storage, and a belief in a layered cosmos. Maya hieroglyphic writing had spread to the Yucatan already in the late 8th century (Grube and Krochock 2007); long-distance trade relations, especially those that brought obsidian from central Mexico and Guatemala, continued (Braswell 2010). At the same time, it is clear that sociopolitical structures among the Postclassic Maya were reconfigured. Major cities controlled significant territories, resulting in a landscape of competing territorial states, including Uxmal, Cobá, and Chichen Itza. And while it is likely that each of these states was ruled by a king, rulers did not appear in inscriptions or art; the ideology of power and control was completely different in this new landscape.

Chichen Itza is usually viewed as typical of Postclassic Maya territorial capitals, and it is the best preserved and most analyzed. On the other hand, there may be atypical elements to Chichen Itza's layout and sociopolitical organization; its coordination of sea trade and its similarity in layout to central Mexican sites may be anomalous for other regions in the Yucatan Peninsula. Written documents at Chichen Itza date as early as 832 CE but may stop at the end of the 9th century, as elsewhere in the Maya lowlands. Like Classic Maya texts, inscriptions from Chichen Itza record the dedications of major buildings; unlike the earlier documents, however, these texts record the building commissioners as groups of noblemen, not as individual kings (Schele and Freidel 1990: 356).

Chichen Itza was laid out with its central structures on an artificially leveled plaza, with paved causeways connecting the major buildings. Three walled precincts contained the major structures of the city, each comprising temples and palatial structures on platforms. The main ceremonial buildings included the nine-stepped El Castillo pyramid, with a four-doored temple on top (Figure 12.9a). Within the final building form were earlier versions of the pyramid and temple; one contained a throne and chacmool statue (Figure 12.9b), representing a prisoner on his back, with a cavity in the middle of the chest, supposedly to hold a heart sacrifice (Miller and Samayoa 1998; Schele and Freidel 1990: 364–70). Near El Castillo is the largest ballcourt in Mesoamerica, measuring 168 by 70 meters. East of El Castillo are additional smaller ballcourts, arranged around a series of stepped platforms with columns at their base and on the summits. The square-sectioned columns feature low relief carvings of hundreds of warriors, elites, priests, and captives, seemingly in procession toward the ritual spaces they adorn. On some of the platforms are additional chacmool statues.

One final space at Chichen Itza deserves mention: the Sacred Cenote, located north of this central group of structures. Sixty meters in diameter and 20 meters deep, this natural sinkhole was still in use when the Spanish arrived, and its use in ritual was documented in their accounts. Postclassic Maya rituals included sacrifice—of humans and valued objects—by throwing items into the water of the cenote. Dredging and excavations since the 19th century have discovered more than 120 human victims, as well as incense made from copal, textiles, wooden objects, and jade. Cenotes, of which there were several at Chichen Itza, were points of communication and appeal to underworld and earthly forces, as well as more practical sources of water (Miller and Samayoa 1998; Romey 2005).

Chichen Itza and contemporary Postclassic centers in the Yucatan were at their peak in the 10th and 11th centuries, with high populations and active building and sculptural programs that promoted a sense of community. Expressions of the singular power of individual rulers were suppressed, apparently in the interest of more corporate forms of identity. For a time, these territorial states contended with one another for short-term territorial gains; eventually, Mayapan established loose control over the entire region for 200 years, until the mid-15th century. When the Spanish arrived in the Yucatan a century later, numerous groups calling themselves "Maya" resisted European dominance for decades.

FIGURE 12.9 Chichen Itza: a. Photo of El Castillo; b. Photo of Chacmool From the Temple of the Warriors

Source: a. Gianni Dagli Orti / The Art Archive at Art Resource, NY; b. Museo Regional de Antropologia Merida, Mexico (Gianni Dagli Orti / The Art Archive at Art Resource, NY)

Postclassic Central Mexico: The Toltec Territorial State

The modern view of the Postclassic Period of central Mexico (see Figure 12.5 for a map) is dominated by the Late Postclassic Aztec Empire, but there were several significant territorial states in the region, established following the decline of Teotihuacan. Best known, though certainly not well understood, was the Toltec state centered on the site of Tula. The Toltecs controlled territory on the west side of the Basin of Mexico, reaching their peak population in the 11th century. Their 16 square kilometer center, Tula, held 60,000 people; their estimated hinterland population, producing much of the subsistence for the capital, was 30,000 to 50,000 (Healan and Cobean 2012).

The Toltecs left no written evidence; much of the perception of their achievements comes from later legends recounted to Spanish colonists by the Aztecs. Major construction at Tula has been dated to 900 to 1150 CE and later, with parallels to Chichen Itza in terms of site layout and decorative plan, though executed in a different artistic style. It is now clear that the initial influences flowed from Chichen Itza to Tula, rather than the other way around (Kristan-Graham and Kowalski 2007). These influences spread economic goods, military techniques, ritual practices, and beliefs rather than an imposed political system. Architectural features shared with Chichen Itza (but also with Teotihuacan) include a north-south, east-west orientation of central architecture that is adjusted to 17 degrees east of true north. The public architecture of the core of the city includes two pyramids, ballcourts, and structures filled with columns at the top of and base of platform mounds. In parallel to Chichen Itza, Tula's columns include reliefs of warriors in procession, while three-dimensional chacmool sculptures occur in several buildings. Unique to Tula, however, are the four colossal anthropomorphic warrior columns that stood at the top of Pyramid B.

The Culmination of the Postclassic Period: The Aztec Empire

By the time the Aztecs established their rule over the Valley of Mexico in the 15th century, centuries of warfare had dominated and altered the region's political map. While it is not clear what caused the decline of Tula and other early Postclassic territorial states, large-scale population movements were a major feature of the period, and the upheaval and competition over lands that preceded the Aztec takeover are another example of political cycling characteristic of Mesoamerica. Various ethnic groups moved into the Valley of Mexico, including the Mexica (more familiarly known as Aztecs), the Acolhua, and the Tepenaca—the three groups comprising the Triple Alliance that commenced in 1430 (Brumfiel 1987). These three powers engaged in wars of conquest and expansion, eventually controlling a discontinuous territory of 135,000 square kilometers, with nearly 500 towns organized into 38 provinces (Marcus 1992: 155; Smith and Sergheraert 2012). Eventually, the Aztecs, from their capital at Tenochtitlan, dominated the region and its population of 1.6 million people (Evans 2001: 238).

According to their origin legend, the Aztecs migrated from northwestern Mexico and chose to settle on the island of Tenochtitlan, in Lake Texcoco, because of a sign from the gods. Archaeological evidence places the date of settlement in the Middle Postclassic Period, following the Toltec decline (Smith 2001). A phase of cooler and wetter climatic conditions at this time encouraged agricultural intensification, while the political system of small territorial states facilitated interregional exchange as well as shifting political relationships of cooperation, conflict, and domination. The Aztecs appear to have adapted quickly to their new circumstances, adopting both Tula and Teotihuacan as ancestral places to which they felt themselves tied by blood and belief.

Aztec social organization, and its archaeological expressions, were similar to earlier culture groups in Mesoamerica. Residence, whether in cities or rural areas, was in extended family compounds with shared patio and work spaces. Both Spanish and Aztec written sources indicate there were two official socioeconomic classes: noble and commoner. There was also a burgeoning middle class of merchants and specialists making prestige goods; slaves constituted a social group on their own, though they could own possessions and gain freedom after a term of service (Berdan 1989; Evans 2001: 238–39). Elites served as the administrative and warrior class (Trigger 2003: 256).

Gender roles in Aztec society appear to have been rigidly defined; Aztec codices indicate that girls and boys began learning proper gender roles from a very early age (Joyce 2007). Aztec inheritance and status were patrilineal, but the mother's lineage could also enhance status (Trigger 2003: 178). In the home, women were responsible for food preparation and textile production, as well as other domestic activities that included preparing tribute payments to the central administration (Brumfiel 1991). But certain other specialized occupations, including priest, were also available to women.

With a population of over 1 million people spread across the Valley of Mexico, the Triple Alliance needed massive food surpluses from the provinces. Agricultural methods in the Late Postclassic included multicropping (the use of the same field for more than one crop over the course of a year), *chinampa* (raised bed), and irrigation farming (Berdan 1989). Written records, kept in both towns and capitals, indicate that elites controlled most land and leased it to farmers; owners received part of the yield, which they consumed in part, and forwarded the remainder to the capital as taxes (Fowler 1987). Some imperial expansion was fueled by the drive for more tribute from conquered territories, paid in food, labor, and crafted items like cloth and prestige goods (Smith 2001).

Internal and long-distance trade also played a major role in the Aztec economy. Merchants might work for private gain or on behalf of the government; it is likely that many merchants did both at the same time (Berdan 1989). The establishment of relative peace after a long period of endemic warfare encouraged trade and economic development. Long-distance trade brought in feathers, stone, and metals, all highly valued by the elite classes. Daily markets in major towns and cities made trade goods and locally produced materials, including food, available to all residents of central Mexico. In rural areas, such markets took place less often but still on a regularly scheduled, predictable basis. Local currencies included cloth and cacao beans (Berdan 1989). Craft production for sale was sometimes based on regionally available resources. In Tenochtitlan, some residential neighborhoods were organized by the craft specialty of their inhabitants; production at the capital included both prestige items like dress and ornament that served as gifts from the ruler to worthy officials, and more broadly available items, like obsidian tools and ceramics (Berdan 1989).

Aztec political organization facilitated the movement of a rich variety of goods. The city-state-centered provinces were ruled by men who were vassals to the Aztec king (Brumfiel 1987). To gain a foothold in a new region, the Aztecs would intervene in local conflicts, allying themselves with one side and eventually claiming tribute from both sides (Hicks 1994). The principal role of the Aztec king was to lead warriors into battle, but he cemented political relations by means of dynastic marriages (Marcus 1992: 225; Wolf 1999: 149). Each new king was "elected" by a council of noblemen; all Aztec kings came from the same lineage but rarely did the crown pass from father to son. Rather, power was contested and uncertain, requiring strategy, calculation, and negotiation (Marcus 1992: 307).

Like their politics, the Aztecs saw the cosmos itself as embattled (Brumfiel 2007). The very movement of the sun and moon across the sky implied to them a battle, with daily victors and losers. To maintain the cosmic balance and guarantee the annual seasonal cycle, the Aztec gods required sacrifices from their people, including a daily sacrifice of human life at the Templo Mayor at Tenochtitlan. At times of greater uncertainty—after eclipses, at the end of the solar year, or in periods of drought—such events became even bloodier spectacles, according to ethnohistoric sources and Spanish witnesses. But the sense that humans and the gods stood in a relationship of reciprocity extended to all citizens of the Aztec Empire; excavations of houses reveal that people sacrificed flowers, incense, and food at home in the process of making requests of individual gods (Brumfiel 2007; Marcus 2007).

Evidence for Aztec ideology and ritual is concentrated at their capital at Tenochtitlan, buried beneath colonial and modern Mexico City. Because of this historic-period overlay, knowledge of the original layout of the city is fragmentary, though enriched each time 21st-century residents put in new buildings, roads, and other infrastructure. Between 150,000 and 200,000 people lived in Tenochtitlan at its early 16th-century acme; few of these were food producers, and many were Aztec elites and provincial rulers, who were required to live for at least part of the year in the capital (Berdan 1989; Brumfiel 1987, 1994a). The Aztec king was a centralizing force, bringing others into his presence for political and ritual performances.

The best-preserved archaeological remains at Tenochtitlan belong to the Templo Mayor (the "main temple"), located in the center of the city, where the Spanish conquerors placed their principal administrative and religious structures as well. The Templo Mayor comprised two temples atop a high platform; excavations within the core structure indicate that construction on the building began in the 14th century and that at least six phases preceded the building's final form. The pyramid form was said to replicate the mythical Serpent Mountain, the place of creation, and rituals atop the southern staircase re-enacted creation's violence, when the newborn sun god, Huitzilopochtli, defeated and dismembered his moon goddess sister, who had arrayed forces to oppose and kill him. A 3.25-meter diameter stone disk found at the base of the staircase depicts the defeated goddess in relief; daily ritual re-enactment by throwing a captive and probably lifeless enemy down these steps guaranteed the sun's continued movement, and its dominance among cosmic forces. While the southern of the two temples was dedicated to Huitzilopochtli, who was also the Aztec god of war, the northern one housed the worship of Tlaloc, the god of rain and agriculture (Matos Moctezuma 1984). Tlaloc also required human sacrifice, including the decapitation of women; a chacmool positioned before his temple may have received heart sacrifices and communicated messages to the god.

When Spanish conquistadors arrived in 1519, Aztec power was at its peak, but so was the terror that power aroused in the empire's neighbors and subjects. Between 1519 and 1521, the Spanish, led by Hernán Cortés, gathered local allies, captured the Aztec king, fought a series of battles, and eventually successfully besieged Tenochtitlan. After the fall of the Aztecs, full conquest of Mexico required several decades. A significant part of the Spanish conquest involved obscuring and destroying evidence of Aztec religion and administration; at the same time, by incorporating Aztecs into their political system, using education and intermarriage, they guaranteed the survival of native cultural practices and beliefs, albeit in hybridized forms.

Conclusion

Complex society in Mesoamerica is first found among the ranked elites of the Preclassic Olmec, Oaxaca Valley, and early Maya population centers. In these areas, access to high-value trade goods may have opened up pathways to power, but individual achievement was largely masked. In all three cases, monumental earth-moving and construction projects led to the creation of landscapes that replicated cosmology and formed settings for the re-enactment of myth. While the basic outline of the belief systems among these groups may have been similar, their political organization and ideological expression varied sharply.

By the Classic Period, conflict and competition came to play major roles in political histories of southwestern, central, and eastern Mesoamerica. The nearness of rivals prevented any one Maya city-state from building a territorial state. Maya kings deployed charismatic force and perceived connections to the gods to hold exclusive power within their limited territories. In contrast, the lack of rivals through most of Teotihuacan's and Monte Albán's primacy produced a different ideology of power in those centers, whose geographical reach anticipated Postclassic territorial states like the Postclassic Maya and the Toltecs. Finally, in the Late Postclassic Period, the Aztecs promoted an ideology of violence that linked their conquests and conflicts to those among the gods.

13

ANDEAN CIVILIZATIONS AND EMPIRES

Introduction

The Inca Empire ruled much of the western portion of the South American continent from the early 1400s CE until it fell to the Spanish in 1536. However, the Inca were not the first complex society to rise in this beautiful but formidable landscape of mountains, valleys, and coast. A host of polities and states preceded the rise of the Inca Empire.

In some cases, Andean rulers and elites held sway over economic concerns, while in other cultures religion played an enormous role in allowing rulers and elites to gain power and influence, especially through long-held ancestor veneration systems. Prominent in some of these cultures was violent engagement with neighbors for purposes of territorial expansion and suppression of internal revolt. The Incas employed many of these same methods and constructed a vast administrative system to rule an enormous area that encompassed hundreds of ethnicities and millions of people.

Geography and Chronology

The Andes, one of the most dramatic mountain ranges in the world, forms the "spine" of South America. They stretch from the most northern edges of the continent to the very southern tip. One of the earliest sites in South America, Monte Verde, is located in southern Chile. Monte Verde was occupied roughly 14,000 years ago and likely signals the earliest modern human occupation of the continent.

Geography and Ecological Setting

The Andes range extends approximately 7,000 kilometers along the western coast of South America, with the northern range found in western Venezuela and the heart of Colombia (Figure 13.1). The central Andes range grows in girth (reaching about 700 kilometers in width) as it forms the majority of the modern countries of Ecuador, Peru, and Bolivia, where it also borders the Amazon rainforest. As the range continues its southern trajectory, it forms the eastern edge of Chile and the western region of Argentina, tailing off to individual mountains in southern Chile just south of Patagonia. The Andes range features several dozen volcanoes that reach heights of up to 6,900 meters (Figure 13.2), and the average height of the mountains throughout the range stands at approximately 4,000 meters. Scattered

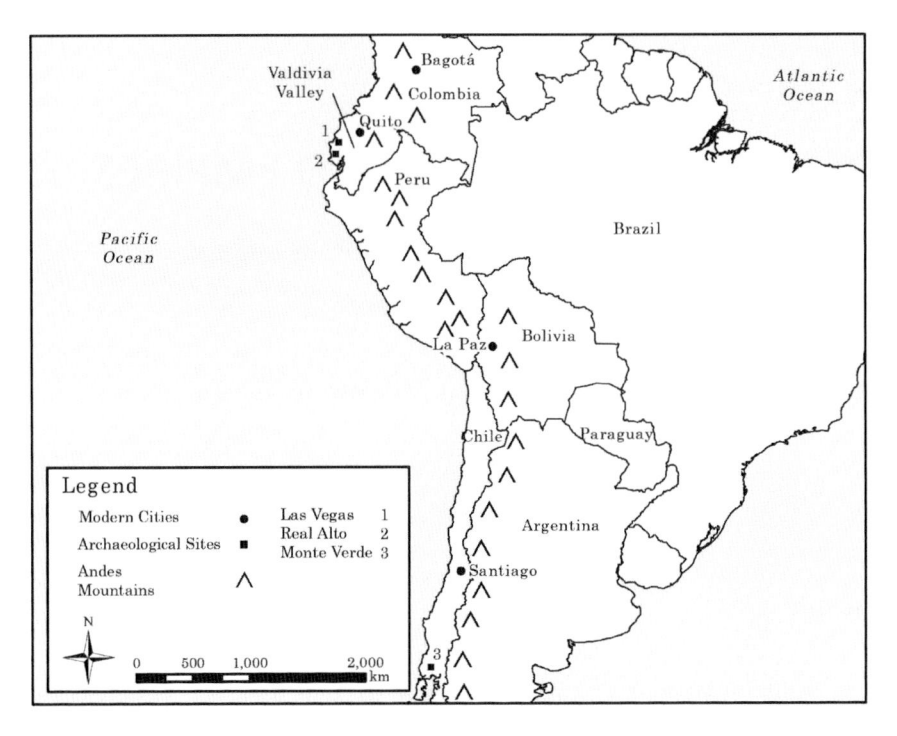

FIGURE 13.1 Map of South American Region and Location of Early Preceramic Sites

Source: B. Spencer

FIGURE 13.2 View of an Andes Volcano (at Villarrica Lake, Chile)

Source: Photo by S.R. Steadman

throughout the Andes are high plateaus where some of the continent's larger cities, including Quito in Ecuador, Bogotá in Colombia, and La Paz in Bolivia, have developed.

The central Andes, the focus of this chapter's discussion, encompass Ecuador, Peru, and Bolivia, stretching over 1.6 million square kilometers, an area that was once almost entirely controlled by the Inca Empire. There are at least three geographical and ecological zones in the central Andes. The western zone includes the coast and western Andean hills that feature a cold, desert climate. East of this coastal desert strip are the higher peaks of the Andes mountain range. On the eastern flanks of the Andes is a strip of tropical rainforest. Beyond this zone, the range plunges downward to the Amazonian basin. It is the combination of the topography and climatological process that creates this varied landscape.

The Andes halt the progress of rain-bearing air masses from the west. This, combined with cool air currents sweeping up the west coast from Antarctica, creates the Andean coastal deserts (McEwan 2006: 20). Lower peaks and valleys allow some rainfall through, creating increased rainfall in higher elevations. Thus, the central Andes provides a variety of ecosystems that require different exploitation strategies. Coastal area crops include chili peppers and fruits; on the western flanks of the Andes, where temperatures are more moderate and rainfall slightly higher, a wider range of plants such as maize, squash, and other edibles can thrive. The higher zones are more suited for growing tubers and grains, and in the high plains are grasses and hills where animals such as the native vicuña thrive and domesticated animals can be pastured; crystal clear lakes at these altitudes provide ample fresh water. The residents of westernmost South America have had to deal with two powerful periodic events visited on them by nature: earthquakes and climatic change created by the El Niño ocean currents (Sandweiss and Richardson 2008). Both of these have had significant effects on the rise, and fall, of Andean cultures.

The Chronological Sequence

Archaeology in the coastal regions of Peru and Ecuador has yielded evidence of seasonal campsites such as Monte Verde dating to between 14,000 and 9,000 years ago that exploited freshwater and marine resources as well as waterfowl. In these early millennia of occupation, variously called Preceramic or Archaic (12,000–1500 BCE) by archaeologists (Moore 2014) the Las Vegas culture (ca. 8000–4000 BCE), in Ecuador, established sedentary communities and experimented with cultivation (Table 13.1). The end date of the Preceramic phase is in some flux as archaeologists retrieve radiocarbon dates and additional data regarding social and technological changes from the Andean region (Janusek 2004). By the later Preceramic, plants and animals were domesticated and the building of larger settlements and ceremonial complexes had commenced. The Preceramic is followed by the Initial Period (ca. 1500–500 BCE), which serves as a "transitional" phase between the development of monumental architecture and growing social complexity and the development of kingdoms in the following Early Horizon Period (500–200 BCE).

In the Early Horizon Period, monumental buildings and decorative art became common, exemplified by Chavín de Huántar. After the Chavín collapse by the 3rd century BCE, several other cultures began to coalesce, and the Early Intermediate Period (200 BCE–600 CE) began. One of most remarkable cultural complexes to arise in the Early Intermediate was the Mochica (ca. 100–800 CE), and contemporary to the Mochica, but further south, was the Nasca culture (ca. 1–700 CE). Significant climatic change around 700 CE may have caused these Peruvian cultures to fade and eventually collapse.

Before and during the Middle Horizon Period (ca. 600–1000 CE), further inland where the climatic changes had less effect, several other Andean kingdoms rose to prominence. The Tiwanaku culture (ca. 100 BCE–1000 CE) built its capital near the shores of Lake Titicaca at the southern boundary of Peru, and just to the north of the Tiwanaku was the Wari culture (ca. 550–1000 CE); though more short-lived than the Tiwanaku, it grew to significant power. For the next several

TABLE 13.1 Chronological Periods and Sites Discussed in Chapter 13

Dates	Period	Sites and Cultures Discussed in Chapter	Cultural Horizons
ca. 12,000–7000 BCE	Early Preceramic	Monte Verde; Las Vegas Culture sites	Hunting and gathering, marine resources exploitation
ca. 7000–3000 BCE	Middle Preceramic	Valdivia	Semisedentary & permanent settlements; domestication of tubers, root crops, maize, and legumes; camelids and cuy are domesticated
ca. 3000–1500 BCE	Late Preceramic	Real Alto; Supe Valley Sites Aspero, Caral; Moxeke Culture, Sechín Alto; Kotosh Religious Tradition	Larger towns; public structures & open plazas in U-shape patterns; platform mounds (*huaca*); elaborate mortuary practices and human sacrifice; long-distance trade; household (kin-based?) religion
ca. 1500–500 BCE	Initial Period	Casma Valley Sites; Kotosh continues	Development of polities; decorated monumental architecture & temples; palaces
ca. 500–200 BCE	Early Horizon	Chavín de Huántar	State temples & deities; duality in cosmology; urban centers
ca. 200 BCE–600 CE	Early Intermediate Period	Mochica; Huacas de Moche; Sipán; El Brujo; Nasca; Cahuachi; Geoglyphs	Royal burials; extensive (ritualized?) warfare; state-sponsored religious practice
ca. 600–1000 CE	Middle Horizon Period	Tiwanaku, Tiahuanaco; Wari, Huari	Central rule of capital cities; establishment of enclaves/colonies
ca. 1000–1400 CE	Late Intermediate Period	Chimú, Chan Chan	Vast storage systems for state-run redistributive economy
ca. 1400–1536 CE	Late Horizon	Inca, Cuzco; Machu Picchu	Royal road system; taxation (*mit'a*) system; state cult and supreme deity; empire

centuries small kingdoms developed across the Andean valleys, trading and vying for additional lands and ushering in the Late Intermediate Period states (ca. 1000–1476 CE) (Bauer and Covey 2002; Covey 2003). One of these was the Chimú, with their capital at Chan Chan. However, by the Late Horizon Period (ca. 1476–1536 CE), most of these smaller kingdoms had been absorbed into the Inca Empire. The Inca Empire grew at a very rapid rate, reaching its zenith a few decades later. The Inca fell to a Spanish invasion of their lands by 1536.

Pre-State Cultures: The Preceramic and Initial Periods

Not surprisingly, the earliest residents of the Central Andes (ca. 12,000–7000 BCE) exploited marine resources, along with the hunting and gathering of a variety of other foods including camelids, wild beans, seeds, and fruits. While there is evidence that people living in the Las Vegas sites of

10,000 years ago began experimenting with squash cultivation (Dillehay 2008), hunting, gathering, and fishing remained the subsistence norm for some time. Michael Moseley has proposed that the vast exploitation of marine resources by the earliest populations of the Central Andes is the central principle that led to the origins of complex society in the region (Moseley 1975; Moseley and Feldman 1988), but this is not universally accepted by archaeologists. By about 7000 BCE, some regions appear to have had semisedentary settlements (Dillehay 2008).

Following the early Las Vegas experimentation with squash, different regions began cultivation of a variety of plants. Those occupying the highlands in the 7th millennium BCE were likely the earliest cultivators, growing a variety of tubers and root crops such as potatoes and quinoa that could survive the colder climates (Pearsall 2008). A second important crop, maize, is documented in Colombia and Ecuador, in the lower elevations, by the 6th millennium BCE. Contemporary to or slightly later than maize were experiments and eventual domestications of other plants including legumes (beans), squash, and even peanut (see Box 13.1).

BOX 13.1 CUYS AND CAMELIDS

The best-known animal domesticates from South America are the llama and alpaca, both camelids. Another domesticated animal found in many Andean sites is the guinea pig (Figure 13.3), known in South America as the *cuy*, which may have served as a sort of household "vacuum," consuming trash and food scraps. Cuy bones are found in central Andean sites as early as 8500 BCE, but these were likely wild; evidence of "hutches" where domesticated animals may have been raised do not appear until the mid-6th millennium BCE, and secure evidence of their domestication dates only as early as 3600 BCE (Stahl 2008). Like the cuy, camelid bones appear in the earliest central Andean sites but probably as a result of hunting. Archaeological evidence suggests that the camelids were being herded and kept in pens by approximately 4000 BCE in the higher-elevation settlements (Stahl 2008). Domestication of these species spread over the following millennia to more lowland regions so that, by 1700 BCE, llama/alpaca herd management was part of nearly every Central Andean community and provided wool for the important Andean textile production activities.

a.

b.

FIGURE 13.3 a. Photo of South American Cuy; b. Photo of South American Alpacas (Camelids)

Source: a. Photo courtesy of Philippe Lavoie (https://commons.wikimedia.org/w/index.php?curid=1508346); b. Photo courtesy of Pedro M. Martínez Corada, CC BY-SA 4.0 (https://commons.wikimedia.org/w/index.php?curid=37822488)

Earliest Settled Communities

By the 5th millennium, people had begun to settle into more permanent communities. The Valdivia culture in southwestern Ecuador grew out of the Las Vegas cultural tradition in the Chanduy Valley (Figure 13.4). By approximately 4400 BCE, the Valdivia culture was producing some of the earliest ceramics in the Americas in small and medium-sized villages (Moore 2014: 189). Pole and thatch ovoid huts were built in a circular or U-shaped arrangement, creating an open space within the center of the village (Damp 1984). People exploited riverine and marine resources; hunted game; and grew maize, beans, peppers and gourds in gardens. Valdivian ceramics are well made and beautifully decorated. Highly decorated bowls feature geometric designs that some have suggested represent the images seen as one enters an altered state (Stahl 1985); they may have been used for consuming intoxicating beverages during ceremonies or rituals. The presence of numerous Valdivian bowls at specific sites points to these as places where ceremonies took place; people from surrounding villages might have traveled there to attend rituals and gatherings (Raymond 2008).

By the 3rd millennium, Valdivian sites (ca. 3000–2400 BCE) had changed rather dramatically from the earlier smaller villages. The site of Real Alto had become a town with numerous houses, public buildings, and a population of as many as a thousand people (Marcos 2003). Domestic structures, still arranged in a U-shape, created an open plaza (Figure 13.5), within which residents had constructed two platform mounds called "Charnel" and "Fiesta" by excavators (Clark, Gibson, and Zeidler 2010). On top of the more northerly Fiesta Mound were

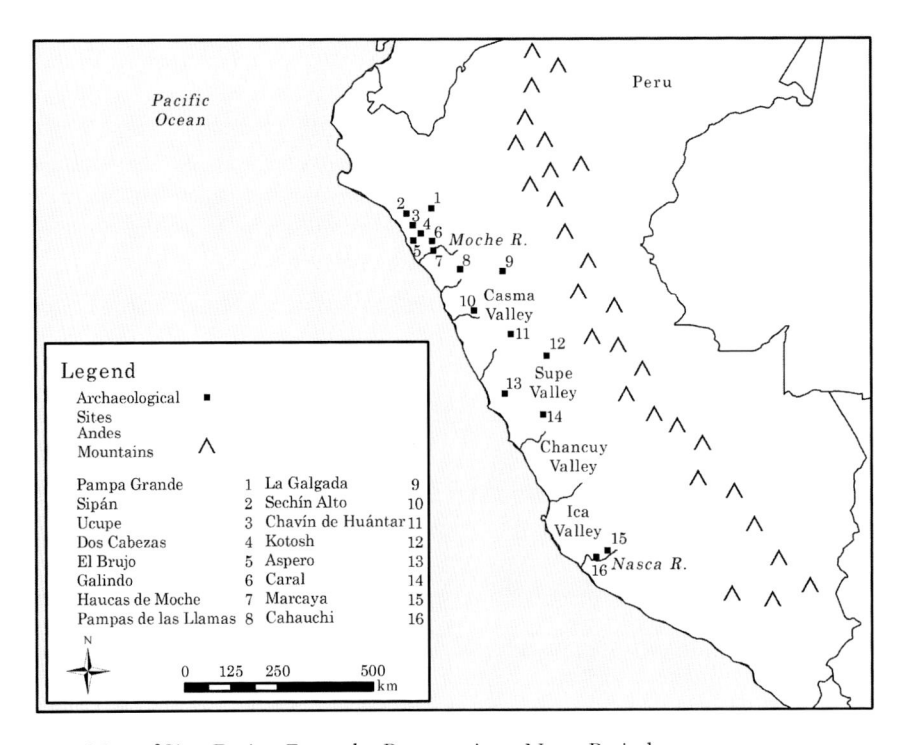

FIGURE 13.4 Map of Sites Dating From the Preceramic to Nasca Period

Source: B. Spencer

structures likely intended for ceremonial use. Food remains, the bowls noted earlier, and other artifacts suggest feasting took place on the mound. Associated with the more southerly Charnel Mound were human burials (Clark, Gibson, and Zeidler 2010). Evidence suggests that Valdivians used boat travel to settle islands off the coast of Ecuador (Zeidler 2008). Valdivian sites continued to grow and develop until the end of the Valdivian culture in ca. 1800 BCE when a volcanic eruption in the region likely affected crop production and made continued residence in the area impossible.

Contemporary with the emergence of monumental architecture at Valdivia is a complex of settlements in the Supe Valley of Peru. Several dozen sites, dating to between 3000 and 1800 BCE, featured settlements of substantial size, monumental architecture, and evidence of trade. Two Supe Valley sites, Aspero and Caral, illustrate the type of economic relationship that may have existed in this region at this time. Aspero was located near the coast at the mouth of the Supe Valley while Caral lies close to 15 kilometers inland. At Aspero residents built at least 17 mounds of stone, adobe, and mud (see Box 13.2) set upon valley hills to give them extra height. On top of many of these huacas were structures that may have been temples. The rooms atop Huaca de los Idolos yielded a number of human figurines; several burials on top of Huaca de los Sacrificios suggest a mortuary cult or perhaps even human sacrifice (Feldman 1987). The effort necessary to construct these mounds was considerable; both Aspero inhabitants and residents in surrounding communities likely contributed to their construction, perhaps at the behest of local elites (Feldman 1987).

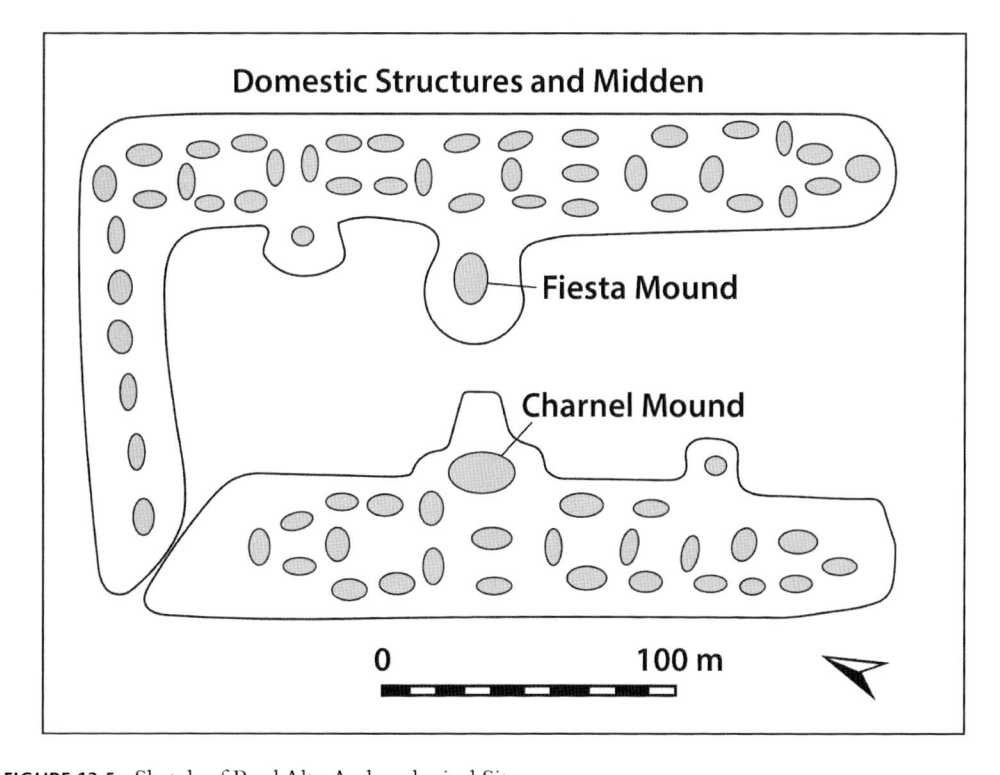

FIGURE 13.5 Sketch of Real Alto Archaeological Site

Source: S.R. Steadman after Clark, Gibson and Zeidler (2010: 212, fig. 11.4)

BOX 13.2 HUACAS

Huaca is a word that refers to sacred places. In the Inca state, huacas could be natural places such as mountains or caves or built places such as ancient cities (McEwan 2006: 158). The sacred aspect of huacas came from the belief that spirits inhabited the world around Andean peoples, and thus, any natural formation could be sacred. An additional layer of importance might be added to a particular place through mythological attributions of ancient important events to certain locations. Because the word refers to sacred and ritual places, many of the monumental structures at ancient Andean sites acquired the name "huaca" such as the Huaca del Sol and Huaca de la Luna at Moche and the Huaca de los Sacrificios at Aspero. In the Inca state, hundreds of huacas were believed to rest on sacred lines called *ceque* that radiated from the Inca capital at Cuzco (Zuidema 1964). Ceremonies and rituals at these places were important events on the Inca calendar.

Caral is a far larger site featuring over 30 stone-built structures; Caral may have been the Supe Valley regional center (Shady Solis 2006). Some of these large structures are set around a central open plaza; the buildings usually have an internal sunken plaza from which one ascends stairs to the rooms at the top. Artifacts found within these structures, such as condor and pelican bone flutes and bones from other animals carved with decorative motifs, indicate that this was a site where ceremonies and rituals were carried out. Human figurines were also recovered from Caral. Residential compounds were associated with these large structures, suggesting that each was "managed" by a family or extended kin group (Shady Solis, Haas and Creamer 2001).

The people at Caral had a robust agriculture-based subsistence system cultivating beans, squash, and sweet potato as well as cotton (Pozorski and Pozorski 2008). At Aspero, residents harvested vast quantities of marine resources in order to supply the inland communities such as Caral with this desirable resource (Sandweiss 2009), likely for subsistence items and cotton grown at places like Caral. Elite control of this exchange system would have afforded them significant power in their communities (Feldman 1987; Moseley 1975). A need to ensure the continued success of subsistence activities may have given leaders at both Aspero and Caral the ability to marshal vast quantities of labor from the people to build ceremonial centers and huacas.

Appearing approximately 4,000 years ago, and lasting until the end of the Initial Period (ca. 1500–500 BCE), the Casma Valley complex of sites, including those of the Moxeke culture, emerges further north on the Peruvian coast and shows a similar level of architectural and political sophistication to that found in the Supe Valley. Five large Moxeke settlements, each featuring monumental architecture, are clustered together in the inland region between 13 and 18 kilometers from the coast. Each center, with Pampa de las Llamas-Moxeke and Sechín Alto the most heavily explored, has massive huacas or buildings that appear to be dedicated to different activities. At Pampa de las Llamas-Moxeke, an enormous mound may have served as a temple; large stone friezes decorated with anthropomorphic images once stood atop the mound and would have been visible from the plazas below.

At Sechín Alto, the largest mound held a building that may have served as an administrative center for managing trade and the valley's irrigation system; as many as 18,000 people may have lived in and around Sechín Alto (Pozorski and Pozorski 2005). An architectural complex at another center was large enough to be termed a "palace" and may have been the leader's residence. Casma Valley elites and leaders controlled a vast territory that included a sophisticated exchange network of valuable resources. A close interrelationship between economy and religion was at the heart of this cultural complex and drove the development of social inequality and the rise of leadership.

There is evidence that household religion was also a norm within the Late Preceramic (ca. 3000–2100 BCE) and Initial Period (1500–500 BCE) cultures. Household religion is in part defined by architecture that belongs to what has become known as the "Kotosh Religious Tradition," named after the site of Kotosh, on the eastern slopes of the Andes; Kotosh architecture has also been discovered at La Galgada to the north, and at Caral in the Supe Valley. The tradition features semi-subterranean single-roomed rectangular structures that include wall niches, benches encircling the interior, and central hearths ventilated to direct air flow (Moore 2014: 239). The location of these chambers in the domestic quarters suggests that they served household needs for religious practice, perhaps for individual families, and may have been complementary to the larger-scale ceremonies carried out at Andean centers.

The later Preceramic and Initial Period cultural systems all faded, some due to climatic change and others due to internal strife, or a combination of both. Each contributed various components to the growing milieu of cultural complexity found in the various cultures across the Central Andes. Power structures during these periods hinged in part on the trade in valuable resources, and the ability of elites to marshal labor for the building of magnificent religious and secular structures.

Growing Complexity: The Early Horizon and Early Intermediate Periods

The Early Horizon phase (ca. 1000–200 BCE) sees growing socioeconomic and political complexity at the amazing Peruvian site of Chavín de Huántar and in the truly remarkable Intermediate Period (200 BCE–600 CE) Mochica and Nasca cultures located at opposite ends of the central Andes regions.

Chavín de Huántar

Chavín de Huántar (ca. 1100–500 BCE) lies at an elevation of just over 3,000 meters and at the junction of two rivers: the Mosna, which runs north/south, and the Huachecsa running east/west (Figure 13.6). Here residents built an impressive complex of temples and plazas. The Mosna generates hot mineral springs, which may have drawn the Chavín builders to this location (Rick 2008). By the Urabarriu cultural phase (ca. 1100–700 BCE), people at Chavín de Huántar commenced building a massive temple archaeologists named the "Old Temple" (Kembel 2008; Rick 2008). During the following Janabarriu cultural phase (ca. 700–500 BCE) there were significant additions to the temple, called by some archaeologists the "New Temple" phase. The last 50 years of the Janabarriu (ca. 550–500 BCE) is known as the "support period" when walls that became unstable, likely resulting from an earthquake, were reinforced (Kembel 2008). It was not long after, perhaps around 500 BCE, that the area was largely abandoned (Rick et al. 2009). The Chavín construction phases consist of complicated and largely constant building and rebuilding of the Chavín monument from at least 900 BCE until its abandonment four centuries later (Rick 2013a, 2013b).

Little is known about the Urabarriu community that began building Chavín. A few hundred residents probably consisted of personnel responsible for upkeep of and service to the temple and craft-workers dedicated to creating carvings and art (Miller and Burger 1995). Local farmers grew tubers; camelid faunal remains indicate herding was an important part of the local economy. The main craft was textile production using camelid wool. Residents traded with mountain and coastal settlements, demonstrated by ceramic styles and mussels, clam shells, and fish bones at Chavín (Burger 1992).

336 Andean Civilizations and Empires

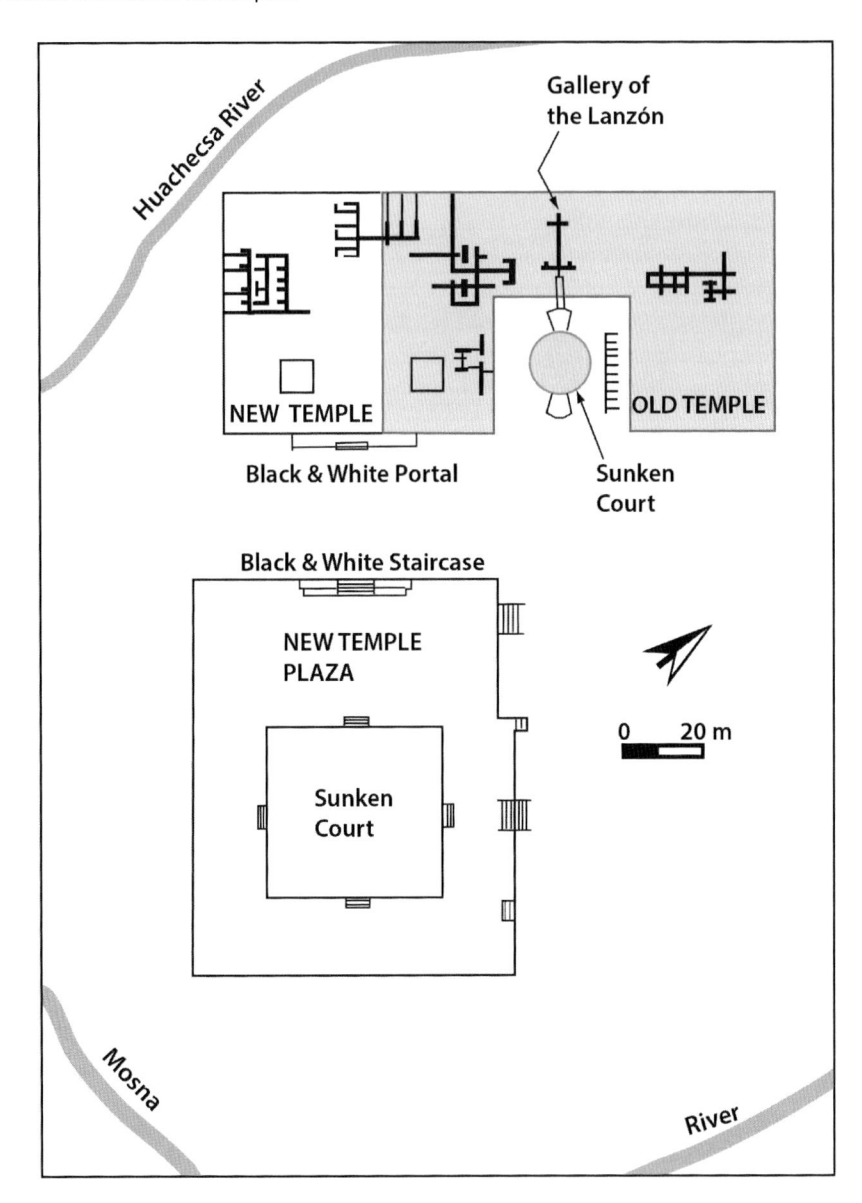

FIGURE 13.6 Plan of Chavín de Huántar Site and Area

Source: S.R. Steadman after Moseley (2001: pp. 164–65, figs. 68–69).

    The Chavín temple was built in the familiar U-shape, with a southern wing that was wider than the northern one, making the overall look of the temple asymmetrical. The walls ranged from 11 to 16 meters high, and the exterior was decorated with rows of different types of stone including granite, sandstone, and limestone creating colorful patterns. Protruding from the walls were sculpted stone heads of mythological beings both anthropomorphic and zoomorphic in form and at least twice the size of human heads (Burger 1992: 131–32). The interior of the temple consists of a set of galleries that underlie both the temple itself and the rectangular fronting plaza. These galleries are mazelike with abrupt turns and multiple levels; according to one scholar, "ritual activities seem

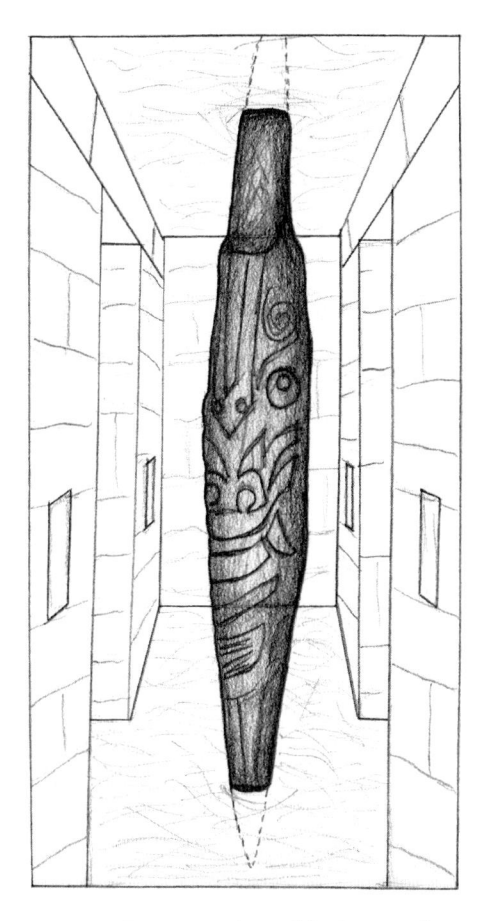

FIGURE 13.7 Representation of the Lanzon Stone

Source: R Jennison

clearly indicated. . . . The dark, mysterious, and highly controllable environments would probably have had a major ambience-setting effect on participants" (Rick 2013a: 153).

Perhaps most important is the Lanzón Gallery in the central part of the temple. Found here was the 4.5-meter tall Lanzón stone carving, which may depict the deity to whom the temple was dedicated (Figure 13.7). The narrower top of this unusually shaped stone was inserted into the gallery ceiling, and the narrow bottom end rests in a notch in the floor. The shape of the stone has been compared to a lance, knife, and even an Andean foot plow. Depicted is a human-like figure with feline fangs, adorned with a necklace and ear plugs and a belt with snake and jaguar images. A duct built into the architecture allows natural light to illuminate the face (Rick 2013a). The distinctive artistic style at this center, featuring highly stylized human and animal themes, is known as the "Chavín Style" and can be recognized at regional sites that were influenced by Chavín religion and culture (Rick 2013b). A second carved stone, known as the Tello Obelisk, was found in an outer courtyard, part of the temple built in the final phase of the building's usage. This 2.5-meter tall stone carving depicts two versions of a cayman-like creature, the crocodile that was ubiquitous in Peruvian rivers until the last century.

Important in Andean cosmology is the notion of duality and the balance of opposites; this may have been expressed at the Chavín temple by the placement of the Lanzón deity at the center of the U-shaped temple, implying his role was as mediator, between the two arms of the temple. The Lanzón deity may have served as the *axis mundi* of the cosmological universe (Burger 1992: 137), making the Chavín temple extremely important for the entire region. The two caymans on the Tello Obelisk may also portray duality, representing two cosmological worlds consisting of earth and water (Urton 2008); the caymans may also be costumed humans engaged in ritual activity (Rick 2008). The representation of plants on the Tello Obelisk may indicate the images had some relationship to agricultural fertility.

The discovery of groups of ceramic vessels in some galleries suggests that they served as storage areas for goods perhaps used at public ceremonies in the plaza. Other galleries contained ritually important items such as conch-shell trumpets, likely stored for ceremonial use (Rick 2013a). Sophisticated drainage and ventilation systems in the galleries are further evidence that they were used on a consistent basis. The presence of numerous human bones, some carved with animal images, others burnt and cut, suggests that human cremation or sacrifice may have been part of the ritual activities (Lumbreras 1993). Chavín seems to have served as a regional temple dedicated to an important deity who may have been responsible for keeping the entire Andean world in balance. Its location at the confluence of two rivers may also indicate that it rested at the center of a sacred geography for the ancient Andeans.

In the Janabarriu phase (ca. 700–500 BCE), the population at Chavín increased to several thousand (Burger 2008), and socioeconomic differentiation becomes archaeologically apparent. Those residents living immediately adjacent to the temple possessed higher quality goods than those living across the rivers. The wealthier households possessed obsidian tools, marine shells from as far away as the Ecuadorian coast, finer imported ceramics, and imported gold jewelry. They also enjoyed the choicest cuts of llama meat. Lower-status households featured chert tools, fewer imported ceramics, fewer coastal imports, and cuts of meat that were less optimal and from older animals (Burger 2008).

At this time, the Chavín complex grew with additional underground galleries; a large plaza with a sunken rectangular courtyard (in which the Tello Obelisk was found), flanked by two additional stone buildings, was built in front of the entire complex to accommodate public ceremonies (Kembel 2008). Ritual seems to have taken place in specially constructed buildings built atop the temple and entered by narrow chambers that would have effectively restricted access to all except specialists and perhaps elites.

In the Janabarriu phase, the extensive long-distance trade and development of economic and status-based social differentiation, in the shadow of a monumental religious building, allow archaeologists to call Chavín a "regional center" and perhaps even a substantial "polity" (Burger 2008). Though regional populations may have cooperated in the building of the Chavín temple, it was emerging elites that likely directed the last major building phase and began to control access to its religious areas (Rick 2004). As noted earlier, an earthquake necessitated a rebuilding period during the latter half of the 6th century BCE. By the 5th century, the region was no long occupied and the temple was abandoned.

The Mochica

North of Chavín de Huántar and on the coast, the Mochica (ca. 100–800 CE) cultural sphere gained prominence in the Early Intermediate Period (ca. 200 BCE–600 CE). Settled approximately 2,000 years ago, the site of Huacas de Moche is situated on the Moche River. Very quickly, small agricultural settlements coalesced into larger centers where large huacas were built and Mochica leaders were established. By 200 CE, Mochica leaders controlled numerous valleys; it is cited by early scholars as the first archaic state society in the Andes (Stanish 2001). Recent scholarship (Castillo and Uceda 2008) has suggested that the Mochica were not a unified "culture" but rather a set of related polities: a Southern Mochica sphere in which two major polities (one at Huacas de Moche and the other at El Brujo) may have been allied and a politically fragmented Northern Mochica sphere in which individual Mochica rulers each controlled a single valley (Chapdelaine 2010a, 2010b). As at Chavín, Mochica elites ruled the region through a combination of religious control as well as a strong hand in the economic strategies of the region.

As irrigation agriculture developed in Mochica regions, elites may have organized labor to build irrigation canals and then reaped the benefits of additional crop yields. Higher populations brought emphasis on craft specialization. Well known for their extraordinary ceramics, Mochica craftmakers also produced items of gold, silver, metal alloys, precious stones, and other materials. Elites and leaders also needed to protect their people in a region and period of growing competition and hostile interaction. Conflict required leaders to recruit and support warriors and to interact and negotiate with neighboring polities to ensure peaceful relations. Concomitant with these developments was an increased concentration on ritual and the building of ceremonial structures at what became Mochica centers. Mochica complex society, therefore, emerged based on the control leaders exerted over economic and religious concerns and the need for those leaders to build effective military mechanisms and political interactions (Castillo and Uceda 2008).

At Huacas de Moche, two large huacas face one another at a distance of 500 meters: the larger, Huaca del Sol, stands near the river; Huaca de la Luna rests nearer the mountains. Huaca del Sol, covering an area roughly 340 by 160 meters, stands 40 meters high today and was almost certainly higher when first built. Inside were platforms, courts, rooms, and burials, though much of the monument was destroyed by colonial period Spanish looting. Huaca de la Luna was decorated with murals depicting deities, rituals, and other images; within it were burials of both adults and children, the latter perhaps sacrificial victims (Bourget 2001). Between the two huacas was the settlement, which may have been home to several thousand people (Chapdelaine 2002).

The town (Figure 13.8) is described as an urban center with significant population (Chapdelaine 2000). Stone and adobe houses were built in compounds possibly reflecting the extended families that lived and cooperated together as is the norm in many Central and South American cultures (Nash 2009). Figurines representing both humans and animals were also found in these houses; some look like the anthropomorphic creatures painted on Mochica ceramics and may have been part of household ritual activities. Residents at Huacas de Moche benefitted from the trade and water management systems controlled by the center's elites, living stable if not luxurious lives at the Southern Mochica center (Chapdelaine 2006).

The commoner class was located in smaller villages outside the center. These farmers also engaged in fishing and could be called to the center for labor when needed. Where the elites and leaders lived is still not clear. Many archaeologists believe that some of the massive huacas at Mochica centers may have supported palaces (Chapdelaine 2006, 2011); alternatively, lower platforms near the huacas may have once supported the houses of the elites. The most secure evidence for the presence of elites and rulers at Mochica centers comes from burial evidence, discussed in more detail later.

Economic and Sociopolitical Structures

The Mochica engaged in significant craft production both within individual households and in workshops. In addition to ceramics and textiles, artisans fashioned metal, wooden, gourd, feather, and stone objects for trade within and beyond Mochica borders (Chapdelaine 2011; Quilter 2002). The Mochica "middle class" in part consisted of the artisans, merchants, and traders. The marine merchant class used wooden boats to ply the islands and coastal regions for raw resources such as shells; ethnohistorical evidence suggests these sea-based merchants worked at the behest of rulers

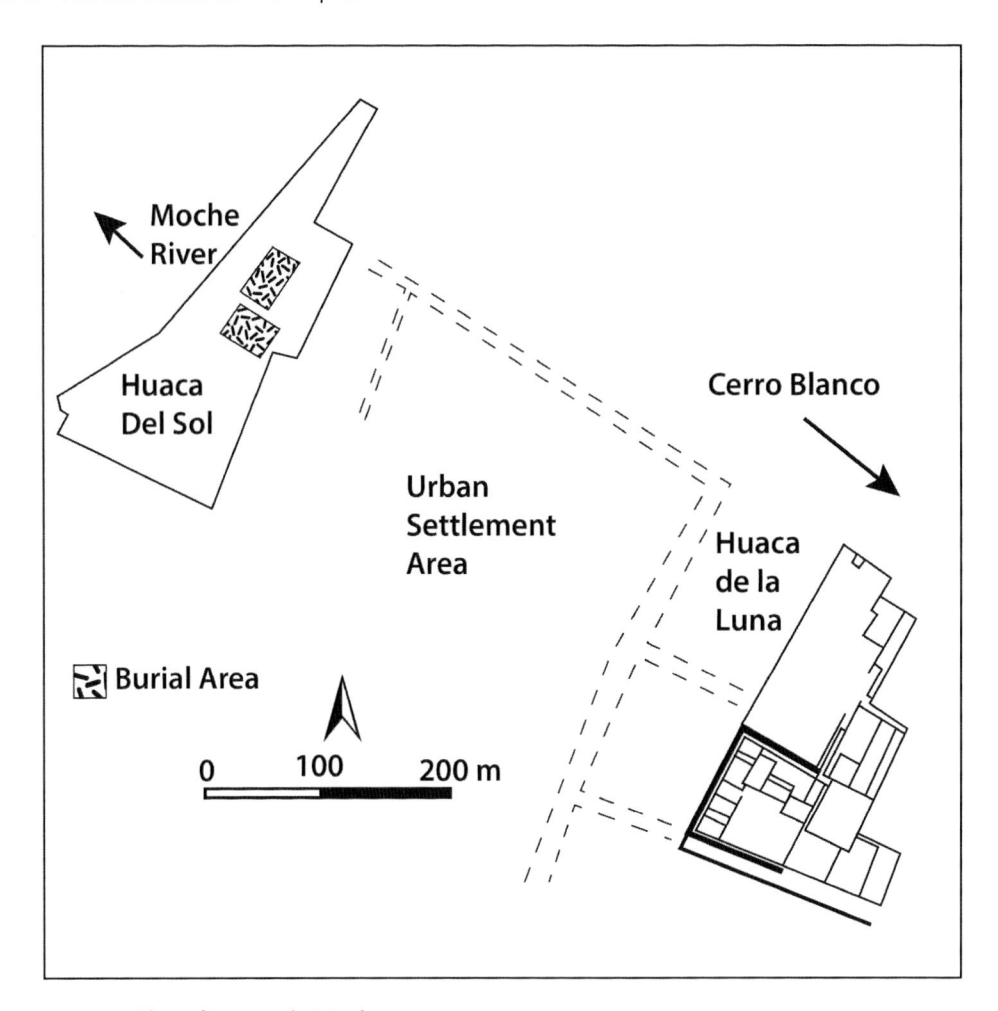

FIGURE 13.8 Plan of Huacas de Moche

Source: S.R. Steadman after Moore (1996: 53, fig. 2.19)

and that their livelihoods depended on royal support (Bawden 1996: 102). The overland trade may have also been largely controlled by Mochica elites. Raw resources such as wool, shell, and metal ore were fashioned into beautiful display items that primarily ended up in the hands, and burials, of the elites. There is also strong evidence to suggest that artisans not only provided their products to elites but were attached to their houses. For instance, a bowl depicts (female) weavers being supervised by a Mochica administrator. At the site of Galindo, the metalworking areas were found very near administrative architecture, situated so that entry into the area was somewhat restricted.

Ceramic production offers an even clearer view into elite control of craft production. At Galindo, there was a ceramic workshop in the domestic quarter producing daily wares, while workshops for producing fine wares were located near the administrative center where artisans could be supervised by administrative elites (Bawden 1996: 98). Fine ware vessels are excellent tools for decoding the complex Mochica religion and ideology, which included many deities, human sacrifice, and fertility rituals (Bourget 2006). Evidence suggests that Mochica elite ideologies were transmitted to the people through the production of ceramics and other luxury goods. Scenes on fine ware ceramics may have been required by the state to conform to state ideologies, emphasizing some rituals and deities over others, depending on the message each polity wished to send to the people (Billman 2010; Chapdelaine 2011; Vaughn 2006). Thus, not just the production of the crafts but their form and decoration may have been under the strict control of Mochica elites and the ruling class.

Mochica culture was stratified into at least three classes. At the bottom were the commoners who carried out farming, fishing, and various required labors; at the top were the elites and leaders, and in between was the large urban middle class, which itself likely consisted of "upper middle" and "lower middle" classes. At the upper end of the middle class, perhaps verging into the upper rung of society, were likely religious personnel and equal or superior to them may have been regional leaders who reported to the royal house. At the uppermost stratum of Mochica society were of course the royal families. Though evidence is minimal, it would seem that Mochica society was patriarchal, with males making many of the important economic decisions and certainly serving as rulers (though see discussion later on the Lady of Huaca Cao Viejo).

Unfortunately, looting, extending back to colonial times and continuing today, has destroyed many Mochica tombs, rendering them unintelligible to archaeologists. A few Mochica centers have escaped the attention of looters. Tombs of elites, sometimes identified as priests, warriors, or rulers, have been excavated at sites such as Dos Cabezas, Sipán, Ucupe, and other locales in the North Mochica region (Alva and Donnan 1993; Bourget 2008; Donnan 2007) (see Box 13.3). In the southern Mochica sphere, some elite tombs have been discovered at Huacas de Moche, as well as at El Brujo (Chapdelaine 2011), though most of the contents of the tombs at these sites are gone. A short description of the undisturbed tombs at Sipán and Dos Cabezas presents a clear picture of the wealth and pageantry associated with elite Mochica burials and of the lives these elites and royal figures must have lived.

BOX 13.3 THE PRIESTESSES OF SAN JOSÉ DE MORO

Excavations at the Mochica site of San José de Moro discovered several high-status female burials in 1991 (Castillo and Donnan 1994; Donnan and Castillo 1992, 1994). These burials contained significant numbers of burial goods and iconography and objects, including goblets, that represented the "sacrifice scenes" in Mochica religion. The women wore elaborate headdresses that are also found on people in ritual scenes painted on ceramics. Several of the main burials were accompanied by additional burials that may have been meant as servants to accompany the priestess into the next world. Whether secular or religious elites, these burials indicate that women may have held important positions in Mochica culture.

In 1987 at the site of Sipán, archaeologist Walter Alva discovered an exceedingly rich tomb situated within a large architectural complex called Huaca Rajada. The dead were entombed in the 3rd century CE below an eroded pyramid. In the first tomb, Alva found over 1000 Mochica pots and the burial of a seated male whose feet had been removed. Below this layer was a 5 by 5 meter tomb containing the burial of an individual who has become known as the Lord of Sipán (Alva and Donnan 1993). This adult male wore richly decorated Mochica clothing, a crescent-shaped headdress of gold, a face mask of the same material, jewelry of gold and turquoise, and metal plates (of gold and silver) meant to protect his body in warfare (Alva and Donnan 1993). He carried a scepter also made of gold, and within the tomb were many objects made of gold, silver, shells, textiles, feathers, and other precious materials. These tomb contents are depicted on Mochica ceramics in scenes where such an individual presides over ceremonies of ritual and sacrifice. The man in this burial was clearly a high-ranking member of Mochica society, perhaps the ruler. Along with the befooted man, likely meant to serve as a guard in perpetuity, were six other burials: two males, likely guards, flanked the main burial; a child was laid at the head of the tomb; three women were either at the feet or head in small coffins made of wood or cane. Food, in the form of meat and liquids, was also placed in the tomb.

Two other tombs at Huaca Rajada display the wealth of Mochica elites. A year later, Alva discovered a second tomb contemporary to the first, also featuring a male burial dubbed "The Priest." This man held a cup and also wore a headdress and a necklace of gold fashioned into beads with human faces in a variety of expressions. A befooted man also accompanied this burial as did two women. The cup held by The Priest is depicted on Mochica ceramics in which a priest collects blood from sacrificial victims and then offers this sacred drink to a Mochica lord, someone like the Lord of Sipán. A final tomb at Sipán contained "The Old Lord," a man similarly outfitted to the first burial in that the footless guard protected his chamber and he was dressed in finery and had many objects buried with him. A gold figurine of a Mochica warrior accompanied him, perhaps a version of the Old Lord in life; a necklace of golden spiders adorned his body. DNA analysis of the Lord and Old Lord indicates they were related, perhaps representing two rulers in the Sipán Dynasty; in fact, a dozen more tombs have been excavated at Sipán in recent years, and many of these elite burials contained relatives of the Sipán lords (Bourget 2008).

At Dos Cabezas, 64 kilometers south of Sipán, Christopher Donnan excavated a set of tombs containing eight individuals, five males and three women. Once again, the tombs (dating to between 450 and 550 CE) were located under a monumental structure. The males in Tombs 1, 2, and 3 were likely entombed at the same time or only days apart; each seems to have had a human female sacrificed and placed in the tomb with him to serve as an attendant. Besides ceramics, the tomb chambers contained copper figurines and other items, and the dead wore full regalia including masks, headdresses, and jewelry and carried shields and weapons (Donnan 2007). A fascinating element of the Dos Cabezas male burials is that each suffered from gigantism; these males stood roughly 30 centimeters taller than other Mochica males (Cordy-Collins and Merbs 2008). This alone suggests that these males were related, demonstrating again that there was dynastic rulership among the Mochica.

Although the vast majority of Mochica elite burials belong to males, a few contain elite females. At El Brujo, in the northern portion of the South Mochica region, a tomb belonging to the "Lady of Huaca Cao Viejo" was found (Benson 2012). This female was in her mid-twenties, and she sported tattoos on her skin. She had been wrapped in cotton, and her tomb contained dozens of items of jewelry as well as some weapons; some clothing had gold sewn onto it (Benson 2012: 124). It is possible that such women served as priestesses in Moche ceremonies. It is notable that both males and females took weapons with them into the afterlife.

Mochica Warfare and Religion

Though warfare is a central theme in Mochica art and iconography, and in material remains within elite tombs, the warfare in which the Mochica engaged may have been more ritualized than actual. For instance, the shields worn by elites, depicted on ceramics and displayed in burials, would not have been sufficient to repel a blow or arrow (Quilter 2002). Warfare was carried out to aid in Mochica religion rather than as part of a political agenda. It is certainly the case that prisoners of war were sacrificed. Mochica ceramics and at least one mural at El Brujo depict precise sequences of events in which a warrior is captured and then stripped nude; a rope around his neck (sometimes there are several prisoners linked by the rope) is used to lead him from the battlefield to a huaca ritual site; the prisoner is then usually struck on the head and/or his throat is cut; in some cases, the blood from the cut is collected, and the lord consumes it from a special goblet such as was found in the burial of "The Priest" (Bourget 2006). That these events took place is proven by the discovery of burials at Huaca de la Luna at the Moche center that featured cut marks on their cervical spines (indicating cuts to the throat) and blows to the head (Quilter 2002; Uceda 2008). Many skeletons showed evidence of healed broken bones resembling what warriors would sustain in combat (e.g., defensive breaks on the arm). After death, these prisoners were dismembered and sometimes left to lie on the platforms at the huacas; occasionally, the body part of one person was inserted into that of another, suggesting a process of "dishonoring" the dead.

Those who argue that Mochica warfare was "actual," and conducted to protect and expand the realm, cite the mistreatment of the dead and the significant theme of warfare expressed through iconography and in violent deaths evidenced in burials. The argument for ritualized warfare stems also from the iconography, which shows Mochica-on-Mochica battle, and on the less than battle-worthy weapons noted earlier. The Mochica may have engaged in ritual combat, in almost a "gladiator"-style warfare in which two warriors of opposing sides fought literally to the death; death came, however, not on the battlefield but in the losing side's sacrifice to the lord. It is perhaps most likely that warfare for *both* political and ritual reasons existed in the Mochica world. Rulers expanded their territories using actual warriors skilled in battle; ritualized warfare and the blood of the vanquished (whether foreign or Mochica) fed the gods and the rulers.

Warfare and religion clearly went hand-in-hand in Mochica culture. However, Mochica religion was complex, evidenced by Mochica deities depicted on vessels and murals. They are generally anthropomorphic but often combine human and animal characteristics, representing priests wearing animal garb at ceremonies or the deities themselves (Bourget 2006). One of the most important deities was the Decapitator God, a human/spider combination, responsible for human sacrifice; this god may have served as a state religious symbol (Donnan 2010). Possibly priests, or even the ruler, impersonated this god at the sacrificial rituals. Other deities were associated with the burial of elites: the "Snake-Belt God" (also referred to as "Wrinkle Face"), the Iguana God, and at least one female goddess of the moon (Benson 2012). Other supernatural beings had animal forms and seem to accompany the anthropomorphic gods in their duties and ceremonies. The clear message is that rulers were closely tied to the gods, and they and their priests may have assumed the mantle of the gods' powers during important ceremonies. Elite control of craft production allowed for the projection of an ideology in which elites and Mochica deities were tied irrevocably in the minds of all who viewed iconographic images on ceramics, murals, and textiles.

Complexity and Mochica Society

The previous discussion offers some notions as to how Mochica rulers maintained their power, but the fine details of sociopolitical structures are still lacking. In fact, as one scholar notes, "One of the most controversial questions in Andean prehistory is the nature of Moche political organizations" (Billman 2010: 182). Clearly, a single state model, with a singular ruler, is no longer the best explanation of the Mochica system (Quilter 2002). The southern Mochica sphere, likely composed of two major polities at Huacas de Moche and El Brujo, conforms more closely to the definition of a "state" in the sense of a center, central ruler, and control over a large expanse of territory. In the northern sphere, evidence suggests the existence of three or more competing polities, each with a center located in a defendable valley (Chapdelaine 2011). A very recent analysis sees the north organized into three regions each with multiple competing polities within them (Castillo 2010). It is no longer correct to think of the Mochica as a single state but rather as a system in which numerous leaders likely competed for land, resources, and power.

The sophisticated Mochica irrigation system ensured sufficient harvests; elites and leaders could organize the labor to build the canals and could call on farmers who used the canals to carry out work such as building huacas (Billman 2010). This led to a second source of power, the building of monumental architecture, both secular and religious, that centralized ceremony and critical activities in spaces controlled by elites and leaders. Leaders and high elites also had residences on or near these monumental structures that tied them visually and ideologically with the state cult, its deities, and all the associated pageantry. State ideologies were transmitted to the people by other visual means, through the production of textiles and ceramics (Billman 2010). All of these factors ensured that rulers were well respected and obeyed while alive and were deserving of sumptuous mortuary gifts and elaborate ritual at their deaths.

During the early 8th century CE, settlements began to empty, and by 800 CE, the Mochica system was at an end. There may have been a variety of factors that caused instability, but environmental change was certainly one of them. El Niño weather patterns brought about torrential floods and intermittent drought, which affected their ability to produce sufficient agricultural products. Huacas de Moche itself seems to have experienced a catastrophic flood. While environmental damage may have been a contributing factor to their slow decline, it was not the entire cause (Chapdelaine 2000). Likely internal conflicts, in part arising over diminishing resources, destabilized some Mochica polities; inability to maintain the critical irrigation systems with a decreasing population, and increasingly hostile relations with neighbors, may also have contributed to a decline; disruptions in trade might have also been an issue. As is noted in Chapter 14, collapse is never a result of a singular cause, and the Mochica system is certainly testament to that.

The Nasca

In southern Peru, the Nasca culture, roughly contemporary to the Moche (ca. 1–700 CE), offers a very different sociopolitical trajectory. The Nasca developed out of the Paracas culture (ca. 750 BCE to 1 CE) that earlier dominated the southern coast. A new ceramic style at the turn of the era marks the archaeological beginning of the Nasca culture. The arid landscapes of the Nasca and Ica valleys were challenging to farm. Sophisticated water management systems and habitation on the mountain slopes, leaving fertile valleys free for farming, allowed the Nasca to establish a stable agricultural economy. Elites seem to have gained their power via their involvement in religious activities and possibly through efforts to maintain water management systems. The dichotomy between farmer and leader, however, was not as extreme as it was for their Mochica neighbors to the north.

The Nasca lived in small, dispersed communities probably peopled by kin-related groups. In addition to these agricultural communities, two other types of settlements existed in the Nasca realm: administrative and ceremonial centers. At administrative centers were large structures with many rooms, some columned and large enough to accommodate a number of people; these may have been the homes of local elites (Proulx 2008). Material goods in these centers and in nearby tombs attest to the wealth of those who occupied the larger centers.

The Nasca built at least one ceremonial center, Cahuachi, on the banks of the Nasca River some 50 kilometers inland. Cahuachi features at least 40 huacas built on the naturally hilly landscape; additional debris piled on top of a hill was then faced with adobe bricks (Silverman 2002). Some of these huacas were used for burial and others had platforms suitable for ritual activity. Individual huacas may have belonged to kin groups, used for burial of members of their lineage and for feasting (Proulx 2008). The largest huaca, the Great Temple, contained a large central plaza, rooms, and internal courtyards. At Cahuachi, water springs from the ground, a startling event in this very arid environment that points to why it was chosen as the ritual center. When first discovered, archaeologists believed Cahuachi was a vast uninhabited pilgrimage site (Silverman 1993, 2002; Silverman and Proulx 2002). Continued investigations, however, have shown that Cahuachi was inhabited, though primarily by elites, perhaps serving as high-level "caretakers" of the sacred center and hosts for the major ceremonies that drew in residents from outlying villages (Vaughn 2009).

Nasca Socioeconomic and Political Structures

The Nasca are justifiably famous for two products: their ceramics and their geoglyphs, the latter discussed in more detail later. Nasca ceramics are polychrome, portraying scenes ranging from daily activities to deities. Ceramics were produced at Cahuachi and possibly other administrative centers and were, as in the Mochica culture, purveyors of ideologies that bound the Nasca together in a belief system (Vaughn 2004, 2009). The Nasca also produced extraordinary textiles, some of which have been found in sealed tombs at Cahuachi and elsewhere. It is clear that craft production was a very important element in the Nasca socioeconomic structure and that these products served as important symbolic items to be included in mortuary rituals and in trade relations. While the Nasca did engage in trade, as demonstrated by the presence of obsidian and shell (Vaughn 2009: 59), it is unclear whether exchange was controlled solely by elites. Obsidian was used in agricultural and other subsistence-related pursuits, but it was also fashioned into ceremonial knives for ritual beheading, discussed later.

Evidence from Nasca villages (see Box 13.4) shows that social ranking was present in outlying agricultural communities. Elite residences at Cahuachi and at other secondary centers further testify to a stratified society. There seems to have been a "sliding scale" of wealth and power in which elites held more, farmers less, but the difference between the two groups was far smaller than in the Mochica culture. It is possible that a "chief" ruled his (or her) somewhat sparsely populated smaller territory from an administrative center (Proulx 2008). Such leaders organized the building of irrigation systems, directed the construction of huacas both at their administrative centers and possibly at Cahuachi, and may have sponsored the creation of geoglyphs. The elites at Cahuachi may have been primarily religious in function (Vaughn 2009), heading up major ceremonies at the Nasca center and perhaps also at the geoglyphs.

BOX 13.4 MARCAYA

Excavations of a Nasca village site called Marcaya offer a clear idea of what these dispersed communities were like (Vaughn 2009). At Marcaya, houses were built of wattle and daub and were set in over 20 "patio groups": small clusters of houses built around a patio, suggesting that kin-related inhabitants cooperated economically in production and subsistence activities. Several of these patio groups were larger with more well-built houses, reflecting some status differentiation at Marcaya. Residents engaged in the production of maize, beans, squash, tubers, peanuts, and potatoes; Nasca residents also participated in camelid pastoralism and traded with coastal communities for marine resources. Besides subsistence goods, families in patio groups produced lithics and textiles, the latter for both household use and possibly for trade.

Warfare and Religion

That the Nasca engaged in warfare seems clear from the images portrayed on their pottery but also from burials of both Nasca warriors and, apparently, victims. Ceramics show Nasca warriors preparing for, or engaging in, battle. They carry a variety of weapons including slings, knives, spearthrowers (atlatls) and spears. The goal in Nasca battle was not to take opposing warriors hostage as the Mochica did but to behead them. Enemy heads then became trophies, perhaps carried around on Nasca warriors' belts (Proulx 2001). These trophy heads, while testifying to the prowess of Nasca warriors, also served an important religious function discussed later. Unclear is who the Nasca fought in these battles. Some argue that most if not all warrior engagements were part of ritualized warfare, carried out for the purposes of trophy head acquisition and thus religious purposes; others argue that the Nasca engaged in warfare to effect territorial expansion (Proulx 2008) or perhaps most likely a combination of both.

Like the Mochica, much of the Nasca belief system is found in the images painted on their ceramics and stitched into their textiles; burial evidence is also an invaluable resource for clues to their complex cosmology. Three aspects of Nasca beliefs will be described here: portrayals on ceramics, the meaning of the trophy heads, and the geoglyphs. As noted earlier, ceramic production may have been controlled by Nasca elites to ensure they bore the correct images displaying the symbolic messages appropriate to Nasca beliefs. The supernatural beings in Nasca religion were born out of nature. Animals and anthropomorphic figures from both land and sea are represented as powerful entities; their role seems to have been to ensure sufficient rainfall, agricultural fertility, and health (Proulx 2006, 2008). A shaman is often portrayed on the ceramics, interceding between the human sphere and the supernatural beings to carry out important rituals. These persons may have formed some of the religious elites who occupied administrative centers or Cahuachi.

The act of beheading victims is shown on Nasca ceramics. Once severed from the body, the skulls were emptied of internal soft tissue, and holes were drilled in the cranium so that they could be carried on a rope; the lips were pinned shut with thorns (Proulx 2001). Trophy heads, primarily recovered from burials, were related in some way to crop fertility; ceramics display images of trophy heads with plants growing out of them and entwining the skulls. Heads were buried in caches and may have functioned as ritual offerings to the supernatural beings responsible for successful agricultural harvests. Some Nasca burials contain headless corpses, including those of women and children (Silverman and Proulx 2002). Recent analysis shows that some of these headless corpses were ethnically Nasca, suggesting either internal conflicts or perhaps ritualized battle or sacrifice (Conlee et al. 2009).

The Nasca geoglyphs were images created on the plains (pampas) and hillsides in the Nasca heartland; the top layer of dark stone was removed to reveal a white alluvial underlayer visible from miles away. Geoglyphs are either geometric, forming lines (some as long as 20 kilometers), triangles, and other shapes, or "biomorphs" (Proulx 2008) of enormous animals including a monkey, spider, whale, and birds (Figure 13.9). The biomorphs correspond to images on Nasca pottery and may represent supernatural beings in their cosmology. The purpose of the geoglyphs has not been satisfactorily solved; they may have served a variety of purposes including as places of ritual where propitiates walked the lines, for astronomical readings of seasonal changes, and for the marking or ritual renewal of underground water sources (Silverman and Proulx 2002). What is clear is that the geoglyphs had a deep religious significance to the Nasca and that labor could be organized, perhaps by religious elites, to create these enormous and impressive monuments.

Complexity in Nasca Society

Nasca leadership may have operated on the basis of allied groups living in adjacent chiefdoms or polities each with a ranked leader; regular ceremonies at Cahuachi or on the pampas, as well as symbolism displayed on ceramics and textiles, may have united all Nasca in their religious and sociopolitical beliefs perhaps even crossing kinship boundaries. That the Nasca were willing to defend their lands and beliefs in warfare is clear. Like the Mochica, the Nasca came to a somewhat ignoble end due in part to the vagaries of weather as well as to internal issues that caused societal dissolution by the 9th century CE.

FIGURE 13.9 Photo of Nasca Geoglyphs Showing the "Hummingbird"
Source: Photo by J. Siegl

Andean Kingdoms in the Middle Horizon Period to the Late Intermediate

While the Mochica and Nasca were located relatively close to the coast, contemporaneous and longer-lived complex societies were located further inland in the Middle Horizon Period (ca. 600–1000 CE). These include the Tiwanaku state located on the shores of Lake Titicaca in Bolivia and the neighboring Wari culture. To the north and closer to the coast, the Chimú state arose just prior to the Late Intermediate Period (ca. 1000–1476 CE).

The Tiwanaku

The site of Tiahuanaco ("Tiwanaku" refers to the state or culture), located about 20 kilometers from the shores of Lake Titicaca (Figure 13.10), emerged as the leading urban center in the region by ca. 200 BCE. Tiwanaku chronology (ca. 100 BCE–1100 CE) is divided into five phases (Janusek 2009), with Tiwanaku I–III (ca. 100 BCE–500 CE) describing the earliest settlements and development of the center. It is during Tiwanaku IV (ca. 500–800 CE) and Tiwanaku V (ca. 800–1100 CE) that the state reached its height (Janusek 2015). By the rise of the Incas a few centuries later, the Tiwanaku culture had weakened due to drought and climatic problems, as well as possible internal unrest.

The Lake Titicaca Basin is situated on a high plateau at an elevation ranging from 3500 to 4000 meters; this region, known as the "altiplano," is quite cold, with alternating very dry and very wet yearly cycles (Kolata 1986). Successful agriculture is a challenge, and the efforts to which the Tiwanaku state went to ensure sufficient food resources were a very important element in the rise of its political and economic power. For instance, residents of the state, likely directed and supported by the elites, reclaimed land from the marshy edges of the lake by creating raised agricultural fields, allowing population to increase and expand socioeconomic development (Kolata 1986).

The site of Tiahuanaco was vast, covering up to 6 square kilometers (Stanish 2003: 172). At its center was a complex of buildings that may have had a religious function (Isbell 2013); outside of this area are other buildings that may have served both religious and secular purposes. Much

348 Andean Civilizations and Empires

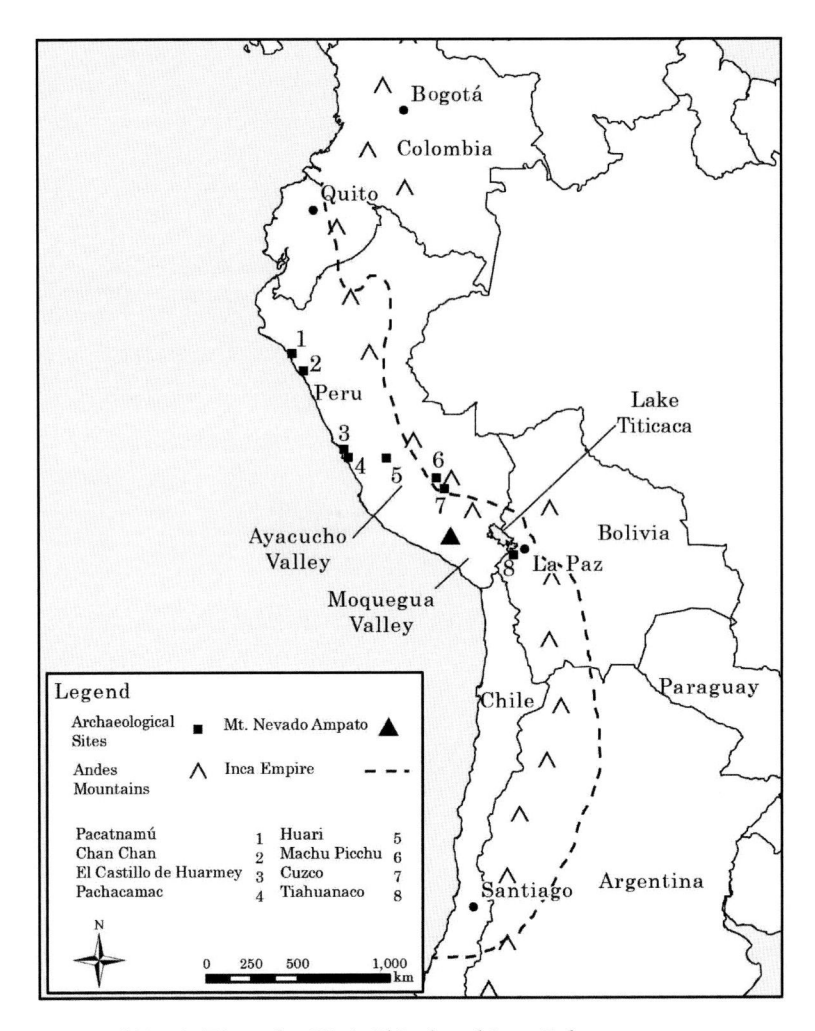

FIGURE 13.10 Map of Sites in Tiwanaku, Wari, Chimú, and Inca Cultures

Source: B. Spencer

controversy surrounds the role Tiahuanaco played: was it a vast city inhabited by thousands of people, or was it a pilgrimage site like Cahuachi with only a caretaker population of elites? Survey and archaeological work has demonstrated that Tiahuanaco was densely populated with perhaps over 10,000 people and possibly as many as 20,000 (Isbell 2008, 2013; Janusek 2004; Stanish 2013). Houses were organized in compounds that may have represented groups engaged in cooperative activities such as ceramic production (Janusek 2015). Labor invested in compounds, and luxury goods within them, indicate that ranking or some level of class stratification was present in the Tiwanaku state; simpler compounds may have housed pilgrims who journeyed to Tiahuanaco (Janusek 2004, 2015).

Tiwanaku Religion

Scattered across the site were many beautiful stone carvings bearing images symbolizing Tiwanaku beliefs. The ceremonial center contained several massive buildings including the Akapana, the Kalasasaya, and the Putuni, the last perhaps a palace or elite dwelling. The Akapana was built in a "cross" shape constructed in several platform layers that allow it to rise 16.5 meters above the ground; a sunken cross-shaped courtyard was placed at the top (Stanish 2003: 172). Though looting affected the Akapana terribly, archaeologists did recover several burials there that may have belonged to religious specialists who lived on the Akapana itself (Janusek 2004). A nearby complex held burials that may have held Tiahuanaco elites; buildings near the ceremonial center may have been their residences (Stanish 2003: 172).

The Kalasasaya was a large building on a platform with a central sunken court; numerous stone carvings portray human-like faces protruding from the courtyard walls. Located there is the Ponce Stela, a stone carving of a human figure with headdress and decorative clothing, carrying two objects in his hands; he may represent a deity known as the "Staff God." Various other stone stelae, as well as the heads protruding from the Kalasasaya walls, may represent different territories conquered by, and incorporated into, the Tiwanaku state (Stanish 2003: 174).

Several other stone monuments at Tiahuanaco give clues to their belief system. The "Gate of the Sun," located within the Kalasasaya, has two massive stone uprights topped by a lintel stone. All are heavily decorated, and the lintel stone portrays three types of anthropomorphic figures, which are likely Tiwanaku deities. These are known as "Staff God," the "Rayed Head" figure, and the "Profile Attendants." The Rayed Head image has 12 rays and may correspond to the solar calendar; 30 Profile Attendants may correspond to the number of days in each month within the 12-month solar calendar (Isbell 2008). At the center of Tiwanaku religion was a focus on the sun, the astronomical calendar, and the fertility of the earth. This trio of images is found on ceramics and textiles, indicating they sat at the center of this ancient cosmology.

Socioeconomic Structure

The Tiwanaku state depended on agricultural production to support itself and its constituents. The raised agricultural fields surrounding the center resulted in a complicated series of canals and irrigation channels emanating from Lake Titicaca and other sources that supplied an otherwise arid landscape. The state may have been responsible for helping to build and maintain the water management system, giving Tiahuanaco elites and leaders a critical role in the socioeconomic system. Trade was also important, with resources such as obsidian, copper, and possibly subsistence items brought into the Tiahuanaco center for elite consumption (Stanish 2003: 196). Elite ownership of camelid herds provided wool for textile production, which may have been the primary export from the center. As was the case in Mochica polities, elites may have also controlled the production and distribution of ceramics, which carried important ideological messages about religious and secular ideals. Tiahuanaco products were found at towns and villages at distances as far away as 150 kilometers from the center, carried by camelid caravans that eventually reached the far outposts of areas under its control (Stanish et al. 2010). Settlements in the Moquegua valley in southern Peru and in northern Chile and central Bolivia demonstrate extensive Tiwanaku ceramics and other material culture; they have been labeled "colonies" by a number of archaeologists (Kolata 1993; Stanish 2013). The export of prestigious items bearing Tiwanaku symbolism helped the center to maintain ties, and perhaps sociopolitical control, of regions far from the ceremonial center of the state.

Other areas around Lake Titicaca engaged in trade with the Tiwanaku state, some as independent polities and others becoming part of the state (Janusek 2004). Perhaps most interesting is Tiwanaku's relationship with its northern neighbor, the Wari. While this state would seem to have been the main competitor to Tiwanaku, evidence suggests that most relations were peaceful and perhaps even beneficial to both.

Complexity in Tiwanaku Society

The Tiwanaku state is perhaps best considered as a set of radiating regions in which differing levels of control were exerted by elites and leaders (Stanish 2003). At the center was the state capital and pilgrimage center to which all residents likely traveled at least once, if not repeatedly, during their lives. The building and maintenance of agricultural fields, irrigation systems, and monumental structures demonstrates the ability to organize vast labor contingents. Tiwanaku control of territories seems to have been varied and complex, with some apparently existing as independent polities and other areas functioning as part of the Tiwanaku state but maintaining indigenous social identities. These regions were intertwined with the center economically and by dedication to the religious ideologies of the Tiwanaku religion, centered at the capital city (Janusek 2002, 2004, 2006). Power and leadership in this ancient state was effected not primarily through force, but by a careful balance of socioeconomic control, including the facilitation of subsistence strategies and distribution of critical and desirable goods, and the successful projection of a unifying religious ideology that tied elites to the cosmology and the continued health and welfare of the people and the state.

The Wari

The Wari cultural complex (ca. 550–1000 CE) was located north of Tiwanaku. Like Tiwanaku, it faded in influence by ca. 1000, in part due to a terrible drought that prevented adequate subsistence production. Its capital, Huari, in the Ayacucho Valley, sits at an elevation of over 2500 meters and may have been the largest city to exist in the pre-modern Andes. The Nasca culture was beginning a downward trajectory by the time the Wari began to coalesce into a state. The Wari sphere of influence encompassed the Nasca and Ica valleys, and the Nasca engaged with it in trade and an exchange of religious beliefs and cosmologies (Conlee 2010). In the same vein, the Wari complex interacted with the southern Moche state to the north but did not usurp the power of local Mochica lords (Chapdelaine 2010b).

Far less is known about the Huari center due to limited archaeological investigation, an unforgiving topography, and a relative lack of monumental remains. The Huari center may have been quite heavily populated with tens of thousands of people (Isbell 2009; Jennings 2010), though its narrow streets and high walls suggest it did not function as a pilgrimage center. The people at Huari lived in the "patio groups" found in many other Andean cultures. Some of the walled compounds in the Huari city center are large and even opulent and may have belonged to the elites of the society (Isbell 2009). Huari residents built with fieldstones and mud, covering the walls with a plaster finish. They repeatedly remodeled and rebuilt external walls of compounds and internal cells, or living areas, attempting to achieve a living situation in line with their needs; the result, however, was a rather chaotic cityscape with no straight pathways through it and no semblance of an "urban grid." Isbell notes that "Approaching Huari, the visitor was confronted by a confusion of enormous architectural blocks, erupting like jagged white teeth from a skeletal jaw of gray volcanic rock" (Isbell 2008: 754).

The landscape around them did not lend itself to easy agricultural production. Massive irrigation systems and hillside terracing were necessary to produce sufficient subsistence for the growing population (Meddens and Branch 2010). Additional lands had to be incorporated into the state that eventually stretched from the northernmost borders of the Tiwanaku state to the southern borders of the Mochica culture.

The Wari acquired goods through trade and also produced fine ceramics and textiles, advancing an iconographic style, as at Tiwanaku, that influenced much of Andean culture until colonial times. The scattered distribution of Wari products across the state suggests that levels of socioeconomic control were uneven or regionally differentiated (Jennings 2010). For instance, in the Moquegua

Valley, Wari people apparently settled among locals and near where Tiwanaku had also established enclaves. This valley may have served as a place where both states could rely on inhabitants to facilitate trade and interaction between the two. In other areas, local ceramics constituted the utilitarian goods while the more finely made Wari ceramics served as the fine and imported wares. Isbell (2010) suggests this pattern could have resulted from marriage practices in which Wari men married local women in outlying villages, perhaps to facilitate Wari trade.

Religion

The Wari temples are D-shaped buildings with doorways in the middle of the straight wall. In comparison to other Andean temples they are quite small, approximately 10 meters across the straight wall; wall niches organized in groups of four may have been for making offerings or displaying objects (Quilter 2014: 206), including possibly human heads, removed from the dead at the time of, or shortly after, burial (Meddens and Branch 2010). As among the Nasca, the human head was an important symbol in Wari cosmology; heads of important Wari individuals, perhaps elites and leaders, or religious personnel, may have been displayed in ritual contexts. Wari burials are some of the best evidence of the social stratification present in the society and the wealth and power held by elites. As many as six social classes may have existed in the Wari heartland (Isbell and Korpisaari 2012). At the Huari center, several tomb complexes, although looted, featured subterranean stone cells (as many as 20 separate cells) into which the dead were placed, once accompanied by items of significant wealth.

Excavations at El Castillo de Huarmey in 2012 revealed an unlooted massive built tomb complex in which four royal women, each with her own tomb chamber, were discovered (Pringle 2014). Surrounding each woman were additional burials of elites, perhaps family, as well as attendants and apparent human sacrifices. Burial goods made of gold, silver, shell, and metal and countless ceramics, textiles, and other items accompanied the dead. After the placement of several dozen interments, a male and female guard, additional sacrifices, were placed at the door; the tombs were then sealed with 30 tons of gravel, and a layer of adobe bricks was laid over the entire complex. An above-ground room was built with the wall niches described earlier; looters report that mummified and wrapped burial remains once rested in the niches, suggesting that ancestor veneration was practiced here (Pringle 2014). It is clear that a Wari royal family lived at this site some distance from the Wari heartland.

Burial methods varied across the Wari sphere of influence, including multiple burials in cave-like rooms dug from bedrock, built cist tombs and chambers, pit graves below floors, charnel rooms, and bundle-wrapped burials (Isbell 2004). These differences likely attest to the presence of varying ethnic groups living in the Wari state. They are also indicative of social class, reflected in the labor investment in tomb construction, the location of the burial, and the number and types of goods placed with the deceased. Wari mortuary cults were adopted by outlying regions as the Wari state expanded. For instance, the Wari often buried their dead in a seated position, which became common in tombs outside the Wari heartland (Isbell 2010). People in more distant regions may have adopted Wari identity through a focus on ancestor veneration, necessitating alterations in burial methods (Isbell 2010). Wari influence through ideologies and ritual beliefs, if not through actual physical control, swept through regions considered part of the Wari sphere.

Sociopolitical Structure

The power structure may have been dispersed rather than centralized in the Wari state (Jennings 2010). Places such as El Castillo de Huarmey and elsewhere, where ethnic Wari elites lived and presumably ruled, may have served as administrative and religious centers in a cooperative and reciprocal relationship with Huari itself but each operating as its own (semi-)independent polity (Topic and Topic 2010). Other regions further to the north were even more independent, featuring little in the way of Wari material culture but still demonstrating aspects of Wari ideological influence in, for instance, burial methods. The movement of ethnic Wari people to these outlying regions, such as Wari men marrying local women, established opportunities for trade and brought Wari beliefs and behaviors into these far-flung regions.

The Chimú

As the Tiwanaku and Wari states began to diminish, another state began to rise where Mochica lords once ruled. The Chimú state (also often referred to as Chimor; ca. 900–1470 CE) was one of the largest and most powerful states in the pre-Inca Late Intermediate Period (ca. 1000–1400 CE) Andes; it was vanquished by the Incas in 1470 CE. The Chimor capital Chan Chan covered as much as 20 square kilometers and held a population of perhaps 40,000 people (Moore and Mackey 2008).

Chan Chan consists of a set of walled compounds, known as *ciudadelas* (Figure 13.11), that likely housed royal families. These included residences, burial areas, open plazas where significant numbers of people could gather (*audencias*), and vast storage areas. Further out from the city center commoners lived in multi-room clustered wattle-and-daub complexes in patio groups (Topic 2009); workshops were interspersed in the commoner residential areas.

Each ciudadela was probably constructed by a royal family when they were in power. Members of the royal ruling family were buried in the ciudadelas constructed by the current king, where he was also eventually interred. Unlike the apparent decentralized political structure in the Wari state, Chimor power seems to have been quite centralized at Chan Chan. Excavations have demonstrated that workshops were located within the ciudadelas; the crafts produced may have been made by retainers to the royal family, producing elite goods to be consumed by only that family or a small circle of upper-echelon elites (Topic 2009).

As Chan Chan grew, it required additional agricultural production, which necessitated an expansion in territory. Throughout the heartland, which included the Moche and surrounding valleys, the Chimor kingdom either maintained or expanded the irrigation canals constructed by the Mochica before them and claimed previously uncultivated land by building raised agricultural fields (J. Moore 1988). They established Chimú communities in these regions to ensure that the capital had secure access to all products of the land (Keatinge 1975; Keatinge and Day 1974). Some communities were engaged in craft production including metalwork and textile production, in addition to their agricultural work. The state ensured that sufficient quantities of food not only made it back to the vast storerooms in the ciudadelas at Chan Chan but also to administrative outposts where important crafts were stored.

In the 13th and 14th centuries, the Chimor kingdom expanded to the north incorporating numerous valleys previously ruled by independent polities. Chimú-style compounds were built in valley centers, likely occupied by Chimú elites who became the new regional rulers and served as administrative bureaucrats for the capital. These compounds held storerooms and plazas, the former for storage of goods retrieved from the newly controlled region, the latter for public ceremonies including feasts that helped the new Chimú rulers to maintain political alliances with the now dethroned local rulers and elites (Moore and Mackey 2008). Chimú rulers and elites appear to have engaged in extensive interaction with polities to their far north and south. The presence of Chimú ceramics and other goods in these regions suggests a lively trade relationship and perhaps a form of indirect control by the Chimor Kingdom.

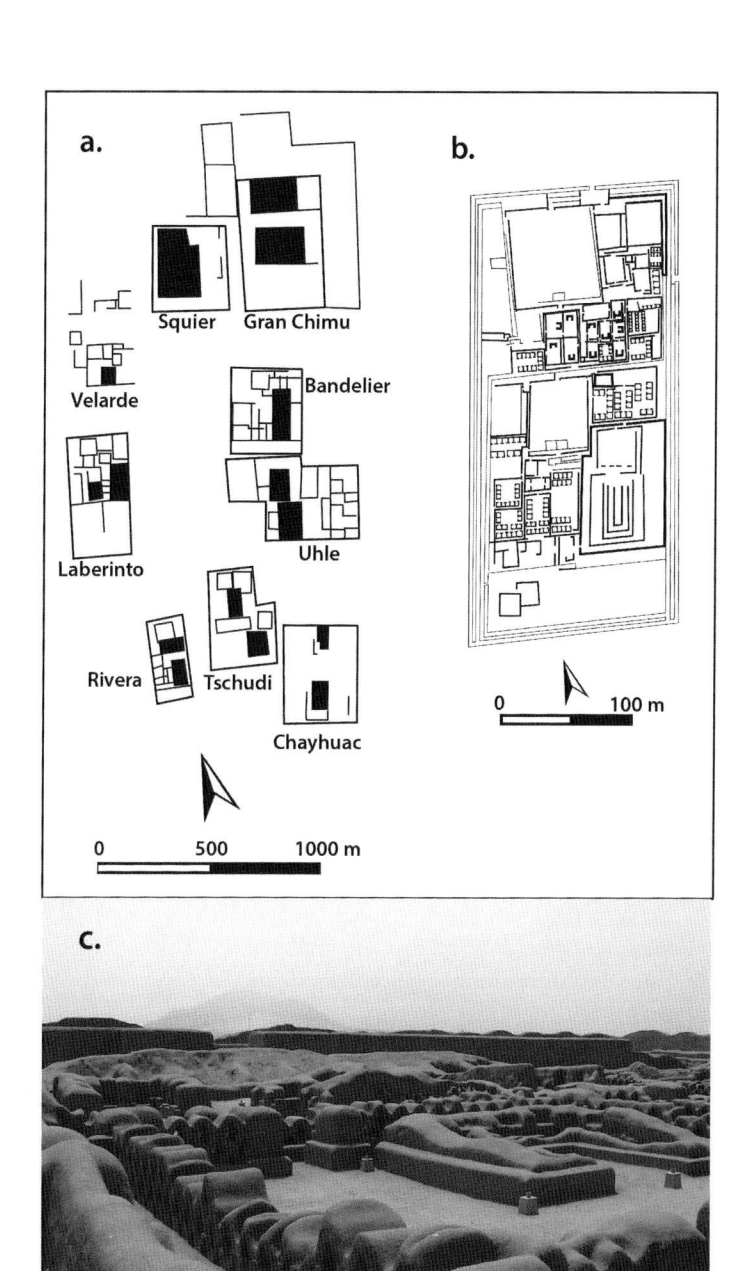

FIGURE 13.11 a. Sketch Plan of the Chan Chan Capital; b. Detail of Ciudadela Rivera; c. Photo of the administrative area of Ciudadela Tschudi

Source: b. S.R. Steadman after Moseley (2001: 269, 272, figs. 124, 128); c. photo courtesy of Martin St-Amant, licensed by Wikipedia—CC-BY-SA-3.0

Socioeconomic and Political Structures

Chimú society was class-based, as demonstrated by the architectural evidence described earlier. At the pinnacle were the royals at Chan Chan and just below were the nobles and elites living in the lavish residences. At the bottom were the commoners who lived in simple houses and buried their dead in plain graves. How conquered elites fit into these social classes is somewhat unclear though they clearly existed above the commoner classes. Within the enormous ciudadelas were platforms under which the king and close family were buried. These were singular burial events preventing the addition of later deceased family members. However, the massive platforms constructed above the tombs provided a place for feasting activities and other ceremonies meant to celebrate the deceased ancestral ruler (Moore 2004).

Chan Chan was a powerful capital city at the pinnacle of a landscape that included administrative centers controlling surrounding and outlying territories. Chimú rulers and elites wielded a great deal of control over the subsistence economy and the production of goods. Not only did the Chimú state maintain water management systems and create additional agricultural lands, but the vast storage areas demonstrate that surplus was given to the state for redistributive purposes. In a land where the climate was not conducive to large-scale food production, the state's ability to guarantee a stable subsistence base provided a critical method for sociopolitical control of a population and territory. The raw materials that flowed into Chan Chan were then distributed to artisans who produced luxury items for Chimú elites. Some items were given to loyal residents and even to the craft-workers themselves, but most were retained as the privilege of elite class.

Religion and Warfare

The relative lack of archaeological investigation at Chimú sites has made the recovery of their religion a bit more challenging. Iconographic representations on ceramics, wall murals, figurines, and textiles, suggest that there were four main deities: the Staff God, the Plumed Headdress Deity, the Chimú Goddess, and the Moon Animal deity (Moore and Mackey 2008). Images of the Staff God and the Chimú Goddess, the latter always depicted in the round, are found both in elite contexts (inside ciudadelas) and in areas where commoners could clearly view representations of these deities. Depictions of the Moon Animal and Plumed Headdress Deity, however, are found on ceramics, textiles, and metal objects more closely associated with elites (Moore and Mackey 2008). Royalty and high elites may have maintained a state cult on behalf of the Chimú population, carried out inside ciudadelas without commoner participation. However, Chimú religion seems to have emphasized ancestor veneration, seen in the continued recognition of deceased kings by family and attendants.

The discovery of several mass graves suggests the Chimor kingdom was not averse to sending messages through violent means. At the site of Pacatnamú (ca. 1270 CE), archaeologists found remains of more than a dozen men deposited in an open ditch near the entry to the city center. They had been stabbed, decapitated, and left in the open ditch to rot, perhaps serving as a message to others who might resist the Chimú rule (Verano 2008). A similar but even more extraordinary discovery was made at the site of Punta Lobos where approximately 200 individuals, mostly male, were found in shallow graves. They had been bound with rope and blindfolded, their throats cut so extensively that knife marks were found on their vertebrae (Verano 2008). This event, dating ca. 1250–1300, was perhaps a mass execution of Punta Lobos males as punishment for a rebellion or other defiance of Chimú power (Verano 2008).

A final example of human sacrifice took place roughly 200 years later at a site called Huanchaquito (now nicknamed "Las Llamas"), just outside Chan Chan. Excavations in 2011 revealed the burial of 43 humans and 76 camelids, all sacrificed and buried in muddy sands near the Peruvian coast (Lobell 2012). Rather than territorial control, archaeologists suggest that these individuals and animals may have been sacrificed to deities who controlled the ocean and the rain; the early 15th century was a time of torrential rains and flooding due to El Niño patterns.

Complexity in Chimú Society

The Chimú state conquered outlying territories and apparently violently repressed rebellion or misbehavior. Chimú religion emphasized a cult of royal ancestors who were critical to the health and survival of the Chimú people and state; the worship of some major Chimú gods and important ritual activities may have been performed by only elites and rulers as proxies for the people. Although the Chimú had suffered climatic vagaries in the early 15th century, the kingdom continued to rule a vast territory on the northern Peruvian coast even as a rival kingdom began to emerge to their south. By 1470, the Chimor kingdom had been conquered by that rival state, the Incas.

The Inca Civilization

After the collapse of the Tiwanaku and Wari states around 1100 CE, the central Andes region south of the Chimor kingdom was occupied by a number of small polities identified, in part, on the basis of ceramic styles (Covey 2008a). Archaeological work shows that some polities occupied a single valley while others spread over several and demonstrated a more complex sociopolitical system. As the decades wore on, settlements in these various polities built fortifications, suggesting that warfare, likely due to territorial expansionary tactics, became more common (Dulanto 2008). Evidence of an Inca political entity appeared by the 13th century in the Cuzco area, annexing neighboring regions and then emerging as a regional power in the 14th century (Bauer 2004; Covey 2008a; Dulanto 2008). By the early 15th century CE, an Inca state, centered at Cuzco, had developed; territory was acquired by Inca rulers through warfare, intimidation, and negotiated alliances (see Box 13.5) (Covey 2008b). During the Late Horizon Period (ca. 1400–1536), the Incas launched an imperial expansion campaign that lasted for more than a century and garnered a state that stretched from the northern borders of modern Ecuador southward to capture the northwest quarter of Argentina and much of northern Chile. The Inca Empire prevailed until the 1530s when the arrival of the Spaniards brought the state to its knees.

BOX 13.5 CHINCHA POLITY

The Chincha polity developed contemporary or prior to the Inca state. Located on the southern Peruvian coast, this culture had developed a complex political structure with numerous lords and thousands of residents by the 14th century (Moore 2015: 404). The sites of La Centinela and Tambo de Mora formed the center of the Chincha polity; the former offered evidence of craft-working and areas devoted to food production and storage, and the latter appears to have been dedicated to ritual and political functions. It was also at La Centinela that the major religious structures could be found, consisting of walled compounds and a large pyramid atop which was a chamber containing a boulder that served as an important oracle for both the Chincha polity and the Inca state (Covey 2006: 198). In part, the Chincha grew economically through long-distance trade. Using ocean-worthy wooden boats, they plied the coastal regions northward into Ecuador, trading their own ceramics and other products for exotic items from far-flung regions. Of great interest to the Chincha were red *Spondylus* shells, which were used in ritual functions (McEwan 2006: 87). Chincha incorporation into the Inca Empire was largely peaceful; a lack of material culture representing Inca statecraft suggests that the Chincha rulers retained a consistent level of power and some autonomy from the Inca right up to the period of Spanish conquest (Covey 2006: 199–201).

Foundation and Expansion

Inca mythology attributes the origins of the Andean peoples to the creator god Viracocha, who was responsible for the emergence of the sun from the sacred waters of Lake Titicaca and for the creation of animals and people. Viracocha created many ethnicities and languages, scattering peoples to the many Andean valleys (Moseley 2001: 13–14). There are several dozen origin myths for the Inca royal lineage, recorded by the Spanish after their arrival in the region. Several places are cited as the point of origin of the Inca people, one of them being Lake Titicaca and another the town of Pacariqtambo (McEwan 2006: 57). The most commonly told myth is associated with the latter location. Here, Viracocha and the sun god Inti created eight siblings who emerged from a cave (near Pacariqtambo); these siblings formed four marriages. One man became the leader and took the name Manco Capac; he led his group to settle Cuzco where he conquered those living there (though his male siblings did not survive the journey). In the Lake Titicaca myth, Manco and his wife were created by Inti; they traveled to Cuzco where the people selected him as king due to his divine nature. In both myths, Manco Capac carried a golden staff that was used to test the ground for the perfect place to settle; Cuzco was that place in each of the creation myths (McEwan 2006: 57–60; Urton 1999). It is from Manco Capac that the Inca royal lineage traced its descent (McEwan 2006: 58). Archaeological investigation places Inca origins in the region of Cuzco (Bauer 2004; Bauer and Smit 2015).

A descendant of these earliest rulers, Viracocha Inca was in power in Cuzco ca. 1438 CE when a rival kingdom known as the Chanca attacked. Cuzco was saved by Viracocha Inca's son Yupanqui who then took the throne from his father and brother. Yupanqui took the name Pachacuti ("Earthshaker") and launched a long series of attacks to expand his kingdom (McEwan 2006: 74). Pachacuti instituted a taxation system, communication and transport routes, and a vast storage system that allowed Inca rulers and elites to extract, store, and reap the benefits of vast quantities of wealth from the conquered countryside. He also created the Inti Sun God cult within the empire. Inca mythology recounts Pachacuti's allegiance to Inti, who was created by the god Viracocha at Lake Titicaca. Inti became the patron god of Cuzco and of the ruler, and from the time of Pachacuti onward, rulers were considered sons of Inti, giving them a divine connection to one of the most important gods in Inca cosmology.

Pachacuti and his successors launched major building projects throughout the expanding state that allowed for more effective Inca rule. One of the major accomplishments of the Inca state, likely begun under Pachacuti, was the construction of the Inca road system (see Box 13.6), encompassing over 40,000 kilometers of roads by the time the Spaniards arrived (Morris and von Hagen 2011: 43). These linked nodes were built by the Incas to serve as administrative centers and way stations. Way-stations and outposts were places where travelers could shelter overnight with their goods and gear. Archaeological survey suggests there may have been as many as 2000 of these way-stations strung along the Inca road system (D'Altroy 2002: 238), built and maintained by local rulers at the Inca state's behest.

BOX 13.6 INCA ROYAL ROAD

The incredible Inca road system consisted of two main highways running on a north-south axis, one through the Andes and the other along the coast (Nair and Protzen 2015). Numerous paths connected these two. The "royal road" through the mountains connected Cuzco to Quito; in some places, this road was 16 meters wide, while most roads ranged between 2 and 10 meters in width (Nair and Protzen 2015). The Inca used their highway system to move troops and goods and to ensure consistent communication between different parts of their empire. Roads were built of stone slabs and steep mountainside paths were sometimes stepped. In the easier-to-traverse coastal regions, the roads were lined with stones to indicate the proper path. The Inca built raised earth pathways across marshy areas and constructed amazing suspension bridges of woven ropes made from plants (Nair and Protzen 2015). These spanned gorges high above rivers. Some of these bridges can still be seen in the Andes region today.

Administrative centers were either built by the state or by local populations, likely under the direction of the Inca state. Larger administrative centers, many located in the highlands, were newly established by the state to ensure control of the region. One center that has been investigated featured over 500 stone-built storehouses; other architectural remains may correspond to a plaza, temples, and elite housing (Morris and von Hagen 2011: 155–57). Ethnohistorical sources note that administrative centers served as home to Inca regional rulers, loyal to the state, who helped advance the economic and political desires of the Inca king. Local ethnic groups were conscripted for service to build and serve these centers; Inca religious beliefs were also transported to these centers, and local populations were expected to immerse themselves in Inca ritual and cosmology.

Two other types of Inca facilities existed on the road system and throughout the empire: imperial enclaves and fortification systems. Imperial enclaves consisted of previously existing large towns or cities in regions that had come under Inca control. In some cases, Inca elites were dispatched to these enclaves to rule alongside local leaders; elite residences were built in both local and Inca styles, and temples dedicated to both local and Inca deities (the latter usually Inti) demonstrate this "cooperative rule" in the enclaves (Morris and von Hagen 2011: 146–47). Incan forts were located primarily in the Inca heartland and at outer reaches of Inca control to the north and east; some were constructed by Inca builders, and others in local styles but probably commissioned by the state. These forts were positioned in places where traffic on the Inca road system could be monitored and hostile advances could be repelled.

A set of important sites was scattered in remote areas of the highlands, on trails leading off the Royal Road. These places featured beautiful stone architecture and vast land holdings, termed "Inca Estates" by many archaeologists (Niles 2015). Most spectacular among these is the site of Machu Picchu set high on the cliffs and offering commanding views of jungle and valleys. The beautiful stonework at this site (Figure 13.12) features a central complex with structures that appear to be largely residential, and the nearby terraces suggest farming was practiced there. However, the presence of fountains and other architectural features, burials of young women, and the utterly remote location imply the purpose of this structure was religious. Additional discoveries of other estates similar to Machu Picchu have led to an alternative interpretation; these beautiful places may have served as rural estates for Inca royalty, each built by a new king after he ascended the throne (D'Altroy 2002). Identifying these sites as royal mountain villas does not preclude the practice of ritual activities, but their primary function may have been to serve as retreats from the Cuzco center.

FIGURE 13.12 Photo of Machu Picchu

Source: Drawing by J. Siegl

The State Capital: Cuzco

Located in the highlands at an elevation of 3,400 meters, Cuzco was an urban center housing tens of thousands of people. The Inca called their realm *Tawantinsuyu*, which translates to "The Four Parts Together" (D'Altroy 2002). Tawantinsuyu refers to four regions to the north and south, and to the east and west, of the capital Cuzco. Each of these four regions was governed by an Inca lord who reported to the king (D'Altroy 2002: 87). The ruling Inca king, known as *Sapa Inca*, resided at Cuzco in a palace he had constructed. Arrayed around him were the palaces of the previous kings within which the mummified remains of each resided, worshipped and cared for by family and servants. The palace complex held the ruler and his *panaqa* ("royal kin group"). The panaqa remained the possession of the dead king rather than being passed to a son or relative who became the Sapa Inca (McEwan 2006: 99). Each new ruler built up his wealth through the system of corvée labor described in more detail later and through the products created by artisans who served his family. The acquisition of new lands and additional taxation of those lands also filled his coffers.

Much of Cuzco was destroyed during years of battle prior to the Spanish defeat of the empire and is also now covered by the modern city. At the center of the city were public areas including plazas and temples, and the palaces that belonged to the deceased and living Inca kings. Also at the center was the *aclla wasi* complex where young women, retrieved from across the Inca Empire, were housed for the purpose of serving the Inca state by becoming servants, wives of the emperor or high-ranking officials, or dedications to serve Inti (McEwan 2006: 101–102; Silverblatt 1987). At or near the center were lesser Inca nobility living in elite residences. Living among them were the craft-workers, known as *yanakuna*, who worked in elite houses serving elite needs (Covey 2009).

Since skilled craft-workers might be found anywhere in the Inca state, some yanakuna were not ethnically Inca, making the city quite diverse. Outside the city, elite housing gave way to rural farming areas.

Like the administrative centers, Cuzco boasted vast storage facilities. Raw resources and finished products filled these facilities, including non-perishable goods such as metalwork, textiles, ritual objects, and ceramics (Covey 2009). It is in Cuzco that the highest-status goods were produced: distinctly Inca and beautifully made. Possession of one of these instantly recognizable items by an official in a more distant provincial administrative center was symbolic of that official's important position in the imperial order. Cuzco served as the political, economic, and religious center of the entire Inca realm.

Economy

The various way-stations, centers, and forts strung along the road system were instrumental in developing and maintaining an extensive economic network within the Inca state. This system depended on the adequate provision of subsistence items, as well as the distribution of luxury goods to leaders and elites in provincial lands. The Inca Empire consisted primarily of farmers, pastoralists, artisans, and traders, who made up well over 90% of the total population (D'Altroy 2002: 181). Smaller communities in the highlands, but also nearer the coast, consisted of one or several *ayllu*, a kin group (based on the male lineage) who worked cooperatively to support all family members. Ayllu might contain thousands of people with some households possessing greater wealth and societal standing than others. The ayllu practiced a reciprocal relationship between households so that within an ayllu a variety of pursuits beyond farming, such as craft production, fishing, or trade, were practiced (D'Altroy 2002). This ensured a balance of activities within the ayllu and the even distribution of necessary goods. The ayllu provided a safety net that was vitally important when males in a household were called away to serve the state as laborers or soldiers. In these times, members of other households in the ayllu would come to help with daily activities or major events such as the harvest. This ayllu system certainly pre-dated the rise of the Inca state, and the Inca left the system largely in place.

The Inca government demanded taxes from its people in the form of goods or labor; taxation served as payment by ayllu for being allowed to live on and work "Inca lands," since, once conquered, all lands belonged to the state. *Mit'a* was a corvée labor system that involved the heads of households taking turns to supply labor to the state. Local regents living in the enclaves or Inca officials living in the administrative centers kept track of ayllu heads of household and terms of service. At the height of Inca power, the mit'a system had as many as 2 million men available to the state at any given time (D'Altroy 2002: 266). Mit'a service lasted for two or three months; if the head of household had a son old enough to serve, that son might be sent in place of the father.

There were many forms of service; being a soldier topped the list, but other work included being a litter-bearer, building structures (and Inca roads), or serving as a farmer on state-run lands, some of which were taken from existing populations who were relocated to elsewhere in the state. In the highlands, state pasture lands held countless camelids, cared for by herders performing mit'a service. Besides meat, their hair provided critical fibers for the much-valued textile production in Inca households. These farming and pasture lands were managed by personnel at the new administrative centers where products from state lands were then kept in the vast storehouses. Such storehouses were critical because of the difficulty of moving large goods from province to province. The challenging terrain and a lack of wheeled vehicles meant that each province needed to have sufficient supplies to outfit elites and support the population. The administrative centers distributed necessary (subsistence) and luxury items as needed (see Box 13.7).

> **BOX 13.7 CHICHA**
>
> Besides the crops themselves, maize could be turned into *chicha*, a fermented drink much prized by the Inca. Subsistence goods, chicha, and other products such as textiles were given as payment and rewards to those loyal to the state. Chicha was an important component in numerous Inca rituals. Ethnohistorical documents indicate that it was consumed in mass quantities at important ceremonies such as the multiday funeral after the death of a Sapa Inca (Kaulicke 2015). Inca control of the production of chicha, mainly in ayllu households, was an important aspect of their power structure.

Artisans who could produce crafts—items of metal, stone, clay, and especially cloth—were of intense interest to Inca royalty and elites. These workers, removed from their ayllus, became full-time artisans attached to the state at the capital or administrative centers or as yanakuna serving elites at Cuzco. These former members of ayllus often lost contact with their families and communities, becoming part of the state machine and fully dependent on provision by it (Morris and von Hagen 2011: 60). The goods produced by the full-time artisans, as well as those acquired from mit'a labor, were the sole possession of the state.

Fine goods were distributed, judiciously, to officials and local rulers in the provinces for their service to the state. Their Inca style was instantly recognizable and the possession of them identified their owners as favored by the state. Metalsmiths crafted objects of gold (sweat of Inti, the sun god) and silver (tears of the Moon deity) for consumption by Inca elites; most of these objects were melted down by Spanish colonists for their own purposes, and thus, only a few survive. Only verbal accounts attest to the thousands of vessels, figurines, and other items of metal that adorned Inca palaces and estates. Another important talent was masonry. Inca architecture, at places such as Cuzco and Machu Picchu, and many administrative centers, is renowned for its beauty and skilled stonework. Inca-style ceramics were of terrific importance and are one way that archaeologists can document the presence of Inca elites in a province. In the heartland territory around Cuzco, Inca pottery is ubiquitous, but in the provinces, it is usually found only in elite houses; occasionally it was discovered in ayllu households, but this is rare and usually indicates service to the state. The discovery of Inca ceramics in the graves of both elites and occasionally commoners shows the symbolic importance of possessing Inca-style ceramics, both in this world and the next. Archaeologists have noted that ayllu production of household wares began to adjust to replicate, on a local level, Inca styles, again demonstrating the importance of the Inca state on every level.

Of paramount importance to the state was the production of textiles. Andean women produced textiles long before the Inca came to power, and they continued in this capacity throughout the existence of the empire. Textiles were of cotton or wool and woven images portrayed important Inca messages of state power and religious ideology. Textile production was part of the mit'a service required by the state, and women in Andean ayllu households were required to produce a certain quota for the state when called upon to do so. Certain communities and ethnic groups were known for their weaving skills and they were most consistently asked to provide to the state. In some cases, skilled weaving communities were uprooted and moved to different provinces, situated near administrative centers where their work could be monitored and the state could provide cotton and wool from the storehouses (D'Altroy 2002: 297).

Keeping track of mit'a, the production and movement of goods, and tax payments was an immense undertaking and required a recording device. Inca administrators employed the *khipu* (Figure 13.13), a textile of threads that could be knotted in a sophisticated system that served as a mnemonic for its owner (Urton 1997, 2015). Khipu existed for at least a millennium before the rise of the empire. However, the Inca made it into a vast system that kept track of both the economic aspects of the empire as well as the very complicated religious calendar. Khipu were dyed in different colors, each of which had a specific meaning. Knots of varying types were tied at different places along the cord, again bearing specific information such as dates and amounts. Sadly, many khipu were destroyed by the Spaniards who believed them to be associated with religious belief

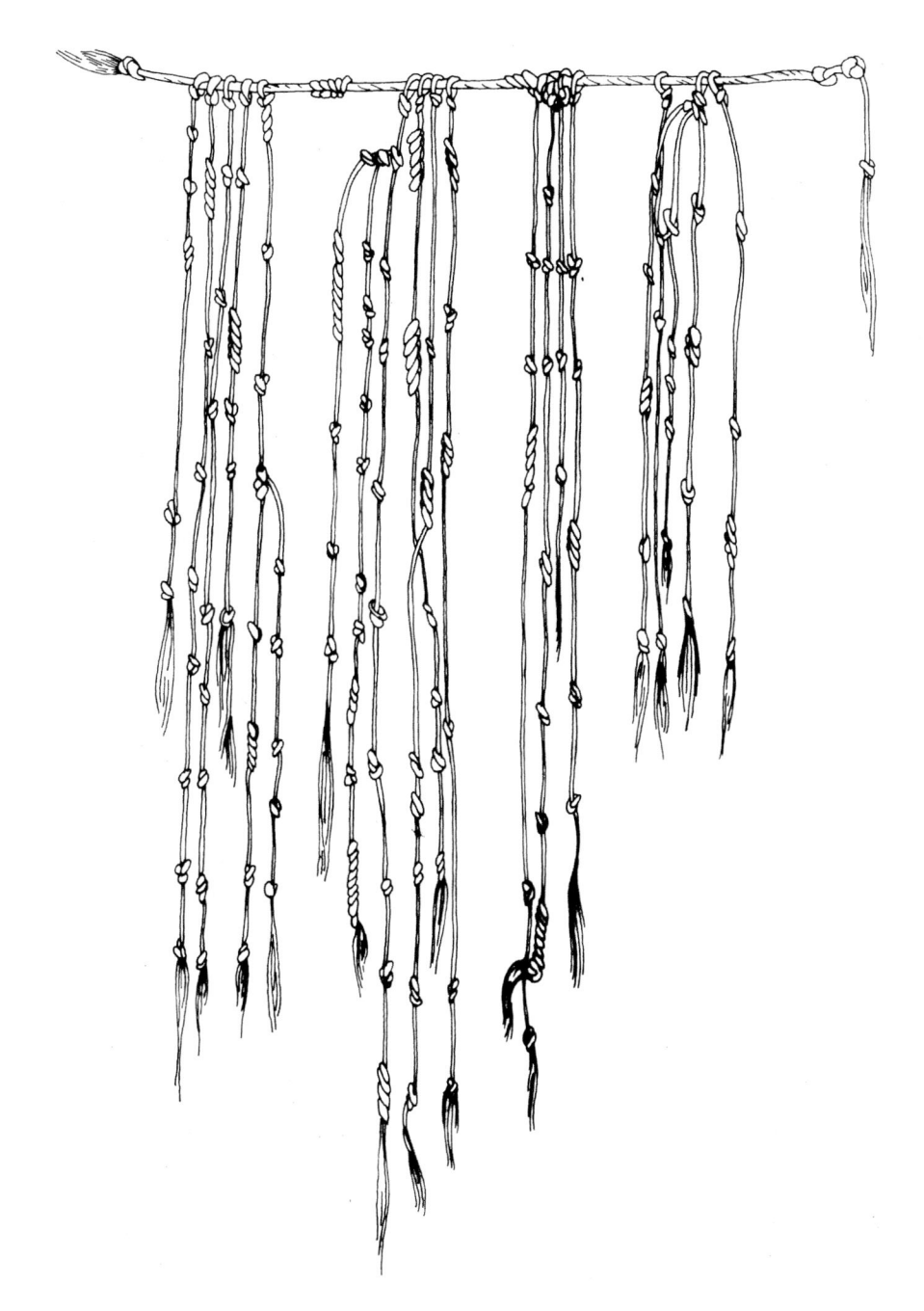

FIGURE 13.13 Drawing of a Khipu

Source: Laurel D. Hackley

rather than the more logistical usage to which they were dedicated. Only a few hundred khipu have been recovered to date.

Religion

Incas allowed conquered peoples to continue local religious practices in their households and communities, as long as the state religion, including Inti, was acknowledged. This tolerance is found at Pachacamac near modern Lima where an important local oracle and temple had existed long before the arrival of the Incas. Rather than destroy this temple and risk the wrath, and rebellion, of the indigenous peoples, the Incas built a Sun Temple there, allowing Inti and the local deity to reside side-by-side (Morris and von Hagen 2011: 65). This site became an important pilgrimage site for local people and for Incas. The incorporation of conquered people's deities and sacred places into the Inca religion was common. Sacred locations were known as huacas (see Box 13.2); huacas could be built or might consist of sacred natural landscape features such as springs, caves, and rock formations. They were located on 41 "*ceque* lines," which were sacred lines emanating from Cuzco across the landscape (Earls and Cervantes 2015; Zuidema 1964). Care of shrines (huacas) on the ceque lines was the responsibility of various kin groups who were required to carry out rituals according to the Inca calendar, a system recorded on khipus (Zuidema 1983). The ceque lines, some extending over 10 kilometers from Cuzco, were also pilgrimage routes so that Andeans could celebrate both Inca and local deities at appropriate times during the year. Some of these pilgrimages continue today (Sallnow 1998). This overlaying a veneer of Inca religion onto local beliefs, as well as "honoring" the local deities by bringing their haucas to Cuzco, allowed the Inca to better manage a diverse and multiethnic empire.

The state temple, dedicated to Inti, was located at Cuzco. The Sapa Inca was considered to be the human manifestation of Inti on earth. Sun temples were built throughout the empire, and residents were expected to acknowledge Inti as supreme, their indigenous deities subordinate to him and other Inca deities. Inti, Viracocha, and a third god, Illapa, created an Inca triad. Illapa, god of lightning, was responsible for weather and thus was critical in a culture that depended heavily on agricultural produce. Mama-Quilla, the goddess of the Moon and wife of Inti, was also very important; the ruler's wife took on the mantle of Mama-Quilla on earth. Many other deities also occupied the Inca pantheon.

The Inca calendar was complex, based on both the solar and lunar cycles, and required numerous rituals and ceremonies on minor or major auspicious days. Prior to Inca rule, most peoples of the Andes operated by the 354-day lunar calendar. With the establishment of the sun god Inti as the major deity in the empire, the solar calendar began to be used, based on a 365-day cycle; the gradual spread of the solar calendar throughout the empire is a good measure of the power of Inca rule through religious ideals.

Held at Cuzco, the *Inti Raymi* was one of the most important ceremonies in the calendar. Occuring at the June solstice and lasting a week, this ceremony celebrated the sun god (D'Altroy 2002: 154). The Inti Raymi, or "Warriors' Cultivation Festival" began at sunrise on the first day in the open plaza of central Cuzco where Inca elites, priests, and the ruling family sang praises to the sun. Also attending were the previous, deceased Inca rulers in the form of statues adorned with the remains of those rulers (hair, fingernails, etc.). Sacrifices of meat and other items were made to the god, and at the end of the period of celebration, the fields were plowed to ready them for the planting season. Another important event was the *Qoya Raymi* or "Queen's Festival," which was a rite of purification (D'Altroy 2002: 155). At the new moon during the rainy season, selected elites and non-elites were required to carry the "evils" (symbolized by items of clothing and other goods) out of the city, which were then passed to a succession of people further and further away from the city. Finally, the goods were let loose in a river where they would be carried out to sea, and thus the city was symbolically cleansed of harm and evil.

Human sacrifice was carried out in Cuzco, at other locations where there were important huacas, and on the landscape, especially on mountaintops. Children and adolescents were sacrificed at regularly scheduled ceremonies to honor the sun god Inti, Illapa, Viracocha, and a few other deities. At times of crisis such as after earthquakes or widespread disease, the death of a ruler, or solar and lunar eclipses, large-scale human sacrifice was also undertaken in order to set the world aright.

Archaeological discoveries of mummies found on Andes mountaintops have made it into the news repeatedly over the last several decades. Several pairs or groups of children, male and female, have been found at these locations. They are often dressed in finery and had figurines made of gold and silver, and sometimes shell, with them (Reinhard and Ceruti 2005) as well as other items such as pottery. It is likely that these were part of a ceremony celebrating a new Inca ruler and that the children were meant to personify Inti and Mama-Quilla, the gold and silver representing the sweat of the sun and tears of the moon. Perhaps the most famous was the "Ice Maiden" discovered in 1996 on Mount Nevado Ampato at a height of 6,310 meters (Reinhard 2005). This young woman, nicknamed "Juanita," was in her teens when she climbed the mountain to the place of her death. The procession of probably over a dozen people likely included priests, assistants who may have been aclla wasi, and other pilgrims. Juanita was adorned with beautiful clothing and many items including pottery, silver and gold statues, shell items, and other goods (Figure 13.14). She ingested chicha and then died from a blow to her head. She was then placed, wrapped in a blanket, in a stone-built pocket at the mountaintop (Reinhard and Ceruti 2005). Chroniclers note that the Inca required beautiful, perfect, virginal sacrifices, and thus Juanita and other young sacrificial girls may

FIGURE 13.14 Artistic Reconstruction of Sacrifice Ritual of Ice Maiden ("Juanita")

Source: M.J. Hughes

have come from the aclla wasi (Ceruti 2004). It is the belief of some archaeologists that mountaintop sacrifice was an ancient tradition of the local Andean populations, pre-dating Inca control of the regions. The Inca may have incorporated this ritual pilgrimage into ceremonies in order to honor the major Inca deities with this most precious of offerings.

The Inca-built shrines and the sacrificial victims high on these peaks reminded all that the Inca ruler was at the helm of the empire, ruling by divine mandate and through imperial control. They are one element in a large toolkit of Inca religious practice that served to incorporate local beliefs while also imposing Inca-mandated cosmology onto every corner of the empire. They were so successful at installing the sun god as the main imperial deity that many peoples across the empire not only accepted Inti as the greatest of the gods but also adjusted to the solar calendar after millennia of using the lunar cycle. That the Inca also practiced ancestor veneration meshed well with local beliefs, and the insistence that all peoples honor royal ancestors housed in Cuzco did not seem unreasonable to commoners across the land; these ancestors were, after all, both royal and divine. Religion clearly played a critical role in imperial control of the vast Inca Andean Empire.

Warfare

The Inca army was drawn from mit'a service when the king intended to launch an offensive. When called to service, the Inca army could exceed 100,000 soldiers. When Manqo Inca, the last king of the empire, attacked Cuzco in an effort to oust the Spaniards in 1536, he mustered as many as 200,000 soldiers to attack the city, but it is likely that the usual size of the army was smaller, perhaps in the 30,000 range (D'Altroy 2002). There is some evidence (from oral and Spanish accounts) to suggest that all boys in the empire were required to train as warriors in the event of their being called to mit'a service. Elites were formally trained as warriors, and some sons from these families served as personal guards for the king or as officers commanding the soldiers.

When going to war, the army was organized according to ethnic group; men serving mit'a from the same region fought together and were tasked with the tactic most suited to their region (e.g., javelin, sling-stones, hand-to-hand combat). Upon successful completion of a campaign, a celebration was held in Cuzco where the king, his generals, and some of the army marched before the residents of Cuzco. If captives were taken, they were sometimes sacrificed, and a ritual in which the king drank chicha from the head of a vanquished foe was also occasionally part of the ceremony (D'Altroy 2002: 229). Those who had distinguished themselves on the battlefield, including commoners, were rewarded with booty gained in battle.

The End of Empire

If not for the arrival of the Spanish invading forces the Inca may well have been at the helm of a vast nation in South America today. This was not to be, however, as the Spanish state had their eyes on the control of the entire South American continent. In the 1520s, the Inca king, Wayna Capac, was undertaking conquests to the north in an effort to expand his newly acquired empire. However, one of the weapons of the Spanish, though not necessarily one they had launched themselves, had already reached the Inca Empire: smallpox. In 1528, Wayna Capac contracted the disease and died as did his chosen heir Ninan Cuyuchi (D'Altroy 2002: 76). The unexpected death of a young ruler and his heir launched a dynastic war between two royal sons (of different mothers), Waskhar and Atawallpa; Atawallpa achieved victory in 1532. As he was celebrating his victory, the Spanish, led by Francisco Pizarro, arrived and captured Atawallpa, demanding a ransom from the Inca people for the return of their king. The Inca were to fill a room approximately 6 by 5 meters in size, up to a height of 2.5 meters, with gold objects, and twice this volume of silver objects (D'Altroy 2002:

315). After the ransom had been paid, the decision was made to kill Atawallpa, and on a July night in 1533, his rule of the Inca came to an end.

This launched a full-scale war, which raged for three more years; the Spaniards gained ground with every passing month. After the death of Atawallpa, Pizarro installed a man named Thupa Wallpa who could serve as a puppet ruler for the Spanish, but he succumbed to disease in 1535. Shortly after, when he took Cuzco Pizarro appointed a "Sapa Inca" who would rule according to Spanish needs, named Manqo Inca. However, Manqo Inca soon turned against his Spanish overlords and organized an attack on them and the capital Cuzco. Leading a huge army he laid siege to Cuzco, destroying much of the city. However, the Spaniards were able to fend off even this immense attack, in part because Manqo Inca's army could not stay in Cuzco for long periods due to the requirements of the agricultural cycle. Eventually, the siege army dwindled enough for the Spaniards to repel Manqo Inca's forces. By 1536, the Inca Empire was at an end, and its lands and people were in the hands of the Spanish crown.

Conclusion

The Inca arose not out of a vacuum but rather following a rich history of powerful and well-constructed states. The Inca built on mechanisms of statecraft that included the skillful control and management of important economic strategies, the establishment of a state religion that intertwined leader with supreme deity, and the use of warfare as both a method to further the control of territories and to keep those within the state acquiescent. To this, the Inca added the creation of a vast communication system that allowed goods, peoples, and ideologies to flow to every corner of the empire. Also critical was the Inca decision to allow various elements of indigenous traditions such as the ayllu system to remain intact. Local communities with indigenous deities and sacred places were incorporated into the state ritual practices. Through these various means, the Inca built an enormous and incredibly vital state.

14

WHY COMPLEX SOCIETIES COLLAPSE

Introduction

This final chapter examines the collapse of complex societies (not coincidentally, the title of a monograph by Joseph Tainter, published in 1988). Archaeologists and ancient historians have long had an interest in how and why societies decline, both in specific cases and in comparative study. Multiple episodes of collapse, sometimes within a single geographical region, have been presented in this book, as collapse is nearly as common as complexity, though it is not limited to state-organized societies. Yet complexity and collapse are completely separate phenomena; no cause for the rise of complexity can be cited as the reason for a society's collapse (Adams 1988). At the same time, complexity (as seen in this book) is an expensive strategy of political centralization and integration, with costs stemming from labor, military, resource, and ideological expenditures (Cowgill 1988; Tainter 1988: 92). For this reason, it is worthwhile to look at the dissolution of such societies in greater detail.

Like complexity, collapse is predominantly a political matter: it is most often recognized by archaeologists as the termination of political structures and interconnections and often as a shift to "simpler" forms of governance. Eisenstadt (1988) points out that it also usually includes a restructuring of social relationships and boundaries, as well as geographic movements, changed degrees of social differentiation, and even new family and religious structures. Complete cultural or demographic collapse or dissolution is extremely rare in history, limited to mass wipe-outs of people due to war, disease, and environmental catastrophe (Bronson 1988; Cowgill 1988). More commonly, political collapse is followed by restructuring, a simultaneous breaking down and building up of societal infrastructure.

Archaeological evidence for and potential causes of societal collapse also vary. Collapse was often a systemic process, with effects visible across a wide array of cultural institutions. Decline in economic specialization, in degrees of socioeconomic stratification, and in centralization and integration may be detectable archaeologically (Tainter 1988: 4). Outright signs of political dominance—ideological display, written records, and monumental architecture—may disappear. Typically, civilizations suffering political collapse do not abandon a territory, but disruption of settlement, indicated by destructions or abandonment at individual sites, squatter occupations, or selective burning of buildings or sections of a site, may be manifested.

The following section will review the collapse of some of the major civilizations examined in this book (in each case, greater detail is available in the corresponding chapter). The point here is not to reiterate that societies collapse; "cycling"—the rise and decline of political systems—is a major feature of many ancient polities. Rather, this re-examination will allow for specific causes proposed for collapse to be reviewed and assessed.

Specific Examples of Collapse and Their Causes

Scholars typically attribute collapse to one of four causes: political or military forces, economic decline, social upheaval, or environmental/natural disasters. Most of these explanations are not mutually exclusive; in the examples that follow, it will be evident that factors built on one another, and often it is difficult, especially in the absence of written records, to determine what happened first, and what resulted from it.

Political Collapse

As noted earlier, to some degree, the results of collapse were predominantly political, with partial or complete disappearance of a governmental apparatus. But scholars also look for potential political causes for collapse, often in the form of external factors (invaders or outsiders eager to bring down a government; overextension of the military on offensive or defensive actions; or internal factors such as rebellion, factionalism, or struggles over succession). These features have played significant roles in the decline of a number of civilizations examined here.

Perhaps the most obvious examples of political collapse are those in which a territory or state succumbed to attack from invaders. Numerous examples of this befell city-states, territorial states, and even empires in ancient Mesopotamia. Ancient China illustrates circumstances in which one political system collapsed, only to be replaced by another, usually dynastic, system, which resulted in a re-emergent state; the defeat of the Late Shang Dynasty by the Western Zhou is one example. Other examples explored in this book include the Hellenistic conquest of Classical Greek city-states and the Gothic invasion of Rome, which ultimately put an end to the western Roman Empire. And the Spanish conquistadors dealt the finishing blows to Aztec and Inca rule in the New World at a time when those empires were experiencing political competition from internal and external sources.

Yet these examples are not all equivalent in either cause or effect. In Mesopotamia, military conflict typically took place between neighbors, meaning that most social and economic activities continued on as before in the territory, with one overlord replacing another and the administrative infrastructure continuing on as before. In other cases, as in the Old Akkadian and Ur III territorial states of Mesopotamia, a foreign enemy took down an already-weak territorial state, and the lands reverted to earlier, more typical city-state organization. In contrast, the Macedonian king Philip II took advantage of Greek city-states weakened by war and internal political factions to create a larger imperial, monarchic structure that still acknowledged the cultural achievements of the Greek past. Similarly, the Goth king, usurping the throne of the final Roman emperor, still called himself by the titles of imperial tradition; like Philip, he saw the opportunity presented by an administratively overstretched empire. Finally, the Spanish conquests of Mexico and Peru took very different forms. In central Mexico, the conquistadors made military alliances with enemies of the Aztecs, capitalizing on local rivalries and instability, as well as on religious fears associated with calendrical turning points. In Peru, European-borne disease devastated Inca populations before the Spanish even arrived in Cuzco, so that Inca resistance, while persistent, eventually broke down; the Inca had already been weakened by warfare resulting from competition over the throne. At the same time, Spanish administrators retained significant elements of Inca political and economic organizations in their governance of this new land.

Claims for internal political causes of collapse are less common, but political dissent and competition certainly contributed to conditions of instability in many ancient societies. Political infighting among leaders in ancient Athens led to strategic miscues in the Greek city's war against Sparta, ultimately opening it to attack and defeat. Weak leadership contributed to phases of Egyptian decline, particularly when lines of succession were unclear or contested; this left Egypt susceptible to outside attack or to environmentally caused catastrophe from which recovery was difficult. Environmental decline also appears to have induced internal dissent and rebellion against the Minoan palaces early in the Late Bronze Age (see later).

Environmental Decline and Natural Disaster

Theories of civilizational decline due to environmental change or natural disaster (especially volcanic eruption) have had enormous influence in archaeology and studies of ancient history. Their popularity seems cyclic (much like complexity itself); common in the early 20th century, these theories went into decline, to be revived again in the 1960s and 1970s with the development of new models for social organization and new methods for recovering environmental data. They are experiencing another renewal in the early 21st century, in part reflecting present-day concerns about environmental decline. Often cited as a prime example of an ancient human-caused environmental crisis is the decline of the civilization that sculpted the colossal stone heads on Rapa Nui (Easter Island). The collapse of the group, perhaps organized as a chiefdom, has been attributed to overexploitation of their rich forested environment in the process of building a ritual landscape of altars and idols (Diamond 2005: 79–119). Reanalysis reveals a more complicated scenario: decline may have begun the moment humans first arrived on the island, as rats from their boats deforested the land, destroying, over several hundred years, its fragile ecosystem. Even after this, a population hung on until disease, introduced by European visitors, devastated it (Hunt and Lipo 2010).

Though the extreme case of Easter Island's purportedly human-caused overexploitation of resources may be dismissed as a misreading of the evidence, numerous examples within this book indicate how deeply human groups are embedded within local environments, and the profound effect environmental crises may have on culture groups at all levels of complexity. A strong case may be put forward for the role of environmental crisis in the decline of Classic Maya civilization, which reached its peak of urban development, monumental construction, and royal display around 800 CE. Within 100 years, most highland and southern lowland Maya centers had been abandoned, and a mass movement of people took place into the Yucatecan lowlands. A common theory in the 1970s and 1980s was that the rapid rise in Maya urban occupation outstripped the ability of the southern lowland subsistence base to support such populations (Culbert 1988). Skeletal analysis has, meanwhile, indicated that a period of malnutrition set in during the 9th century; what is unclear is whether human action caused long-term damage to the environment, cutting yields, or if conditions of climate change limited production. Recent evidence for water shortages at the time of collapse suggests the latter (Lucero 2002); no governmental support could stop the resulting drift of people from cities to villages and then from the south to the north (Freter 1994). Yet much of Maya culture was retained in post-Classic southern Mexico.

Other examples from this book illustrate cases where environmental decline was followed, sooner or later, by political decline and collapse. A convincing scenario has been put forth in which the volcanic eruption on Santorini in the Aegean Sea led eventually to the destruction, one by one, of the Minoan palaces of the Neopalatial Period. The eruption itself took place 50 to 100 or more years before the palaces were burned; its immediate effect on Crete was a decades-long suppression of crop yields, which took a toll on the economic, physiological, and psychological health of the population. The selective burning of only the seats of political power in the Neopalatial Period on

Crete suggests that the populations took their own revenge on the leaders who could no longer provide them with sufficient support.

The Minoans were not the last group to succumb to environmentally driven collapse in the Mediterranean region. The collapse of Mycenaean, Hittite, and Levantine societies at the end of the Late Bronze Age was affected by the migration of groups coming from more inland areas of Europe under circumstances of apparent subsistence stress. This series of migrations had a domino effect on the established city-states and empires, which were already under some pressure from internal and external conflicts. A similar set of environmentally caused subsistence pressures may have brought the decline of the Indus Valley civilization in Pakistan, and earlier Mesopotamian states. In the Andes, several polities and early states, the Mochica and Nasca in particular, were severely weakened by climatic factors, including flooding created by powerful El Niño currents that also impacted successful agricultural yields. The uncertainty created by environmental changes manifested themselves in internal strife and eventually the economic and political dissolution of both systems. Though it hung on until they were conquered by the Incas, the Chimor kingdom may have become weakened by environmental factors as well.

In other instances, political systems that were already in decline were dealt a final blow by climatic or environmental deterioration. A good example of this comes from Old Kingdom Egypt. Here, the same long-term desiccation that contributed to the overturning of the Old Akkadian state and other 3rd millennium BCE political regimes of the Near East was confronted by political dynasties that had already lost a great deal of their centralized power to the growing influence of provincial governors. A series of low Nile floods, caused by a decline in Indian Ocean monsoons, provided additional evidence for Egyptians that their kings had lost the confidence and support of the gods, the pillar of Egyptian royal power. Although there is no evidence of outright rebellion, the unifying force of kingship slipped away; when centralized power re-emerged in Middle Kingdom Egypt, the ideological basis for kingship was reconfigured, and a larger portion of the population had access to the gods.

Finally, there must have been numerous cases of environmental decline in the ancient world that had little or no impact on political systems, though their effects on populations may have been significant. These are cases where a local environmental change—caused by a natural disaster like flooding or volcanic eruption—was adjusted to and compensated for by population movement, resource redistribution, or other measures. Many of these events may be undetectable in written sources (an exception being the eruption of Mt. Vesuvius in 79 CE and its destruction of Pompeii and Herculaneum), and their archaeological effects may be similarly obscured. Examples include local catastrophes that led to the abandonment of cities in the Greek world in the Classical and Hellenistic Periods. While populations moved out of settlements affected by earthquake, silting of harbors, and other natural forces (as well as by war), they could be incorporated into neighboring towns and regions thanks to a perception of shared culture and kin (Mackil 2004).

Economic and Social Collapse

Compared with the preponderance of evidence for political and environmental contributions to civilizational collapse, examples of decline caused by social and economic forces are relatively few in number. Most often, the effects of decline or collapse are apparent in social and economic life: changes in religious beliefs or practices, disappearance of social differentiation, changes in family structure or gender roles, reduction or cessation of trade or in supplies of key resources, or changes to subsistence practices.

But economic and social forces play a contributory role in collapse, even when they may not be primary causes. The collapse of the Khmer Empire is perhaps one of the best illustrations of economic and social factors contributing to the dissolution of a state. The Khmer centers, such as Angkor Thom, relied on a constant infusion of wealth in order to maintain the canals (used for transport and irrigation) critical to the empire. However, the Khmer kings spent so much wealth and corvée labor on other structures, such as their own temples and mausolea, that little was left to tend to the more prosaic but vital imperial needs. Much of the wealth and work provided to the Khmer leaders came from the commoners; taxation was a major contributor to elite coffers and labor came from the farmers and artisans in the empire. As the economy declined, tax rates may have climbed, causing social unrest among those who not only had to pay the taxes but had to provide labor for imperial projects as well. Though the final Khmer kings no longer required their people to build massive stone temples and likely regulated taxes more effectively, the damage had been done, and a weakened and smaller Khmer kingdom was easily overrun by neighboring states by the 15th century.

Roman history featured several phases of social unrest and political change without complete decline. In Republican Rome, growing inequality between patricians and plebeians in the 5th century BCE, combined with instances of public abuse of poor men and women (especially women) by elites, led to internal dissent that verged on rebellion. Government reforms were required to set the state back on solid footing, though the long-term effects did little to alleviate the suffering of the poor. Later slave revolts, sometimes held up as causes for major Roman decline, appear to have been largely localized affairs, with few ramifications for Roman societies as a whole (Bowersock 1988: 174). A better case might be made for the idea that the high economic cost of maintaining the Roman Empire eventually became too great, resulting in sections breaking away (Tainter 1988: 129). Internal dissent that led to a stoppage of vital trade relations has been postulated as an explanation of the decline of Teotihuacan as well (Millon 1988).

Conclusion: Is There Collapse?

In the majority of the case studies in this book, and in the examples cited here, political decline and/or collapse was not accompanied by mass depopulation or the disappearance of a culture. Instead, governmental disintegration marked a new stage of development and was typically followed by the establishment of new leaders and new (though not necessarily radically different) institutions.

Scholars therefore envision episodes of collapse as regenerative (Schwartz 2005), assuming that populations survived and environments remained sustaining. Even after phases of environmental decline, populations retaining their cultural identities that relocated to new areas adapted to their new neighbors and circumstances. Loss of complexity does not have to imply loss of life or of society; human groups have remarkable resilience, an idea that lends hope in all dark times (McAnany and Yoffee 2010).

BIBLIOGRAPHY

Abrams, Elliot M. 2009 "Hopewell Archaeology: A View from the Northern Woodlands." *Journal of Archaeological Research* 17: 169–204.
Abrams, Elliot M. and AnnCorinne Freter 2005 "Tribal Societies in the Hocking Valley." In *The Emergence of Moundbuilders: The Archaeology of Tribal Societies in Southeastern Ohio*, edited by E.M. Abrams and A. Freter, pp. 174–95. Athens: Ohio University Press.
Acosta Ochoa, Guillermo 2012 "Ice Age Hunter-Gatherers and the Colonization of Mesoamerica." In *The Oxford Handbook of Mesoamerican Archaeology*, edited by D.L. Nichols and C.A. Pool, pp. 129–40. Oxford: Oxford University Press.
Adams, Barbara 1996 "Elite Graves at Hierakonpolis." In *Aspects of Early Egypt*, edited by J. Spencer, pp. 1–15. London: British Museum Press.
Adams, Ellen 2004 "Power and Ritual in Neopalatial Crete: A Regional Comparison." *World Archaeology* 36: 26–42.
——— 2007 "'Time and Chance': Unraveling Temporality in North-Central Neopalatial Crete." *American Journal of Archaeology* 111: 391–421.
Adams, Robert M. 1969 "The Study of Ancient Mesopotamian Settlement Patterns and the Problem of Urban Origins." *Sumer* 25: 111–24.
——— 1988 "Contexts of Civilizational Collapse: A Mesopotamian View." In *The Collapse of Ancient States and Civilizations*, edited by N. Yoffee and G.L. Cowgill, pp. 20–43. Tucson: University of Arizona Press.
——— 2004 "The Role of Writing in Sumerian Agriculture: Asking Broader Questions." In *Assyria and Beyond: Studies Presented to Mogens Trolle Larsen*, edited by J.G. Dercksen, pp. 1–8. Leiden: Nederlands Instituut voor het Nabije Oosten.
——— 2005 "Critique of Guillermo Algaze's 'The Sumerian Takeoff'." *Structure and Dynamics: eJournal of Anthropological and Related Sciences* 1.1: Article 9.
Adams, Robert M. and Hans J. Nissen 1972 *The Uruk Countryside*. Chicago: University of Chicago Press.
Adovasio, J.M., J. Donahue and R. Stuckenrath 1990 "The Meadowcroft Rockshelter Radiocarbon Chronology 1975–1990." *American Antiquity* 55.2: 348–54.
Agrawal, D.P. 2007 *The Indus Civilization: An Interdisciplinary Perspective*. New Delhi: Aryan Books.
Agrawal, D.P. and J.S. Kharakwal 2003 *Bronze and Iron Ages in South Asia*. New Delhi: Aryan Books International.
Ahler, Steven R. 1998 "Early and Middle Archaic Settlement Systems in the Modoc Locality, Southwest Illinois." *Illinois Archaeology* 10.1–2: 1–109.
Aimers, James J. 2007 "What Maya Collapse? Terminal Classic Variation in the Maya Lowlands." *Journal of Archaeological Research* 15: 329–77.
Akkermans, Peter M.M.G. and Glenn M. Schwartz 2003 *The Archaeology of Syria: From Complex Hunter-Gatherers to Early Urban Societies (ca. 16,000–300 B.C.)*. Cambridge: Cambridge University Press.

Alberti, Benjamin 2002 "Gender and the Figurative Art of Late Bronze Age Knossos." In *Labyrinth Revisited: Rethinking 'Minoan' Archaeology*, edited by Y. Hamilakis, pp. 98–117. Oxford: Oxbow Books.

Aldenderfer, Mark 1993 "Ritual, Hierarchy, and Change in Foraging Societies." *Journal of Anthropological Archaeology* 12: 1–40.

Algaze, Guillermo 2001 "Initial Social Complexity in Southwestern Asia." *Current Anthropology* 42: 199–233.

——— 2004 "Trade and the Origins of Mesopotamian Civilization." *Bibliotheca Orientalis* 61: 5–19.

——— 2008 *Ancient Mesopotamia at the Dawn of Civilization: The Evolution of an Urban Landscape*. Chicago: University of Chicago Press.

Allen, Mark W. 2006 "Transformations in Maori Warfare: Toa, Pa, and Pu." In *The Archaeology of Warfare: Prehistories of Raiding and Conquest*, edited by E.N. Arkush and M.W. Allen, pp. 184–213. Gainesville: University Press of Florida.

——— 2008 "Hillforts and the Cycling of Maori Chiefdoms: Do Good Fences Make Good Neighbors?" In *Global Perspectives on the Collapse of Complex Systems*, edited by J.A. Railey and R.M. Reycraft, pp. 65–81. Albuquerque: Maxwell Museum of Anthropology.

——— 2016 "Food, Fighting, and Fortifications in Pre-European New Zealand: Beyond the Ecological Model of Maori Warfare." In *The Archaeology of Food and Warfare: Food Insecurity in Prehistory*, edited by A.M. VanDerwarker and G.D. Wilson, pp. 41–60. Cham: Springer International.

Allen, Sarah 1984 "The Myth of the Xia Dynasty." *Journal of the Royal Asiatic Society* 2: 242–56.

——— 2007 "Erlitou and the Formation of Chinese Civilization: Toward a New Paradigm." *Journal of Asian Studies* 66.2: 461–96.

Alt, Susan M. 2006 "The Power of Diversity: The Roles of Migration and Hybridity in Culture Change." In *Leadership and Polity in Mississippian Society*, edited by B.M. Butler and P.D. Welch, pp. 289–308. Center for Archaeological Investigations Occasional Paper No. 33. Carbondale: Southern Illinois University Press.

Alt, Susan M., ed. 2010a *Ancient Complexities: New Perspectives in Precolumbian North America*. Salt Lake City: University of Utah Press.

——— 2010b "Complexity in Action(s): Retelling the Cahokia Story." In *Ancient Complexities: New Perspectives in Precolumbian North America*, edited by S.M. Alt, pp. 119–37. Salt Lake City: University of Utah Press.

Alva, Walter and Christopher B. Donnan 1993 *The Royal Tombs of Sipán*. Los Angeles: Fowler Museum of Cultural History.

Anderson, William L. 1991 *Cherokee Removal: Before and After*. Athens: University of Georgia.

Appadurai, Arjun 1986 "Introduction: Commodities and the Politics of Value." In *The Social Life of Things: Commodities in Cultural Perspective*, edited by A. Appadurai, pp. 3–63. Cambridge: Cambridge University Press.

Arnold, Jeanne E. 1993 "Labor and the Rise of Complex Hunter-Gatherers." *Journal of Anthropological Archaeology* 12: 75–119.

——— 2000 "Revisiting Power, Labor Rights, and Kinship: Archaeology and Social Theory." In *Social Theory in Archaeology*, edited by M.D. Schiffer, pp. 14–30. Salt Lake City: University of Utah Press.

——— 2009 "The Role of Politically Charged Property in the Appearance of Institutionalized Leadership: A View from the North American Pacific Coast." In *The Evolution of Leadership: Transitions in Decision Making from Small-Scale to Middle-Range Societies*, edited by K.J. Vaughn, J.W. Eerkens and J. Kantner, pp. 121–46. Santa Fe: School for Advanced Research Press.

Arnold, Philip J., III 2012 "Not Carved in Stone: Building the Gulf Olmec from the Bottom Up." In *The Oxford Handbook of Mesoamerican Archaeology*, edited by D.L. Nichols and C.A. Pool, pp. 188–99. Oxford: Oxford University Press.

Arroyo, Bárbara 2012 "Archaeology of the Maya Highlands." In *The Oxford Handbook of Mesoamerican Archaeology*, edited by D.L. Nichols and C.A. Pool, pp. 245–54. Oxford: Oxford University Press.

Ashmore, Wendy 1992 "Deciphering Maya Architectural Plans." In *New Theories on the Ancient Maya*, edited by E.C. Danien and R.J. Sharer, pp. 173–84. Philadelphia: University Museum.

Asthana, Shashi 1993 "Harappan Trade in Metals and Minerals: A Regional Approach." In *Harappan Civilization: A Recent Perspective*, Second edition, edited by G.L. Possehl, pp. 271–85. New Delhi: American Institute of Indian Studies.

Atwood, Roger 2009 "Maya Roots." *Archaeology* 62.4: 18, 58–60, 65–66.

Baby, Raymond S. 1971 "Prehistoric Architecture: A Study of House Types in the Ohio Valley." *The Ohio Journal of Science* 71.4: 193–98.

Baby, Raymond S. and Suzanne M. Langlois 1979 "Seip Mound State Memorial: Nonmortuary Aspects of Hopewell." In *Hopewell Archaeology: The Chillicothe Conference*, edited by D.S. Brose and N.B. Greber, pp. 16–18. Kent: Kent State University Press.

Bachhuber, Christoph 2006 "Aegean Interest on the Uluburun Ship." *American Journal of Archaeology* 110: 345–63.

Bacus, Elisabeth A. 2004 "Social Identities in Bronze Age Northeast Thailand: Intersections of Gender, Status and Ranking at Non Nok Tha." In *Uncovering Southeast Asia's Past: Selected Papers from the 10th International Conference of the European Association of Southeast Asian Archaeologists*, edited by E.A. Bacus, I.C. Glover and V.C. Pigott, pp. 105–15. Singapore: Nus Press.

Baines, John 1983 "Literacy and Ancient Egyptian Society." *Man* N.S. 18: 572–99.

——— 1988 "Literacy, Social Organization, and the Archaeological Record: The Case of Early Egypt." In *State and Society: The Emergence and Development of Social Hierarchy and Political Centralization*, edited by J. Gledhill, B. Bender and M.T. Larsen, pp. 192–214. London: Unwin Hyman.

——— 1995 "Palaces and Temples of Ancient Egypt." In *Civilizations of the Ancient Near East*, edited by J.M. Sasson, pp. 303–17. New York: Charles Scribner's Sons.

Baines, John and Norman Yoffee 1998 "Order, Legitimacy, and Wealth in Ancient Egypt and Mesopotamia." In *Archaic States*, edited by G.M. Feinman and J. Marcus, pp. 199–260. Santa Fe: School of American Research Press.

Bala, Madhu 2004 "Kalibangan: Its Periods and Antiquities." In *Indus Civilization Sites in India: New Discoveries*, edited by D.K. Chakrabarti, pp. 34–43. Mumbai: Marg Publications.

Bang, Peter Fibiger 2013 "The Roman Empire II: The Monarchy." In *The Oxford Handbook of the State in the Ancient Near East and Mediterranean*, edited by P.F. Bang and W. Scheidel, pp. 412–72. Oxford: Oxford University Press.

Banning, E.B. 1997 "Spatial Perspectives on Early Urban Development in Mesopotamia." In *Urbanism in Antiquity: From Mesopotamia to Crete*, edited by W.E. Aufrecht, N.A. Mirau, and S.W. Gauley, pp. 17–34. Sheffield: Sheffield Academic Press.

Barber, Ian G. 1996 "Loss, Land and Monumental Landscaping: Towards a New Interpretation of the 'Classic' Maori Emergence." *Current Anthropology* 37: 868–80.

Bard, Kathryn A. 1992 "Origins of Egyptian Writing." In *The Followers of Horus: Studies Dedicated to Michael Allen Hoffman 1944–1990*, edited by R. Friedman and B. Adams, pp. 297–306. Oxford: Oxbow.

——— 1994 *From Farmers to Pharaohs: Mortuary Evidence for the Rise of Complex Society in Egypt*. Sheffield: Sheffield Academic Press.

——— 2008 *An Introduction to the Archaeology of Ancient Egypt*. Oxford: Blackwell Publishing.

Barker, Graeme 2006 *The Agricultural Revolution in Prehistory: Why Did Foragers Become Farmers?* Oxford: Oxford University Press.

Barnes, Gina L. 1993 *China, Korea, and Japan: The Rise of Civilization in East Asia*. London: Thames and Hudson.

Barrett, Tim 2013 "Confucius: The Key to Understanding China." In *Demystifying China: New Understandings of Chinese History*, edited by N. Standen, pp. 41–47. Lanham: Rowman & Littlefield Publishers, Inc.

Bar-Yosef, Ofer 1986 "The Walls of Jericho: An Alternative Interpretation." *Current Anthropology* 27: 157–62.

——— 1989 "The PPNA in the Levant—An Overview." *Paléorient* 15.1: 57–63.

Bar-Yosef, Ofer and Richard H. Meadow 1995 "The Origins of Agriculture in the Near East." In *Last Hunters-First Farmers: New Perspectives on the Prehistoric Transition to Agriculture*, edited by T.D. Price and A.B. Gebauer, pp. 39–94. Santa Fe: School of American Research Press.

Bar-Yosef, Ofer and François R. Valla 1991 "The Natufian Culture—An Introduction." In *The Natufian Culture in the Levant*, edited by O. Bar-Yosef and F.R. Valla, pp. 1–10. Ann Arbor: International Monographs in Prehistory.

Baud, Michel 2010 "The Old Kingdom." In *A Companion to Ancient Egypt*, edited by A.B. Lloyd, pp. 63–80. Oxford: Blackwell Publishing Ltd.

Bauer, Brian S. 2004 *Ancient Cuzco: Heartland of the Inca*. Austin: University of Texas Press.

Bauer, Brian S. and R. Alan Covey 2002 "Processes of State Formation in the Inca Heartland (Cuzco, Peru)." *American Anthropologist* 104.3: 846–64.

Bauer, Brian S. and Douglas K. Smit 2015 "Separating the Wheat from the Chaff: Inka Myths, Inka Legends, and the Archaeological Evidence for State Development." In *The Inka Empire: A Multidisciplinary Approach*, edited by I. Shimada, pp. 67–80. Austin: University of Texas Press.

Bauer, Josef 1998 "Der vorsargonische Abschnitt der mesopotamischen Geschichte." In *Mesopotamien. Späturuk-Zeit und Frühdynastische Zeit*, edited by J. Bauer, R.K. Englund and M. Krebernik, pp. 431–585. Freiburg: Universitätsverlag.

Baumbach, Lydia 1983 "An Examination of the Personal Names in the Knossos Tablets as Evidence for the Social Structure of Crete in the Late Minoan II Period." In *Minoan Society: Proceedings of the Cambridge Colloquium 1981*, edited by O. Krzyszkowska and L. Nixon, pp. 3–10. Bristol: Bristol Classical Press.

Bawden, Garth 1996 *The Moche*. Oxford: Blackwell.

Beacham, Richard C. 1999 *Spectacle Entertainments of Early Imperial Rome*. New Haven: Yale University Press.

Beaudry, Mary P. 1984 *Ceramic Production and Distribution on the Southeastern Maya Periphery*. Oxford: British Archaeological Reports.

Beaulieu, Paul-Alain 1989 *The Reign of Nabonidus King of Babylon 556–539 B.C.* New Haven: Yale University Press.

Beck, Robin A., Jr. 2006 "Persuasive Politics and Domination at Cahokia and Moundville." In *Leadership and Polity in Mississippian Society*, edited by B.M. Butler and P.D. Welch, pp. 19–42. Center for Archaeological Investigations Occasional Paper No. 33. Carbondale: Southern Illinois University.

Becker, Marshall Joseph 1973 "Archaeological Evidence for Occupational Specialization among the Classic Period Maya at Tikal, Guatemala." *American Antiquity* 38: 397–406.

——— 1983 "Indications of Social Class Differences based on the Archaeological Evidence for Occupational Specialization among the Classic Maya at Tikal, Guatemala." *Revista Española de Antropologia Americana* 13: 29–46.

Bellina, Bérénice and Ian Glover 2004 "The Archaeology of Early Contact with India and the Mediterranean World, from the Fourth Century BC to the Fourth Century AD." In *Southeast Asia from Prehistory to History*, edited by I. Glover and P. Bellwood, pp. 68–88. London: RoutledgeCurzon.

Bellwood, Peter 1987 *The Polynesians: Prehistory of an Island People*. Revised edition. London: Thames and Hudson.

——— 2004 "The Origins and Dispersals of Agricultural Communities in Southeast Asia." In *Southeast Asia from Prehistory to History*, edited by I. Glover and P. Bellwood, pp. 21–40. London: RoutledgeCurzon.

——— 2005 *First Farmers: The Origins of Agricultural Societies*. Oxford: Blackwell Publishing.

——— 2006 "Asian Farming Diasporas? Agriculture, Languages, and Genes in China and Southeast Asia." In *Archaeology of Asia*, edited by M.T. Stark, pp. 96–118. Oxford: Blackwell Publishing.

——— 2013 *First Migrants: Ancient Migration in Global Perspective*. West Sussex: Wiley-Blackwell.

Bendall, Lisa M. 2001 "The Economics of Potnia in the Linear B Documents: Palatial Support for Mycenaean Religion." In *Potnia: Deities and Religion in the Aegean Bronze Age*, edited by R. Laffineur and R. Hägg, pp. 445–52. Aegaeum 22. Liège: Université de Liège.

——— 2003 "A Reconsideration of the Northeastern Building at Pylos: Evidence for a Mycenaean Redistributive Center." *American Journal of Archaeology* 107: 181–231.

Bender, Barbara 1978 "Gatherer-Hunter to Farmer: A Social Perspective." *World Archaeology* 10: 204–22.

——— 1990 "The Dynamics of Nonhierarchical Societies." In *The Evolution of Political Systems: Sociopolitics in Small-Scale Sedentary Societies*, edited by S. Upham, pp. 247–63. Cambridge: Cambridge University Press.

Ben-Schlomo, David, Eleni Nodarou and Jeremy B. Rutter 2011 "Transport Stirrup Jars from the Southern Levant: New Light on Commodity Exchange in the Eastern Mediterranean." *American Journal of Archaeology* 115: 329–55.

Benson, Elizabeth P. 2012 *The Worlds of the Moche on the North Coast of Peru*. Austin: University of Texas Press.

Benson, Larry V., Timothy R. Pauketat and Edward R. Cook 2009 "Cahokia's Boom and Bust in the Context of Climate Change." *American Antiquity* 74.3: 467–83.

Bentz, Martin 1998 *Panathenäische Preisamphoren. Eine athenische Vasengattung und ihre Funktion vom 6.-4. Jahrhundert v. Chr.* Basel: Vereinigung der Freunde antiker Kunst.

Berdan, Frances F. 1989 "Trade and Markets in Precapitalist States." In *Economic Anthropology*, edited by S. Plattner, pp. 78–107. Stanford: Stanford University Press.

Bernbeck, Reinhard 1995 "Lasting Alliances and Emerging Competition: Economic Developments in Early Mesopotamia." *Journal of Anthropological Archaeology* 14: 1–25.

Betancourt, Philip P. 1999 "Discontinuity in the Minoan-Mycenaean Religions: Smooth Development or Disruptions and War?" In *Polemos: Le contexte guerrier en Égée à l'âge du bronze*, edited by R. Laffineur, pp. 219–25. Aegaeum 19. Liège: Université de Liège.

——— 2006 *The Chrysokamino Metallurgy Workshop and Its Territory*, edited by P.P. Betancourt. Hesperia Supplement 36. Athens: American School of Classical Studies.

——— 2007 *Introduction to Aegean Art*. Philadelphia: INSTAP Academic Press.

Bettinger, Robert L. 2001 "Holocene Hunter-Gatherers." In *Archaeology at the Millennium: A Sourcebook*, edited by G.M. Feinman and T.D. Price, pp. 137–95. New York: Kluwer Academic/Plenum Publishers.

Bhan, Kuldeep K., V.H. Sonawane, P. Ajithprasad and S. Pratapchandran 2005 "A Harappan Trading and Craft Production Centre at Gola Dhoro (Bagasra)." *Antiquity* 75 (Online Project).

Bietak, Manfred 1995 "Connections between Egypt and the Minoan World: New Results from Tell el-Dab'a/Avaris." In *Egypt, the Aegean and the Levant: Interconnections in the Second Millennium B.C.*, edited by W.V. Davies and L. Schofield, pp. 19–28. London: British Museum Press.

——— 2000 "'Rich Beyond the Dreams of Avaris: Tell el-Dab'a and the Aegean World—A Guide for the Perplexed': A Response to Eric H. Cline." *Annual of the British School at Athens* 95: 185–205.

Bietak, Manfred, Nannó Marinatos and Clairy Palivou 2007 *Taureador Scenes in Tell El-Dab'a (Avaris) and Knossos*. Wien: Verlag der österreichischen Akademie der Wissenschaften.

Billman, Brian R. 2010 "How Moche Rulers Came to Power: Investigating the Emergence of the Moche Political Economy." In *New Perspectives on Moche Political Organization*, edited by J. Quilter and L.J. Castillo, pp. 181–200. Washington: Dumbarton Oaks.

Bird, Douglas W. and Rebecca Bliege Bird 2009 "Competing to be Leaderless: Food Sharing and Magnanimity among Martu Aborigines." In *The Evolution of Leadership: Transitions in Decision Making from Small-Scale to Middle-Range Societies*, edited by K.J. Vaughn, J.W. Eerkens and J. Kantner, pp. 21–49. Santa Fe: School for Advanced Research Press.

Blanton, Richard E., Jill Appel, Laura Finsten, Steve Kowalewski, Gary Feinman and Eva Fisch 1979 "Regional Evolution in the Valley of Oaxaca, Mexico." *Journal of Field Archaeology* 6: 369–90.

Blanton, Richard E., Gary M. Feinman, Stephen A. Kowalewski and Linda M. Nicholas 1999 *Ancient Oaxaca: The Monte Albán State*. Cambridge: Cambridge University Press.

Blanton, Richard E., Gary M. Feinman, Stephen A. Kowalewski and Peter N. Peregrine 1996 "A Dual-Processual Theory for the Evolution of Mesoamerican Civilization." *Current Anthropology* 37: 1–14.

Blomster, Jeffrey P. 2002 "What and Where Is Olmec Style? Regional Perspectives on Hollow Figurines in Early Formative Mesoamerica." *Ancient Mesoamerica* 13: 171–95.

Bocek, Barbara 1991 "Prehistoric Settlement Pattern and Social Organization on the San Francisco Peninsula, California." In *Between Bands and States*, edited by S.A. Gregg, pp. 58–86. Center for Archaeological Investigations Occasional Paper No. 9. Carbondale: Southern Illinois University.

Boulotis, Christos 1987 "Nochmals zum Prozessionsfresko von Knossos: Palast und Darbringung von Prestige-Objekten." In *The Function of the Minoan Palaces*, edited by R. Hägg and N. Marinatos, pp. 145–56. Stockholm: Paul Aströms Förlag.

Bourget, Steve 2001 "Children and Ancestors: Ritual Practices at the Moche Site of Huaca de la Luna, North Coast of Peru." In *Ritual Sacrifice in Ancient Peru*, edited by E.P. Benson and A.G. Cook, pp. 93–118. Austin: University of Texas Press.

——— 2006 *Sex, Death, and Sacrifice in Moche Religion and Visual Culture*. Austin: University of Texas Press.

——— 2008 "The Third Man: Identity and Rulership in Moche Archaeology and Visual Culture." In *The Art and Archaeology of the Moche: An Ancient Andean Society of the Peruvian North Coast*, edited by S. Bourget and K.L. Jones, pp. 263–88. Austin: University of Texas Press.

Bowersock, G.W. 1988 "The Dissolution of the Roman Empire." In *The Collapse of Ancient States and Civilizations*, edited by N. Yoffee and G.L. Cowgill, pp. 165–75. Tucson: University of Arizona Press.

Bowne, Eric E. 2013 *Mound Sites of the Ancient South: A Guide to the Mississippian Chiefdoms*. Athens: University of Georgia Press.

Bradley, Douglas E. 2001 "Gender, Power, and Fertility in the Olmec Ritual Ballgame." In *The Sport of Life and Death: The Mesoamerican Ballgame*, edited by E.M. Whittington, pp. 32–39. Charlotte: The Mint Museum of Art.

Branigan, Keith 1988 "Some Observations on State Formation in Crete." In *Problems in Greek Prehistory*, edited by E.B. French and K.A. Wardle, pp. 63–71. Bristol: Bristol Classical Press.

Braswell, Geoffrey E. 2010 "The Rise and Fall of Market Exchange: A Dynamic Approach to Ancient Maya Economy." In *Archaeological Approaches to Market Exchange in Ancient Societies*, edited by C.P. Garraty and B.L. Stark, pp. 127–40. Boulder: University Press of Colorado.

Braun-Holzinger, Eva Andrea 1991 *Mesopotamische Weihgaben der Frühdynastischen bis Altbabylonischen Zeit.* Heidelberg: Heidelberger Orientverlag.

Brennan, Tamira 2010 "The South Cape Site: A Fortified Mississippian Village in Southeast Missouri." *Missouri Archaeological Society Quarterly* 27: 12–19.

Bronson, Bennet 1988 "The Role of Barbarians in the Fall of States." In *The Collapse of Ancient States and Civilizations*, edited by N. Yoffee and G.L. Cowgill, pp. 196–218. Tucson: University of Arizona Press.

Broodbank, Cyprian 2000 *An Island Archaeology of the Early Cyclades.* Cambridge: Cambridge University Press.

Brown, James A. 1997 "The Archaeology of Ancient Religion in the Eastern Woodlands." *Annual Review of Anthropology* 26: 465–85.

——— 2006 "Where's the Power in Mound Building? An Eastern Woodlands Perspective." In *Leadership and Polity in Mississippian Society*, edited by B.M. Butler and P.D. Welch, pp. 197–213. Center for Archaeological Investigations Occasional Paper No. 33. Carbondale: Southern Illinois University.

——— 2007 "On the Identity of the Birdman within Mississippian Period Art and Iconography." In *Ancient Objects and Sacred Realms: Interpretations of Mississippian Iconography*, edited by F.K. Reilly III and J.F. Garber, pp. 56–106. Austin: University of Texas Press.

Brumfiel, Elizabeth M. 1987 "Elite and Utilitarian Crafts in the Aztec State." In *Specialization, Exchange and Complex Societies*, edited by E.M. Brumfiel and T.K. Earle, pp. 102–18. Cambridge: Cambridge University Press.

——— 1991 "Weaving and Cooking: Women's Production in Aztec Mexico." In *Engendering Archaeology*, edited by J.M. Gero and M.W. Conkey, pp. 224–55. Oxford: Basil Blackwell.

——— 1994a "Ethnic Groups and Political Development in Ancient Mexico." In *Factional Competition and Political Development in the New World*, edited by E.M. Brumfiel and J.W. Fox, pp. 89–102. Cambridge: Cambridge University Press.

——— 1994b "Factional Competition and Political Development in the New World: An Introduction." In *Factional Competition and Political Development in the New World*, edited by E.M. Brumfiel and J.W. Fox, pp. 3–13. Cambridge: Cambridge University Press.

——— 2007 "Huitzilopochtli's Conquest: Aztec Ideology in the Archaeological Record." In *The Archaeology of Identities: A Reader*, edited by T. Insoll, pp. 265–80. London: Routledge.

Brumfiel, Elizabeth M. and Timothy K. Earle 1987 "Specialization, Exchange, and Complex Societies: An Introduction." In *Specialization, Exchange and Complex Societies*, edited by E.M. Brumfiel and T.K. Earle, pp. 1–9. Cambridge: Cambridge University Press.

Bryan, Betsy 2010 "New Kingdom Sculpture." In *A Companion to Ancient Egypt*, edited by A.B. Lloyd, pp. 913–43. Oxford: Blackwell Publishing Ltd.

Buckley, Stephen A., Katherine A. Clark and Richard P. Evershed 2004 "Complex Organic Chemical Balms of Pharaonic Animal Mummies." *Nature* 431: 294–99.

Burger, Richard L. 1992 *Chavín and the Origins of Andean Civilization.* London: Thames and Hudson.

——— 2008 "Chavín de Huántar and Its Sphere of Influence." In *Handbook of South American Archaeology*, edited by H. Silverman and W.H. Isbell, pp. 681–703. New York: Springer.

Burks, Jarrod and N'omi B. Greber 2009 "Exploring the Features Found During the 1971–1977 Seip Earthworks Excavation." *Midcontinental Journal of Archaeology* 34.1: 143–70.

Butzer, Karl W. 1995 "Environmental Change in the Near East and Human Impact on the Land." In *Civilizations of the Ancient Near East*, edited by J.M. Sasson, pp. 123–51. New York: Charles Scribner's Sons.

Byrd, Brian F. 1994 "Public and Private, Domestic and Corporate: The Emergence of the Southwest Asian Village." *American Antiquity* 59: 639–66.

Callender, Gae 1998 *Egypt in the Old Kingdom: An Introduction.* South Melbourne: Longman.

Cameron, M.A.S. 1978 "Theoretical Interrelations among Theran, Cretan and Mainland Frescoes." In *Thera and the Aegean World I: Papers Presented at the Second International Scientific Congress, Santorini, Greece, August 1978*, edited by C. Doumas, pp. 579–92. London: Thera and the Aegean World.

——— 1987 "The 'Palatial' Thematic System in the Knossos Murals: Last Notes on Knossos Frescoes." In *The Function of the Minoan Palaces*, edited by R. Hägg and N. Marinatos, pp. 321–28. Stockholm: Paul Åströms Förlag.

Campbell, Roderick B. 2009 "Toward a Networks and Boundaries Approach to Early Complex Polities: The Late Shang Case." *Current Anthropology* 50.6: 821–48.

Canby, Jeanny Vorys 2001 *The "Ur-Nammu" Stela.* Philadelphia: University of Pennsylvania Museum of Archaeology and Anthropology.

Cantarella, Eva 2002 "Marriage and Sexuality in Republican Rome: A Roman Conjugal Love Story." In *The Sleep of Reason: Erotic Experience and Sexual Ethics in Ancient Greece and Rome*, edited by M.C. Nussbaum and J. Sihvola, pp. 269–82. Chicago: University of Chicago Press.
——— 2003 "Fathers and Sons in Rome." *Classical World* 96: 281–98.
Carneiro, Robert L. 1970 "A Theory of the Origin of the State." *Science* 169: 733–38.
——— 1981 "The Chiefdom as Precursor of the State." In *The Transition to Statehood in the New World*, edited by G. Jones and R. Kautz, pp. 370–79. Cambridge: Cambridge University Press.
Carr, Christopher and D. Troy Case 2005 "The Nature of Leadership in Ohio Hopewellian Societies." In *Gathering Hopewell: Society, Ritual, and Ritual Interaction*, edited by C. Carr and D.T. Case, pp. 19–50. New York: Springer.
Carter, Jane B. and Laura J. Steinberg 2010 "*Kouroi* and Statistics." *American Journal of Archaeology* 114: 103–28.
Cartledge, Paul 1998 "The Machismo of the Athenian Empire—Or the Reign of the Phaulus?" In *When Men Were Men: Masculinity, Power and Identity in Classical Antiquity*, edited by L. Foxhall and J. Salmon, pp. 54–67. London: Routledge.
Castillo, Luis Jaime 2010 "Moche Politics in the Jequetepeque Valley: A Case for Political Opportunism." In *New Perspectives on Moche Political Organization*, edited by J. Quilter and L.J. Castillo, pp. 83–109. Washington: Dumbarton Oaks.
Castillo, Luis Jaime and Santiago Uceda Castillo 2008 "The Mochicas." In *Handbook of South American Archaeology*, edited by H. Silverman and W.H. Isbell, pp. 707–29. New York: Springer.
Castillo, Luis Jaime and Christopher B. Donnan 1994 "La Occupación Moche de San José de Moro, Jequetepeque." In *Moche: Propuestas y Perspectivas*, edited by S. Uceda and E. Mujica, pp. 93–146. Lima: Universidad Nacional de la Libertad, Trujillo.
Catling, H.W. 1976–77 "Excavations at the Menelaion, Sparta, 1973–1976." *Archaeological Reports* 23: 24–42.
Ceruti, Constanza 2004 "Human Bodies as Objects of Dedication at Inca Mountain Shrines (North-Western Argentina)." *World Archaeology* 36.1: 103–22.
Chakrabarti, Dilip K. 2001 "The Archaeology of Hinduism." In *Archaeology and World Religion*, edited by T. Insoll, pp. 33–60. London: Routledge.
——— 2004 "Internal and External Trade of the Indus Civilization." In *Indus Civilization Sites in India: New Discoveries*, edited by D.K. Chakrabarti, pp. 29–33. Mumbai: Marg Publications.
Chang, Kwang-Chih 1974 "Urbanism and the King in Ancient China." *World Archaeology* 6.1: 1–14.
——— 1980 *Shang Civilization*. New Haven: Yale University Press.
——— 1983 *Art, Myth, and Ritual: The Path to Political Authority in Ancient China*. Cambridge: Harvard University Press.
——— 1986 *The Archaeology of Ancient China*. New Haven: Yale University Press.
——— 2005 "The Rise of Kings and the Formation of City-States." In *The Formation of Chinese Civilization, An Archaeological Perspective*, edited by S. Allen, pp. 125–39. New Haven: Yale University Press.
Chapdelaine, Claude 2000 "Struggling for Survival: The Urban Class of the Moche Site, North Coast Peru." In *Environmental Disaster and the Archaeology of Human Response*, edited by G. Bawden and R.M. Reycraft, pp. 121–42. Maxwell Museum of Anthropology Papers no. 7. Albuquerque: University of New Mexico Press.
——— 2002 "Out on the Streets of Moche: Urbanism and Sociopolitical Organization at a Moche IV Urban Center." In *Andean Archaeology I: Variations in Sociopolitical Organization*, edited by W.H. Isbell and H. Silverman, pp. 53–88. New York: Kluwer Academic/Plenum.
——— 2006 "Looking for Moche Palaces in the Elite Residences of the Huacas of Moche Site." In *Palaces and Power in the Americas: From Peru to the Northwest Coast*, edited by J. Christie and P. Sarro, pp. 23–43. Austin: University of Texas Press.
——— 2010a "Moche Political Organization in the Santa Valley: A Case of Direct Rule through Gradual Control of the Local Population." In *New Perspectives on Moche Political Organization*, edited by J. Quilter and L.J. Castillo, pp. 252–79. Washington: Dumbarton Oaks.
——— 2010b "Moche and Wari during the Middle Horizon on the North Coast of Peru." In *Beyond Wari Walls: Regional Perspectives on Middle Horizon Peru*, edited by J. Jennings, pp. 213–32. Albuquerque: New Mexico Press.
——— 2011 "Recent Advances in Moche Archaeology." *Journal of Archaeological Research* 19: 191–231.
Chapin, Anne 2010 "Frescoes." In *The Oxford Handbook of the Bronze Age Aegean (ca. 3000–1000 BC)*, edited by E.H. Cline, pp. 223–36. Oxford: Oxford University Press.

Chapman, Robert 2003 *Archaeologies of Complexity*. London: Routledge.
––––––– 2010 "Downsizers, Upgraders, Cultural Constructors, and Social Producers." In *Ancient Complexities: New Perspectives in Precolumbian North America*, edited by S.M. Alt, pp. 205–19. Salt Lake City: University of Utah Press.
Charles, Douglas K. and Jane E. Buikstra 2009 "Archaic Mortuary Sites in the Central Mississippi Drainage: Distribution, Structure, and Behavioral Implications." In *Archaic Hunters and Gatherers in the American Midwest*, edited by J.L. Phillips and J.A. Brown, pp. 117–43. Walnut Creek: Left Coast Press.
Chase, Arlen F. and Diane Z. Chase 2012 "Complex Societies in the Southern Maya Lowlands: Their Development and Florescence in the Archaeological Record." In *The Oxford Handbook of Mesoamerican Archaeology*, edited by D.L. Nichols and C.A. Pool, pp. 255–67. Oxford: Oxford University Press.
Chase, Diane Z. 1992 "Postclassic Maya Elites: Ethnohistory and Archaeology." In *Mesoamerican Elites: An Archaeological Assessment*, edited by A.F. Chase and D.Z. Chase, pp. 118–34. Norman: University of Oklahoma Press.
Chávez, R.E., et al. 2001 "Site Characterization by Geophysical Methods in the Archaeological Zone of Teotihuacan, Mexico." *Journal of Archaeological Science* 28: 1265–76.
Childe, V. Gordon 1936 *Man Makes Himself*. London: Watts.
––––––– 1950 "The Urban Revolution." *The Town Planning Review* 21: 3–17.
Chirikure, Shadreck and Innocent Pikirayi 2008 "Inside and Outside the Dry Stone Walls: Revisiting the Material Culture of Great Zimbabwe." *Antiquity* 82: 976–93.
Christakis, Kostis S. 2011 "Redistribution and Political Economies in Bronze Age Crete." *American Journal of Archaeology* 115: 197–205.
Chrysoulaki, Stella and Lefteris Platon 1987 "Relations between the Town and Palace of Zakros." In *The Function of the Minoan Palaces*, edited by R. Hägg and N. Marinatos, pp. 77–84. Stockholm: Paul Aströms Förlag.
Clark, John E. and Michael Blake 1994 "The Power of Prestige: Competitive Generosity and the Emergence of Rank Societies in Lowland Mesoamerica." In *Factional Competition and Political Development in the New World*, edited by E.M. Brumfiel and J.W. Fox, pp. 17–30. Cambridge: Cambridge University Press.
Clark, John E., Jon L. Gibson and James Zeidler 2010 "First Towns in the Americas: Searching for Agriculture, Population Growth, and Other Enabling Conditions." In *Becoming Villagers: Comparing Early Village Societies*, edited by M.S. Bandy and J.R. Fox, pp. 205–45. Tucson: University of Arizona Press.
Clark, Sharri R. 2003 "Representing the Indus Body: Sex, Gender, Sexuality, and the Anthropomorphic Terracotta Figurines from Harappa." *Asian Perspectives* 42.2: 304–28.
Clarke, John R. 1991 *The Houses of Roman Italy, 100 B.C.-A.D. 250: Ritual, Space, and Decoration*. Berkeley: University of California Press.
Clay, R. Berle 2009 "Where Have all the Houses Gone? Webb's Adena House in Historical Context." *Southeastern Archaeology* 28.1: 43–63.
Cline, Eric H. 2008 "Troy as a 'Contested Periphery': Archaeological Perspectives on Cross-Cultural and Cross-Disciplinary Interactions concerning Bronze Age Anatolia." In *Anatolian Interfaces: Hittites, Greeks and Their Neighbours*, edited by B.J. Collins, M.R. Bachvarova and I.C. Rutherford, pp. 11–19. Oxford: Oxbow Books.
Cline, Eric H. and Assaf Yasur-Landau 2007 "Musings from a Distant Shore: The Nature and Destination of the Uluburun Ship and Its Cargo." *Tel Aviv* 34: 125–41.
Cobb, Charles R. 2003 "Mississippian Chiefdoms: How Complex?" *Annual Review of Anthropology* 32: 63–84.
Coe, Michael D. 1989 "The Olmec Heartland: Evolution of Ideology." In *Regional Perspectives on the Olmec*, edited by R.J. Sharer and D.C. Grove, pp. 68–82. Cambridge: Cambridge University Press.
Cohen, Andrew C. 2005 *Death Rituals, Ideology, and the Development of Early Mesopotamian Kingship: Toward a New Understanding of Iraq's Royal Cemetery of Ur*. Leiden: Brill.
Coldstream, J.N. 1991 "The Geometric Style: Birth of the Picture." In *Looking at Greek Vases*, edited by T. Rasmussen and N. Spivey, pp. 37–56. Cambridge: Cambridge University Press.
Collins, Paul 2000 *The Uruk Phenomenon: The Role of Social Ideology in the Expansion of the Uruk Culture during the Fourth Millennium*. Oxford: British Archaeological Reports.
Collon, Dominique 1988 *First Impressions: Cylinder Seals of the Ancient Near East*. London: British Museum Publications.
Conlee, Christina A. 2010 "Nasca and Wari: Local Opportunism and Colonial Ties During the Middle Horizon." In *Beyond Wari Walls: Regional Perspectives on Middle Horizon Peru*, edited by J. Jennings, pp. 96–112. Albuquerque: New Mexico Press.

Conlee, Christina A., Michele R. Buzon, Aldo N. Gutierrez and Antonio Simonetti 2009 "Identifying Foreigners versus Locals in a Burial Population from Nasca, Peru: An Investigation Using Strontium Isotope Analysis." *Journal of Archaeological Science* 36: 2755–64.

Coningham, Robin and Ruth Young 2015 *The Archaeology of South Asia: From the Indus to Asoka, c. 6500 BCE-200 CE*. Cambridge: Cambridge University Press.

Connelly, Joan Breton 2014 *The Parthenon Enigma*. New York: Knopf.

Cook, Constance A. 1997. "Wealth and the Western Zhou." *Bulletin of the School of Oriental and African Studies* 60.2: 253–94.

Coon, Matthew S. 2009 "Variation in Ohio Hopewell Political Economies." *American Antiquity* 74.1: 49–76.

Coppa, A., L. Bondioli, A. Cucina, D.W. Frayer, C. Jarrige, J.-F. Jarrige, G. Quivron, M. Rossi, M. Vidale and R. Macchiarelli 2006 "Early Neolithic Tradition of Dentistry." *Nature* 440: 755–56.

Cordy-Collins, Alana and Charles F. Merbs 2008 "Forensic Iconography: The Case of the Moche Giants." In *The Art and Archaeology of the Moche: An Ancient Andean Society of the Peruvian North Coast*, edited by S. Bourget and K.L. Jones, pp. 93–111. Austin: University of Texas Press.

Cork, Edward 2011 *Rethinking the Indus: A Comparative Re-Evaluation of the Indus Civilisation as an Alternative Paradigm in the Organisation and Structure of Early Complex Societies*. BAR International Series 2213. Oxford: BAR International.

Cornell, T.J. 1995 *The Beginnings of Rome: Italy and Rome from the Bronze Age to the Punic Wars (c. 1000–264 BC)*. London: Routledge.

Cosmopoulos, Michael B. 2003 "Mycenaean Religion at Eleusis: The Architecture and Stratigraphy of Megaron B." In *Greek Mysteries: The Archaeology and Ritual of Ancient Greek Secret Cults*, edited by M.B. Cosmopoulos, pp. 1–24. London: Routledge.

Covey, R. Alan 2003 "A Processual Study of Inka State Formation." *Journal of Anthropological Archaeology* 22: 333–57.

——— 2006 *How the Incas Built Their Heartland*. Ann Arbor: University of Michigan Press.

——— 2008a "Multiregional Perspectives on the Archaeology of the Andes during the Late Intermediate Period (c. A.D. 1000–1400)." *Journal of Archaeological Research* 16: 287–338.

——— 2008b "The Inca Empire." In *Handbook of South American Archaeology*, edited by H. Silverman and W.H. Isbell, pp. 809–30. New York: Springer.

——— 2009 "Domestic Life and Craft Specialization in Inka Cusco and Its Rural Hinterland." In *Domestic Life in Prehispanic Capitals: A Study of Specialization, Hierarchy, and Ethnicity*, edited by L.R. Manzanilla and C. Chapdelaine, pp. 243–54. Memoirs of the Museum of Anthropology, No. 46. Ann Arbor: University of Michigan.

Cowgill, George L. 1988 "Onward and Upward with Collapse." In *The Collapse of Ancient States and Civilizations*, edited by N. Yoffee and G.L. Cowgill, pp. 244–76. Tucson: University of Arizona Press.

——— 1992a "Social Differentiation at Teotihuacan." In *Mesoamerican Elites: An Archaeological Assessment*, edited by A.F. Chase and D.Z. Chase, pp. 206–20. Norman: University of Oklahoma Press.

——— 1992b "Toward a Political History of Teotihuacan." In *Ideology and Pre-Columbian Civilizations*, edited by A.A. Demarest and G.W. Conrad, pp. 87–114. Santa Fe: School of American Research Press.

——— 2003 "Teotihuacan: Cosmic Glories and Mundane Needs." In *The Social Construction of Ancient Cities*, edited by M.L. Smith, pp. 37–55. Washington: Smithsonian Books.

——— 2007 "The Urban Organization of Teotihuacan, Mexico." In *Settlement and Society: Essays Dedicated to Robert McCormick Adams*, edited by E. Stone, pp. 261–95. Los Angeles: Cotsen Institute of Archaeology, UCLA.

Crawford, Gary W. 2006 "East Asian Plant Domestication." In *Archaeology of Asia*, edited by M.T. Stark, pp. 77–95. Oxford: Blackwell Publishing.

Crielaard, Jan Paul 1995 "How the West Was Won: Euboeans vs. Phoenicians." In *Trade and Production in Premonetary Greece: Aspects of Trade*, edited by C. Gillis, C. Risberg and B. Sjöberg, pp. 125–27. Jonsered: Paul Astroms Forlag.

Crown, Patricia L., Thomas E. Emerson, Jiyan Gu, W. Jeffrey Hurst, Timothy R. Pauketat and Timothy Ward 2012 "Ritual Black Drink Consumption at Cahokia." *Proceedings of the National Academy of Sciences* 109.35: 13944–49.

Crown, Patricia L., W. Jeffrey Hurst and Bruce D. Smith 2009 "Evidence of Cacao Use in the Prehispanic American Southwest." *Proceedings of the National Academy of Sciences of the United States of America* 106: 2110–13.

Crumley, Carole L. 1995 "Heterarchy and the Analysis of Complex Societies." In *Heterarchy and the Analysis of Complex Societies*, edited by R. Ehrenreich, C. Crumley and J. Levy, pp. 1–5. Archaeological Papers of the American Anthropological Association, No. 6. Washington: American Anthropological Association.

Culbert, T. Patrick 1988 "The Collapse of Classic Maya Civilization." In *The Collapse of Ancient States and Civilizations*, edited by N. Yoffee and G.L. Cowgill, pp. 69–101. Tucson: University of Arizona Press.

Cyphers, Ann 1999 "From Stone to Symbols: Olmec Art in Social Context at San Lorenzo Tenochtitlán." In *Social Patterns in Pre-Classic Mesoamerica*, edited by D.C. Grove and R.A. Joyce, pp. 155–81. Washington: Dumbarton Oaks Research Library and Collection.

Cyphers, Ann and Judith Zurita-Noguera 2012 "Early Olmec Wetland Mounds: Investing Energy to Produce Energy." In *Early New World Monumentality*, edited by R.L. Burger and R.M. Rosenswig, pp. 138–73. Gainesville: University Press of Florida.

Dalan, Rinita A., George R. Holley, William I. Woods, Harold W. Watters Jr. and John A. Koepke 2003 *Envisioning Cahokia: A Landscape Perspective*. DeKalb: Northern Illinois University Press.

D'Altroy, Terence N. 2002 *The Incas*. Oxford: Blackwell Publishers.

Damp, Jonathan E. 1984 "Architecture of the Early Valdivia Village." *American Antiquity* 49.3: 573–85.

Dancey, William S. and Paul J. Pacheco 1997 "A Community Model of Ohio Hopewell Settlement." In *Ohio Hopewell Community Organization*, edited by W.S. Dancey and P.J. Pacheco, pp. 3–40. Kent: Kent State University Press.

Davidson, Janet 1984 *The Prehistory of New Zealand*. Auckland: Longman Paul.

——— 1987 "The Paa Maaori Revisited." *Journal of the Polynesian Society* 96.1: 7–26.

Davies, Vivian and Renée Friedman 1998 *Egypt Uncovered*. New York: Stewart, Tabori & Chang.

Davis, Ellen N. 1983 "The Iconography of the Ship Fresco from Thera." In *Ancient Greek Art and Iconography*, edited by W.G. Moon, pp. 3–14. Madison: University of Wisconsin Press.

——— 1995 "Art and Politics in the Aegean: The Missing Ruler." In *The Role of the Ruler in the Prehistoric Aegean*, edited by P. Rehak, pp. 11–20. Aegaeum 11. Liège: Université de Liège.

Davis, Whitney 1992 *Masking the Blow: The Scene of Representation in Late Prehistoric Egyptian Art*. Berkeley: University of California Press.

——— 1993 "Narrativity and the Narmer Palette." In *Narrative and Event in Ancient Art*, edited by P.J. Holliday, pp. 14–54. Cambridge: Cambridge University Press.

Day, Jane Stevenson 2001 "Performing on the Court." In *The Sport of Life and Death: The Mesoamerican Ballgame*, edited by E.M. Whittington, pp. 64–77. Charlotte: The Mint Museum of Art.

Day, Peter M. and David E. Wilson 1998 "Consuming Power: Kamares Ware in Protopalatial Knossos." *Antiquity* 72: 350–58.

——— 2002 "Landscapes of Memory, Craft and Power in Prepalatial and Protopalatial Knossos." In *Labyrinth Revisited: Rethinking 'Minoan' Archaeology*, edited by Y. Hamilakis, pp. 143–66. Oxford: Oxbow Books.

Day, Peter M., Maria Relaki and Edward W. Faber 2006 "Pottery Making and Social Reproduction in the Bronze Age Mesara." In *Pottery and Society: The Impact of Recent Studies in Minoan Pottery*, edited by M.H. Wiener, J.L. Warner, J. Polonsky and E.E. Hayes, pp. 22–72. Boston: Archaeological Institute of America.

DeBoer, Warren R. 1997 "Ceremonial Centres from the Cayapas (Esmeraldas, Ecuador) to Chillicothe (Ohio, U.S.A.)." *Cambridge Archaeological Journal* 7: 225–53.

de la Fuente, Beatriz 1981 "Toward a Conception of Monumental Olmec Art." In *The Olmec and Their Neighbors: Essays in Memory of Matthew W. Stirling*, edited by E.P. Benson, pp. 83–94. Washington: Trustees for Harvard University.

DeMarrais, Elizabeth, Luis Jaime Castillo and Timothy Earle 1996 "Ideology, Materialization, and Power Strategies." *Current Anthropology* 37: 15–32.

Demel, Scott J. and Robert L. Hall 1998 "The Mississippian Town Plan and Cultural Landscape of Cahokia, Illinois." In *Mississippian Towns and Sacred Spaces: Search for an Architectural Grammar*, edited by R.B. Lewis and C. Stout, pp. 200–26. Tuscaloosa: University of Alabama Press.

de Miroschedji, Pierre 2002 "The Socio-Political Dynamics of Egyptian-Canaanite Interaction in the Early Bronze Age." In *Egypt and the Levant: Interrelations from the 4th through the Early 3rd millennium BCE*, edited by E.C.M. van den Brink and T.E. Levy, pp. 39–57. London: Leicester University Press.

Demoule, Jean-Paul and Catherine Perlès 1993 "The Greek Neolithic: A New Review." *Journal of World Prehistory* 7: 355–416.

de Polignac, François 1994 "Mediation, Competition, and Sovereignty: The Evolution of Rural Sanctuaries in Geometric Greece." In *Placing the Gods: Sanctuaries and Sacred Space in Ancient Greece*, edited by S.E. Alcock and R. Osborne, pp. 3–18. Oxford: Clarendon Press.

Diakonoff, I.M. 1969 "The Rise of the Despotic State in Ancient Mesopotamia." In *Ancient Mesopotamia: Socio-Economic History: A Collection of Studies by Soviet Scholars*, edited by I.M. Diakonoff, pp. 173–203. Moscow: "Nauka" Publishing House.

Diamond, Jared 2005 *Collapse: How Societies Choose to Fail or Succeed*. New York: Penguin.

Di Cosmo, Nicola 1999 "The Northern Frontier in Pre-Imperial China." In *The Cambridge History of Ancient China*, edited by M. Loewe and E.L. Shaughnessy, pp. 885–966. Cambridge: Cambridge University Press. (Published online in 2008.)

——— 2009 "Han Frontiers: Toward an Integrated View." *Journal of the American Oriental Society* 129.2: 199–214.

Diehl, Richard A. 1981 "Olmec Architecture: A Comparison of San Lorenzo and La Venta." In *The Olmec and Their Neighbors: Essays in Memory of Matthew W. Stirling*, edited by E.P. Benson, pp. 69–81. Washington: Trustees for Harvard University.

Dillehay, Tom D. 2008 "Profiles in Pleistocene History." In *Handbook of South American Archaeology*, edited by H. Silverman and W.H. Isbell, pp. 29–43. New York: Springer.

Dodson, Aidan 2010 "Mortuary Architecture and Decorative Systems." In *A Companion to Ancient Egypt*, edited by A.B. Lloyd, pp. 804–25. Oxford: Blackwell Publishing Ltd.

Dodson, Aidan and Dyan Hilton 2004 *The Complete Royal Families of Ancient Egypt*. London: Thames and Hudson.

Dolce, Rita 2000 "Political Supremacy and Cultural Supremacy: A Hypothesis of Symmetrical Alternations between Upper Mesopotamia and Northern Syria in the Fourth and Third Millennia BC." In *Landscapes: Territories, Frontiers and Horizons in the Ancient Near East. Part II. Geography and Cultural Landscapes*, edited by L. Milano, S. de Martino, F.M. Fales and G.B. Lanfranchi, pp. 103–21. Padua: Sargon srl.

Dong, Guanghui, Xin Jia, Robert Elston, Fahu Chen, Shuicheng Li, Lin Wang, Linhai Cai and Chengbang An 2013 "Spatial and Temporal Variety of Prehistoric Human Settlement and Its Influencing Factors in the Upper Yellow River Valley, Qinghai Province, China." *Journal of Archaeological Science* 40: 2538–46.

Donnan, Christopher B. 2007 *Moche Tombs at Dos Cabezas*. Monograph 59. Los Angeles: Cotsen Institute of Archaeology.

——— 2010 "Moche State Religion: A Unifying Force in Moche Political Organization." In *New Perspectives on Moche Political Organization*, edited by J. Quilter and L.J. Castillo, pp. 47–69. Washington: Dumbarton Oaks Research Library and Collections.

Donnan, Christopher B. and Luis Jaime Castillo 1992 "Finding the Tomb of a Moche Priestess." *Archaeology* 45.6: 38–42.

——— 1994 "Excavaciones de tumbas de sacerdotisas Moche en San José de Moro, Jequetepeque." In *Moche: Propuestas y Perspectivas*, edited by S. Uceda and E. Mujica, pp. 415–24. Lima: Universidad Nacional de la Libertad, Trujillo.

Doumas, Christos G. 1983 *Thera: Pompeii of the Ancient Aegean. Excavations at Akrotiri 1967–79*. London: Thames and Hudson Ltd.

Drennan, Robert D. and Christian E. Peterson 2012 "Challenges for Comparative Study of Early Complex Societies." In *The Comparative Archaeology of Complex Societies*, edited by M.E. Smith, pp. 62–87. Cambridge: Cambridge University Press.

Drews, Robert 1993 *The End of the Bronze Age: Changes in Warfare and the Catastrophe ca. 1200 B.C.* Princeton: Princeton University Press.

Driessen, Jan 2002 "Towards an Archaeology of Crisis: Defining the Long-Term Impact of the Bronze Age Santorini Eruption." In *Natural Disasters and Cultural Change*, edited by R. Torrence and J. Grattan, pp. 250–63. London: Routledge.

Driessen, Jan and Colin F. Macdonald 1997 *The Troubled Island: Minoan Crete before and after the Santorini Eruption*. Aegaeum 17. Liège: Université de Liège.

duBois, Page 2009 "Slavery." In *The Oxford Handbook of Hellenic Studies*, edited by G. Boys-Stones, B. Graziosi and P. Vasunia, pp. 316–27. Oxford: Oxford University Press.

Dulanto, Jalh 2008 "Between Horizons: Diverse Configurations of Society and Power in the Late Pre-Hispanic Central Andes." In *Handbook of South American Archaeology*, edited by H. Silverman and W.H. Isbell, pp. 761–82. New York: Springer.

Earle, Timothy K. 1978 *Economic and Social Organization of a Complex Chiefdom: The Halelea District, Kaua'i, Hawaii*. Museum of Anthropology Papers No. 63. Ann Arbor: University of Michigan.

—— 1987 "Chiefdoms in Archaeological and Ethnohistorical Perspective." *Annual Review of Anthropology* 16: 279–308.

—— 1990 "Style and Iconography as Legitimation in Complex Chiefdoms." In *The Uses of Style in Archaeology*, edited by M. Conkey and C. Hastorf, pp. 73–81. Cambridge: Cambridge University Press.

—— 1991a "Property Rights and the Evolution of Chiefdoms." In *Chiefdoms: Power, Economy, and Ideology*, edited by T. Earle, pp. 71–99. Cambridge: Cambridge University Press.

—— 1991b "The Evolution of Chiefdoms." In *Chiefdoms: Power, Economy, and Ideology*, edited by T. Earle, pp. 1–15. Cambridge: Cambridge University Press.

—— 2000 "Archaeology, Property, and Prehistory." *Annual Review of Anthropology* 29: 39–60.

—— 2001 "Institutionalization of Chiefdoms: Why Landscapes Are Built." In *From Leaders to Rulers*, edited by J. Haas, pp. 105–24. New York: Kluwer Academic/Plenum Publishers.

Earls, John C. and Gabriela Cervantes 2015 "Inka Cosmology in Moray: Astronomy, Agriculture, and Pilgrimage." In *The Inka Empire: A Multidisciplinary Approach*, edited by I. Shimada, pp. 121–47. Austin: University of Texas Press.

Eerkens, Jelmer W. 2009 "Privatization of Resources and the Evolution of Prehistoric Leadership Strategies." In *The Evolution of Leadership: Transitions in Decision Making from Small-Scale to Middle-Range Societies*, edited by K.J. Vaughn, J.W. Eerkens and J. Kantner, pp. 73–94. Santa Fe: School for Advanced Research Press.

Eisenstadt, Shmuel 1979 "Observations and Queries about Sociological Aspects of Imperialism in the Ancient World." In *Power and Propaganda: A Symposium on Ancient Empires*, edited by M.T. Larsen, pp. 21–33. Copenhagen: Akademisk Forlag.

—— 1988 "Beyond Collapse." In *The Collapse of Ancient States and Civilizations*, edited by N. Yoffee and G.L. Cowgill, pp. 236–43. Tucson: University of Arizona Press.

Elson, Christina 2012 "Cultural Evolution in the Southern Highlands of Mexico from the Emergence of Social Inequality to the Decline of Classic-Period States." In *The Oxford Handbook of Mesoamerican Archaeology*, edited by D.L. Nichols and C.A. Pool, pp. 230–44. Oxford: Oxford University Press.

Emerson, Thomas E. 1997a *Cahokia and the Archaeology of Power*. Tuscaloosa: University of Alabama Press.

—— 1997b "Cahokia Elite Ideology and the Mississippian Cosmos." In *Cahokia: Domination and Ideology in the Mississippian World*, edited by T.R. Pauketat and T.E. Emerson, pp. 190–228. Lincoln: University of Nebraska Press.

—— 2002 "An Introduction to Cahokia 2002: Diversity, Complexity, and History." *Midcontinental Journal of Archaeology* 27.2: 127–48.

—— 2003 "Materializing Cahokia Shamans." *Southeastern Archaeology* 22.2: 135–54.

—— 2007 "Cahokia and the Evidence for Late-Pre-Columbian War in the North American Midcontinent." In *North American Indigenous Warfare and Ritual Violence*, edited by R.J. Chacon and R.G. Mendoza, pp. 129–48. Tucson: University of Arizona Press.

Emerson, Thomas E., Susan M. Alt, and Timothy R. Pauketat 2008 "Locating American Indian Religion at Cahokia and Beyond." In *Religion, Archaeology, and the Material World*, edited by L. Fogelin, pp. 216–36. Center for Archaeological Investigations Occasional Paper no. 36. Carbondale: Southern Illinois University Press.

Emerson, Thomas E. and Steven L. Boles 2010 "Contextualizing Flint Clay Cahokia Figurines at the East St. Louis Mound Center." *Illinois Archaeology* 22.2: 473–90.

Emerson, Thomas E. and Andrew C. Fortier 1986 "Early Woodland Cultural Variation, Subsistence, and Settlement in the American Bottom." In *Early Woodland Archaeology*, edited by K. Farnsworth and T. Emerson, pp. 475–522. Kampsville: Kampsville Seminars in Archaeology.

Emerson, Thomas E. and Eve Hargrave 2000 "Strangers in Paradise? Recognizing Ethnic Mortuary Diversity on the Fringes of Cahokia." *Southeastern Archaeology* 19.1: 1–23.

Emerson, Thomas E., Eve Hargrave, and Kristin Hedman 2003 "Death and Ritual in Early Rural Cahokia." In *Theory, Method, and Practice in Modern Archaeology*, edited by R.J. Jeske and D.K. Charles, pp. 163–81. Westport: Praeger.

Emerson, Thomas E. and Kristin M. Hedman 2015 "The Dangers of Diversity: The Consolidation and Dissolution of Cahokia, Native North America's First Urban Polity." In *Beyond Collapse: Archaeological Perspectives on Resilience, Revitalization, and Transformation in Complex Societies*, edited by R.K. Faulseit. Occasional Paper No. 42, Center for Archaeological Investigations, pp. 147–78. Carbondale: Southern Illinois University Press.

Emerson, Thomas E. and Randall E. Hughes 2000 "Figurines, Flint Clay Sourcing, the Ozark Highlands, and Cahokian Acquisition." *American Antiquity* 65.1: 79–101.

Emerson, Thomas E., Randall E. Hughes, Mary R. Hynes, and Sarah U. Wisseman 2003 "The Sourcing and Interpretation of Cahokia-Style Figurines in the Trans-Mississippi South and Southeast." *American Antiquity* 68.2: 287–313.

Emerson, Thomas E. and Dale L. McElrath 2001 "Interpreting Discontinuity and Historical Process in Mid-continental Late Archaic and Early Woodland Societies." In *The Archaeology of Traditions: Agency and History Before and After Columbus*, edited by T.R. Pauketat, pp. 195–217. Gainesville: University Press of Florida.

Emerson, Thomas E. and Timothy R. Pauketat 2008 "Historical-Processual Archaeology and Culture Making: Unpacking the Southern Cult and Mississippian Religion." In *Belief in the Past: Theoretical Approaches to the Archaeology of Religion*, edited by D.S. Whitley and K. Hays-Gilpin, pp. 167–88. Walnut Creek: Left Coast Press.

Englund, Robert K. 1998 "Texts from the Late Uruk Period." In *Mesopotamien. Späturuk-Zeit und Frühdynastische Zeit*, edited by J. Bauer, R.K. Englund and M. Krebernik, pp. 15–233. Freiburg: Universitätsverlag.

Enmarch, Roland 2010 "Middle Kingdom Literature." In *A Companion to Ancient Egypt*, edited by A.B. Lloyd, pp. 663–84. Oxford: Blackwell Publishing Ltd.

Eppihimer, Melissa 2010 "Assembling King and State: The Statues of Manishtushu and the Consolidation of Akkadian Kingship." *American Journal of Archaeology* 114: 365–80.

Evans, Susan Toby 2001 "Aztec Noble Courts: Men, Women, and Children of the Palace." In *Royal Courts of the Ancient Maya. Vol. 2. Data and Case Studies*, edited by T. Inomata and S.D. Houston, pp. 237–73. Boulder: Westview Press.

——— 2012 "Time and Space Boundaries: Chronologies and Regions in Mesoamerica." In *The Oxford Handbook of Mesoamerican Archaeology*, edited by D.L. Nichols and C.A. Pool, pp. 114–26. Oxford: Oxford University Press.

Evans-Pritchard, E.E. 1940 *The Nuer: A Description of the Modes of Livelihood and Political Institutions of a Nilotic People*. Oxford: Clarendon.

Eyre, Christopher J. 1995 "The Agricultural Cycle, Farming, and Water Management in the Ancient Near East." In *Civilizations of the Ancient Near East*, edited by J.M. Sasson, pp. 175–84. New York: Charles Scribner's Sons.

Fairservis, Walter A., Jr. 1961 *The Harappan Civilization: New Evidence and More Theory*. American Museum Novitates 2055, pp. 1–35. New York: American Museum of Natural History.

——— 1967 *The Origin, Character and Decline of an Early Civilization*. American Museum Novitates 2302, pp. 9–48. New York: American Museum of Natural History.

Faltings, Dina A. 2002 "The Chronological Frame and Social Structure of Buto in the Fourth Millennium BCE." In *Egypt and the Levant: Interrelations from the 4th through the Early 3rd Millennium BCE*, edited by E.C.M. van den Brink and T.E. Levy, pp. 165–70. London: Leicester University Press.

Fargher, Lane F. and Richard Blanton 2007 "Revenue, Voice, and Public Goods in Three Pre-Modern States." *Comparative Studies in Society and History* 49.4: 848–82.

Fash, Barbara W. 2005 "Iconographic Evidence for Water Management and Social Organization at Copán." In *Copán: The History of an Ancient Maya Kingdom*, edited by E.W. Andrews and W.L. Fash, pp. 103–38. Santa Fe: School of American Research Press.

Feinman, Gary M. 1998 "Scale and Social Organization: Perspectives on the Archaic State." In *Archaic States*, edited by G.M. Feinman and J. Marcus, pp. 99–133. Santa Fe: School of American Research Press.

——— 2001 "Mesoamerican Political Complexity: The Corporate-Network Dimension." In *From Leaders to Rulers*, edited by J. Haas, pp. 151–75. New York: Kluwer Academic/Plenum Publishers.

Feldman, Robert A. 1987 "Architectural Evidence for the Development of Nonegalitarian Social Systems in Coastal Peru." In *The Origins and Development of the Andean State*, edited by J. Haas, S. Pozorski and T. Pozorski, pp. 9–14. Cambridge: Cambridge University Press.

Feng, Li 2003 "'Feudalism' and Western Zhou China: A Criticism." *Harvard Journal of Asiatic Studies* 63.1: 115–44.

Fentress, Marcia A. 1984 "The Indus 'Granaries': Illusion, Imagination and Archaeological Reconstruction." In *Studies in the Archaeology and Palaeoanthropology of South Asia*, edited by K.A.R. Kennedy and G.L. Possehl, pp. 89–98. New Delhi: American Institute of Indian Studies.

Ferris, I.M. 2000 *Enemies of Rome: Barbarians through Roman Eyes*. Phoenix Mill: Sutton Publishing Limited.

Fiedel, Stuart J. 2001 "What Happened in the Early Woodland?" *Archaeology of Eastern North America* 29: 101–42.

Firth, Raymond 1929 *Primitive Economics of the New Zealand Maori*. Wellington: A.R. Shearer, Government Printer.
Flad, Rowan K. 2007 "Rethinking Specialization in the Context of Salt Production in Prehistoric Sichuan." In *Rethinking "Specialized" Production: Archaeological Analyses of the Social Meaning of Manufacture*, edited by Z.X. Hruby and R.K. Flad, pp. 107–28. Arlington: American Anthropological Association.
——— 2008 "Divination and Power: A Multiregional View of the Development of Oracle Bones in Early China." *Current Anthropology* 49.3: 403–37.
——— 2013 "The Sichuan Basin Neolithic." In *A Companion to Chinese Archaeology*, edited by A.P. Underhill, pp. 125–46. West Sussex: Wiley-Blackwell.
Flannery, Kent V. 1976 "The Early Mesoamerican House." In *The Early Mesoamerican Village*, edited by K.V. Flannery, pp. 16–24. New York: Academic Press.
——— 1998 "The Ground Plans of Archaic States." In *Archaic States*, edited by G.M. Feinman and J. Marcus, pp. 15–57. Santa Fe: School of American Research Press.
Flannery, Kent and Joyce Marcus 2005 *Excavations at San José Mogote I: The Household Archaeology*. Memoirs of the Museum of Anthropology, University of Michigan, No. 40. Ann Arbor: Regents of the University of Michigan.
——— 2012 *The Creation of Inequality: How Our Prehistoric Ancestors Set the Stage for Monarchy, Slavery, and Empire*. Cambridge: Harvard University Press.
Foias, Antonia E. 2013 *Ancient Maya Political Dynamics*. Gainesville: University Press of Florida.
Foley, Robert A. 2001 "Evolutionary Perspectives on the Origins of Human Social Institutions." *Proceedings of the British Academy* 110: 171–95.
Fortier, Andrew C. 1983 "Settlement and Subsistence at the Go-Kart North Site: A Late Archaic Titterington Occupation in the American Bottom." In *Archaic Hunters and Gatherers in the American Midwest*, edited by J.L. Phillips and J.A. Brown, pp. 243–60. New York: Academic Press.
——— 2001 "A Tradition of Discontinuity: American Bottom Early and Middle Woodland Culture History Reexamined." In *The Archaeology of Traditions: Agency and History Before and After Columbus*, edited by T.R. Pauketat, pp. 174–94. Gainesville: University Press of Florida.
——— 2008 "The Archaeological Contexts and Themes of Middle Woodland Symbolic Representation in the American Bottom." *Illinois Archaeology* 20: 1–47.
Fortier, Andrew C., Thomas E. Emerson and Dale L. McElrath 2006 "Calibrating and Reassessing American Bottom Culture History." *Southeastern Archaeology* 25.2: 170–211.
Fortier, Andrew C. and Douglas K. Jackson 2000 "The Formation of a Late Woodland Heartland in the American Bottom, Illinois cal A.D. 640–900." In *Late Woodland Societies: Tradition and Transformation across the Midcontinent*, edited by T.E. Emerson, D.L. McElrath, and A.C. Fortier, pp. 123–47. Lincoln: University of Nebraska Press.
Foster, William C. 2012 *Climate and Culture Change in North America AD 900–1600*. Austin: University of Texas Press.
Fowler, Don 1987 "Uses of the Past: Archaeology in the Service of the State." *American Antiquity* 52: 229–48.
Fowler, Melvin L. 1974 *Cahokia: Ancient Capital of the Midwest*. Addison-Wesley Module in Anthropology No. 48. Reading: Addison-Wesley.
——— 1975 "A Precolumbian Urban Center on the Mississippi." *Scientific American* 23.2: 92–101.
——— 1991 "Mound 72 and Early Mississippian at Cahokia." In *New Perspectives on Cahokia: Views from the Periphery*, edited by J.B. Stoltman, pp. 1–28. Monographs in World Archaeology, No. 2. Madison: Prehistory Press.
——— 1997 *The Cahokia Atlas: A Historical Atlas of Cahokia Archaeology*. Revised edition. Urbana-Champaign: University of Illinois.
Fox, Aileen 1976 *Prehistoric Fortifications in the North Island of New Zealand*. New Zealand Archaeological Association Monograph No. 6. London: Longman Publishing Group.
Foxhall, Lin 2007 *Olive Cultivation in Ancient Greece: Seeking the Ancient Economy*. Oxford: Oxford University Press.
Freed, Rita E. 2010 "Sculpture of the Middle Kingdom." In *A Companion to Ancient Egypt*, edited by A.B. Lloyd, pp. 882–912. Oxford: Blackwell Publishing Ltd.
Freidel, David A. 1986 "Maya Warfare: An Example of Peer Polity Interaction." In *Peer Polity Interaction and Socio-Political Change*, edited by C. Renfrew and J. Cherry, pp. 93–108. Cambridge: Cambridge University Press.

———— 1992 "The Trees of Life: *Ahau* as Idea and Artifact in Classic Lowland Maya Civilization." In *Ideology and Pre-Columbian Civilizations*, edited by A.A. Demarest and G.W. Conrad, pp. 115–33. Santa Fe: School of American Research Press.
Freter, AnnCorinne 1994 "The Classic Maya Collapse at Copan, Honduras: An Analysis of Maya Rural Settlement Trends." In *Archaeological Views from the Countryside: Village Communities in Early Complex Societies*, edited by G.M. Schwartz and S.E. Falconer, pp. 160–76. Washington: Smithsonian Institution Press.
Friedman, Florence Dunn 1995 "The Underground Relief Panels of King Djoser at the Step Pyramid Complex." *Journal of the American Research Center in Egypt* 32: 1–42.
Friedman, Renée 1996 "The Ceremonial Centre at Hierakonpolis Locality HK29A." In *The Followers of Horus: Studies Dedicated to Michael Allen Hoffman 1944–1990*, edited by R. Friedman and B. Adams, pp. 16–35. Oxford: Oxbow.
Frifelt, Karen 1989 "'Ubaid in the Gulf Area." In *Upon This Foundation: The 'Ubaid Reconsidered*, edited by E.F. Henrickson and I. Thuesen, pp. 405–17. Copenhagen: University of Copenhagen.
Fuller, Dorian Q. and Charlene Murphy 2014 "Overlooked But Not Forgotten: India as a Center for Agricultural Domestication." *General Anthropology* 21.2: 1–8.
Fung, Christopher 2000 "The Drinks Are on Us: Ritual, Social Status, and Practice in Dawenkou Burials, North China." *Journal of East Asian Archaeology* 2.1–2: 67–92.
Gabriel, Kathryn 1991 *Roads to Center Place: A Cultural Atlas of Chaco Canyon and the Anasazi*. Boulder: Johnson Books.
Galloy, Joseph M. 2011 "A Once and Future City: The Spendor of Prehistoric East St. Louis." In *The Making of an All-America City: East St. Louis at 150*, edited by M. Abbott, pp. 5–14. St. Louis: Virginia Publishing.
Gangal, Kavita, M.N. Vahia and R. Adhikari 2010 "Spatio-Temporal Analysis of the Indus Urbanization." *Current Science* 98.6: 846–52.
Gao, Qiang and Yun Kuen Lee 1993 "A Biological Perspective on Yangshao Kinship." *Journal of Anthropological Archaeology* 12: 266–98.
Garlake, P.S. 1973 *Great Zimbabwe*. New York: Stein and Day.
Gauss, Walter 2010 "Aegina Kolonna." In *The Oxford Handbook of the Bronze Age Aegean (ca. 3000–1000 BC)*, edited by E.H. Cline, pp. 737–51. Oxford: Oxford University Press.
Geertz, Clifford 1980 *Negara: The Theatre State in Nineteenth-Century Bali*. Princeton: Princeton University Press.
Gelb, I.J. 1973 "Prisoners of War in Early Mesopotamia." *Journal of Near Eastern Studies* 32: 70–98.
Giardina, Andrea 2007 "The Transition to Late Antiquity." In *The Cambridge Economic History of the Greco-Roman World*, edited by W. Scheidel, I. Morris and R. Saller, pp. 743–68. Cambridge: Cambridge University Press.
Gibson, Jon 2000 *The Ancient Mounds of Poverty Point: Place of Rings*. Gainesville: University Press of Florida.
———— 2010 "Poverty Point Redux." In *Archaeology of Louisiana*, edited by M.A. Rees, pp. 77–96. Baton Rouge: Louisiana State University Press.
Gillespie, Susan D. 1999 "Olmec Thrones as Ancestral Altars: The Two Sides of Power." In *Material Symbols: Culture and Economy in Prehistory*, edited by J.E. Robb, pp. 224–53. Carbondale: Southern Illinois University.
Gilman, Antonio 1991 "Trajectories toward Social Complexity in the Later Prehistory of the Mediterranean." In *Chiefdoms: Power, Economy, and Ideology*, edited by T. Earle, pp. 71–99. Cambridge: Cambridge University Press.
Glover, Ian 1996 "The Southern Silk Road: Archaeological Evidence for Early Trade between India and Southeast Asia." In *Ancient Trade and Cultural Contacts in Southeast Asia*, edited by A. Srisuchat, pp. 57–94. Bangkok: National Culture Commission.
———— 1998 "The Role of India in the Late Prehistory of Southeast Asia." *Journal of Southeast Asian Archaeology* 18: 21–49.
Goebel, Ted, Michael R. Waters and Dennis H. O'Rourke 2008 "The Late Pleistocene Dispersal of Modern Humans in the Americas." *Science* 319.5869: 1497–1502.
Goldhill, Simon 1990 "The Great Dionysia and Civic Ideology." In *Nothing to Do with Dionysos? Athenian Drama in Its Social Context*, edited by J.J. Winkler and F.I. Zeitlin, pp. 97–129. Princeton: Princeton University Press.
Good, I.L., J.M. Kenoyer and R.H. Meadow 2009 "New Evidence for Early Silk in the Indus Civilization." *Archaeometry* 51.3: 457–66.

Goodison, Lucy 2009 "'Why All This about Oak or Stone?' Trees and Boulders in Minoan Religions." In *Archaeologies of Cult: Essays on Ritual and Cult in Crete in Honor of Geraldine C. Gesell*, edited by A.L. d'Agata and A. Van de Moortel, pp. 51–7. Hesperia Supplement 42. Princeton: American School of Classical Studies at Athens.

Graziadio, Giampaolo 1991 "The Process of Social Stratification at Mycenae in the Shaft Grave Period: A Comparative Examination of the Evidence." *American Journal of Archaeology* 95: 403–40.

Greber, N'omi B. 1997 "Two Geometric Enclosures in the Paint Creek Valley: An Estimate of Possible Changes in Community Patterns through Time." In *Ohio Hopewell Community Organization*, edited by W.S. Dancey and P.J. Pacheco, pp. 207–28. Kent: Kent State University Press.

——— 2005 "Adena and Hopewell in the Middle Ohio Valley: To Be or Not to Be?" In *Woodland Period Systematics in the Middle Ohio Valley*, edited by D. Applegate and R.C. Mainfort, Jr., pp. 19–39. Tuscaloosa: University of Alabama Press.

——— 2006 "Enclosures and Communities in Ohio Hopewell: An Essay." In *Recreating Hopewell: New Perspectives on Middle Woodland in Eastern North America*, edited by D.K. Charles and J.E. Buikstra, pp. 74–105. Gainesville: University Press of Florida.

——— 2009 "Final Data and Summary Comments." *Midcontinental Journal of Archaeology* 34.1: 171–86.

Gregg, Susan A. 1988 *Foragers and Farmers: Population Interaction and Agricultural Expansion in Prehistoric Europe*. Chicago: University of Chicago Press.

Grinin, Leonid 2011 "Complex Chiefdom: Precursor of the State or Its Analogue?" *Social Evolution and History: Studies in the Evolution of Human Societies* 10.1: 234–75.

Grove, David C. 1981 "Olmec Monuments: Mutilation as a Clue to Meaning." In *The Olmec and Their Neighbors: Essays in Memory of Matthew W. Stirling*, edited by E.P. Benson, pp. 49–68. Washington: Trustees for Harvard University.

——— 1999 "Public Monuments and Sacred Mountains: Observations on Three Formative Period Sacred Landscapes." In *Social Patterns in Pre-Classic Mesoamerica*, edited by D.C. Grove and R.A. Joyce, pp. 255–99. Washington: Dumbarton Oaks Research Library and Collection.

Grove, David C. and Susan D. Gillespie 1992 "Ideology and Evolution at the Pre-State Level: Formative Period Mesoamerica." In *Ideology and Pre-Columbian Civilizations*, edited by A.A. Demarest and G.W. Conrad, pp. 15–36. Santa Fe: School of American Research Press.

Grube, Nikolai and Ruth J. Krochock 2007 "Reading between the Lines: Hieroglyphic Texts from Chichén Itzá and Its Neighbors." In *Twin Tollans: Chichén Itzá, Tula, and the Epiclassic to Early Postclassic Mesoamerican World*, edited by J.K. Kowalski and C. Kristan-Graham, pp. 205–49. Washington: Dumbarton Oaks Research Library and Collection.

Guedes, Jade d'Alpoim, Ming Jiang, Kunyu He, Xiaohong Wuy and Zhanghua Jiang 2013 "Site of Baodun Yields Earliest Evidence for the Spread of Rice and Foxtail Millet Agriculture to South-west China." *Antiquity* 87: 758–71.

Hallager, Birgitta P. and Erik Hallager 1995 "The Knossian Bull—Political Propaganda in Neo-Palatial Crete?" In *Politeia: Society and State in the Aegean Bronze Age*, edited by R. Laffineur and W.-D. Niemeier, pp. 547–59. Aegaeum 12. Liège: Université de Liège.

Hallager, Erik 2010 "Crete." In *The Oxford Handbook of the Bronze Age Aegean (ca. 3000–1000 BC)*, edited by E.H. Cline, pp. 149–59. Oxford: Oxford University Press.

Halstead, Paul 1981 "From Determinism to Uncertainty: Social Storage and the Rise of the Minoan Palace." In *Economic Archaeology: Towards an Integration of Ecological and Social Approaches*, edited by A. Sheridan and G. Bailey, pp. 187–213. Oxford: British Archaeological Reports.

——— 1997 "Storage and States on Prehistoric Crete: A Reply to Strasser (JMA 10 [1997] 73–100)." *Journal of Mediterranean Archaeology* 10: 103–7.

Hammer, Catherine 2000 "Women, Ritual, and Social Standing in Roman Italy." In *The Villa of the Mysteries in Pompeii: Ancient Ritual, Modern Muse*, edited by E.K. Gazda, pp. 38–49. Ann Arbor: Kelsey Museum of Archaeology.

Hannestad, Niels 1979 "Rome—Ideology and Art: Some Distinctive Features." In *Power and Propaganda: A Symposium on Ancient Empires*, edited by M.T. Larsen, pp. 361–90. Copenhagen: Akademisk Forlag.

Hansen, Mogens Herman 2008 "Analyzing Cities." In *The Ancient City: New Perspectives on Urbanism in the Old and New World*, edited by J. Marcus and J.A. Sabloff, pp. 67–76. Santa Fe: School for Advanced Research.

Harl, Joseph L. 2009 "Archaic Period of East-Central Missouri." In *Archaic Societies: Diversity and Complexity across the Midcontinent*, edited by T.E. Emerson, D.L. McElrath and A.C. Fortier, pp. 377–400. Lincoln: University of Nebraska.

Harmanşah, Ömür 2013 *Cities and the Shaping of Memory in the Ancient Near East*. Cambridge: Cambridge University Press.

Harrison, Peter D. 1986 "Tikal: Selected Topics." In *City-States of the Maya: Art and Architecture*, edited by E.P. Benson, pp. 45–71. Denver: Rocky Mountain Institute for Pre-Columbian Studies.

Hart, C.W.M. 1965 *The Tiwi of North Australia*. New York: Holt, Rinehart and Winston.

Hassan, Fekri A. 1998 "The Earliest Goddesses of Egypt: Divine Mothers and Cosmic Bodies." In *Ancient Goddesses: The Myths and the Evidence*, edited by L. Goodison and C. Morris, pp. 98–112. Madison: University of Wisconsin Press.

Hastorf, Christine 1990 "One Path to the Heights: Negotiating Political Inequality in the Sausa of Peru." In *The Evolution of Political Systems: Sociopolitics in Small-Scale Sedentary Societies*, edited by S. Upham, pp. 146–76. Cambridge: Cambridge University Press.

Hatzopoulos, M.B. 2011a "Macedonia and Macedonians." In *Brill's Companion to Ancient Macedon: Studies in the Archaeology and History of Macedon, 650 BC–300 AD*, edited by R. Lane Fox, pp. 43–49. Leiden: Brill.

——— 2011b "Macedonians and Other Greeks." In *Brill's Companion to Ancient Macedon: Studies in the Archaeology and History of Macedon, 650 BC–300 AD*, edited by R. Lane Fox, pp. 51–78. Leiden: Brill.

Haviland, William A. 1967 "Stature at Tikal, Guatemala: Implications for Ancient Maya Demography and Social Organization." *American Antiquity* 32: 316–25.

——— 2003 "Settlement, Society, and Demography at Tikal." In *Tikal: Dynasties, Foreigners, and Affairs of State: Advancing Maya Archaeology*, edited by J. Sabloff, pp. 111–42. Santa Fe: School of American Research Press.

Haviland, William A. and Hattula Moholy-Nagy 1992 "Distinguishing the High and Mighty from the Hoi Polloi at Tikal, Guatemala." In *Mesoamerican Elites: An Archaeological Assessment*, edited by A.F. Chase and D.Z. Chase, pp. 50–60. Norman: University of Oklahoma Press.

Hayden, Brian 1995 "A New Overview of Domestication." In *Last Hunters, First Farmers: New Perspectives on the Prehistoric Transition to Agriculture*, edited by T.D. Price and A.B. Gebauer, pp. 273–99. Santa Fe: School of American Research Press.

Hayes, W.C. 1953 *The Scepter of Egypt*. Cambridge: Harvard University Press.

——— 1975a "Chronology: Egypt to the End of the Twentieth Dynasty." In *Cambridge Ancient History*, Third Edition, Vol. 1, Part 2, edited by I.E.S. Edwards, C.J. Gadd, N.G.L. Hammond and E. Sollberger, pp. 173–93. Cambridge: Cambridge University Press.

——— 1975b "The Middle Kingdom in Egypt: Internal History from the Rise of the Heracleopolitans to the Death of Ammenemes III." In *Cambridge Ancient History*, Third Edition, Vol. 1, Part 2, edited by I.E.S. Edwards, C.J. Gadd, N.G.L. Hammond and E. Sollberger, pp. 464–531. Cambridge: Cambridge University Press.

Hays, Christopher T. 2010 "Adena Mortuary Patterns in Central Ohio." *Southeastern Archaeology* 29.1: 106–20.

Headrick, Annabeth 2007 *The Teotihuacan Trinity: The Sociopolitical Structure of an Ancient Mesoamerican City*. Austin: University of Texas Press.

Healan, Dan M. and Robert H. Cobean 2012 "Tula and the Toltecs." In *The Oxford Handbook of Mesoamerican Archaeology*, edited by D.L. Nichols and C.A. Pool, pp. 372–84. Oxford: Oxford University Press.

Hegmon, Michelle 1991 "The Risks of Sharing and Sharing as Risk Reduction: Interhousehold Food Sharing in Egalitarian Societies." In *Between Bands and States*, edited by S.A. Gregg, pp. 309–29. Center for Archaeological Investigations Occasional Paper No. 9. Carbondale: Southern Illinois University.

Heitman, Carrie C. 2015 "The House of Our Ancestors: New Research on the Prehistory of Chaco Canyon, New Mexico, A.D. 800–1200." In *Chaco Revisited: New Research on the Prehistory of Chaco Canyon, New Mexico*, edited by C.C. Heitman and S. Plog, pp. 215–48. Tucson: University of Arizona Press.

Helms, Mary W. 1993 *Craft and the Kingly Ideal: Art, Trade, and Power*. Austin: University of Texas Press.

Hendon, Julia A. 1991 "Status and Power in Classic Maya Society: An Archaeological Study." *American Anthropologist* 93: 894–918.

——— 2010 *Houses in a Landscape: Memory and Everyday Life in Mesoamerica*. Durham: Duke University Press.

Hendrickx, Stan and Frank Förster 2010 "Early Dynastic Art and Iconography." In *A Companion to Ancient Egypt*, edited by A.B. Lloyd, pp. 826–52. Oxford: Blackwell Publishing Ltd.

Hendrix, Elizabeth 2003 "Painted Early Cycladic Figures: An Exploration of Context and Meaning." *Hesperia* 72: 405–46.

Hermann, Edward W., G. William Monaghan, William F. Romain, Timothy M. Schilling, Jarrod Burks, Karen L. Leone, Matthew P. Purtill and Alan C. Tonetti 2014 "A New Multistage Construction Chronology for the Great Serpent Mound, USA." *Journal of Archaeological Science* 50: 117–25.

Heyden, Doris 1981 "Caves, Gods, and Myths: World-View and Planning in Teotihuacan." In *Mesoamerican Sites and World-Views*, edited by E.P. Benson, pp. 1–39. Washington: Dumbarton Oaks Research Library and Collections.

Hicks, Frederic 1994 "Alliance and Intervention in Aztec Imperial Expansion." In *Factional Competition and Political Development in the New World*, edited by E.M. Brumfiel and J.W. Fox, pp. 111–16. Cambridge: Cambridge University Press.

Higham, Charles 1989 *The Archaeology of Mainland Southeast Asia*. Cambridge: Cambridge University Press.

——— 1994 "A Review of Archaeology in Mainland Southeast Asia." *Journal of Archaeological Research* 4.1: 3–49.

——— 2001 *The Civilization of Angkor*. London: Phoenix.

——— 2002a *Early Cultures of Mainland Southeast Asia*. Chicago: Art Media Resources.

——— 2002b "Languages and Farming Dispersals: Austroasiatic Languages and Rice Cultivation." In *Examining the Language/Farming Dispersal Hypothesis*, edited by P. Bellwood and C. Renfrew, pp. 223–32. Cambridge: McDonald Institute for Archaeological Research.

——— 2004 "Mainland Southeast Asia from the Neolithic to the Iron Age." In *Southeast Asia from Prehistory to History*, edited by I. Glover and P. Bellwood, pp. 41–67. London: RoutledgeCurzon.

——— 2010 "The Iron Age of Thailand: Trends to Complexity." In *50 Years of Archaeology in Southeast Asia: Essays in Honour of Ian Glover*, edited by B. Bellina, E.A. Bacus, T.O. Pryce and J.W. Christie, pp. 129–39. Bangkok: River Books.

Higham, Charles, Thomas Higham, Roberto Ciarla, Katerina Douka, Amphan Kijngam and Fiorella Rispoli 2011 "The Origins of the Bronze Age in Southeast Asia." *Journal of World Prehistory* 24: 227–74.

Higham, Charles and Rachanie Thosarat 2004 "Ban Non Wat: The First Three Seasons." In *Uncovering Southeast Asia's Past: Selected Papers from the 10th International Conference of the European Association of Southeast Asian Archaeologists,* edited by E.A. Bacus, I.C. Glover and V.C. Pigott, pp. 98–104. Singapore: Nus Press.

Hiltebeitel, Alf 1978 "The Indus Valley 'Proto-'Siva,' Reexamined through Reflections on the Goddess, the Buffalo, and the Symbolism of Vāhanas." *Anthropos* 73: 767–97.

Hirth, Kenneth G. 1978 "Interregional Trade and the Formation of Prehistoric Gateway Communities." *American Antiquity* 43: 35–45.

——— 1998 "The Distributional Approach: A New Way to Identify Marketplace Exchange in the Archaeological Record." *Current Anthropology* 39: 451–76.

——— 2009 "Craft Production in a Central Mexican Marketplace." *Ancient Mesoamerica* 20: 89–102.

——— 2010 "Finding the Mark in the Marketplace: The Organization, Development, and Archaeological Identification of Market Systems." In *Archaeological Approaches to Market Exchange in Ancient Societies*, edited by C.P. Garraty and B.L. Stark, pp. 227–47. Boulder: University Press of Colorado.

Hitchcock, Louise A. 2000 *Minoan Architecture: A Contextual Analysis*. Jonsered: Paul Aströms Förlag.

——— 2010a "Minoan Architecture." In *The Oxford Handbook of the Bronze Age Aegean (ca. 3000–1000 BC)*, edited by E.H. Cline, pp. 189–99. Oxford: Oxford University Press.

——— 2010b "Mycenaean Architecture." In *The Oxford Handbook of the Bronze Age Aegean (ca. 3000–1000 BC)*, edited by E.H. Cline, pp. 200–9. Oxford: Oxford University Press.

Hively, Ray and Robert Horn 1984 "Hopewellian Geometry and Astronomy at High Bank." *Astroarchaeology* 7: 85–100.

Hodos, Tamar 2006 *Local Responses to Colonization in the Iron Age Mediterranean*. London: Routledge.

Hoffman, Michael A. 1979 *Egypt before the Pharaohs*. New York: Knopf.

Hole, Frank 1989 "Patterns of Burial in the Fifth Millennium." In *Upon this Foundation: The 'Ubaid Reconsidered*, edited by E.F. Henrickson and I. Thuesen, pp. 148–80. Copenhagen: University of Copenhagen.

Holt, Julie Z. 2009 "Rethinking the Ramey State: Was Cahokia the Center of a Theater State?" *American Antiquity* 74.2: 231–54.

Hommel, Peter and Margaret Sax 2014 "Shifting Materials: Variability, Homogeneity and Change in the Beaded Ornaments of the Western Zhou." *Antiquity* 88: 1213–28.

Hommon, Robert J. 2013 *The Ancient Hawaiian State: Origins of a Political Society.* Oxford: Oxford University Press.
Honeychurch, William 2015 *Inner Asia and the Spatial Politics of Empire: Archaeology, Mobility, and Culture Contact.* New York: Springer.
Honghai, Chen 2013 "The Qijia Culture of the Upper Yellow River Valley." In *A Companion to Chinese Archaeology*, edited by A.P. Underhill, pp. 105–24. West Sussex: Wiley-Blackwell.
Hopkins, Keith 2008 "The Political Economy of the Roman Empire." In *The Dynamics of Ancient Empires*, edited by I. Morris and W. Scheidel, pp. 178–204. New York: Oxford University Press.
Hornblower, Simon 1983 *The Greek World, 479–323 BC.* London: Methuen.
Houby-Nielsen, Sanne 2000 "Child Burials in Ancient Athens." In *Children and Material Culture*, edited by J.S. Derevenski, pp. 151–66. London: Routledge.
Houston, Stephen D. 2004 "Writing in Early Mesoamerica." In *The First Writing: Script Invention as History and Process*, edited by S.D. Houston, pp. 274–309. Cambridge: Cambridge University Press.
Hua, Sun 2013 "The Sanxingdui Culture of the Sichuan Basin." In *A Companion to Chinese Archaeology*, edited by A.P. Underhill, pp.147–68. West Sussex: Wiley-Blackwell.
Hudson, Charles, Marvin Smith, David Hally, Richard Polhemus and Chester B. DePratter 1985 "Coosa: A Chiefdom in the Sixteenth-Century Southeastern United States." *American Antiquity* 50: 723–37.
Huffman, Thomas 1987 *Symbols in Stone: Unravelling the Mystery of Great Zimbabwe.* Johannesburg: Witwatersrand University.
——— 2005 *Mapungubwe: Ancient African Civilisation on the Limpopo.* Johannesburg: Wits University Press.
——— 2009 "Mapungubwe and Great Zimbabwe: The Origin and Spread of Social Complexity in Southern Africa." *Journal of Anthropological Archaeology* 28: 37–54.
——— 2010a "State Formation in Southern Africa: A Reply to Kim and Kusimba." *African Archaeological Review* 27: 1–11.
——— 2010b "Revisiting Great Zimbabwe." *Azania: Archaeological Research in Africa* 45.3: 321–28.
——— 2011 "Debating Great Zimbabwe." *South African Archaeological Bulletin* 66.193: 27–40.
Hull, Sharon, Mostafa Fayek, F. Joan Mathien and Heidi Roberts 2013 "Turquoise Trade of the Ancestral Puebloan: Chaco and Beyond." *Journal of Archaeological Science* 45: 187–95.
Humphrey, Caroline and Stephen Hugh-Jones 1992 "Introduction: Barter, Exchange and Value." In *Barter, Exchange and Value: An Anthropological Approach*, edited by C. Humphrey and S. Hugh-Jones, pp. 1–20. Cambridge: Cambridge University Press.
Hunt, Terry L. and Carl P. Lipo 2010 "Ecological Catastrophe, Collapse, and the Myth of 'Ecocide' on Rapa Nui (Easter Island)." In *Questioning Collapse: Human Resilience, Ecological Vulnerability, and the Aftermath of Empire*, edited by P.A. McAnany and N. Yoffee, pp. 21–44. Cambridge: Cambridge University Press.
Huot, Jean-Louis 1989 "Ubaidian Villages of Lower Mesopotamia: Permanence and Evolution from 'Ubaid 0 to 'Ubaid 4 as Seen from Tell el 'Oueili." In *Upon this Foundation: The 'Ubaid Reconsidered*, edited by E.F. Henrickson and I. Thuesen, pp. 19–42. Copenhagen: University of Copenhagen.
Hurwit, Jeffrey M. 1993 "Art, Poetry, and the Polis in the Age of Homer." In *From Pasture to Polis: Art in the Age of Homer*, edited by S. Langdon, pp. 14–42. Columbia: University of Missouri Press.
Ikram, Salima 1995 *Choice Cuts: Meat Production in Ancient Egypt.* Orientalia Lovaniensia Analecta 69. Leuven: Peeters.
Ingold, Tim 1979 *Hunters, Pastoralists, and Ranchers: Reindeer Economics and Their Transformations.* Cambridge: Cambridge University Press.
Inomata, Takeshi 2001 "King's People: Classic Maya Courtiers in a Comparative Perspective." In *Royal Courts of the Ancient Maya. Vol. 1. Theory, Comparison, and Synthesis*, edited by T. Inomata and S.D. Houston, pp. 27–53. Boulder: Westview Press.
——— 2006 "Politics and Theatricality in Mayan Society." In *Archaeology of Performance: Theaters of Power, Community, and Politics*, edited by T. Inomata and L.S. Coben, pp. 187–221. Lanham: AltaMira Press.
Inomata, Takeshi, Daniela Triadan, Kazuo Aoyama, Victor Castillo and Hitoshi Yonenobu 2013 "Early Ceremonial Constructions at Ceibal, Guatemala, and the Origins of Lowland Maya Civilization." *Science* 340: 467–71.
Isaac, Barry L. 1996 "Approaches to Classic Maya Economies." *Research in Economic Anthropology* 17: 297–334.
Isbell, William H. 2004 "Mortuary Preferences: A Huari Case Study from Middle Horizon Peru." *Latin American Antiquity* 15: 3–32.

——— 2008 "Wari and Tiwanaku: International Identities in the Central Andean Middle Horizon." In *Handbook of South American Archaeology*, edited by H. Silverman and W.H. Isbell, pp. 731–59. New York: Springer.

——— 2009 "Huari: A New Direction in Central Andean Urban Revolution." In *Domestic Life in Prehispanic Capitals: A Study of Specialization, Hierarchy, and Ethnicity*, edited by L.R. Manzanilla and C. Chapdelaine, pp. 197–219. Memoirs of the Museum of Anthropology, No. 46. Ann Arbor: University of Michigan.

——— 2010 "Agency, Identity, and Control: Understanding Wari Space and Power." In *Beyond Wari Walls: Regional Perspectives on Middle Horizon Peru*, edited by J. Jennings, pp. 233–54. Albuquerque: New Mexico Press.

——— 2013 "Nature of an Andean City: Tiwanaku and the Production of Spectacle." In *Visions of Tiwanaku*, edited by A. Vranich and C. Stanish, pp. 167–96. Monograph 78. Los Angeles: Cotsen Institute of Archaeology Press.

Isbell, William H. and Antti Korpisaari 2012 "Burial in the Wari and the Tiwanaku Heartlands: Similarities, Differences, and Meanings." *Diálogo Andino* 39: 91–22.

Iseminger, William R. 2010 *Cahokia Mounds: America's First City*. Charleston: The History Press.

Izzet, Vedia E. 1996 "Engraving the Boundaries: Exploring Space and Surface in Etruscan Funerary Architecture." In *Approaches to the Study of Ritual: Italy and the Ancient Mediterranean*, edited by J.B. Wilkins, pp. 55–72. London: Accordia Research Centre, University of London.

——— 2001 "Form and Meaning in Etruscan Ritual Space." *Cambridge Archaeological Journal* 11.2: 185–200.

Jackowski, Christian, Stephan Bolliger and Michael J. Thali 2008 "Common and Unexpected Findings in Mummies from Ancient Egypt and South America as Revealed by CT." *Radiographics* 28.5: 1477–92.

Jackson, Sarah E. 2013 *Politics of the Maya Court: Hierarchy and Change in the Late Classic Period*. Norman: University of Oklahoma Press.

Jacques, Claude 1986 "Sources on Economic Activities in Khmer and Cham Lands." In *Southeast Asia in the 9th to 14th Centuries*, edited by D.G. Marr and A.C. Milner, pp. 327–34. Singapore: Institute of Southeast Asian Studies and Research School of Pacific Studies.

Jacques, Claude and Philippe Lafond 2007 *The Khmer Empire: Cities and Sanctuaries Fifth to the Thirteenth Centuries*. Bangkok: River Books.

Jaffe, Yitzchak 2013 "Materializing Identity–A Statistical Analysis of the Western Zhou Liulihe Cemetery." *Asian Perspectives* 51.1: 47–67.

Jakobsen, V.A. 1969 "The Social Structure of the Neo-Assyrian Empire." In *Ancient Mesopotamia: Socio-Economic History: A Collection of Studies by Soviet Scholars*, edited by I.M. Diakonoff, pp. 277–95. Moscow: "Nauka" Publishing House.

Jameson, Michael 1990 "Domestic Space in the Greek City-State." In *Domestic Architecture and the Use of Space*, edited by S. Kent, pp. 92–113. Cambridge: Cambridge University Press.

Jansen, M. 1989 "Water Supply and Sewage Disposal at Mohenjo-Daro." *World Archaeology* 21.2: 177–92.

——— 2010 "Architectural Measurements in the Indus Cities: The Case Study of Mohenjo-Daro." In *The Archaeology of Measurement: Comprehending Heaven, Earth and Time in Ancient Societies*, edited by I. Morley and C. Renfrew, pp. 125–29. Cambridge: Cambridge University Press.

Janusek, John W. 2002 "Out of Many, One: Style and Social Boundaries in Tiwanaku." *Latin American Antiquity* 13: 35–61.

——— 2004 "Tiwanaku and Its Precursors: Recent Research and Emerging Perspectives." *Journal of Archaeological Research* 12.2: 121–83.

——— 2006 "The Changing 'Nature' of Tiwanaku Religion and the Rise of an Andean State." *World Archaeology* 38.3: 469–92.

——— 2009 "Residence and Ritual at Tiwanaku: Hierarchy, Specialization, Ethnicity, and Ceremony." In *Domestic Life in Prehispanic Capitals: A Study of Specialization, Hierarchy, and Ethnicity*, edited by L.S. Manzanilla and C. Chapdelaine, pp. 149–69. Ann Arbor: University of Michigan.

——— 2015 "Tiwanaku Urban Origins: Distributed Centers and Animate Landscapes." In *Early Cities in Comparative Perspective, 4000 BCE–1200 CE*, Cambridge World History Volume III, edited by N. Yoffee, pp. 229–52. Cambridge: Cambridge University Press.

Jarrige, Jean-François and Catherine Jarrige 2006 "Premiers pasteurs et agriculteurs dans le sous-continent Indo-Pakistanais." *Comptes Rendus Palevol* 5: 463–72.

Jarrige, Jean-François, Catherine Jarrige and Gonzague Quivron 2005 "Mehrgarh Neolithic: The Updated Sequence." In *South Asian Archaeology, 2001*, edited by C. Jarrige and V. Lefevre, pp. 128–41. Paris: Editions Recherche sur les Civilisations.

Jeffries, Richard W. 2008 *Holocene Hunter-Gatherers of the Lower Ohio River Valley*. Tuscaloosa: University of Alabama Press.

Jennings, Justin 2010 "Beyond Wari Walls." In *Beyond Wari Walls: Regional Perspectives on Middle Horizon Peru*, edited by J. Jennings, pp. 1–18. Albuquerque: New Mexico Press.

Jessup, Helen I. 2010 "South-East Asia: The Khmer 802–1566." In *The Great Empires of Asia*, edited by J. Masselos, pp. 72–103. Berkeley: University of California.

Johnson, Allen W. and Timothy Earle 1987 *The Evolution of Human Societies: From Foraging Group to Agrarian State*. Stanford: Stanford University Press.

Johnson, Gregory A. 1973 *Local Exchange and Early State Development in Southwestern Iran*. Ann Arbor: University of Michigan.

Jones, Donald W. 1999 *Peak Sanctuaries and Sacred Caves in Minoan Crete: A Comparison of Artifacts*. Jonsered: Paul Aströms Förlag.

Joyce, Arthur A. 2000 "The Founding of Monte Albán: Sacred Propositions and Social Practices." In *Agency in Archaeology*, edited by M.-A. Dobres and J.E. Robb, pp. 71–92. London: Routledge.

Joyce, Arthur A. and Marcus Winter 1996 "Ideology, Power, and Urban Society in Pre-Hispanic Oaxaca." *Current Anthropology* 37: 33–47.

Joyce, Rosemary A. 2007 "Girling the Girl and Boying the Boy: The Production of Adulthood in Ancient Mesoamerica." In *The Archaeology of Identities: A Reader*, edited by T. Insoll, pp. 77–86. London: Routledge.

Judge, W. James and Linda S. Cordell 2006 "Society and Polity." In *The Archaeology of Chaco Canyon: An Eleventh-Century Pueblo Regional Center*, edited by S.H. Lekson, pp. 189–210. Santa Fe: School of American Research Press.

Jung, Reinhard 2010 "End of the Bronze Age." In *The Oxford Handbook of the Bronze Age Aegean (ca. 3000–1000 BC)*, edited by E.H. Cline, pp. 171–84. Oxford: Oxford University Press.

Kanawati, Naguib 1980 *Governmental Reforms in Old Kingdom Egypt*. Warminster: Aris and Phillips.

Kantner, John 2004 "Great-House Communities and the Chaco World." In *In Search of Chaco: New Approaches to an Archaeological Enigma*, edited by D.G. Noble, pp. 70–77. Santa Fe: School of American Research Press.

——— 2009 "Identifying the Pathways to Permanent Leadership." In *The Evolution of Leadership: Transitions in Decision Making from Small-Scale to Middle-Range Societies*, edited by K.J. Vaughn, J.W. Eerkens and J. Kantner, pp. 249–81. Santa Fe: School for Advanced Research Press.

Kantner, John and Kevin J. Vaughn 2012 "Pilgrimage as Costly Signal: Religiously Motivated Cooperation in Chaco and Nasca." *Journal of Anthropological Archaeology* 31: 66–82.

Kaulicke, Peter 2015 "Inka Conceptions of Life, Death, and Ancestor Worship." In *The Inka Empire: A Multidisciplinary Approach*, edited by I. Shimada, pp. 247–61. Austin: University of Texas Press.

Keatinge, Richard W. 1975 "Urban Settlement Systems and Rural Sustaining Communities: An Example from Chan Chan's Hinterland." *Journal of Field Archaeology* 2.3: 215–27.

Keatinge, Richard W. and Kent C. Day 1974 "Chan Chan: A Study of Pre-Columbian Urbanism and Management of Land and Water Resources in Peru." *Archaeology* 27: 228–35.

Keesling, Catherine M. 2003 *The Votive Statues of the Athenian Acropolis*. Cambridge: Cambridge University Press.

Kehoe, Alice B. 1998 *The Land of Prehistory: A Critical History of American Archaeology*. London: Routledge.

——— 2002 "Theaters of Power." In *The Dynamics of Power*, edited by M. O'Donovan, pp. 259–72. Center for Archaeological Investigations Occasional Paper No. 30. Carbondale: Southern Illinois University Press.

Kehoe, Dennis P. 2007 "The Early Roman Empire: Production." In *The Cambridge Economic History of the Greco-Roman World*, edited by W. Scheidel, I. Morris, and R. Saller, pp. 543–69. Cambridge: Cambridge University Press.

Keightley, David N. 1978a *Sources of Shang History: The Oracle-Bone Inscriptions of Bronze Age China*. Berkeley: University of California Press.

——— 1978b "The Religious Commitment: Shang Theology and the Genesis of Chinese Political Culture." *History of Religions* 17.3/4: 211–25.

——— 1988 "Shang Divination and Metaphysics." *Philosophy East and West* 38: 367–97.

——— 2000 *The Ancestral Landscape: Time, Space, and Community in Late Shang China (ca. 1200–1045 B.C.)*. China Research Monograph 53. Berkeley: University of California Press.

——— 2014 *These Bones Shall Rise Again: Selected Writings on Early China*. Albany: State University of New York Press.

Keith, Kathryn 2003 "The Spatial Patterns of Everyday Life in Old Babylonian Neighborhoods." In *The Social Construction of Ancient Cities*, edited by M.L. Smith, pp. 56–80. Washington: Smithsonian Books.

Kelder, Jorrit 2005 "Greece during the Late Bronze Age." *Jaarbericht van het Vooraziatisch-egyptisch genootschap 'Ex Oriente Lux'* 39: 131–79.

Keller, Cynthia and Christopher Carr 2005 "Gender, Role, Prestige, and Ritual Interaction across the Ohio, Mann, and Havana Hopewell Regions, as Evidenced by Ceramic Figurines." In *Gathering Hopewell: Society, Ritual, and Ritual Interaction*, edited by C. Carr and D.T. Case, pp. 428–60. New York: Springer.

Kellum, Barbara 1996 "The Phallus as Signifier: The Forum of Augustus and Rituals of Masculinity." In *Sexuality in Ancient Art: Near East, Egypt, Greece, and Italy*, edited by N.B. Kampen, pp. 170–83. Cambridge: Cambridge University Press.

Kelly, John E. 1990 "Range Site Community Patterns and the Mississippian Emergence." In *The Mississippian Emergence*, edited by B.D. Smith, pp. 67–112. Washington: Smithsonian Institution Press.

——— 1991 "The Evidence for Prehistoric Exchange and Its Implications for the Development of Cahokia." In *New Perspectives on Cahokia: Views from the Periphery*, edited by J.B. Stoltman, pp. 65–91. Monographs in World Archaeology, No. 2. Madison: Prehistory Press.

——— 1997 "Stirling-Phase Sociopolitical Activity at East St. Louis and Cahokia." In *Cahokia: Domination and Ideology in the Mississippian World*, edited by T.R. Pauketat and T.E. Emerson, pp. 141–66. Lincoln: University of Nebraska Press.

——— 2002 "Woodland Period Archaeology in the American Bottom." In *The Woodland Southeast*, edited by D.G. Anderson and R.C. Mainfort, Jr., pp. 134–61. Tuscaloosa: University of Alabama Press.

——— 2006 "The Ritualization of Cahokia: The Structure and Organization of Early Cahokia Crafts." In *Leadership and Polity in Mississippian Society*, edited by B.M. Butler and P.D. Welch, pp. 236–63. Center for Archaeological Investigations Occasional Paper No. 33. Carbondale: Southern Illinois University Press.

Kembel, Silvia Rodriguez 2008 "The Architecture at the Monumental Center of Chavín de Huántar: Sequence, Transformations, and Chronology." In *Chavín: Art, Architecture and Culture*, edited by W. Conklin and J. Quilter, pp. 35–81. Los Angeles: Cotsen Institute of Archaeology.

Kemp, Barry 1967 "The Egyptian 1st Dynasty Royal Cemetery." *Antiquity* 41: 22–32.

——— 1989 *Ancient Egypt: Anatomy of a Civilization*. London: Routledge.

Kenoyer, Jonathan Mark 1989 "Socio-Economic Structures in the Indus Civilization as Reflected in Specialized Crafts and the Question of Ritual Segregation." In *Old Problems and New Perspectives in the Archaeology of South Asia*, edited by J.M. Kenoyer, pp. 183–92. Wisconsin Archaeological Reports, Vol. 2. Madison: University of Wisconsin.

——— 1992 "Harappan Craft Specialization and the Question of Urban Segregation and Stratification." *Eastern Anthropologist* 45.1–2: 39–54.

——— 1994 "The Harappan State: Was it or Wasn't It?" In *From Sumer to Meluhha: Contributions to the Archaeology of South and West Asia in Memory of George F. Dales, Jr.*, edited by J.M. Kenoyer, pp. 71–80. Wisconsin Archaeological Reports, Vol. 3. Madison: University of Wisconsin.

——— 1997a "Early City-States in South Asia: Comparing the Harappan Phase and Early Historic Period." In *The Archaeology of City-States: Cross-Cultural Approaches*, edited by D.L. Nichols and T.H. Charlton, pp. 51–70. Washington: Smithsonian Institution Press.

——— 1997b "Trade and Technology of the Indus Valley: New Insights from Harappa, Pakistan." *World Archaeology* 29.2: 262–80.

——— 1998 *Ancient Cities of the Indus Valley Civilization*. Karachi: Oxford University Press.

——— 2005 "Uncovering the Keys to the Lost Indus Cities." *Scientific American Special Edition* 15.1: 25–33.

——— 2008 "Indus Urbanism: New Perspectives on its Origin and Character." In *The Ancient City: New Perspectives on Urbanism in the Old and New World*, edited by J. Marcus and J.A. Sabloff, pp. 183–208. Santa Fe: School for Advanced Research.

——— 2010 "Measuring the Harappan World: Insights into the Indus Order and Cosmology." In *The Archaeology of Measurement: Comprehending Heaven, Earth and Time in Ancient Societies*, edited by I. Morley and C. Renfrew, pp. 106–24. Cambridge: Cambridge University Press.

Kenoyer, J. Mark, T. Douglas Price and James H. Burton 2013 "A New Approach to Tracking Connections between the Indus Valley and Mesopotamia: Initial Results of Strontium Isotope Analyses from Harappa and Ur." *Journal of Archaeological Science* 40: 2286–97.

Khai, Vo Si 2003 "The Kingdom of Fu Nan and the Culture of Oc Eo." In *Art and Archaeology of Fu Nan: Pre-Khmer Kingdom of the Lower Mekong Valley*, edited by J.C.M. Khoo, pp. 36–84. Bangkok: Orchid Press.

Kidder, Tristram R. 2006 "Climate Change and the Archaic to Woodland Transition (3000–2500 Cal B.P.) in the Mississippi River Basin." *American Antiquity* 71.2: 195–231.

Kim, Nam C. and Chapurukha M. Kusimba 2008 "Pathways to Social Complexity and State Formation in the Southern Zambezian Region." *African Archaeological Review* 25: 131–52.

Kim, Nam C., Lai Van Toi and Trinh Hoang Hiep 2010 "Co Loa: An Investigation of Vietnam's Ancient Capital." *Antiquity* 84: 1011–27.

Kim, Seung-Og 1994 "Burials, Pigs, and Political Prestige in Neolithic China." *Current Anthropology* 35.2: 119–41.

King, Adam and J.A. Freer 1995 "The Mississippian Southeast: A World-System Perspective." In *Native American Interactions: Multiscalar Analyses and Interpretations in the Eastern Woodlands*, edited by M. Nassaney and K. Sassaman, pp. 266–88. Knoxville: University of Tennessee Press.

Kipp, Rita Smith and Edward M. Schortman 1989 "The Political Impact of Trade in Chiefdoms." *American Anthropologist* 91: 370–85.

Kirch, Patrick V. 2000 *On the Road of the Winds: An Archaeological History of the Pacific Islands before European Contact*. Berkeley: University of California Press.

——— 2001 *Hawaiki, Ancestral Polynesia: An Essay in Historical Anthropology*. Cambridge: Cambridge University Press.

——— 2010 *How Chiefs became Kings: Divine Kingship and the Rise of Archaic States in Ancient Hawai'i*. Berkeley: University of California Press.

Kleiner, Diane E.E. 1978 "The Great Friezes of the Ara Pacis Augustae: Greek Sources, Roman Derivatives, and Augustan Social Policy." *Mélanges de l'École Française de Rome. Antiquite* 90: 753–85.

Kluckholm, Clyde 1942 "Myths and Rituals: A General Theory." *Harvard Theological Review* 35.1: 45–79.

Knapp, A. Bernard 1988 "Copper Production and Eastern Mediterranean Trade: The Rise of Complex Society on Cyprus." In *State and Society: The Emergence and Development of Social Hierarchy and Political Centralization*, edited by J. Gledhill, B. Bender and M.T. Larsen, pp. 149–69. London: Unwin Hyman.

Knapp, Michael, K. Ann Horsburgh, Stefan Prost, Jo-Ann Stanton, Hallie R. Buckley, Richard K. Walter and Elizabeth A. Matisoo-Smith 2012 "Complete Mitochrondrial DNA Genome Sequences from the First New Zealanders." *Proceedings of the National Academy of Science* 109.45: 18350–54.

Koehler, E. Christiana 2010 "Prehistory." In *A Companion to Ancient Egypt*, edited by A.B. Lloyd, pp. 25–47. Oxford: Blackwell Publishing Ltd.

Kolata, Alan L. 1986 "The Agricultural Foundations of the Tiwanaku State: A View from the Heartland." *American Antiquity* 51.4: 748–62.

——— 1993 *Tiwanaku: Portrait of an Andean Civilization*. Cambridge: Blackwell Publishers.

Kolb, Michael J. 1994 "Monumentality and the Rise of Religious Authority in Precontact Hawai'i." *Current Anthropology* 34.5: 521–47.

Kolb, Michael J. and Boyd Dixon 2002 "Landscapes of War: Rules and Conventions of Conflict in Ancient Hawai'i (and Elsewhere)." *American Antiquity* 67.3: 514–34.

Koldehoff, Brad 2006 "Hopewellian Figurines from the Southern American Bottom." *Illinois Archaeology* 18: 185–93.

Koldehoff, Brad and Joseph M. Galloy 2006 "Late Woodland Frontiers in the American Bottom." *Southeastern Archaeology* 25.2: 275–300.

Kottaridi, A. 2011 "The Palace at Aegae." In *Brill's Companion to Ancient Macedon: Studies in the Archaeology and History of Macedon, 650 BC–300 AD*, edited by R. Lane Fox, pp. 297–333. Leiden: Brill.

Kristan-Graham, Cynthia and Jeff Karl Kowalski 2007 "Chichén Itzá, Tula, and Tollan: Changing Perspectives on a Recurring Problem in Mesoamerican Archaeology and Art History." In *Twin Tollans: Chichén Itzá, Tula, and the Epiclassic to Early Postclassic Mesoamerican World*, edited by J.K. Kowalski and C. Kristan-Graham, pp. 13–83. Washington: Dumbarton Oaks Research Library and Collection.

Kristiansen, Kristian 1991 "Chiefdoms, States, and Systems of Social Evolution." In *Chiefdoms: Power, Economy, and Ideology*, edited by T. Earle, pp. 16–43. Cambridge: Cambridge University Press.

Krzyzaniak, Lech 1979 "Trends in the Socio-Economic Development of Egyptian Predynastic Societies." In *Acts of the First International Congress of Egyptology*, edited by W.F. Reineke, pp. 407–12. Berlin: Akademie Verlag.

Kuhn, Steven L. and Mary C. Stiner 2006 "Middle Palaeolithic 'Creativity': Reflections on an Oxymoron?" In *Creativity in Human Evolution and Prehistory*, edited by S. Mithen, pp. 143–64. London: Routledge.

Kuijt, Ian 2001 "Place, Death, and the Transmission of Social Memory in Early Agricultural Communities of the Near Eastern Pre-Pottery Neolithic." In *Social Memory, Identity, and Death: Anthropological Perspectives on Mortuary Rituals*, edited by M.S. Chesson, pp. 80–99. Archeological Papers of the American Anthropological Association 10. Arlington: American Anthropological Association.

——— 2008 "The Regeneration of Life: Neolithic Structures of Symbolic Remembering and Forgetting." *Current Anthropology* 49: 171–97.
Kusimba, Chapurukha M. and Sibel B. Kusimba 2009 "Leadership in Middle-Range African Societies." In *The Evolution of Leadership: Transitions in Decision Making from Small-Scale to Middle-Range Societies*, edited by K.J. Vaughn, J.W. Eerkens and J. Kantner, pp. 223–47. Santa Fe: School for Advanced Research Press.
Kyle, Donald G. 1992 "The Panathenaic Games: Sacred and Civic Athletics." In *Goddess and Polis: The Panathenaic Festival in Ancient Athens*, edited by J. Neils, pp. 77–101. Hanover: Hood Museum of Art.
Lal, B.B. 1979 "Kalibangan and Indus Civilization." In *Essays in Indian Prehistory*, edited by D.P. Agrawal and D. Chakrabarti, pp. 65–97. Delhi: B.R. Publishing.
Lane Fox, Robin 2011 "Philip of Macedon: Accession, Ambitions, and Self-Representation." In *Brill's Companion to Ancient Macedon: Studies in the Archaeology and History of Macedon, 650 BC–300 AD*, edited by R. Lane Fox, pp. 335–66. Leiden: Brill.
Lapatin, Kenneth 2002 *Mysteries of the Snake Goddess: Art, Desire, and the Forging of History*. Boston: Houghton Mifflin.
Larsen, Mogens Trolle 1979 "The Tradition of Empire in Mesopotamia." In *Power and Propaganda: A Symposium on Ancient Empires*, edited by M.T. Larsen, pp. 75–103. Copenhagen: Akademisk Forlag.
——— 1987 "Commercial Networks in the Ancient Near East." In *Centre and Periphery in the Ancient World*, edited by M. Rowlands, M. Larsen and K. Kristiansen, pp. 47–56. Cambridge: Cambridge University Press.
Lass, Barbara 1998 "Crafts, Chiefs, and Commoners: Production and Control in Precontact Hawaii." In *Craft and Social Identity*, edited by C.L. Costin and R.P. Wright, pp. 19–30. Arlington: American Anthropological Association.
Lawler, Andrew 2013 "Mohenjo-Daro's New Story: What May be the Bronze Age's Largest City Lies on the Plains of Pakistan." *Archaeology* 66.1: 32–37.
Leacock, Eleanor 1982 "Relations of Production in Band Society." In *Politics and History in Band Societies*, edited by E. Leacock and R.B. Lee, pp. 159–70. Cambridge: Cambridge University Press.
Leblanc, Steven A. 1999 *Prehistoric Warfare in the American Southwest*. Salt Lake City: University of Utah Press.
Lee, Mirielle 2000 "Deciphering Gender in Minoan Dress." In *Reading the Body: Representations and Remains in the Archaeological Record*, edited by A.E. Rautman, pp. 111–23. Philadelphia: University of Pennsylvania Press.
Lee, Richard B. 1984 *The Dobe !Kung*. New York: Holt, Rinehart and Winston.
Lee, Richard B. and Irven DeVore, eds. 1968 *Man the Hunter*. Chicago: Aldine.
Lee, Yun Kuen 2004 "Control Strategies and Polity Competition in the Lower Yi-Luo Valley, North China." *Journal of Anthropological Archaeology* 23: 172–95.
——— 2007 "Centripetal Settlement and Segmentary Social Formation of the Banpo Tradition." *Journal of Anthropological Archaeology* 26: 630–75.
Lefkowitz, Mary R. 1983 "Influential Women." In *Images of Women in Antiquity*, edited by A. Cameron and A. Kuhrt, pp. 49–64. Detroit: Wayne State University Press.
Lehner, Mark 2010 "Villages and the Old Kingdom." In *Egyptian Archaeology*, edited by W. Wendrich, pp. 85–101. West Sussex: Wiley-Blackwell.
Leick, Gwendolyn 2001 *Mesopotamia: The Invention of the City*. London: Penguin.
Lekson, Stephen H. 1999 *The Chaco Meridian: Centers of Political Power in the Ancient Southwest*. Walnut Creek: AltaMira Press.
——— 2005 "Complexity." In *Southwest Archaeology in the Twentieth Century*, edited by L.S. Cordell and D.D. Fowler, pp. 157–73. Salt Lake City: University of Utah Press.
——— 2006 "Chaco Matters: An Introduction." In *The Archaeology of Chaco Canyon: An Eleventh-Century Pueblo Regional Center*, edited by S.H. Lekson, pp. 3–44. Santa Fe: School of American Research Press.
——— 2009 *A History of the Ancient Southwest*. Santa Fe: School for Advanced Research Press.
——— 2010 "The Good Gray Intermediate: Why Native Societies of North America Can't Be States." In *Ancient Complexities: New Perspectives in Precolumbian North America*, edited by S.M. Alt, pp. 153–76. Salt Lake City: University of Utah Press.
——— 2012 "Chaco's Hinterlands." In *The Oxford Handbook of North American Archaeology*, edited by T.R. Pauketat, pp. 597–607. Oxford: Oxford University Press.
——— 2015 "Chaco as Altepetl: Secondary States." In *The Southwest in the World* (http://stevelekson.com/2011/07/22/what-was-chaco/).
Leprohon, Ronald J. 1995 "Royal Ideology and State Administration in Pharaonic Egypt." In *Civilizations of the Ancient Near East*, edited by J.M. Sasson, pp. 273–87. New York: Charles Scribner's Sons.

Lewis, Mark E. 2007 *The Early Chinese Empires: Qin and Han*. Cambridge: Belknap Press.
Liancheng, Lu 2005 "The Eastern Zhou and the Growth of Regionalism." In *The Formation of Chinese Civilization, An Archaeological Perspective*, edited by S. Allen, pp. 203–47. New Haven: Yale University Press.
Liancheng, Lu and Yan Wenming 2005 "Society during the Three Dynasties." In *The Formation of Chinese Civilization, An Archaeological Perspective*, edited by S. Allen, pp. 141–201. New Haven: Yale University Press.
Liendo Stuardo, Rodrigo 2007 "The Problem of Political Integration in the Kingdom of Baak: A Regional Perspective for Settlement Patterns in the Palenque Region." In *Palenque: Recent Investigations at the Classic Maya Center*, edited by D.B. Marken, pp. 85–106. Lanham: AltaMira Press.
Lim, Richard 2010 "The Later Roman Empire." In *The Oxford Handbook of Roman Studies*, edited by A. Barchiesi and W. Scheidel, pp. 547–63. Oxford: Oxford University Press.
Liu, Li 1996 "Settlement Patterns, Chiefdom Variability, and the Development of Early States in North China." *Journal of Anthropological Archaeology* 15: 237–88.
——— 1999 "Who Were the Ancestors? The Origins of Chinese Ancestral Cult and Racial Myths." *Antiquity* 73: 602–13.
——— 2000 "Ancestor Worship: An Archaeological Investigation of Ritual Activities in Neolithic North China." *Journal of East Asian Archaeology* 1.1–2: 129–64.
——— 2003 "'The Products of Minds as Well as of Hands': Production of Prestige Goods in the Neolithic and Early State Periods of China." *Asian Perspectives* 42.1: 1–40.
——— 2009a "State Emergence in Early China." *Annual Review of Anthropology* 38: 217–32.
——— 2009b "Academic Freedom, Political Correctness, and Early Civilisation in Chinese Archaeology: The Debate on Xia-Erlitou Relations." *Antiquity* 83: 831–43.
Liu, Li and Xingcan Chen 2003 *State Formation in Early China*. London: Duckworth.
——— 2012 *The Archaeology of China: From the Late Paleolithic to the Early Bronze Age*. Cambridge: Cambridge University Press.
Liu, Li and Hong Xu 2007 "Rethinking Erlitou: Legend, History and Chinese Archaeology." *Antiquity* 81: 886–901.
Liverani, Mario 1979 "The Ideology of the Assyrian Empire." In *Power and Propaganda. A Symposium on Ancient Empires*, edited by M.T. Larsen, pp. 363–83. Copenhagen: Akademisk Forlag.
Lobell, Jarrett A. 2012 "A Society's Sacrifice." *Archaeology* 65.1: 43–47.
Loewe, Michael 2007 "The First Emperor and the Qin Empire." In *The First Emperor: China's Terracotta Army*, edited by J. Portal, pp. 59–79. Cambridge: Harvard University Press.
López Austin, Alfredo, Leonardo López Luján and Saburo Sugiyama 1991 "The Temple of Quetzalcoatl at Teotihuacan: Its Possible Ideological Significance." *Ancient Mesoamerica* 2: 93–105.
Lü, Houyuan, Yumei Li, Jianping Zhang, Xiaoyan Yang, Maolin Ye, Quan Li, Can Wang and Naiqin Wu 2014 "Culinary Archaeology: Millet Noodles in Late Neolithic China." *Chinese Science Bulletin* 59.35: 5136–52.
Lucero, Lisa J. 2002 "The Collapse of the Classic Maya: A Case for the Role of Water Control." *American Anthropologist* 104: 814–26.
Lumbreras, Luis 1993 *Chavín de Huántar: Excavaciones en la Galería de las Ofrendas*. Materialien zur allgemeinen und vergleichenden Archäologie 51. Mainz am Rhein: Philipp von Zabern.
Lupack, Susan 2010 "Minoan Religion." In *The Oxford Handbook of the Bronze Age Aegean (ca. 3000–1000 BC)*, edited by E.H. Cline, pp. 251–62. Oxford: Oxford University Press.
Mackay, Christopher S. 2000 "Sulla and the Monuments: Studies in His Public Persona." *Historia: Zeitschrift für Alte Geschichte* 49: 161–210.
Mackay, E.J. 1938 *Further Excavations at Mohenjo-Daro, Being an Official Account of Archaeology Excavations Carried Out by the Government of India between the Years of 1927 and 1931*. New Delhi: Government Press.
Mackil, Emily 2004 "Wandering Cities: Alternatives to Catastrophe in the Greek Polis." *American Journal of Archaeology* 108: 493–516.
Mainfort, Robert C., Jr. 1989 "Adena Chiefdoms? Evidence from the Wright Mound." *Midcontinental Journal of Archaeology* 14.2: 164–78.
——— 2005 "Some Comments on Woodland Taxonomy in the Middle Ohio Valley." In *Woodland Period Systematics in the Middle Ohio Valley*, edited by D. Applegate and R.C. Mainfort, Jr., pp. 221–30. Tuscaloosa: University of Alabama Press.
Malik, S.C. 1979 "Changing Perspectives of Archaeology and Interpreting Harappan Society." In *Essays in Indian Prehistory*, edited by D.P. Agrawal and D. Chakrabarti, pp. 187–204. Delhi: B.R. Publishing.

Mallah, Qasid H., Nilofer Shaikh and G.M. Veesar 2002 "Complementary Role of the Rohri Hills and the Thar Desert in the Development of Indus Valley Civilization: New Research." *Asia Pacific: Perspectives* 2.1: 21–31.

Manguin, Pierre-Yves 2004 "The Archaeology of Early Maritime Polities of Southeast Asia." In *Southeast Asia from Prehistory to History*, edited by I. Glover and P. Bellwood, pp. 282–313. London: RoutledgeCurzon.

Mann, Michael E. 1986 *The Sources of Social Power. Vol. I: A History of Power from the Beginning to A.D. 1760*. Cambridge: Cambridge University Press.

Mann, Michael E., Zhihua Zhang, Scott Rutherford, Raymond S. Bradley, Malcolm K. Hughes, Drew Shindell, Caspar Ammann, Greg Faluvegi and Fenbiao Ni 2009 "Global Signatures and Dynamical Origins of the Little Ice Age and Medieval Climate Anomaly." *Science* 326.5957: 1256–60.

Manning, Joseph G. 2007 "Hellenistic Egypt." In *The Cambridge Economic History of the Greco-Roman World*, edited by W. Scheidel, I. Morris and R. Saller, pp. 434–59. Cambridge: Cambridge University Press.

——— 2013. "Egypt." In *The Oxford Handbook of the State in the Ancient Near East and Mediterranean*, edited by P.F. Bang and W. Scheidel, pp. 61–93. Oxford: Oxford University Press.

Manning, Sturt W. and David A. Sewell 2002 "Volcanoes and History: A Significant Relationship? The Case of Santorini." In *Natural Disasters and Cultural Change*, edited by R. Torrence and J. Grattan, pp. 264–91. London: Routledge.

Manzanilla, Linda 1996 "Corporate Groups and Domestic Activities at Teotihuacan." *Latin American Antiquity* 7: 228–46.

——— 2001 "State Formation in the New World." In *Archaeology at the Millennium: A Sourcebook*, edited by G.M. Feinman and T.D. Price, pp. 381–413. New York: Kluwer Academic/Plenum Publishers.

——— 2002 "Houses and Ancestors, Altars and Relics: Mortuary Patterns at Teotihuacan, Central Mexico." In *The Space and Place of Death*, edited by H. Silverman and D.B. Small, pp. 55–65. Arlington: American Anthropological Association.

——— 2009 "Corporate Life in Apartment and Barrio Compounds at Teotihuacan, Central Mexico: Craft Specialization, Hierarchy, and Ethnicity." In *Domestic Life in Prehispanic Capitals: A Study of Specialization, Hierarchy, and Ethnicity*, edited by L.R. Manzanilla and C. Chapdelaine, pp. 21–42. Ann Arbor: University of Michigan.

Manzanilla, L., L. Barba, R. Chávez, A. Tejero, G. Cifuentes and N. Peralta 1994 "Caves and Geophysics: An Approximation to the Underworld of Teotihuacan, Mexico." *Archaeometry* 36: 141–57.

Marcos, Jorge G. 2003 "A Reassessment of the Ecuadorian Formative." In *Archaeology of Formative Ecuador*, edited by J.S. Raymond and R.L. Burger, pp. 7–32. Washington: Dumbarton Oaks Research Library and Collection.

Marcus, Joyce 1992 *Mesoamerican Writing Systems: Propaganda, Myth, and History in Four Ancient Civilizations*. Princeton: Princeton University Press.

——— 1998 "The Peaks and Valleys of Ancient States: An Extension of the Dynamic Model." In *Archaic States*, edited by G.M. Feinman and J. Marcus, pp. 59–94. Santa Fe: School of American Research Press.

——— 1999 "Men's and Women's Ritual in Formative Oaxaca." In *Social Patterns in Pre-Classic Mesoamerica*, edited by D.C. Grove and R.A. Joyce, pp. 67–96. Washington: Dumbarton Oaks Research Library and Collection.

——— 2007 "Rethinking Ritual." In *The Archaeology of Ritual*, edited by E. Kyriakidis, pp. 43–76. Los Angeles: Cotsen Institute of Archaeology, UCLA.

Marcus, Joyce and Gary M. Feinman 1998 "Introduction." In *Archaic States*, edited by G.M. Feinman and J. Marcus, pp. 3–13. Santa Fe: School of American Research Press.

Margueron, Jean-Claude 1982 *Recherches sur les palais mésopotamiens de l'age du Bronze*. Paris: Librairie Orientaliste Paul Geuthner.

Marinatos, Nannó 1987 "Public Festivals in the West Courts of the Palaces." In *The Function of the Minoan Palaces*, edited by R. Hägg and N. Marinatos, pp. 135–43. Stockholm: Paul Aströms Förlag.

——— 1993 *Minoan Religion: Ritual, Image, and Symbol*. Columbia: University of South Carolina Press.

Martin, Simon 2003 "In Line of the Founder: A View of Dynastic Politics at Tikal." In *Tikal: Dynasties, Foreigners, and Affairs of State: Advancing Maya Archaeology*, edited by J. Sabloff, pp. 3–45. Santa Fe: School of American Research Press.

Matheny, Ray T. 1986 "Early States in the Maya Lowlands during the Late Preclassic Period: Edzna and El Mirador." In *City-States of the Maya: Art and Architecture*, edited by E.P. Benson, pp. 1–44. Denver: Rocky Mountain Institute for Pre-Columbian Studies.

Matos Moctezuma, Eduardo 1984 "The Templo Mayor of Tenochtitlan: Economics and Ideology." In *Ritual Human Sacrifice in Mesoamerica: A Conference at Dumbarton Oaks, October 13th and 14th, 1979*, edited by E.H. Boone, pp. 133–64. Washington: Dumbarton Oaks.

——— 2001 "The Ballcourt in Tenochtitlan." In *The Sport of Life and Death: The Mesoamerican Ballgame*, edited by E.M. Whittington, pp. 78–87. Charlotte: The Mint Museum of Art.

Matthews, Roger 2000 *The Early Prehistory of Mesopotamia 500,000 to 4,500 BC*. Brepols: Turnhout.

Mauss, Marcel 1967 *The Gift*. Translated by I. Cunnison. New York: W.W. Norton & Co.

McAnany, Patricia A. and Shannon Plank 2001 "Perspectives on Actors, Gender Roles, and Architecture at Classic Maya Courts and Households." In *Royal Courts of the Ancient Maya. Vol. 1. Theory, Comparison, and Synthesis*, edited by T. Inomata and S.D. Houston, pp. 84–129. Boulder: Westview Press.

McAnany, Patricia A. and Norman Yoffee 2010 "Why We Question Collapse and Study Human Resilience, Ecological Vulnerability, and the Aftermath of Empire." In *Questioning Collapse: Human Resilience, Ecological Vulnerability, and the Aftermath of Empire*, edited by P.A. McAnany and N. Yoffee, pp. 1–17. Cambridge: Cambridge University Press.

McAnany, Patricia A., Ben Thomas, Polly Peterson, Steve Morandi and Eleanor Harrison 2002 "Praise the Ajaw and Pass the Kakaw: Xibun Maya and the Political Economy of Cacao." In *Ancient Maya Political Economies*, edited by M.A. Masson and D.A. Freidel, pp. 123–39. Walnut Creek: AltaMira Press.

McCallum, Lucinda Rasmussen 1987 Decorative Program in the Mycenaean Palace of Pylos: The Megaron Frescoes. Unpublished PhD dissertation, University of Pennsylvania.

McCord, Beth K. and Donald R. Cochran 2008 "The Adena Complex: Identity and Context in East-Central Indiana." In *Transitions: Archaic and Early Woodland Research in the Ohio Country*, edited by M.P. Otto and B.G. Redmond, pp. 334–59. Athens: Ohio University Press.

McDowell, A.G. 1999 *Village Life in Ancient Egypt: Laundry Lists and Love Songs*. Oxford: Oxford University Press.

McElrath, Dale L., Thomas E. Emerson, Andrew C. Fortier and James L. Phillips 1984 "Late Archaic Period." In *American Bottom Archaeology: A Summary of the FAI-270 Project. Contributions to the Culture History of the Mississippi River Valley*, edited by C.J. Bareis and J.W. Porter, pp. 34–58. Urbana: University of Illinois.

McElrath, Dale L. and Andrew C. Fortier 2000 "The Early Late Woodland Occupation of the American Bottom." In *Late Woodland Societies: Tradition and Transformation across the Midcontinent*, edited by T.E. Emerson, D.L. McElrath and A.C. Fortier, pp. 92–121. Lincoln: University of Nebraska Press.

McElrath, Dale L., Andrew C. Fortier, Brad Koldehoff and Thomes E. Emerson 2009 "The American Bottom: An Archaic Cultural Crossroads." In *Archaic Societies: Diversity and Complexity across the Midcontinent*, edited by T.E. Emerson, D.L. McElrath and A.C. Fortier, pp. 317–75. Lincoln: University of Nebraska.

McEwan, Gordon F. 2006 *The Incas: New Perspectives*. New York: W.W. Norton & Company.

McIntosh, Jane R. 2002 *A Peaceful Realm: The Rise and Fall of the Indus Civilization*. Cambridge: Westview Press.

——— 2008 *The Ancient Indus Valley: New Perspectives*. Santa Barbara: ABC/Clio.

McIntosh, Roderick 1998 "Riddle of Great Zimbabwe." *Archaeology* 51.4: 44–49.

Meadow, Richard H. 1984 "Animal Domestication in the Middle East: A View from the Eastern Margin." In *Animals and Archaeology 3. Early Herders and their Flocks*, edited by J. Clutton-Brock and C. Grigson, pp. 309–37. Oxford: British Archaeological Reports.

Meddens, Frank and Nicholas Branch 2010 "The Wari State, Its Use of Ancestors, Rural Hinterland, and Agricultural Infrastructure." In *Beyond Wari Walls: Regional Perspectives on Middle Horizon Peru*, edited by J. Jennings, pp. 155–70. Albuquerque: New Mexico Press.

Mee, C.B. 1998 "Anatolia and the Aegean in the Late Bronze Age." In *The Aegean and the Orient in the Second Millennium: Proceedings of the 50th Anniversary Symposium, Cincinnati, 18–20 April 1997*, edited by E.H. Cline and D. Harris-Cline, pp. 137–48. Aegaeum 18. Liège: Université de Liège.

Mee, C.B. and W.G. Cavanagh 1984 "Mycenaean Tombs as Evidence for Social and Political Organization." *Oxford Journal of Archaeology* 3.3: 45–64.

Mehrer, Mark W. 1995 *Cahokia's Countryside: Household Archaeology, Settlement Patterns, and Social Power*. DeKalb: Northern Illinois University.

Meskell, Lynn 1999 "Archaeologies of Life and Death." *American Journal of Archaeology* 103: 181–99.

Michalowski, Piotr 2008 "The Mortal Kings of Ur: A Short Century of Divine Rule in Ancient Mesopotamia." In *Religion and Power: Divine Kingship in the Ancient World and Beyond*, edited by N. Brisch, pp. 33–45. Chicago: University of Chicago.

Midant-Reynes, Béatrix 2000 *The Prehistory of Egypt: From the First Egyptians to the First Pharaohs*. Translated by I. Shaw. Oxford: Blackwell Publishers Ltd.

Miksic, John N. 2003 "The Beginning of Trade in Ancient Southeast Asia: The Role of Oc Eo and the Lower Mekong Delta." In *Art and Archaeology of Fu Nan: Pre-Khmer Kingdom of the Lower Mekong Valley*, edited by J.C.M. Khoo, pp. 1–33. Bangkok: Orchid Press.

Militello, Pietro 2007 "Textile Industry and Minoan Palaces." In *Ancient Textiles: Production, Craft and Society*, edited by C. Gillis and M.-L.B. Nosch, pp. 36–45. Oxford: Oxbow Books.

Miller, George R. and Richard L. Burger 1995 "Our Father the Cayman, Our Dinner the Llama: Animal Utilization at Chavín de Huántar, Peru." *American Antiquity* 60.3: 421–58.

Miller, Heather M.-L. 2007 "Associations and Ideologies in the Locations of Urban Craft Production at Harappa, Pakistan (Indus Civilization)." In *Rethinking Craft Specialization in Complex Societies: Archaeological Analyses of the Social Meaning of Production*, edited by Z.X. Hruby and R.K. Flad, pp. 37–51. Archeological Papers of the American Anthropological Association, No. 17. Arlington: American Anthropological Association.

Miller, Mary 2001 "The Maya Ballgame: Rebirth in the Court of Life and Death." In *The Sport of Life and Death: The Mesoamerican Ballgame*, edited by E.M. Whittington, pp. 78–87. Charlotte: The Mint Museum of Art.

Miller, Mary and Marco Samayoa 1998 "Where Maize May Grow: Jade, Chacmools, and the Maize God." *RES: Anthropology and Aesthetics* 33: 54–72.

Millon, René 1970 "Teotihuacán: Completion of Map of Giant Ancient City in the Valley of Mexico." *Science* 170: 1077–82.

——— 1981 "Teotihuacan: City, State, and Civilization." In *Supplement to the Handbook of Middle American Indians. Vol. 1. Archaeology*, edited by J.A. Sabloff, pp. 198–243. Austin: University of Texas Press.

——— 1988 "The Last Years of Teotihuacan Dominance." In *The Collapse of Ancient States and Civilizations*, edited by N. Yoffee and G.L. Cowgill, pp. 102–64. Tucson: University of Arizona Press.

Mills, Barbara J. 2002 "Recent Research on Chaco: Changing Views on Economy, Ritual, and Society." *Journal of Archaeological Research* 10.1: 65–117.

——— 2004 "Key Debates in Chacoan Archaeology." In *In Search of Chaco: New Approaches to an Archaeological Enigma*, edited by D.G. Noble, pp. 123–30. Santa Fe: School of American Research Press.

——— 2012 "The Archaeology of the Greater Southwest: Migration, Inequality, and Religious Transformations." In *The Oxford Handbook of North American Archaeology*, edited by T.R. Pauketat, pp. 547–60. Oxford: Oxford University Press.

——— 2015 "Unpacking the House: Ritual Practice and Social Networks at Chaco." In *Chaco Revisited: New Research on the Prehistory of Chaco Canyon, New Mexico*, edited by C.C. Heitman and S. Plog, pp. 249–71. Tucson: University of Arizona Press.

Milner, George R. 1991 "American Bottom Mississippian Culture: Internal Developments and External Relations." In *New Perspectives on Cahokia: Views from the Periphery*, edited by J.B. Stoltman, pp. 29–47. Monographs in World Archaeology, No. 2. Madison: Prehistory Press.

——— 1998 *The Cahokia Chiefdom: The Archaeology of a Mississippian Society*. Washington: Smithsonian Institution.

——— 1999 "Warfare in Prehistoric and Early Historic Eastern North America." *Journal of Archaeological Research* 7: 105–51.

——— 2004 *The Moundbuilders: Ancient Peoples of Eastern North America*. London: Thames and Hudson.

Molloy, Barry P.C. 2012 "Martial Minoans? War as Social Process, Practice and Event in Bronze Age Greece." *Annual of the British School at Athens* 107: 87–142.

Monroe, Christopher M. 2009 *Scales of Fate: Trade, Tradition, and Transformation in the Eastern Mediterranean ca. 1350–1175 BCE*. Münster: Ugarit-Verlag.

——— 2010 "Sunk Costs at Late Bronze Age Uluburun." *Bulletin of the American Schools of Oriental Research* 357: 19–33.

Moore, A.M.T. 1991 "Abu Hureyra I and the Antecedents of Agriculture on the Middle Euphrates." In *The Natufian Culture in the Levant*, edited by O. Bar-Yosef and F.R. Valla, pp. 277–94. Ann Arbor: International Monographs in Prehistory.

Moore, Elizabeth 1988 *Moated Sites in Early North East Thailand*. BAR International Series 400. Oxford: BAR International.

——— 1997 "Circular Sites at Angkor: A Radar Scattering Model." *Journal of the Siam Society* 85: 107–19.

Moore, Jerry D. 1988 "Prehistoric Raised Field Agriculture in the Casma Valley, Peru." *Journal of Field Archaeology* 15.3: 265–76.

——— 1996 *Architecture and Power in the Ancient Andes: The Archaeology of Public Buildings*. Cambridge: Cambridge University Press.

——— 2004 "The Social Basis of Sacred Spaces in the Prehispanic Andes: Ritual Landscapes of the Dead in Chimú and Inka Societies." *Journal of Archaeological Method and Theory* 11.1: 83–124.

——— 2014 *A Prehistory of South America: Ancient Cultural Diversity on the Least Known Continent*. Boulder: University Press of Colorado.

——— 2015 "Inca Sacred Space: Landscape, Site and Symbol in the Andes." *Journal of Historical Geography* 49: 110–11.

Moore, Jerry D. and Carol J. Mackey 2008 "The Chimú Empire." In *Handbook of South American Archaeology*, edited by H. Silverman and W.H. Isbell, pp. 783–807. New York: Springer.

Moorey, P.R.S. 1977 "What Do We Know about the People Buried in the Royal Cemetery?" *Expedition* 20: 24–40.

Moran, William L. 2000 *The Amarna Letters*. Baltimore: Johns Hopkins University Press.

Morenz, Ludwig D. and Lutz Popko 2010 "The Second Intermediate Period and the New Kingdom." In *A Companion to Ancient Egypt*, edited by A.B. Lloyd, pp. 101–19. Oxford: Blackwell Publishing Ltd.

Morris, Craig and Adriana von Hagen 2011 *The Incas: Lords of the Four Quarters*. London: Thames & Hudson.

Morris, Ian 1987 *Burial and Ancient Society: The Rise of the Greek City-State*. Cambridge: Cambridge University Press.

——— 1992 *Death-Ritual and Social Structure in Classical Antiquity*. Cambridge: Cambridge University Press.

——— 1997 "Homer and the Iron Age." In *A New Companion to Homer*, edited by I. Morris and B. Powell, pp. 534–59. Leiden: Brill.

——— 2008 "The Greater Athenian State." In *The Dynamics of Ancient Empires*, edited by I. Morris and W. Scheidel, pp. 99–177. New York: Oxford University Press.

Morse, Dan F. 1997 *A Paleoindian Dalton Cemetery in Arkansas*. Washington: Smithsonian Institution Press.

Moseley, Michael E. 1975 *The Maritime Foundations of Andean Civilization*. Menlo Park: Cummings Publishing.

——— 2001 *The Incas and Their Ancestors: The Archaeology of Peru*. Revised edition. London: Thames and Hudson.

Moseley, Michael E. and Robert A. Feldman 1988 "Fishing, Farming, and the Foundations of Andean Civilisation." In *The Archaeology of Prehistoric Coastlines*, edited by G. Bailey and J. Parkington, pp. 125–34. Cambridge: Cambridge University Press.

Moulherat, Christophe, Margareta Tengberg, Jérôme-F. Haquet and Benoît Mille 2002 "First Evidence of Cotton at Neolithic Mehrgarh, Pakistan: Analysis of Mineralized Fibres from a Copper Bead." *Journal of Archaeological Science* 29: 1393–1401.

Mughal, M. Rafique 1990 "The Harappan 'Twin Capitals' and Reality." *Journal of Central Asia* 13.1: 155–62.

Muller, Jon 1997 *Mississippian Political Economy*. New York: Plenum Press.

Mumford, Gregory D. 2010 "Settlements—Distribution, Structure, Architecture: Pharaonic." In *A Companion to Ancient Egypt*, edited by A.B. Lloyd, pp. 326–49. Oxford: Blackwell Publishing Ltd.

Munn, Nancy D. 1986 *The Fame of Gawa*. Durham: Duke University Press.

Munoz, Samuel E., Sissel Schroeder, David A. Fike and John W. Williams 2014 "A Record of Sustained Prehistoric and Historic Land Use from the Cahokia Region, Illinois, USA." *Geology* 42: 499–502.

Murnane, William J. 1977 *Ancient Egyptian Coregencies*. Chicago: University of Chicago Press.

——— 2012 *The Ancient Egypt Guide*. Third Edition, revised by Aidan Dodson. Northhampton: Interlink Books.

Murray, Carrie 2011 "Constructions of Authority through Ritual: Considering Transformation in Ritual Space as Reflecting Society in Iron Age Etruria." In *State Formation in Italy and Greece: Questioning the Neoevolutionist Paradigm*, edited by N. Terrenato and D.C. Haggis, pp. 199–216. Oxford: Oxbow Books.

Nafplioti, Argyrio 2009 "Mycenae Revisited Part 2. Exploring the Local versus Non-local Geographical Origin of the Individuals from Grave Circle A: Evidence from Strontium Isotope Ratio (87Sr/86Sr) Analysis." *Annual of the British School at Athens* 104: 279–91.

Nagy, Gregory 1997 "The Shield of Achilles: Ends of the *Iliad* and Beginnings of the Polis." In *New Light on a Dark Age: Exploring the Culture of Geometric Greece*, edited by S. Langdon, pp. 194–207. Columbia: University of Missouri Press.

Nair, Stella and Jan-Pierre Protzen 2015 "The Inka Built Environment." In *The Inka Empire: A Multidisciplinary Approach*, edited by I. Shimada, pp. 215–31. Austin: University of Texas Press.

Nakassis, Dimitri 2012 "Prestige and Interest: Feasting and the King at Mycenaean Pylos." *Hesperia* 81: 1–30.

Nakassis, Dimitri, Michael L. Galaty and William A. Parkinson 2010 "State and Society." In *The Oxford Handbook of the Bronze Age Aegean (ca. 3000–1000 BC)*, edited by E.H. Cline, pp. 239–50. Oxford: Oxford University Press.

Nash, Donna J. 2009 "Household Archaeology in the Andes." *Journal of Archaeological Research* 17: 205–61.

Ndoro, Webber 2005 "Great Zimbabwe." *Scientific American* 15.1: 74–79.

Neils, Jenifer 2001 *The Parthenon Frieze.* Cambridge: Cambridge University Press.

Neitzel, Jill E., ed. 1999 *Great Towns and Regional Polities in the Prehistoric American Southwest and Southeast.* Albuquerque: University of New Mexico Press.

Neitzel, Jill E. 2007 "Architectural Studies of Pueblo Bonito: The Past, the Present, and the Future." *The Architecture of Chaco Canyon, New Mexico*, edited by S.H. Lekson, pp. 127–54. Salt Lake City: University of Utah Press.

——— 2010 "Landscapes of Complexity in the U.S. Southwest: The Hohokam, Chacoans, and Peer Polity Interaction." In *Ancient Complexities: New Perspectives in Precolumbian North America*, edited by S.M. Alt, pp. 153–76. Salt Lake City: University of Utah Press.

Nelson, Sarah M. 2003 "Feasting the Ancestors in Early China." In *The Archaeology and Politics of Food and Feasting in Early States and Empires*, edited by T.L. Bray, pp. 65–89. New York: Kluwer Academic/Plenum Publishers.

Nichols, Deborah L. and Christopher A. Pool 2012 "Mesoamerican Archaeology: Recent Trends." In *The Oxford Handbook of Mesoamerican Archaeology*, edited by D.L. Nichols and C.A. Pool, pp. 1–28. Oxford: Oxford University Press.

Niemeier, Wolf-Dietrich 1991 "Minoan Artisans Travelling Overseas: The Alalakh Frescoes and the Painted Plaster Floor at Tel Kabri (Western Galilee)." In *Thalassa: L'Égée préhistorique et la mer*, edited by R. Laffineur and L. Basch, pp. 189–201. Aegaeum 7. Liège: Université de Liège.

Niles, Susan A. 2015 "Considering Inka Royal Estates: Architecture, Economy, History." In *The Inka Empire: A Multidisciplinary Approach*, edited by I. Shimada, pp. 233–46. Austin: University of Texas Press.

Nissen, Hans J. 1985 "The Emergence of Writing in the Ancient Near East." *Interdisciplinary Science Reviews* 10: 349–61.

——— 1995 "Kulturelle und politische Vernetzungen im vorderen Orient des 4. und 3. vorchristlichen Jahrtausends." In *Beiträge zur Kulturgeschichte Vorderasiens*, edited by U. Finkbeiner, R. Dittmann and H. Hauptmann, pp. 473–90. Mainz: Verlag Philipp von Zabern.

——— 2002 "Uruk: Key Site of the Period and Key Site of the Problem." In *Artefacts of Complexity: Tracking the Uruk in the Near East*, edited by J.N. Postgate, pp. 1–16. Warminster: British School of Archaeology in Iraq.

Noreña, Carlos F. 2010 "The Early Imperial Monarchy." In *The Oxford Handbook of Roman Studies*, edited by A. Barchiesi and W. Scheidel, pp. 533–46. Oxford: Oxford University Press.

Nu, He 2013 "The Longshan Period Site of Taosi in Southern Shanxi Province." In *A Companion to Chinese Archaeology*, edited by A.P. Underhill, pp. 255–77. West Sussex: Wiley-Blackwell.

Nylander, Carl 1979 "Achaemenid Imperial Art." In *Power and Propaganda. A Symposium on Ancient Empires*, edited by M.T. Larsen, pp. 345–59. Copenhagen: Akademisk Forlag.

O'Brien, Patricia J. 1989 "Cahokia: The Political Capital of the 'Ramey' State?" *North American Archaeologist* 25: 188–97.

——— 1991 "Early State Economics: Cahokia, Capital of the Ramey State." In *Early State Economics*, edited by H.J.M. Claessen and P. van de Velde, pp. 143–75. Brunswick: Transaction Publishers.

O'Connor, David 2002 "Context, Function and Program: Understanding Ceremonial Slate Palettes." *Journal of the American Research Center in Egypt* 39: 5–25.

O'Reilly, Dougald J.W. 2007 *Early Civilizations of Southeast Asia.* Lanham: AltaMira Press.

Oakley, John H. 2000 "Some 'Other' Members of the Athenian Household: Maids and their Mistresses in Fifth-Century Athenian Art." In *Not the Classical Ideal: Athens and the Construction of the Other in Greek Art*, edited by B. Cohen, pp. 227–47. Leiden: Brill.

Oates, Joan 1960 "Ur and Eridu, the Prehistory." *Iraq* 22: 32–50.

——— 1983 "Ubaid Mesopotamia Reconsidered." In *The Hilly Flanks and Beyond*, edited by T.C. Young, Jr., P.E.L. Smith and P. Mortensen, pp. 251–81. Chicago: Oriental Institute.

Oates, Joan and David Oates 2001 *Nimrud: An Assyrian Imperial City Revealed.* London: British School of Archaeology in Iraq.

Olsen, Barbara 1998 "Women, Children and the Family in the Late Aegean Bronze Age: Differences in Minoan and Mycenaean Constructions of Gender." *World Archaeology* 29: 380–92.

Oppenheim, A. Leo 1954 "The Seafaring Merchants of Ur." *Journal of the American Oriental Society* 74: 6–17.
Orlin, Eric M. 2002 *Temples, Religion, and Politics in the Roman Republic*. Boston: Brill.
Ortíz C., Ponciano and María del Carmen Rodríguez 1999 "Olmec Ritual Behavior at El Manatí: A Sacred Space." In *Social Patterns in Pre-Classic Mesoamerica*, edited by D.C. Grove and R.A. Joyce, pp. 225–54. Washington: Dumbarton Oaks Research Library and Collection.
Osborne, Robin 1988 "Death Revisited; Death Revised: The Death of the Artist in Archaic and Classical Greece." *Art History* 11: 1–16.
——— 1996 *Greece in the Making, 1200–479 B.C.* London: Routledge.
——— 2000 "An Other View: An Essay in Political History." In *Not the Classical Ideal: Athens and the Construction of the Other in Greek Art*, edited by B. Cohen, pp. 23–42. Leiden: Brill.
——— 2001 "Why did Athenian Pots Appeal to the Etruscans?" *World Archaeology* 33: 277–95.
Pacheco, Paul J. and William Dancey 2006 "Integrating Mortuary and Settlement Data on Ohio Hopewell Society." In *Recreating Hopewell: New Perspectives on Middle Woodland in Eastern North America*, edited by D.K. Charles and J.E. Buikstra, pp. 3–25. Gainesville: University Press of Florida.
Palaima, Thomas G. 1987 "Preliminary Comparative Textual Evidence for Palatial Control of Economic Activity in Minoan and Mycenaean Crete." In *The Function of the Minoan Palaces*, edited by R. Hägg and N. Marinatos, pp. 301–6. Stockholm: Paul Aströms Förlag.
——— 1995 "The Nature of the Mycenaean Wanax: Non-Indo-European Origins and Priestly Functions." In *The Role of the Ruler in the Prehistoric Aegean*, edited by P. Rehak, pp. 119–39. Aegaeum 11. Liège: Université de Liège.
——— 2010 "Linear B." In *The Oxford Handbook of the Bronze Age Aegean (ca. 3000–1000 BC)*, edited by E.H. Cline, pp. 356–72. Oxford: Oxford University Press.
Palmer, Ruth 1995 "Linear A Commodities: A Comparison of Resources." In *Politeia: Society and State in the Aegean Bronze Age*, edited by R. Laffineur and W.-D. Niemeier, pp. 133–54. Aegaeum 12. Liège: Université de Liège.
Parkinson, William A. 1999 "Chipping Away at a Mycenaean Economy: Obsidian Exchange, Linear B, and Palatial Control in Late Bronze Age Messenia." In *Rethinking Mycenaean Palaces: New Interpretations of an Old Idea*, edited by M.L. Galaty and W.A. Parkinson, pp. 73–85. Los Angeles: Cotsen Institute of Archaeology, UCLA.
Parkinson, William A., ed. 2002 *The Archaeology of Tribal Societies*. Ann Arbor: International Monographs in Prehistory.
Parpola, Asko 1984 "New Correspondences between Harappan and Near Eastern Glyptic Art." In *South Asian Archaeology, 1981*, edited by B. Allchin, pp. 176–95. Cambridge: Cambridge University Press.
Parsons, Jeffrey R. and Yoko Sugiura Y. 2012 "Teotihuacan and the Epiclassic in Central Mexico." In *The Oxford Handbook of Mesoamerican Archaeology*, edited by D.L. Nichols and C.A. Pool, pp. 309–23. Oxford: Oxford University Press.
Pauketat, Timothy R. 1994 *The Ascent of Chiefs: Cahokia and Mississippian Politics in Native North America*. Tuscaloosa: University of Alabama Press.
——— 1997 "Cahokian Political Economy." In *Cahokia: Domination and Ideology in the Mississippian World*, edited by T.R. Pauketat and T.E. Emerson, pp. 30–51. Lincoln: University of Nebraska Press.
——— 1998 "Refiguring the Archaeology of Greater Cahokia." *Journal of Archaeological Research* 6: 45–89.
——— 2000 "The Tragedy of the Commoners." In *Agency in Archaeology*, edited by M.-A. Dobres and J.E. Robb, pp. 113–29. London: Routledge.
——— 2002 "A Fourth-Generation Synthesis of Cahokia and Mississippianization." *Midcontinental Journal of Archaeology* 27: 149–70.
——— 2004 *Ancient Cahokia and the Mississippians*. Cambridge: Cambridge University Press.
——— 2007 *Chiefdoms and Other Archaeological Delusions*. Lanham: AltaMira Press.
——— 2013 *An Archaeology of the Cosmos: Rethinking Agency and Religion in Ancient America*. London: Routledge.
Pauketat, Timothy R. and Thomas E. Emerson 1991 "The Ideology of Authority and the Power of the Pot." *American Anthropologist* 93: 919–41.
——— 1997 "Reflections from the Countryside on Cahokian Hegemony." In *Cahokia: Ideology and Domination in the Mississippian World*, edited by T. Pauketat and T. Emerson, pp. 167–89. Lincoln: University of Nebraska Press.
Pauketat, Timothy R., Andrew C. Fortier, Susan M. Alt, and Thomas E. Emerson 2013 "A Mississippian Conflagration at East St. Louis and its Political-Historical Implications." *Journal of Field Archaeology* 38.3: 210–26.

Pauketat, Timothy R., Lucretia S. Kelly, Gayle J. Fritz, Neal H. Lopinot, Scott Elias, and Eve Hargrave 2002 "The Residues of Feasting and Public Ritual at Early Cahokia." *American Antiquity* 67.2: 257–79.

Payne, Claudine 2006 "The Foundations of Leadership in Mississippian Chiefdoms: Perspectives from Lake Jackson and Upper Nodena." In *Leadership and Polity in Mississippian Society*, edited by B.M. Butler and P.D. Welch, pp. 91–111. Center for Archaeological Investigations Occasional Paper No. 33. Carbondale: Southern Illinois University Press.

Pearsall, Deborah M. 2008 "Plant Domestication and the Shift to Agriculture in the Andes." In *Handbook of South American Archaeology*, edited by H. Silverman and W.H. Isbell, pp. 105–20. New York: Springer.

Peatfield, Alan 1992 "Rural Ritual in Bronze Age Crete: The Peak Sanctuary at Atsipadhes." *Cambridge Archaeological Journal* 2: 59–87.

Pedley, John Griffiths 1998 *Greek Art and Archaeology*. Second edition. Upper Saddle River: Prentice Hall.

Pelly, David F. 2001 *The Sacred Hunt*. Seattle: University of Washington.

Peña, J. Theodore 2011 "State Formation in Southern Coastal Etruria: An Application of the Kipp-Schortman Model." In *State Formation in Italy and Greece: Questioning the Neoevolutionist Paradigm*, edited by N. Terrenato and D.C. Haggis, pp. 179–98. Oxford: Oxbow Books.

Peregrine, Peter 1992 *Mississippian Evolution: A World-System Perspective*. Monographs in World Archaeology, No. 9. Madison: Prehistory Press.

——— 1995 "Networks of Power: The Mississippian World-System." In *Native American Interactions: Multiscalar Analyses and Interpretations in the Eastern Woodlands*, edited by M. Nassaney and K. Sassaman, pp. 247–65. Knoxville: University of Tennessee Press.

Perlès, Catherine 2001 *The Early Neolithic in Greece: The First Farming Communities in Europe*. Cambridge: Cambridge University Press.

Peters, Joris and Klaus Schmidt 2004 "Animals in the Symbolic World of Pre-Pottery Neolithic Göbekli Tepe, South-Eastern Turkey: A Preliminary Assessment." *Anthropozoologica* 39.1: 179–218.

Peterson, Christian E. and Gideon Shelach 2012 "Jiangzhai: Social and Economic Organization of a Middle Neolithic Chinese Village." *Journal of Anthropological Archaeology* 31: 265–301.

Pfaffenberger, Bryan 1988 "Fetishised Objects and Humanised Nature: Towards an Anthropology of Technology." *Man* N.S. 23: 236–52.

Pikirayi, Innocent 2001 *The Zimbabwe Culture: Origins and Decline of Southern Zambezian States*. Walnut Creek: AltaMira Press.

Pikirayi, Innocent and Shadreck Chirikure 2011 "Debating Great Zimbabwe." *Azania: Archaeological Research in Africa* 46.2: 221–31.

Piperno, Dolores and Bruce D. Smith 2012 "The Origins of Food Production in Mesoamerica." In *The Oxford Handbook of Mesoamerican Archaeology*, edited by D.L. Nichols and C.A. Pool, pp. 151–64. Oxford: Oxford University Press.

Platon, Lefteris 2010 "Kato Zakros." In *The Oxford Handbook of the Bronze Age Aegean (ca. 3000–1000 BC)*, edited by E.H. Cline, pp. 509–17. Oxford: Oxford University Press.

Plog, Stephen 2015 "Understanding Chaco: Past, Present, and Future." In *Chaco Revisited: New Research on the Prehistory of Chaco Canyon, New Mexico*, edited by C.C. Heitman and S. Plog, pp. 3–29. Tucson: University of Arizona Press.

Plog, Stephen and Carrie Heitman 2010 "Hierarchy and Social Inequality in the American Southwest, A.D. 800–1200." *Proceedings of the National Academy of Sciences* 107.48: 19619–26.

Pohl, Mary E.D. and John M.D. Pohl 1994 "Cycles of Conflict: Political Factionalism in the Maya Lowlands." In *Factional Competition and Political Development in the New World*, edited by E.M. Brumfiel and J.W. Fox, pp. 138–57. Cambridge: Cambridge University Press.

Pollini, John 1993 "The Gemma Augustea. Ideology, Rhetorical Imagery, and the Creation of a Dynastic Narrative." In *Narrative and Event in Ancient Art*, edited by P.J. Holliday, pp. 258–98. Cambridge: Cambridge University Press.

Pollock, Susan 1991 "Of Priestesses, Princes and Poor Relations: The Dead in the Royal Cemetery of Ur." *Cambridge Archaeological Journal* 1: 71–89.

——— 1999 *Ancient Mesopotamia: The Eden That Never Was*. Cambridge: Cambridge University Press.

——— 2007 "The Royal Cemetery of Ur: Ritual, Tradition, and the Creation of Subjects." In *Representations of Political Power: Case Histories from Times of Change and Dissolving Order in the Ancient Near East*, edited by M. Heinz and M.H. Feldman, pp. 89–110. Winona Lake: Eisenbrauns.

Pool, Christopher A. 2009 "Asking More and Better Questions: Olmec Archaeology for the Next Katun." *Ancient Mesoamerica* 20: 241–52.
——— 2012 "The Formation of Complex Societies in Mesoamerica." In *The Oxford Handbook of Mesoamerican Archaeology*, edited by D.L. Nichols and C.A. Pool, pp. 169–87. Oxford: Oxford University Press.
Possehl, Gregory L. 1990 "Revolution in the Urban Revolution: The Emergence of Indus Urbanization." *Annual Review of Anthropology* 19: 261–82.
——— 1998 "Sociocultural Complexity without the State: The Indus Civilization." In *Archaic States*, edited by G.M. Feinman and J. Marcus, pp. 261–91. Santa Fe: School of American Research Press.
——— 2002 *The Indus Civilization: A Contemporary Perspective*. Walnut Creek: AltaMira Press.
——— 2005 "Mohenjo-Daro: The Symbolic Landscape of an Ancient City." In *Structure and Meaning in Human Settlements*, edited by T. Atkin and J. Rykwert, pp. 67–84. Philadelphia: University of Pennsylvania Museum of Archaeology and Anthropology.
Powell, Barry B. 1997a "From Picture to Myth, from Myth to Picture: Prolegomena to the Invention of Mythic Representation." In *New Light on a Dark Age: Exploring the Culture of Geometric Greece*, edited by S. Langdon, pp. 154–93. Columbia: University of Missouri Press.
——— 1997b "Homer and Writing." In *A New Companion to Homer*, edited by I. Morris and B. Powell, pp. 3–32. Leiden: Brill.
Powis, Terry G., et al. 2002 "Spouted Vessels and Cacao Use among the Preclassic Maya." *Latin American Antiquity* 13: 85–106.
Pozorski, Shelia and Thomas Pozorski 2008 "Early Cultural Complexity on the Coast of Peru." In *Handbook of South American Archaeology*, edited by H. Silverman and W.H. Isbell, pp. 607–31. New York: Springer.
Pozorski, Thomas and Shelia Pozorski 2005 "Architecture and Chronology at the Site of Sechín Alto, Casma Valley, Peru." *Journal of Field Archaeology* 30.2: 143–61.
Preziosi, Donald and Louise A. Hitchcock 1999 *Aegean Art and Architecture*. Oxford: Oxford University Press.
Price, Simon 1987 "From Noble Funerals to Divine Cult: The Consecration of Roman Emperors." In *Rituals of Royalty: Power and Ceremonial in Traditional Societies*, edited by D. Cannadine and S. Price, pp. 56–105. Cambridge: Cambridge University Press.
Pringle, Heather 2014 "Untouched." *National Geographic* 225.6: 54–77.
Proulx, Donald A. 2001 "The Ritual Use of Trophy Heads in Ancient Nasca Society." In *Ritual Sacrifice in Ancient Peru*, edited by E.P. Benson and A.G. Cook, pp. 119–36. Austin: University of Texas Press.
——— 2006 *A Sourcebook of Nasca Ceramic Iconography*. Iowa City: University of Iowa Press.
——— 2008 "Paracas and Nasca: Regional Cultures on the South Coast of Peru." In *Handbook of South American Archaeology*, edited by H. Silverman and W.H. Isbell, pp. 563–85. New York: Springer.
Pullen, Daniel J. 2011 "Before the Palaces: Redistribution and Chiefdoms in Mainland Greece." *American Journal of Archaeology* 115: 185–95.
Purcell, Nicholas 2010 "Urbanism." In *The Oxford Handbook of Roman Studies*, edited by A. Barchiesi and W. Scheidel, pp. 579–93. Oxford: Oxford University Press.
Pwiti, Gilbert 2004 "Economic Change, Ideology and the Development of Cultural Complexity in Northern Zimbabwe." *Azania: Archaeological Research in Africa* 39.1: 265–82.
Quilter, Jeffrey 2002 "Moche Politics, Religion, and Warfare." *Journal of World Prehistory* 16.2: 145–95.
——— 2014 *The Ancient Central Andes*. London: Routledge.
Quirke, Stephen 1991 "Royal Power in the 13th Dynasty." In *Middle Kingdom Studies*, edited by S. Quirke, pp. 123–39. New Malden: SIA Publishing.
Rabett, Ryan and Graeme Barker 2010 "Late Pleistocene and Early Holocene Forager Mobility in Southeast Asia." In *50 Years of Archaeology in Southeast Asia: Essays in Honour of Ian Glover*, edited by B. Bellina, E.A. Bacus, T.O. Pryce, and J.W. Christie, pp. 67–77. Bangkok: River Books.
Rafferty, Sean M. 2006 "Evidence of Early Tobacco in Northeastern North America?" *Journal of Archaeological Science* 33.4: 453–58.
——— 2008 "Smoking Pipes and Early Woodland Mortuary Ritual." In *Transitions: Archaic and Early Woodland Research in the Ohio Country*, edited by M.P. Otto and B.G. Redmond, pp. 271–83. Athens: Ohio University Press.
Ramage, Nancy H. and Andrew Ramage 1996 *Roman Art: Romulus to Constantine*. Englewood Cliff: Prentice Hall.
Rao, S.R. 1973 *Lothal and the Indus Civilization*. London: Asia Publishing House.

Rathje, William L., David A. Gregory and Frederick M. Wiseman 1978 "Trade Models and Archaeological Problems: Classic Maya Examples." In *Mesoamerican Communication Routes and Cultural Contacts*, edited by T.A. Lee, Jr. and C. Navarrete, pp. 147–75. Provo: Brigham Young University.

Ratnagar, Shereen 1981 *Encounters, the Westerly Trade of the Harappan Civilization*. Delhi: Oxford University Press.

——— 2001 *Understanding Harappa: Civilization in the Greater Indus Valley*. New Delhi: Tulika.

——— 2004 *Trading Encounters: From the Euphrates to the Indus in the Bronze Age*. Oxford: Oxford University Press.

Rautman, Alison E. 2013 "Social Integration and the Built Environment of Aggregated Communities in the North American Puebloan Southwest." In *From Prehistoric Villages to Cities: Settlement Aggregation and Community Transformation*, edited by J. Birch, pp. 111–33. London: Routledge.

Rawson, Beryl 2010 "Family and Society." In *The Oxford Handbook of Roman Studies*, edited by A. Barchiesi and W. Scheidel, pp. 610–23. Oxford: Oxford University Press.

Raymond, J. Scott 2008 "The Process of Sedentism in Northwestern South America." In *Handbook of South American Archaeology*, edited by H. Silverman and W.H. Isbell, pp. 79–90. New York: Springer.

Reade, J.E. 1978 "Kassites and Assyrians in Iran." *Iran* 16: 137–43.

——— 1979 "Ideology and Propaganda in Assyrian Art." In *Power and Propaganda: A Symposium on Ancient Empires*, edited by M.T. Larsen, pp. 329–43. Copenhagen: Akademisk Forlag.

Redhouse, D.I. and Simon Stoddart 2011 "Mapping Etruscan State Formation." In *State Formation in Italy and Greece: Questioning the Neoevolutionist Paradigm*, edited by N. Terrenato and D.C. Haggis, pp. 162–78. Oxford: Oxbow Books.

Redmond, Elsa M. and Charles S. Spencer 2012 "Chiefdoms at the Threshold: The Competitive Origins of the Primary State." *Journal of Anthropological Archaeology* 31: 22–37.

Rees, Roger 1993 "Images and Image: A Re-Examination of Tetrarchic Iconography." *Greece & Rome* Second Series 40: 181–200.

Reinhard, Johan 2005 *The Ice Maiden: Inca Mummies, Mountain Gods, and Sacred Sites in the Andes*. Washington: National Geographic.

Reinhard, Johan and Constanza Ceruti 2005 "Sacred Mountains, Ceremonial Sites, and Human Sacrifice among the Incas." *Archaeoastronomy* 19: 1–43.

Renfrew, Colin 1972 *The Emergence of Civilisation: The Cyclades and the Aegean in the 3rd Millennium B.C.* London: Methuen and Co. Ltd.

Reusser, Christoph 2002 *Vasen für Etrurien. Verbreitung und Funktionen attischer Keramik im Etrurien des 6. und 5. Jahrhunderts vor Christus*. Zürich: Akanthos.

Revell, Louise 2009 *Roman Imperialism and Local Identities*. Cambridge: Cambridge University Press.

Rice, Don S. 1993 "Eighth-Century Physical Geography, Environment, and Natural Resources in the Maya Lowlands." In *Lowland Maya Civilization in the Eighth Century A.D.: A Symposium at Dumbarton Oaks, 7th and 8th October 1989*, edited by J.A. Sabloff and J.S. Henderson, pp. 11–63. Washington: Dumbarton Oaks Research Library and Collection.

Rice, Prudence M. 1987 "Economic Change in the Lowland Maya Late Classic Period." In *Specialization, Exchange and Complex Societies*, edited by E.M. Brumfiel and T.K. Earle, pp. 76–85. Cambridge: Cambridge University Press.

Richards, Janet 2010 "Kingship and Legitimation." In *Egyptian Archaeology*, edited by W. Wendrich, pp. 55–84. West Sussex: Wiley-Blackwell.

Rick, John W. 2004 "The Evolution of Authority and Power at Chavín de Huántar, Peru." *Archaeological Papers of the American Anthropological Association* 14.1: 71–89.

——— 2008 "Context, Construction, and Ritual in the Development of Authority at Chavín de Huántar." In *Chavín: Art, Architecture and Culture*, edited by W. Conklin and J. Quilter, pp. 3–34. Los Angeles: Cotsen Institute of Archaeology.

——— 2013a "Architecture and Ritual Space at Chavín de Huántar." In *Chavín: Peru's Enigmatic Temple in the Andes*, edited by P. Fux, pp. 151–66. Zurich: Scheidegger and Spiess.

——— 2013b "Religion and Authority at Chavín de Huántar." In *Chavín: Peru's Enigmatic Temple in the Andes*, edited by P. Fux, pp. 167–76. Zurich: Scheidegger and Spiess.

Rick, John W., Christian Mesia, Daniel Contreras, Silvia R. Kembel, Rosa M. Rick, Matthew Sayre and John Wolf 2009 "La Cronología de Chavín de Huántar y sus Implicancias para el Periodo Formativo." *Boletín de Arqueología PUCP* 13: 87–132.

Ringle, William M. 2014 "Plazas and Patios of the Feathered Serpent." In *Mesoamerican Plazas: Arenas of Community and Power*, edited by K. Tsukamoto and T. Inomata, pp. 168–92. Tucson: University of Arizona Press.

Roaf, Michael 1974 "The Subject Peoples on the Base of the Statue of Darius." *Cahiers de la Délégation Archéologique Française en Iran* 4: 73–160.

——— 1984 "Ubaid Houses and Temples." *Sumer* 43: 80–90.

——— 1990 *Cultural Atlas of Ancient Mesopotamia*. New York: Facts on File.

Robins, Gay 1993 *Women in Ancient Egypt*. Cambridge: Harvard University Press.

Roller, Lynn E. 1999 *In Search of God the Mother: The Cult of Anatolian Cybele*. Berkeley: University of California Press.

Romain, William F. 2000 *Mysteries of the Hopewell: Astronomers, Geometers, and Magicians of the Eastern Woodlands*. Akron: University of Akron Press.

——— 2004 "Journey to the Center of the World: Astronomy, Geometry, and Cosmology of the Fort Ancient Enclosure." In *The Fort Ancient Earthworks: Prehistoric Lifeways of the Hopewell Culture in Southwestern Ohio*, edited by R. Connolly and B. Lepper, pp. 66–83. Columbus: Ohio Historical Society.

Romey, Kristin M. 2005 "Watery Tombs." *Archaeology* 58.4: 42–9.

Root, Margaret Cool 1979 *The King and Kingship in Achaemenid Art*. Leiden: Brill.

Roscoe, Paul 2000 "Costs, Benefits, Typologies, and Power: The Evolution of Political Hierarchy." In *Hierarchies in Action: Cui Bono?* edited by M.W. Diehl, pp. 113–33. Center for Archaeological Investigations Occasional Paper No. 27. Carbondale: Southern Illinois University.

Rose, Charles Brian 2010 "Iconography." In *The Oxford Handbook of Roman Studies*, edited by A. Barchiesi and W. Scheidel, pp. 49–76. Oxford: Oxford University Press.

Rowland, Ingrid 2008 "Marriage and Mortality in the Tetnies Sarcophagi." *Etruscan Studies* 11: 151–64.

Rowlands, Michael 1987 "Power and Moral Order in Precolonial West-Central Africa." In *Specialization, Exchange and Complex Societies*, edited by E.M. Brumfiel and T.K. Earle, pp. 52–63. Cambridge: Cambridge University Press.

Ruby, Bret J., Christopher Carr and Douglas K. Charles 2005 "Community Organizations in the Scioto, Mann, and Havana Hopewellian Regions: A Comparative Perspective." In *Gathering Hopewell: Society, Ritual, and Ritual Interaction*, edited by C. Carr and D.T. Case, pp. 119–76. New York: Springer.

Runnels, Curtis and Priscilla Murray 2001 *Greece before History: An Archaeological Companion and Guide*. Stanford: Stanford University Press.

Säflund, Gösta 1981 "Cretan and Theran Questions." In *Sanctuaries and Cults in the Aegean Bronze Age*, edited by R. Hägg and N. Marinatos, pp. 190–208. Stockholm: Paul Aströms Förlag.

Sahlins, Marshall D. 1958 *Social Stratification in Polynesia*. Seattle: University of Washington Press.

——— 1963 "Poor Man, Rich Man, Big-Man, Chief: Political Types in Melanesia and Polynesia." *Comparative Studies in Society and History* 5.3: 285–303.

——— 1985 *Islands in History*. Chicago: University of Chicago Press.

Sallnow, M.J. 1998 "Communitas Reconsidered: The Sociology of Andean Pilgrimage." In *Religion in Culture and Society*, edited by J.R. Bowen, pp. 182–200. Boston: Allyn and Bacon.

Sanders, William T. and David Webster 1988 "The Mesoamerican Urban Tradition." *American Anthropologist* 90: 521–46.

Sandweiss, Daniel H. 2009 "Early Fishing and Inland Monuments: Challenging the Maritime Foundations of Andean Civilization?" In *Andean Civilization: A Tribute to Michael E. Moseley*, edited by J. Marcus and P.R. Williams, pp. 39–54. Cotsen Institute of Archaeology Monograph 63. Los Angeles: Cotsen Institute of Archaeology.

Sandweiss, Daniel H. and James B. Richardson III 2008 "Central Andean Environments." In *Handbook of South American Archaeology*, edited by H. Silverman and W.H. Isbell, pp. 93–104. New York: Springer.

Sarcina, A. 1979 "The Private House at Mohenjo-Daro." In *South Asian Archaeology 1977*, edited by M. Taddei, pp. 433–62. Istituto Universitario Orientale, Seminario di Studi Asiatici, 6. Naples: Istituto Universitario Orientale.

Sassaman, Kenneth E. 2005 "Poverty Point as Structure, Event, Process." *Journal of Archaeological Methods and Theory* 12.4: 355–64.

——— 2010 *The Eastern Archaic, Historicized*. Lanham: AltaMira Press.

Saunders, Joe W. 2010 "Middle Archaic and Watson Brake." In *Archaeology of Louisiana*, edited by M.A. Rees, pp. 63–76. Baton Rouge: Louisiana State University Press.

Saunders, Joe, Thurman Allen, Dennis LaBlatt, Reca Jones, and David Griffing 2001 "An Assessment of the Antiquity of the Lower Jackson Mound." *Southeastern Archaeology* 20.1: 67–77.

Saunders, Joe W., Rolfe D. Mandel, C. Garth Sampson, Charles M. Allen, E. Thurman Allen, Daniel A. Bush, James K. Feathers, Kristen J. Gremillion, C.T. Hallmark, H. Edwin Jackson, Jay K. Johnson, Reca Jones, Roger T. Saucier, Gary L. Stringer and Malcolm F. Vidrine 2005 "Watson Brake, A Middle Archaic Mound Complex in Northeast Louisiana." *American Antiquity* 70.4: 631–68.

Schele, Linda 1986 "Architectural Development and Political History at Palenque." In *City-States of the Maya: Art and Architecture*, edited by E.P. Benson, pp. 110–37. Denver: Rocky Mountain Institute for Pre-Columbian Studies.

Schele, Linda and David Freidel 1990 *A Forest of Kings: The Untold Story of the Ancient Maya*. New York: William Morrow and Co., Inc.

Schele, Linda and Mary Ellen Miller 1986 *The Blood of Kings: Dynasty and Ritual in Maya Art*. New York: George Braziller, Inc.

Schilling, Timothy 2013 "The Chronology of Monks Mound." *Southeastern Archaeology* 32: 14–28.

Schmandt-Besserat, Denise 1992 *Before Writing*. Austin: University of Texas Press.

Schneider, Thomas 2010 "Foreigners in Egypt: Archaeological Evidence and Cultural Context." In *Egyptian Archaeology*, edited by W. Wendrich, pp. 143–63. West Sussex: Wiley-Blackwell.

Schoep, Ilse 2002 *The Administration of Neopalatial Crete: A Critical Assessment of the Linear A Tablets and Their Role in the Administrative Process*. Salamanca: Ediciones Universidad de Salamanca.

——— 2006 "Looking Beyond the First Palaces: Elites and the Agency of Power in EM III-MM II Crete." *American Journal of Archaeology* 110: 37–64.

Schwartz, Glenn M. 2005 "From Collapse to Regeneration." In *After Collapse: The Regeneration of Complex Societies*, edited by G.M. Schwartz and J.J. Nichols, pp. 3–17. Tucson: University of Arizona Press.

Sebastian, Lynne 1992 *The Chaco Anasazi: Sociopolitical Evolution in the Prehistoric Southwest*. Cambridge: Cambridge University Press.

——— 2006 "The Chaco Synthesis." In *The Archaeology of Chaco Canyon: An Eleventh-Century Pueblo Regional Center*, edited by S.H. Lekson, pp. 393–422. Santa Fe: School of American Research Press.

Seeman, Mark F. 1979 "The Hopewell Interaction Sphere: The Evidence of Inter-Regional Trade and Structural Complexity." *Indiana Historical Society, Prehistoric Research Series* 5: 237–438.

——— 1988 "Ohio Hopewell Trophy Skull Artifacts as Evidence for Competition in Middle Woodland Societies circa 50 B.C.-A.D. 350." *American Antiquity* 53: 565–77.

Service, Elman 1962 *Primitive Social Organization*. New York: Random House.

Shady Solis, Ruth 2006 "America's First City? The Case of Late Archaic Caral." In *Andean Archaeology III: North and South*, edited by W. Isbell and H. Silverman, pp. 28–66. New York: Springer.

Shady Solis, Ruth, Jonathan Haas and Winifred Creamer 2001 "Dating Caral, A Preceramic Site in the Supe Valley on the Central Coast of Peru." *Science* 292: 723–26.

Shaffer, Jim G. 1993 "Harappan Culture: A Reconsideration." In *Harappan Civilization: A Recent Perspective*, Second edition, edited by G.L. Possehl, pp. 41–50. New Delhi: American Institute of Indian Studies.

Shanks, Michael 1999 *Art and the Greek City State: An Interpretive Archaeology*. Cambridge: Cambridge University Press.

Shaw, Leslie 2012 "The Elusive Maya Marketplace: An Archaeological Consideration of the Evidence." *Journal of Archaeological Research* 20: 117–55.

Shaw, Maria C. 1995 "Bull Leaping Frescoes at Knossos and Their Influence on the Tell el-Dab'a Murals." In *Trade, Power and Cultural Exchange: Hyksos Egypt and the Eastern Mediterranean World 1800–1500 B.C.*, edited by M. Bietak, pp. 91–120. Ägypten und Levante 5. Wien: Österreichischen Akademie der Wissenschaften.

Shelton, Kim 2010 "Mainland Greece." In *The Oxford Handbook of the Bronze Age Aegean (ca. 3000–1000 BC)*, edited by E.H. Cline, pp. 139–48. Oxford: Oxford University Press.

Shoko, Tabona 2007 *Karanga Indigenous Religion in Zimbabwe*. Burlington, VT: Ashgate.

Shoocongdej, Rasmi 2010 "Subsistence-Settlement Organisation During the Late Pleistocene-Early Holocene: The Case of Lang Kamnan Cave, Western Thailand." In *50 Years of Archaeology in Southeast Asia: Essays in Honour of Ian Glover*, edited by B. Bellina, E.A. Bacus, T.O. Pryce and J.W. Christie, pp. 51–65. Bangkok: River Books.

Silverblatt, Irene 1987 *Moon, Sun, Witches: Gender Ideologies and Class in Inca and Colonial Peru*. Princeton: Princeton University Press.

Silverman, Helaine 1993 *Cahuachi in the Ancient Nasca World*. Iowa City: University of Iowa Press.

——— 2002 *Ancient Nasca Settlement and Society*. Iowa City: University of Iowa Press.

Silverman, Helaine and Donald A. Proulx 2002 *The Nasca*. Oxford: Blackwell Publishers.
Simmons, Alan H. 2007 *The Neolithic Revolution in the Near East: Transforming the Human Landscape*. Tucson: University of Arizona Press.
Simon, Mary L. 2014 "Reevaluating the Introduction of Maize into the American Bottom and Western Illinois." *Midwest Archaeological Conference, Inc. Occasional Papers* 1: 97–134.
Simon, Mary L. and Kathryn E. Parker 2006 "Prehistoric Plant Use in the American Bottom: New Thoughts and Interpretations." *Southeastern Archaeology* 25.2: 212–57.
Sit, Victor F.S. and Fengxuan Xue 2010 *Chinese City and Urbanism: Evolution and Development*. Singapore: World Scientific Publishing Company.
Sivan, Hagith 2010 "Christianity." In *The Oxford Handbook of Roman Studies*, edited by A. Barchiesi and W. Scheidel, pp. 782–96. Oxford: Oxford University Press.
Slater, Philip A., Kristin M. Hedman and Thomas E. Emerson 2014 "Immigrants at the Mississippian Polity of Cahokia: Strontium Isotope Evidence for Population Movement." *Journal of Archaeological Science* 44: 117–27.
Smith, Michael E. 2001 "The Aztec Empire and the Mesoamerican World System." In *Empires: Perspectives from Archaeology and History*, edited by S.E. Alcock, et al., pp. 128–54. Cambridge: Cambridge University Press.
Smith, Michael E. and Maëlle Sergheraert 2012 "The Aztec Empire." In *The Oxford Handbook of Mesoamerican Archaeology*, edited by D.L. Nichols and C.A. Pool, pp. 449–58. Oxford: Oxford University Press.
Smith, W. Stevenson 1998 *The Art and Architecture of Ancient Egypt*. Third edition. New Haven: Yale University Press.
Smyth, Michael P. 1996 "Storage and the Political Economy: A View from Mesoamerica." *Research in Economic Anthropology* 17: 335–55.
Sneath, David 2007 "The Decentralised State: Nomads, Complexity and Sociotechnical Systems in Inner Asia." In *Socialising Complexity: Structure, Interaction and Power in Archaeological Discourse*, edited by S. Kohring and S. Wynne-Jones, pp. 228–44. Oxford: Oxbow Books.
Snellgrove, David L. 2004 *Angkor–Before and After: A Cultural History of the Khmers*. Bangkok: Orchid Press.
Sofaer, Anna 2007 "The Primary Architecture of the Chacoan Culture: A Cosmological Expression." In *Anasazi Architecture and American Design*, edited by B.H. Morrow and V.B. Price, pp. 88–132. Albuquerque: University of New Mexico Press.
Soler-Arechalde, A.M., et al. 2006 "Archaeomagnetic Investigation of Oriented Pre-Columbian Lime-Plasters from Teotihuacan, Mesoamerica." *Earth Planets Space* 58: 1433–39.
Soles, Jeffrey 1995 "The Functions of a Cosmological Center: Knossos in Palatial Crete." In *Politeia: Society and State in the Aegean Bronze Age*, edited by R. Laffineur and W.-D. Niemeier, pp. 405–14. Aegaeum 12. Liège: Université de Liège.
Spencer, Charles S. 2010 "Territorial Expansion and Primary State Formation." *Proceedings of the National Academy of Science* 107.16: 7119–7126.
Squier, Ephraim G. and Edwin H. Davis 1848 *Ancient Monuments of the Mississippi Valley: Comprising the Results of Extensive Original Surveys and Explorations*. Washington: Smithsonian Institution.
Srinivasan, Doris 1984 "Unhinging Siva from the Indus Civilization." *Journal of the Royal Asiatic Society of Great Britain and Ireland* 116.1: 77–89.
Stadelman, Rainer 1995 "Builders of the Pyramids." In *Civilizations of the Ancient Near East*, edited by J.M. Sasson, pp. 719–34. New York: Charles Scribner's Sons.
Stahl, Peter W. 1985 "The Hallucinogenic Basis of Early Valdivia Phase Ceramic Bowl Iconography." *Journal of Psychoactive Drugs* 17.2: 105–23.
——— 2008 "Animal Domestication in South America." In *Handbook of South American Archaeology*, edited by H. Silverman and W.H. Isbell, pp. 121–30. New York: Springer.
Stanish, Charles 2001 "The Origin of State Societies in South America." *Annual Review of Anthropology* 30: 41–64.
——— 2003 *Ancient Titicaca: The Evolution of Complex Society in Southern Peru and Northern Bolivia*. Berkeley: University of California Press.
——— 2009 "The Evolution of Managerial Elites in Intermediate Societies." In *The Evolution of Leadership: Transitions in Decision Making from Small-Scale to Middle-Range Societies*, edited by K.J. Vaughn, J.W. Eerkens, and J. Kantner, pp. 97–119. Santa Fe: School for Advanced Research Press.
——— 2013 "What Was Tiwanaku?" In *Visions of Tiwanaku*, edited by A. Vranich and C. Stanish, pp. 151–66. Monograph 78. Los Angeles: Cotsen Institute of Archaeology Press.

Stanish, Charles, Edmundo de la Vega, Michael Moseley, Patrick R. Williams, Cecilia Chávez, Benjamin Vining and Karl LaFavre 2010 "Tiwanaku Trade Patterns in Southern Peru." *Journal of Anthropological Archaeology* 29: 524–32.

Stark, Barbara L. and John K. Chance 2012 "The Strategies of Provincials in Empires." In *The Comparative Archaeology of Complex Societies*, edited by M.E. Smith, pp. 192–237. Cambridge: Cambridge University Press.

Stark, Miriam 1998 "The Transition to History in the Mekong Delta: A View from Cambodia." *International Journal of Historical Archaeology* 2.3: 175–203.

——— 2003 "Angkor Borei and the Archaeology of Cambodia's Mekong Delta." In *Art and Archaeology of Fu Nan: Pre-Khmer Kingdom of the Lower Mekong Valley*, edited by J.C.M. Khoo, pp. 89–106. Bangkok: Orchid Press.

——— 2004 "Pre-Angkorian and Angkorian Cambodia." In *Southeast Asia from Prehistory to History*, edited by I. Glover and P. Bellwood, pp. 89–119. London: RoutledgeCurzon.

——— 2006 "Early Mainland Southeast Asian Landscapes in the First Millennium A.D." *Annual Review of Anthropology* 35: 407–32.

Stark, Miriam, B.P. Griffin, P. Church, J. Ledgewood, M. Dega, C. Mortland, N. Dowling, J. Bayman, S. Bong, V. Tea, C. Chhan and K. Latinis 1999 "Results of the 1995–1999 Field Investigations at Angkor Borei, Cambodia." *Asian Perspectives* 38.1: 7–36.

Steadman, Sharon R. 2009 *The Archaeology of Religion: Cultures and Their Beliefs in Worldwide Context*. Walnut Creek: Left Coast Press.

——— 2015 *The Archaeology of Domestic Architecture and the Human Use of Space*. Walnut Creek: Left Coast Press.

Stein, Gil J. 1994 "Economy, Ritual, and Power in Ubaid Mesopotamia." In *Chiefdoms and Early States in the Near East: The Organizational Dynamics of Complexity*, edited by G. Stein and M.S. Rothman, pp. 35–46. Madison: Prehistory Press.

——— 1999 *Rethinking World-Systems: Diasporas, Colonies, and Interaction in Uruk Mesopotamia*. Tucson: University of Arizona Press.

Stein, Gil J. and Rana Özbal 2007 "A Tale of Two Oikumenai: Variation in the Expansionary Dynamics of 'Ubaid and Uruk Mesopotamia." In *Settlement and Society: Essays Dedicated to Robert McCormick Adams*, edited by E. Stone, pp. 329–42. Los Angeles: Cotsen Institute of Archaeology, UCLA.

Stein, John R. and Stephen H. Lekson 1992 "Anasazi Ritual Landscapes." In *Anasazi Regional Organization and the Chaco System*, edited by D.E. Doyel, pp. 87–100. Anthropological Papers No. 5. Albuquerque: University of New Mexico Maxwell Museum of Anthropology.

Steinkeller, Piotr 1987 "The Administrative and Economic Organization of the Ur III State: The Core and the Periphery." In *The Organization of Power. Aspects of Bureaucracy in the Ancient Near East*, edited by M. Gibson and R.D. Biggs, pp. 19–41. Chicago: Oriental Institute.

——— 1993 "Early Political Development in Mesopotamia and the Origins of the Sargonic Empire." In *Akkad: The First World Empire. Structure, Ideology, Traditions*, edited by M. Liverani, pp. 107–29. Padua: Sargon srl.

——— 2004 "The Function of Written Documentation in the Administrative Praxis of Early Babylonia." In *Creating Economic Order: Record-Keeping, Standardization, and the Development of Accounting in the Ancient Near East*, edited by M. Hudson and C. Wunsch, pp. 65–88. Bethesda: CDL Press.

Stephens, Susan 2009 "Hellenistic Culture." In *The Oxford Handbook of Hellenic Studies*, edited by G. Boys-Stones, B. Graziosi and P. Vasunia, pp. 86–97. Oxford: Oxford University Press.

Stewart, Andrew 1983 "Stesichoros and the François Vase." In *Ancient Greek Art and Iconography*, edited by W.G. Moon, pp. 53–74. Madison: University of Wisconsin Press.

——— 1990 *Greek Sculpture: An Introduction*. New Haven: Yale University Press.

Stone, Elizabeth C. 1987 *Nippur Neighborhoods*. Chicago: University of Chicago Press.

Stone, Elizabeth C. and Paul Zimansky 2004 *The Anatomy of a Mesopotamian City: Survey and Soundings at Mashkan-shapir*. Winona Lake: Eisenbrauns.

Strasser, Thomas F. 1997 "Storage and States on Prehistoric Crete: The Function of the Koulouras in the First Minoan Palaces." *Journal of Mediterranean Archaeology* 10: 73–100.

Strezewski, Michael 2009 "The Concept of Personhood in a Mississippian Society." *Illinois Archaeology* 21: 166–90.

Stronach, David 1990 "The Garden as a Political Statement: Some Case Studies from the Near East in the First Millennium B.C." In *In Honor of Richard Nelson Frye: Aspects of Iranian Culture* (Bulletin of the Asia

Institute, n.s. 4), edited by C.A. Bromberg, B. Goldman, P.O. Skjaervo and A.S. Shabazi, pp. 171–80. Ames: Iowa State University Press.

Stuart, David E. 2014 *Anasazi America: Seventeen Centuries on the Road from Center Place*. Second edition. Albuquerque: University of New Mexico Press.

Sugiyama, Saburo 1993 "Worldview Materialized in Teotihuacan, Mexico." *Latin American Antiquity* 4.2: 103–29.

——— 2012 "Ideology, Polity, and Social History of the Teotihuacan State." In *The Oxford Handbook of Mesoamerican Archaeology*, edited by D.L. Nichols and C.A. Pool, pp. 215–29. Oxford: Oxford University Press.

Sun, Yan 2003 "Bronzes, Mortuary Practice and Political Strategies of the Yan during the Early Western Zhou Period." *Antiquity* 77: 761–70.

Sutton, Douglas G. 1990 "Organisation and Ontology: The Origins of the Northern Maori Chiefdom." *Man* N.S. 25.4: 667–92.

Sutton, Robert F., Jr. 1992 "Pornography and Persuasion on Attic Pottery." In *Pornography and Representation in Greece and Rome*, edited by A. Richlin, pp. 3–35. New York: Oxford University Press.

Sweet, Ronald F.G. 1997 "Writing as a Factor in the Rise of Urbanism." In *Urbanism in Antiquity: From Mesopotamia to Crete*, edited by W.E. Aufrecht, N.A. Mirau and S.W. Gauley, pp. 35–49. Sheffield: Sheffield Academic Press.

Tainter, Joseph A. 1988 *The Collapse of Complex Societies*. Cambridge: Cambridge University Press.

Taladoire, Eric 2001 "The Architectural Background of the Pre-Hispanic Ballgame: An Evolutionary Perspective." In *The Sport of Life and Death: The Mesoamerican Ballgame*, edited by E.M. Whittington, pp. 96–115. Charlotte: The Mint Museum of Art.

Tanner, Harold M. 2010 *China: A History (Volume I): From Neolithic Cultures through the Great Qing Empire (10,000 BCE—1799 CE)*. Indianapolis: Hackett Publishing.

Thomas, David H. and Matthew C. Sanger, eds. 2010 *Trend, Tradition, and Turmoil: What Happened to the Southeastern Archaic?* New York: Anthropological Papers of the American Museum of Natural History.

Thorp, Robert L. 2006 *China in the Early Bronze Age: Shang Civilization*. Philadelphia: University of Pennsylvania Press.

Toll, H. Wolcott 2004 "Artifacts in Chaco: Where They Came from and What They Mean." In *In Search of Chaco: New Approaches to an Archaeological Enigma*, edited by D.G. Noble, pp. 32–40. Santa Fe: School of American Research Press.

——— 2006 "Organization of Production." In *The Archaeology of Chaco Canyon: An Eleventh-Century Pueblo Regional Center*, edited by S.H. Lekson, pp. 117–51. Santa Fe: School of American Research Press.

Topic, John R. 2009 "Domestic Economy as Political Economy at Chan Chan, Perú." In *Domestic Life in Prehispanic Capitals: A Study of Specialization, Hierarchy, and Ethnicity*, edited by L.R. Manzanilla and C. Chapdelaine, pp. 221–42. Memoirs of the Museum of Anthropology, No. 46. Ann Arbor: University of Michigan.

Topic, Theresa L. and John R. Topic 2010 "Contextualizing the Wari-Huamachuco Relationship." In *Beyond Wari Walls: Regional Perspectives on Middle Horizon Peru*, edited by J. Jennings, pp. 188–212. Albuquerque: New Mexico Press.

Trainor, Kevin 2001 "Theravada Buddhism." In *Buddhism, The Illustrated Guide*, edited by K. Trainor, pp. 120–31. Oxford: Oxford University Press.

Trigger, Bruce G. 1983 "The Rise of Egyptian Civilization." In *Ancient Egypt: A Social History*, edited by B.G. Trigger, pp. 1–70. Cambridge: Cambridge University Press.

——— 1989 *A History of Archaeological Thought*. Cambridge: Cambridge University Press.

——— 2003 *Understanding Early Civilizations*. Cambridge: Cambridge University Press.

Trubitt, Mary Beth D. 2000 "Mound Building and Prestige Goods Exchange: Changing Strategies in the Cahokia Chiefdom." *American Antiquity* 65.4: 669–90.

Uceda, Santiago 2008 "The Priests of the Bicephalus Arc: Tombs and Effigies Found in Huaca de la Luna and Their Relation to Moche Rituals." In *The Art and Archaeology of the Moche*, edited by S. Bourget and K.L. Jones, pp. 153–78. Austin: University of Texas Press.

Underhill, Anne P. 2000 "An Analysis of Mortuary Ritual at the Dawenkou Site, Shandong, China." *Journal of East Asian Archaeology* 2.1–2: 93–127.

——— 2002 *Craft Production and Social Change in Northern China*. New York: Kluwer Academic/Plenum Publishers.

Underhill, Anne P. and Junko Habu 2006 "Early Communities in East Asia: Economic and Sociopolitical Organization at the Local and Regional Levels." In *Archaeology of Asia*, edited by M.T. Stark, pp. 121–48. Oxford: Blackwell Publishing.

Ur, Jason A. 2002 "Settlement and Landscape in Northern Mesopotamia: The Tell Hamoukar Survey 2000–2001." *Akkadica* 123: 57–88.

Uriarte, María Teresa 2006 "The Teotihuacan Ballgame and the Beginning of Time." *Ancient Mesoamerica* 17: 17–38.

Urton, Gary 1997 *The Social Life of Numbers: A Quechua Ontology of Numbers and Philosophy of Arithmetic*. Austin: University of Texas Press.

——— 1999 *Inca Myths*. Austin: University of Texas Press.

——— 2008 "The Body of Meaning in Chavín Art." In *Chavín: Art, Architecture, and Culture*, edited by W.J. Conklin and J. Quilter, pp. 215–34. Los Angeles: Cotsen Institute of Archaeology.

——— 2015 "The State of Strings: *Khipu* Administration in the Inka Empire." In *The Inka Empire: A Multidisciplinary Approach*, edited by I. Shimada, pp. 149–64. Austin: University of Texas Press.

Vahia, Mayank and Srikumar M. Menon 2013 "A Possible Harappan Astronomical Observatory at Dholavira." *Journal of Astronomical History and Heritage* 16.3: 261–68.

Valentine, Benjamin, George D. Kamenov, Jonathan M. Kenoyer, Vasant Shinde, Veena Mushrif-Tripathy, Erik Otarola-Castillo and John Krigbaum 2015 "Evidence for Patterns of Selective Urban Migration in the Greater Indus Valley (2600–1900 BC): A Lead and Strontium Isotope Mortuary Analysis." *PLoS ONE* 10.4: 1–20.

van de Mieroop, Marc 2004 *A History of the Ancient Near East ca. 3000–323 B.C.* Oxford: Blackwell Publishing.

VanDerwarker, Amber M. 2006 *Farming, Hunting, and Fishing in the Olmec World*. Austin: University of Texas Press.

Van Dyke, Ruth M. 2004 "Chaco's Sacred Geography." In *In Search of Chaco: New Approaches to an Archaeological Enigma*, edited by D.G. Noble, pp. 78–85. Santa Fe: School of American Research Press.

——— 2007 "Great Kivas in Time, Space, and Society." In *The Architecture of Chaco Canyon, New Mexico*, edited by S.H. Lekson, pp. 93–126. Salt Lake City: University of Utah Press.

——— 2012 *The Chaco Experience: Landscape and Ideology at the Center Place*. Santa Fe: School for Advanced Research.

Van Liere, W.J. 1980 "Traditional Water Management in the Lower Mekong Basin." *World Archaeology* 11.3: 265–80.

van Meijl, Toon 1995 "Maori Socio-Political Organization in Pre- and Proto-History: On the Evolution of Post-Colonial Constructs." *Oceania* 65.4: 304–22.

Vaughn, Kevin J. 2004 "Households, Crafts, and Feasting in the Ancient Andes: The Village Context of Early Nasca Craft Consumption." *Latin American Antiquity* 15.1: 61–88.

——— 2006 "Craft Production, Exchange, and Political Power in the Pre-Incaic Andes." *Journal of Archaeological Research* 14: 313–44.

——— 2009 *The Ancient Andean Village: Marcaya in Prehispanic Nasca*. Tucson: University of Arizona Press.

Verano, John W. 2008 "Trophy Head-Taking and Human Sacrifice in Andean South America." In *Handbook of South American Archaeology*, edited by H. Silverman and W.H. Isbell, pp. 1047–60. New York: Springer.

Vickery, Michael 1998 *Society, Economics and Politics in Pre-Angkor Cambodia*. Tokyo: Center for East Asian Cultural Studies for UNESCO.

Vidale, Massimo 2000 *The Archaeology of Indus Crafts: Indus Craftspeople and Why We Study Them*. Rome: Istituto Italiano per l'Africa e l'Oriente.

——— 2010 "Aspects of Palace Life at Mohenjo-Daro." *South Asian Studies* 26.1: 59–76.

Vivian, R. Gwinn and Adam S. Watson 2015 "Reevaluating and Modeling Agricultural Potential in the Chaco Core." In *Chaco Revisited: New Research on the Prehistory of Chaco Canyon, New Mexico*, edited by C.C. Heitman and S. Plog, pp. 30–65. Tucson: University of Arizona Press.

von Falkenhausen, Lothar 2006 "The External Connections of Sanxingdui." *Journal of East Asian Archaeology* 5.1–4: 191–245.

——— 2008 "Stages in the Development of 'Cities' in Pre-Imperial China." In *The Ancient City: New Perspectives on Urbanism in the Old and New World*, edited by J. Marcus and J.A. Sabloff, pp. 209–28. Santa Fe: School for Advanced Research.

Wall, S.M., J.H. Musgrave and P.M. Warren 1986 "Human Bones from a Late Minoan IB House at Knossos." *Annual of the British School in Athens* 81: 333–88.

Wallerstein, Immanuel 1974 *The Modern World System: Capitalist Agriculture and the Origins of the European World Economy in the Sixteenth Century*. New York: Academic Press.

Walter, Richard, Ian Smith and Chris Jacomb 2006 "Sedentism, Subsistence, and Socio-Political Organization in Prehistoric New Zealand." *World Archaeology* 38.2: 274–90.

Walz, Gregory R., Brian Adams, Paul P. Kreisa, Kevin P. McGowan and Jacqueline M. McDowell 1998 "The Strong Site and the Dennis Hollow Phase: A New Perspective on Middle Archaic Chronology, Technology and Subsistence." *Illinois Archaeology* 10.1–2: 155–94.

Wang, Jihuai 1987 "An Archaeological Outline of Qijia Agricultural Discovery and Research." *Agricultural Archaeology* 1: 71–75 (translated by E. Wong and B. Gordon).

Wangping, Shao 2000 "The Longshan Period and Incipient Chinese Civilization." *Journal of East Asian Archaeology* 2.1–2: 195–226.

—— 2005 "The Formation of Civilization: The Interaction Sphere of the Longshan Period." In *The Formation of Chinese Civilization, An Archaeological Perspective*, edited by S. Allen, pp. 85–123. New Haven: Yale University Press.

Warren, Peter 1981 "Minoan Crete and Ecstatic Religion: Preliminary Observations on the 1979 Excavations at Knossos." In *Sanctuaries and Cults in the Aegean Bronze Age*, edited by R. Hägg and N. Marinatos, pp. 155–67. Stockholm: Paul Aströms Förlag.

Watrous, L. Vance 1998 "Egypt and Crete in the Early Middle Bronze Age: A Case of Trade and Cultural Diffusion." In *The Aegean and the Orient in the Second Millennium: Proceedings of the 50th Anniversary Symposium, Cincinnati, 18–20 April 1997*, edited by E.H. Cline and D. Harris-Cline, pp. 19–28. Liège: Université de Liège.

—— 2004 "State Formation (Middle Minoan IA)." In *The Plain of Phaistos: Cycles of Social Complexity in the Mesara Region of Crete*, edited by L.V. Watrous, D. Hadzi-Vallianou and H. Blitzer, pp. 253–76. Los Angeles: Cotsen Institute of Archaeology.

Webb, Clarence H. 1968 "The Extent and Content of Poverty Point Culture." *American Antiquity* 33.3: 297–321.

—— 1971 "Archaic and Poverty Point Zoomorphic Locust Beads." *American Antiquity* 36.1: 105–14.

Webb, William S. and Charles E. Snow 1974 *The Adena People*. Reprint. Knoxville: University of Tennessee Press.

Weber, Stephen A. 1999 "Seeds of Change: Palaeoethnobotany and the Indus Civilisation." *Antiquity* 73: 813–26.

—— 2003 "Archaeobotany at Harappa: Indications for Change." In *Indus Ethnobiology*, edited by S. Weber and W.R. Belcher, pp. 175–98. Lanham: Lexington Books.

Wegner, Josef 2010 "Tradition and Innovation: The Middle Kingdom." In *Egyptian Archaeology*, edited by W. Wendrich, pp. 119–42. West Sussex: Wiley-Blackwell.

Weiberg, Erika and Martin Finné 2013 "Mind or Matter? People-Environment Interactions and the Demise of Early Helladic II Society in the Northeastern Peloponnese." *American Journal of Archaeology* 117: 1–31.

Weinstein, James M. 1981 "The Egyptian Empire in Palestine: A Reassessment." *Bulletin of the American Schools of Oriental Research* 241: 1–28.

Wendorf, Fred and Romauld Schild 1998 "Nabta Playa and Its Role in Northeastern African Prehistory." *Journal of Anthropological Archaeology* 17: 97–123.

Wengrow, David 2006 *The Archaeology of Early Egypt: Social Transformations in North-East Africa, 10,000 to 2650 BC*. Cambridge: Cambridge University Press.

Westenholz, Joan Goodnick 1989 "Enheduanna, En-Priestess, Hen of Nanna, Spouse of Nanna." In *dumu-e₂-dub-ba-a: Studies in Honor of Ake W. Sjöberg*, edited by H. Behrens, D. Loding and M.T. Roth, pp. 539–56. Philadelphia: Occasional Publications of the Samuel Noah Kramer Fund.

Wheeler, R.E. Mortimer 1968 *The Indus Civilization*. Third edition. Cambridge: Cambridge University Press.

Whiteley, Peter 2015 "Chacoan Kinship." In *Chaco Revisited: New Research on the Prehistory of Chaco Canyon, New Mexico*, edited by C.C. Heitman and S. Plog, pp. 272–304. Tucson: University of Arizona Press.

Whitley, James 2009 "Archaeology." In *The Oxford Handbook of Hellenic Studies*, edited by G. Boys-Stones, B. Graziosi, and P. Vasunia, pp. 720–33. Oxford: Oxford University Press.

Wilcox, David R. 1991 "The Mesoamerican Ballgame in the American Southwest." In *The Mesoamerican Ballgame*, edited by V. Scarborough and D.R. Wilcox, pp. 101–25. Tucson: University of Arizona Press.

—— 1999 "A Peregrine View of Macroregional Systems in the North American Southwest." In *Great Towns and Regional Polities in the Prehistoric Southwest and Southeast*, edited by J.E. Neitzel, pp. 115–42. Albuquerque: University of New Mexico Press.

Wilkinson, Toby A.H. 1996 *State Formation in Egypt: Chronology and Society.* Oxford: British Archaeological Reports.
——— 1999 *Early Dynastic Egypt.* London: Routledge.
——— 2003 *Genesis of the Pharaohs: Dramatic New Discoveries Rewrite the Origins of Ancient Egypt.* London: Thames and Hudson.
——— 2010 *The Rise and Fall of Ancient Egypt.* New York: Random House.
Willems, Harco 2010 "The First Intermediate Period and the Middle Kingdom." In *A Companion to Ancient Egypt*, edited by A.B. Lloyd, pp. 81–100. Oxford: Blackwell Publishing Ltd.
Wills, Wirt H. 2001 "Ritual and Mound Formation During the Bonito Phase in Chaco Canyon." *American Antiquity* 66.3: 433–52.
Wilson, Gregory D., Jon Marcoux and Brad Koldehoff 2006 "Square Pegs in Round Holes: Organizational Diversity between Early Moundville and Cahokia." In *Leadership and Polity in Mississippian Society*, edited by B.M. Butler and P.D. Welch, pp. 43–72. Center for Archaeological Investigations Occasional Paper, No. 33. Carbondale: Southern Illinois University Press.
Windes, Thomas C. 2004 "The Rise of Early Chacoan Great Houses." In *In Search of Chaco: New Approaches to an Archaeological Enigma*, edited by D.G. Noble, pp. 14–21. Santa Fe: School of American Research Press.
Winter, Irene 1981 "Royal Rhetoric and the Development of Historical Narrative in Neo-Assyrian Reliefs." *Studies in Visual Communication* 7.2: 2–38.
——— 1985 "After the Battle is Over: The Stele of the Vultures and the Beginning of Historical Narrative in the Art of the Ancient Near East." In *Pictorial Narrative in Antiquity and the Middle Ages*, edited by H.L. Kessler and M.S. Simpson, pp. 1–32. Washington: National Gallery of Art.
——— 1987 "Women in Public: The Disk of Enheduanna, the Beginning of the Office of en-Priestess, and the Weight of Visual Evidence." In *La femme dans le proche-orient antique*, edited by J.M. Durand, pp. 189–201. Paris: Editions Recherche sur les Civilisations.
——— 1989 "The Body of the Able Ruler: Toward an Understanding of the Statues of Gudea." In *dumu-e$_2$-dub-ba-a: Studies in Honor of Ake W. Sjöberg*, edited by H. Behrens, D. Loding and M.T. Roth, pp. 573–83. Philadelphia: Occasional Publications of the Samuel Noah Kramer Fund.
——— 1996 "Sex, Rhetoric, and the Public Monument: The Alluring Body of Naram-Sîn of Agade." In *Sexuality in Ancient Art: Near East, Egypt, Greece, and Italy*, edited by N.B. Kampen, pp. 11–26. Cambridge: Cambridge University Press.
——— 1997 "Art *in* Empire: The Royal Image and the Visual Dimensions of Assyrian Ideology." In *Assyria 1995*, edited by S. Parpola and R.M. Whiting, pp. 359–81. Helsinki: The Neo-Assyrian Text Corpus Project.
——— 2000 "*Le Palais imaginaire*: Scale and Meaning in the Iconography of Neo-Assyrian Cylinder Seals." In *Images as Media: Sources for the Cultural History of the Near East and the Eastern Mediterranean (Ist millennium BCE)*, edited by C. Uehlinger, pp. 51–87. Orbis Biblicus et Orientalis 175. Fribourg: University Press.
Wittfogel, Karl A. 1957 *Oriental Despotism: A Comparative Study of Total Power.* New Haven: Yale University Press.
Wolf, Eric R. 1999 *Envisioning Power: Ideologies of Dominance and Crisis.* Berkeley: University of California Press.
Wood, Frances 2007 *China's First Emperor and His Terracotta Warriors.* New York: St. Martin's Press.
Woolf, Greg 2012 *Rome: An Empire's Story.* Oxford: Oxford University Press.
Woolley, C. Leonard 1934 *Ur Excavations II: The Royal Cemetery.* London: Trustees of the British Museum.
Wright, Henry T. 1977 "Recent Research on the Origin of the State." *Annual Review of Anthropology* 6: 379–97.
Wright, Henry T. and Gregory A. Johnson 1975 "Population, Exchange, and Early State Formation in Southwestern Iran." *American Anthropologist* 77: 267–89.
Wright, James C. 1994 "The Spatial Configuration of Belief: The Archaeology of Mycenaean Religion." In *Placing the Gods: Sanctuaries and Sacred Space in Ancient Greece*, edited by S.E. Alcock and R. Osborne, pp. 37–78. Oxford: Clarendon Press.
Wright, Rita P. 1991 "Women's Labor and Pottery Production in Prehistory." In *Engendering Archaeology: Women and Prehistory*, edited by J.M. Gero and M.W. Conkey, pp. 194–223. Oxford: Blackwell Publishing.
——— 2010 *The Ancient Indus: Urbanism, Economy, and Society.* Cambridge: Cambridge University Press.
Xu, Jay 1996 "The Cemetery of the Western Zhou Lords of Jin." *Artibus Asiae* 56.3/4: 193–231.
——— 2006 "Defining the Archaeological Cultures at the Sanxingdui Site." *Journal of East Asian Archaeology* 5.1–4: 149–90.
Yang, Xiaoyan, Zhengkai Xie and Maolin Ye 2003 "Prehistoric Disasters at Lajia Site, Qinghai, China." *Chinese Science Bulletin* 48.17: 1877–81.

Yanping, Zhu 2013 "The Early Neolithic in the Central Yellow River Valley, c. 7000–4000 BC." In *A Companion to Chinese Archaeology*, edited by A.P. Underhill, pp. 171–93. West Sussex: Wiley-Blackwell.

Yao, Alice 2010 "Recent Developments in the Archaeology of Southwestern China." *Journal of Archaeological Research* 18: 203–39.

Yerkes, Richard W. 1989 "Mississippian Craft Specialization on the American Bottom." *Southeastern Archaeology* 8.2: 93–106.

Yoffee, Norman 1993 "Too Many Chiefs? (or, Safe Texts for the '90s)." In *Archaeological Theory: Who Sets the Agenda?* edited by N. Yoffee and A. Sherratt, pp. 60–78. Cambridge: Cambridge University Press.

——— 1997 "The Obvious and the Chimerical: City-States in Archaeological Perspective." In *The Archaeology of City-States: Cross-Cultural Approaches*, edited by D.L. Nichols and T.H. Charlton, pp. 255–63. Washington: Smithsonian Institution Press.

——— 2005 *Myths of the Archaic State: Evolution of the Earliest Cities, States, and Civilizations.* Cambridge: Cambridge University Press.

——— 2010 "The Unbearable Lightness of Complexity." In *Ancient Complexities: New Perspectives in Precolumbian North America*, edited by S.M. Alt, pp. 220–25. Salt Lake City: University of Utah Press.

Yoffee, Norman, Suzanne K. Fish and George R. Milner 1999 "Comunidades, Ritualities, Chiefdoms: Social Evolution in the American Southwest and Southeast." In *Great Towns and Regional Polities in the Prehistoric American Southwest and Southeast*, edited by J.A. Neitzel, pp. 261–71. Albuquerque: University of New Mexico Press.

Young, Biloine W. and Melvin L. Fowler 2000 *Cahokia, the Great Native American Metropolis.* Urbana: University of Illinois Press.

Young, Lisa 2012 "Diversity in First-Millennium AD Southwestern Farming Communities." In *The Oxford Handbook of North American Archaeology*, edited by T.R. Pauketat, pp. 561–70. Oxford: Oxford University Press.

Yung-ti, Li 2006 "On the Function of Cowries in Shang and Western Zhou China." *Journal of East Asian Archaeology* 5.1–4: 1–26.

Zanker, Paul 1988 *The Power of Images in the Age of Augustus.* Translated by A. Shapiro. Ann Arbor: University of Michigan Press.

Zeidler, James A. 2008 "The Ecuadorian Formative." In *Handbook of South American Archaeology*, edited by H. Silverman and W.H. Isbell, pp. 459–88. New York: Springer.

Zhao, Zhijun 2010 "New Data and New Issues for the Study of Origin of Rice Agriculture in China." *Archaeological and Anthropological Sciences* 2: 99–105.

Zhimin, An 1992 "The Bronze Age in Eastern Parts of Central Asia." In *History of Civilizations of Central Asia. Volume I: The Dawn of Civilization: Earliest Times to 700 B.C.*, edited by A.H. Dani and V.M. Masson, pp. 308–25. Paris: UNESCO Publishing.

Zhongpei, Zhang 2005 "The Yangshao Period: Prosperity and the Transformation of Prehistoric Society." In *The Formation of Chinese Civilization An Archaeological Perspective*, edited by S. Allen, pp. 43–83. New Haven: Yale University Press.

Zhou Daguan 2007 *A Record of Cambodia: The Land and Its People.* Translated by P. Harris. Chang Mai: Silkworm Books.

Zuidema, R. Tom 1964 *The Ceque System of Cuzco: The Social Organization of the Capital of the Inca.* Leiden: Brill.

——— 1983 "Hierarchy and Space in Incaic Social Organization." *Ethnohistory* 30: 49–75.

INDEX

Note: Page numbers in *italics* denote references to Figures, Tables and Plates.

Abu Hureyra 55
Abydos 94, 98
Achaemenid Empire 84
Acolhua 324
Acropolis 153
Adams, Robert M. 2, 60–1, 64
Adena cultural complex 269, 275
Aegean Sea 118
Aegean Sea region: chronological periods *120–1*; chronological sequence 119–22; Classical Age 150–4; Early Bronze Age 123–6; geography and ecological setting 118–19; map of *119*; Minoan influence on 134; in Neolithic Period *120*, 122–3; pre-state societies 122–5; in Protopalatial period 126–9; *see also* Classical Greece
Aeneid 169
Aeotearoa 42
Agora 152–3
agora areas 146–7
agricultural administration 133–4
agricultural fertility 23, 31–2, 284, 292, 294, 338
agricultural production 170–1
agricultural surpluses 99, 101
agriculture, origins of 3
Ah Cacaw 317
Ahhiyawans 142
ahupua'a system 47, 48
Ahuramazda 85
Ain Ghazal 56
Akapana 349
Akhenaten 110–11
Akhetaten 75, 108, *111*
Akkadian kings 70
Akkadian writing system 84
Akrotiri 134
Alexander the Great 84, 117, 121, 154–5
Algaze, Guillermo 64

ali'i akua (god-kings) 50
ali'i class 48–9
altars 302
Alva, Walter 341, 342
Amarna Letters 75, 77
Amenhotep III 110
Amenhotep IV 110
American Bottom: in Archaic State 269–70; chronology 268–9, *268*; described 267; geography and ecological setting 266–8; in Late Archaic 270–3; in Late Woodland Period 283–4; map of *266*; material culture 274; mound-building 271–3; in Terminal Late Woodland Period 284; Watson Brake mounds 271, *271*; *see also* Mississippian system
American Southwest, map of *33*; *see also* Chaco Canyon
Amratian 91–2
Amri-Nal phase sites 178
Amun-Re 108–9
ancestor veneration 213, 218, 228, 249, 255, 293
Andean civilizations: the Chimú state 352–5; chronology 329–30, *330*; cosmology 337–8; the Mochica 338–44; Nasca culture 344–6; pre-state cultures 330–5; *see also* Incan Civilization
Andes, the: geography and ecological setting 327–9; map of *328*; volcano *328*
Angkor Borei 246, 247
Angkor Thom 258, *259*
Angkor Wat 252, 255–6
animal domestication 52–3, 89, 122–3, 176, 180, 208, 242, 309, 329, 331
animal husbandry 179
animal imagery 281
animal mummies 113, *114*
animal offerings/sacrifice 224–5, 242
animal symbolism 7

Antigonus 155
Anu temple precinct 61
Anyang city 222, 223
Ao 221
apotropaic figures 80
Apsaras 256, *257*, 262
Ara Pacis 169
Archaic Period *120*, 121, 146–52, *148*, *268*, 299–300, *300*
archaic state 23–7, 47
Arch of Constantine 171
art and architecture: in Archaic Period Greece 147–8; of Augustus 167; in Chalcolithic Period Near East 59–60; in Chenla Empire 249–50; Classical period 153–4; in Early Dynastic Period Near East 65–6; in Fourth Dynasty 102; in Geometric Period 145, *145*; in Hellenistic Age 156; Minoan influence on 134; in the Mochica 342–3; in Naqada I phase 91–2; of Naqada III phase 94; of Neo-Assyrian Period 79–82; from Neo-Babylonian Period 83; in Olmec culture 301–2; of Persian Empire 84–5; of Principate 170; public art 80, 84, 165, 167; of Roman world 166, 169; royal art 80, *81*, 85; in Teotihuacan 309; of Trajan 170; Ubaid 60
artificial water systems 253; *see also* water management systems
Aspero site 333, 334
Assur 79, 80
Assurbanipal 78, 79
Assurnasirpal II 78, 79
Assyrian State 76–7
Assyrian steles 85
Atawallpa 364
Aten 110–11
Athenian democracy 151–2
Athens 144–5, 148, 149–50
Attic painters 160
Attic pottery 148, *148*, 154
Augustus 161, 166–9
Au Lac Kingdom 244
Avaris 107
Avenue of the Dead 307
ayllu 359
Aztec society 324–6

Babylonian Dynasty 73; *see also* Old Babylonian Period
Badarian Period 90–1
Baines, John 69
ballcourt 318, 323
Ban Chiang 242
Ban Na Di 242
Banpo 208
Banquet Stele 79
Banteay Srei 253
Banteay Srei Temple *254*
Baodun cultural complex 210
barays 253
barter transactions 11
basileus 140

Basketmaker cultures 34
Bayon 258, *258*
BBB Motor site 284, 288, 292
beaded burial 286, 293–4
bianfa style hair braid 215, *216*
biomorphs 346
bird imagery 31, *32*, 215
Birger figurine *293*
black drink 293
Black Obelisk 82
Block 6 180
bloodletting rituals 319, *319*
Bonampak 321
Bronze Age: Aegean Sea region 123–43; China 206–7; Italy 157; Southeast Asia *240*, 241–3
bronze foundry 217–18
bronze metallurgy 211, 215, 221, 231
bronze vessels 231
Buddhism 243, 247, 251, 255, 263
Building J Monte Albán 305–6
bull imagery 199
bureaucracy 13–14; *see also* political differentiation
burial mounds 270–3, 275, 277–80, 282–3, 285–7
burial practices 98, 157, 217, 351; *see also* cemeteries; cremation; inhumation burials

Cahokia Mississippian culture *see* Mississippian system
Cahuachi 344–5
Calendar Round 321
calendrical systems 321, 362
Cambodian house on stilts *239*
Cambyses II 116
camelids 331
canal irrigation *see* irrigation canals/agriculture; water management systems
Caral site 333–4
Carneiro, Robert 4
Carr Creek Culture 274
Carter, Howard 113
caste system 202
Cat Mummy *114*
cattle domestication 89–90
cattle symbolism 7
cemeteries 158; *see also* burial practices
ceramics *see* pottery
chacmool *323*
Chacoan culture: complexity of 40–1; elite power 39–40; Great Houses of 34–8, *35*; household religion 40; leadership structures 38; masonry-built structures 34–5; matrilineal kinship 35; origins of 34–5; population of 35–6; ritual practices 39–40; society of 35–8
Chaco Canyon: economic structures 39; map of *33*; Pueblo del Arroyo Great House *36*; as regional polity 41; as secondary state 41; warfare 38
Chalcolithic Period, Near East *54*, 59–60
Champa kingdom 252
Chan Chan 352–5, *353*
Chang, Kwang-Chih 226

Chapman, Robert 294–5
charnel houses 280
Charnel Mound 333, *333*
Chavín de Huántar 329, 335–8, *336*
Chengziyai site 210–11
Chenla Empire 239, 249–51, 255
Chenla kings 250–1, 262
Chetro Ketl 36
chicha 360
Chichen Itza 322–3, *323*
chiefdoms: Cahokia Mississippian complex 294–5; centralization of society and 13; Chaco Canyon 40–1; defined 294; described 20–3; Funan culture 239, 246; Great Zimbabwe 28; Harappan 201; Hawaiian 46–7, 49; Iron Age Southeast Asia 243–6; Khmer Empire 262; Mississippian culture 268, 281, 284; Polynesian culture 42; *see also* regional polity
Chiefdoms and other Archaeological Delusions (Pauketat) 4
Childe, V. Gordon 3
Chimor kingdom 352
Chimú Goddess 354
Chimú state, the 330, 352–5
China: Bronze Age 213–19; chronology 206–7, *206*–7; climatic zones 206; Erligang culture 219–22; Erlitou culture 216–19; geography and ecological setting 204–6; Great Wall *233*, 234, 235–6; irrigation canals/agriculture 205–6; Jiangzhai Village 208–9; Late Neolithic 207–13; Late Shang 222–9; map of *205*; metallurgical methods 211; national boundaries 204; Sanxingdui culture 213–16; Silk Road 233–4, 236; writing origins 222–3; *see also* Imperial China
Chincha polity 355–6
chocolate drinking 313–14
Christianity, emergence of 171–2
Churchill, Winston 173
circumscription theory 4
citadels 135–6, 139, 180, *181*, 185, 194, 199; *see also* fortified settlements
citizen-farmer 164
city planning 182–7
Ciudadela complex 307–8
ciudadelas (walled compounds) 352
Ciudadela Tschudi *353*
Civil Wars 165–6
Classical Age 150–4
Classical Greece: Archaic Period 146–52; Athens 144–5; chronological periods *120*–1; collapse of Mycenaean places 121; colonization 146; complexity of 152–4; geography and ecological setting 118; Geometric Period 144–6; in Hellenistic Period 154–7; map of *119*, *143*; Olympian gods 147–8; pan-Hellenic identity 146; in Protogeometric Period 143–4; slaves 152, 154; trade in 145–6; unification 155
Classical Period Greece *121*, 154, 305–10
Classic Maya: bloodletting rituals 319, *319*; calendrical systems 321; chocolate drinking 313–14; collapse of 321–2; economy of 312–13; elite power in 314; environmental crisis 368; map of *312*; palaces 315; Palenque 317; political organization 315–18; religious beliefs 318–21; social organization 314; Tikal 315–17; warfare 321
Classic Period Mesoamerica *300*, 305–10
clay tablets 63
Cleopatra VII 112
Clovis Culture 268–9
Coffin Texts 104, 115
collapse, defined 366
collective land ownership 19
College of Priests 180, 194
Co Loa 244
colonialism 63
Colossal Winged Lion *81*
Column of Trajan 170
complexity: of Chacoan culture 40–1; in Chimú Society 355; in Classical Athens 152–4; critiques of 4; defined 4; in Early Dynastic Mesopotamia 68–9; in farming societies 18; of Great Zimbabwe 32–3; of Hawaiian society 50; of Late Bronze Age Near East 77–8; of Mochica society 343–4; in Mycenaean Age 141; in Nasca Society 346; in Protopalatial period 129; in Tiwanaku Society 350; of Uruk Period 64
complex societies: defined 1; economic systems 8–12; history of 1–2; kinship relationships 6–7; political systems 12–15; religious belief systems 7–8
Confucius 232, 235–6
Constantine 171–2
Cook, James 46
Corinthian pottery 148, *148*
corridor houses 125
Cortés, Hernán 326
corvée labor 9, 14, 24, 101, 359
cosmology 20, 292, 305–7, 337–8, 351
Council of 500 151
craft production: in Aztec society 325; in Chenla Empire 250; in Erlitou culture 217–18; as family business 188; at Great Zimbabwe 33; as guild structure 189; and Harappan trade network 187–90; in Hawaiian society 49; jade-based 214–15; in Mississippian culture 291, 296; of the Mochica 339; of the Nasca 345; in Neolithic Period Indus Valley 177; tax obligations and 10; technology and 9–10; in Teotihuacan 309; in Yangshao Period 208; at Yinxu settlement 224
craft-workers 39, 49, 92, 102, 217–18, 335, 358–9
craft workshops 25, 181–2
cremation 142, 144, 157–8, 170, 276, 280, 338; *see also* burial practices
Crete 118, *119*, 125–6, 128–32, 140, 368–9
crop fertility 346
cultivation *see* plant cultivation
cultural institutions, defined 6–7
Curia 164
cuy 331

Cuzco 358–9, 362
Cyclades 118
Cycladic Folded-Arm Figurine *124*
cycling characteristics 324, 367
Cyclopean style 139
cylinder seals 63, 82
Cyrus 83, 84
Cyrus Cylinder 83

Damb Sadaat site 178
Danta Pyramid 311
Danzantes building 305–6
Danzante slabs 305–6, *306*
Darius I 84, 85
Dark Age/Early Iron Age Greece *120*
debt-bondage 164, 262; *see also* slaves
Decapitator God 343
deep pits 126
Deir el-Bahri 104–5
Deir el-Medina 115
Delian League 152
Delphi 148, 154
delta region 90
democratic reforms 154
Dennis Hollow phase 269
dentistry, Neolithic 176
Devarâja ceremony 251
Dholavira 185–6, 190
Dholavira Observatory *185*
differentiation: to balanced diet 192; in death 90; economic 11–12; at Great Zimbabwe 33; of Harappan people 191–3; of Hawaii culture 47–8; in Maori society 44; in Mesoamerica 300; political 13–14; socioeconomic 213; state society and 25; *see also* socioeconomic differentiation
Dimini 123
"Ding" bronze cauldron *230*
Diocletian 171
distribution of goods 23, 24, 218, 290, 313
divination 212, 213, 227–8
Djoser 99
domestic architecture 66, 69, 177, 178
domesticated animals *see* animal domestication
domesticated grain/plants 90, 122–3, 241; *see also* plant cultivation
Dominate period 166
Dong Son bronze dagger 245
Dong Son culture 243–4
Donnan, Christopher 342
Dos Cabezas 342
drainage and sewage systems 186
Dur-Sharrukin 79

Eanna precinct 61, *62*
Eannatum 67
Early Archaic Period North America 269
Early Bronze Age: Aegean Sea region *120*, 123–6; China *206*
Early Cycladic Period 124
Early Dynastic Period *54*, 58, 64–9, *88*, 95–9

Early Empires Period *240*
Early Harappan Period 175, *175*, 177–9
Early Helladic 125
Early Holocene era 207
Early Horizon Period 329, *330*, 335–8
Early Indus Period 175
Early Intermediate Period 329, *330*, 338
Early Iron Age: Italy 157–60; Southeast Asia *240*, 243–6
Early Kingdoms Period 239
Early Minoan Period 125–6
Early Preceramic Period Andean region *330*
Early Shang Period 219–20
Early Woodland Period 274–6
earthen mounds *see* burial mounds
Easter Island 368
Eastern Han Period 235
Eastern Zhou state *207*, 232
East St. Louis site 289–90, 292
economic collapse 369–70
economic development 56, 177
economic differentiation, described 11–12
economic inequality 12
economic organization 133–4, 139–40, 149–50
economic power/structures: in archaic states 24; at Chaco Canyon 39; in Classical Period Greece 154; described 2–3, 8–12; Incan 359–62; in Mississippian culture 290–1; non-subsistence resources 9; in Old Babylonian Period 75; privately held businesses 83; in Qin Dynasty 232–4; regional polity and 21–2; resources 8–9; subsistence 8
economic strategies: in foraging societies 17; in Neo-Assyrian Empire 78–9; in sedentary villages 19
Edzna 311
effigy mounds 282
effigy pipes 280, *280*, 281
egalitarian 16–17
Egypt: climatic fluctuation in 87–8; cult centers 108–9; Early Dynastic 95–9; economic decline of 115; Eighteenth Dynasty 107–8, 110; Eleventh Dynasty 103, 104; Fifteenth Dynasty 107; Fifth Dynasty 102–3; First Intermediate 103; under foreign rule 116–17; Fourteenth Dynasty 107; Fourth Dynasty 101, 102; geography and ecological setting 86–8; Great Sphinx 102; International Age 107–8; international relationships 108; irrigation canals/agriculture 104; kingdoms 89; kings in first dynasty 93; Late Period 116–17; material culture 86, 91, 92, 107, 116; Middle Kingdom 103–6; monumental architecture/structures 99, 115; in Naqada I phase 91; in Naqada II phase 92–3; Neolithic *88*, 89–91; New Kingdom 107–15; Old Kingdom 100–3, 369; Predynastic 91–4; Ptolemaic Dynasty *88*, 117; pyramids 99–102; royal burial complexes 98; royal power 110; Second Intermediate 106–7; Seventeenth Dynasty 107; Sixth Dynasty 102, 103; sun worship 101, 102; Third Dynasty 99–100; Third Intermediate 116; Thirteenth

Dynasty 105–6; Twelfth Dynasty 105; unification of 91, 93–5, 103–4, 107; warfare 108; writing 94
Eighteenth Dynasty 107–8, 110
Eisenstadt, Samuel 366
Elamite writing system 84
El Brujo 342
El Castillo pyramid 323
Eleventh Dynasty 103, 104
elite power: in Classic Maya 314; competition of 149; on Crete 129; as critical player in religious ritual 26; factions 149–50; gift-giving 231; at Great Zimbabwe 30–1; of Harappan people 200; in Hawaiian society 48; in Late Shang Period 227; in pre-Columbian Mississippian culture 26; at Pueblo Bonito 38
El Manatí site 303
El Mirador 311
Emerson, Thomas 295
empire, defined 78
Enheduanna 70
environmental decline 368–9
Epipaleolithic Period *54*, 55
Eridu 60
Erligang culture 219–22
Erlitou culture 216–19
Esarhaddon 78, 83
Etruria 158
Etruscan Mural *159*
Etruscans 122, 158–60
Euboia island 144
Evans, Arthur 126, 128

Fajada Butte 36, *37*
Falling Springs 270
farming societies 18
feasting rituals 213
Feathered Serpent Pyramid 308, *308*
female sacrifices 294
Fertile Crescent 52
feudal system 229
Fiesta Mound 332–3, *333*
Fifteenth Dynasty 107
Fifth Dynasty 102–3
figural art/figurines: bianfa style hair braid 215, *216*; Cahokian *293*; Cycladic Folded-Arm Figurine *124*; in Geometric Period 145; of Harappan people 194–7, *196*; in Mississippian culture 292; in Naqada I phase 91–2; in Naqada II phase 93; at Poverty Point 273
fire altars 194
First Intermediate Period *88*, 103
Five Towers *256*
Flannery, Kent V. 2
Florence Culture 274–5
food production: in Chimú Society 354; in Chincha polity 355; in Neolithic Period Near East 58; in Olmec culture 304; in sedentary villages 18; wild foods *vs.* 8
foraging societies 16–18
Formative Period *300*

fortified settlements: in Early Cycladic Period 124; in Early Helladic Period 125; in Late Uruk Period 61; in Maori communities 43; in Mississippian culture 290; at Mycenaean centers 135–6, 139; in Neo-Babylonian Period 83
Fort Shalmaneser 79
Forum 164
Fourteenth Dynasty 107
Fourth Dynasty 101, 102
Fowler, Melvin 286
Fox Mound 286
Franchthi Cave 122
Fu Hao 223, 224
Funan Kingdom 239, 246–9
funerary architecture 125

Galindo site 340
Ganweriwala 184
Gaozu, Emperor 234
Geertz, Clifford 295
gendered differentiation 208, 242
gender roles 17, 73, 191, 250, 325, 369
geoglyphs 346, *347*
Geometric Period 144–6
Gerzean 92–3
gift-giving 11, 25, 231
Gilgamesh 66
Giza 101–2, *101*
Göbekli Tepe 58
god-kings 50
Grandstand Fresco 131
Grave Circle A 136
Grave Circle B 136
Great Bath at Mohenjo Daro 180, *181*, 194, *195*
Great Courtyard 180
Great Enclosure 30, 31
Great House communities at Chaco Canyon 34–8, *35*, *36*
Great Mica Grave 280
Great Sphinx 102
Great Temple at Cahuachi 344
Great Wall of China *233*, 234, 235–6
Great Zimbabwe: complexity of 32–3; craft production 33; differentiation 33; elite power in 30–1; Great Enclosure 30, 31; Hill Complex 30, 31; household religion in 31; map of *29*; origins of 28–9; regional polity of 28; religious beliefs 31–2; social stratification 33; warfare 33
Greece *see* Classical Greece
Gudea 72
Guila Naquitz 300

Halaf culture 59
Hammurabi 73
Hammurabi's Law Code Stele 73–4
Han Dynasty *207*, 234–5, 246
Hanging Gardens 83
hapū 44
Harappan civilization: agrarian nature of 179; caste system 202; chiefdom status of 201; chronology

175–6, *175*; city planning 182–7; craft production 187–90; demise of 201; Dholavira 185–6; in Early Harappan Period 177–9; elite power in 200; geography and ecological setting 173–5; health of 192–3; kin relationships 193; map of *174*; Mohenjo Daro 180–2; multicropping 180; in Neolithic Period *175*, 176–7; public architecture 186–7; religious beliefs 194–9; river use for trade 189; seals *191*, *192*, 197–9, 201; socioeconomic differentiation 191–3; sociopolitical organization of 199–201; state-level society 201–2; trade 187–90; warfare 199–200; weight system 189
Harappan demise *175*
Harappan seals *191*, *192*, 197–9, *198*, 201
Hariharalaya 251
Hassuna 59
Hatshepsut 111–12
Hawaii, pre-contact 46–50
Hawaiian Feathered Cape *49*
Hawaiiki 42
Hayden site 270
he decorative vessel *218*
Hellenistic Age *121*, 154–7
Herodotus 86, 152
Heroön 144
Hesiod 141, 147
Hierakonpolis 91, 92–3
hieroglyphic writing 94, 127
Higham, Charles 244
Hill Complex *30*, 31
Hinduism 199, 203, 243, 247, 251, 255
Hittites 142
Hoabinhian phase 241
Homer 140, 141–2
Hopewell earthen mounds 277–80, *279*
Hopewell Period 277–81
Hopewell Period effigy *278*
Hopewell pipes 277
Horus 94
House 1 194
household religion: of Chacoan culture 40; described 7; at Great Zimbabwe 31; kivas and 39–40; in Late Preceramic Period 335; in sedentary villages 20
House of the Tiles *124*, 125
Huaca de la Luna 339
Huaca del Sol 339
Huaca Rajada 341–2
huacas 334, 362
Huacas de Moche 338, *340*
Huari center 350
Hu Hai 234
Huitzilopochtli 326
human sacrifice 217, 221, 225, 323, 325–6, 354–5, 363–4, *363*
Hummingbird geoglyph *347*
hunter-gatherers 17–18, 28, 34, 175, 207, 239, 241, 269–70
hut-urns 158
hydraulic hypothesis 3

Hyksos Period 106–7
Hymn of Aten 110

Ice Maiden 363–4, *363*
ideological power 2
IEMP Model 2
Iguana God 343
Iliad (Homer) 141
Illapa 362
Imhotep 99
Imperial China 232–6
Inca Empire 330
Incan civilization: administrative centers 357; calendar 362; Chincha polity 355–6; collapse of 364–5; Cuzco 358–9; economic structures 359–62; foundation and expansion 356–7; in Late Horizon Period 355; pottery 360; religious beliefs 362–4; road system 356–7; warfare 364; way stations 356
Inca Royal Road 357
Indrapura 251
Indravarman III 262–3
Indus River 173
Indus script 190–1
Indus Valley civilization 179–80
inequality 12
inheritance customs 21, 24, 250, 314, 325
inhumation burials 68, 136, 144–5, 157–9, 170, 242, 276, 282
Initial Period *330*
integration 14–15, 25
International Age 75–8, 107–8
Inti 356
Inundation, The 86–7
Iron Age 122, 239
irrigation canals/agriculture: in Aztec society 325; in Chimú Society 352; in China 205–6; in Egypt 104; in Hawaiian society 47; in Khmer Empire 370; in Maya culture 312–13; in Mesopotamia 52, 59, 66; in Mochica system 339, 344; in Nasca Society 345; at Sechín Alto 334; in Tiwanaku Society 350; in Uruk Period 64; *see also* water management systems
Ishanapura 249
Ishtar Gate 83
Isin-Larsa Period 73
Italian Iron Age *121*
Italian Neolithic and Bronze Age *121*
Italy: Bronze Age 157; chronology 121–2, *121*; map of *143*; *see also* Roman Empire
iwi 44

Janabarriu phase 335, 338
Jayadevi 250, 251
Jayavarman I 250, 251, 262
Jayavarman II 240, 251, 262
Jayavarman IV 255
Jayavarman V 252
Jayavarman VII 252, 253, 255, 258, 263
Jericho 56

jia decorative vessel *218*
Jiangzhai Village 208–9, *209*
Johnson, Gregory A. 64
jua decorative vessel *218*
Julius Caesar 166, 167

K1 pit at Sanxingdui 214–15
K2 pit at Sanxingdui 214–15
K2 settlement southeast Africa 29
Kalasasaya 349
Kalhu 79
Kalibangan 194
Kamares Ware 126–7
Kamehameha I, King 46
Kaminaljuyú 311
Kampong Phluk Village *239*
Kane 50
kapu 50
Karnak 108, 110
Kassite State 76
Kato Zakro palace 132–3
kauwā people 48
Kenoyer, Jonathan Mark 184, 186, 199, 202
keyhole architecture 283
Khafre 101
Khasekhemwy 98–9
khipu (knotted ropes) 15, 360–2, *361*
khlon sruk 260
khlon visaya 260
Khmer Empire: collapse of 262–3, 369–70; daily life in 261–2; founding of 251; irrigation canals/agriculture 370; kingship 252; landscape 252–3; legal system 261; religious belief systems 251, 253–8, 263; royal court 260–1; rulers absolute power over population 8; slaves 262; socioeconomic structure 258–62; trade 261
Khmer Empire Period *240*
Khmer People Roasting a Pig *259–60*
Khmer People Roasting Food at a Picnic *259–60*
Khok Phanom Di 241
Khufu 101–2
king before god image 74
Kingdom of Great Zimbabwe *see* Great Zimbabwe
king vis-à-vis gods 255
K'inich Janaab Pakal 317, 320–1
kin relationships: of Harappan people 193; in Mississippian culture 288; in Shang culture 226
kinship: in archaic state 23–4; in early Yangshao phase 209; in foraging societies 17; matrilineal 35; patrilineal 44; regional polity and 21; role of 7; in sedentary villages 18–19
kinship structure: described 6–7; of Hawaii culture 47–8; of Maori society 44
kivas *36*, 39–40
Kleisthenes 151
Knossos 129–32
Knossos Palace 130–2, *130*
Knossos tablets 139
kore statues 149, *150*
Kot Diji phase 178
Kotosh Religious Tradition 335

koulouras 126
kouros statues 149, *150*
Kū 50
Kula Ring 11
Kush 116

labor: corvée system 9; described 9; rights to other's 24; tax obligations met through 9
Labras Lake phase 270
La Centinela 355
Lady of Huaca Cao Viejo tomb 342
Lady Xok 319
Lagash 65
Lajia culture 211
Lake Titicaca 329, 347, 349, 356
land management 229–30
land ownership 19, 24
land use 122
Lanzón Gallery 337–8
Lanzón stone *337*
Las Vegas culture 329
Late Archaic Period 269, 270
Late Bronze Age: Aegean Sea region 157; China *207*; Near East 75–8
Late Helladic society 121, 137–43
Late Horizon Period 330, *330*, 355
Late Intermediate Period *330*, 352–5
Late Neolithic Period: China *206*, 210–13; Egypt 90–1
Late Period Egypt *88*, 116–17
Late Preceramic Period *330*, 335
Late Shang Period 222–9
Late Uruk Period 60, 63–4
Late Woodland Period 283–4
Late Yangshao phase 210
La Venta phase 301–2
lawagetas 140
Law Code Stele of Hammurabi 73–4, *74*
law codes 73–4
leadership structures: in archaic states 24–7; in Chacoan culture 38; development of 18; generosity in 25; of Maori society 44; in Minoan society 127–8; in Protopalatial period 127–8; in sedentary villages 19–20; urbanism and 25; in Uruk Period 64
legalism 232, 234, 261
Lekson, Stephen 41, 294
Lerna 125
Levant 90
Libyan dynasties 116
Liliuokalani, Queen 46
Linear A 127, 134
Linear B tablets 139
lingam stone 247–8, *248*
Liu Bang 234–6
Long Count Calendar 321
Longshan/Dawenkou cultures 210–13
Lono 50
Lord of Sipán 341
Lothal settlement 189
Lower Egypt 91

Lower Jackson Mound 273
Luxor 108

Maadi 92
Macedonian Empire 155–7
Machu Picchu 357, *358*
maize agriculture 300
Maize God 318
mana 50
Manco Capac 356
Manda settlement 189
Mandate of Heaven 229
Manetho 89
Mann, Michael 2
Manqo Inca 364, 365
Maori ariki 46
Maori society of New Zealand 42–6
Mapungubwe 29–30, *29*
Marcaya site 345
Marion culture 274
maritime trade 77
Mark Antony 167
market exchange 11
masonry-built structures 360
mastaba tombs 100
material culture: of the Adena 275; of American Bottom 274; in Early Cycladic Period 124; in Early Dynastic Period 66–7; Egyptian 86, 91, 92, 107, 116; Etruscan 158; Halaf 59; in Hawaiian society 47; at Hayden site 70; in Hopewell Tradition 277; in Kot Dijian phase 78; in Late Uruk Period 60, 63–4; in Late Woodland Period 283; in the Levant 55; in Maori society 44; in Middle Archaic Period 269–70; Mycenaean 143; in Neopalatial Period 134; Samarran 59; in Shang culture 229; Teotihuacan 307; of Tiwanaku culture 349; Wari culture 52
materialization, in small-scale society 26
matrilineal kinship 35, 193, 242, 250, 262, 288
matrilocal residential practice 35, 193, 284, 288
Mature Harappan Period 175–6, *175*, 179–80
Mauss, Marcel 10
Maya culture: in Early Classic Period 310; environment 310; irrigation canals/agriculture 312–13; Postclassic Period 322–6; Preclassic Period 310–11; public architecture 311; pyramids 311; ritual practice 314; social differentiation 311, 314; *see also* Classic Maya
Mayapan 323
Meadowcroft Rock Shelter 268
Medieval Warm Period 267–8
Mehrgarh Phase 176–7
Memphis 98, 107
Menes 95
Menkaure 101
Mentuhotep II 103, 104
Merneptah 115
Mesoamerica: Aztec Empire 324–6; chronology 299, *300*; in Classical Period 305–10; cosmological structure 305–7; cycling characteristics 324; differentiation 300; geography and ecological setting 298; map of *299*; Maya Culture 322–4; Monte Albán 305–7; monumental architecture/structures 300–1; Olmec culture 301–4; Postclassic Period 324–6; Teotihuacan 307–10; *see also* Classic Maya; Maya Culture
Mesoamerican ballgame 302–3, 318
Mesopotamia: in Archaic Period 299–300; Assur 79; Assyrian State 76–7; in Chalcolithic Period 59–60; chronological periods *54*; chronological sequence 54–5; complexity 68–9; deportations 79; Early Dynastic Period 64–9; in Epipaleolithic 55; geography and ecological setting 52–3; in International Age 75–8; irrigation canals/agriculture 52, 59, 66; Kassite State 76; in Late Bronze Age 75–8; map of *53*; Mitanni State 76; monumental architecture/structures 56; Neo-Assyrian Empire 78–83; Neo-Babylonian Empire 83; in Neolithic Period 55–9; Neo-Sumerian revival 72; Old Akkadian Period 69–71; Old Babylonian Period 73–5; Persian Empire 84–5; in pottery (Ceramic) Neolithic Period 58; in Pre-Pottery (Aceramic) Neolithic 56–7; royal dynasties 54–5; tablet collections 73; temples 58; territorial states 54, 65, 69–78; in Ubaid Period 62–3; Ur III Dynasty 72; urbanization 64; Uruk colonies 63; Uruk Period 60–4
metallurgical methods 211
metalsmiths 360
Mexica 324
Middle Archaic Period North America 269
Middle Assyrian state 76
Middle Bronze Age *206*
Middle Horizon Period 329, *330*
Middle Kingdom Period *88*, 103–6
Middle Mississippi River Valley 266
Middle Neolithic Period China *206*, 208–9
Middle Preceramic Period Andean Region *330*
Middle Shang Dynasty Period 221
Middle Uruk Period 64
Middle Woodland Period 276–81
military conflict 367
military power 3
Mills, Barbara 34
Ming Dynasty 234
Minoans: forgeries 131; hieroglyphs 127; leadership structures 127–8; palaces 135; trade 134
Mississippi Period *268*, 269
Mississippian system: burial mounds 285–7; collapse of 296–7; complexity factor 294–5; craft production 291, 296; economic structures 290–1; housing 287–8; kin relationships 288; religious beliefs 291–4; rise of 284–5; ritual practice 292; sociopolitical structure 294–6; as state-level society 295; Stirling phase 284; as theater state 295; trade in 288–9; warfare 289–90; *see also* American Bottom
Mitanni State 76
mit'a system 359–60, 364
Mitchell Mounds 288
moated mounds 242–3
mobile agriculturalists 8

mobile foraging societies 16–18
Mochica, the 329, 338–44
Mohenjo Daro settlement 180–2, *181*, *183*, 200
Monks Mound 285, *286*
Monte Albán 305–7, *306*
Monte Verde 329
monumental architecture/structures: in archaic states 23; corridor houses 125; corvée labor and 14; in Early Dynastic Period 66; in Egypt 99, 115; funerary architecture 125; House of the Tiles *124*, 125; in the Levant 134; in Maori society 44–5; in Mesoamerica 300–1; in Mesopotamia 56; among the Mochica 344; in Olmec culture 301–2; in Pre-Pottery (Aceramic) Neolithic 56; in Protopalatial period 126–7; in Rome 162, 169; step pyramid 99–100
monumentality 14, 113, 125
Moon Animal 354
Moorehead phase 296
Moquegua Valley 350–1
Morgan, Lewis Henry 1
Morris, Ian 145
mortuary cult 293
mortuary practices *see* burial practices
mortuary ritual 242
Moseley, Michael 331
Motley Mound 273
mound-building 269
Mound 72 Cahokia 286–7, 290, 293–4
Mound City 280
Mt. Meru 253, 255, 256
Mt. Vesuvius 369
Moxeke culture 334–5
multicropping 180, 325
mummification 113, *114*
Mundo Perdido complex 316
Mwari 31–2
Mycenaean society: complexity of 141; decline in 141–3; fortified settlements at 139; monumental tombs 137; religious beliefs 140–1; shaft graves 136–7, *136*; social differentiation in 140; social organization in 140; sociopolitical complexity in 141
Myths of the Archaic state (Yoffee) 4

Nabonidus 83
Nabopolassar 83
Nabta Playa 89–90
Nakbe 311
Naqada I Period 91–2
Naqada II Period 92–3
Naqada III phase 93–4
Naram-Sin 70–1
Naram-Sin stele 70–1, *71*
Narmer 93
Narmer Palette 95, 96–7, *96*, *97*
Nasca culture 329, 344–6, 350
natural disasters 368, 369
naturalistic worldview 20, 26
Neak Ta 255
Nefertari 112

Nefertiti 110, *111*, 112
Neo-Assyrian Empire 78–83, 116
Neo-Babylonian Empire 83
Neolithic Period: in the Aegean *120*, 122–3; in China 207–13; craft production 177; dentistry in 176; in Egypt *88*, 89–91; food production 58; in Harappan civilization *175*, 176–7; social stratification 177; in Southeast Asia *240*, 241; in Southwest Asia 55–9; technology in 56
Neopalatial Period 34, *120*, 129–35
Neo-Sumerian revival 72
New Kingdom Period *88*, 107–15
New Temple phase 335
New Zealand, colonization of 46
Nile River 86–7
Nile Valley: chronological periods 88–9, *88*; geography and ecological setting 86–8; map of *87*
Ninan Cuyuchi 364
Nineveh 79
Ningirsu 67
Nissen, Hans J. 60–1
Nochta site 269–70
Noen U-Loke 244
Non Nok Tha 242
North American societies *see* Chaco Canyon; Mississippian system

Oaxaca Valley 304, 305
Oc Eo 246, 247
Octavian Caesar 160–1, 166–9
Ohio River 266–7
Ohio Valley *see* Adena cultural complex
Old Akkadian Dynasty 65, 69–71
Old Babylonian Period 73–5
Old Kingdom Period *88*, 100–3, 369
Olmec culture 301–4
Olmec head *301*
Olympia 154
Olympian Gods 147–8, 153
oracle bones 212, *212*, 213, 227
Ordos bronze culture 220–1
Orientalizing subphase 146
Osiris 102

paa 43
Pacariqtambo 356
Pacatnamú site 354
Pachacamac 362
Pachacuti 356
Pakal 317, 320–1
palaces: in Classic Maya 315; destruction of Minoan 135; in Early Shang Period 219–20; at Kato Zakro 132–3; at Knossos 129–32, *130*; in Late Helladic III 138–9; Minoan 135; Neo-Assyrian 79–82; in New Kingdom Period 108; Pylos Palace *138*
Palace without a Rival, The 79
Palenque 317
Paleoindian Period *268*, 269
Palermo Stone 98
palisades 289–90

Pampa de las Llamas-Moxeke 334
panaqa 358
Panathenaic vases 160
Pan Geng 223
pan-Hellenic games 148, 154
pan-Hellenic identity 146
Paracas culture 344
Parthenon 153
pastoralists 176, 179–80
paterfamilias 165
Patrick phase 283
patrilineal inheritance 44, 314
Pauketat, Timothy 4, 295
Peaceful Realm, A (McIntosh) 200
peak sanctuaries 133
Peloponnesian War 152
Peñasco Blanco Great House 36
People's Republic of China (PRC) *see* China
Pepy II 103
Pergamon 156
Persian Empire 84–5, 116–17
Persian Wars 151, 152
Phaistos 126
Philip II 155, 156, 367
Phnom Kulen 251
Phoenicians 146
pietas 165
pilgrimage fair model 40
Pillared Hall 180–1
Ping, Emperor 235
pipal tree *198*, 199
Pithekoussai 146
Pizarro, Francisco 364, 365
plant cultivation 176, 179, 207–8, 283, 331; *see also* domesticated grain/plants
plastered skull 56, *57*
Plumed Headdress Deity 354
Pnyx 153
political collapse 366, 367–8
political complexity 13–15
political differentiation 13–14
political leadership 303
political organization: in archaic states 24–5; in Aztec society 325; centralization 13; defined 12–13; described 12–15; of Mochica Society 343–4; in Neopalatial Period 133–4; of Roman Empire 163–5; in sedentary villages 19–20; in Terminal Late Woodland Period 284
political power 3, 93
political units 13
Pollock, Susan 61
polygynous households 314
Polynesian cultures: Hawaiian society 46–50; Maori population 42–6; map of *43*
Ponce Stela 349
Popol Vuh 318
Possehl, Gregory L. 202
Postclassic Period 299, *300*, 322–6
pottery: in Archaic Period Greece *148*, 149; Corinthian 148, *148*; in Early Harappan Period 178; figural decoration on 145; Inca-style 360; of the Mochica 340–1; in Protopalatial period 126–7; in Ubaid Period 62–3; Uruk 62–3; in Valdivia culture 332
Pottery (Ceramic) Neolithic Period *54*, 58
pottery technology 90
Poverty Point 272–3, *272*
power: in archaic states 24–5; consolidation by emerging leaders 7; regional polity and 22; in Teotihuacan 308–9; through labor control 9; of writing 104
Prairie Lake phase 270
Preceramic Period Andean Region 330–5, *332*
Preceramic sites, map of *328*
Preclassic Period 299, 300–5, *300*
Predynastic Period *88*, 91–4
Pre-Pottery (Aceramic) Neolithic Period *54*, 56–7
priestesses of San José de Moro 341
Priest-King statue 197
priests *see* religious specialists
Prima Porta statute 167, *168*
Principate Period 166, 170–1
private land ownership 19
private rituals 22
private tombs 106, 115
Protogeometric Period 143–4
Protopalatial Period *120*, 126–9
proto-Shiva seal *198*, 199
Ptolemaic Dynasty *88*, 117
Ptolemy I 117, 155
public architecture 186–7, 311
public art 80, 84, 165, 167; *see also* art and architecture
public religion 22
Pueblo I phase settlement 34
Pueblo II phase settlement 34–5
Pueblo III phase settlement 35
Pueblo Bonito Great House *35*, 36, 38
Pueblo del Arroyo Great House *36*
Pulcher Mounds 288
Punta Lobos site 354
purity *see* ritual purity
Pylos 138–9
Pylos Palace *138*
Pylos tablets 140
Pyramid of the Moon 308
Pyramid of the Sun 308
pyramids: at Chichen Itza 323; at Giza 101–2, *101*; Maya culture 311; step 99–100; in Teotihuacan 308
Pyramid Texts 102–3, 104
pyromancy 227–8

Qijia culture 211
Qin Dynasty *207*, 232–4
Qoya Raymi 362
Queen's Festival 362

Rajendravarman II 255
Ramesses II 108, 115
Ramesses III 115
Range site 283

Rapa Nui 368
Rayed Head figure 349
Real Alto site 332–3, *333*
reciprocity 10–11, 39, 325
reciprocity-redistribution system 40, 41
redistribution of goods 11, 22, 24, 29, 39, 64
Reforms of Uruinimgina 69
regionalization 175, 178–9, 201
regional polity: of Chacoan culture 41; described 20–3; economic structures and 21–2; of Great Zimbabwe 28; in Oaxaca Valley 304; in Preclassic Period 305; religious beliefs and 22–3
Rehman Dheri site 178
religious belief systems: in archaic states 26–7; of Chimú 354–5; in Classic Maya 318–21; in Crete 128–9; described 7–8; in Early Dynastic Period 98; in foraging societies 17–18; in Funan culture 247–9; at Great Zimbabwe 31–2; Greek influence in Etruria 160; of Harappan people 194–9; Hawaiian 50; of Inca culture 362–4; of Khmer Empire 251, 253–8, 263; in Mississippian culture 291–4; of the Mochica 343; in Mycenaean society 140–1; in Neopalatial Period 133; private 22; in Protopalatial period 128–9; public 22; regional polity and 22–3; in sedentary villages 20; Shang Dynasty 227–9; sun worship 101, 102; of Tiwanaku 348–9; tobacco and 276; in Wari temples 351; *see also* household religion
religious specialists 7, 17–18, 20, 26–7, 294; *see also* shamans
religious statuary 66, *67*
religious structures 27, 44–5, 128–9, 133, 186–7; *see also* monumental architecture/structures; temples
renewal ritual 276
Republic Rome 370
Res Gestae (Deeds) 167
residential neighborhoods 75, 200, 287–8, 309
rice cultivation 179, 241, 252, 260–1
rights of property 19
rights to labor 7, 21–2
risk management strategies 17, 19, 24
rites of intensification 292
ritual practice: animal offerings 242; animal sacrifice 224; Aztec ideology 326; bloodletting 319, *319*; of Chacoan culture 39–40; feasting rituals 213; human sacrifice 217, 221, 225; in Late Shang Period 227; in Maori society 45; in Maya culture 314; in Mississippian culture 292; in Pre-Pottery (Aceramic) Neolithic 56–7; private 22; Sed festival 100; in a state system 26; *see also* household religion; religious belief systems
ritual purity 48, 194, 199, 202–3
Roman Empire: Christianity and 171–2; Civil War Period 165–6; collapse of 172; Dominate Period 166; Early Iron Age 157–60; map of *163*; monumental architecture/structures 162, 169; political organization of 163–5; Principate Period 166, 170–1; Third-Century Crisis 166; warfare 170
Roman Republic *121*, 151, 162
Rome: architectural design of 161–2; as aristocratic system of rule 163; civil war 165–6; Curia 164; economy of 164; Forum 164; origins of 160–2; patrician Senate 163; plan of *161*; social organization of 164–5; territorial expansion of 162–3; Third-Century Crisis 166, 171
Romulus 160
Round Top 286
royal art 80, *81*, 85; *see also* art and architecture
royal burials 68, 100, 104–5, 113
Royal Cemetery at Ur 68
royal court 260–1
royal power 227–9

Sacred Cenote 323
Sacred Hot Springs *45*
sacrificial burials 217
Sahlins, Marshall 1
Samarra 59
Sambor Prei Kuk 249
sanctuaries 128–9, 148; *see also* religious structures; temples
Sand Prairie phase 296
San José de Moro 341
San José Mogote 304
San Lorenzo phase 301
Santorini 135, 368
Sanxingdui culture 213–16
Sanxingdui settlement *214*
Sapa Inca 358, 362
Saqqara 98, 100
sarcophagus lid of Pakal 320–1, *320*
Sargon I 70
Sargon II 78
Sargonid Dynasty 78
Sassaman, Kenneth E. 274
satrapies 84
Schliemann, Heinrich 141
Scorpion Macehead 94
sculptural imagery 82
sculpture 149, 156
seals: of Harappan civilization 197–9, 201; Harappan Script on *191*; Harappan seal with unicorn *192*; in Protopalatial period 127; proto-Shiva seal *198*
Sechín Alto 334
Second Intermediate Period *88*, 106–7
sedentary foragers 8, 13
sedentary villages 18–20
Sed ritual 100
Seip Mound 279–80
Seleucus I 155
Sennacherib 78, 83
Senwosret III as a Sphinx 105, *106*
serekh 94
Serpent Mound 282–3, *282*
Service, Elman 1
Sesklo 123
settlement patterns: defined 13; in Early Dynastic Period 65; in Geometric Period 145; in Iron Age 122; leadership and 284; of Neopalatial Period 130, 133; in Oaxaca Valley 305; in southeast Asia 239, 241; in Uruk Period 64
settlements *see* fortified settlements

Seventeenth Dynasty 107
shaft graves 136–7, *136*
Shalmaneser III 78, 79, 83
shamans 7, 17–18, 20, 346; *see also* religious specialists
Shamash 74
Shang Di 228
Shang Dynasty 204, 219, 225–6
Shang religion 227–9
Shang Yang 232
shifting cultivation 18
Shi Huangti 232–4
Shi Huangti tomb *235*
Shiva-linga 248, 251, 253
Shiva/Shakti deities *198*, 199, 203, 243, 247–9, 251, 253
Shulgi 72
Silk Road 233–4, 236
Sipán site 341–2
sipapu 40
Sixth Dynasty 102, 103
Siyaj K'ak' 316
slash-and-burn cultivation techniques 283
slaves: at Angkor Borei 247; in Aztec society 325; in Classical Greece 152, 154; in Early Dynastic Period 69; foreign-born 149; in Funan culture 249; in Khmer Empire 262; in Late Helladic society 140; in Roman Republic 164–5, 171
small-scale sedentary village structures 18–20
Snake-Belt God 343
snake imagery 31
social identity 6–7, 18–19, 23–4
social order 14
social organization 140, 158, 164–5, 314
social power 2–3, 141
social status 90, 193–4, 213
social stratification: in Andean region 335; at Banpo 208; burials as best evidence of 351; in Erligang settlements 221; of Erlitou culture 217; at Great Zimbabwe 33; in Late Archaic 270; in Late Neolithic Period 210–11; in Lower Egypt 91; of the Mochica 341; in Neolithic Period 177; origins of 17; in Southeast Asia 244; at Yinxu settlement 226
societal collapse 366, 369–70
societies, types of 1–2
socioeconomic differentiation: in Andean region 338; in Bronze Age settlements 243; in China 213; in death 90; in Janabarriu phase 338; in Maya culture 311, 314; in Mycenaean society 140; in Oaxaca Valley 304; in Preclassic Period 304; in Yangshao Period 209
socioeconomic structure 20–1, 42, 46–7, 260–3, 345, 349, 354
sociopolitical integration 14
sociopolitical organization: of Archaic Period 149–50; of Baodun culture 210; at Chichen Itza 322–3; of Harappan people 199–201; of Maori society 46; Mississippian culture 294–6; in Shang society 225–6; of Wari state 351–2
Sotka Koh settlement 190

Southeast Asia: Bronze Age farmers 241–2; chronology 239–40, *240*; Early Iron Age 243–6; geography and ecological setting 237–9; later Iron Age 246–51; map of *238*; in Neolithic Period 241; settlement patterns 239, 241; social stratification 244; trade 134
Southern Ceremonial Complex 296
Spanish conquests 364–5, 367
Sparta 149, 151–2
spatial differentiation 147
Sponemann site 284, 288, 292
Spring and Autumn Period 232
Stadelman, Rainer 101–2
Staff God deity 349, 354
Stalin, Joseph 8
standard megaron plan 123, *123*
Standard of Ur 68
standing army 14, 71–3, 173, 199, 225, 261; *see also* warfare
Stark, Miriam 249, 255
statuary 82, 302–3
status differentiation *see* differentiation
Stein, John R. 60
Stele of the Vultures 67, 69
Stele of Ur-Nammu 72
steles 70–1, 85
step pyramid 99–100
Stirling phase 284
stone statuary 196–7
stoneware bangle production 187–8
subsistence economy 8, 42–3, 65, 354
Sumer 65
sun circles 286, 289
Sun Temple at Cuzco 362
sun temples in Egypt 102
sun worship 101, 102, 215
Supe Valley sites 333
surplus: agricultural 99; in foraging societies 17; in sedentary villages 19
Suryavarman I 252
Suryavarman II 252, 255–6
Sutkagen-Dor settlement 190
sweat lodges 288
Syria 63
systems theory in archaeology 2–3

tablet collections 73
tamrvac 260
Taosi site 210–11
tapu 45
Tawantinsuyu 358
technological production 9
technology: in Archaic Period 148; craft specialization and 9–10; defined 9; iron 245; in Neolithic Period 56; in Predynastic Period 91
technology change 10
Tell el-Amarna 75, 110
Tello Obelisk 337–8
temples: in Archaic Period 147; in Chenla Empire 249; in Early Dynastic Period 58, 66; Etruscan 158–9; in Geometric Period 144; in Mesopotamia

58; in New Kingdom Period 108, *109*; in Uruk City 61–2; *see also* religious structures; sanctuaries
Templo Mayor 325, 326
Tenochtitlan 324, 326
Teotihuacan 307–10, *308*
Tepenaca 324
Terminal Late Woodland Period 284
terracotta soldiers in Qin Emperor Shi Huangti's tomb *235*
territorial states: in International Age 75–8; in Mesopotamia 65; in Neo-Sumerian Period 72; of Old Akkadian Period 69–71; in Old Babylonian Period 73–5; in southwest Asia *54*, 55
tetrarchy structure 171
textile production 133, 360
Theater of Dionysus 153
Theogony (Hesiod) 147
Thera 135
Third-Century Crisis 166, 171
Third Dynasty 99–100
Third Intermediate Period *88*, 116
Thirteenth Dynasty 105–6
tholos tombs 125–6
Thuc Phan 244
Thupa Wallpa 365
Thutmose I 111
Thutmose II 111
Thutmose III 108, 111–12
Tiahuanaco site 347–8
Tiberius 169
Tiglath-Pileser III 78, 79
Tigre Pyramid 311
Tikal 315–17, *316*
Titterington phase 270
Tiwanaku culture 329, 347–50, *348*
Tiye 112
Tlaloc 326
tobacco 276
Toltec state 324
tomb-robbing 113–14
Tomb U-j 94, *95*
Tonle Sap Lake 238, *239*
trade: in the Adena 275; in Aztec economy 325; in Early Dynastic Period 98; in Egypt 92–3; with Erlitou culture 219; in Geometric Period 145–6; Harappan network 187–90; in Khmer Empire 261; in Late Helladic III period 140; Minoan participation in 134; in Mississippian culture 288–9, 290–1; movement of goods 189–90; in Naqada II phase 92–3; of the Nasca 345; overland 340; in southeast Asia 244
transhumance 92
Transitional Period *175*
tribal political structures 19–20
tripartite shrine 131
Trojan War 141, 142
trophy skulls 281
Troy 142
Truman Road site 270
Tula site 324

Tutankhamun 111, 113–14
Twelfth Dynasty 105
Two Ladies Name 93
Tylor, Edward 1

Uaxactun 316
Ubaid Period 59–60, 62–3
Uluburun wreck 77
unification: in Early Dynastic Period Mesopotamia 65; of Egypt 91, 93–5, 103–4, 107; of Greek culture 155; in Old Akkadian Period 70; in Persian Empire 84
Upper Egypt 91; *see also* Egypt
Ur 68, 190
Ur III Dynasty 72
Urabarriu community 335
urbanism 25, 158–60
Ur-Nammu 72
Uruk City 61–3
Uruk Period *54*, 60–4
Uruk-Period colonialism 63

Valdivia culture 332–4
Valley of the Kings 113
value 9
vase-painting 153–4
Veii 159
Vergina 156
Vestal Virgins 151
victual mummies 113
village agriculturalists 13
Villanovan Culture 158
Viracocha 356
Vishnu 256
votive statuary 66, *67*, 70, 72, 82, 134

Wallerstein, Immanuel 3–4
wanax 140
Wang Mang 235
warfare: in Cahokia 289–90; at Chaco Canyon 38; of Chimú 354–5; in Classic Maya 321; in Egypt 108; at Great Zimbabwe 33; of Harappan people 199–200; in Hawaiian society 49; in Hellenistic Period 156; of Inca culture 364; in Late Woodland Period 284; in Maori society 45–6; among the Mochica 342–3; of the Nasca 345–6; in Rome 170; in Shang society 225–6
Wari culture 329, 350–2
Warka Vase 62
Warring States *207*
Warring States Period 232, 234
Warriors' Cultivation Festival 362
Washukanni 76
water management systems 186, 252, 311, 344, 349
Watson Brake mounds 271, *271*
Wayna Capac 364
wealth inequality 12
weight system 189
Wen, King 229
West Baray 252
Western Han Empire 235

Western Zhou state *207*, 231–2
whānau 44
White Temple 61, *62*
Wittfogel, Karl 3
Wolf, Eric 2
woodhenges 286
Woodland Phase *268*, 269, 274–6
Woolley, Leonard 68
Wright, Henry T. 64
Wright, Rita P. 193
Wrinkle Face God 343
writing: in archaic states 23; Chinese 222–3, *223*; Coffin Texts 104, 115; in Egypt 94; government success and 15; hieroglyphic 94, 127; Indus Script 190–1; in Olmec Preclassic Period 304; pictographs *223*; power of 104; in Protopalatial period 127; Pyramid Texts 102–3, 104
writing systems 84, 190–1
Wu, Emperor 235–6, 246
Wu, King 229
Wu Ding 223

Xerxes I 84
Xia Dynasty 216, 229
Xibeigang Royal Cemetery *226*, 227

yanakuna 358–9
Yangshao cultural complex 208–9
Yanshi settlement 219–20, *220*
Yashovarman I 255
Yaxchilan 319
Ying Zheng 232
Yinxu settlement 223, 224, *225*, 226, 227
Yoffee, Norman 4, 69, 295
Yupanqui 356

Zhengzhou settlement 219–22
Zhou Daguan 260
Zhou Dynasty bronze cauldron *230*
Zhou State 207, 229–33
Zhukaigou culture 220–1
ziggurats 72, 83
Zi lineage 225, 228–9